With

& best wishes.

Tolley's
Tax Guide
1992/93

by

Arnold Homer

Rita Burrows

Tolley Publishing Company Ltd
A UNITED NEWSPAPERS PUBLICATION

Tenth Edition August 1992

Published by
Tolley Publishing Co Ltd
Tolley House
2, Addiscombe Road
Croydon Surrey CR9 5AF
England
081-686 9141

Printed in Great Britain
at the Bath Press, Avon

About this book

This is the tenth edition of Tolley's Tax Guide, which is one of the range of Tolley annuals on all aspects of taxation.

The Guide is updated annually to incorporate the changes in law and practice that occur each year, and is published soon after the passing of the main Finance Act.

The aim of the book is to provide clear and concise guidance on all aspects of taxation that are likely to be encountered from day to day by businessmen, practitioners, professional advisers and private individuals. It deals with income tax, corporation tax, capital gains tax, inheritance tax, value added tax and stamp duty. There are also chapters on poll tax and business rates, national insurance contributions and statutory sick pay and statutory maternity pay. There are numerous examples to demonstrate how the provisions work in practice.

The authors use their wide practical experience to bring out the tax planning opportunities in the various areas, and these are highlighted as 'tax points' at the end of most chapters.

This edition gives the position for the tax year 1992/93 and covers all legislation, statements of practice and other relevant sources of information including the provisions of the Finance Act 1992 and the Finance (No 2) Act 1992. Where appropriate the position for earlier years is also explained.

All chapters have been revised to incorporate the many changes that have taken place since the previous edition, and there is a useful summary of the main changes.

The general law, as opposed to tax law, is not always the same in Scotland and in Northern Ireland as in England and Wales. Except where otherwise stated, this book is concerned with the law in England and Wales. Readers in Scotland and Northern Ireland should take advice if in any doubt.

The assistance of professional colleagues is gratefully acknowledged by the authors.

Any comments on this publication will as always be welcomed by the publishers.

TOLLEY PUBLISHING COMPANY LIMITED

Contents

Employment

CONTENTS

CONTENTS

Tax and the family

Choosing your investment

Miscellaneous

Abbreviations

ACT	=	Advance Corporation Tax
Board	=	Board of Inland Revenue
CAA 1990	=	Capital Allowances Act 1990
CGT	=	Capital Gains Tax
CTT	=	Capital Transfer Tax
DSS	=	Department of Social Security
EC	=	European Community
ESC	=	Extra-Statutory Concession
FA	=	Finance Act
F(No 2)A	=	Finance (No 2) Act
IHT	=	Inheritance Tax
IHTA 1984	=	Inheritance Tax Act 1984
MIRAS	=	Mortgage Interest Relief At Source
NI	=	National Insurance
PAYE	=	Pay As You Earn
PEP	=	Personal Equity Plan
PPC	=	Personal Pension Contribution
RAP	=	Retirement Annuity Premium
reg	=	regulation
s	=	section
SA 1891	=	Stamp Act 1891
SAYE	=	Save As You Earn
Sch	=	Schedule
SI	=	Statutory Instrument
SMP	=	Statutory Maternity Pay
SP	=	Inland Revenue Statement of Practice
SSCBA 1992	=	Social Security Contributions and Benefits Act 1992
SSP	=	Statutory Sick Pay
TA 1988	=	Income and Corporation Taxes Act 1988
TCGA 1992	=	Taxation of Chargeable Gains Act 1992
TMA 1970	=	Taxes Management Act 1970
VAT	=	Value Added Tax
VATA 1983	=	Value Added Tax Act 1983

Table of rates and allowances

(Correct to 17 July 1992)

Income and corporation tax

Personal allowances (see chapter 2 for full description)

	1990/91 £	1991/92 £	1992/93 £
Personal allowance—under 65	3,005	3,295	3,445
—65 to 74	3,670	4,020	4,200
—75 and over	3,820	4,180	4,370
Married couple's allowance—under 65	1,720	1,720	1,720
—65 to 74	2,145	2,355	2,465
—75 and over	2,185	2,395	2,505
Income limit for age-related allowances	12,300	13,500	14,200
Additional personal allowance for children	1,720	1,720	1,720
Widow's bereavement allowance	1,720	1,720	1,720
Blind person's allowance	1,080	1,080	1,080

Income tax rates on taxable income (see chapter 2)

Rate	1990/91 Band £	Tax £	1991/92 Band £	Tax £	1992/93 Band £	Tax £
Lower (20%)	—	—	—	—	0–2,000	400
Basic (25%)	0–20,700	5,175	0–23,700	5,925	2,001–23,700	5,425
Higher (40%)	Over 20,700		Over 23,700		Over 23,700	

Car benefit scale rates (see chapter 10)

1990/91

	Car benefit Age of car at end of year	
Original market value up to £19,250	Under 4 years	4 years or more
(a) with a cylinder capacity of:	£	£
up to 1,400 cc	1,700	1,150
1,401 cc to 2,000 cc	2,200	1,500
2,001 cc or more	3,550	2,350
(b) without a cylinder capacity but original market value:		
up to £5,999	1,700	1,150
£6,000 to £8,499	2,200	1,500
£8,500 to £19,250	3,550	2,350
Original market value over £19,250		
£19,251 to £29,000	4,600	3,100
£29,001 or more	7,400	4,900

1991/92

	Car benefit Age of car at end of year	
Original market value up to £19,250	Under 4 years	4 years or more
(a) with a cylinder capacity of:	£	£
up to 1,400 cc	2,050	1,400
1,401 cc to 2,000 cc	2,650	1,800
2,001 cc or more	4,250	2,850
(b) without a cylinder capacity but original market value:		
up to £5,999	2,050	1,400
£6,000 to £8,499	2,650	1,800
£8,500 to £19,250	4,250	2,850
Original market value over £19,250		
£19,251 to £29,000	5,500	3,700
£29,001 or more	8,900	5,900

1992/93

Original market value up to £19,250	Car benefit Age of car at end of year	
	Under 4 years £	4 years or more £
(a) with a cylinder capacity of:		
up to 1,400 cc	2,140	1,460
1,401 cc to 2,000 cc	2,770	1,880
2,001 cc or more	4,440	2,980
(b) without a cylinder capacity but original market value:		
up to £5,999	2,140	1,460
£6,000 to £8,499	2,770	1,880
£8,500 to £19,250	4,440	2,980
Original market value over £19,250		
£19,251 to £29,000	5,750	3,870
£29,001 or more	9,300	6,170

TABLE OF RATES AND ALLOWANCES

Car fuel scale rates (see chapter 10)

1990/91 and 1991/92

	Fuel benefit	
	Petrol	Diesel
(a) with a cylinder capacity of:	£	£
up to 1,400 cc	480	480
1,401 cc to 2,000 cc	600	600
2,001 cc or more	900	900
(b) without a cylinder capacity but original market value:		
up to £5,999	480	480
£6,000 to £8,499	600	600
£8,500 or more	900	900

1992/93

	Fuel benefit	
	Petrol	Diesel
(a) with a cylinder capacity of:	£	£
up to 1,400 cc	500	460
1,401 cc to 2,000 cc	630	460
2,001 cc or more	940	590
(b) without a cylinder capacity but original market value:		
up to £5,999	500	500
£6,000 to £8,499	630	630
£8,500 or more	940	940

Fixed profit car scheme (FPCS) (see chapter 10)

1990/91

cc	First 4,000 business miles	Additional business miles
Up to 1,000	24.5p	9.5p
1,001 to 1,500	30p	11.5p
1,501 to 2,000	34p	13.5p
Over 2,000	43p	16.5p

1991/92

cc	First 4,000 business miles	Additional business miles
Up to 1,000	24.5p	11p
1,001 to 1,500	30p	13p
1,501 to 2,000	34p	16p
Over 2,000	45p	20.5p

1992/93

cc	First 4,000 business miles	Additional business miles
Up to 1,000	25p	14p
1,001 to 1,500	30p	17p
1,501 to 2,000	38p	21p
Over 2,000	51p	27p

Official rate of interest – beneficial loans (see chapter 10)

From 6 June 1992	10.5% p.a.
From 6 March 1992 to 5 June 1992	10.75% p.a.
From 6 October 1991 to 5 March 1992	11.25% p.a.
From 6 August 1991 to 5 October 1991	11.75% p.a.
From 6 July 1991 to 5 August 1991	12.25% p.a.
From 6 May 1991 to 5 July 1991	12.75% p.a.
From 6 April 1991 to 5 May 1991	13.5% p.a.
From 6 March 1991 to 5 April 1991	14.5% p.a.
From 6 November 1990 to 5 March 1991	15.5% p.a.
From 6 November 1989 to 5 November 1990	16.5% p.a.
From 6 July 1989 to 5 November 1989	15.5% p.a.
From 6 January 1989 to 5 July 1989	14.5% p.a.
From 6 October 1988 to 5 January 1989	13.5% p.a.
From 6 August 1988 to 5 October 1988	12% p.a.
From 6 May 1988 to 5 August 1988	9.5% p.a.
From 6 December 1987 to 5 May 1988	10.5% p.a.
From 6 September 1987 to 5 December 1987	11.5% p.a.
From 6 June 1987 to 5 September 1987	10.5% p.a.
From 6 April 1987 to 5 June 1987	11.5% p.a.

Interest on overdue tax/Repayment Supplement (see chapters 2 and 3)

From 6 October 1991	9.25% p.a.
From 6 July 1991 to 5 October 1991	10% p.a.
From 6 May 1991 to 5 July 1991	10.75% p.a.
From 6 March 1991 to 5 May 1991	11.5% p.a.
From 6 November 1990 to 5 March 1991	12.25% p.a.
From 6 November 1989 to 5 November 1990	13% p.a.
From 6 July 1989 to 5 November 1989	12.25% p.a.
From 6 January 1989 to 5 July 1989	11.5% p.a.
From 6 October 1988 to 5 January 1989	10.75% p.a.
From 6 August 1988 to 5 October 1988	9.75% p.a.
From 6 May 1988 to 5 August 1988	7.75% p.a.
From 6 December 1987 to 5 May 1988	8.25% p.a.
From 6 September 1987 to 5 December 1987	9% p.a.
From 6 June 1987 to 5 September 1987	8.25% p.a.
From 6 April 1987 to 5 June 1987	9% p.a.

Corporation tax rates (see chapter 3)

Year beginning	Full rate	Small companies					
		rate	upper profit limit	marginal relief			
				upper profit limit	relief fraction	effective marginal rate	
1 April 1987	35%	27%	£100,000	£500,000	1/50	37%	
1 April 1988	35%	25%	£100,000	£500,000	1/40	37.5%	
1 April 1989	35%	25%	£150,000	£750,000	1/40	37.5%	
1 April 1990	34%	25%	£200,000	£1,000,000	9/400	36.25%	
1 April 1991	33%	25%	£250,000	£1,250,000	1/50	35%	
1 April 1992	33%	25%	£250,000	£1,250,000	1/50	35%	

Capital gains are included in profits and therefore chargeable at the corporation tax rate applicable.

The advance corporation tax (ACT) rate is 1/3rd with effect from 6 April 1988. It was 27/73rds during 1987/88.

Capital gains tax (see chapter 4)

Rate: After 5 April 1988, gains are chargeable to capital gains tax
   (a) for individuals, at the rates that would apply if they were the top slice of income;
   (b) for discretionary and accumulation trusts, at a rate equivalent to the total of the basic and additional rates of income tax (35% for 1992/93);
   (c) for other trusts and for personal representatives, at a rate equivalent to the basic rate of income tax (25% for 1992/93).

Annual exemption (Individuals)		
1990/91, 1989/90 and 1988/89	£5,000
1991/92	£5,500
1992/93	£5,800

Retail prices index (for indexation allowance)

	1982	1983	1984	1985	1986	1987
January		82.61	86.84	91.20	96.25	100.0
February		82.97	87.20	91.94	96.60	100.4
March	79.44	83.12	87.48	92.80	96.73	100.6
April	81.04	84.28	88.64	94.78	97.67	101.8
May	81.62	84.64	88.97	95.21	97.85	101.9
June	81.85	84.84	89.20	95.41	97.79	101.9
July	81.88	85.30	89.10	95.23	97.52	101.8
August	81.90	85.68	89.94	95.49	97.82	102.1
September	81.85	86.06	90.11	95.44	98.30	102.4
October	82.26	86.36	90.67	95.69	98.45	102.9
November	82.66	86.67	90.95	95.92	99.29	103.4
December	82.51	86.89	90.87	96.05	99.62	103.3

	1988	1989	1990	1991	1992
January	103.3	111.0	119.5	130.2	135.6
February	103.7	111.8	120.2	130.9	136.3
March	104.1	112.3	121.4	131.4	136.7
April	105.8	114.3	125.1	133.1	138.8
May	106.2	115.0	126.2	133.5	139.3
June	106.6	115.4	126.7	134.1	139.3
July	106.7	115.5	126.8	133.8	
August	107.9	115.8	128.1	134.1	
September	108.4	116.6	129.3	134.6	
October	109.5	117.5	130.3	135.1	
November	110.0	118.5	130.0	135.6	
December	110.3	118.8	129.9	135.7	

The index was re-referenced in January 1987 from 394.5 to 100. The figures above which relate to months before January 1987 have been worked back from the new base and are not, therefore, those produced at the time by the Department of Employment.

National insurance contribution rates

Employers and employees (see chapter 13)

	6/4/91 –5/4/92	6/4/92 –5/4/93
Lower earnings limit per week (LEL)	£52.00	£54.00
Upper earnings limit per week (UEL)	£390.00	£405.00

Employees pay no contributions if their weekly earnings are below LEL. Otherwise, they are liable as below.

Not contracted out
Employee

—earnings up to LEL	2.0%	2.0%
—balance of earnings up to UEL	9.0%	9.0%

Employer (% payable on **all** earnings)

—earnings up to LEL	—	—
—earnings LEL to £89.99 pw (1991/92 LEL to £84.99 pw)	4.6%	4.6%
—earnings £90 to £134.99 pw (1991/92 £85.00 to £129.99 pw)	6.6%	6.6%
—earnings £135.00 to £189.99 pw (1991/92 £130.00 to £184.99 pw)	8.6%	8.6%
—earnings £190.00 pw and above (1991/92 £185 pw and above)	10.4%	10.4%

Contracted out
Reduction in 'not contracted out' contributions
  (but applied only to part of earnings falling
  between LEL and UEL)

—employee	2.0%	2.0%
—employer	3.8%	3.8%

Reduced rate for certain married women and widows
% payable on **all** earnings up to UEL

providing earnings exceed LEL	3.85%	3.85%

Self-employed (see chapter 24)

	1991/92	1992/93
Class 2 contributions per week	£5.15	£5.35
Class 4 contributions		
rate	6.3%	6.3%
on profits between	£5,900 and £20,280	£6,120 and £21,060

TABLE OF RATES AND ALLOWANCES

Employers' national insurance contributions on company cars and fuel (see chapter 13)

1991/92 (annual contributions due)

Cars under four years old at 5/4/92

	Annual business mileage		
	2,500 or less	2,501–17,999	18,000 and above
Original market value up to £19,250:			
up to 1,400 cc	£319.80	£213.20	£106.60
1,401 cc to 2,000 cc	£413.40	£275.60	£137.80
over 2,000 cc	£663.00	£442.00	£221.00
Original market value over £19,250:			
£19,251 to £29,000	£858.00	£572.00	£286.00
£29,001 or more	£1,388.40	£925.60	£462.80

Cars over four years old at 5/4/92

	Annual business mileage		
	2,500 or less	2,501–17,999	18,000 and above
Original market value up to £19,250:			
up to 1,400 cc	£218.40	£145.60	£72.80
1,401 cc to 2,000 cc	£280.80	£187.20	£93.60
over 2,000 cc	£444.60	£296.40	£148.20
Original market value over £19,250:			
£19,251 to £29,000	£577.20	£384.80	£192.40
£29,001 or more	£920.40	£613.60	£306.80

Fuel

	Annual business mileage	
	Below 18,000	18,000 and above
Up to 1,400 cc	£49.92	£24.96
1,401 cc to 2,000 cc	£62.40	£31.20
Over 2,000 cc	£93.60	£46.80

1992/93 (annual contributions due)

Cars under four years old at 5/4/93

	Annual business mileage		
	2,500 or less	2,501–17,999	18,000 and above
Original market value up to £19,250:			
up to 1,400 cc	£333.84	£222.56	£111.28
1,401 cc to 2,000 cc	£432.12	£288.08	£144.04
over 2,000 cc	£692.64	£461.76	£230.88
Original market value over £19,250:			
£19,251 to £29,000	£897.00	£598.00	£299.00
£29,001 or more	£1,450.80	£967.20	£483.60

Cars over four years old at 5/4/93

	Annual business mileage		
	2,500 or less	2,501–17,999	18,000 and above
Original market value up to £19,250:			
up to 1,400 cc	£227.76	£151.84	£75.92
1,401 cc to 2,000 cc	£293.28	£195.52	£97.76
over 2,000 cc	£464.88	£309.92	£154.96
Original market value over £19,250:			
£19,251 to £29,000	£603.72	£402.48	£201.24
£29,001 or more	£962.52	£641.68	£320.84

Fuel (petrol)

	Annual business mileage	
	Below 18,000	18,000 and above
Up to 1,400 cc	£52.00	£26.00
1,401 cc to 2,000 cc	£65.52	£32.76
Over 2,000 cc	£97.76	£48.88

Fuel (diesel)

	Annual business mileage	
	Below 18,000	18,000 and above
Up to 2,000 cc	£47.84	£23.92
Over 2,000 cc	£61.36	£30.68

Statutory sick pay from 6 April 1992 (see chapter 14)

Average weekly earnings	£190.00 and over	£54.00–£189.99
SSP weekly rate	£52.50	£45.30

Statutory maternity pay from 6 April 1992 (see chapter 14)

Higher rate	9/10ths of employee's average weekly earnings
Lower rate	£46.30 per week

Main state benefits (see chapter 10)

Taxable (weekly rates)	9.4.90 –7.4.91 £	8.4.91 –5.4.92 £	From 6.4.92 £
Retirement pension*			
—single	46.90	52.00	54.15
—wife non-contributor	28.20	31.25	32.55
Old person's pension*			
—higher rate	28.20	31.25	32.55
Widow's benefits			
—widowed mother's allowance	46.90	52.00	54.15
—widow's pension (standard rate)	46.90	52.00	54.15
Industrial death benefit*** widow's pension			
—higher permanent rate	46.90	52.00	54.15
—lower permanent rate	14.07	15.60	16.25
Invalidity allowance**			
—higher rate	10.00	11.10	11.55
—middle rate	6.20	6.90	7.20
—lower rate	3.10	3.45	3.60
Invalid care allowance*			
—single	28.20	31.25	32.55
—adult dependant	16.85	18.70	19.45
Unemployment benefit under pension age			
—single	37.35	41.40	43.10
—adult dependant	23.05	25.55	26.60
over pension age			
—single	46.90	52.00	54.15
—adult dependant	28.20	31.25	32.55

Main state benefits (see chapter 10) (continued)

Non-taxable (weekly rates)	9.4.90 –7.4.91 £	8.4.91 –5.4.92 £	From 6.4.92 £
Child benefit			
—eldest child	7.25	8.25/9.25†	9.65
—other children	7.25	7.25/7.50†	7.80
Maternity allowance	35.70	40.60	42.25
One parent benefit	5.60	5.60	5.85
Child addition to benefits	9.65	10.70	10.85
Sickness benefit			
under pension age			
—single	35.70	39.60	41.20
—adult dependant	22.10	24.50	25.50
over pension age			
—single	45.00	49.90	51.95
—adult dependant	27.00	29.95	31.20
Mobility allowance	26.25	29.10	—
Disability living allowance			
care component			
—higher rate	—	—	43.35
—middle rate	—	—	28.95
—lower rate	—	—	11.55
mobility component			
—higher rate	—	—	30.30
—lower rate	—	—	11.55
Attendance allowance			
—higher rate	37.55	41.65	43.35
—lower rate	25.05	27.80	28.95
Invalidity pension			
—single	46.90	52.00	54.15
—adult dependant	28.20	31.25	32.55
Severe disablement allowance*			
—single (standard rate)	28.20	31.25	32.55
—adult dependant	16.85	18.70	19.45

* A taxable age addition of 25p per week is payable to persons aged 80 or over with any one of these benefits.
** Taxable only if paid with retirement pension.
*** For deaths before 11 April 1988 only.
† Higher rates apply after 6 October 1991.

NB: This table does not include the following income-related benefits:

income support
family credit
housing benefit
community charge benefit
disability working allowance

Value added tax (see chapter 7)

Standard rate (from 1/4/91)   17.5%

Registration threshold taxable supplies	from 20/3/91	from 11/3/92
—in last four quarters	More than £35,000	More than £36,600
—in next 30 days	More than £35,000	More than £36,600

Deregistration limits taxable supplies	from 1/5/91	from 1/5/92
—in the next year	£33,600 or less	£35,100 or less

VAT – fuel scale rates – private motoring (from 6/4/92)

Return period	Car's cc	Scale benefit (VAT inclusive)	Vat @ 17.5%
Petrol		£	£
Quarterly	to 1,400	125	18.62
	1,401–2,000	158	23.53
	over 2,000	235	35.00
Monthly	to 1,400	42	6.26
	1,401–2,000	53	7.89
	over 2,000	78	11.62
Diesel			
Quarterly	to 2,000	115	17.13
	over 2,000	148	22.04
Monthly	to 2,000	38	5.66
	over 2,000	49	7.30

Where business mileage is at least 4,500 per quarter or 1,500 per month, scale charge is approximately halved.

Inheritance tax (see chapter 5)

Tables of rates (from 18/3/86)

Transfers on and after 18/3/86 and before 17/3/87

Cumulative chargeable transfers (gross)	On death Rate %	On death Cumulative total tax	Lifetime transfers Rate %	Lifetime transfers Cumulative total tax
0– £71,000	Nil	Nil	Nil	Nil
£71,000– £95,000	30	£7,200	15	£3,600
£95,000–£129,000	35	£19,100	17.5	£9,550
£129,000–£164,000	40	£33,100	20	£16,550
£164,000–£206,000	45	£52,000	22.5	£26,000
£206,000–£257,000	50	£77,500	25	£38,750
£257,000–£317,000	55	£110,500	27.5	£55,250
£317,000 and above	60		30	

Transfers on and after 17/3/87 and before 15/3/88

Cumulative chargeable transfers (gross)	On death Rate %	On death Cumulative total tax	Lifetime transfers Rate %	Lifetime transfers Cumulative total tax
0– £90,000	Nil	Nil	Nil	Nil
£90,000–£140,000	30	£15,000	15	£7,500
£140,000–£220,000	40	£47,000	20	£23,500
£220,000–£330,000	50	£102,000	25	£51,000
£330,000 and above	60		30	

From 15 March 1988, there has been a single rate of inheritance tax of 40% (20% for lifetime transfers), applicable to the excess of gross cumulative chargeable transfers over a 'nil rate' threshold. The thresholds since that date have been as follows:

Transfers on and after 15/3/88 and before 6/4/89	£110,000
Transfers on and after 6/4/89 and before 6/4/90	£118,000
Transfers on and after 6/4/90 and before 6/4/91	£128,000
Transfers on and after 6/4/91 and before 10/3/92	£140,000
Transfers on and after 10/3/92	£150,000

Main Tax Changes

Because of the General Election there have been two Finance Acts this year. There are a large number of changes to virtually all the taxes, which are outlined below. General points for each tax are shown separately, and points that relate to specific chapters bear the same chapter heading.

March 1993 will be the last Spring Budget. Budgets will thereafter be introduced in December each year, commencing December 1993, with the changes becoming law around April/May of the following year. This should enable PAYE increases in personal allowances to be introduced from the beginning of the tax year.

Income tax

This year sees the re-introduction of a reduced rate of tax, the first £2,000 of taxable income of individuals being charged at the lower rate of 20%. The lower rate does not apply to personal representatives or to trustees. The basic rate remains unchanged at 25% and the higher rate at 40%, but the basic rate band has been reduced from £23,700 to £21,700, so that higher rate tax still applies to taxable income above £23,700.

The tax deduction rate for any payments from which tax is deducted at source is still 25%, and non-taxpayers and those liable at only 20% will still be able to retain the 25% tax deducted from MIRAS interest, employees' personal pension contributions, private medical insurance premiums for those over 60 and qualifying payments by trainees for vocational training.

The under 65s married couple's allowance, and allowances linked to it, i.e. additional personal allowance for single parents, widow's bereavement allowance and maintenance relief for divorced and separated couples, have again been frozen at £1,720 but other personal allowances have been increased as shown on page xix.

From 1993/94 all or half of the basic married couple's allowance (not any age addition) will be able to be transferred to a wife. If you want to do this for 1993/94, you need to make a claim *before* 6 April 1993.

Corporation tax

The corporation tax rates for the year to 31 March 1993 remain unchanged at 25% on profits of up to £250,000 and 33% on profits of over £1,250,000 (reduced in both cases where there are associated companies), with an effective marginal rate of 35% on profits lying between those two figures.

The 'Pay and File' system is expected to apply to accounts ending after 30 September 1993. Companies will have to pay tax, estimated if necessary, nine months after the end of the accounting period, or suffer interest on the amount they should have paid, and file their accounts within twelve months after the end of the accounting period, or be liable to penalties for late filing.

Capital gains tax

The annual exemption is increased from £5,500 to £5,800 for individuals and personal representatives and from £2,750 to £2,900 for most trusts. Gains of individuals are charged at their marginal income tax rate, and thus may be charged at 20% to the extent that taxable income is below £2,000. Discretionary trusts normally pay tax at 35% and other trusts at 25%.

Inheritance tax

For transfers on and after 10 March 1992, the inheritance tax nil rate threshold is increased from £140,000 to £150,000, the tax rate on the excess over that amount remaining at 40%.

From the same date, the rates of business and agricultural property relief have been increased from 50% and 30% to 100% and 50%, with shares on the Unlisted Securities Market being treated in the same way as other unquoted securities for these reliefs.

Stamp duty

The date for the abolition of most stamp duties has still not been fixed but it is now expected to be around April 1993. Stamp duty will continue to apply to land and buildings and charges on the premium and rent of new leases. The increase from £30,000 to £250,000 in the threshold for certified transactions only applied to documents executed between 20 December 1991 and 19 August 1992 inclusive.

Value added tax

From 11 March 1992, the VAT registration threshold is increased from £35,000 to £36,600, and the de-registration limit is increased from £33,600 to £35,100 from 1 May 1992.

The maximum rate of default surcharge has been reduced from 30% to 20% for defaults on or after 1 April 1992, and the serious misdeclaration penalty for assessments raised on or after 11 March 1992 is reduced from 20% to 15%. In addition the penalty will not normally be imposed unless the net tax underdeclared or over-reclaimed exceeds £2,000.

The partial exemption rules have been changed so that the input tax on overheads is recovered according to the values of taxable and total supplies. There is now a single monthly de minimis limit of £600 for exempt supplies.

Employers will not have to account for VAT where employees receive a lower salary in return for private use of a company car, but VAT will apply where employees make a payment for private use.

A large number of changes will apply from 1 January 1993 because of the introduction of the EC Single Market.

Poll tax and business rates (chapter 8)
The uniform business rate for 1992/93 is 40.2p. The transitional increases in the uniform business rate will not be made in 1992/93, and the increase will be limited to the rate of inflation. Rates reductions that are being phased in will be more generous in 1992/93, and the full balance of the reduction will be given in 1993/94. Transitional relief will no longer be lost on a change of occupier.

Dealing with the Revenue (chapter 9)
From 6 April 1992, the turnover limit below which you can send three-line accounts to the Revenue is increased from £10,000 to £15,000.

Employments—income chargeable and allowable deductions (chapter 10)
For 1992/93 the scale charges for employees' private use of an employer's car and for private petrol are increased as shown on pages xxi and xxii. A lower scale charge has been introduced for diesel fuel. It is intended to base the scale charges on car values rather than engine sizes, and the change is expected to take effect from 6 April 1993. The tax-free mileage allowances under the Fixed Profit Car Scheme have been increased as shown on page xxiii.

The average monthly limit of tax and national insurance payments which permits employers to pay their PAYE quarterly instead of monthly is increased from £400 to £450 from 6 April 1992.

Interest will be charged from 6 April 1993 on unpaid PAYE and national insurance contributions for 1992/93 that remain outstanding after 19 April 1993.

National insurance contributions (chapters 13 and 24)
National insurance contributions and earnings and profit levels are increased as shown on page xxvii. The Class 1A contributions payable by employers on the provision of cars and fuel for employees' private use are shown on pages xxviii and xxix.

The combined employer/employee contracting-out rebate is to be reduced from 5.8% to 4.8% from 6 April 1993.

Statutory sick pay and statutory maternity pay (chapter 14)
The limit of total national insurance payments in 1991/92 entitling an employer to recover 100% of SSP in 1992/93 (80% for the first six weeks' incapacity) is increased from £15,000 to £16,000.

Pension schemes (chapters 16 and 17)
The pension scheme earnings cap (up to which earnings may attract tax relief and on which occupational pensions are based) is increased from £71,400 to £75,000 from 6 April 1992.

Capital allowances (chapter 22)
The 'expensive cars' limit is increased from £8,000 to £12,000 for cars bought after 10 March 1992, giving a maximum annual writing-down allowance of £3,000. The restriction on allowable deductions for car lease payments is similarly linked to a figure of £12,000.

For expenditure on or after 10 March 1992, capital expenditure on licensed computer software qualifies for plant and machinery allowances.

For enterprise zone buildings first used on or after 16 December 1991, the 100% allowance will be available to someone buying a building within two years of first use.

Encouraging business efficiency (chapter 29)
The business expansion scheme is to be withdrawn at the end of 1993 and will not apply to shares issued after that time. In the meantime the rules have been altered to facilitate mortgage rescue schemes.

Your family home (chapter 30)
A new 'rent a room' relief has been introduced from 6 April 1992, under which owner-occupiers and leasehold tenants will be exempt from tax on rent of up to £3,250 from letting furnished rooms in their homes.

A country life: farms and woodlands (chapter 31)
From 1 January 1993, farmers will be able to opt to become 'flat rate farmers', so that they need not register for VAT but will be able to add a fixed flat rate percentage to their sale prices to compensate for the input VAT they have suffered. Those to whom they sell will be able to recover the compensation amount as if it were VAT.

Husband, wife and children (chapter 33)
There are a number of points of detail to be aware of concerning the right from 1993/94 to transfer all or half of the basic married couple's allowance to the wife.

Investing in stocks and shares (chapter 38)
From 6 April 1992, investors can put the full £6,000 permitted Personal Equity Plan investment into qualifying unit and investment trusts.

The overseas element (chapter 41)
The law of domicile is shortly to be changed, and it will be easier to change your domicile when you go abroad, but more difficult to retain a foreign domicile when you come to live in the UK.

Various changes have been made as a result of bringing UK law into line with EC directives, and as a result of the introduction of the Single Market from 1 January 1993.

Charities and charitable trusts (chapter 43)
The limit for tax-allowable one-off donations to charity by individuals and close companies is reduced from £600 to £400 for gifts on or after 7 May 1992.

1
Introduction

Tax is a topic that rarely excites much enthusiasm, but most people feel they need to know something about it. If you are an employee you may want to know why some extra earnings in a particular week or month seem to get heavily taxed, or how the taxman arrives at your tax code. If you are a pensioner with a pension from your employer, you may feel that what you get on one hand as an increase in your state pension is taken away on the other by extra tax on your occupational pension. In these difficult economic days, many businessmen feel they can no longer leave tax entirely to their accountants and increasingly want to know more about it, to see if savings can be made by arranging things differently. And if you are an accountant you are hard pressed to keep up with the multitude of changes in all directions, not just tax.

Clearly one relatively short book cannot provide the answer to everyone's problems. What this guide can do, however, is to explain in straightforward terms how tax liabilities are calculated and what reliefs and deductions are available. It also highlights areas where there are several taxes to be considered in relation to a single transaction. One of the obvious areas is if you are a self-employed individual who is going to 'go limited'. You need to think about income tax, capital gains tax, value added tax, stamp duty, inheritance tax and the national insurance implications. Chapter 27 considers all these aspects together. Other chapters adopt a similar approach.

One of the aims of the Government in recent years has been to simplify the tax system. Another objective has been to reduce the level of direct taxation. This year has seen the reintroduction of a lower rate of tax on the first slice of taxable income. This in itself adds complexity to the system, so that the second objective conflicts with the first. And even though direct taxes are reduced, much of the Government's revenue is raised through the indirect taxes, notably value added tax. Major changes lie ahead on the value added tax front, because of the introduction of the Single Market on 1 January 1993. The value added tax law in this country must follow the various European Community directives, and if there is any conflict, European law takes precedence. All of this makes it more difficult for progress to be made on tax simplification.

Nevertheless, proposals for streamlining the tax treatment in various areas are still being introduced. Companies will be moving on to a 'Pay and File' system in 1993, which broadly requires them to pay tax (estimated if necessary) nine months after the end of the accounting period, and file their accounts not later than twelve months after the end of the period. It is also intended that the tax system for the self-employed should be streamlined, with something similar to 'Pay and File' being introduced for individuals. This is currently the subject of a consultation process, and no firm proposals have yet been put forward. It is, however, the clear intention that the complicated 'previous year basis of assessment' that is currently used for the self-employed will come to an end.

Whatever changes are made, taxes will remain one of life's certainties, and they will make their impact in some form or another on all of us. This book will help you to understand how the tax system works, how it will affect you in particular situations, such as starting a new business or changing jobs, and how the tax rules can be used to your best advantage. The first part of the book contains a brief outline of all the various taxes, including the poll tax. The following sections deal with specific subject areas, such as 'Employment', 'Pensions', 'Tax and the family', 'Choosing your investment' and 'Trades, professions and vocations'. Any special tax saving opportunities or possible problems are highlighted in the form of 'Tax points' at the end of each chapter.

Avoiding tax is not the same as illegally evading tax. If you break the law, you can not only be required to pay the tax you should have paid plus interest and penalties, but you could be facing a criminal prosecution. You must therefore make sure that you seek professional advice where appropriate.

For those who need to look at a topic in more depth, there are statutory references to help track down the relevant legislation. The main statutes are the Income and Corporation Taxes Act 1988, the Taxation of Chargeable Gains Act 1992, the Value Added Tax Act 1983, the Inheritance Tax Act 1984 and the Capital Allowances Act 1990. In addition there are annual Finance Acts (sometimes, as this year, two in a year) which alter some of the existing provisions and bring in new ones, and various statutory instruments. A major source of information is the explanatory booklets put out by the various Government Departments. And there are also published Statements of Practice and Extra-statutory Concessions, which explain the Revenue's views on particular aspects and sometimes allow matters to be treated more sympathetically than the strict letter of the law allows. These are, however, based on the Revenue's views of what the law means, and in many instances the wording of the relevant statutory provision is not clear. Alternatively, the meaning of the law may not be in doubt, but the facts of the case may be. You may therefore have a disagreement with the Revenue on the meaning of the law, or on establishing facts, or on a mixture of the two.

You may for example live in mixed business and private accommodation and you and the tax inspector may not be able to agree on the business proportion of your expenditure. This is a dispute on a matter of fact. On the other hand, you may claim a deduction from your wages for additional accommodation and living expenses incurred when your work requires you to live away from home for long periods. There will be no dispute about how much you have spent, but the inspector may consider that the expense is not 'wholly, exclusively and necessarily incurred in the performance of the duties of the employment'. This is a question of law, and it has in fact been the subject of an appeal which the Revenue won, on the grounds that the expenditure was not incurred 'in the performance of the duties of the employment' but to put the employee in a position to perform his duties, which is not the same thing. If a dispute cannot be resolved by negotiation, the Revenue will issue an assessment based on their view, but you have the right to appeal against the assessment to the Appeal Commissioners. There are two types of Commissioners, the General Commissioners, who are usually local business people acting in a voluntary unpaid capacity, and the Special Commissioners, who are full-time civil servants based in London who travel on circuit to the different parts of the country. Most appeals are heard by the General Commissioners, but some specialised appeals have to go to the Special Commissioners. You cannot make a non-specialised appeal to the Special Commissioners unless there are points in dispute. If it is merely a delay appeal where the Revenue have not received the information needed to settle it, it will be heard by the General Commissioners. The Commissioners' decisions are not currently reported, but in 1993 it is expected that selected decisions of the Special Commissioners will be published, and provisions will be introduced to enable the Special Commissioners (not the General Commissioners) to award costs where one party to the appeal has acted unreasonably.

The distinction between questions of law and fact is important, because what the Appeal Commissioners decide on questions of fact is generally binding on both the taxpayer and the Revenue. Their decisions on points of law, however, can be referred by the losing party to the High Court, then to the Court of Appeal (or the equivalent Scottish or Irish Courts) and finally, if leave is granted, to the House of Lords. You should, however, think very carefully before taking an appeal on a question of law to the Commissioners, because it may take a very long time before it is settled, it will cost you a lot of time and money, and at the end of the day you may find yourself on the losing side with the Revenue's costs to pay as well. The Revenue will not always look for costs to be awarded to them, and will sometimes agree in advance that they will pay their own costs in any event, if the case deals with a point of principle that is of widespread importance. But that could still leave you with your own costs to bear. In addition, many taxpayer victories are short-lived, because the law is then changed to what the Revenue think it ought to be.

The Revenue have yet another weapon in their armoury, in that they can challenge 'a series of transactions with a tax avoidance motive' so that any intermediate steps are ignored and only the end result is taken into account. This has not only blocked some complicated tax avoidance schemes, but has also led to the need for caution to be exercised even when considering modest tax-saving plans. Advance planning by way of a series of trans-actions is still possible providing they are not so pre-planned and inter-linked that they can only really be regarded as a single transaction.

The aim of this book is to help you to understand the tax system, and to organise your affairs in such a way that the taxman puts 'the smallest possible shovel into your stores'. A Swedish economist has recently worked out that 24 May is 'Tax Freedom Day' in the UK in 1992, by which he means that the average person will pay the proportion of his income represented by the period from 1 January to 23 May to the taxman and the rest is his own. Although that may be as useful as telling you that on average you are fine when you have one hand in the fire and the other in an ice-bucket, it obviously makes sense to aim at bringing your own particular 'Tax Freedom Day' forward.

2
Income tax: general principles

Basis of charge

A judge once said 'Income tax, if I may be pardoned for saying so, is a tax on income. It is not meant to be a tax on anything else'. That begs the question of what 'income' means. Nowhere in the tax legislation is there a single definition. Instead, the legislation classifies amounts received under various headings, called Schedules (sometimes subdivided into 'Cases'), and an item must come within one of these headings to be charged as income. Sometimes the tax law requires capital receipts to be treated as income. For example, when a landlord charges a tenant a lump sum for granting him a lease for up to fifty years, part of the lump sum is taxed as income. But unless there is a specific provision, an amount cannot be charged to income tax unless it has the quality of income rather than capital. There is a separate heading, Schedule D, Case VI, which deals with items of an income nature that are not covered elsewhere, and also certain capital items that the legislation regards as income.

The distinction between income and capital used to be very important because the top income tax rate was twice as much as the capital gains tax rate. From 6 April 1988, gains have been charged at the same rates as income, after an exemption for the first slice, currently £5,800 (see chapter 4).

Exempt income

Certain types of income are specifically exempt from tax, notably the following, which are dealt with in the chapter indicated:

	Chapter
The first £70 interest (husband and wife £70 each) from national savings bank ordinary accounts.	37
Increase in value of national savings certificates.	36
Premium bond prizes.	36
Bonuses and profits on life assurance policies (subject to detailed anti-avoidance rules).	40
The capital part of the yearly amount received from a purchased life annuity.	34

Some social security benefits (but others are taxable).	10
Prizes and bettings winnings.	4
Save As You Earn account bonuses.	36
Shares allocated to you by your employer under an approved profit sharing scheme.	11
Profit-related pay, up to a maximum of £4,000.	12
Local authority home improvement grants.	
Housing benefit.	
Educational grants and scholarships.	
Statutory redundancy pay, pay in lieu of notice and certain larger amounts received from your employer on termination of your employment.	15
Maintenance payments under arrangements made after 14 March 1988, and the first £1,720 (for 1992/93) of maintenance payments under earlier arrangements.	33

Persons chargeable

Each individual, whether man, woman or child, is chargeable in respect of his/her own income, although a child's income may be treated as the parent's if it derives from the parent (see page 378). Before 6 April 1990 the income of a married woman was normally treated as her husband's income. Personal representatives and trustees are chargeable in respect of estate and trust income. Companies pay corporation tax instead of income tax (see chapter 3).

Income tax is charged broadly on the income of UK residents, whether it arises in the UK or abroad, subject to certain deductions for earnings abroad and for individuals who are not ordinarily resident or not domiciled in the UK. Non-residents are liable to income tax only on income that arises in the UK. Double tax relief is available where income is taxed both in the UK and abroad. For detailed provisions on the overseas aspect, see chapter 41.

Calculation of taxable income

Income is classified under various headings called 'Schedules', some of the schedules being subdivided into 'Cases'. Each schedule has its own rules as to how income is calculated and what deductions are allowed.

When the total income from all sources has been calculated, certain payments, called charges on income, may be deducted, and also certain allowances, such as the personal allowance or married couple's allowance. The balance is taxable at the rates in the table on page xix.

The tax due is accounted for in various ways, some being deducted at source before the income is received, some collected by employers through the PAYE system and some collected directly from the taxpayer.

The income tax year runs from 6 April in one year to 5 April in the next, but the income charged to tax in any tax year is not always the amount arising during that tax year because of the different rules for measuring different types of income. The total income arrived at using these different rules is known as 'statutory total income'.

The detailed rules for calculating income from the various sources are dealt with in the appropriate chapters, but are summarised in the following table. Note that there is no Schedule B. It was a charge on the occupation of woodlands, but it was abolished from 6 April 1988 (see chapter 31).

Schedule and Case	Type of income	Basis of assessment	Normal due date of payment
Schedule A	Rents from UK land and buildings	Rent due in tax year, whether received or not, less allowable expenses	1 January in tax year
Schedule C	Income from UK and foreign Government Stocks, paid through UK paying agent such as a bank	Income received in the tax year	Basic rate tax deducted by payer and accounted for to the Revenue. Excess over basic rate due 1 December in next tax year
Schedule D			
Case I	Profits of trade	Normally profits of accounting year ended in previous tax year, with special rules for opening and closing years, on change of accounting date and on change of partners	Equal instalments on 1 January in tax year and 1 July following
Case II	Profits of profession or vocation		
Case III	Interest, annuities or other annual amounts received	Income received in tax year where tax is deducted by the payer or where interest is received gross from a building society or bank (other than the National Savings Bank). For other interest received gross, including National	As for Schedule C if tax is deducted at source, otherwise 1 January in tax year

Schedule and Case	Type of income	Basis of assessment	Normal due date of payment
		Savings Bank interest, normally the amount received or credited in the previous tax year, with special rules for opening and closing years. There is no relief for expenses	
Case IV	Income from foreign securities ⎤	Normally the amount arising in previous tax year with special rules for opening and closing years, subject to percentage deductions where the income is from a pension. Based on amount remitted to UK if taxpayer resident but not ordinarily resident and/or not domiciled in UK	Normally 1 January in year of assessment but as for Case I for foreign businesses
Case V	Income from foreign possessions ⎦		
Case VI	Income not assessable under any other Schedule or Case	Profits or gains arising in the tax year, less appropriate expenses	1 January in tax year
Schedule E			
Case I	Earnings of employee resident and ordinarily resident in UK, other than 'foreign emoluments' earned wholly abroad. (Foreign emoluments are earnings of non-UK-domiciled employee from	All earnings in the tax year whether duties are performed in the UK or abroad, but special rules apply to earnings during long absences abroad	Normally under PAYE system, otherwise 30 days after issue of assessment, or as provided for the particular item

2 INCOME TAX: GENERAL PRINCIPLES

Schedule and Case	Type of income	Basis of assessment	Normal due date of payment
	non-UK-resident employer)		
Case II	Earnings of employee not resident or resident but not ordinarily resident in UK	Earnings for UK duties	PAYE system if possible, otherwise collected directly, usually by 4 instalments
Case III	'Foreign emoluments' earned wholly abroad by person resident and ordinarily resident in UK	Remittances in tax year. No charge if not remitted	Tax is normally collected after end of tax year
	Earnings abroad of person resident but not ordinarily resident in UK		
Schedule F	Dividends and distributions of UK-resident company	Dividends and distributions in the tax year plus accompanying tax credits	Tax credit covers basic rate tax. Excess over basic rate due 1 December following tax year

Often it is not possible to issue assessments in time for tax to be paid by the dates in the above table. Where assessments are issued late, the due date of payment of tax is thirty days after the issue of the assessment. To speed up the collection of tax, the Revenue will often charge tax on a provisional basis and then make the appropriate adjustments when the true figures are known.

Interest on loans to companies (sometimes called debentures) and most government stocks is received after deduction of tax. The same applies from 6 April 1991 to interest received from building societies and banks (other than the National Savings Bank) unless the investor certifies that he is entitled to receive interest gross (for details, see chapter 37). The main other items of interest received before deduction of tax are National Savings Bank interest, interest on 3½% War Loan and interest on loans by one private individual to another.

Charges on income and other deductions

These are payments you have made that are treated under the tax rules as allowable deductions in arriving at your taxable income. The main items are:

Allowable interest payments (see page 12).

Maintenance payments to former or separated spouse (maximum deduction for 1992/93—£1,720, unless obligation existed at 15 March 1988).

One half of class 4 national insurance contributions paid by the self-employed.

Covenanted payments to charity, and gifts to charity of at least £400 each, net of tax (£600 net for gifts before 7 May 1992).

Private medical insurance premiums paid by or on behalf of those aged 60 and over and their spouses (from 6 April 1990).

Payments by individuals for their own vocational training (from 6 April 1992—see chapter 10).

Before 15 March 1988, most non-charitable covenants also qualified for tax relief. The same applied to maintenance payments between divorced or separated couples or to their children. Relief is still available for non-charitable covenants entered into on or before 14 March 1988 and for maintenance payments to children or to a former or separated spouse where there was an existing obligation at 15 March 1988 (see chapters 33 and 34).

You save tax on charges at your highest rate of tax except for mortgage interest (from 6 April 1991) and non-charitable covenants, which do not qualify for higher rate relief.

Some charges are paid in full, and you get relief by having your tax code or income tax assessment adjusted. Other charges are paid net of basic rate tax and they do not normally affect the tax you pay unless you are liable to tax at the 40% rate, in which case you will get any extra relief to which you are entitled by an adjustment in your coding or income tax assessment. The way the Revenue give you the extra relief is by increasing the band of income chargeable at the basic rate. The end result is that the amount of tax you suffer is the same whether charges are paid net or gross. See example 1.

Charges that are paid net of basic rate tax are:

Interest under the MIRAS scheme (mortgage interest relief at source).

Covenanted payments and qualifying gifts to charity.

Payments under pre-15 March 1988 covenants.

Private medical insurance premiums.

Payments for qualifying vocational training (from 6 April 1992).

Charges that are paid in full are:

Class 4 national insurance contributions.

Maintenance payments, under arrangements made both before and after 14 March 1988 (but see page 383 for exceptions).

Allowable interest outside the MIRAS scheme.

Example 1	£1,600 maintenance paid in full		£1,600 gross, £1,200 net, covenanted payment to charity	
Income	28,845		28,845	
Less charges	1,600			
	27,245		28,845	
Personal reliefs, say	3,445		3,445	
Taxable income	23,800		25,400	
Tax payable				
At lower rate	2,000 @ 20%	400	2,000 @20%	400
At basic rate	21,700 @ 25%	5,425	21,700 ⎱@25%	5,825
Extension re charitable covenant			1,600 ⎰	
Balance of	100 @ 40%	40	100 @40%	40
	23,800		25,400	
		5,865		6,265
Less retained when paying charitable covenant £1,600 @ 25%		—		400
Net tax suffered		£5,865		£5,865

Allowing you to deduct tax when paying charges on income is a convenient way of giving you tax relief without the Revenue getting directly involved. You are, however, not entitled to that tax relief unless in the first place you are a taxpayer up to that amount. If you are not, the Revenue will issue an assessment under TA 1988, s 350 to recover from you any tax relief you have deducted to which you are not entitled. This does not apply to the basic rate tax deducted under the MIRAS scheme, from private medical insurance premiums and from qualifying payments for vocational training (from 6 April 1992), which may be retained whether you are a taxpayer or not.

If you are self-employed, or are not in your employer's pension scheme, you may pay premiums under a personal pension policy. Such premiums are deductible from your earnings and are not a charge on your general income. Self-employed people pay the premiums gross and obtain a deduction against their taxable profits. But if you are an employee, the premiums are paid net of basic rate tax in the same way as MIRAS interest, and any higher rate relief you are entitled to is given by coding adjustment. You may also retain the tax deducted whether you are a taxpayer or not. For the detailed provisions, see chapter 17.

Allowable interest (TA 1988, ss 353–379)

Not all interest payments are deductible in calculating taxable income. Most allowable interest payments are dealt with in context in the appropriate chapters, but they can be summarised as follows:

(a) On up to £30,000 of borrowing for purchase of your only or main residence in the UK, or of a home for future occupation if you live in job-related accommodation (see chapter 30). From 6 April 1991, relief is given only at the basic rate of tax and not at the higher rate.

(b) Bridging loans when you change your only or main residence, up to £30,000, in addition to (a) above, strictly for a period of one year, but generally extended by Revenue concession to two years (see chapter 30). Relief is again restricted to the basic rate, but see chapter 30 for special rules for pre-6 April 1991 loans.

(c) On borrowing for purchase or improvement of property in the UK let for more than 26 weeks out of 52 and, when not so let, available for letting or not available because of repairs or improvements or use by owner as qualifying main residence. The interest is allowed as a deduction from rent and not as a charge on general income. (Less restrictive rules apply to furnished holiday lettings – see page 365.)

(d) On a loan for the purchase of a partnership share, for introducing capital to a partnership or for lending money to it, providing that you are not a limited partner and providing you are still a partner when the interest is paid (see pages 231 and 269).

(e) On a loan to buy shares in or lend money to a trading company controlled by its directors or by five or fewer people, so long as, at the time the interest is paid, either you own more than 5% of the issued ordinary share capital or you own any part of the ordinary share capital, however small, and work for the greater part of your time in the management or conduct of the company or an associated company. (But if you or your spouse claim relief under the Business Expansion Scheme in respect of shares acquired on or after 14 March 1989, you cannot also claim interest relief on a loan to buy the shares.)

(f) On a loan to buy plant or machinery (for example a car) for use in your partnership or employment. Relief is available for interest paid in the tax year of purchase and the next three tax years. Where there is part private use, relief is restricted accordingly (see chapter 10).

2 INCOME TAX: GENERAL PRINCIPLES

(g) On a loan to personal representatives of a deceased person to pay inheritance tax (see chapter 35).

(h) Where you are 65 years of age or over, on a loan secured on your home to purchase an income for life (called a life annuity). From 6 April 1991, relief is given only at the basic rate of tax and not at the higher rate.

(j) On a loan to acquire shares in an employee-controlled trading company.

(k) On a loan to acquire a share or shares in a co-operative.

Interest is allowable on loans which replace other loans in the above list (but care is needed when considering replacing a home loan—see chapter 30).

Relief is only available as the interest is paid. It is not spread over the period of accrual and will not be allowed if it is never paid.

Bank overdraft interest is never allowed as a deduction from *total* income. Relief is only available where the overdraft is part of the funding of a trade and therefore allowable as an expense in arriving at trading profits.

Personal allowances (TA 1988, ss 256–265)

In addition to relief for charges, you may claim the following allowances in arriving at the amount of income on which tax is paid.

Personal allowance

Every individual who is a UK resident (and some non-residents—see page 464) is entitled to a personal allowance, whether he or she is single or married.

The allowance depends on your age, and is increased in and after the tax years in which you reach age 65 and age 75, as follows:

Under 65	Age 65 to 74	Age 75 and over
£3,445	£4,200	£4,370

The higher allowances for those aged 65 and over are, however, subject to an income limit (see page 14).

Married couple's allowance

A married man is entitled to a married couple's allowance, and this allowance is increased in and after the tax years in which the older spouse reaches age 65 and age 75, as follows:

Elder under 65	Elder aged 65 to 74	Elder aged 75 and over
£1,720	£2,465	£2,505

Again, an income limit applies to the higher allowances for those aged 65 and over (see page 14).

The married couple's allowance commences in the year of marriage, but in that year it is reduced by one-twelfth (£143.33 for 1992/93 if both are under 65) for each complete tax month (ending on the 5th) before the wedding date. If in the year of marriage a man is entitled to the additional allowance as a single parent (see below), he can claim that allowance instead of the reduced married couple's allowance. The married couple's allowance is given in full in the year of divorce, separation or death of either spouse. A widow will get the benefit of any unused married couple's allowance in the year of her husband's death.

Where a married man's income is too low to use the married couple's allowance, he may notify his tax inspector that the excess is to be transferred to his wife. Income for this purpose is counted before deducting MIRAS interest, relief under the Business Expansion Scheme (see page 325), personal pension premiums paid by employees, medical insurance premiums paid from 6 April 1990 on behalf of someone over 60, or (from 6 April 1992) qualifying payments for vocational training.

Commencing in 1993/94, a married woman will be entitled as of right to half the basic married couple's allowance (not any extra married couple's allowance given to the over 65s), if she makes a claim to that effect. Alternatively the couple may jointly claim for the *whole* of the basic allowance to be given to the wife. In either case, the claim must be made *before* the beginning of the relevant tax year, i.e. before 6 April 1993 for 1993/94 (except in the year of marriage, when the claim may be made within that tax year). The allowance will then be allocated in the chosen way until the claim is withdrawn, or where a joint claim has been made for the whole allowance to go to the wife, until the husband makes a fresh claim for half of the allowance. The withdrawal or the husband's claim must also be made before the beginning of the tax year for which the revised allocation is to take effect. If no claim to allocate half or all the allowance to the wife is made, the normal provisions will apply.

Claims must be made on a prescribed form, which will be available from the Revenue from Summer 1992. If either husband or wife has insufficient income to use the married couple's allowance they are entitled to (including any additional allowance available to the husband because one of them is over 65), that spouse may notify the Revenue (within six years after the end of the relevant tax year) that the unused amount is to be transferred to the other.

Income limit for age allowances

Your increased personal allowance because of age is reduced by £1 for every £2 by which your net total income (after deducting charges, including the gross amount of any MIRAS interest) exceeds £14,200, but the allowance cannot fall below £3,445.

The married couple's age allowance is similarly reduced by half of the excess of the husband's total income over £14,200 which has not already been taken into account to reduce his personal allowance, but again it cannot fall below £1,720. The wife's income is not taken into account at all, even if the allowance is given because of her age rather than the husband's, or if the allowance is transferred to the wife because the husband's income is too low to use it.

A single person or married woman will lose the benefit of age allowance if income is higher than the following:

Age 65 to 74	£15,710
Age 75 and over	£16,050

A married man will lose the benefit of married couple's age allowance, and his own age allowance if relevant, if his own income is higher than the following:

Husband under 65, wife 65 to 74	£15,690
Husband under 65, wife 75 or over	£15,770*
Husband 65 to 74, wife under 75	£17,200
Husband 65 to 74, wife 75 or over	£17,280
Husband 75 or over	£17,620

* Increased to the figure shown on page 17 where the transitional provisions apply.

Transitional provisions

Because of the introduction of independent taxation of husband and wife from 6 April 1990, some husbands may not get the same level of allowances as they would have had if the old system had continued. There are two transitional provisions to ensure that the allowances do not actually fall.

First, where a husband's 1990/91 income was less than his personal allowance, then in addition to transferring the married couple's allowance, part of his unused personal allowance could be transferred to the wife in that year if the joint allowances would otherwise have been less than the joint allowances given in 1989/90. For 1991/92 and later years, transitional relief is due only if the husband can transfer the full married couple's allowance *and* the wife was entitled to transitional relief in the previous year. The transitional relief is the smaller of:

(a) the transitional relief given in the previous year less any current year increase in the personal and married couple's allowances given to the wife, and

(b) the excess of the husband's personal allowance over his income for the year.

This means that in 1991/92 and later years the transitional relief will preserve the total allowances at a minimum of the 1989/90 level. If the husband's income increases above the 1989/90 level the total allowances will increase accordingly, up to the point where they are the same as the normal joint allowances for husband and wife. See examples 2, 3 and 4.

Example 2

Allowances available to a couple in 1989/90 were married man's allowance of £4,375 and wife's earned income relief of £2,785, totalling £7,160. All of this amount was given against the wife's income because the husband's only income was a tax-exempt educational grant.

In 1990/91 the husband still had no taxable income, so that his personal allowance was unused.

He could transfer the married couple's allowance of £1,720 plus £2,435 of his unused personal allowance. The total allowances given in 1990/91 were thus the same as in 1989/90:

To husband—personal allowance		—
To wife —personal allowance	3,005	
married couple's allowance	1,720	
part of husband's personal allowance	2,435	7,160

Example 3

Facts as in example 2, with husband still having no taxable income for 1991/92 and 1992/93, so that his personal allowance is unused.

Transitional relief is as follows:

	1991/92 £	1992/93 £
Lower of:		
(a) 2,435 − (3,295 − 3,005)	2,145	
(b)	3,295	2,145
Lower of:		
(a) 2,145 − (3,445 − 3,295)	1,995	
(b)	3,445	1,995
Wife's allowances are:		
Personal allowance	3,295	3,445
Married couple's allowance	1,720	1,720
Transitional relief	2,145	1,995
	7,160	7,160

Example 4

Facts as in example 3, except that husband's income in 1992/93 is £3,200, so that £245 of his personal allowance is unused.

In 1992/93 he may transfer the married couple's allowance of £1,720 plus the lower of:

(a) £2,145 less £150 (1992/93 increase in allowances)   £1,995
(b) Husband's unused personal allowance   £245

The transferred amount is therefore £245 and the total allowances in 1992/93 will be the same as those available to other married couples:

To husband—personal allowance		3,200
To wife —personal allowance	3,445	
married couple's allowance	1,720	
transitional relief	245	5,410
		£8,610

If a couple married in 1989/90, the transitional rules are modified to give essentially the same position, i.e. that the total allowances given in 1990/91 were not less than the total allowances given in 1989/90 (even though the incomes of husband and wife were never in fact added together for tax purposes), and transitional relief for 1991/92 and later years depends on the transitional relief given in 1990/91.

If a husband is entitled to the special personal allowance under the second transitional provision dealt with below, that special allowance is taken into account for 1991/92 onwards instead of the normal personal allowance in calculating whether transitional relief is also due under the first provision.

The second transitional provision is only available in 1992/93 to certain married men under 65 whose wives were 75 or over in 1989/90. Where the husband's 1990/91 personal allowance and married couple's age allowance amounted to less than his 1989/90 married age allowance, he can claim an increased personal allowance of £3,540 in 1992/93, the allowance being subject to the age allowance income limit of £14,200. The benefit of the increased personal allowance and married couple's age allowance will be lost when the husband's income reaches £15,960.

A husband who was under 65 with a wife aged 65 to 74 in 1989/90 can no longer benefit from the transitional provisions, because his 1989/90 married age allowance of £5,385 is less than the combined allowances he is now entitled to.

Additional personal allowance for single parents etc.

Relief of £1,720 is available for a claimant who is single, widowed, divorced

17

or separated if he or she has one or more qualifying children resident with him or her for all or part of the year. If the child is your own child (including a stepchild or an adopted child who was under 18 when adopted), the child must either be under 16 at the beginning of the tax year or be in full-time education (or undergoing a minimum two-year full-time training for a trade, profession or vocation). If the child is not your own child, then in addition to the requirement for the child to be under 16 or in full-time education or training, you must maintain the child for all or part of the year, and the allowance for a child who is not your own is not available in any event if the child is over 18 at the beginning of the tax year. The relief is apportioned where there are two or more claimants in respect of the same child, but if, say, separated parents each claim for a different child, the full relief is available to each if the conditions are satisfied (except that the husband cannot claim the allowance in the tax year of separation). If, however, an unmarried couple live together as man and wife, they are entitled from 6 April 1989 to only one allowance between them, no matter how many qualifying children there are.

A man entitled to the married couple's allowance can claim the additional relief only if his wife has throughout the year been totally incapacitated by physical or mental infirmity.

Widow's bereavement allowance

In the tax year in which her husband dies and in the following tax year (unless she marries before the beginning of it) a widow is entitled to a bereavement allowance of £1,720. The allowance is available against any of her income for the whole year.

Blind person's relief

Relief of £1,080 is available to a blind person. A married couple who are both blind may each claim the allowance. A married blind person may transfer unused blind person's relief to the spouse (whether or not the spouse is blind).

Life assurance relief (TA 1988, ss 266–274 and Schs 14 and 15)

Life assurance relief is no longer available for contracts made after 13 March 1984 but it continues for policies made on or before that date. The relief is currently at the rate of 12½% of qualifying premiums subject to a limit on allowable premiums of either one-sixth of total income or £1,500, whichever is greater.

Relief is obtained by deduction at source when the premium is paid, and, as with interest relief under the MIRAS scheme and private medical insurance premiums, the relief may be retained whether you are a taxpayer or not.

There were many restrictions on what policies qualified for relief, and there are anti-avoidance rules under which the Revenue recover excess relief. The provisions are dealt with in detail in chapter 40. Life cover for a limited period (term assurance) is available with tax relief on the premium at the highest rate you pay, under the 'personal pension scheme' provisions (see chapter 17).

Income of married couples and children

Up to 5 April 1990, the income of married couples was added together for tax purposes, although they could ask to be assessed separately (which gave them some independence but did not save tax) or to have the wife's earned income taxed separately (which could save tax if the earnings were high enough). As from 6 April 1990, the income of married couples is taxed independently. For the detailed provisions on taxation of husband and wife, see chapter 33.

Children are assessable individuals in their own right and the personal allowance is available against any income they have, however young they are. The income of unmarried children under 18 is, however, regarded as that of the parent if it comes from the parent, either directly or indirectly, unless the total of any such income is £100 a year or less from 6 April 1991—previously £5 a year. The limit applies separately to income provided by each parent. So each parent could provide a capital sum for, say, a building society or bank deposit account in the child's name and avoid income tax on the income arising if the gross amount is within the permitted limit. But if income from sources provided by the parent should exceed the limit, the whole of the income and not just the excess over £100 would be charged on the parent. Surpluses on children's savings bonds (see chapter 36) and friendly society policies (see chapter 40) do not fall to be treated as the parent's income. It is also possible to establish a settlement of capital on children in some circumstances under which the income may escape being treated as the parent's—see chapter 42.

Postponement applications and interest on overdue tax (TMA 1970, ss 55, 86, 88)

Tax is due for payment either on the normal due date indicated in the table shown above (page 7 onwards) or 30 days after the issue of the assessment if later. The due date of payment may be affected if you appeal against an assessment and apply for postponement of all or part of the tax charged. If postponement is not applied for, tax is due on the normal due date despite the appeal.

If tax is to be postponed, a separate postponement application must be made within thirty days after the date of the assessment. Late applications may be made if your circumstances change.

It is, however, not sufficient in a postponement application to say that the tax may be excessive. The application must state by how much you believe you have been overcharged and your reasons for that belief. This is almost the same as advancing your arguments on the appeal itself so you need to think carefully before making postponement applications.

Following an agreement between you and your tax inspector as to how much tax may be postponed, or following a decision of the appeal commissioners if you do not agree, the inspector will issue a notice stating how much tax is payable immediately, the tax being due within thirty days after issue of that notice or on the normal due date if later. If the outcome of the appeal is that all or part of the tax postponed is payable, it is due for payment thirty days after the appeal is settled (or the normal due date, if later).

Interest arises when tax is not paid on the due date, but if it amounts to £30 or less it is generally ignored. The interest is not deductible for tax purposes. The rate is adjusted frequently in line with commercial interest rates. Recent rates are as follows.

9.25% p.a. from 6 October 1991
10% p.a. from 6 July 1991 to 5 October 1991
10.75% p.a. from 6 May 1991 to 5 July 1991
11.5% p.a. from 6 March 1991 to 5 May 1991
12.25% p.a. from 6 November 1990 to 5 March 1991
13% p.a. from 6 November 1989 to 5 November 1990
12.25% p.a. from 6 July 1989 to 5 November 1989

The Revenue publishes tables of interest rate factors to help with the necessary calculations, and these are updated when rates change.

Interest is charged from the 'reckonable date', which normally means the date when the tax is actually due for payment. Where any of the tax has been postponed, however, interest may run from an earlier date, which is either 30 days after the issue of the original assessment or, if later:

For Schedules A and D 1 July after the tax year (e.g. 1 July 1993 for 1992/93).

For higher rates on taxed income 1 June in next but one tax year (e.g. 1 June 1994 for 1992/93).

Interest will, however, run from the normal due date where the reason for an assessment being made late is the fraudulent or negligent conduct of the taxpayer. (See chapter 9.)

Certificates of tax deposit

Certificates of tax deposit may be purchased by individuals, partnerships, personal representatives, trustees or companies, subject to an initial deposit of £2,000, with minimum additions of £500. The certificates may be used to pay any tax except PAYE, VAT and tax deducted from payments to sub-contractors. Interest accrues daily for a maximum of six years, and provision is made for varying interest rates during the term of the deposit. A lower rate of interest applies if the deposit is withdrawn for cash rather than used to settle tax liabilities. The interest is charged to tax under Schedule D, Case III. Tax deposit certificates are a way of ensuring that liquid resources are earmarked for the payment of tax when due.

Repayment claims

Repayment claims will arise where the taxpayer's income is wholly or mainly subject to deduction of tax at source so that it has not been possible to take the personal allowances into account in calculating the tax originally payable. This is particularly likely to apply in the case of old people entitled to age allowance and to students with income from their parents which was covenanted before 15 March 1988. The number of repayment claims will increase as a result of the introduction of a 20% rate of tax. See example 5.

Example 5

Income of widow aged 67 in 1992/93 is £2,816 widow's pension, £2,300 occupational pension and £900 net building society interest. The age allowance given against the occupational pension was (4,200 − 2,816) = £1,384, and tax charged on the balance of £916 at 20% amounted to £183.

A repayment claim arises as follows:

		£	Tax paid £
Pension		2,816	—
Occupational pension		2,300	183
Building society interest (net)	900		
Tax thereon	300	1,200	300
		6,316	483
Age allowance		4,200	
Taxable income		2,116	
Tax thereon:			
£2,000 @ 20%		400	
116 @ 25%		29	429
Repayment due			£54

Repayment claims will also arise in other circumstances, for example when relief is claimed for trading losses of new businesses against the income of the previous three years.

Repayment supplement (TA 1988, s 824)

A tax-free repayment supplement is paid to individuals receiving a repayment of at least £25 more than one year after the end of the tax year to which it relates. Recent rates are the same as those for interest on overdue tax as shown on page 20.

The supplement runs from the end of the tax year following the year for which the repayment is made (or from the end of the tax year in which the tax was paid if later) to the next 5th of the month after the repayment date. See example 6. The Revenue publishes tables of interest rate factors to help with the necessary calculations, and these are updated when rates change. Where the tax or any part of it has been paid late, repayments will be treated as relating to tax paid later rather than earlier.

Example 6

Self-employed person paid tax for 1989/90 on due dates, 1 January and 1 July 1990, totalling £5,000. A repayment of £1,000 is subsequently made on 24 May 1992. The repayment supplement added to the repayment is reckoned from 6 April 1991 and amounts to:

£1,000 × 11.5% × 1 mth to 5.5.91	9.58
£1,000 × 10.75% × 2 mths to 5.7.91	17.92
£1,000 × 10% × 3 mths to 5.10.91	25.00
£1,000 × 9.25% × 8 mths to 5.6.92	61.67
	£114.17

If the second instalment of tax for 1989/90 had not been paid until May 1991, that is in 1991/92, the supplement would have been calculated from 6 April 1992 and would have been:

£1,000 × 9.25% × 2 mths to 5.6.92	£15.42

Responsibility to provide information to the Revenue

Apart from returns made by employers in respect of earnings of their employees, there are various reporting requirements, such as by banks and building societies as to interest paid, payers of commissions and royalties, and those who receive profits and income belonging to other people (for example interest or rent collected by solicitors or other agents).

3
Corporation tax: general principles

Basis of charge (TA 1988, s 6)

Corporation tax is charged on the profits of companies and of unincorporated bodies that are not partnerships, for example members' clubs. The term profits includes all sources of income (other than dividends from UK companies) and also capital gains.

Corporation tax is charged on the world profits of UK-resident companies. Non-resident companies carrying on a trade, profession or vocation in the UK through a branch or agency are charged on the income arising from the branch or agency and on capital gains on the disposal of assets in the UK used for the purposes of the trade, profession or vocation or otherwise for the branch or agency. The overseas aspect is dealt with in chapter 41.

Calculation of profits (TA 1988, ss 9, 345, 468F)

A company's taxable income is computed using income tax Schedules and Cases (see page 6), but always on the basis of the current accounting period (see below) and never on the preceding year basis that sometimes applies for income tax. Where income, such as interest on government stock and building society interest, has had income tax deducted at source, the gross amount is nonetheless included in the company's profits for corporation tax. The income tax deducted is recovered either by set-off against the company's liability to account for income tax it has deducted from its own payments, or by set-off against its corporation tax liability, or, if that is insufficient, by repayment. Bank interest received by a company is received in full, so there is no income tax to recover. The only source of income that escapes corporation tax is dividends or other distributions from UK-resident companies. Such dividends, with their related tax credits, are called franked investment income and their tax treatment is dealt with below. Dividends from authorised unit trusts in respect of periods after 31 December 1990 are treated not as franked investment income but as income net of income tax, so that the gross amount is chargeable to corporation tax and the income tax deemed to have been suffered may be recovered as described above.

In computing the company's trading profits, capital allowances are deducted as trading expenses, and balancing charges treated as trading receipts (see chapter 22). Pre-trading expenditure of a revenue nature incurred not more than five years before commencement of trading is treated as incurred on the day the trade commences.

A company's chargeable gains are computed using capital gains tax principles (see chapter 4). The amount of the gains used to be reduced by a specified fraction before being included in profits chargeable to corporation tax. This had the result of giving an effective tax rate of 30%, which was the same as that for individuals. Gains made on or after 17 March 1987 are not subject to this reduction and are charged at the same rate as the rate on the company's income profits.

Companies are not entitled to any annual capital gains exemption.

Charges on income (TA 1988, ss 338, 339, 349, 350 and Sch 16)

Having arrived at the company's total profits (both income and capital), charges on income are deducted to arrive at the profits chargeable to corporation tax. Charges usually comprise the payments from which the company has deducted income tax at source, e.g. interest payments (other than bank interest), patent royalties and covenanted payments to charity. On rare occasions, bank interest may be treated as a charge where not allowed as a business expense. One-off donations to charity are also sometimes treated as a charge (see page 490).

The full amount of the charges paid (that is, before the income tax deduction at source) is deducted from profits, and the company has to account to the Revenue for the income tax it has deducted (subject to a set-off for any income tax suffered on its income). The income tax is accounted for on a quarterly basis to 31 March, 30 June, 30 September and 31 December, the tax being due within fourteen days after the quarter ends. Where a company's accounting year does not end on one of the four calendar quarter days the company has five return periods, the first running from the first day of the account to the next calendar quarter day and the last ending at the end of the accounting period.

If the charges exceed profits, the excess may be carried forward as a trading loss provided that the charges are wholly and exclusively for the purposes of the trade (which usually means all charges except charitable covenants and one-off charitable donations). This aspect is dealt with in chapter 26 on company losses.

Periods of account and chargeable accounting periods (TA 1988, s 12)

A company's profits are computed for a chargeable accounting period, which normally means the period for which the company's accounts are made up, no matter how short it is. If, however, a company makes up an account for a period greater than 12 months, it is split into one or more chargeable accounting periods of 12 months plus a chargeable accounting period covering the remainder of the period of account.

In arriving at the split of profits for an account exceeding twelve months, the trading profit is usually split on a time basis. Capital allowances are calculated for each chargeable accounting period, so that if for example an account was made up for the fifteen months from 1 January 1992 to 31 March 1993 and plant was bought in February 1993, the first writing-down allowance would be given against the profit of the three months to 31 March 1993.

Other sources of income, such as rents and bank interest, are allocated to the chargeable accounting period in which they arise (with no apportionment over the period during which they accrue). There are, however, some anti-avoidance provisions where rent is received from an associated company—see page 360. Chargeable gains are allocated to the chargeable accounting period in which the disposal occurs, and charges on income to the chargeable accounting period in which they are paid.

If a company ceases to trade, the date of cessation marks the end of a chargeable accounting period even if the period of account continues to the normal accounting date. The commencement of winding-up also marks the end of a chargeable accounting period.

Losses (TA 1988, ss 393, 393A, 394, 396)

When a company incurs a trading loss, it may set the loss against any other profits of the same accounting period, both income and capital, and then, if it wishes, carry any balance back against the total profits of accounting periods ended within the previous three years, latest first, proportionately restricted to exclude profits of an accounting period falling partly outside those three years. (The carry-back was restricted to a length of time equal to the loss period for accounting periods ended before 1 April 1991.) Any balance of loss remaining (or the whole loss if the company does not wish to claim the current set-off and carry-back) is carried forward to set against later profits of the same trade. The detailed provisions are in chapter 26, which also deals with terminal losses arising on cessation of trade and transfer of trading losses within groups.

If a company sustains losses on other sources of income, for example on rented property, the income tax rules for set-off apply, with the set-off being confined to the same source of income (and in the case of rented property, depending on the type of lease—see chapter 32).

Capital losses can only be set against capital gains of the same chargeable accounting period, any excess being carried forward to set against future gains.

Rate of tax (TA 1988, s 8)

Corporation tax rates are fixed for financial years ending 31 March. Financial years are identified by the calendar year in which they commence, so the financial year 1992 is the year to 31 March 1993. The rate for the financial year 1992 is 33%. A lower small companies rate applies where profits are below a stipulated threshold (see below). For details of the rates in recent years, see page xxv.

Where the tax rate changes during a company's chargeable accounting period, the total profits are apportioned on a time basis and charged at the respective rates in calculating the corporation tax bill for the period.

Small companies rate (TA 1988, s 13)

Where a company's profits are below a stipulated amount, a lower rate of tax is charged. This lower rate used to be charged only on the company's income, but since 16 March 1987 it has been charged on the capital gains as well. The small companies rate has been 25% since 1 April 1988. There is a special definition of profits for the small companies rate. It includes not only the profits chargeable to corporation tax (which are called the 'basic profits') but also dividends received from other UK companies plus their related tax credits (the dividends plus the credits being called 'franked investment income'). The inclusion of franked investment income in the calculations means that it is not possible for a company with a large amount of income in that form to obtain the benefit of the small companies rate on only a small amount of profits chargeable to corporation tax.

Where the profits as defined lie between the stipulated amount and an upper maximum, marginal relief is available. The marginal relief is given by calculating tax on the basic profits at the full corporation tax rate and reducing it by an amount arrived at by the following formula:

$$(M - P) \times \frac{I}{P} \times F$$

where M = Upper maximum
P = Profits as defined for small companies rate purposes (see above)
I = Basic profits, i.e. the income and gains chargeable to corporation tax
F = Small companies marginal relief fraction

The upper and lower limits for the financial years 1991 and 1992 are £1,250,000 and £250,000 and the marginal relief fraction is one-fiftieth. Earlier limits and fractions are shown on page xxv.

The marginal relief ensures that the corporation tax rate on the profits is gradually increased to the full level, but the effect is that profits lying between the lower and upper limits suffer a tax rate in excess of the full rate. This marginal rate is 35% for the financial years 1991 and 1992 where there is no franked investment income. (Where there is franked investment income the marginal rate is less.) See example 1.

Example 1

Year to 31 March 1993

Company with no franked investment income has the following profits chargeable to corporation tax: £

  (i) £250,000 @ 25%   62,500

or

(ii) £260,000 @ 33%   85,800

Marginal relief $(1,250,000 - 260,000) \times \dfrac{260,000}{260,000} \times \dfrac{1}{50}$ 19,800   66,000

Additional corporation tax on extra £10,000 profits (35%)   £3,500

To the extent that a company is able to reduce its profits within the marginal tranche, it can thus save tax at the marginal rate.

The lower and upper limits are annual limits and they are scaled down proportionately if an accounting period is less than 12 months. They are also scaled down where for any part of a chargeable accounting period a company has associated companies. Associated companies include both companies associated through being members of the same group and companies controlled by the same persons. If, for example, the same persons control five companies, the limits for each company for the year to 31 March 1993 are £50,000 and £250,000. If four have profits of £60,000 and one £40,000 the small companies rate will only apply to the last one, and the others will have profits subject to the marginal rate. On the other hand if, say, there were two companies associated with each other and one's profits were £1,500,000 and the other's £125,000, the company with £125,000 profits would qualify for small companies rate even though the combined profits greatly exceeded the upper maximum.

If a company's accounting period does not end on 31 March and there is a change either in the marginal relief fraction or in the marginal relief limits or both, the profit figures have to be apportioned to apply the respective figures for the different financial years.

The small companies rate was previously applied automatically where relevant. The Revenue have announced (in Statement of Practice SP 1/91, issued 6 March 1991) that the relief must be specifically claimed, by a statement in the company's return, computation or accompanying correspondence and, except for unincorporated associations such as members' clubs, the statement should indicate how many associated companies there are. If there are none, this should be stated.

Date of payment of tax (TA 1988, s 10 and Sch 30)

Corporation tax is payable nine months after the end of the chargeable accounting period. Companies established before April 1965, when corporation tax started, used to be entitled to retain the same time interval as they had for income tax so long as the trade remained the same. Income tax was payable by companies on 1 January in the next income tax year following their accounting year end, so if a company made up accounts to 31 December 1964, tax was due on 1 January 1966 and the time interval was one year plus one day.

The Finance Act 1987 provided that the due date of payment for old established companies was to be shortened to nine months after the end of the accounting period, the same as for post-April 1965 companies. This was done in three equal steps commencing with the first accounting period beginning after 16 March 1987. For an old established company with a 31 December year end, the position will have been as follows:

12 months to 31 December 1987	Tax due 1 January 1989
12 months to 31 December 1988	Tax due 1 December 1989
12 months to 31 December 1989	Tax due 1 November 1990
12 months to 31 December 1990	Tax due 1 October 1991

Assessments are not always issued on time, and in no case is tax due earlier than thirty days after the date of issue of the assessment. This does not, however, affect the date from which interest is charged if there is fraudulent or negligent conduct.

Interest on overdue tax and repayment supplement (TMA 1970, s 86; TA 1988, s 825)

Interest is charged on overdue corporation tax (see page xxiv for the rates), and the interest is not allowable in calculating taxable profits. The interest runs from the due date of payment unless an application has been made for postponement of tax pending an appeal, in which case any of the postponed tax that remains chargeable after settlement of the appeal attracts interest either from the actual due date of payment or, if earlier, from six months after the normal due date (unless the original assessment was issued very late, in which case interest would run from 30 days after that assessment if it was later than six months after the normal due date). Interest will always run from the normal due date in cases of fraudulent or negligent conduct. See chapter 9.

Where a company has overpaid tax and a repayment of not less than £100 is made more than twelve months after the date the company was due to pay the tax, it attracts a tax-free repayment supplement (see page xxiv for the rates). The supplement is given for each complete tax month in the period commencing one year after the company's due date of payment and ending at the end of the tax month in which the repayment is made, unless the company paid the tax more than a year after the due date. In that event the supplement runs for each complete tax month from the next anniversary of the due date that falls after the date the tax was paid, i.e. a year's supplement is lost for each full year between the due date and the date when the tax was paid. See example 2.

Example 2

Company formed in 1980 prepares accounts to 30 September annually. Corporation tax for the year to 30 September 1990 is due 9 months later, that is 1 July 1991.

If tax is paid on	Repayment supplement on tax overpaid runs from
1.7.1991	6.7.1992
30.11.1991	6.7.1992
31.8.1992	6.7.1993

Pay and File (TMA 1970, ss 11, 87A, 91, 94; F(No 2)A 1987, ss 82–86; TA 1988, s 826)

A new system is to be introduced, called 'Pay and File', which is designed to do away with estimated assessments, appeals and delay hearings. The system is expected to apply to accounts ended after 30 September 1993.

Companies will be required to pay tax on their own estimate of the amount due, within nine months after the end of the accounting period, and to file a statutory return, accounts and computations, within twelve months after the end of the accounting period.

When the liability has been agreed, an assessment will be issued and any over/under payment will be settled. Interest on the over/under payment will run from the due date of payment. But the rate of interest on a repayment will be lower than that charged on an underpayment. Repayments arising from carrying back surplus ACT will only attract interest from the normal due date of payment for the period in which the surplus ACT arose.

The inspector will still be able to issue an estimated assessment where a return has not been made, or where he is not satisfied with a return.

An amended return will be required if amendments, revision or withdrawal of claims are necessary.

Penalties will be charged for late returns unless the company can show a reasonable excuse. The penalty will depend on how late the return is. There are fixed penalties for each late return, ranging from £100 to £1,000, and also tax-based penalties if a return is more than six months late (for example filed later than 30 June 1995 for the year to 31 December 1993) and any tax remained unpaid nine months after the due date of payment.

Franked investment income (TA 1988, s 238)

Dividends and other distributions of company profits are not allowable deductions in calculating the profits chargeable to corporation tax. Where dividends from UK-resident companies are received by a company, they do not have to be included in that company's profits chargeable to corporation tax because the underlying profits of the paying company have already suffered corporation tax before the dividend was paid. In the hands of the receiving company the dividends plus their related tax credits are termed 'franked investment income'. Such income may be passed on as dividends to the receiving company's own shareholders without tax consequences for the receiving company, and the shareholders then get the benefit of the paying company's tax credit.

Dividend payments and other distributions (TA 1988, ss 14, 20, 231, 238, 239, 241, 246 and Sch 13)

When a company pays dividends or makes other qualifying distributions (see below), such as distributions in kind instead of cash, it has to pay over in advance some of the corporation tax on the profits of the period in which the dividend is paid, except to the extent that it is passing on a dividend from another company as indicated above. The advance payment of corporation tax (ACT) is at the rate of 25/75ths (one third) of the dividend, and thus represents 25% of the sum of the dividend plus the ACT. Although this payment reduces the company's liability to corporation tax, it is also passed on to the shareholder in the form of a tax credit to satisfy the shareholder's liability to income tax at the basic rate on the dividend. If the shareholder is not liable to tax the credit is repaid to him.

Within fourteen days after the end of each calendar quarter ended 31 March, 30 June, 30 September and 31 December the company has to account to the Revenue for the ACT on dividends paid during the quarter. If the company's accounting period does not end on one of those dates, there are five return periods, the fifth ending at the end of the accounting period, with the ACT due within fourteen days thereafter.

In order to compute the amount of ACT payable, franked payments (that is, dividends paid plus related tax credits) are compared with franked investment income (that is, dividends received plus related tax credits) and the company is liable to pay ACT at the rate of 25% on the excess payments (if any), since only to that extent is it regarded as distributing its own profits to its shareholders, as distinct from passing on someone else's through the dividend received.

Where there is a change in the rate of advance corporation tax, the previous rate is used for a dividend paid between 1 and 5 April inclusive. If the change occurs during an accounting period in which a dividend has been paid before 6 April and a dividend has been paid or received on or after that date, the parts before and after the change are treated as separate accounting periods for ACT purposes.

If a company's franked investment income exceeds its franked payments, the excess, known as surplus franked investment income, may be carried forward and a later dividend payment made out of it. It may alternatively be used to obtain a repayment where a company has made a trading loss. This is dealt with in chapter 26.

As the name indicates, advance corporation tax is an advance payment of the company's liability to pay corporation tax, and, subject to a maximum set-off limit, it reduces the corporation tax on the profits of the accounting period in which the dividend is paid. The set-off limit is an amount equal to basic rate income tax on the company's profits chargeable to corporation tax.

Where the basic rate changes during the accounting period, the set-off limit is arrived at by applying the different rates to a proportionate part of the profits, as shown in example 3. ACT was not previously allowed to be set against that part of the corporation tax that related to capital gains, but for accounting periods commencing on or after 17 March 1987 the ACT may be set against the tax on both income and gains. This benefits shareholders, because companies wishing to pass on a capital profit had previously not been able to offset the ACT on the dividend against the tax on the capital profit, so that there was effectively a double tax charge.

Example 3

Assume the full rate of corporation tax and the small company rate profit limits remain unchanged for the year to 31 March 1994 but the basic rate of income tax and the small companies rate are reduced to 20%.

Company has following profits in year to 30 September 1993:

	£
Income from trading, etc.	1,400,000
Capital gains	100,000
Profits chargeable to corporation tax	£1,500,000
Corporation tax payable @ 33%	£495,000

Maximum ACT set-off:
Basic rate income tax % × profits chargeable to
corporation tax, i.e. £1,500,000

6/12 × £1,500,000 × 25%	187,500
6/12 × £1,500,000 × 20%	150,000
	£337,500

Surplus ACT (TA 1988, s 239)

If the amount of ACT paid exceeds the permitted set-off, the excess—called surplus ACT—may be carried back and set against the corporation tax liability of accounting periods commencing in the previous six years, latest first, but again subject to the maximum relief limit for those years. The carry-back claim must be made within two years after the end of the accounting period in which the surplus ACT arises. Any balance of ACT remaining unrelieved may be carried forward without time limit.

Example 4

	Year to 31 March		
	1991	1992	1993
	(FY 1990)	(FY 1991)	(FY 1992)
	£	£	£
Profits chargeable to corporation tax	80,000	100,000	95,000
Maximum ACT set-off (25% of profits)	20,000	25,000	23,750
Corporation tax payable at			
small companies rate of 25%	20,000	25,000	23,750
Less ACT paid in year, say	(13,000)	(13,400)	(41,450)
Surplus ACT carried back	(6,100)	(11,600)	17,700
Mainstream corporation tax payable	£900	NIL	NIL

A company may find itself with surplus ACT for an earlier year as a result of carrying back a trading loss, but be unable to claim to carry back the surplus because the time limit has expired. When such ACT is carried forward to a later year, it may then be included in a carry-back claim for that later year.

Example 5

A company claims to carry back a loss of the year to 31 December 1993, and as a result ACT that was originally within the permitted set-off limit becomes surplus ACT in the year to 31 December 1990. A claim to set the surplus ACT off against corporation tax payable for the six years back to 1984 cannot be made for 1990, but a claim to carry back surplus ACT for, say, 1992, made within the two-year time limit, i.e. by 31 December 1994, could include the 1990 surplus ACT that had been carried forward into that year, so that the surplus could then be carried back to 1986.

Where ACT is carried back, the tax for the earlier period will usually already have been paid, so that a tax repayment will result. In calculating any repayment supplement arising, the ACT cannot be treated as having been paid in the earlier period and the supplement will run only from one year after the due date for corporation tax in respect of the accounting period in which the surplus ACT arose.

The balance of corporation tax payable after the set-off of ACT is popularly called mainstream corporation tax.

With the small companies rate being the same as the basic rate of income tax, and now that ACT can be offset against the tax on capital gains, a company chargeable at small companies rate will have no mainstream tax charge where the maximum ACT set-off is made.

Qualifying and non-qualifying distributions (TA 1988, ss 14, 234, 238)

The legislation distinguishes between 'qualifying distributions' and 'non-qualifying distributions'. Qualifying distributions attract an ACT liability as indicated above. Non-qualifying distributions are broadly those that confer a future rather than a current claim on the company's assets, such as a bonus issue of redeemable shares. The company has no tax liability on such a distribution, but the shareholder is liable where appropriate to the excess of higher rate over basic rate tax. The company is required to notify the Revenue within fourteen days after the end of the quarter in which the non-qualifying distribution is made.

When the shares are redeemed, the redemption is a qualifying distribution liable to ACT, but the tax paid by the shareholder on the non-qualifying distribution may be set against that due on the later qualifying distribution.

Where a company supplies goods or services to a shareholder for more than cost but at a price concession, a distribution does not arise because there is no cost to the company, as distinct from a reduction in profit margins, so that no part of the company profits has been distributed.

Company liquidations (TA 1988, ss 12, 342)

When a company goes into liquidation this is usually preceded by a cessation of trade. The cessation of trade denotes the end of a chargeable accounting period, and a chargeable accounting period also ends at the commencement of winding-up.

Problems can arise when a company that has been making trading losses realises chargeable gains on the sale of its assets, because if the gains are realised after the trade ceases there will be no current trading losses to offset them, but it is not possible to part with the assets until the trade has ceased. This problem can be avoided if the contract for sale of the assets takes place before ceasing to trade, with completion taking place subsequently. The contract date is the relevant disposal date for capital gains purposes, and any trading losses occurring in the accounting period in which the trade ceases will then be available to reduce the gains. The gains cannot, however, be reduced by trading losses brought forward (see chapter 26 for the detailed provisions on company losses).

Close companies (TA 1988, ss 13A, 414–422; FA 1989, ss 103–107 & Sch 12)

A close company is a company under the control of five or fewer participators (which broadly means shareholders, although it is defined more widely), or under the control of its directors. In considering what rights an individual has in a company, the rights of his 'associates' are included, which covers close family, partners and the trustees of any family settlements.

As well as being subject to the normal corporation tax rules, close companies are subject to additional requirements.

Benefits in kind to participators are treated as distributions (except where already treated as earnings under the Schedule E benefits rules, see chapter 10) and loans to participators attract a tax liability. These provisions are dealt with in chapter 12.

If the company is a 'close investment-holding company', tax is charged at the full rate of corporation tax (currently 33%) rather than at the lower small companies rate, whatever the level of the company's profits. A company is not a close investment-holding company if it is a trading company (including companies that deal in land, shares or securities) or a member of a trading group, or if it carries on the business of property investment on a commercial basis.

Close company liquidations

Where a close trading company ceases to trade and goes into liquidation, it will not be treated as a close investment-holding company for the accounting period beginning at the commencement of winding-up, providing it was within the definition of a close trading company for the previous accounting period. This provision will be of little benefit to most companies, since there will almost always be a gap between ceasing to trade and commencing winding-up, so that the 33% rate will apply to the period in which the winding-up commences as well as to later chargeable accounting periods until the winding-up is completed.

Groups of companies (TA 1988, ss 240, 247, 248, 347, 402–413; TCGA 1992, ss 170–175, 178–181)

The Taxes Acts do not treat a group of companies as a taxable entity. The corporation tax position of each company in the group is computed independently (small companies rate and various other limits being scaled down according to the number of associated companies). There are, however, various provisions that recognise the group structure and give special treatment in the appropriate circumstances.

Holding company and its 51% subsidiaries

(a) ACT paid by the holding company on dividends (not other distributions) may be surrendered to one or more subsidiaries for use against the subsidiary's corporation tax liability for the corresponding or future accounting periods. It cannot be carried back by a subsidiary.

(b) A subsidiary cannot surrender ACT to its holding company, but it can avoid paying ACT in the first place, because an election may be made for a subsidiary to pay a dividend to its holding company (or to a fellow subsidiary) without accounting for ACT. Such a dividend is termed 'group income'. The receiving company will thus have no tax credit passed to it and will pay ACT in the normal way as and when it passes the dividend on to its own shareholders. These provisions also apply to dividends paid by a trading company to a consortium of UK resident companies who own 75% or more of its issued ordinary share capital.

(c) Charges on income may be paid gross by any group company to another.

Holding company and its 75% subsidiaries

(a) Trading losses (and charges in excess of other profits) can be surrendered to other group members for use against total profits (including capital gains) of the corresponding accounting period. These provisions—called group relief—are dealt with in chapter 26.

(b) Chargeable assets for capital gains purposes are transferred to another group company without a chargeable gain arising, the transferee company assuming the base cost and acquisition date of the transferor company. In this way assets to be sold outside the group can first be centralised in one company for setting off losses against profits. Otherwise there is no facility for chargeable gains of one group company to be relieved by capital losses of another.

(c) A chargeable gain made by one group company on a business asset qualifying for rollover relief may be rolled over or held over against an acquisition by another group company. Rollover relief is dealt with in chapter 4.

The group provisions have frequently been manipulated in order to make tax savings over and above what the provisions are intended to allow, and there are numerous anti-avoidance provisions, including provisions in the 1992 legislation to strengthen the rules denying group relief for losses where there are 'arrangements' under which some or all of a company's shares could be disposed of to another party.

Encouraging business efficiency

Various measures are available to enable companies to operate in a tax-efficient manner and to stimulate investment in new and expanding ventures:

Business expansion scheme.
Purchase of own shares by company.
Demergers.

These are dealt with separately in chapter 29. The business expansion scheme is being withdrawn at the end of 1993.

4
Capital gains tax: general principles

Introduction

Capital gains tax was introduced with effect from 6 April 1965. The law has been consolidated in the Taxation of Chargeable Gains Act 1992, which received Royal Assent on 6 March 1992. All references in this chapter are to that Act unless otherwise stated.

Basis of charge (ss 1–6, 35 and Sch 3)

Capital gains tax applies when chargeable assets are disposed of. Gains and losses are calculated on each asset. In general, the cost of an asset acquired before 31 March 1982 is taken to be its value on that date, although there are provisions to use original cost in some circumstances. An allowance, called indexation allowance, is made to adjust for inflation, and the gains and losses are then aggregated to give the net chargeable gains or allowable losses for the year. The first £5,800 of gains in 1992/93 is exempt and the balance is charged at income tax rates as if it were the top slice of the taxpayer's income (although personal allowances, charges on income, etc.

Example 1

Net gains in 1992/93 £15,800 less annual exemption £5,800 = £10,000.

If taxpayer's taxable income is	Capital gains tax payable is		£
Nil, because income is equal to or less than available allowances	2,000 @ 20%	400	
	8,000 @ 25%	2,000	2,400
£6,000	10,000 @ 25%		2,500
£15,000	8,700 @ 25%	2,175	
	1,300 @ 40%	520	2,695
£24,000	10,000 @ 40%		4,000

37

cannot be offset against chargeable gains)—see example 1. If losses exceed gains, the excess is carried forward to set against later chargeable gains.

For certain trusts, the capital gains tax rate is only 25%, but there are anti-avoidance provisions to prevent this being exploited by higher rate tax-payers—see page 479.

Trading losses

From 1991/92 onwards, sole traders and partners may set off surplus trading losses against their capital gains in certain circumstances—see chapter 25 for the detailed provisions.

Persons liable (ss 2, 9–12)

Those who are resident or ordinarily resident in the UK are liable on all gains wherever they arise, if UK domiciled, and on gains arising in, or remitted to, the UK if domiciled elsewhere. Non-residents carrying on a trade, profession or vocation in the UK are liable on gains arising on the disposal of business assets in the UK. The overseas aspect is dealt with in chapter 41.

Husband and wife (ss 2, 58)

From 6 April 1990, gains of husband and wife are calculated and charged separately, each being entitled to the annual exemption (£5,800 for 1992/93). Losses of one may no longer be set against the other's gains. Disposals between husband and wife in a tax year when they are living together are, however, not chargeable. The acquiring spouse is treated as having acquired the asset when the other spouse acquired it, at its original cost plus indexation allowance to the date of transfer. It should therefore be possible through advance planning and transfers of assets between them to ensure that one spouse is not left with unrelieved losses while the other has gains in excess of the exemption.

Companies (s 8 and TA 1988, s 6)

Gains are computed on capital gains tax principles but are charged to cor-poration tax and not capital gains tax. The annual exemption is not avail-able. The effective rate of tax on a company's gains used to be 30%. This was achieved by reducing the chargeable gains by a specified fraction and then including the reduced amount in profits chargeable to corporation tax at the full rate. Since 17 March 1987 gains have been charged at normal corpor-ation tax rates. Recent corporation tax rates are shown on page xxv.

Chargeable assets and exempt assets (ss 21–27, 51, 251–255)

All forms of property are chargeable unless specifically exempt. A charge may also arise when a capital sum is realised without any disposal taking place (for example if compensation is received for damage to an asset, although if the compensation is used to restore the asset no gain arises).

Where a loss arises on money lent, the loss is not normally allowable unless the debt is a 'debt on a security', which usually means secured or unsecured loan stock, and even then special provisions apply (see page 437). Special provisions also apply to losses on certain other loans (see page 53).

Where an asset is exempt no chargeable gain or allowable loss can normally arise, although there are some special rules about losses on chattels. See the table below for exempt assets and for the chapter in this book which deals with them.

Exempt assets	TCGA 1992 reference	See chapter
An individual's only or main residence (providing various conditions are satisfied, otherwise part or all of the gain may be chargeable)	222, 223	30
Chattels which are wasting assets, unless used in a business	45	39
Non-wasting and business chattels where disposal proceeds do not exceed £6,000	262	39
Government securities and qualifying company loan stock	115	38
SAYE contracts, savings certificates and premium bonds	121	36
Prizes and betting winnings	51	
Private motor cars, including veteran and vintage cars	263	
Sterling currency, and foreign currency for an individual's own spending and maintenance of assets abroad	21, 269	39
Decorations for valour if disposed of by the original holder or legatees but not by a purchaser	268	
Compensation or damages for personal or professional wrong or injury	51	
Life assurance policies but only in the hands of the original owner or beneficiaries	210	40
Gifts of assets that are considered by the Treasury to be of national, historic or scientific interest, but breach of any conditions imposed will nullify the CGT exemption	258	
Gifts to charities	257	43

Computation of gains and losses (ss 2, 15–17, 35–57 and Schs 2–4)

Gains and losses are worked out by deducting from the sale proceeds or, in some instances, from the market value (see page 51) the following amounts:

Original cost and incidental costs of acquisition
Expenditure that has increased the value of the asset
Incidental costs of disposal
Indexation allowance (see below)

See example 2.

Example 2
In April 1992, Mr A sells for £20,000 a painting which he bought in April 1983 for £8,000. The indexation allowance due (see below) is 64.7%, i.e. £5,176.

	£
Sale proceeds	20,000
Cost of painting	8,000
Unindexed gain	12,000
Indexation allowance	5,176
Chargeable gain	£6,824

This gain will be added to Mr A's other gains for the tax year, and the total gains will be reduced by the annual exemption.

Effect of capital allowances (s 41)

Gains on some assets that qualify for capital allowances are exempt from capital gains tax, such as on items of movable plant and machinery bought and sold for less than £6,000. Allowable losses can, however, arise on such items—see page 445. Where a chargeable asset has qualified for capital allowances, the allowances are not deducted from the cost in computing a gain, so that there will be a gain before indexation allowance only if the asset is sold for more than original cost. Capital allowances are, however, taken into account in computing a loss. They are deducted from the cost of the asset in arriving at the cost for capital gains tax, so that there will not normally be a loss before indexation is taken into account, but the indexation allowance will usually create an allowable loss.

Where the asset was acquired before 31 March 1982 and the value at 31 March 1982 is used to compute the gain or loss, the 31 March 1982 value is reduced by the capital allowances given in computing the allowable loss.

For examples, see pages 254–256.

Indexation allowance (ss 53, 54)

No allowance was made for the effects of inflation until the introduction of an indexation allowance in 1982. The indexation allowance applies to disposals on or after 6 April 1982 (1 April 1982 for companies). It is calculated by applying to each item of expenditure the increase in the retail prices index between the month when the expenditure was incurred, or March 1982 if later, and the month of disposal of the asset. The index increase is expressed as a decimal and rounded (up or down) to three decimal places.

The movement in the index is published monthly and the figure for each month since March 1982 is tabled on page xxvi.

Where the expenditure was incurred before 31 March 1982 and the disposal is on or after 6 April 1988, the indexation calculation is made by reference to the value of the asset at 31 March 1982 if the taxpayer has elected to be treated as if he had acquired all the assets he owned on 31 March 1982 at their market value on that day (see below). If the election has not been made, the 31 March 1982 value will still be used to calculate the indexation allowance unless using original cost would give a higher figure, in which case the higher figure is taken. For disposals between 6 April 1985 (1 April 1985 for companies) and 5 April 1988 a taxpayer had to make a specific written election if he wanted to base indexation allowance on 31 March 1982 value. The election had to be made within two years from the end of the tax year (or company accounting period) in which the disposal occurred. For disposals before 6 April 1985, the indexation allowance was based on cost (or sometimes on 6 April 1965 value—see below). It was not given until an asset had been held for twelve months, and applied from that 12-month anniversary (or 31 March 1982 if later). The indexation allowance could not turn a gain into an allowable loss or increase an allowable loss. Both of these restrictions were removed for disposals after 5 April 1985 (31 March 1985 for companies) and the right to base indexation allowance on 31 March 1982 value was introduced from that date.

Assets held on 31 March 1982 (ss 35, 36 and Schs 3, 4)

Originally, capital gains tax applied to gains or losses made on or after 6 April 1965, and there were special rules relating to assets already owned on that date to ensure that when they were disposed of, pre-6 April 1965 gains and losses were excluded. The Finance Act 1988 provided that as from 6 April 1988, only gains or losses on or after 31 March 1982 are to be taken into account. Taxpayers may make an irrevocable election (a rebasing election) to regard all assets owned on 31 March 1982 (except plant and machinery on which capital allowances have been, or could have been, claimed) as having been acquired at their market value on that day. The election could have been made by 5 April 1990, whether or not any disposals were made before then. Otherwise, it must be made within two years after the end of the tax year or company accounting period in which the first disposal is made after 5 April 1988. Most disposals that normally result in no chargeable gain or allowable loss are not treated as triggering the time limit (see Revenue Statement of Practice SP 4/92, issued 14 May 1992).

If the election is not made, the 31 March 1982 value is still used to calculate gains and losses, unless using original cost would show a lower gain or

41

lower loss, in which case the lower figure is taken. If one method shows a gain and the other a loss the result is treated as neither a gain nor a loss.

For many assets it may be costly to find out their value at 31 March 1982, but this has to be done whether the election to use 31 March 1982 value is made or not. The election does simplify the calculations and it makes it unnecessary to maintain old records.

There are many instances in the capital gains legislation where tax on gains may be deferred to a later time, either by treating the gains as reducing other expenditure, or by treating them as arising at a later time. Where gains were deferred before 31 March 1982, the effect of using 31 March 1982 value to calculate later gains is that these deferred gains will escape tax altogether, since the cost from which the deferred gain was deducted is no longer used. Where an asset acquired after 31 March 1982 but before 6 April 1988 is disposed of after 5 April 1988, and the gain relates wholly or partly, directly or indirectly, to an asset acquired before 31 March 1982 (in other words, where a claim for deferral was made between 31 March 1982 and 5 April 1988 that related to an asset acquired before 31 March 1982), a claim may be made for one half of the gain to be exempt from tax (see example 3).

The main occasions when this relief applies are:

Rollover and holdover relief on replacement of business assets or compulsorily acquired land (see page 48).

Holdover of gains where assets were acquired by gift, including the charge when the donee emigrates (see page 52).

Rollover of gains on the transfer of a business to a company (see page 309).

Example 3

1979 Taxpayer acquires business asset No. 1 for £5,000.

1984 Asset No. 1 is sold at a gain of £2,000 and asset No. 2 is acquired for £8,000. The gain is rolled over.

1986 Asset No. 2 is sold at a gain of £5,000 (after taking into account gain rolled over on asset No. 1) and asset No. 3 is acquired for £20,000. The gain is rolled over.

1992 Asset No. 3 is sold for £33,000. Available indexation allowance is, say, 41%.

Gain on sale of asset No. 3 is as follows:

	£	£
Sale proceeds 1992		33,000
Cost 1986	20,000	
Less half of rolled over gain of £5,000 (other half being exempt)	2,500	
	17,500	
Indexation allowance 41%	7,175	24,675
Chargeable gain		£8,325

Assets held on 6 April 1965 (s 35 and Sch 2)

Assets already owned on 6 April 1965, the original start date for capital gains tax, will be treated as acquired at market value on 31 March 1982 if the appropriate election is made (see above). If it is not, the position is a bit more complicated, because the old special rules for those assets must be considered in conjunction with the new. The old rules for calculating the position on assets owned on 6 April 1965 contained separate provisions for land with development value, for quoted securities and for all other assets.

The gain or loss on land with development value was calculated by comparing the proceeds either with the original cost or with the value at 6 April 1965, whichever showed the lower gain or loss after taking indexation allowance into account. If one method showed a gain and the other a loss there was neither gain nor loss. The same rules applied to quoted securities, except that it was possible to elect for quoted securities to be treated as having been acquired on 6 April 1965 at their value on that date. The detailed provisions are in chapter 38.

Where an asset other than quoted securities or land with development value was acquired before 6 April 1965, only the time proportion of the gain falling after 6 April 1965 was chargeable, although the earliest date that could be used in a time apportionment calculation was 6 April 1945. You could elect to work out the gain by using the 6 April 1965 value as the cost instead of using time apportionment, but once made this election was irrevocable, even if it resulted in more tax being payable. Where the allowable expenditure had been incurred on different dates, the overall gain was first apportioned in proportion to the respective blocks of expenditure. The time apportionment formula was then applied to those gains where the expenditure was incurred before 6 April 1965, gains where the expenditure was incurred after that date being wholly chargeable.

Following the changes in the Finance Act 1988, if the rebasing election has not been made, the above rules are modified to bring the 31 March 1982 value into the calculation. The calculation is first made using the old rules for assets owned on 6 April 1965, and the result is compared with the result using 31 March 1982 value. The lower gain or loss is then taken and if one calculation shows a gain and the other a loss, the result is neither gain nor loss. If, however, the old 6 April 1965 rules have already resulted in a no gain/no loss result, that position is not disturbed.

In making the calculations for assets acquired before 31 March 1982, the indexation allowance is always based on the higher of 31 March 1982 value and cost (or 6 April 1965 value if appropriate) no matter which of those figures is being taken into account in the calculation itself. It is the Revenue view that indexation allowance should be deducted before applying any time apportionment but they have recently lost a case on this point in the Court of Appeal. The calculations in examples 4 and 5 are based on the Court of Appeal decision, but it could still be reversed in the House of Lords. The outcome will mainly be relevant where disposals have occurred between 6 April 1985 and 5 April 1988, during which time you could claim to base indexation allowance on 31 March 1982 value although the cost itself could not be uplifted. After 5 April 1988 the result using 31 March 1982 value will almost always show a more favourable result than the old rules, so that the point at which the indexation allowance is deducted in the time apportionment calculation is irrelevant.

Example 4

Cost of antique 6.4.57	£4,000
Value at 6.4.65	£4,500
Value at 31.3.82	£9,000
Sale proceeds 6.4.92	£15,000

Indexation allowance March 1982 to April 1992 74.7%

If no election to use 31.3.82 value for all assets
Calculation using old rules

	£	£
Sale proceeds	15,000	15,000
Cost	(4,000)	
6.4.65 value		(4,500)
Overall gain	£11,000	

Time proportion since 6.4.65 $\dfrac{27}{35} \times 11,000 =$ 8,486

Indexation allowance @ 74.7% on 31.3.82 value of £9,000	(6,723)	(6,723)
Gain	£1,763 or	£3,777

Therefore no election would be made to use 6.4.65 value and gain under old rules is £1,763.

Calculation using new rules	£
Sale proceeds	15,000
31.3.82 value	(9,000)
Indexation allowance 74.7%	(6,723)
Loss under new rules	£723

The transaction would therefore be treated as no gain/no loss, since there is a gain using the old rules and a loss using the new rules.

If election made to use 31.3.82 value for all assets

Calculation would be as second calculation above, giving an allowable loss of £723.

Example 5

Mr B sells a freehold investment property, the relevant particulars being:

	£
Sale proceeds less expenses, 6 April 1992	36,000
Cost, 5 April 1955	5,500
Cost of extension, 5 April 1983	500
Market value at 6 April 1965	7,900
Market value at 31 March 1982	25,000

The retail prices index was as follows:
March 1982, 79.44; April 1983, 84.28; April 1992, 138.8

A. Using old 6.4.65 rules

(i) Time apportionment method

	£	£
Sale proceeds less expenses		36,000
Less cost		
5.4.55	5,500	
5.4.83	500	6,000
		30,000

Apportion gain to expenditure		
5.4.55 cost 5,500/6,000 × £30,000		27,500
5.4.83 cost 500/6,000 × £30,000		2,500
		£30,000

Time apportionment on gain of £27,500

$$\frac{6.4.65-6.4.92}{5.4.55-6.4.92} = \frac{27}{37} \times 27,500 \qquad\qquad 20,068$$

Gain wholly after 6.4.65		2,500
		£22,568

Less indexation allowance
On 31.3.82 value substituted for 5.4.55 cost

$$£25,000 \times \left(\frac{138.8 - 79.44}{79.44} = .747 \right) \qquad 18,675$$

On 5.4.83 cost

$$£500 \times \left(\frac{138.8 - 84.28}{84.28} = .647 \right) \qquad 324 \quad 18,999$$

Chargeable gain	£3,569

example 5 continued overleaf

example 5 continued

(ii) 6 April 1965 market value election

Sale proceeds less expenses		36,000
Less 6.4.65 market value	7,900	
Expenditure after 6.4.65	500	8,400
Unindexed gain		£27,600
Less indexation allowance		
On 31.3.82 value substituted for 6.4.65 value		
(as before)	18,675	
On 5.4.83 cost (as before)	324	18,999
Chargeable gain		£8,601

The election is not beneficial so the chargeable gain
  using the old rules is   £3,569

B. Using 31.3.82 value

	£	£
Sale proceeds less expenses		36,000
Less 31.3.82 value	25,000	
Extension cost 5.4.83	500	25,500
		10,500
Less Indexation allowance as before		
On 31.3.82 value	18,675	
On 5.4.83 cost	324	18,999
Loss		£8,499

If no election is made to use 31.3.82 value for all assets, the disposal
will be treated as giving no gain/no loss, since there is a gain using
6.4.65 rules and a loss using 31.3.82 value.

If the election is made to use 31.3.82 value for all assets there will
be an allowable loss of £8,499.

Part disposals (ss 42, 242)

Where part only of an asset is disposed of, the cost of the part disposed of is
worked out by taking the proportion of the overall cost that the sale proceeds bear to the sum of the sale proceeds plus the market value of what
remains unsold. The indexation allowance is calculated on the apportioned
part of the cost and not on the total. Where a part disposal took place

between 31 March 1982 and 5 April 1988, then on any later disposal the appropriate proportion of the value at 31 March 1982 is used instead of the proportion of original cost.

Where part of a holding of land is sold for £20,000 or less, and the proceeds represent not more than 20% of the value of the land, the taxpayer may claim not to be treated as having made a disposal, but the amount received reduces the allowable cost of the remaining land for a future disposal. The indexation allowance on a subsequent disposal is calculated on the full cost in the usual way, but is then reduced to take account of the previous part disposal. This claim may not be made if other disposals of land are made in the same year, and the total proceeds for all disposals of land exceed £20,000.

Leases (s 240 and Sch 8)

The grant of a lease at a premium gives rise to a capital gains tax liability, and also an income tax liability if the term is 50 years or less. The calculation of the income and capital elements is shown in chapter 32. Where a tenant assigns a lease at a premium to another tenant, the premium is charged to tax in the normal way if the lease has more than 50 years to run at the time of the assignment. If, however, it has 50 years or less to run, it is a wasting asset and the cost has to be depreciated over that 50 years according to a table in Sch 8 which ensures that the cost is depreciated more slowly during the early part of the 50-year period than during the later years.

Annual exemption (s 3 and Sch 1)

The annual exemption is £5,800 for 1992/93, available to each of husband and wife. Provision is made for the exempt amount to be increased each year in line with increases in the retail prices index unless Parliament decides otherwise, and this has resulted in the increase of £300 compared with the 1991/92 figure of £5,500. Although your gains and losses in the same year must be netted off, brought-forward losses need not be set against gains covered by the exemption. So if, say, you have net gains in the current year of £5,600 and brought forward losses of £4,000, the £4,000 losses are carried forward intact. If the gains are £7,000, only £1,200 of the brought-forward losses is used to reduce the gains to the exempt £5,800, leaving £2,800 to be carried forward.

For the annual exemption available to personal representatives and trustees, see pages 55 and 56.

Reliefs

Specific reliefs are available for:

(a) replacement of business assets;
(b) retirement of a sole trader, partner or family company director;
(c) gifts of certain assets;

(d) transfer of a business to a company;
(e) assets of negligible value; and
(f) relief for losses on certain loans.

These are dealt with in the following paragraphs, except for (d) which is dealt with in chapter 27.

Replacement of business assets and compulsorily purchased land (ss 152–160, 247)

Where a chargeable gain arises on the disposal of a qualifying business asset and the proceeds (or deemed proceeds if the asset is given away) are matched by the acquisition of another business asset within the period commencing one year before and ending three years after the disposal, a claim may be made for the gain to be deferred. The replacement asset need not be used in the same trade where one person carries on two or more trades either successively or at the same time. The relief applies to land and buildings, fixed plant and machinery, ships, aircraft, hovercraft, satellites, space stations and spacecraft including launch vehicles, goodwill and milk and potato quotas. The replacement asset does not have to be in the same category as the asset disposed of, providing both are qualifying assets, and the proceeds of a single disposal could be applied in acquiring several qualifying assets or vice versa.

If only part of the sale proceeds is used to acquire replacement assets within the rollover period, the remaining part of the gain is chargeable immediately, treating the gain as the last part of the proceeds to be used.

If the replacement asset has a life of more than 60 years (e.g. freehold land or goodwill) the gain is rolled over and treated as reducing the cost of the replacement asset. Indexation allowance on the replacement asset is calculated on the cost less the rolled over gain.

If, however, a gain has been rolled over in this way against a replacement asset acquired before 31 March 1982, the effect of using 31 March 1982 value as the cost of such an asset is that the rolled over gain escapes tax altogether.

If the replacement is a depreciating asset with a life of less than 60 years (which in fact applies to most of the business assets qualifying for relief) the gain does not reduce the tax cost of the replacement (so the calculation of the indexation allowance is not affected) but it is held over for a maximum of ten years. It becomes chargeable when the replacement asset is sold or ceases to be used in a business carried on by the taxpayer, or, at latest, ten years after acquisition of the replacement asset. The gain will not crystallise at that point, however, if at or before that time a non-depreciating asset has been acquired against which a claim is made for the gain to be rolled over instead. The held-over gain will escape tax altogether if the disposal to which it relates was made on or before 31 March 1982 and the time when it would otherwise have become chargeable is after 5 April 1988.

The time limit for the original rollover or holdover claim is six years from the end of the tax year to which the claim relates. Where a holdover claim is being replaced by a rollover claim as a result of the later acquisition of a non-depreciating asset (which could in fact be up to thirteen years after the disposal giving rise to the gain that had been held over), it is thought that the time limit for the claim to switch from holdover to rollover relief is a further six years from the end of the year in which the non-depreciating asset was acquired, although this is not made clear in the legislation. The Revenue will, where appropriate, assess gains at the normal time, but the taxpayer will be able to postpone payment of the tax on the production of satisfactory evidence that he intends to acquire qualifying assets within the time limit. He would, of course be liable to interest on overdue tax if the replacement was not in fact acquired.

Rollover relief is also available where an asset owned personally and used in the owner's partnership or family trading company is disposed of and replaced. The payment of rent does not affect the availability of the relief.

Rollover relief is only available on investment property in two instances. If the property is the subject of compulsory purchase (or compulsory acquisition by a lessee), the relief is available provided that the replacement is not a capital gains tax exempt dwelling-house (see page 366). The relief is also available on property let as furnished holiday accommodation (see chapter 32).

See page 42 for the treatment of disposals after 5 April 1988 that are affected by deferred gains on assets acquired before 31 March 1982. See chapter 41 for the overseas aspect of rollover relief.

Retirement relief (ss 163, 164 and Sch 6)

Where an individual aged 55 or over (60 for disposals before 19 March 1991) disposes of all or part of his business or partnership share, or of shares in his family trading company in which he is a full-time working director, retirement relief is available in respect of aggregate gains (net of losses) on 'chargeable business assets', which means assets (including goodwill, but not including shares and other assets held as investments) that are used for the purposes of a trade, profession, vocation, office or employment, other than an asset on which no chargeable gain or loss would be made if it was disposed of. Plant or machinery is a chargeable business asset unless it is movable plant or machinery with a cost and value of £6,000 or less (when it would be an exempt chattel). Private type cars are excluded since they are exempt. All or part of the gains arising on the business assets are exempt up to a maximum of £150,000, and all or part of gains between £150,000 and £600,000 are reduced by 50%. (The limits were £125,000 and £500,000 for disposals before 19 March 1991.) A husband and wife can each get relief on gains of up to £600,000 providing each satisfies the necessary conditions. 'Family company' means either one in which the individual owns not less than 25% of the voting rights or one in which he and his family

Example 6

In June 1992, Mr C has gains of £400,000 on disposal of business assets on retirement at age 63 from a business he has owned throughout the previous six years.

In business six years out of ten, therefore upper limit for relief is $6/10 \times £600,000 = £360,000$

		£
Gains are		400,000
Relief: Fully exempt $6/10 \times 150,000$	90,000	
$50\% \times (360,000 - 90,000)$	135,000	225,000
Chargeable gains		£175,000
If gains had been		200,000
Relief would be: Fully exempt		
$6/10 \times 150,000$	90,000	
$50\% \times (200,000 - 90,000)$	55,000	145,000
Leaving chargeable gains of		£55,000

which would be further reduced by the annual exemption if not otherwise used.

together own more than 50%, with his own share being at least 5%. The relief is also given where an individual has to retire before age 55 because of ill health, which must be evidenced by a medical certificate on forms provided by the Revenue. The forms have to be submitted to the medical officer acting for the Revenue, who may require a further medical examination to be made.

The available relief is reduced proportionately where the business has not been owned for the whole of the previous ten years, or, in the case of family companies, where the director has not been a full-time working director for that period. Where, however, a director ceases full-time working some time before he disposes of his shares, then providing he works for at least ten hours a week on average in the period before disposal, the relief will be given by reference to the length of time for which he was a full-time working director. The minimum period of ownership or full-time directorship to enable relief to be claimed is one year (called the qualifying period). See example 6 above. In working out how long the business has been owned, the date of disposal is strictly the contract date, but by concession the completion date may be taken instead where business activities have continued up to completion. Where someone has been in business for two or more separate periods, with an intervening gap not exceeding two years, the periods are added together to determine the qualifying period (but if they overlap, the overlap is counted only once). Any part of the resulting period that goes back earlier than ten years is disregarded. It does not affect the relief if part of the qualifying period relates to a self-employed business and part to full-time directorship of a family company. Note that it is the length of time the *interest in the business* has been owned that determines the available relief, not the time for which the assets themselves have been owned.

Where the disposal is of shares in a family company, the gain on the shares is reduced in the proportion of the company's chargeable business assets to the total chargeable assets to arrive at the gain qualifying for relief. Chargeable assets are all assets on which a chargeable gain or allowable loss would arise if the company disposed of them (or which would be treated as disposed of for neither gain nor loss). Current assets are therefore excluded. On a disposal of shares in a family holding company of a trading group, it is the group's assets that are taken into account, and inter-group shareholdings are ignored.

Property let commercially as furnished holiday accommodation (see chapter 32) qualifies as a business asset for this relief.

The relief may also be given where a director, partner or employee disposes of assets owned by him which have been used for the purposes of the business or employment, or where trustees dispose of settled property consisting of assets qualifying for relief in which a beneficiary has an interest in possession. The relief is, however, restricted if rent is paid, and charging a full market rent during any part of the ten-year qualifying period would deny the relief altogether for that part of the period, except for that fraction of premises let to a partnership that corresponds to the owner's share in the partnership, since he cannot let to himself.

Gifts and transactions with connected persons (ss 17–19, 67, 165–169, 258–261, 281, 286 and Sch 7)

For capital gains tax, a gift of a chargeable asset is regarded as a disposal at open market value (except for husband/wife transfers), and the chargeable gain or allowable loss is computed in the usual way, with indexation allowance being taken into account. There are, however, some special rules for both gains and losses.

Not only gifts but all transactions between connected persons, or not at arm's length, are regarded as at open market value except for husband/wife transactions, which are not normally chargeable (see page 38). Broadly, a person is connected with his or his wife's close relatives and their spouses, with business partners and their spouses and relatives (except in relation to normal commercial transactions), and, if he is the trustee of a settlement, with the settlor (if an individual) and with any person connected with the settlor. Companies under the same control are connected with each other and with the persons controlling them.

Where an asset is disposed of to a connected person (other than the individual's husband or wife) and a loss arises, the loss may not be set against general gains but only against a later gain on a transaction with the same connected person. Where someone disposes of assets on different occasions within a period of six years to one or more persons connected with him, and their value taken together is higher than their separate values, then the disposal value for each of the transactions is a proportionate part of the aggregate value, and all necessary adjustments will be made to earlier tax charges.

For many years, it was possible to defer gains on most gifts made by individuals or trustees to individuals or trustees. It has also been possible to defer gains on gifts of business assets to companies. One of the reasons for the deferral of capital gains tax was that inheritance tax was payable on gifts. But most lifetime gifts are now exempt from inheritance tax unless the donor dies within seven years, so the general gifts relief for capital gains tax is no longer available for disposals after 13 March 1989. The relief for gifts of business assets continues and relief is also available for certain other assets.

The gifts that now qualify for relief are as follows:

(a) Business assets, which comprise
    (i) Assets used in the donor's business or in his family company (defined as for retirement relief—see page 49);
    (ii) Farm land and buildings that would qualify for inheritance tax agricultural property relief—see page 71; note that this enables relief to be claimed on agricultural land held as an investment, providing the appropriate conditions are satisfied;
    (iii) Shares or securities in trading companies that are neither quoted on the Stock Exchange nor dealt in on the Unlisted Securities Market;
    (iv) Shares or securities in the donor's family trading company (relief being restricted proportionately if not all the company's assets are business assets);

(b) Gifts of heritage property (works of art, historic buildings etc.);

(c) Gifts to funds for the maintenance of heritage property;

(d) Gifts to political parties;

(e) Gifts that are *immediately* chargeable to inheritance tax or would be had they not been covered by the inheritance tax annual exemption. This mainly covers gifts into and out of discretionary trusts but also covers any other gifts that are within the inheritance tax annual exemption (see page 60).

Where gifts relief is claimed, the donor is not charged to tax on the gain and the value at which the donee is treated as having acquired the asset is reduced by the gain, so that the donee will make a correspondingly larger gain (or smaller loss) when he disposes of the asset. There are provisions to ensure that the gifts relief is not used to avoid tax altogether, for example where the donee is not resident in the UK. If the donee is resident at the time of the gift but becomes not resident and not ordinarily resident in the

UK before disposing of the asset, the gain is then charged to tax. There is no time limit on this provision for trustees, but for individuals it only applies to a change of residence within six years after the end of the tax year in which the gift was made. It does not apply at all to trustees becoming resident and not ordinarily resident in the UK after 18 March 1991 because there are new rules for the tax treatment of such trustees—see page 472.

Gifts relief is also available where assets are not given outright but are disposed of for less than their value, but the gain arising may then only be deferred to the extent to which it exceeds the amount received.

Claims for gifts relief to apply must be made by the donor and donee jointly except where the donees are trustees, in which case only the donor need make the claim.

Where part of a gain on a gift is covered by retirement relief, gifts relief may be claimed on the balance. Where a gift on which the gifts holdover relief is claimed attracts inheritance tax, either immediately or as a result of the donor's death within seven years, the donee's base cost for capital gains tax is increased by the inheritance tax (but not so as to create a loss on future disposal).

Where gifts relief is not available, tax may be paid by ten annual instalments on gifts of land, a controlling shareholding in a company, or minority holdings of shares or securities in a company that are neither quoted on the Stock Exchange nor dealt in on the Unlisted Securities Market. Interest will, however, be charged on the full amount outstanding and not just on any instalment which is paid late.

See page 42 for the treatment of disposals after 5 April 1988 that are affected by deferred gains on assets acquired before 31 March 1982.

Assets of negligible value (s 24(2))

Where the value of an asset has become negligible, a claim may be made for the asset to be treated as sold and reacquired at that value, establishing an allowable loss accordingly. Although, strictly, you should be treated as having disposed of the asset on the date of the claim, there is a Revenue concession (D28) allowing you to choose a deemed disposal date falling within the two years before the tax year or company accounting period in which the claim is made, providing the asset was of negligible value on that date and when the claim is made (whether or not it was of negligible value before that deemed disposal date).

Relief for losses on loans (ss 251–255)

The normal rules for working out allowable losses do not apply to ordinary debts. They do, however, apply to the loss of money lent if the loan is marketable loan stock or a similar security *other than* a qualifying corporate bond (see page 436). The loans qualifying for relief under the normal rules will therefore mainly be non-sterling loan stock, loan stock that is convertible into shares, and loan stock acquired before 14 March 1984.

Qualifying corporate bonds are exempt from capital gains tax, and if a loss arises it will not normally be an allowable loss. There are, however, special rules to allow the relief described below in certain circumstances—see page 437.

Relief is available to the lender or guarantor for losses on loans or guarantees that do not qualify under the normal rules outlined above if the borrower is a UK resident and uses the money lent wholly for the purposes of a trade carried on by him. Upon an appropriate claim by the lender or guarantor, an irrecoverable loan or payment under guarantee gives rise to an allowable loss for CGT, provided that the debt or the rights acquired by the guarantor following the guarantee payment are not assigned. There is no indexation allowance on the allowable loss. If any amount is subsequently recovered (whether from the borrower or from any co-guarantor) it will be treated as a capital gain.

Relief is not available if the loss arises because of something the lender, or guarantor, has done or failed to do, or where the amount has become irrecoverable in consequence of the terms of the loan, nor is it available where the claimant and borrower are husband and wife or companies in the same group.

Due date of payment and interest on overdue tax (s 7 and TMA 1970, ss 86, 88)

The normal due date of payment of capital gains tax is 1 December after the end of the tax year, or 30 days after the issue of the assessment if later. Where an appeal is made against an assessment, tax is still due on the normal due date unless a postponement application is made, when the tax not to be postponed becomes payable 30 days after the date the Revenue agree the amount that cannot be postponed if that gives a later date than the normal due date. If any postponed tax ultimately becomes payable following settlement of the appeal, it is due for payment 30 days after the issue of the revised assessment following settlement of the appeal (or on the normal due date if later). Interest normally runs from the due date of payment, but where tax has been postponed the date from which interest runs is put back to 30 days after the date the non-postponed tax was agreed (if that is after the 1 December date), subject to its never being later than 1 June in the next but one tax year after that to which the tax relates (unless the original assessment was issued very late, in which case interest would run from 30 days after that assessment if it was later than the 1 June date). In cases of substantial delay in submitting a return, interest runs from the date the tax ought to have been paid (see chapter 9). In this connection, the Revenue will usually regard a delay as substantial if a return has not been made by 31 October in the tax year following that in which the gain arose and they were not otherwise made aware of the gain or given sufficient information to enable an assessment to be raised. (Revenue Statement of Practice SP 6/89). The rates of interest in recent years are given on page xxiv.

Payment by instalments (s 280)

Capital gains tax may be paid by instalments where the proceeds are being received by instalments over 18 months or more and paying tax in one sum would cause hardship. The instalments run over eight years, or until the last instalment of the price is received if sooner, with relief for bad debts being available if part of the amount due proves irrecoverable. Interest is charged on any instalments paid late (but only on the instalment and not on the full amount outstanding).

Capital gains tax is also payable by instalments on certain gifts – see page 53.

Quoted and unquoted securities

Special rules apply to the treatment of both quoted and unquoted securities. These are dealt with in detail in chapter 38.

No gain / no loss disposals

Special provisions apply to certain disposals, the main ones being:

(a) Transfers on company reconstructions (s 139).
(b) Transfers within a 75% group of companies (s 171).
(c) Husband / wife transfers (s 58).
(d) Transfers by personal representatives to legatees (s 62).

The disposal is effectively treated as giving rise to neither gain nor loss, and the transferee's acquisition cost is the original cost plus indexation allowance to date.

Death (ss 3(7), 62)

No capital gains tax charge arises on death. If losses arise in the year of death these may be carried back and set against gains assessable in the three previous tax years, latest first (with the set-off being made only against any gains not covered by the annual exemption in those years).

The personal representatives or legatees are treated as acquiring the assets at the market value at the date of death. When personal representatives dispose of assets at values in excess of the values at death, gains arising will be charged to tax (and exemptions the deceased could have claimed may not be available, for example on a private residence) but they may claim the annual exemption, currently £5,800, in respect of disposals by them in the tax year of death and in each of the following two tax years.

Where within two years after a death the persons entitled to the estate vary the way in which it is distributed, and notify the Revenue within six months after the variation, the variation is not regarded as a disposal by those originally entitled but as having been made by the deceased at the date of death so that no CGT charge arises on any increase in value since death.

Trusts (ss 3, 68–98 and Schs 1, 5)

Trustees are chargeable persons for capital gains tax. They are entitled to an annual exemption of £2,900 for 1992/93, this being divided where there are associated trusts, but with each trust getting a minimum exemption of £580. The exemption is usually increased each year in line with the retail prices index, as it has been for 1992/93 (see page 47).

When assets are placed in trust, and when they are transferred to beneficiaries other than on the death of a life tenant, a disposal at market value is treated as taking place, but gains may sometimes be rolled over under the gifts relief provisions dealt with on page 52. When a life interest ends other than on the death of a life tenant, this is not a chargeable event for capital gains tax. When a life tenant dies and someone else becomes entitled to the life interest, or a beneficiary becomes absolutely entitled to trust assets following a life tenant's death, the trustees are not treated as making either chargeable gains or allowable losses, but the market value of the trust property at that time becomes the future base value for capital gains tax, either in the hands of the trustees or of the beneficiary.

The detailed provisions on the capital gains position of trusts are dealt with in chapter 42, except for the overseas element, which is dealt with in chapter 41.

Options and futures (ss 114, 143–148)

There are special rules concerning options connected with employment (see chapter 11). The rules for other options depend on the type of option.

The following options are not treated as wasting assets.

> Quoted options to subscribe for new shares
> Traded options to buy or sell shares or other financial instruments quoted on a recognised stock exchange or futures exchange (such as the London International Financial Futures and Options Exchange – LIFFE) and 'over the counter' financial options
> Options to acquire assets for use by the option holder in his business.

This means that when they are disposed of or abandoned, an allowable loss or chargeable gain may arise.

Other options are treated as wasting assets, so that their cost wastes away over their life, restricting loss relief accordingly if they lapse or become valueless. If such options are abandoned, no allowable loss can arise. The forfeiture of a deposit is treated as the abandonment of an option.

Whether an option is treated as a wasting asset or not, it is generally treated as a separate chargeable asset, so that the full amount of the consideration for the option is chargeable as a gain. This separate treatment does not apply if the option is exercised. In that case the price paid for the option is incorporated with the cost of the asset to form a single transaction both as regards the seller and the buyer.

In relation to shares, the above provisions are modified to bring options within the share pooling provisions. Purchased options of the same series will therefore be pooled if an acquisition is not matched with a disposal on the same day or within the next nine days, and indexation allowance will then be available. If an option is exercised, the shares acquired will merge with any existing pool of shares of the same class in the same company, and the indexed cost of the option will form part of the pool cost. The disposal of an option to buy or sell gilt-edged securities or qualifying corporate bonds is exempt.

Although both individuals and institutions invest in traded options, the commodity and financial futures market is essentially for the professionals and the institutional investors. The gains and losses of banks and building societies on futures and traded options are treated as trading transactions. The transactions of insurance companies and investment trusts are some-times capital and sometimes revenue, and investment trusts are exempt from tax on the capital transactions. Authorised unit trusts and pensions funds are exempt on both capital and trading transactions.

Deferred consideration

An increasing number of transactions are being structured along lines where only part of the consideration is received at the time of the sale, with further amounts depending upon later events, for example profit perfor-mance in the case of the sale of a family company. This aspect is dealt with briefly in chapter 28.

5
Inheritance tax: general principles

Introduction

Inheritance tax is the latest in the line of taxes on lifetime and death gifts. It used to be called capital transfer tax, and it was introduced in 1975 to replace estate duty. The law is contained in the Inheritance Tax Act 1984 (abbreviated in this book to IHTA 1984) and subsequent Finance Acts.

Basis of charge (IHTA 1984, ss 1–8)

Inheritance tax is charged on certain lifetime gifts, on wealth at death and on certain transfers into and out of trusts. Some lifetime transfers are wholly exempt from tax (see page 60). Those lifetime transfers which are liable to tax are called chargeable transfers. Some lifetime transfers are only liable if the donor dies within seven years of making them, and these are called potentially exempt transfers (see page 62). If the donor survives seven years, the potentially exempt transfer becomes an exempt transfer. If he dies within seven years it becomes a chargeable transfer. Whether a transfer is an immediately chargeable transfer or becomes chargeable because of the donor's death within seven years, no tax will even so be payable if the transfer is below the 'nil rate' threshold (see below).

A running total is kept of chargeable lifetime transfers and tax is only payable when a statutory threshold is reached, currently £150,000 (applicable from 10 March 1992). The rate of tax used to rise progressively through various bands, but since 15 March 1988 there has been only a single rate of 40%. To encourage lifetime giving, chargeable lifetime transfers are charged at only half rate, i.e. at 20% (see page 59). The scales of rates for earlier years are shown on page xxxiii. Transfers are excluded from the running total seven years after they are made. Before 18 March 1986 the period was ten years. The existing running total at that date was amended to exclude transfers made more than seven years previously.

The threshold is increased annually, at least in line with increases in the retail prices index. These increases do not enable tax paid on earlier transfers to be recovered.

When someone dies, he is treated as making a final transfer of the whole of his estate and the tax charged on the estate depends on the total of chargeable lifetime transfers within the previous seven years and on any potentially exempt transfers which become chargeable at death because the donor has not survived the seven-year period.

If a transfer is chargeable during the lifetime of the donor, the rate of tax charged at that time on any excess over the nil rate threshold is at one half of the scale rate, i.e. currently 20%. If the donor dies within the next seven years the tax is recomputed at the full scale rate applicable at the date of death (and using the nil rate threshold applicable at the date of death), but is then reduced if the donor has survived the gift by more than three years (see page 64). The tax on potentially exempt transfers which become chargeable because of the death of the donor within seven years may also be less than the full scale rate, the reduction depending on the time that has elapsed since the gift was made.

The seven-year survivorship period is therefore relevant for three reasons.

(a) Tax paid on chargeable lifetime transfers is recomputed if death occurs within seven years.
(b) Chargeable lifetime transfers are excluded from the running total after seven years.
(c) Lifetime transfers which are potentially exempt are completely exempt after seven years, but will be chargeable if death occurs within seven years.

Before 18 March 1986 the tax on a lifetime transfer was only increased to the full death rate if the donor died within three years and not seven as under the current provisions. The running total of transfers that determined how much tax was payable, however, covered the previous ten years and not seven. These provisions continued to apply to transfers made before 18 March 1986 but are not relevant to deaths occurring after 17 March 1989 (i.e. three years from 18 March 1986).

Persons liable (IHTA 1984, ss 6, 48, 158, 159, 267)

UK domiciled individuals are chargeable in respect of property anywhere in the world and non-UK domiciled individuals in respect of property in the UK. Husband and wife are separate chargeable persons, so any limits on exempt transfers apply separately to each of them and each can make transfers free of tax up to the statutory threshold.

Domicile is a legal term that is not easy to define but essentially it means the country you regard as 'home'. The term has an extended meaning for inheritance tax, and a person is treated as UK domiciled if:

(a) he was UK domiciled on or after 10 December 1974 and within the three years preceding the transfer; or
(b) he was resident in the UK on or after 10 December 1974 and in at least 17 of the 20 tax years up to and including the year of transfer.

Double taxation relief is given where the transfer of assets attracts tax overseas as well as in the UK.

Treatment of lifetime transfers

Where a transfer is made in lifetime, it may be an exempt transfer, or a potentially exempt transfer, or a chargeable transfer.

Exempt transfers

Certain transfers are exempt only if they are made in lifetime. They are as follows.

Small gifts to same person (IHTA 1984, s 20)

Any outright lifetime gifts to any one person in any one tax year are exempt if the total gifts to that person do not exceed £250 in that year.

Gifts in consideration of marriage (IHTA 1984, s 22)

A gift of up to £5,000 by a parent, of £2,500 by a grandparent, of £2,500 by one party to the marriage to the other, or of £1,000 by another person, is exempt providing it is a lifetime gift made in consideration of the marriage. If the gift is into a marriage settlement it must be primarily for the benefit of the married couple, their children or their children's spouses.

Normal expenditure out of income (IHTA 1984, s 21)

To obtain exemption the gift must be part of the donor's normal expenditure, and must not, taking one year with another, reduce the donor's available net income (after all other transfers) below that required to maintain his usual standard of living. The exemption will often apply to life assurance policy premiums paid for the benefit of another.

Waivers of remuneration and dividends (IHTA 1984, ss 14, 15)

A waiver or repayment of remuneration does not attract inheritance tax. Nor does a waiver of dividends made within twelve months before any right to the dividend arises.

Capital transfers for family maintenance (IHTA 1984, ss 11, 51)

It may sometimes be necessary to make transfers of capital in order to provide for your family, for example following the dissolution of a marriage when the usual exemption for transfer between husband and wife (see below) has ceased to apply, or to make reasonable provision for a dependent relative. Such transfers may be made without attracting liability.

Annual transfers not exceeding £3,000 (IHTA 1984, s 19)

The first £3,000 of lifetime transfers in any tax year are exempt. Any unused portion of the exemption may be carried forward for one year only for use in the following tax year after the exemption for that following tax year has been used.

The intention of the legislation was that the annual exemption would not be used in the first instance to exempt a transfer that would otherwise be a potentially exempt transfer, and would therefore be fully available against transfers that were immediately chargeable. But if a potentially exempt transfer had become chargeable because of the donor's death within seven years, the annual exemption could have been used against it if not already used. It has been recognised that there is a defect in the law, and that the first £3,000 of transfers in any year not covered by any other exemption utilise the annual exemption, and only any balance will be either potentially exempt or chargeable. The annual exemption will therefore not have to be considered when computing the tax or extra tax payable on death, having already been taken into account in calculating the amount chargeable or potentially exempt in lifetime.

Other exemptions are available whether the transfer is made in lifetime or on death, as follows.

Transfers between husband and wife (IHTA 1984, s 18)

These are exempt, except where a husband or wife domiciled in the UK transfers to a foreign domiciled spouse, when transfers are only exempt up to £55,000.

Gifts to charities (IHTA 1984, s 23)

Gifts to charities, either outright or to be held on trust for charitable purposes, are wholly exempt.

Gifts to political parties (IHTA 1984, s 24)

Gifts to qualifying political parties are wholly exempt. To qualify, a party must either have at least two MPs in the House of Commons, or one MP and at least 150,000 votes in its favour at the last general election.

Gifts to housing associations (IHTA 1984, s 24A)

Gifts of land on or after 14 March 1989 to registered housing associations are exempt.

Gifts for national purposes (IHTA 1984, s 25)

These are exempt.

Conditional exemption for heritage property (IHTA 1984, s 26)

Providing various undertakings are given, for example public access, conditional exemption applies to the lifetime or death transfer of property which is designated by the Treasury as of national, scientific, historic, artistic, architectural or scenic interest (e.g. works of art and historic buildings). If there is any breach of an undertaking, inheritance tax becomes payable by the donee.

Maintenance funds for heritage property (IHTA 1984, s 27)

Transfers into a settlement established for the maintenance, repair or preservation of heritage property are exempt providing a Treasury direction is made in respect of the property.

Mutual transfers

Where a potentially exempt transfer (see below) or a chargeable transfer is made and the donee then makes a gift back to the donor, there are provisions to avoid a double charge to tax as a result of the donor's death within seven years.

Potentially exempt transfers (IHTA 1984, s 3A)

Where a transfer is not covered by exemptions, it is nonetheless not in the first instance treated as a chargeable transfer where

(i) it is made by an individual on or after 18 March 1986, and

(ii) it is a gift to another individual or into an accumulation and maintenance trust or trust for disabled persons.

For transfers on and after 17 March 1987, the following transfers are also not initially treated as chargeable transfers:

(i) the creation by an individual of a trust fund in which someone is entitled to the income for life (called an interest in possession) and further gifts into such a trust, and

(ii) the termination of such a life interest during the lifetime of the person entitled to the income, followed either by another life interest or by someone becoming absolutely entitled to the trust property.

A transfer in one of these categories is called a potentially exempt transfer and is only relevant in the calculation of inheritance tax if the donor dies within seven years after the gift.

A potentially exempt transfer which becomes a chargeable transfer because of the donor's death within seven years is brought into account at the value of the gift at the time of the transfer, although the nil rate threshold and rate of tax used are those in force at the date of the donor's death.

It is therefore possible to crystallise the value of the transfer by giving in lifetime and this may be particularly useful where there are appreciating assets, since any later growth in value is in the hands of the donee. The capital gains tax effect must also be considered, however, because a lifetime gift will be a chargeable disposal for capital gains tax unless the gifts relief is available (see page 52), whereas if the asset is held until death the increase in value up to that time escapes capital gains tax.

Retaining a benefit (FA 1986, s 102 and Sch 20)

Property is treated as continuing to belong to a donor if he continues to enjoy any benefit from the gifted property. If the donor still retains a benefit at the time of his death, the property is treated as remaining in his estate and is taxed accordingly. See example 1.

These rules can result in a double tax charge and there are special rules to eliminate any double charges that occur.

Example 1

A donor gives away his house but continues to live in it. He will be treated as making a second gift at the time when he ceases to occupy the house or pays a proper rent for his occupation so that inheritance tax may be payable if he does not then survive for a further seven years.

The same applies where a donor gives away £50,000, but continues to receive the interest on it. He will be treated as making a second gift when he ceases to receive the interest.

Chargeable lifetime transfers (IHTA 1984, ss 2, 3, 5)

A chargeable transfer is any transfer of value other than an exempt transfer or a potentially exempt transfer (which will, however, become a chargeable transfer if the donor does not survive for seven years).

A transfer of value is any transfer of money or other assets made by a person which reduces the value of his estate, and this decrease in the value of the estate is the value transferred. Commercial transactions and other arm's length transactions are not, however, treated as transfers of value.

Now that most lifetime gifts are potentially exempt, the main examples of chargeable lifetime transfers are transfers into and out of discretionary trusts, in which no-one has a right to the income, and transfers involving companies.

The starting point in valuing a transfer is the value of the donor's estate.

A person's estate is the total of all the property to which he is beneficially entitled. As well as his own property, it includes:

 (i) an interest as a joint tenant. Such an interest is automatically transferred to the other joint tenant(s) on his death, but it still forms part of his estate for tax purposes. (This differs from a share as a tenant in common, which means each person has a separate share which he may dispose of as he wishes, and which therefore counts as his own property for all purposes.); and

(ii) the capital supporting the income which he is entitled to receive from a trust fund (called an interest in possession).

The inclusion of the capital in a trust fund in a person's estate means that on his death, he is deemed to make a chargeable transfer of the capital in the fund, although the tax on that amount is paid by the trustees.

On the other hand, there is no charge to tax when someone entitled to the income from a trust fund is allocated part of the supporting capital, because the capital is treated as being part of his estate already.

Special provisions apply to discretionary trusts, where no-one is entitled as of right to the income from the fund, and the trustees merely have a discretion as to when, and possibly to whom, they pay it. Favourable treatment is given to discretionary trusts that are accumulation and maintenance trusts for minor children. The treatment of the various types of trust is dealt with in detail in chapter 42.

If a lifetime gift is chargeable and the donor pays the tax, his estate is reduced not only by the gift itself but also by the tax he pays. The reduction in his estate is found by grossing up the amount of the gift to allow for the tax which he has to pay.

Example 2

Donor makes a chargeable lifetime transfer of £8,000 when the nil threshold had already been used, so that the rate of tax is 20%. He pays the tax.

The reduction in his estate is £8,000 × 100/80 = £10,000.

Being: The chargeable transfer	10,000
Tax payable @ 20%	2,000
Leaving for the donee	£8,000

If any capital gains tax is payable by the recipient of the gift, it is deducted from the value of the gift in calculating the decrease in the donor's estate.

Position on death (IHTA 1984, s 4)

When someone dies, the value of his estate becomes liable to inheritance tax. The death also affects chargeable transfers made in the seven years before death, on which additional tax may now be payable, and potentially exempt transfers made within the seven years before death, which now become chargeable transfers.

Chargeable transfers made within the seven years before death (IHTA 1984, s 7)

Tax on the original lifetime transfers will have been calculated at half the scale rates, and any potentially exempt transfers made within the previous seven years will not have been included in the running total in making that calculation. Tax is now recalculated using the full scale rates in force at the date of death. Any potentially exempt transfers that were made earlier than the chargeable lifetime transfer but within seven years before death are, however, now brought into that running total (see example 4 on page 67). The tax is then reduced according to the length of time by which the donor has survived the gift. The percentage of the full scale rate payable following the reduction is as follows (see example 3).

Time between chargeable gift and death	% payable
Up to 3 years	100
More than 3 but less than 4 years	80
More than 4 but less than 5 years	60
More than 5 but less than 6 years	40
More than 6 but less than 7 years	20

The donee is primarily liable to pay the amount by which the tax at the appropriate percentage of the full scale rate exceeds the tax paid on the gift in lifetime. If, however, the lifetime tax exceeds the death tax, no repayment is available.

If the value of the gifted asset has fallen between the time of the gift and death, the lower value may be used to calculate the tax, unless the asset was tangible movable property with a predictable life of 50 years or less (for example, a car). The sale proceeds; if lower than the value when given

---

Example 3

The only chargeable transfer made by a taxpayer is a transfer to a discretionary trust of £160,000 (after exemptions) on 30 September 1992. The tax payable is:

	150,000	—
	10,000 @ 20% (half rate)	2,000
	£160,000	£2,000

Assuming that the tax rate and threshold remain unchanged, so that £4,000 is in fact the amount of tax at the full scale rate, the effect of the tapering relief is as follows.

If taxpayer dies on	Time between gift and death	% of £4,000 payable	Amounting to
			£
10.10.93	Less than 3 yrs	100	4,000
31.12.95	3 to 4 yrs	80	3,200
31.1.98	5 to 6 yrs	40	1,600

Extra tax if death occurs on 10.10.93 will be £2,000.
Extra tax if death occurs on 31.12.95 will be £1,200, i.e. £3,200 less £2,000.

No extra tax will be due if death occurs on 31.1.98 because the reduced tax of £1,600 is less than the tax already paid of £2,000.

The rate of tax on death would not, in fact, be double the earlier lifetime rate as in this example, because of the indexation of the threshold.

away, may also be used where the donee has sold the asset before the donor's death in an arm's length, freely negotiated sale, to an unconnected person.

Potentially exempt transfers made within the seven years before death

If a donor has survived a potentially exempt transfer by seven years, it becomes an exempt transfer and is not taken into account at all. Any potentially exempt transfer made within the seven years before death becomes chargeable. It is treated as if it had been a chargeable transfer at the date of the original gift, and is added to the running total of transfers made within the seven years before it (including any earlier potentially exempt transfers that now become chargeable because they were also made within seven years before the donor's death). The tax is calculated at the full scale rate in force at the date of death, but the reduced rates of tax for transfers between four and seven years before death shown on page 65 apply, and also the relief where the value of the gifted asset has fallen before the death. If the potentially exempt transfer falls within the nil rate threshold, then no tax will be charged on it – and no reduced rates of tax can therefore apply – but it is nonetheless taken into account to calculate how much tax is payable on any later transfers and on the death estate.

It was intended by the legislation that a potentially exempt transfer which became a chargeable transfer could qualify for the annual exemption for the year in which it was made, plus any unused amount for the previous year. It has now been decided that the law is defective and there can be no question of the annual exemption later becoming available on a potentially exempt transfer since it will already have been taken into account at the time of the transfer (see page 61).

The estate at death

In order to calculate the tax payable on the estate at death, the value of the estate is added to the total of the chargeable lifetime transfers made in the seven years before death, plus the potentially exempt transfers made in the seven years before death that have now become chargeable. See example 4.

Transfers of 'excluded property' are ignored in valuing the death estate (IHTA 1984, ss 3, 5, 6, 48). The most common forms of excluded property are:

(i) property situated overseas where the owner is not domiciled in the UK; and
(ii) reversionary interests in trust funds (which means the right to the capital when the present beneficiary's right to the income comes to an end).

The way in which the death estate is valued, and the reliefs which are available, are dealt with below. The exemptions available are dealt with on pages 60–62.

Example 4

At 17 March 1986 a taxpayer had made chargeable lifetime transfers (after deducting available exemptions) of £40,000 on 30 June 1983 and £30,000 on 31 December 1985. He made the following gifts on 30 September 1989.

£5,000 to a national charity
£70,000 to his sister

On 30 October 1989, he transferred £60,000 to a discretionary trust, the trustees paying the tax out of the £60,000.

He died on 28 December 1992 leaving an estate of £200,000 divided equally between his two adult children.

The capital transfer tax/inheritance tax position is as follows.

Transfers at 17.3.86 (on which CTT will have been paid)

	£	£
On 30.6.83	40,000	
On 31.12.85	30,000	70,000

Gifts on 30.9.89

Gift of £5,000 to national charity is exempt.		
Gift to sister	70,000	
Annual exemption	(3,000)	
Annual exemption from previous year	(3,000)	
Potentially exempt gift to sister	64,000	—
Gift on 30.10.89 to discretionary trust		60,000
		130,000

Tax payable by trustees at half of scale rate on FA 1989 scale i.e. 20% on (£130,000–£118,000) = £2,400

At 1.7.90, exclude transfers more than seven years before, i.e. 30.6.83	40,000
	£90,000

Following taxpayer's death on 28.12.92, potentially exempt transfer on 30.9.89 becomes chargeable, and tax from seven years before death (but not before 18.3.86) must be recalculated, using full scale rates in force at 28.12.92, with tapering relief if appropriate. Tax on gifts *before* 18 March 1986 is only recalculated if donor dies within *three* years (see page 59), so no extra tax could arise on the 31

December 1985 gift. Such gifts are, however, still included in the cumulative total for any gifts made within the following seven years.

Gift on 30.9.89

Transfers in previous seven years	70,000
Potentially exempt transfer now chargeable	64,000
	134,000

No tax payable by sister since total transfers are below nil threshold.

Gift on 30.10.89

Discretionary trust	60,000
	194,000

Tax payable by trustees @ 40% on (£194,000 − 150,000)	17,600	
Less tapering relief (3 to 4 yrs, 20%)	3,520	
	14,080	
Less paid on lifetime transfer	2,400	
	£11,680	

At 1.7.90, exclude transfers more than seven years before, i.e. 30.6.83	40,000
	154,000
Estate at death 28.12.92	200,000
	£354,000

Tax on estate of £200,000 @ 40% = £80,000, payable by personal representatives before dividing the estate between the children.

Valuation of property (IHTA 1984, ss 160–198)

The value of property for inheritance tax is the amount it might reasonably be expected to fetch if sold in the open market. The price is not, however, to be reduced on the grounds that the whole property is placed on the market at one time.

If the asset to be transferred will give rise to a capital gains tax liability, and the donee agrees to pay that tax, then the value transferred is reduced by the capital gains tax paid. However, capital gains tax may sometimes not arise on gifts because of the availability of gifts holdover relief. See page 52.

Valuation on death

Apart from life assurance policies (see below) the value of property to be included in the estate at death is that immediately prior to death. Changes in the value of the estate as a result of the death are taken into account, for example the increased value of life assurance policies and the reduction in the value of goodwill which depends upon the personal qualities of the deceased. Allowance is made for reasonable funeral expenses. In the case of overseas property, allowance is also made for additional expenses incurred because of its situation, subject to a limit of 5% of the value of the property.

Quoted securities and land transferred on death

Where an estate on death includes quoted securities and they are sold, before being transferred to the beneficiaries, within twelve months after death for less than their value at death, then the total sales proceeds before expenses may be substituted for the death value. Similarly, if the estate includes land which is sold within three years after death, before being transferred to the beneficiaries, relief is available for the reduction in value by comparing the total sale proceeds before expenses with the value at death.

Related property

In some instances, if an asset is divided up, the total value of the parts may be less than the value of the whole. If a part:

(a) belongs to a spouse, or
(b) was the subject of an exempt transfer by the taxpayer to a charity, political party or national heritage body and is still owned by that body or has been so owned at any time within the previous five years,

the special provisions concerning related property apply.

If it produces a higher value than its unrelated value, the value of a part of related property is taken as an appropriate portion of the total value of all the property. See example 5.

Example 5

The shareholders of Related Ltd, an unquoted company, are Mr R 40%, Mrs R 25%, others 35%. Shareholdings are valued as follows:

65%	£58,500
40%	£24,000
25%	£15,000

Inheritance tax values are:

Mr R 40/65 × £58,500 £36,000 (being greater than £24,000)
Mrs R 25/65 × £58,500 £22,500 (being greater than £15,000)

If related property is sold within three years after death to an unconnected person, a claim may be made for the tax at death to be recomputed using its unrelated value (not its sale value).

Life assurance policies

The valuation of life assurance policies depends on whether the transfer is during the lifetime or on the death of the donor. Policies transferred in lifetime are valued at the greater of the surrender value and the premiums paid. Sometimes it is the policy premiums, rather than the policy itself, which are transfers of value (e.g. where a policy is written in trust for another person and the premiums are paid by the person whose life is assured) and in such cases each premium payment will be a potentially exempt transfer unless it is already exempt as a gift out of income or as a small gift or because of the annual exemption.

On death the maturity value of a policy taken out by a person on his own life will be included in his estate unless it has been assigned to someone else in lifetime, or it has been written in trust for the benefit of someone else.

Associated operations (IHTA 1984, s 268)

There are rules to enable the Revenue to treat a series of connected operations as a single transfer made at the time of the last of them.

Business property relief (IHTA 1984, ss 103–114; FA 1987, s 58 and Sch 8; F(No 2)A 1992, Sch 14) and agricultural property relief (IHTA 1984, ss 115–124A; FA 1987, s 58 and Sch 8; F(No 2)A 1992, Sch 14)

Business property relief is available on valuing transfers of business property, providing certain conditions as to the length of ownership and type of business are satisfied. For transfers on and after 10 March 1992, and any recalculation of tax on earlier transfers following a death on or after that date, the relief has been increased from 50% or 30% to the following rates:

A business or interest in a business (including a partnership share) 100%
Transfers out of unquoted shareholdings of more than 25% 100%
Transfers out of a controlling shareholding in a quoted company (including control through 'related property' holdings) 50%
Transfers out of unquoted shareholdings of 25% or less 50%
Land or buildings, machinery or plant used for a business carried on by:
  a company of which the donor has control; or
  a partnership in which the donor was a partner; or
  the donor, being settled property in which he had an interest in possession 50%

With effect from 10 March 1992, shares on the Unlisted Securities Market are treated as unquoted shares.

The property transferred must normally have been owned by the donor throughout the previous two years. For unquoted shareholdings, the donor must have owned more than 25% of the voting power *throughout* the two years before the transfer in order to get the 100% rate of relief. Business property relief is not available where the business consists of dealing in stocks and shares (except market makers on the Stock Exchange and discount houses), dealing in land and buildings or holding investments (including land which is let).

The relief is applied automatically without a claim and is given after agricultural property relief (see below) but before available exemptions.

Agricultural property relief is available on the transfer of agricultural property so long as various conditions are met. As with business property relief, the rates of relief have been increased from 50% or 30% to the rates shown below for transfers on and after 10 March 1992, and for any recalculation of tax on earlier transfers following a death on or after that date. The relief only applies to the agricultural value of the property, and in arriving at that value any loan secured on the agricultural property must be deducted.

The agricultural property must at the time of the transfer have been either occupied by the donor for agriculture throughout the two years ending with the date of transfer or owned by the donor throughout the previous seven years and occupied for agriculture by him or another throughout that period. Note that this enables relief to be given on agricultural investment property. In certain circumstances these rules are modified if the property transferred was acquired as a replacement for other agricultural property.

Relief is available both on the transfer of agricultural property itself, and on the transfer of shares out of a controlling holding in a farming company to the extent of the underlying agricultural value.

Relief is given at the rate of 100% where the donor had the right to vacant possession immediately before the transfer (or the right to obtain vacant possession within the next twelve months) and 50% on tenanted agricultural property. Transitional provisions enable relief to be claimed at the 100% rate on tenanted agricultural property where the donor had been beneficially entitled to his interest in the property since before 10 March 1981 and would have been entitled to the higher rate of relief (then 50%) under the former provisions for agricultural relief which operated before that date.

Where agricultural property satisfies the conditions for business property relief, agricultural property relief is given first and business property relief is given on the non-agricultural value. As with business property relief, agricultural property relief is given without the need for a claim.

Binding contract for sale (IHTA 1984, ss 113, 124)

Property does not qualify for business or agricultural relief if it is subject to a binding contract for sale (except in cases of a conversion of an unincorporated business to a company, or a company reconstruction). A 'buy and sell' agreement made by partners or company directors to take effect on their death is considered by the Revenue to constitute such a contract, but it is understood that a double option agreement whereby the deceased's personal representatives have an option to sell and the surviving partners or directors an option to buy would not be so treated.

Calculation of tax on lifetime transfers following death within seven years (IHTA 1984, ss 113A, 124A; FA 1987, s 58 and Sch 8)

Many lifetime gifts of agricultural and/or business property will be potentially exempt when they are made. The gift will later become chargeable if the donor dies within seven years.

There will also be occasions where the transfer was chargeable at the time (such as a transfer into a discretionary trust, or a gift involving a limited company), but because the donor dies within seven years, the charge has to be recomputed at the full scale rates (allowing for tapering relief).

In computing the tax payable as a result of the death, business and agricultural property relief is applicable so long as:

 (i) the original property (or qualifying property which has replaced it) was owned by the donee throughout the period beginning with the date of the transfer and ending with the death of the donor (this condition will be regarded as satisfied if there is a period of no more than twelve months between the sale of one qualifying property and the acquisition of another); and
(ii) immediately before the death of the donor, the property (or any replacement property) is qualifying business or agricultural property (this may not apply because, for example, there might have been a change of use, or at the time of death there might be a binding contract for sale). In order for unquoted shares to be qualifying business property they must still be unquoted when the donor dies.

If the donee died before the donor, the periods at (i) and (ii) are from the date of the gift to the date of death of the donee.

Proportionate relief is available where only part of the property continues to qualify, for example, where part of the property has been sold.

To the extent that a transfer of business or agricultural property is covered by the annual exemption, it would appear that that part of the transfer, as reduced by the business or agricultural relief, should be totally exempt and no recalculation should be necessary if the donor dies within seven years. The Revenue do not, however, share that view. The point is now academic where the available relief is at the 100% rate.

The availability of the 100% relief, coupled with the fact that there is an effective capital gains tax free uplift in values on a taxpayer's death, adds a new dimension to estate planning, because where the 100% relief applies there will be no tax benefit from making potentially exempt transfers in lifetime. On the other hand, it cannot be certain that the tax regime will remain as favourable as it now is.

Growing timber (IHTA 1984, ss 125–130)

Where an estate on death includes growing timber, an election may be made to leave the timber (but not the land on which it stands) out of account in valuing the estate at death. The relief is dealt with in chapter 31.

Quick succession relief (IHTA 1984, s 141)

Where a donee dies shortly after receiving a chargeable transfer, the transfer has increased his estate at death and therefore attracts tax in his estate as well as possibly having been taxed at the time of the earlier transfer. Relief is given where the death occurs within five years after the earlier transfer. There is no requirement to retain the actual asset obtained by that transfer.

The total tax on the chargeable estate is calculated in the normal way and reduced by the quick succession relief. The relief is the following percentage of the tax paid (if any) on the previous transfer, reduced in the proportion of value received by the deceased after tax over the earlier chargeable transfer:

Period between transfer and death	Percentage relief
Less than 1 year	100%
1–2 years	80%
2–3 years	60%
3–4 years	40%
4–5 years	20%

Quick succession relief is also available where there are successive charges within five years on trust property in which there is an interest in possession. The rates of relief are the same as those quoted above, with the percentage relief depending on the period between the successive charges.

It may be that at the time the donee dies, the transfer to him is still classed as a potentially exempt transfer because the donor is still alive, but the donor may then die, after the donee but within the seven-year period, so that the potentially exempt transfer becomes chargeable in the donor's estate. Quick succession relief will then be available in the donee's estate. The liability to pay any tax due on the transfer will be that of the personal representatives of the donee.

Survivorship clauses (IHTA 1984, s 92)

Although the tax on successive transfers may be reduced by quick succession relief where death occurs within five years after the first transfer, this is not so beneficial as the value not being included at all. It is possible to include a survivorship clause in a will stipulating that assets do not pass to the intended beneficiary unless he/she survives the deceased by a prescribed period, limited to a maximum of six months. This avoids the double charge to tax.

Deeds of family arrangement (IHTA 1984, ss 17, 142)

The way in which a deceased's estate is distributed, either under a will or on intestacy, may be varied by those entitled to it, and legacies may be disclaimed wholly or in part. Where this happens within two years after the death, the variation or disclaimer is not a separate transfer of value provided that written notice is given to the Revenue within six months after the date of the instrument of variation or disclaimer. This must be signed by those making it, and by the personal representatives if it results in additional tax being paid by them. Inheritance tax will then be payable as if the revised distribution had operated at death.

Interest-free loans

Where a loan is made free of interest there is no transfer of capital and it is usually possible to regard the interest forgone as being normal expenditure out of income and thus exempt. If, however, a loan is made for a fixed period, or is not repayable on demand, it may be treated as a transfer of value equal to the difference between the amount lent and the present value of the future right to repayment.

Date of payment and interest on overdue tax (IHTA 1984, ss 226–236)

The normal due dates of payment are as follows.

Chargeable lifetime transfers between 6 April and 30 September	Chargeable lifetime transfers between 1 October and 5 April	Death – including additional tax on chargeable lifetime transfers and tax on potentially exempt transfers which become chargeable
30 April in following year	6 months after end of month in which transfer was made	6 months after end of month in which death occurs

The personal representatives must, however, pay any tax for which they are liable at the time they apply for probate, even if this is before the due date as shown above.

Interest is payable on overdue tax, recent rates being as follows.

> 8% p.a. from 6 July 1991
> 9% p.a. from 6 May 1991 to 5 July 1991

10% p.a. from 6 March 1991 to 5 May 1991
11% p.a. from 6 July 1989 to 5 March 1991
9% p.a. from 6 October 1988 to 5 July 1989
8% p.a. from 6 August 1988 to 5 October 1988

Interest on overdue tax is not deductible in arriving at income tax payable by the personal representatives and interest on overpaid tax is tax-free. Over-payments carry interest from the date of payment at the same rate as that charged on overdue tax.

Where tax has not been paid because a transfer was conditionally exempt, the due date is six months after the end of the month in which the event by reason of which it is chargeable occurs (e.g. breach of an undertaking in respect of heritage property).

Payment by instalments

Tax may be paid by equal yearly instalments over ten years on certain assets transferred on death, and also on chargeable lifetime transfers if the *donee* pays the tax. The option to pay by instalments also applies to a potentially exempt transfer of qualifying property which becomes a chargeable transfer on the death of the donor within seven years after the gift, so long as the donee still owns the gifted property (or, for transfers on and after 17 March 1987 of property qualifying for business or agricultural relief, replacement property) at the time of the donor's death. The first instalment is due on chargeable lifetime transfers on the normal due date and in the case of tax payable in consequence of death, six months after the end of the month in which the death occurred.

The instalment option applies to land wherever situated, to a business or interest in a business, to timber when it becomes chargeable after being left out of account on a previous death, to controlling shareholdings, and to unquoted shares if certain conditions are met. For events on and after 17 March 1987, the instalment option on unquoted shares is not available for tax payable in consequence of the donor's death, unless the shares are still unquoted when the donor dies (or, if earlier, when the donee dies).

Interest normally runs only from the date the instalment falls due and not on the full amount of the deferred tax. This does not apply in the case of land, other than land included in a business or partnership interest and agricultural land, nor in the case of shares in an investment company. Interest in those two cases is charged on the total amount remaining unpaid after the normal due date, the interest being added to each instalment as it falls due.

If the property is sold, the outstanding tax becomes payable immediately.

Liability for tax (IHTA 1984, ss 199–214, 237)

On lifetime transfers of property which are immediately chargeable, other than transfers of property in a trust fund, primary liability for payment rests with the donor. The donor and donee may, however, agree between them who is to pay, the transfer having to be grossed up if the donor pays (see example 2 on page 64).

In the case of lifetime transfers of property which is within a discretionary trust, the primary liability is that of the trustees.

On death, the personal representatives are liable to pay the tax on the assets coming into their hands, while the liability for tax on trust property which becomes chargeable at death rests with the trustees. See the example on page 481.

Where, as a result of the death of the donor within seven years, additional tax becomes payable on a lifetime transfer, or a potentially exempt transfer becomes liable to tax, the primary responsibility for paying the tax is that of the donee. The personal representatives are only liable if the tax remains unpaid twelve months after the end of the month in which the donor died, or to the extent that the tax payable exceeds the value of the gifted property held by the donee.

In addition to the persons mentioned, certain other people may be liable to pay inheritance tax, but usually only where tax remains unpaid after the due date. Where tax is unpaid the Inland Revenue are usually able to take a legal charge on the property concerned.

The person who is liable to pay inheritance tax is not necessarily the person who ultimately bears the tax. The trustees of a settlement are liable to pay any tax arising on the transfer of trust funds, but the next person to enjoy the income or to receive the capital bears the tax because the trust funds are correspondingly lower. Personal representatives are liable to pay the tax on the assets of the deceased at death, but the residuary legatees (those who receive the balance of the estate after all other legacies) will suffer the tax by a reduction in the amount available for them, the other legatees receiving their legacies in full unless the will specifies that any particular legacy should bear its own tax.

Use of insurance

There are many instances in the inheritance tax provisions where the potential liability to tax is not known at the time of the transfer, notably when potentially exempt transfers are made, but also when chargeable transfers are made, because if the donor dies within seven years, additional tax may be payable. Temporary insurance cover may be taken out on the life of the donor to provide for the possible tax liability, with the policies being tailored to take account of the reduction in potential liability once the donor has survived the gift by three years.

6
Stamp duty

Background

Stamp duty is a fixed or ad valorem charge on documents. It has been charged since the seventeenth century, and present legislation is based on the Stamp Act 1891 as amended by numerous subsequent Finance and other Acts. It is administered by the Commissioners of Inland Revenue through the Office of the Controller of Stamps.

A separate tax—stamp duty reserve tax—was introduced by Finance Act 1986 to charge certain transactions which escape stamp duty. Regulations for the administration of stamp duty reserve tax were made by statutory instrument (SI 1986 No 1711) and these were amended on 27 May 1988 by SI 1988 No 835. From a date yet to be fixed (expected to be April 1993 at the earliest), stamp duty will only be charged on land and buildings, and all other stamp duties, including stamp duty reserve tax, will be abolished.

Stamp duty

'Heads' and basis of charge (mainly in SA 1891, Sch 1)

Stamp duty is charged on certain documents completed in the UK or relating to UK property or transactions. No duty arises on transactions which are carried out orally.

Generally, documents should be stamped before they take effect, although in practice the Commissioners permit stamping within thirty days without charging any penalty.

Duty is either fixed or ad valorem depending on the head of charge under which the transaction falls. Some of the main heads of charge and rates of duty (some of which are on a sliding scale) are given in the table on page 78.

There are many other heads, a number of which attract only a fixed duty of 50p. There are numerous exemptions and reliefs from each head. Many of the nominal fixed duties were repealed by the Finance Act 1985 and further documents were exempted after 30 April 1987 by SI 1987 No 516, including

Head of charge	Rate of duty
Bearer instruments	
Inland bearer instruments (other than deposit certificates for overseas stock)	1½%
Overseas bearer instruments (other than deposit certificates for overseas stock or bearer instruments by usage)	1½%
Bearer instruments excluded above	10p per £50 or part
Conveyances or transfers on sale	
Stock and marketable securities	½%
Other transfers (including house purchase)	1%
Duty on 'certified transactions': not exceeding £30,000 (temporarily increased to £250,000 from 20 December 1991 to 19 August 1992)	Nil
Various share transactions	
Such as takeovers, mergers, demergers, schemes of reconstruction and amalgamation (except where there is no real change in ownership), purchase by a company of its own shares	½%
Shares converted into depositary receipts or put into duty free clearance systems	1½%
Leases	
For definite term less than 1 year of furnished dwelling house at rent in excess of £500 per annum	£1
For any other definite or indefinite term (rent)	Ad valorem duty from 0 to 24% on sliding scale by reference to average rent
For any other definite or indefinite term (premium)	As for conveyances or transfers on sale

Stamp duty on all categories other than Conveyances or transfers on sale of land and buildings and Leases is to be abolished in or around April 1993.

gifts. The 50p duty on a deed (i.e. a document under seal) not liable to other duties was also repealed by the Finance Act 1985. The fixed duties that remain are retained to enable the Stamp Office to scrutinise documents that may be liable to ad valorem duty.

Adjudication and valuation (SA 1891, s 12)

Adjudication is the process whereby the Commissioners assess the amount of duty, if any, payable on a document. Adjudication may be voluntary or compulsory. Any person may voluntarily request the Commissioners to express their opinion as to whether a document is chargeable, and if so, to state the amount of duty payable. In certain instances legislation provides that adjudication is compulsory, for example where exemption from duty is claimed on a company reconstruction without change in ownership.

Having considered the document the Commissioners will either stamp it 'adjudged not chargeable with any stamp duty' or they will assess the duty due and on receipt will stamp the document 'adjudged duly stamped'. An adjudication stamp is normally conclusive evidence of due stamping.

Letters of allotment

Sales of renounceable letters of allotment are chargeable to stamp duty reserve tax at ½% (see page 81) until its abolition.

Conveyances and transfers on sale (FA 1963, s 55 and Sch 11; FA 1958, s 34; FA 1987, ss 50, 55; FA 1990, ss 107–109, 111)

Documents relating to sales of all types of property are currently covered under this heading, including house sales and transactions such as the release of an interest in property or the surrender of a lease. It also includes shared ownership schemes run by local authorities and housing associations under which those who cannot afford the full amount needed to buy their house are able partly to buy and partly to rent the property. But no duty is payable where property can be handed over without a document of title, for example ordinary trading stock or plant and equipment. Stamp duty on all share transactions is to be abolished some time in 1993.

The exemption from duty for transactions up to £30,000, (£250,000 for documents executed between 20 December 1991 and 19 August 1992 inclusive) applies only to certified transactions. A certificate cannot be given for a lease where the rent exceeds £300 per annum (£2,500 per annum for leases executed between 20 December 1991 and 19 August 1992 inclusive) or for the transfer of stock or marketable securities, or units in a unit trust. An instrument is certified at a particular amount if it contains a statement that the transaction contained therein does not form part of a larger transaction or series of transactions whose value exceeds the certified amount. Where land is purchased for less than £30,000 (or £250,000 where relevant) and a house is subsequently built on it, no stamp duty is payable. But if the purchase of the land and the erection of the house are really a single transaction, stamp duty must be paid on the combined amount.

Certificates are also required for the following transactions (see below):

(a) Equality money paid on an exchange or partition.
(b) Premiums paid under leases.

No duty is payable in connection with British Government stock, including gilt warrants, nor in respect of a conveyance, transfer or lease to the Crown.

Exchange or partition

Where a document effects an exchange or partition of freehold land, and consideration ('equality money') exceeding £100 is given, ad valorem duty is payable on the equality money at conveyance on sale rates. Where the equality money is less than £100, a fixed duty of 50p is payable.

When the housing market is depressed, many house builders are prepared to accept a purchaser's existing house on a trade-in basis. Where they do so considerable savings on stamp duty can be made, as duty will only become payable if the equality money exceeds £30,000 (or £250,000 where relevant), provided that a certificate of value is obtained—see above.

Premiums on leases of land and buildings

Where a premium is paid on a lease for a definite term exceeding one year or for an indefinite term, the premium is treated as the consideration on a conveyance or transfer on sale and chargeable accordingly. The exemption for certified transactions up to £30,000 (or £250,000 where relevant) only applies to the premium, however, if the rent payable under the lease does not exceed £300 (or £2,500 where relevant) per annum.

Surrenders of leases

Where a lease is surrendered, duty is payable on any consideration paid by the landlord as for a conveyance on sale. If no consideration passes, a fixed duty of 50p is charged. Where the provisions of a lease can only be altered by surrender and re-grant, for example the alteration of the term, the re-granted lease will bear the appropriate duty but no duty will be paid on the surrender of the old lease.

Gifts (SA 1891, s 57)

There is no stamp duty on gifts unless the gift is of mortgaged property, in which case stamp duty is charged on the amount of the mortgage, as if it were a sale.

Trusts

No stamp duty is charged on the creation of a trust by will.

There will be a 50p stamp on any written declaration of trust in lifetime. Property that is vested in the trustees by way of conveyance or transfer will usually be exempt from duty as a gift. Property that can be vested in some other way, for example cash, does not require a document and will not attract duty. If the trust is declared in writing prior to the transfer, there will be a 50p declaration of trust stamp.

Once a trust has been created, the trustees are subject to stamp duty in the same way as any other person. Thus, if they purchase land, they will pay the stamp duty on the conveyance.

If a new trustee is subsequently appointed, the deed of appointment does not attract duty.

There is no duty on a transfer of trust property to a beneficiary.

Deeds of family arrangement
Transfers of property on break-up of marriage (FA 1985, ss 83, 84)

All qualifying deeds of family arrangement (see chapter 35) and deeds conveying property under a divorce court order or on separation are exempt from duty.

Company takeovers (FA 1986, ss 75–77)

Transactions currently attract duty at ½%.

Foreign exchange currency rules (FA 1985, s 88)

All foreign currency amounts on which duty is payable are converted to sterling at the rate applying on the date of the document.

Interest and penalties (SA 1891, s 15)

Where documents are submitted late for stamping, the maximum penalty is £10 plus an amount equal to the duty payable. The penalty will usually be mitigated so that the total penalty does not exceed the equivalent of interest at 12% to 15% for a delay of up to three months, 15% to 20% for three to six months delay and 20% to 25% for six to twelve months delay.

Stamp duty reserve tax (FA 1986, s 86; FA 1987, s 56 and Sch 7; FA 1990, ss 110, 111)

Stamp duty reserve tax at the rate of ½% applies to share transactions which escape duty, for example, sales of renounceable letters of allotment and transactions within the same Stock Exchange account, but it is to be abolished some time in 1993 along with stamp duty on share transactions. The tax does not apply to gilt-edged stocks, traded options and futures, non-convertible loan stocks, foreign securities not on a UK register, purchases by a charity, transfers of units to unit trust managers and of units in foreign unit trusts, and the issue of new securities. There are also special exemptions for Stock Exchange market makers, for broker-dealers who buy and sell shares within seven days and for principal traders on the London International Financial Futures and Options Exchange (LIFFE). Liability to stamp duty reserve tax normally arises two months after the date of the transaction, unless stamp duty has become payable in the meantime, and the tax is payable by the end of the next following month. If duty is paid after reserve tax has been paid, the reserve tax is refunded (plus income tax free interest on refunds over £25). The reserve tax liability on renounceable letters of allotment, however, arises on the date of the transaction itself, with the tax due at the end of the following month. The accountable persons include market makers, brokers and dealers.

Stamp duty reserve tax also applies to shares converted into depositary receipts or put into a duty free clearing system, and the rate of tax on these transactions is 1½%. The tax is only payable, however, to the extent that it exceeds any ad valorem stamp duty on the transaction, and where the ad valorem duty exceeds the amount of reserve tax, no reserve tax is payable.

Interest and penalties (SI 1986/1711 Parts IX & X)

Interest is charged on overdue reserve tax, and there are various penalties for defaults, including a mitigable penalty of £50, plus £10 a day following a declaration by the Commissioners, where the appropriate notice of liability has not been given and the tax has not been paid.

7
Value added tax: general principles

Basis of charge (VATA 1983, ss 1, 2)

Value added tax (VAT) is charged on the supply of goods and services in the UK and on the import of goods and certain services into the UK. It applies where the supplies are taxable supplies made in the course of business by a taxable person. Significant changes are being made to the UK system as a result of the introduction by the European Community of the Single Market on 1 January 1993. These are outlined on page 92.

References in this chapter are to Value Added Tax Act 1983 unless otherwise stated, but many of the detailed regulations are by statutory instrument, making the legislation cumbersome and often difficult to follow.

Taxable supplies (s 3 and Schs 2 and 4)

All supplies of goods and services (including goods taken for own use) are taxable supplies, apart from items which are specifically exempt (see below). Goods for own use are valued at cost. Business gifts are taxable supplies except where the gift is valued at £10 or less and does not form part of a series of gifts to the same person. They are valued at cost, except for gifts to an educational establishment, for which market value may be used. There is no value added tax on gifts of services.

Exempt supplies (see below) between connected persons are valued at open market value.

Exempt supplies (s 17 and Sch 6)

Exempt supplies are broadly supplies of:

Land	Betting, lotteries and gaming (except
Insurance	takings from gaming and amuse-
Postal services (but not telephones)	ment machines)
Education	Health services
Finance services	Burial and cremation

Who is a taxable person? (Sch 1)

From 11 March 1992, you are liable to be registered for VAT at the end of any month if the taxable turnover of all your business activities in the year ended on the last day of that month has exceeded £36,600 (unless you can satisfy Customs and Excise that your taxable turnover in the next twelve months will not exceed £35,100). You are required to notify Customs and Excise within 30 days of the end of the month in which the yearly limit was exceeded and will be registered from the beginning of the next month or such earlier date as is agreed with Customs and Excise.

Liability to register also arises at any time if your taxable supplies in the next 30 days are expected to exceed £36,600. You must notify Customs and Excise within the 30 days and you will be registered from the beginning of the 30 days.

Example 1

Your turnover for the year ended 30 November 1992 was £37,000, having been below the yearly limit at the end of previous months. You must notify liability to register by 30 December 1992 and will be registered from 1 January 1993 unless you can show that your turnover in the year to 30 November 1993 will not exceed £35,100.

Example 2

On 15 November 1992 you start trading and expect your first month's turnover to be £37,000. You must notify liability to register by 15 December 1992 and will be registered from 15 November 1992.

From 1 January 1993, farmers will be able to avoid VAT registration if they opt to become 'flat rate farmers'—for details, see page 351.

See also below as regards voluntary registration and selling a business as a going concern.

Notification is made on form VAT 1 and a certificate of registration VAT 4 is then issued showing the VAT registration number.

There are provisions for groups of companies to have group registration if they wish (see page 92).

Customs and Excise have discretion to exempt you from registration if you make only zero-rated supplies (see below), and do not wish to be registered. In that event you must notify Customs and Excise within 30 days of a material change in the nature of supplies made, or within 30 days after the end of the quarter in which the change occurred if it is not more precisely identifiable.

There are provisions to prevent the splitting of businesses in order to stay below the VAT registration threshold. Customs and Excise have the power to direct that where two or more persons are carrying on separate business activities which are effectively parts of the same business, they are to be treated for VAT purposes as the same business, e.g. where one spouse is a publican and the other runs the catering within the public house.

Cancellation of registration

From 1 May 1992, you will no longer be liable to be registered if your tax-exclusive turnover in the next twelve months will be £35,100 or less, unless the reason for turnover not exceeding £35,100 is that you will cease making taxable supplies in that year, or will suspend making them for 30 days or more.

You must notify Customs and Excise within 30 days of ceasing to make taxable supplies, upon which your registration will be cancelled from that date or a later date agreed with Customs and Excise. VAT will be payable on the business assets at their value at the time of deregistration, unless no input tax was recovered on their acquisition, or the business is transferred as a going concern (see page 89), or the total VAT does not exceed £250.

Rates of tax (s 9)

VAT is currently charged at only two rates, a standard rate of 17½% and the zero rate. The VAT fraction on tax-inclusive supplies is 7/47.

Zero rate (s 16 and Sch 5)

The main zero-rated items are:

Food, except where supplied in the course of catering, or where it is pet food, or a 'non-essential' item such as chocolate, ice cream, alcoholic and fruit drinks or crisps

Water and sewerage services (but see below)

Books (but not stationery)

Construction of buildings for residential or charitable use (and for commercial use, but only if construction commenced before 1 August 1989)

Children's clothing and footwear

Fuel and power (except petrol) (but see below)

Transport (but not taxis or hire cars)

Drugs and medicines on prescription

Exports and international services (but see page 92 re the European Community)

Fuel and power is zero-rated only if it is supplied for domestic or charitable use and not where it is supplied for commercial use. Similarly, water and

sewerage services are standard-rated when supplied for industrial purposes.

How the system works (ss 14, 15)

Each person in the chain between the first supplier and the final consumer
is charged tax on taxable supplies to him (input tax) and charges tax on
taxable supplies made by him (output tax). He pays over to Customs and
Excise the excess of output tax over input tax, or recovers the excess of input
tax over output tax. The broad effect of the scheme is that businesses are not
affected by VAT except in so far as they are required to administer it, and
the burden of the tax falls on the consumer. This is, however, modified by
the rules relating to turnover thresholds and exemption, because businesses
that do not make taxable supplies have to recover VAT suffered by them in
the prices they charge and businesses that are partially exempt similarly
have to recover unrecovered VAT in their charges. There is also some VAT
paid by fully taxable businesses that cannot be recovered, such as the scale
VAT charges on the provision of petrol for employees' private use, so that
unrecovered VAT will enter into the business expenditure.

VAT repayments are likely to arise where most supplies are zero-rated. The
effect of the zero rate is that the person is making taxable supplies, albeit
charged at a nil rate, and can therefore recover input tax suffered. If you
make exempt supplies you are outside the scheme and cannot recover input
tax (except under the partial exemption rules—see below).

If you offer a cash discount you charge VAT only on the discounted amount
whether the discount is taken or not.

You can recover input tax not only on goods for resale but also on expenses
such as telephones and stationery and on capital items. You cannot, however, recover input tax on cars, other than for resale, or on business entertaining. Companies cannot recover input tax on repairs, refurbishments and
other expenses relating to domestic accommodation provided for directors
or their families. Output tax must be charged on all taxable supplies, including, for example, sales of fixed assets like plant and machinery. Where
business cars are sold, VAT is only payable to the extent that the selling
price exceeds the cost.

If your business petrol bills include petrol for private use by you or your
employees, an adjustment must be made in respect of the non-business
proportion. For commercial vehicles, the adjustment is made by disallowing
the private proportion of the input tax. For cars, a private use scale charge
applies, based on the income tax fuel benefit for directors and higher-paid
employees (see page xxxii). The scale charge is reduced by one-half where
the business travel of the car user is 4,500 miles or more in a quarterly return
period or 1,500 miles or more in a monthly return period. The VAT charged
on car fuel bills is thus fully recoverable, but a tax-inclusive supply equal to
the car fuel scale amount is regarded as made in each return period for the
appropriate number of cars. The scale charges do not apply if you notify

Customs that you are not going to claim an input tax deduction for *any* fuel (including fuel used in commercial vehicles).

Second-hand goods (s 18)

In general, second-hand goods sold in the course of business are taxable on the full selling price, but there are special schemes for cars, caravans and motor cycles, boats and outboard motors, works of art and antiques, aircraft, electronic organs, firearms, horses and ponies. Subject to certain conditions, VAT is charged under the special schemes only on the excess of selling price over cost.

Imports (s 19)

VAT is chargeable on imports when they are entered for home use. The importer has to pay VAT on the goods on importation, and then gets a credit for the input tax on his next return. If the goods are for resale, output tax will be accounted for in the normal way when they are sold. No VAT is payable on goods temporarily imported for repair, processing or modification, then re-exported. Goods which have been temporarily exported and are re-imported by the same person after repair, process, or modification will bear VAT only on the value of the repair, etc. plus freight and insurance.

From 1 January 1993 there will be separate rules for the European Community—see page 92.

Voluntary registration

Voluntary registration may be applied for even though your turnover is below the statutory limits. Customs and Excise used to have a discretion as to whether to register someone in these circumstances but they are now required to do so. Once you are registered, you will then charge VAT on your supplies and recover input tax suffered. This may be beneficial if your customers are mainly taxable persons, but not where they are the general public. Registration will bring the burden of complying with the administrative requirements of the scheme, so may not be thought worthwhile even though a price advantage may arise. See example 3.

Example 3

You are in business as a handyman and pay input tax of £750 on phone, stationery etc. Your turnover is £15,000, including £750 to cover the tax suffered.

If you register voluntarily for VAT, you need only charge £14,250 for the same supplies and your turnover will then be:

£14,250 + 17½% VAT £2,494 = £16,744.

You will pay to Customs and Excise £2,494 less £750 = £1,744, leaving you with £15,000 as before. If your customers are the general public your prices to them will be £1,744 higher, but if they are taxable persons they will recover £2,494, so that their net price will be £14,250.

Intending trader registration

If you are in business and are not currently making taxable supplies, but intend to do so in the future, you may apply for registration and Customs and Excise are required to register you. This enables you to recover any input tax suffered even though no taxable supplies are being made.

Exemption and partial exemption (SI 1985/886 Pt V; SI 1992/645)

If you make only exempt supplies you do not charge VAT but you cannot recover input tax charged to you, so your prices must include an element to recover the VAT suffered. Some businesses make both taxable and exempt supplies and are thus partially exempt.

In these circumstances, there are rules to determine how much of your input tax can be recovered. You can recover all the input tax directly attributable to your taxable supplies, and none of the input tax directly attributable to exempt supplies or supplies that are outside the scope of VAT. As to the remainder of the input tax that relates to overheads, input tax is deductible in the proportion that taxable supplies bear to total supplies. The proportion is expressed as a percentage, rounded up to the nearest whole number. Alternatively, a 'special method' can be agreed with Customs and Excise. Certain exempt supplies can be ignored in these calculations, but only where they are supplies of capital goods used for the business or are 'incidental' to the business activities. Input tax relating to certain other exempt supplies can be treated as relating to taxable supplies. There is a right of appeal against the proportion of input tax which is recoverable.

If you are partially exempt you can recover all input tax suffered despite the exempt supplies if your exempt input tax does not exceed £600 a month on average.

Capital goods scheme (SI 1985/886 Pt VA; SI 1989/2355)

Input tax recovery on certain capital items acquired on or after 1 April 1990 does not depend just on the initial use of the asset but must be adjusted over a longer period where use changes between exempt and taxable supplies.

The assets concerned are computer hardware of a tax-exclusive value of £50,000 or more per item, and land and buildings of a tax-exclusive value of £250,000 or more. The adjustment period is ten years except for computers and leases for less than ten years, where the adjustment period is five years. The adjustments will be reflected in the capital allowances computations (see page 260).

Changes in circumstances

Where your circumstances change, you are required to notify Customs and Excise within 30 days of the change. Some changes require cancellation of your registration, others merely an amendment.

Your registration will require cancellation when you cease business, or take in a partner, or revert from a partnership to a sole proprietor, or incorporate or disincorporate your business, or cease to make taxable supplies. In some circumstances it is possible to transfer your registration number to the new business.

Many changes require amendment to your registration, such as changes in the composition of a partnership, change of business name, changes in a group of companies, change of address and so on.

Selling a business as a going concern

If a VAT registered trader sells all or part of a business as a going concern, the seller does not normally have to account for VAT on the sale consideration, and the purchaser does not have any input tax to reclaim where the sale is to another taxable person or to someone who becomes a taxable person immediately after the sale. This does not apply to the transfer of land and buildings on which the option to tax has been exercised or to commercial buildings and civil engineering works that are unfinished or less than three years old unless the purchaser has also opted to tax and has so notified Customs by the date of the transfer. (For details of the option to tax, see page 368.) If the purchaser is not already registered, the rules for deciding whether he is liable are the same as those outlined on page 84, except that the seller's supplies in the previous twelve months are treated as made by the purchaser. The purchaser must notify his liability within 30 days of the transfer, and will be registered from the date of the transfer. If the seller was not VAT registered, his turnover would not have to be taken into account by the purchaser in deciding when registration was necessary.

These rules do not apply when you merely sell assets, rather than an identifiable part of the business which is capable of separate operation. The sale of a family company is dealt with in chapter 28.

Anti-avoidance provisions have been introduced in relation to transfers to partly exempt groups (see page 92).

Records and returns (Sch 7)

You are required to supply tax invoices in respect of taxable supplies, to keep a VAT account showing the results for each tax period, and to make returns to Customs and Excise showing the VAT payable or repayable.

Tax invoices (SI 1985/886)

Where you make standard-rated supplies to another taxable person, you must provide and keep a copy of a tax invoice showing the following:

    Identifying number
    Tax point (see below)
    Your name, address and VAT registration number

Customer's name and address
Type of supply (e.g. sale, hire-purchase, rental)
Description of goods or services supplied, and for each type of
    goods, the quantity, rate of tax and tax exclusive amount payable
Total amount payable excluding VAT
Rate of cash discount offered
Total tax chargeable

Retailers may provide a less detailed invoice omitting the customer's name and address and the amount (but not the rate) of VAT, if the tax inclusive price is £100 or less. Copies of these less detailed invoices need not be kept.

Tax point (time of supply) (ss 4, 5)

The basic tax point is normally when goods are made available or services are performed, unless they are invoiced and/or paid for earlier, in which case the earlier date is the tax point. Where goods or services are invoiced within fourteen days after supply, the later date is the tax point, and if you invoice monthly you can adopt a monthly tax point.

Special schemes for retailers

The normal VAT procedure requires records to be kept of every separate transaction. Retailers would find it virtually impossible to keep such detailed records, so there are various special schemes—twelve in all—which enable retailers to calculate output tax in a way that suits their particular circumstances.

Lost goods (Sch 7(4)) and bad debts (s 22 and FA 1990, s 11)

If goods are lost or destroyed before being sold, output tax is not chargeable.

But once a supply has been made, tax is chargeable. If a customer fails to pay, then, for supplies on and after 1 April 1989, VAT may be reclaimed on any debt which is more than one year old and has been written off in your accounts. VAT must be accounted for on any part of the debt that is later recovered.

These provisions replace earlier bad debt relief under which you could not normally have relief for VAT which you had charged unless the debtor was formally declared insolvent. Under the present scheme, the claim in the insolvency will be the VAT inclusive amount, because you have to account for VAT on any debt recoveries.

Cash accounting

Businesses with a tax-exclusive turnover of not more than £300,000 can avoid the problems and delay in recovering VAT on bad debts by applying to use the cash accounting system, providing any outstanding VAT does not exceed £5,000 (£1,000 before 1 April 1992). Once a business has been admitted to the scheme, it will be allowed to stay in it unless turnover exceeds £375,000. Tax invoices still have to be issued but output tax will not have to be accounted for until cash is received. On the other hand, input tax will not be recoverable until suppliers are paid. Application to use the system should be made to Customs and Excise on form VAT 621.

VAT account, tax periods and tax returns (FA 1985, ss 19, 20; SI 1988/886)

The results for each tax period must be summarised in a VAT account. Returns are made to Customs and Excise on form VAT 100 for each tax period, showing the VAT payable or repayable and certain statistical information (including, from 1 January 1992, specific entries for European Community sales and purchases). The return is due within one month after the end of the tax period. Customs will usually extend this period by seven days where payment is made by credit transfer. A person making late returns twice in any twelve-month period will receive a 'surcharge liability notice'. If he defaults again within the following twelve months, he will be liable to a 'default surcharge' of 5% of the unpaid tax (or £30 if higher) rising by a further 5% for each subsequent default up to a maximum of 30%, reduced to a maximum of 20% for defaults on or after 1 April 1992 (but the reduction is not retrospective and surcharges already assessed at 25% or 30% will stand). If a trader has evidence (e.g. a certificate of posting) that the return and tax due were posted one working day prior to the due date, it will be regarded as posted on time (and if the due date is a weekend or bank holiday, a default will not be recorded if the return and tax are received on the next following working day).

Where there is an unreasonable delay on the part of Customs in making a VAT repayment, a repayment supplement amounting to an extra 5% (or £30 if more) will be added to the repayment.

A tax period is normally three months, but if you regularly claim VAT repayments (for example because you make mainly zero-rated supplies) you may have a one-month period if you wish. The advantage of earlier repayments in those circumstances must be weighed against the disadvantage of having to complete twelve returns annually.

Quarterly return dates are staggered over the year depending on your business classification. You can ask for the dates to be changed to coincide with your accounting period.

Annual accounting

Businesses with an annual tax-exclusive turnover of not more than £300,000 that have been registered for at least one year may apply (on form VAT 600) to join the annual accounting scheme. They will then agree a provisional VAT liability with Customs and Excise based on the position for the previous year. The agreed figure will be divided by ten. Nine equal monthly payments will then be made by direct debit starting four months after the beginning of the year. The annual return and balancing payment will have to be made within a further two months.

Monthly payments on account for large VAT payers (s 38C; FA 1992, s 6)

Traders who paid more than £2m VAT in the year to 31 March 1991 will be required from October 1992 to make payments on account in the first two months of each quarter, based on 1/12th of their total liability for the 12 months to the previous 31 March, 30 April or 31 May as the case may be. The payments will be calculated and notified to the trader by Customs, and the trader will make any necessary adjustment on his quarterly return. The first payment will be due on 30 November 1992, 31 December 1992 or 31 January 1993 depending on the VAT return periods.

Group registration (ss 29, 29A)

Two or more resident UK companies, and non-resident companies with an established place of business in the UK, may apply to be treated as a group if one of them controls each of the others, or if an individual, partnership or company controls all of them. Only one VAT return is then required.

Where there is no group registration, VAT has to be added to charges for supplies from one to the other, such as management charges, and care must be taken to ensure that this is not overlooked. There are provisions to ensure that unfair advantages are not obtained by group treatment.

Where a business is transferred as a going concern to a partly exempt group, the transfer is treated as a supply to and by the group. The group will therefore have to account for output tax, and will only be able to recover its allowable proportion of input tax according to the partial exemption rules (see page 88). This does not apply if the person who transferred the assets to the group acquired them more than three years previously. Nor does it apply to items covered by the capital goods scheme (see page 88).

European Community Single Market

From 1 January 1993, supplies between European Community countries will no longer be regarded as imports and exports, but as 'acquisitions' and 'supplies'. Supplies to VAT registered customers will be zero-rated by the seller, but VAT will be accounted for by the customer at his country's VAT rate, i.e. the country of destination. (At a later stage, not before 1 January 1997, it is intended to move to a charge based on the country of origin.) Special rules will apply to mail order to private individuals, to private motor vehicles, motor cycles, boats and aircraft, and to supplies to non-VAT registered businesses and institutions, under which VAT will be charged at the rate of the purchaser's country. Other supplies to non-VAT registered individuals will be at the rate applicable in the seller's country. The seller must state both his own and the customer's VAT number on VAT invoices.

In addition to making his normal VAT returns, he will also have to submit a return of all supplies to VAT registered customers in the EC for each calendar quarter (known as aggregate sales lists). Larger businesses will have to submit monthly returns.

Assessments (Sch 7(4); FA 1985, ss 21, 22)

If a taxpayer fails to make returns, or the Commissioners feel returns are incomplete or incorrect, they may issue assessments of the amount of tax due. Such assessments must normally be issued before the expiry of two years from the end of the return period, or, if later, one year after the facts come to light. In no case can assessments be made later than six years after the end of the return period, except in cases of fraudulent or negligent conduct, when the period is increased to 20 years. Where the taxpayer has died, no assessment can be made later than three years after death, or relate to a period more than six years before death. If a taxpayer does not submit a return and instead pays the tax shown on an estimated assessment, the Commissioners may fix an estimated assessment for a later period at a higher figure than they otherwise would have done.

Interest, penalties and surcharge (FA 1985, ss 14–18)

In addition to their right to take criminal proceedings (for other than regulatory offences) which could lead to a fine or imprisonment or both, Customs and Excise have the power to charge interest on overdue tax in certain circumstances, and there are severe penalties, some of them mandatory, for late, incorrect or incomplete returns, or for failure to notify liability to be registered for VAT or unauthorised issue of VAT invoices, or for failure to keep proper records (which now have to be retained for six years instead of three). As indicated on page 91, there is also a default surcharge for persistent late submission of VAT returns.

The serious misdeclaration penalty for errors in VAT returns that was introduced on 1 April 1990 caused widespread concern, and the penalty was reduced from 30% to 20% of the misdeclared VAT for assessments on or after 20 March 1991 relating to return periods beginning on or after 1 April 1990, and has been further reduced to 15% for assessments raised on or after 11 March 1992.

There is a 'period of grace', so that errors in one VAT return discovered and corrected in the next following return will not normally be penalised (even if the error was discovered by Customs). Nor will errors that are corrected by a compensating error in the next following return, such as input VAT claimed in the return before the correct return, or output VAT accounted for in the return following the correct return. Subject to these relaxations, the system works as follows.

If a taxpayer finds he has made mistakes in earlier returns causing tax to be overpaid or underpaid and the net errors discovered in the return period are

£1,000 or less, he corrects them by adjusting the amount of VAT payable or repayable in that return. Providing this is done voluntarily, no penalty will apply and no interest will be charged on the overdue amount. Net errors totalling more than £1,000 in a return period cannot be adjusted in the return and must be separately notified (on form 652) and if tax has been underpaid, interest will be charged on the overdue amount, but again no penalty will be charged if the errors are disclosed voluntarily.

Unless covered by this errors procedure, or the taxpayer can show a reasonable excuse, a serious misdeclaration penalty equal to 15% of the misdeclared VAT will apply if tax is understated on a return and the underdeclaration equals or exceeds

(a) 30% of the true amount of tax for that period, or
(b) the greater of £10,000 and 5% of the true amount of tax for that period.

Even so, the penalty will not normally be imposed unless the net tax underdeclared or overclaimed in a return period exceeds £2,000.

In very serious cases Customs may impose a persistent misdeclaration penalty, but it will not apply as well as the serious misdeclaration penalty.

With such a wide range of possible penalties that may be incurred, you need to be careful that your VAT accounting procedures will enable you to account for VAT correctly and on time.

Interest to taxpayer following Customs error (ss 38A and 38B)

Taxpayers now have a legal right to interest where tax has been overpaid or underclaimed as a result of error by Customs. Previously, any compensation paid was at Customs discretion.

Administration and appeals (Sch 8)

VAT is under the control of the Commissioners of Customs and Excise, operating through the VAT Central Unit and through local VAT offices under Collectors of Customs and Excise. If you disagree with a decision of Customs and Excise as to the VAT payable or various other matters, such as registration or cancellation of registration, use of a retailer's scheme, calculation of output tax etc., you may appeal to an independent VAT tribunal within thirty days of the decision. Normally, any tax in dispute must be paid before the tribunal hearing, but this requirement may be waived to avoid hardship. VAT tribunals normally hear appeals in public. If you are dissatisfied with the tribunal decision, further appeal is possible to the High Court, the Court of Appeal, and, where leave is granted, to the House of Lords. Taking an appeal to the courts may, however, result in costs being awarded against you if the appeal fails.

8
Poll tax and business rates

Introduction

This chapter gives an outline of poll tax and business rates. Points of detail relating to specific areas are dealt with in the appropriate chapter, in particular second homes in chapter 30 and let property in chapter 32. The proposed replacement of the poll tax by the council tax will not take place until April 1993.

The poll tax, or community charge to give it its official name, was introduced in England and Wales on 1 April 1990 to replace domestic rates, having been introduced in Scotland a year earlier. It does not apply in Northern Ireland. There are differences in the Scottish system and this chapter deals mainly with the system for England and Wales. There is a brief comment on the position in Scotland at the end of the chapter (on page 104).

There is a community charge reduction scheme to cushion the effect on individuals suffering large increases under the new system. Those on low incomes can claim community charge benefit to help pay the charge, but most people will have to pay at least 20% of the normal charge. Those on income support get an extra amount to cover the poll tax, but it is based on an estimated national average and will not always cover the amount payable.

At the same time as the introduction of the poll tax, the uniform business rate was introduced, under which businesses all over the country (except for those served by the City of London Corporation) pay rates on their rateable values at a uniform level fixed by central government. The introduction of this system was preceded by a property revaluation. Future annual increases in the business rate will not exceed the increase in the retail prices index. There are transitional provisions to limit gains and losses for individual businesses over the first few years.

Community charge register

Each council has a community charge registration officer, who draws up the community charge register and keeps it up to date. Most of the information comes from householders, but is also drawn from other sources, such as from educational establishments, who provide term-time addresses of full-time students. Requests to householders for information may be made annually or at less frequent intervals, but information can be requested at any time if the registration officer thinks the record is out of date. There are penalties for failing to supply information. You need to notify the registration officer of a change of circumstances affecting your entry, for example moving house, and if you have moved into a different charge area you would have to tell both the old and new registration officers.

Each person is provided with a copy of information on him that is held on the register. A list of the names and addresses of those on the register and of properties designated for the collective charge (see below) is published and members of the public may inspect the list, but may not take copies. You may ask for your name to be excluded from the public list if you think its inclusion may lead to a threat of violence.

Types of community charge

Personal community charge	payable by all those over 18 (unless they are exempt) to the council where their only or main home is. Where someone has more than one home, the decision as to the main home is made by the community charge registration officer, but it may be appealed against.
Standard community charge	payable on a domestic property that is not someone's only or main residence, such as second or holiday homes, empty houses and flats that are normally let. Where a property is divided into self-contained units, each unit is looked at separately. The amount payable may be up to twice the personal community charge.
Collective community charge	payable on property designated as liable to the charge by the community charge registration officer because it is short-stay accommodation used mainly by people from whom it would be difficult to collect the personal charge.

Personal community charge

Anyone who is over 18 has to pay the personal community charge to the council where their only or main home is, unless they are exempt. The charge is fixed for the year to 31 March, but it is worked out on a daily basis and if you are liable for only part of a year, e.g. because you become 18 during the year, you will pay a proportionate amount. If you move house to a different authority, you will be liable to pay the old authority for the number of days from 1 April that you lived in your old house, excluding the day you moved out, and the new authority for the remainder of the year, commencing with the day you moved in. If you have already paid your old council in advance, you will get a refund.

The following are exempt from the personal charge.

(a) Dependent children—i.e. 18 and 19-year olds who are still at school or in full-time further education such as an A-level course (but not students in full-time advanced education, who will normally pay 20%—see page 102 under 'Students') and 18-year olds for whom someone gets child benefit.

(b) Long-term hospital patients, and people being looked after in residential-care homes, nursing homes and hostels providing high levels of care, such as hospices, or alcohol or drug rehabilitation centres. Exemption dates from the time when the hospital etc. is the person's only or main residence.

(c) People who are severely mentally impaired—i.e. those entitled to invalidity pension, disability living allowance at the higher or middle rate, disability working allowance following the receipt of invalidity benefit or severe disablement allowance, unemployability supplement or allowance, severe disablement allowance, attendance allowance, constant attendance allowance or an increase for attendance in their disablement pension, where they have a doctor's certificate stating that they have 'severe impairment of . . . intelligence and social functioning from whatever cause'.

(d) Convicted and remand prisoners, except those in prison for non-payment of fines or of the community charge.

(e) Members of religious communities who depend on the community for their needs, do not draw state benefits and have no personal income or capital (but an occupational pension from a former job is ignored).

(f) People with no fixed abode, i.e. those sleeping rough (but they will be liable to collective charge contributions for any days they stay in a designated property—see page 99).

(g) People staying in certain hostels or night shelters provided for those with no fixed abode and no settled way of life, such as Salvation Army Hostels. (Such people are also exempt from collective charge contributions—see page 100.)

(h) Low-paid residential care workers, e.g. those employed by Community Service Volunteers.

(j) Foreign diplomats and foreign service personnel (and usually their dependants).

People whose sole or main residence is property designated for the collective community charge (see page 99) do not pay the personal charge as well.

Exemptions are automatic providing the conditions are satisfied, and may be backdated for up to two years where exemption is claimed late.

Backdating is not discretionary and refunds must be made where an exempt person has paid the charge.

Some people who are not exempt may get help with paying the poll tax—see pages 100 and 101 under 'Community charge benefit' and 'Community charge reduction scheme'.

Standard community charge

You pay the personal community charge to the council where you have your only or main home. Where a house, flat or self-contained unit is no-one's only or main home, the standard charge is payable, except as indicated below. The standard charge only applies to domestic property. The payer is usually the owner, who might be an individual (of any age) or a company or other organisation, including overseas residents. A tenant with a lease for six months or more is liable if the property is not his home. The most common examples of property that will attract the standard charge are second homes, holiday homes and empty residential property owned by landlords.

The standard charge can be anything up to twice the personal poll tax. In certain cases, the Government decides the multiple but otherwise it may be fixed at 0, ½, 1, 1½ or 2, as the local council decides. As with the personal poll tax, the standard charge is worked out on a daily basis if someone is liable for only part of the year.

The Government has specified a multiple of 0, i.e. no charge will be made, on the following unoccupied property.

(a)   Unfurnished property needing structural repairs to make it habitable. The exemption will cover up to six months after the work is substantially completed.

(b)   Newly built or structurally altered property, for up to six months after the work is substantially completed.

(c)   Any unfurnished property, for the first six months. If, before the end of six months, the property is reoccupied for less than six weeks, no new exempt period starts, but the balance of the original six months is available. If the property is reoccupied for six weeks or more, a fresh six month period starts.

(d)   Property where the person liable previously occupied the property as his main residence and is now exempt from the personal poll tax as a hospital patient or person in residential care etc. or because he is in prison (other than for not paying fines or personal poll tax). Such property may remain furnished.

(e)   Property empty following a death, for up to six months after granting of probate or administration.

(f)   Property whose occupation is prohibited by law, e.g. following compulsory purchase.

(g)   Property left vacant for a minister of religion.

(h)   Property that is empty (but not necessarily unfurnished) because the occupier is now living elsewhere to receive care because of old age, disablement, illness, alcohol/drug dependence or mental disorder.

(j)   Property empty because the occupier is resident elsewhere to look after someone needing care as indicated in (h) above.

(k)   Property owned by and previously used as the main residence of a student paying the 20% personal poll tax at his term-time address.

(l)   Mortgaged property repossessed by the lender for which the borrower remains liable to the charge.

(m)   Property within the same grounds as the owner's only or main residence and difficult to let separately from it.

A maximum multiplier of one half is specified for the following unoccupied property.

(n)   Property whose owner is required to live in job-related accommodation (such as a caretaker or a tenant of licensed premises).

(o)   Unfurnished property that can only be occupied by those working in agriculture.

For the following properties, the multiplier cannot exceed 1.

(p)   Properties where year-round occupation is prohibited—usually holiday properties. (There would be no charge if the property was already in one of the 'nil charge' classes, and if it is your only or main home you will pay the personal poll tax and not the standard charge.) Caravans on protected sites were to have been within this category, but are now exempt from the standard charge. For the detailed provisions on caravans, see page 370. There is no charge for a touring caravan normally kept at your home.

(q)   Domestic property that is part of larger premises where the other part is in non-domestic (usually business) use and the domestic property is either difficult to let separately or cannot be let because of a prohibition imposed before 31 January 1991.

Subject to certain conditions, councils may create other categories of property for which no charge or a lower charge is made. Where property is not covered by any of the specific provisions, however, some councils may fix the multiple at 2, in which case you will pay an amount equal to twice the personal poll tax.

Collective community charge

The collective community charge is intended to be the exception rather than the rule. It applies to short-stay accommodation where most of the residents have no permanent home. But you may have to pay both personal poll tax and a collective charge contribution if for example you have a permanent home and you also stay for a period at a collective charge property.

A community charge registration officer will designate property as liable to the collective charge if he decides that most of the residents are likely to be short-term and that it would be difficult to register them for and collect the personal poll tax. The sort of properties that may be designated are lodging houses, bed and breakfast hotels, hostels and bedsitter accommodation.

The collective charge will not apply if the property is a night shelter or a hostel providing a high level of care (such as a drug rehabilitation centre), or if most of the residents are full-time students. Nor will it apply to non-domestic property such as ordinary hotels and guest houses where the owners pay business rates.

The charge for each qualifying resident for each day they are in the property (including the day of arrival and excluding the day of departure) is the daily equivalent of the personal poll tax. The landlord must pay over this amount monthly, less 5% to cover his administration expenses. He recovers the charge by collecting contributions from the tenants (at least once a month).

The collective charge does not apply to anyone exempt from the personal poll tax, except those who normally sleep rough, who will be liable for any days they spend in property designated for the collective charge. No charge applies to full-time students but if the property is their term-time address they will pay 20% of the personal poll tax for that area in the normal way (see page 102 under 'Students'). Students whose term-time address is in Northern Ireland where poll tax is not payable will, however, be liable to the collective charge for any days they spend in designated property. Many tenants will be entitled to claim benefit to help them to pay the charge (see below under 'Community charge benefit').

The landlord must keep records of tenants' names, periods of occupation and amounts payable for at least a year after the contribution period, and is liable to fines if he does not. The landlord himself will usually pay the personal poll tax, as will staff who live in separate quarters. But where staff quarters are included in the collective charge arrangements, staff will pay contributions like the tenants.

Community charge benefit

Community charge benefit up to a maximum of 80% of the charge is available for people on low incomes. Those on income support will get the maximum, and those who were getting housing benefit but not income support will get relief on a sliding scale up to 80%, as will others on a low income. Where people have savings of £16,000 or more, no benefit will be payable. Those who are on income support will get an additional allowance towards the 20% of the poll tax that remains payable, but this is based on a national average poll tax figure and may or may not cover the remaining amount.

Although poll tax is charged on each individual, the right to benefit depends on the income and savings of a couple where they are married or living together as husband and wife.

The benefit for those who were getting housing benefit will usually be worked out by councils without the need for a claim. The DSS will give claim forms to those getting income support but not housing benefit. Other people who may be entitled need to ask for a claim form. A couple make a joint claim. The benefit is given by reducing the amount of the poll tax charge.

Benefit is available not only for the personal poll tax but also for collective charge contributions (but not for the standard charge). Claims are made in the same way, but the benefit is given either in the form of a voucher, or in cash, or, if the claimant agrees, direct to the landlord. Where someone is liable both to personal poll tax and the collective charge, they may claim benefit towards both.

Students who pay only 20% of the poll tax are not entitled to benefit.

Community charge reduction scheme (previously called transitional relief)

Relief for the personal poll tax, but not the standard or collective charge, will be given in 1992/93 to those whose poll tax burden is significantly higher than the rates they used to pay. The relief is given automatically. The relief for 1992/93 is based on the community charge for that year and the 1989/90 assumed rates bill (i.e. the rateable value × the average domestic rate poundage as set by the Government). The reduction scheme limits the amount by which the total poll tax for the household can exceed the 1989/90 assumed rates to £52 for a single person or a couple plus a further £52 for each additional chargepayer. The available reduction is split evenly between the chargepayers.

Example 1

Poll tax £250, assumed rates £460, three chargepayers in property.

	£
Total poll tax 3 × £250	750
Assumed rates	460
Increase	290
Restricted to £52 for first two	
chargepayers + £52 for third	104
Reduction available	£186

i.e. £62 per chargepayer, so that each person will pay £(250 − 62) = £188 (less community charge benefit if applicable).

The reduction is given to whoever lives in the property on 1 April 1992, even if they did not live there in 1989/90.

Relief is also given to non-ratepayers (or non-rate paying couples) who on 1 April 1990 were over 65 (men) or over 60 (women) or were disabled. People in this category will normally pay not more than £52. No relief is available if the person has moved since 31 March 1990, unless the move was caused by fire, flood, unsafe property etc.

Students

Students in full-time advanced education (which broadly means post-A-level courses) have to pay only 20% of the personal poll tax, and it is payable to the council where their term-time address is. Educational establishments will provide students with a certificate showing that they qualify for the student reduction. The reduction applies from the day the student starts the course to the day it ends, and covers holiday periods even though the student may then be living elsewhere. Where someone leaves school and goes to university etc. and there is a gap between the parent receiving child benefit (which usually ends for summer leavers on the first Monday in September) and the start of the course, the full amount of poll tax used to be due for the days before the course starts, but the child could then claim community charge benefit (see page 100) and was therefore only normally liable at 20% of the full rate for that period as well. For 1992 leavers, the rules have been changed so that their exemption continues until the start of their course.

If a student has no current term-time address (because for example he has given it up during the holidays) he will be treated as continuing to live at his last term-time address, and a student who does not yet have a term-time address is treated as living at his sole or main residence under the normal rules.

Full-time students who spend a year abroad will not be liable to the poll tax during their absence. Overseas students on a full-time course in England or Wales, on the other hand, will be liable to 20% of the personal poll tax at their term-time address. This also applies to foreign language assistants who have a certificate from the Central Bureau for Educational Visits and Exchanges. Students whose term-time address is in Northern Ireland will not pay the personal poll tax, but if they spend time in a collective charge property in England or Wales they will pay collective charge contributions for that period.

Student nurses on academic courses at universities etc., or on Project 2000 training courses, will only have to pay the 20% charge, but not other student nurses, who will pay the full amount less any community charge benefit they are entitled to.

A student who owns property but lives elsewhere during term-time will be liable to the standard charge on his own property unless it is someone else's only or main residence.

Students in full-time education who were ratepayers and who qualify for the community charge reduction (see page 101) will only get 20% of the relief they would have had if they paid the full charge.

Paying the poll tax

Each person liable to the poll tax receives a separate bill, and those who are liable to both personal poll tax and the standard charge will receive two bills. The rules of the scheme provide for payment of the personal and standard charges to be made in ten instalments, but councils may offer alternatives, and may offer discount for early payment. Changes in liability are taken into account as and when they occur, and appropriate adjustments made.

Where a couple are living together and are married or living as husband and wife, each is responsible for payment of the other's personal poll tax and standard charge as well as their own. If a couple separate, this liability ceases from the date of separation. There is no liability to pay a partner's charge unless the person liable has failed to pay and the council have issued a bill to the other partner.

If you fail to pay on time, you may lose the right to pay by instalments, and action may be taken against you for recovery. An attachment of earnings order may be made, requiring your employer to deduct the outstanding poll tax from your salary and account for it to the council. If you don't pay at all, you may be sent to prison.

Appeals

Appeals may be made about register entries, refusal of student discount, designation of your property for the collective charge, and the amount of a bill or penalty. The appeal is first made to the council or registration officer, then to a Valuation and Community Charge Tribunal.

Business rates

From 1 April 1990, businesses pay a uniform business rate (also called the national non-domestic rate) on their rateable values. (This does not apply to those served by the City of London Corporation, for whom there are special arrangements.) A revaluation was made prior to the start of the new system and future revaluations will be made every five years. The level of the rate for 1992/93 has been fixed at 40.2 pence in the pound (compared to 38.6 pence for 1991/92). Annual increases cannot be more than the increase in the Retail Prices Index.

There are transitional arrangements for those facing large increases or decreases. There will, however, be no increases other than for inflation of 4.1% in 1992/93. The phasing-in of increases will resume in 1993/94. The phasing-in of large decreases has been made more generous for 1992/93, and from 1993/94 the phasing-in will no longer apply and businesses will get the full benefit of the decreases. The maximum reductions for 1992/93 will be 22% of the 1991/92 inflation adjusted figures, giving a minimum liability of 81.198% of the 1991/92 figure (or a maximum 27% reduction if the rateable value is less than £15,000 in Greater London or £10,000 elsewhere, giving a minimum liability of 75.993% of the 1991/92 figure). Properties with a rateable value of less than £500 do not come within the transitional arrangements.

If a property changed hands, the transitional relief used to cease and the new occupier paid the full rate. Note that this applied, for example, when a sole trader died (even if the spouse inherited), when a business was incorporated and when a trade was transferred within a group of companies. From 11 March 1992, a new owner will be entitled to take over the previous owner's entitlement to transitional relief. The phasing-in of decreases has never been affected by a change of owner.

Empty property will attract only half the normal rates bill, and then only after it has been empty for three months. And no rates will be payable on empty factories and warehouses, or on empty properties with a rateable value of less than £1,000.

Self-catering holiday accommodation will normally be subject to the business rate if available for short-term letting for 140 days or more in a year.

If you offer bed and breakfast, you will not be liable to business rates if you intend to offer such accommodation for not more than six people, you intend to live in the property at the same time and the property's main use is still as your home. Before 1 April 1991, business rates were payable if the accommodation was offered for more than 100 days a year.

Those in mixed business and private accommodation pay the business rate on the non-domestic part and personal poll tax if the private part is their only or main residence (or the standard charge if it is no-one's only or main residence).

The business rate is collected by individual local councils but it is paid into a national pool from which each council gets a sum based on the number of poll tax payers in its area. Money is therefore transferred from areas with high rates and low domestic population to areas with high domestic population and low rates.

For 1990/91 only, there was a safety net whereby areas whose poll tax would otherwise have been lower than the average rates bill contributed to areas whose bills would have been higher. For the following three years, areas that received protection from the safety net pool will receive it from the Government.

Poll tax in Scotland

The poll tax was introduced in Scotland on 1 April 1989 and there are some significant differences there compared with the system in England and Wales.

In Scotland there is a community water charge system running parallel to the poll tax system, collected under the same three heads of personal, standard and collective charges. There is also a provision for those liable to the standard community charge to recover it from tenants with a lease of less than twelve months, or from licensees.

In Scotland the collective community charge is paid on an annual basis, and depends on the collective charge multiplier, which is worked out according to bedspaces, likely occupancy levels etc. Clearly these figures may change, but the multiplier will only change at intervals of at least three months, so that the multiplier may not reflect the actual number of people liable to pay the charge.

Someone paying the collective community charge contribution never has to pay the personal poll tax as well.

Those who are entitled to community charge benefit do not get benefit towards the community water charge, although those on income support get an adjustment in their allowance for both the poll tax and the water charge.

The normal payment method is by twelve monthly instalments rather than ten as in England and Wales, although with the same provisions for other methods to be offered.

People in Scotland cannot be jailed for not paying the poll tax.

Proposed council tax

The poll tax is to be replaced by the council tax from 1 April 1993. The amount of council tax will depend on the value of the property, property being allocated to one of eight bands A to H. Values will be based on open market values on 1 April 1991, but on a broad basis, without adjustments to take account of the condition of the property. Transitional provisions will ensure that there are no unreasonable increases as a result of the changeover.

There will be only one charge for the household, no matter how many people live there, except that a single householder will automatically be entitled to a 25% discount.

Empty property and second homes will be liable to a 50% charge, and the same exemptions will be available as currently apply to the standard community charge (see page 98). Flats over shops will be separately valued for the council tax.

Those whose income is at or below income support level will get a 100% discount, and there will be a sliding scale of reductions for others on low incomes. Students, student nurses, apprentices and youth trainees will automatically be entitled to personal discounts.

9
Dealing with the Revenue

Revenue officials

Income tax, corporation tax and capital gains tax are administered by the Commissioners of Inland Revenue (also called the Board of Inland Revenue). The Board operates through its appointed officials, inspectors of taxes and collectors of taxes. Inspectors are responsible for sending out tax returns, making assessments and dealing with disputes. Collectors are responsible for collecting tax due as notified to them by the inspectors. Inheritance tax is also administered by the Board of Inland Revenue, but through the Capital Taxes Office. Stamp duties are administered by the Board through the Office of the Controller of Stamps.

Returns by individuals of income and capital gains (TMA 1970, ss 7, 8, 11A, 113)

Tax returns are usually required to be submitted annually, although PAYE taxpayers with no other sources of income may receive them less frequently. The Revenue will accept approved computer produced returns and photocopies of returns and other tax forms (Revenue Statement of Practice SP 5/87). The official time for the submission of a return is 30 days from its issue. If you do not receive a return and you have income (other than wages or salary) or gains chargeable to tax, you must notify the inspector within twelve months after the end of the tax year. It is sensible to keep a photocopy of your return so that you have a full record of the information you have provided.

A return is usually labelled with an income tax year, and requires details of income, allowable outgoings and capital gains of the tax year before and allowances claimed for the tax year itself.

The 1993/94 return, to be issued after 5 April 1993, will thus require details of:

    Your income from all sources for 1992/93
    Your allowable outgoings for income tax during 1992/93
    Capital gains—details of chargeable assets disposed of during 1992/93
    Claim for allowances for 1993/94

Following the introduction of independent taxation of husband and wife from 6 April 1990, both now get their own return to fill in.

You should attach explanatory schedules to your return where necessary. Some special points you need to be aware of when completing your return are as follows.

Trade, profession or vocation

It is often appropriate, particularly so that the submission of a return is not delayed, to use the expressions 'As agreed', or 'To be agreed', or, if you are a partner, 'See partnership returns and accounts'. This is especially so for new businesses, or where there are changes in accounting dates and changes in partners. If a separate trade or partnership is carried on abroad, give details separately. You should not, however, delay the submission of supporting accounts and tax computations, since the return is strictly incomplete until these have been supplied to the Revenue, and interest and penalties may arise.

If, however, your turnover is less than £15,000 (£10,000 for accounts submitted before 6 April 1992), you do not have to send in your accounts (although you must still keep proper records in case the Revenue asks to see them) and you can just show your turnover, purchases and expenses, with the resulting net profit, in the spaces provided on the return.

If you are in partnership, show separately any interest which you pay and capital allowances which you claim for providing your own equipment (perhaps a car or office furniture) for use in the partnership.

Employments etc.

Show each one separately, and attach a schedule if need be. Enter the gross pay from the certificate of pay and tax given to you by your employer. This information will be sent to the Revenue by your employer, but entering it will help you to check any assessment or summary of your tax position you receive from the Revenue. If you receive any benefits (e.g. car provision), expenses allowances or reimbursements it is usually appropriate to say 'See employer's return', since the employer will have to make a detailed return. You should, however, ask the employer for a copy of it, since you are responsible for declaring the detailed items, and you should therefore query any items with which you disagree, and ensure that the return has been submitted if you are relying on it to supply the Revenue with the full details required.

Under the heading 'Expenses in employment', as well as making specific claims, such as for professional subscriptions and items which either you or a trade association have agreed with the Revenue, insert a general heading 'Reimbursed expenses per employer's return', since this effectively cancels the payment to you by the employer of expenses properly incurred in the performance of your duties.

If you have received a lump sum or pay in lieu of notice upon your ceasing to be employed, this should be shown. The sum may not be taxable, or only partly so (see chapter 15), but it needs to be declared.

Tips and income from activities associated with the employment should be shown, whether they are paid by the employer or by someone else.

If you are entitled to a deduction for duties carried on abroad (see chapter 41), the periods of absence should be shown, clearly stating days of departure and return.

This section of the return covers income as an office holder as well as that from a conventional employment. Thus an honorarium, or any excess of a general expenses allowance over the expenses incurred, should be declared.

Social security pensions and benefits

Precise details of the type of benefit received should be shown, since some benefits are taxable while others are not (see chapter 10).

From 6 April 1990, wives are entitled to a personal allowance in their own right, which can be used against any pensions or other income they have, whether the pensions are earned by their own contributions or by their husband's. But where a husband gets an addition to his pension because he has a non-working wife under 60, that counts as his income. It is not the wife's income until it is actually paid to her.

Dividends from UK companies and tax credits

The amount to show is the dividend received in the year to 5 April and the tax credit, which is shown on the dividend counterfoil. The total of the two will be included in the summary of your tax position prepared by the Revenue to see whether you are liable to higher rate tax. Unit trust income distributions will be included here. If you have acquired new units, you will usually have received with your income an amount called 'equalisation'.

This is not income and should not be included. It should be deducted from the acquisition cost of the units for capital gains tax purposes, since it represents a reduction in the cost of your units to cancel the accrued income included in your purchase price when you bought them.

Interest from which tax has been deducted

The interest from which tax has been deducted at source that is shown under this heading is from banks, building societies and other deposit takers such as local authorities.

Interest from which tax has not been deducted

National Savings:

Show the interest received or credited on National Savings Bank accounts and on deposit or income bonds and capital bonds in the year to 5 April. On a National Savings Bank account, take care to show whether the interest is on an ordinary account or an investment account. It is only the first £70 of *ordinary* account interest that is exempt from tax (for each of husband and wife). The full interest should be shown whether exempt or not. The Revenue will deduct the exempt amount when assessing you or including the amount in a summary of your tax position.

Other UK banks, building societies and deposit takers:

Show bank and building society interest on which you have certified that you are not liable to tax because your total income is covered by allowances and you are thus entitled to receive interest gross (see chapter 37) separately from interest paid in full for any other reason (see page 414).

Other UK sources:

Other interest received in full, such as on War Loan, British Savings Bonds and loans to private individuals is shown under this heading.

Property in the UK

If the new 'rent a room' relief (available from 1992/93 onwards—see page 334) applies to rent received, all you need do is state on the return that you have exempt 'rent a room' receipts.

Where the relief does not apply, make sure that the income is inserted opposite the appropriate type of letting. The rent to include is that due in the year ended 5 April, less allowable expenses (see chapter 32 for details). Furnished holiday lettings are treated as trades even though the income is declared under this section. Any interest paid that relates to furnished holiday lettings is deducted in arriving at the income (subject to any restriction for private use) (see chapter 32). Interest on other let property is usually deducted in a different part of the return, unless you are a substantial landlord and have included it in your rent account here (see page 112). If you are the landlord and you pay your wife an amount for her assistance in rent collecting and administration which has been agreed with the Revenue as a proper deduction, this payment should be shown as her income in the employments section of her return.

When you have several properties and some show profits whilst others show losses, the setting-off of losses against taxable profits is not always straightforward (see chapter 32) and it is best to give the Revenue comprehensive details so that they can check your own conclusions and not later be able to say that they were incorrectly or insufficiently informed.

If your total gross letting income before expenses is below £15,000 (£10,000 for returns submitted before 6 April 1992), you do not need to provide a detailed statement showing how the total allowable expenses stated in the return were arrived at, although you must still retain detailed records yourself in case any query is raised.

Other dividends, trust income, etc. already taxed

Enter the full amount of the income before deduction of basic rate income tax. The amount of that income will be clearly shown on the certificate accompanying your income. If you have purchased an annuity from a life assurance company, the income will include a non-taxable element to compensate you for having parted with capital in order to receive an income. This capital element should not be included in the amount entered on your return. The life assurance company and the Revenue will have agreed its amount and it will be clearly shown on the counterfoil accompanying your income. If you have entered into a life assurance contract in order in due course to replace the capital you have spent in purchasing the annuity, the life assurance company will only account to you for the difference between the amount due to you under the annuity and the life assurance premium. This net amount is not the amount to show as income. The income is the income element of the annuity *before adding* the capital element and *before deducting* the life assurance premium.

Settlements

Include any income to which you are entitled in the year ended 5 April. The trustees should give you a certificate showing the amount, which will either have been paid to you or will have been credited to you and made available for you to draw. You should also show any lump sums which you have received, although these will not necessarily be taxable. Again the trustees should indicate what is taxable income in your hands. On the other hand, you may yourself have settled assets on your infant unmarried children, perhaps by making bank or building society investments in their name. Any such income remains yours for tax purposes and must be shown in your return, unless it amounts in total to £100 or less (increased from £5 from 6 April 1991).

Payments from estates (in the course of administration)

If you are entitled to a share of the capital from an estate, the amounts you receive will be a combination of that capital and the income which it has generated. The personal representatives, who will themselves have paid basic rate income tax on the income, will give you either a certificate of the income, or estate accounts showing your income share. The amount before basic rate tax should be shown.

You may sometimes be entitled to income under a trust created by will rather than a share of the capital, in which case the personal representatives will first of all complete the administration of the estate then transfer the residue to a trust fund. Income which you receive during the administration period is regarded as net of basic rate tax, for example £750 net in 1992/93 is equivalent to £1,000 gross, and the gross amount should be shown. In the tax year when the administration is completed, the personal representatives will transfer to you a final amount of income up to the date of the completion of the administration, together with an income certificate. The amount of income should be shown on the return, but the Revenue will then reallocate the entire income during the administration period on a time basis, making appropriate amendments to your taxable income for this and earlier years. Any income you receive from the trustees after the residue has been transferred to them will be entered under the heading 'Other dividends, trust income, etc. already taxed'.

Untaxed income from abroad

The word 'untaxed' relates to UK tax. If tax has been paid abroad you will need to make a claim for relief to be given for it in arriving at how much UK tax you will have to pay. If UK tax has been deducted, for example by the Bank of England when acting as paying agent, the income should not be shown here but under the heading 'Other dividends, trust income, etc. already taxed' (see above).

All other profits or income

The return form usually asks specifically for details of maintenance, alimony, accrued income charges, taxable gains on life assurance policies and excess life assurance relief (see chapter 40).

The amount of maintenance or alimony received in the year to 5 April should be shown. If the maintenance was received under arrangements made before 15 March 1988, the first £1,720 of maintenance from a divorced or separated spouse is exempt from tax (that amount having remained unchanged for 1990/91, 1991/92 and 1992/93). If the arrangements were made after that date, maintenance is wholly exempt. Whether it is wholly or partly exempt, however, the full amount should be shown.

Tax used to be deducted at source from some maintenance payments but since 6 April 1989, virtually all payments are made in full (see page 383).

The life assurance company will issue a certificate of taxable gains which arise from your drawing a sum from a policy (partial surrender) or cashing it (maturity or complete surrender). The gains should be shown in the return of income for the year ended 5 April in which the policy year ends.

Following the introduction of the accrued income scheme (see page 410) you are also required to show, in the return for the tax year in which the next interest payment on the stock fell due, the amount of any accrued income charges on your purchases or sales of stock. The amounts will usually be shown on the contract notes. Do not show the accrued income if you are exempt from the charge because the nominal value of all your stock does not exceed £5,000 in the tax year or years concerned.

This section is not confined to the items mentioned. It relates to any other income or profits. If in doubt as to whether an item should be included you should either seek appropriate professional advice or clear the point in writing with the Revenue.

If you have ceased to trade in an earlier year but have received some late income which was not included in your accounts, the amount should be included here.

Income from personal activities, for example from writing the occasional article or from an occasional commission, where the extent is insufficient to be regarded as from a profession or vocation, should be included in this section.

Where occasional profit items are included, relief may be available for losses on the same or other occasional activities. Include details and ask the Revenue to calculate and give relief for the losses against the profit items.

Private medical insurance for people over 60

If you pay higher rate tax, you must supply a certificate from the insurer of premiums you have paid. The premiums can be paid, and relief obtained, by a relative, so long as the insured person (or one of an insured married couple) is over 60—see page 394.

Interest paid on loans for the purchase or improvement of property in the UK

This section of the return covers interest relating to your only or main residence and interest on let property. Home improvement loans no longer qualify for relief unless they were made before 6 April 1988, so the return deals separately with loans before and after that date. Married couples should show separately how much interest each of them pays on their residence. They may choose to have tax relief allocated in a different way from the way in which they actually pay the interest (see chapter 30), in which case they should mark the appropriate box.

Building society interest paid:

The society will advise the Revenue of the interest paid, and will usually have deducted tax relief at the basic rate in charging the interest to your account. The return asks you to tick a box if you did not get basic rate relief in this way, usually because the loan was in excess of £30,000 and MIRAS relief (mortgage interest relief at source) was not given on the first £30,000.

If you were entitled to tax relief at the higher rate for interest paid up to 5 April 1991, the society will on request give you a certificate showing the interest paid (MIRAS 5), and this is sometimes asked for by the Revenue if they have not been advised direct by the society at the time they wish to summarise your tax position.

The return also asks for information about loans paid off during the year.

All other lenders:

Some banks are in the MIRAS scheme and again you may have had relief at the basic rate by deduction from the interest charged to your account. If you did not get relief in this way, or if you need evidence to obtain tax relief at the higher rate up to 5 April 1991, the lender should be asked for a certificate of the interest paid.

Let property (other than furnished holiday lets):

The interest is deductible from the rents from all let properties. If you are a substantial landlord, you may well have included the interest paid as an expense in your rent account under the income section of the return. But if you have not, the interest actually paid by you in the year to 5 April should be shown here, accompanied by a certificate from the lender.

The property must be let for at least 26 weeks out of a consecutive 52 weeks (not necessarily the tax year) in order for the interest to qualify for relief, and it must be loan interest, not overdraft interest.

You may have borrowings which do not fit straightforwardly into any of the above, but on which tax relief may be due, for example interest which you have paid on a bridging loan while you had two houses, interest on established loans at 5 April 1988 to assist with the purchase of a property occupied rent-free by a dependent relative or in respect of a property occupied by your former marriage partner from whom you are separated or divorced, or interest on borrowing to assist in the purchase of a property which you intend to occupy in the future but which is for the moment not your *main* residence because you have to live on your employer's premises (for example if you are a minister of religion) or on the premises where you carry on your self-employment (for example as a public-house tenant or a tenant farmer). If so, give full details of the circumstances and the interest paid, if necessary in a schedule or covering letter.

Interest on other loans

You can claim a deduction for interest paid for the purposes listed on pages 12 and 13. The interest must be on a loan. Overdraft interest does not qualify for relief except as a business expense. A certificate of the interest paid in the year ended 5 April must be attached.

Other outgoings

Gift Aid donations and covenanted payments to charities:

All such payments should be shown net of tax. Donations under Gift Aid of a minimum of £400 net each qualify for tax relief (£600 net each if paid before 7 May 1992). For details, see chapter 43.

Other covenants, bonds of annuity, settlements, accrued income purchased etc:

Show the full amount before tax. The payees under a covenant will often require from you a certificate of the tax deducted in order to deal with their own tax position. From 15 March 1988, new non-charitable covenants do not qualify for tax relief.

Any accrued income reliefs you are entitled to (see page 411) should be shown in the return for the tax year in which the next interest payment on the stock fell due. You should also enter details of that interest so that the relief may be given against it.

Alimony or maintenance:

Enter here those payments which are enforceable against you because of an order of the court or under a written agreement. The Revenue will require to see the court order or written agreement. If the maintenance arrangements were made after 15 March 1988, you will usually only get tax relief on maintenance to your spouse, not to children, and only on the first £1,720. Maintenance under earlier arrangements, both to a spouse and by court order to children, qualifies for relief in full. Virtually all maintenance is now paid without tax being deducted at source (see page 383). For payments due from 6 April 1992 onwards, relief is due under maintenance orders made in other countries in the European Community.

Capital gains

Chargeable assets disposed of:

In the case of quoted securities it is helpful to include here a schedule showing the movements through purchases, sales, bonus and rights issues, thus reconciling opening and closing holdings. The calculation of the chargeable gains on these and other assets is dealt with in the appropriate chapters, the date of disposal being the contract date in all cases.

Other information required:

You are now also required to supply details of payments made or benefits provided to you by trustees of non-resident or dual-resident settlements, and of chargeable gains of settlements by reference to which you are chargeable as settlor (see pages 472, 473 and 479).

Chargeable assets acquired:

Details of chargeable assets acquired are not now requested on returns. It is still, however, important to retain precise records of acquisitions and additional expenditure on chargeable assets, so that the capital gains tax on a future disposal can be accurately calculated.

The indexation allowance depends upon dates of purchase and sale, so make sure you record them accurately.

Claims for allowances

Some particular points are noted below.

Special personal allowance

The increased personal allowance available to some married men with older wives is only beneficial for 1992/93 to men under 65 whose wives were over 75 on 5 April 1990, enabling the husbands to claim an allowance of up to £3,540 instead of £3,445 (see page 17). With the indexation of allowances, this special allowance is unlikely to be relevant at all for 1993/94.

Married couple's allowance

If you have married since the beginning of the previous tax year, give the date of marriage. This will enable the Revenue to work out your married couple's allowance. Married couple's allowance is not available for years after the year in which you separate. If you separated before 6 April 1990, however, but are still wholly maintaining your wife by unenforceable contributions, the married couple's allowance is still available while you remain married, although the Revenue will usually require proof that you are maintaining her.

For 1993/94 onwards, all or half of the married couple's allowance may be transferred to the wife (see page 14) but you need to make a claim *before 6 April 1993*. Forms will be available from tax offices from Summer 1992.

Additional personal allowance

The question asking whether any other person is claiming the allowance is a reminder that the allowance may be split if two people claim it for the same child, and in these circumstances you should agree the split with the other claimant. It is not possible for an unmarried couple who are living together to claim two additional personal allowances, so the name of a partner has to be shown also.

From 6 April 1993, the allowance will not be available to a wife in the year of separation if the full married couple's allowance has been transferred to her in that year (see page 381).

Surplus allowances

If your income may be too low to use your married couple's allowance (or blind person's allowance), or if you may be able to transfer unused allowances under the transitional provisions on the changeover to independent tax (see chapter 33) you have to notify the Revenue. Put a cross in the box asking for a transfer notice form.

Personal pension payments

These are dealt with in chapter 17. Employees paying new personal pension contributions or free-standing additional voluntary contributions get basic rate tax relief when they pay their contributions, so the payments are shown net. Contributions paid by an employer to an employee's own scheme are also shown. All pension payments by the self-employed, and retirement annuity payments under the old rules by employees, are paid in full and are shown gross. It is best to attach a schedule unless there are only one or two payments. The supporting certificate (SEPC or PPCC) should be attached for the first of regular premiums and for isolated premiums. Your date of birth has to be stated in order that the Revenue can see if, because of your age, you qualify for a higher rate of relief than the minimum 17½% of earnings. Two years' premiums have to be stated, those for the year to the previous 5 April so that the Revenue can see if further relief for that year is due because of payments in the year, and the anticipated payments for the year to 5 April next so that provisional relief can be given in assessments or codings.

Inheritance tax

Most lifetime transfers are 'potentially exempt' but a return to the Capital Taxes Office must be made by either transferor or transferee of those which remain chargeable, unless they do not exceed £10,000 and do not bring the cumulative total to more than £40,000. Returns are strictly not required until twelve months after the end of the month in which the transfer takes place, but interest on overdue tax runs from earlier dates, so returns should be lodged accordingly (see chapter 5).

(If not obvious from other entries, it is advisable for your income tax return to show substantial gifts received or made, thus explaining movements in capital and consequent variation in income. An election for gifts holdover relief for capital gains tax might also need to be made—see chapter 4.)

In the case of death, the return is made in conjunction with the application for a grant of probate (where there is a will) or of administration (where there is no will or where the named executors cannot or will not act). Again, a twelve-month return period is allowed, but interest runs from six months after the end of the month of death, and the need to obtain a grant in order to deal with the affairs of the deceased ensures an earlier return in most cases.

The return at death has to include details of earlier transfers, whether chargeable or potentially exempt at the time, which are required for the calculation of the tax payable (see chapter 5). It is therefore essential that full records of lifetime gifts are kept.

An account need not be submitted for a deceased's estate not exceeding £125,000 (£115,000 before 1 July 1991) provided that no trust is involved, that not more than £15,000 is situated outside the UK, and that there have been no transfers within the seven years before death or gifts where a benefit has been reserved. The Revenue reserve the right to call for an account later.

Late submission of returns

The submission of a return later than the officially allowed 30 days will not usually attract a penalty, but if a return is not made by 31 October after the end of the tax year, thus preventing an assessment being issued in time for the tax to be paid on the normal due date, the Revenue have announced (Revenue Statement of Practice SP 6/89) that the taxpayer will be required to pay interest from the date on which the tax would have been payable had a return been made on time, unless the Revenue had been provided with sufficient information by 31 October to enable them to raise an adequate estimated assessment. This is particularly relevant for capital gains and new sources of income, which the Revenue are less likely to be aware of in the absence of a return, than continuing sources of income where an estimated assessment can be raised.

Corporation tax returns (TMA 1970, s 11)

Although strictly a company should send in a return of its profits on form CT1Z within one month of receipt, giving details of its income, capital gains and losses and charges on income, most companies usually just send in their accounts and computations. Indeed, around two-thirds of corporation tax assessments are initially estimated and appealed against. This system will change from 1 October 1993, when 'Pay and File' is to be introduced, under which companies will be required to pay tax (estimated if necessary) nine months after the year end, or suffer interest on the underpayment, and file a statutory return together with accounts and computations twelve months after the year end, or pay penalties if they do not. The Pay and File system is outlined on page 29.

Under company law, public companies must file accounts with the Registrar of Companies not later than seven months after the end of the accounting period, the time limit for private limited companies being ten months. From 1 July 1992, automatic late filing penalties will apply for public companies, ranging from £500 if accounts are up to three months late to £5,000 if accounts are more than twelve months late, the figures for private companies being £100 to £1,000.

Assessments and additional assessments; error or mistake claims

Income tax, corporation tax, capital gains tax (TMA 1970, ss 29–41)

Assessments to income tax, corporation tax and capital gains tax are based on returns of income and gains made to the inspector of taxes, or are estimated where a return has either not been made or the Revenue doubts its accuracy.

If the Revenue discover that any profits or gains chargeable to tax have not been assessed, or have been insufficiently assessed, they may make an additional assessment. They will, however, not normally reopen an already agreed assessment, even if tax has been undercharged, unless the taxpayer failed to supply them with full information in reaching that agreement.

The normal time limit for making an assessment or additional assessment is six years from the end of the tax year to which it relates. If a taxpayer dies, new or additional assessments cannot be made later than three years after the tax year of his death.

Special rules apply in cases of fraudulent or negligent conduct. These are dealt with on page 120 below.

If an individual or company makes an error or mistake in a return causing an overpayment of tax, relief may be claimed at any time up to six years after the tax year in which the assessment was made. Such a claim is not possible where no return has been submitted. Furthermore, when such a claim is made, it may encourage the Revenue to reconsider other aspects of the tax-payer's affairs if they think fit.

Inheritance Tax (formerly Capital Transfer Tax) (IHTA 1984, s 221)

Notification of the amount of inheritance tax due is contained in a notice of determination issued by the Revenue. Adjustments for tax underpaid or overpaid, plus interest, may be made subsequently but not later than the end of six years from the date of payment, or if later, from the date payment was due. In cases of fraudulent or negligent conduct, the period of six years starts at the time the fraud etc. became known to the Revenue.

Stamp duty (Stamp Act 1891, s 12)

The Revenue may be required to state whether an instrument is liable to stamp duty and if so how much duty is payable. There is a right of appeal to the High Court.

Repayment and remission of tax because of official error

Unless a specific time limit is stated, the normal time limit for claiming reliefs is six years from the end of the relevant tax year. Repayments will, however, be made on claims made outside the time limit where the overpayment was caused by an error by the Revenue or another Government department, providing the facts are not in dispute.

Where the Revenue discover that they have undercharged a taxpayer, although they have been given full information at the proper time, they may, by concession, not collect some or all of the underpayment according to the following scale:

Taxpayer's gross income	Proportion of underpayment not collected
Up to £12,000	All
£12,001 to £14,500	¾
£14,501 to £18,500	½
£18,501 to £22,000	¼
£22,001 to £32,000	1/10
Over £32,000	No remission

The income limits are increased by £3,300 for taxpayers who, at the date of notification, are aged 65 or over or who receive the national insurance retirement or widow's pension, and inspectors of taxes have some discretion where capital is not readily realisable or if the income limits are marginally exceeded and the taxpayer has large or exceptional family responsibilities.

Due dates of payment and interest on overdue tax

Due dates of payment and interest provisions vary for the different taxes and are dealt with in detail for each tax in chapters 2 to 7.

Appeals (Income tax, corporation tax, capital gains tax—TMA 1970, s 31; Inheritance tax—IHTA 1984, s 222; Stamp duty—Stamp Act 1891, s 13)

Normally appeals must be made within thirty days after the date of issue of the assessment, except in relation to stamp duty where the prescribed period is twenty-one days. The appeal must state the grounds on which it is made (for example that the tax is estimated and not in accordance with information supplied or to be supplied). Late appeals may be allowed if the Revenue is satisfied that there was a good reason for the delay.

Postponement of payment of tax

Tax still has to be paid on the normal due dates even though an appeal has been lodged, except that in relation to income tax, corporation tax and capital gains tax an application may be made to postpone payment of all or part of the tax. The postponement application is separate from the appeal itself and must state the amount of tax which it is considered has been overcharged and the grounds for that belief. The amount to be postponed will then be agreed with the inspector or decided by the Appeal Commissioners (see below). Any tax not postponed will be due thirty days after the date of the decision as to how much tax may be postponed, or on the normal due date if later.

The appeal itself may be settled by negotiation with the inspector or, failing that, by following the appeal procedure to the Commissioners and thence if necessary to the courts. Once the appeal has been finally settled, any underpaid tax will be payable within thirty days after the inspector issues a notice of the amount payable. Any overpaid tax will be repaid. Although a postponement application may successfully delay payment of tax, it will not stop interest being charged against the taxpayer on any postponed tax which later proves to be payable (see the due date and interest provisions in chapters 2 to 4).

Appeal procedures

If an appeal is not settled between the taxpayer and the inspector, it is listed for hearing by the Appeal Commissioners. There are two types of appeal commissioners, General Commissioners and Special Commissioners. Certain specialised appeals are heard by the special commissioners and other appeals normally by the general commissioners. It is possible for a taxpayer to seek to have a non-specialised appeal heard by the special commissioners (but not a delay appeal where the Revenue have simply not been given the information they need, and there are no points in dispute) and there are provisions for the transfer of proceedings between the two bodies of commissioners. The decisions of the commissioners on matters of fact are normally binding on both parties. If either the taxpayer or the Revenue are dissatisfied with a decision on a point of law, they may ask the commissioners to 'state a case' for the opinion of the High Court. Further appeal is then possible to the Court of Appeal and, where leave is granted, to the House of Lords. It should be noted, however, that the decision to take an appeal to the commissioners on a point of law must be weighed very carefully because of the likely heavy costs involved, particularly if the taxpayer should be successful at the earlier stages and lose before a higher court. Provisions are to be introduced (probably in April 1993) to enable the Special Commissioners (not the General Commissioners) to award costs if either party to an appeal has acted unreasonably, and for selected decisions of the Special Commissioners to be reported.

Additional and extended time limit assessments to income tax, corporation tax and capital gains tax (TMA 1970, ss 34–36)

The Revenue are able to issue an additional assessment for a year within the normal six-year time limit without alleging that the taxpayer is at fault. They may 'discover' that an assessment is inadequate through considering facts already in their hands, such as by comparing gross profit rates from year to year, or through new facts, such as the existence of a previously undisclosed bank deposit account, or even because they change their minds on how something should be interpreted. They have, however, stated that they will not normally reopen an assessment they later find to be incorrect if they had been given full and accurate information and either the point was specifically agreed or the view implicit in the computation submitted was a tenable one. To reopen years outside the six-year time limit, the Revenue have to show fraudulent or negligent conduct. In that event, assessments may be made at any time up to 20 years after the chargeable period concerned. If the Revenue consider a case to be one of fraudulent or negligent conduct, then, unless they are considering a prosecution, they will usually invite the taxpayer to co-operate in establishing the understated income or gains. If he does so, they will then not normally have to resort to their statutory powers to call for documents and to enter and search premises.

Establishing the tax lost

The Revenue investigation will include some or all of the following for the appropriate period, the effect of one on another being considered:

(a) A full review of the business accounts.
(b) A detailed reconstruction of the private affairs, establishing whether increases in private wealth can be substantiated; or a less time consuming review ensuring that lodgements into bank and building society accounts can be explained.
(c) A business model based on a sample period, adapted for changing circumstances and compared with the results shown by the business accounts.
(d) A living expenses review and comparison with available funds to establish prima facie additional income.

At the conclusion of the review, if the need for a revision of profits, income or gains has been established, the calculation of tax underpaid follows automatically.

Interest and penalties (TMA 1970, ss 88, 88A, 95, 96, 98, 98A; FA 1989, ss 157, 158, 165)

Where the taxpayer has been at fault, interest runs from the date on which the tax ought to have been paid. The Revenue have statutory powers to impose penalties when it has been established that tax has been lost through a taxpayer's fraudulent or negligent conduct. These powers are quite separate from their powers to take criminal proceedings for an offence against the Crown. Following the abolition of the composite rate scheme, a new penalty of up to £3,000 has been introduced for culpable errors in relation to certificates of non-liability to tax.

Penalties are additional to payment of tax and interest, and the maximum penalties are shown in the table below.

The Revenue have power to reduce both interest and penalties. They will rarely reduce interest, but will usually accept a smaller penalty where a settlement is made with a taxpayer without formal proceedings being taken.

Non-compliance	Maximum penalty
Failure to notify liability within one year after end of tax year (TMA 1970, ss 7, 10, 11A)	The equivalent of the tax payable
Failure to submit income tax or capital gains tax returns within required period (TMA 1970, s 93)	£300, and £60 a day for every day failure continues after the £300 penalty has been imposed, plus an amount equal to the tax charged if failure continues beyond the end of the year following that in which the notice to submit the return was served
Failure to submit corporation tax return (TMA 1970, s 94)	£50, and £10 a day for every day failure continues after Commissioners or a Court have made an order for delivery of the return, plus an amount equal to the tax charged if the failure continues beyond the end of the period of two years from the date the notice to submit the return was served
Negligence or fraud in any return or accounts (TMA 1970, ss 95, 96)	An amount equal to the tax lost
Negligence or fraud in relation to a certificate of non-liability to tax, or failure to comply with any undertaking in such a certificate (TMA 1970, s 99A)	£3,000

Alternative to interest and penalty proceedings

Instead of formal proceedings being taken for interest and penalties, the taxpayer will usually be invited to make an offer to the Board of Inland Revenue in consideration of their not taking such proceedings. If that offer is thought reasonable and likely to be accepted by the Board, it will be submitted to them by the Revenue department which has been conducting the enquiry. Offers may sometimes be accepted by the District Inspector on behalf of the Board.

The amount of the offer will in fact be negotiated between the Revenue and the taxpayer and will comprise the calculated tax and interest plus a penalty loading, the penalty being reduced principally on three counts:

(a) Whether the initial disclosure was voluntarily made by the taxpayer or induced or partly induced by communication from the Revenue.
(b) The size and gravity of the offence.
(c) The degree of co-operation by the taxpayer.

The acceptance of a taxpayer's offer by the Board creates a binding contract, and if the taxpayer fails to pay, the Revenue are able to proceed for the amount due under the contract itself without any reference to the taxation position, although the terms of the contract allow them to repudiate it if they wish in the case of non or late payment, and further interest will be charged if payments due under the contract are delayed. This established procedure is used in the vast majority of cases, and has points both in the taxpayer's and in the Revenue's favour, in that the taxpayer may be treated less harshly than if proceedings were taken, and the Revenue are spared the trouble of taking those proceedings.

Special situations

Death of a taxpayer limits the Revenue's right to reopen earlier tax years to the six years before that in which he died, and moreover restricts their right to raise new or additional assessments to the three years after the end of the tax year in which the death occurs, whatever the reason for the unpaid tax (TMA 1970, s 40).

Partnerships involve a joint income tax liability on trading profits (but not on other income or chargeable gains), no partner (even though innocent) being able to settle separately with the Revenue in respect of his share of the trading profits. Where a partner has died, the principle of joint liability will cause his share of profits to remain subject to review while the liability of his estate is limited to the six earlier years, putting an added burden on the surviving partners for the years before the normal six years.

Companies and company directors. While the liabilities of a company and its directors are entirely separate, their financial affairs will be looked at together if they are suspected of being at fault. Unexplained wealth increases or funding of living expenses will generally be regarded as extractions from the company, and, under his duty to preserve the company's assets, the director must account to the company for the extracted funds. The director does not have to pay income tax on the extracted funds, but is required to account to the company for the extractions, the company's accounts having to be rewritten accordingly and the extractions being subject to tax at corporation tax rates where they represent additional company profits. The company is also accountable for tax at the basic rate on the grossed-up equivalent of the extractions unless they are repaid or covered by an amount already standing to the credit of the director. The tax liability attracts interest and is reckoned in the tax due to the Revenue when calculating penalties. Where the extractions do not represent additional taxed profits, but simply untaxed sums taken from the company, income tax will be payable by the director on the calculated benefit which he has enjoyed from the interest-free use of the company's money.

Tax points

- If your wife pays tax at a higher rate than you, you can save tax from 1993/94 onwards by transferring all or half of the married couple's allowance to her. But you need to make the claim *before* the beginning of the tax year, e.g. before 6 April 1993 for 1993/94.

- Companies need to try to get their tax affairs up to date now, so that they are not already behind at the start of the new Pay and File system, with its automatic interest and penalty provisions. Pay and File applies to the first account ending on or after 1 October 1993. Companies should also be aware of the new company law penalties for late filing of accounts.

- If you delay sending in a return which will trigger a tax liability of which the Revenue are otherwise unaware, this will invariably cause the Revenue to seek interest and perhaps penalties. Neither the interest nor the penalties are allowable in calculating your tax liability.

- If, in the case of a new business, the submission of accounts to the Revenue is delayed, not only will interest on overdue tax and sometimes penalties apply, but the Revenue may seek to review the accounts in depth, also involving their looking at your personal financial affairs to confirm the accuracy of the business accounts.

- If you are guilty of known irregularities, a payment on account of the tax eventually to be accounted for will reduce the interest charge and also help to demonstrate your co-operation.

- If you are aware of irregularities in your affairs, you should disclose them fully to the Revenue before they make a challenge. You will thereby obtain the maximum penalty reduction when an offer in settlement is eventually made.

- Whilst the Revenue will usually settle for a cash sum comprising tax, interest and penalties, it should never be forgotten that they may also take criminal proceedings in cases which they believe amount to provable fraud. They may still seek a civil money penalty on those aspects not brought before the court or where the taxpayer has been acquitted of fraud and they feel able to prove negligence (Revenue Statement of Practice SP 2/88).

- The Revenue and Customs and Excise have jointly issued a 'Taxpayer's Charter' setting out what standards they expect from a taxpayer, those which the taxpayer should expect from them, and the taxpayer's rights.

- If your business accounts or taxation affairs generally are under Revenue investigation, you will find useful the Inland Revenue pamphlets IR72 and IR73. They are no substitute for appropriate professional representation but are helpful in explaining procedures.

● The rates of interest on overdue tax vary frequently. A table is given at page xxiv, and the Revenue produce from time to time a table showing the interest factor to use in calculating interest arising on tax found to be due for earlier years.

● Where a tax payment is made through the GIRO system, the date stamped by the branch bank on the payslip is treated as the payment date.

● Following the abolition of the composite rate scheme, you can now receive bank and building society interest gross if you are not liable to tax. But you must not certify that you are entitled to this treatment unless you have *no tax liability at all*. Merely being entitled to a re-payment of some of the tax paid for the year is not enough. There is a new penalty for false declarations.

10
Employments—income chargeable and allowable deductions

Basis of charge (TA 1988, ss 19, 134)

Income from an employment or from the holding of an office such as a directorship is charged to tax under Schedule E, tax normally being collected through the PAYE scheme. It is often hard to decide whether someone is employed or self-employed. See chapter 19 for further details. If you get it wrong, the payer may be held responsible for non-compliance with the PAYE and national insurance regulations and the payee will find significant differences in the allowable expenses, the timing of tax payments and the liability for national insurance contributions. Most agency workers are required to be treated as employees. Responsibility for the operation of PAYE usually rests with the agency but the client is responsible if he pays the worker direct. Sub-contractors in the construction industry are treated as self-employed but are subject to special rules (see chapter 44).

Pensions and social security benefits (TA 1988, ss 150, 167)

Tax is also charged under Schedule E on pensions, whether from your employer or from the state, and on many other social security benefits, but certain benefits are exempt. A summary of the main taxable and exempt state benefits is given in the table on page 126. See pages xxx and xxxi for the current amounts payable. Where taxable, the charge is on the amount due in the tax year, whether or not received. See page 390 for further details.

Persons liable (TA 1988, s 19)

The extent of an individual's liability to tax on earnings depends on his country of residence, ordinary residence and domicile. Broadly, residence normally requires you to be in the country at some time in the tax year, ordinary residence means habitual residence and domicile is the country you regard as your permanent home.

Someone who is resident, ordinarily resident and domiciled in the UK is normally charged to tax on his world-wide earnings, although earnings during 'long' absences abroad may escape tax.

SUMMARY OF MAIN STATE BENEFITS	
TAXABLE	EXEMPT
Retirement pensions Widow's pension and widowed mother's allowance Statutory sick pay Statutory maternity pay Industrial death benefit paid as pension Job release allowance for periods beginning earlier than one year before pension age Income support to unemployed Income support to strikers Unemployment benefit Invalid care allowance	Wounds or disability pensions War widow's pension Disability living allowance Maternity allowance Widow's payment Job release allowance to men aged 64 or over or women aged 59 or over Child benefit and allowances Attendance allowance Sickness benefit Invalidity benefit Severe disablement allowance Disability working allowance Family credit Housing benefit Income support (other than as listed as taxable) Christmas bonus for pensioners Industrial injury benefits

Visitors to the UK are liable to tax on the amount they earn in the UK. If a visitor is not in the UK long enough to be classed as resident, he is not entitled to personal allowances. The provisions charging visitors to tax may be varied by double taxation agreements.

The detailed treatment of earnings abroad for both UK citizens and visitors is dealt with in chapter 41, which also explains residence, ordinary residence and domicile more fully and deals with the question of double taxation.

Assessable earnings (TA 1988, ss 131, 169–184, 202A, 202B; FA 1989, ss 37–40)

The rules for calculating earnings for national insurance contributions are not the same as those for tax and, in particular, national insurance contributions are not usually charged on benefits in kind. For details, see chapter 13.

Tax is charged on 'emoluments', which covers wages, salaries, commissions, bonuses, tips and certain benefits in kind. The emoluments must be 'in the nature of a reward for services rendered, past, present or future'. (See chapter 11 for profit-related pay, up to £4,000 of which is exempt from tax, and chapter 15 for lump sum payments received on ceasing employment or taking up employment.)

If your employer pays a bill that you are legally liable to pay, this counts as the equivalent of a payment of salary. This point needs particular care, otherwise something that was thought to be a benefit in kind provided by the employer may in fact be the settlement by the employer of the debt under a contract entered into by the employee. In that event it should be subject to the deduction of PAYE at the time of payment, and national insurance contributions would also be payable. If it was overlooked, it must be reported at the year end on P9D or P11D (see page 141).

Tax used to be charged on earnings of the tax year, whether received in that year or not. For most employees, the amount received in a tax year and the amount earned for the year are the same. But many company directors and those who receive periodic payments such as commissions often receive amounts some time after the period to which they relate. From 6 April 1989, all directors and employees are charged to tax on the amount received in the tax year, no matter what period the earnings relate to.

There were special provisions to cover the change from the earnings basis to the receipts basis. Where an amount was charged to tax in 1988/89 or an earlier year on the earnings basis and also in 1989/90 on the receipts basis, a claim could be made by 5 April 1991 for the 1988/89 or earlier year's taxable earnings to be reduced accordingly. In some circumstances the Revenue will extend this time limit (see Revenue Statement of Practice SP 1/92).

Certain expenses incurred may be deducted in arriving at the taxable earnings, as indicated later in this chapter.

Employees earning £8,500 per annum or more and directors—P11D employees (TA 1988, s 167)

The rules for reckoning assessable earnings are more onerous if you are an employee earning £8,500 per annum or more or if you are a director. All directors are covered by these special rules unless they (together with their close family and other associates) own not more than 5% of the ordinary share capital and either work full-time for the company or are employed by a charity or an organisation which does not have a profit making objective. Directors who are excluded on these grounds are nonetheless included if they earn £8,500 per annum or more.

Employees and directors covered by the special rules are called P11D employees in the remainder of this chapter (P11D being the form employers complete for such employees at the year end).

Other employees

If you are not a P11D employee, you are not normally taxed on benefits unless they can be turned into cash, and the assessable amount is the cash which could be obtained. For example, if you are given a suit which cost your employer £180 but which is valued second-hand at only £20, you are assessed only on £20. You escape tax on the benefit of use of a car, unless you have the choice of giving up the car for extra wages. In that event the car could be turned into cash at any time by taking up the offer, so you would be treated as having extra wages accordingly. Some benefits are chargeable on all employees.

Benefits are dealt with in more detail later in this chapter.

Allowable expenses and deductions (TA 1988, ss 197B-197F, 198, 201, 202, 577, 590-612; CAA 1990, s 27)

Allowable expenses are those incurred wholly, exclusively and necessarily in the performance of the duties of your employment and for travelling in the performance of those duties. Relatively few expenses satisfy this stringent rule. Some expenses which would not are specifically allowable by statute or by concession.

Travelling expenses from home to work are not allowed since they are not incurred in performing your duties. Travelling expenses on business journeys are allowed, and if you travel directly from home on a business journey away from your normal place of work, the allowable expense is the lower of the cost of the journey from home and what it would have cost to travel from your workplace. You can normally claim the full cost of subsistence when away from home, because it is recognised that you have continuing financial commitments at home. The Revenue are not strictly obliged to allow anything, since subsistence by its very nature can never satisfy the 'wholly, exclusively and necessarily' condition.

Where you use your own car for business, you can claim the business proportion of the running expenses (calculated on a mileage basis) and also capital allowances, and relief for interest on a loan to buy the car (see below). If your employer pays you a mileage allowance, this will be taxable, but your employer may obtain a dispensation from the Revenue to enable the mileage allowance to be ignored, and you will not then need to make an expenses claim. If there is a profit element in the mileage allowance this may be adjusted through your tax coding. Some employers use a scheme known as the 'Fixed Profit Car Scheme' (FPCS) by arrangement with the Revenue, under which the profit element in a business mileage allowance is identified according to bands of business mileage and agreed 'tax-free' rates fixed by reference to engine size. The rates are shown on page xxiii.

It is always open to an employee to calculate his expenses on the strict statutory basis if he wishes. The FPCS does not cover interest on money borrowed to buy the car—relief for interest must be claimed separately.

For most manual workers, flat rate expenses allowances have been negotiated for the upkeep of tools and special clothing, although this does not preclude a higher claim being made. The cost of normal clothing is not allowed even if it costs more than you would normally pay and you would not wear the clothes outside work.

If it is *necessary* for you to work at home you will be able to claim a proportion of the cost of light, heat, phone calls etc. The allowable proportion of such expenses is generally the subject of negotiation with the inspector.

Other allowable expenses include contributions to an approved pension scheme, charitable donations up to £600 a year under the payroll giving scheme, and most professional subscriptions that are relevant to your job. The cost of business entertaining is not allowed, but the disallowance may fall on you or on your employer depending on how payment is made. The disallowance falls on you if it is paid out of your salary or out of a round sum allowance. If you receive a specific entertaining allowance from your employer or are specifically reimbursed for entertaining expenses, no charge will fall on you and the disallowance falls on your employer.

You can claim a deduction against your earnings for:

Contributions to a personal pension plan (see chapter 17).
Capital allowances if you buy equipment that is necessarily provided for use in your job, restricted by any private use proportion (CAA 1990, ss 27, 79). (If it is a car, there is no 'necessarily' requirement and you can claim an allowance for the business use anyway.)
Interest on money borrowed to finance the purchase of such equipment (restricted by any private use proportion)—for the tax year of purchase and the three following tax years (TA 1988, s 359(3)).

Expenses payments and reimbursed expenses

The strict application of the rule for allowable expenses would require all expenses payments to employees to be treated as wages, leaving the employee to claim relief for the allowable part. To avoid a lot of unnecessary work, expenses payments that do no more than cover expenses that are 'wholly, exclusively and necessarily incurred in the performance of the duties of the employment' are not treated as pay under the PAYE scheme except for P11D employees. If, however, the whole allowance is not spent, the balance counts as pay.

For P11D employees, expenses allowances are treated as pay unless the employer obtains from the Revenue a dispensation enabling them to be excluded. The most common expenses for which a dispensation is granted are travelling and subsistence allowances on an agreed scale. Dispensations are never given for round sum expenses allowances.

For both P11D employees and other employees, there are special rules for payments connected with relocation, as follows.

Removal and relocation expenses

There are two concessions for expenses payments by an employer that are connected with an employee's relocation. Reasonable removal expenses are not assessable, including temporary subsistence whilst new accommodation is being sought and also interest on a bridging loan—see page 342 (concession A5). Providing various conditions are met, payments towards higher accommodation costs of a revenue nature, such as rent and net mortgage interest, when an employee is moved to a higher cost housing area, are not taxed up to a maximum of £18,060 (for moves on or after 1 November 1991), spread over a limited period and tapering as the years progress (concession A67).

Sale of home to relocation company

Where an employee sells his home to a relocation company and has a right to share in any profits when the company later sells the home, the employee will be exempt from capital gains tax on the later amount to the same extent as he was exempt on the original sale, providing the later sale occurs within three years. (Part of the original gain may have been chargeable because the home had not always been the main residence, or had been let etc., in which case the same proportion of the later amount will be chargeable.)

Benefits in kind for all employees—specific charges

Benefits assessed on all employees and directors, no matter how much they earn, are the provision of living accommodation and vouchers (see below). There is also a tax charge if a loan made to you by reason of your employment is written off—see page 164.

Living accommodation (TA 1988, ss 145, 146, 163)

If your employer provides you with living accommodation you are charged to tax on its annual value (i.e. letting value) less any rent you pay. (Annual values were based on gross rating values, and will continue on the same basis for the time being, although domestic rates have been abolished. Employers are to estimate annual values where no rateable value is available, for example on new property.) There is no charge, however, if

(a) you are a representative occupier, for example a caretaker, or
(b) it is customary in your employment to be provided with living accommodation, or
(c) the accommodation is provided for security reasons.

Except where the accommodation provided by a company falls within (c) above, a director cannot qualify for exemption unless he does not own more than 5% of the ordinary share capital and either he works full-time for the company or the company is a charity or an organisation which does not have a profit making objective.

If you were exempt under one of the above headings the exemption also covered the payment of rates by your employer. If your employer pays your personal community charge, however, it will count as part of your pay for tax and national insurance.

Employees who are not P11D employees escape tax on the provision of other benefits such as heating, lighting and the use of furniture, because they cannot be converted into cash.

If you are a P11D employee, you are chargeable on the value of other benefits relating to the accommodation whether or not you are chargeable on the letting value, but if you are exempt from the charge on letting value the charge for other benefits cannot exceed 10% of your taxable earnings excluding those benefits.

The charge for living accommodation is increased where the accommodation cost more than £75,000. The formula for calculating the extra charge over and above the letting value is:

((Cost less £75,000) × appropriate %) less rent paid in excess of letting value, if any.

The appropriate percentage is the official rate of interest chargeable on beneficial loans, as at the beginning of the tax year. Beneficial loans are dealt with on page 134.

Vouchers (TA 1988, ss 141–144)

The vouchers rules apply to all employees and are wide-ranging.

Cash vouchers are treated as pay under the PAYE scheme at the time the voucher is provided.

The cost of providing transport vouchers (for example season tickets), vouchers for childcare and other vouchers (including cheques) and the cost of goods or services obtained through the provision of employer's credit cards, although not treated as pay under the PAYE scheme at the time they are provided, are nonetheless taxable, and your employer is required to provide details to the Revenue at the year end. Employees of passenger transport undertakings like British Rail who are not P11D employees are exempt from tax on transport vouchers.

There is still, by Revenue concession, a derisory exemption of 15p per day for luncheon vouchers, providing they are available to all employees, non-transferable and used for meals only. Any excess over 15p is taxable, details being notified to the Revenue by your employer at the year end. No tax arises on free canteen meals that are provided to staff generally so the luncheon voucher rules discriminate against employers who are too small to have their own canteen.

Non-cash vouchers and credit tokens used to obtain a car parking space at or near your place of work are not assessable.

Benefits in kind for P11D employees (TA 1988, ss 153–168, 197A and Schs 6 and 7)

If you are a P11D employee, you are charged to tax on all expenses payments received (unless covered by a dispensation, see page 129) and on the cash equivalent of virtually all benefits provided either direct to you or to your family or household.

The main benefits that are not chargeable to tax are:

Meals in a staff canteen providing they are available to staff generally;

Employer's contributions to an approved pension scheme;

The provision of car parking facilities at or near the workplace, including paying or reimbursing the employee for such provision;

From 6 April 1990, childcare for children under 18 provided (other than on domestic premises) by the employer alone or with other employers, local authorities etc., but with each employer being partly responsible for finance and management. The exemption does *not* cover cash allowances, vouchers, or payment by the employer of the employee's childcare bills, which will be taxable for all employees no matter what they earn.

Payment for the provision of medical treatment or insurance is chargeable unless it relates to treatment outside the UK when on a business trip.

The cash equivalent of a benefit is normally the cost to your employer (including VAT where appropriate, whether recovered or not) less any amount made good by you to the employer. In a recent court case concerning a schoolmaster who paid reduced fees for his son, it was held that the full cost of a place at the school must be taken into account in measuring the benefit, rather than the extra cost of one more pupil. (The full cost would still usually be lower than the fee charged to other pupils, because it excludes the school's profit.) The case is subject to appeal, but if finally upheld, it will have implications for many others receiving benefits (for example, airline staff taking up empty seats). The Revenue will not normally require employers to change the basis adopted for 1992/93 and earlier years, but benefits first provided in or after 1991/92, and existing benefits from 1993/94, must be valued on an average cost basis (unless the decision is reversed in the House of Lords). The Revenue will, however, be prepared to consider employers' practical suggestions on how the average cost is to be arrived at.

Scholarships to employees' children are caught unless they are fortuitous awards paid from a trust fund or scheme under which not more than 25% of the total payments relate to employees. There is an exception for scholarships awarded before 15 March 1983 where the first payment was before 6 April 1984, but the exception does not apply after 5 April 1989 unless the child is still at the same educational establishment.

Special rules apply to share option and incentive schemes (see chapter 11), the provision of cheap loans and the use of cars (see below).

Where you are allowed the use of any asset that belongs to your employer, other than living accommodation (see page 130) or a car, you are charged to tax annually on the private element of 20% of its cost (10% if the asset was first provided before 6 April 1980). If the asset is later given to you, you are charged to tax on the higher of its market value at the date of the gift and the original market value less the intervening benefits assessments, whether made on you or on other directors/employees. See example 1.

Example 1

Television set cost employer £500. Used by director for two years, then given to him or any other P11D employee when market value is £50.

Assessments:

For use of asset, 20% × £500 =   £100 per annum

On gift of asset, higher of £50 and
                         £500 − (2 × £100)
                         = £300, i.e.   £300

If, as well as allowing you to use an asset, your employer meets expenses on it, for example pays the running expenses of a boat or aeroplane, you bear tax on the private element of those expenses as well.

Note that these rules for charging for the use of an asset apply for the private use (including home to work travel) of a vehicle other than a car, for example a company van.

Motor cars (TA 1988, ss 157–159A, 197A and Sch 6)

The benefit of private use of a car belonging to or leased by your employer is charged on a scale basis, with an additional charge being made if you are also provided with car fuel for private use. There is a lower fuel charge for diesel cars. The scale charges are shown at pages xx–xxii.

Any contribution you make to your employer for the use of the car is deducted from the car scale charge, but there is no reduction in the car fuel charge for a contribution to the cost of fuel for private journeys. To escape the fuel charge you must reimburse the whole cost of private fuel to the employer, or pay for it yourself in the first place.

If your annual business miles are 18,000 or more both the car scale charge and the fuel scale charge are halved.

If your annual business miles are 2,500 or less you are charged one and a half times the car scale benefit, but the fuel scale charge is not increased.

If you are provided with more than one car (for example a car for your spouse) the second and subsequent cars are charged at one and a half times the scale benefit whether you do 2,500 business miles in them or not, but again the fuel scale charge for the additional car(s) is not increased.

The scale charges cover the whole benefit obtained from the use of a car, except the expense of providing a chauffeur, which is charged in addition. If a car is provided for only part of the year (for example in the year when you start or cease employment) the scale charge is proportionately reduced. It is also proportionately reduced if the car is incapable of being used for a period of thirty consecutive days or more. Where a car is replaced during the year by one with a different scale charge, the appropriate proportion of each scale figure is charged, and the 18,000 and 2,500 mile limits referred to above are also reduced proportionately and considered in relation to the use of each car.

The provision of a car for private use and of private fuel now attracts employers' (but not employees') national insurance contributions—see page 171. Your employer will also have to account for value added tax on private fuel—see page 86.

It is possible to escape tax on the benefit of use of a car if it is a pool car as defined, but the conditions are restrictive. A pool car is one where the private use is merely incidental to the business use, the car is not normally kept overnight at an employee's home, and the car is not ordinarily used by only one employee to the exclusion of other employees.

The provision of a car telephone used to be included in the scale charge but mobile phones, including car phones, are subject to a fixed benefits charge of £200 per annum from 6 April 1991. The benefit will be reduced pro rata if the telephone is not available for the whole of the year. The benefits charge will not be made if there is no private use of the phone or if the employee is required to and does make good the full cost of any private use. This will require payment not only for the calls but a proper proportion of other costs, i.e. rental, installation costs, maintenance etc.

The increased car scale charges and the imposition of employers' national insurance contributions both on the provision of the car and on private fuel have led some employers to consider offering employees extra salary instead of a car. Care needs to be taken in such cases. If the employee has an ongoing opportunity to swap the car for cash at any time, the cash alternative would replace the scale charge for the car if it was higher. But making an initial choice between car and cash when starting employment, and when renegotiating the employment contract, should not give rise to any problem. Customs attempted to impose a VAT charge on the cash equivalent, but failed in a tribunal case, and from 1 April 1992 VAT only applies where an employee actually makes a payment for private use.

Cheap loans (TA 1988, ss 160, 161 and Sch 7)

If by reason of your employment you are provided with a loan interest-free or at a rate of interest below the official rate, you are charged to tax on an amount equal to interest at the official rate less any interest paid. The official rate of interest is varied by Treasury Order and is kept in line with typical mortgage rates (see page xxiv).

There is no charge if the benefit amounts to £300 or less in the tax year (£200 before 6 April 1991), or if you would have been entitled to tax relief on the interest if you had paid it. Under this provision there has been no tax charge on loans of up to £30,000 to buy your only or main residence. Following the withdrawal of higher rate relief on mortgage interest, the interest on the first £30,000 of a home loan will no longer be wholly excluded, but will be taxed at 15% to the extent that your income exceeds the basic rate band. A coding adjustment will normally be made for this purpose.

If the loan is written off, you are charged to tax whether you are still employed or not (see page 164).

Forms P11D

These forms are required at the year end under the PAYE regulations. They summarise the benefits and expenses payments in respect of directors and employees earning £8,500 per annum or more. They are increasingly subject to close scrutiny and testing by the Revenue as to their accuracy, for example through visits to business premises and directors' homes, and a close inspection of the position as regards loans to directors. Financial and taxation services provided for directors and annual Christmas parties are two examples of benefits under scrutiny, although expenditure of up to £50 (VAT-inclusive) per employee attending an annual dinner can be disregarded. Care should therefore be taken to ensure that all sections of the form are correctly completed, and in particular that all expenses of the employee met by the employer are declared, a claim being made by the employee in his annual tax return for a corresponding deduction if the expenses are allowable for tax.

Substantial penalties may be imposed for failure to submit a form P11D, or for submitting an incorrectly completed form (see page 141).

Training

External training courses

By concession, the meeting by an employer of the cost of external training courses, either of general education where the employee is under 21 when the course starts, or otherwise job-related, does not give rise to a liability to tax on the employee concerned, including additional travelling costs and subsistence where the employee is absent from his normal place of work for less than twelve months. (Similarly, where the employee himself bears the cost of an external training course which he attends whilst still being paid his full salary, that cost, including travel and subsistence in some circumstances, is deductible in calculating taxable earnings where the course is of at least four weeks' duration, takes place in the UK, and is job-related.)

Retraining costs (TA 1988, ss 588, 589)

Where a retraining course in the UK for up to one year is made generally available to appropriate employees, the employee is not assessed on the course costs and any incidental travelling expenses paid for by the employer. The employee must have been employed full-time for at least two years, must leave the employment within two years after the end of the course, and must not be re-employed within two years after leaving.

Vocational training (FA 1991, ss 32, 33; SI 1992/746)

A MIRAS-style tax relief was introduced from 6 April 1992 for payments made by trainees for their own training. Basic rate tax relief is given at source on the payments, and may be retained by both taxpayers and non-taxpayers. Any higher rate tax relief due must be claimed and will be given by coding adjustment or in an assessment. The training organisations are able to reclaim the basic rate tax from the Revenue.

The relief applies to study and examination fees paid by UK resident trainees for training leading to National Vocational Qualifications or Scottish Vocational Qualifications at levels 1 to 4.

The relief is available even if the course is unrelated to the trainee's present work or the trainee has no current job. It is not, however, available if any other public financial assistance is received in respect of the course, or if any other tax relief or deduction is available for the expenditure.

Summary of main benefits provisions

BENEFIT	TAX CHARGE	
	P11D EMPLOYEES	OTHER EMPLOYEES
Use of car	Scale charge Scale charge reduced by half if business miles 18,000 or more Scale charge increased by half if business miles 2,500 or less, and also for second and subsequent cars	Not assessable
Car fuel for private motoring	Scale charge (reduced by half if business miles 18,000 or more)	Cost to employer
Car parking facilities	Not assessable	Not assessable
Mobile telephone	Fixed scale charge of £200	Not assessable
Living accommodation	Letting value (unless job-related)	Letting value (unless job-related)
Provision of services and use of furniture in living accommodation	Cost of services plus 20% p.a. of cost of furniture (but charge cannot exceed 10% of other reckonable earnings from the employment if exempt from living accommodation charge)	Not assessable
Use of other assets (including vans)	20% of cost	Not assessable

| BENEFIT | TAX CHARGE | |
	P11D EMPLOYEES	OTHER EMPLOYEES
Vouchers other than luncheon vouchers	Full value	Full value
Use of employers' credit cards	Cost of goods and services obtained	Cost of goods and services obtained
Medical insurance	Cost to employer	Not assessable
Beneficial loans (unless interest would have qualified for tax relief)	Interest at official rate (see page 134) less any interest paid, but no charge if benefit £300 or less. See also page 134 re mortgage interest	Not assessable
Loans written off	Amount written off	Amount written off
Creche facilities	Not assessable	Not assessable
Free or subsidised canteen meals	Not assessable if available to all employees	Not assessable
Pension provision under approved schemes	Not assessable	Not assessable

Example 2

An employee is paid a salary of £16,000 in 1992/93.

He is provided with a 2-year old 1500 cc company car which is completely run by the employer, including the provision of private petrol and a mobile phone for business and private use. He did 10,000 business miles and 5,000 private miles.

He received an overnight allowance which amounted to £649 and in respect of which a dispensation had been granted to his employer by the Revenue.

He paid hotel and meal bills on business trips amounting to £1,539 and spent £250 on entertaining customers. These expenses were reimbursed by his employer. Telephone bills amounting to £250 were paid by his employer, of which £150 was agreed by the Revenue to be for business use.

He received a round sum expenses allowance of £1,200 out of which allowable expenses of £200 are agreed.

Following Revenue agreement of an expenses claim by the employee the assessable earnings are:

	£	£
Salary		16,000
Scale charge for use of car		2,770
Scale car fuel charge		630
Mobile phone charge		200
Overnight allowance (covered by dispensation)		—
Hotel and meal bills reimbursed		1,539
Entertaining expenses reimbursed		250
Telephone account paid by employer		250
Round sum expenses allowance		1,200
		22,839
Less: Hotel and meal bills reimbursed	1,539	
Entertaining expenses reimbursed (disallowed to employer)	250	
Proportion of telephone account agreed as relating to employment	150	
Other allowable expenses	200	2,139
Assessable emoluments		£20,700

National insurance

As well as the salary, pay for national insurance will include:

Overnight allowance unless the scheme satisfies the national insurance subsistence payments rules (broadly it must be based on a proper estimate of costs and the employee must claim for each subsistence payment).

Telephone bills, except for identified and logged business calls (unless the telephone contract is in the employer's name).

Round sum expenses allowance (except to the extent of any identified business expenses).

In addition to paying Class 1 national insurance contributions on the salary, the employer will pay Class 1A contributions on the car and fuel scale charges at 10.4% of (2,770 + 630 =) £3,400, i.e. £353.60, due for payment in June 1993.

Value added tax

The employer will pay output VAT on the car fuel of £23.53 per VAT quarter, unless no VAT input tax is being claimed on fuel for *any* motor vehicle.

PAYE

Tax under Schedule E is normally collected through the PAYE scheme, and no assessment is necessary unless there is a significant under- or overpayment. Employers deduct tax (usually on a cumulative basis) and national insurance contributions (on a non-cumulative basis except for company directors) from the weekly or monthly pay (including statutory sick pay and statutory maternity pay), using tables supplied by the Revenue. The total amount deducted in each tax month (ending on the 5th), together with the employer's national insurance contributions, less the amount recoverable for statutory sick pay and statutory maternity pay, is due for payment within fourteen days, i.e. by the 19th. Interest will be charged from 6 April 1993 on unpaid PAYE and national insurance contributions for 1992/93 which remain outstanding after 19 April 1993. If during the tax year the cumulative tax paid by an employee exceeds the cumulative amount due the excess is refunded to him by the employer, who then deducts it from the amount due to the Revenue.

From 6 April 1992, employers who expect their average total monthly payment for PAYE and national insurance contributions (and subcontractors' deductions where applicable) to be less than £450 may pay quarterly instead of monthly. (The figure was £400 before 6 April 1992.) New employers must notify the Revenue accordingly but existing employers need not do so unless they receive a demand from the Collector.

For details on national insurance contributions, including those relating to directors, see chapter 13. For details of statutory sick pay and statutory maternity pay, see chapter 14.

All the necessary documentation is supplied by the Revenue. Basic guidance is provided on the P8 cards.

Code numbers

The tax calculation is made using code numbers notified by the Revenue on form P9 or using the specified emergency procedure where no code number is received. Once a code number is issued it remains in force from year to year until the Revenue notify a change.

Your code represents the tax allowances you are entitled to, such as personal allowances and allowable expenses in employment, less a deduction to cover small items of other income like national savings bank interest, or to adjust underpayments in earlier years. The code number is the amount of your allowances less the last digit. For example if your allowances total £3,445 your code number is 344. The code effectively spreads your tax allowances evenly over the tax year. This means that if in any pay period you earn some extra pay, there is no extra tax-free allowance to set against it, so that the whole of the extra suffers tax.

Most codes are three numbers followed by a suffix L, H, P, or V. L denotes personal allowance and H personal allowance plus married couple's allowance or additional personal allowance. P denotes age allowance 65-74 and V age allowance 65-74 plus married couple's age allowance 65-74. The suffixes enable the Revenue to implement changes in these allowances by telling employers to increase the codes by a specified amount. Some codes have suffix T, which means that the code is only to be changed if a specific notification is received from the tax office. A code T may be requested by a taxpayer who wishes his status to remain private.

Some codes have a prefix D or F instead of a suffix. The number following the D or F prefix relates to the tax rate to be used. Prefix D is used if you have more than one employment and your total income will attract higher rate tax. Your allowances are given against the earnings from your main employment and tax is deducted in other employments according to the D code in use. The D code procedure represents an estimate of higher rate tax liability and an adjustment is necessary at the year end when the precise income is known. Prefix F enables tax to be collected on an excess of an employed pensioner's state pension over available allowances. Other codes are BR, which means basic rate tax applies, OT, which means no allowances are available, and NT, which means no tax is to be deducted.

At present, the benefits charges on P11D employees sometimes exceed the tax allowances they are entitled to, so that the full amount of tax due cannot be collected during the year. From 6 April 1993, K codes will be introduced, under which any excess benefits will be added to taxable pay, enabling broadly the correct amount of tax to be collected through PAYE. The K codes will also replace the F codes mentioned above.

Tax tables

Tables A, LR, B and C work on a cumulative basis. Table A shows the cumulative free pay each tax week or month for the various code numbers, Tables LR and B the tax due on taxable pay to date at the lower rate of 20% and the basic rate of 25% up to the basic rate limit and Table C the tax due at the higher rate. Tables D and F are non-cumulative, Table D being a higher rate tax ready reckoner, for use with Table C, for D codes and Table F a tax ready reckoner for F codes.

Records and year end returns

Employers must keep records of pay, tax, employees' and employer's national insurance contributions and the amount of any statutory sick pay and statutory maternity pay (see chapter 14). Details must be provided to the Revenue at the year end for all those who are or have been employed in that year.

Employers may either use deductions working sheets P11 (New) supplied by the Revenue and official end of year return forms P14, or use their own pay records and notify the totals on forms P14, or use their own pay records with substitute end of year returns, or keep computerised records and make end of year returns on magnetic tape.

Form P14 is in three parts, two being sent to the Revenue (one of which is for the Department of Social Security) and the third constituting the form

P60 for the employee showing the total pay and tax deducted in the year. The forms to be sent to the Revenue at the year end are—

Two copies of form P14 (or substitutes)

Form P35 showing the total tax, national insurance contributions, statutory sick pay and statutory maternity pay adjustments for all employees and former employees

Forms P11D showing details of expenses payments and benefits provided to current and former employees earning £8,500 per annum or more and directors

Forms P9D showing expenses payments in excess of £25 to non-P11D employees that have not been treated as pay (other than reimbursed business expenses and expenses paid in accordance with a scale agreed with the Tax Office) and certain other benefits such as the excess of luncheon vouchers over 15p per day.

The time limit for sending in forms P14 and P35 is 19 May, and for sending in forms P11D and P9D, 6 June.

Employers' Class 1A national insurance contributions on the provision of cars and private fuel to employees (see page 171) are calculated annually from the P11D entries. For 1991/92, payment had to be made to the Collector of Taxes with the PAYE remittance due on 19 June 1992 (19 July 1992 if you are a small employer making quarterly returns—see page 139) and the payment will be recorded on year end form P35 after 5 April 1993, so that where an employee leaves, records will still need to be maintained for the appropriate period. DSS allowed a direct payment, outside the PAYE system, to be made for 1991/92 by employers with ten or more cars, but it is not yet known whether or to what extent this will be available in later years. If a business changes hands, the liability for payment of the Class 1A national insurance contributions falls on the successor.

From 1995, automatic penalties may be imposed on employers who are late sending in end of year forms P14 and P35, or who send in incorrect returns. The provisions are being gradually introduced before then, and currently the Revenue may take proceedings for an initial penalty of up to £1,200 for every 50 employees, and further penalties if the returns are still not sent in, or are incorrect. In 1992/93, no penalty proceedings will be taken if 1991/92 returns were submitted by 19 July 1992. The penalties for late filing of forms P11D and P9D apply to each form and are an initial penalty of up to £300 plus up to £60 a day if the failure continues. If an employer fraudulently or negligently provides incorrect information in a P11D or P9D he is liable to a penalty of up to £3,000 for each form.

Changing jobs

When you leave your job, your employer should give you two copies of form P45 and send one copy to the Revenue. The P45 shows the total pay and tax to date in the tax year and the code number in use. You pass on the form to your new employer when you start another job so that he can continue to deduct tax on the correct basis. Wages in lieu of notice and statutory redundancy pay are not treated as pay, but they may be subject to tax under special rules (see chapter 15).

If you do not produce form P45 to your new employer he will ask you to complete form P46, stating either that this is your first job since leaving school and you have not claimed unemployment benefit, or that this is your only or main job. The P46 procedure enables employers to deduct tax on a cumulative basis straight away for school leavers, so that they get the benefit of the single personal allowance from the beginning of the tax year. Other new employees will usually be allocated a single person's allowance, code 344L, on a non-cumulative basis (called week 1 or month 1 basis), which means they get only one week's (or month's) proportion of the allowance against each week's (month's) pay. If you do not complete either statement on form P46, the employer will deduct tax at the basic rate from the whole of your pay.

Forms P46 are sent to the Revenue unless the employee completes one of the two statements and earns less than £66.50 a week. Forms P46 for such employees must be retained by the employer, together with details of the employee's name, address and amount of pay. If the employee earns more than the national insurance threshold of £54 a week, a deductions working sheet must be prepared.

Poll tax

If an employer pays an employee's personal poll tax, the payment will be treated as pay for tax and national insurance.

In some circumstances, an employee may become liable to the standard community charge (levied on domestic property that is not someone's only or main residence). The Revenue have confirmed that where an employer pays an employee's standard charge there will be no tax liability for the employee where the standard charge has arisen as a result of the relocation of the employee, or as a result of the employee being in temporary accommodation while working away for up to twelve months. The DSS have made a similar statement, so such payments do not attract national insurance contributions.

If an employee has not paid his poll tax, an employer may be required to make deductions from his pay under an attachment of earnings order, and may deduct £1 (in Scotland, 50p) by way of administration charge each time a deduction is made. Employers must send in the deductions to their local council within 14 days. They are liable to fines for non-compliance with the regulations.

Tax points

- When the new K codes start on 6 April 1993, collecting tax on an excess of benefits over tax allowances, some P11D employees will find themselves with much higher tax deductions in the first year, because the code is also adjusting for an underpayment brought forward relating to the benefits of the previous year.

- The benefits in kind charges on P11D employees are sometimes less than the real value of the benefit received, and there is usually no national insurance liability in respect of benefits in kind. It is thus often more effective to pay a lower salary plus benefits rather than a higher cash figure with the employee providing the benefits himself out of taxed earnings and the employer having a correspondingly higher national insurance liability.

- Benefits do, however, limit the employee's free choice of what to spend his money on, so sometimes the cash may be preferred.

- Cars used to be one of the most tax-effective perks but the increased scale charges and the VAT and national insurance charges have led some employers to consider schemes to replace cars by extra wages. Think carefully before offering such a scheme—see page 134.

- Check whether it is still tax-efficient to pay an employee's private petrol. Look at the VAT charge and the national insurance contributions as well as the income tax effect. It may be cheaper to pay the employee extra wages to compensate him for buying his own private petrol.

- Home to work travelling expenses are not allowable but the home and the workbase may be the same place. Those holding part-time employments, such as consultants and tribunal members, should seek to establish when they accept their employments that their place of employment is at their home or other workbase, making their travelling expenses from that base allowable.

- Employers must be very careful to comply with the requirements of the PAYE scheme. For example, failing to apply the P46 procedure properly for new employees who do not produce form P45 could render the employer liable to account for tax which was not deducted from the amount paid.

  Forms P11D must be properly completed and sent in promptly for each employee earning £8,500 per annum or more and each director; severe penalties apply if they are not.

- The Revenue have a programme of visits to employers for the purpose of inspecting records to ensure compliance with PAYE regulations, including reporting requirements. They have issued a leaflet IR71 explaining their procedure, which is available from tax offices.

- The definition of 'earnings at the rate of £8,500 per annum' includes certain car expenses met by the employer as well as the car and car fuel scale charges. This brings some employees whose salary is less than £8,500 into the P11D reporting net.

- Remember that an employee's contribution for the private use of a car reduces the scale charge, but a contribution towards car fuel is not taken into account unless it covers the whole cost of private fuel.

- If an employer arranges for his employees earning less than £8,500 per annum to eat at a local café which sends the bill to the employer, the café effectively becomes the works canteen and the employee avoids tax on the provision of the meals.

- An arrangement under which your employer is wholly or partly responsible for the finance and management of a childcare scheme is necessary to exempt those benefits from tax. If he simply pays or reimburses your childcare bills, you will pay tax on the benefit.

- If a car is provided for a relative of a P11D employee, the benefit could be charged at 1½ times the scale rate on the P11D employee, but will be charged on the car user if the user is also an employee and the duties of the employment are such that the car is required in the performance of those duties (e.g. where the employee is a commercial traveller) and would be provided to any employee in equivalent circumstances.

- You are charged to tax on benefits arising from your employment even though your employer is not the payer. The most common example is tips. Another example is where one of your employer's suppliers pays for you to have a foreign holiday as a sales achievement reward. Details of all such benefits should be shown on your tax return, although you may find that the person making an award has an agreement with the Revenue under which the tax liability falls on him rather than on you.

- Many businesses promote goodwill by providing their customers' employees with entrance to sporting and cultural events, and with entertainment at those events. Such benefits are exempt providing they are not procured by the employer and are not related to services per-formed or to be performed in the employment.

- Gifts (other than cash gifts) of up to £100 in a tax year to an employee from a third party are now exempt by concession, unless they are procured by the employer or relate to services that are part of the employee's normal duties.

- The Revenue frequently reviews the list of professional subscriptions which are allowable in computing the taxable pay of an employee. You should therefore keep a watchful eye on this if your own subscription has not so far been allowed.

- It is important to keep proper records of business mileage if you need to establish that it exceeds 2,500 miles or 18,000 miles per annum as the case may be. Not to do so may prove expensive, particularly now that employers' national insurance contributions are payable on the income tax scale figures.

- If you *occasionally* work very late, you are not charged to tax if your employer pays for your transport home. Those who regularly work late get no such exemption.

- 'Payment' for PAYE purposes can be triggered much earlier than when money changes hands, especially as regards directors.

11
Share options, share incentives, and profit-related pay

Background

There is a minefield of legislation in this area, some intended to encourage genuine incentives through worker participation but much of it aimed at preventing the avoidance of income tax by directors or employees through the acquisition of shares in the company or group by which they are employed.

There are three sets of provisions designed to give favourable tax treatment to schemes to acquire shares if the necessary conditions are satisfied:

SAYE linked share option schemes (see page 147)
Discretionary share option schemes (see page 148)
Approved profit sharing schemes (see page 151)

The profit-related pay provisions enable employees to receive a limited amount of tax-free pay related to profit performance (see page 153).

There are provisions relating to Employee Share Ownership Plan trusts (see page 152) which enable companies to set up trusts that have more flexibility than approved profit sharing schemes, although without the tax benefits of the approved schemes.

Subject to certain restrictions, employers can get tax relief for the costs of setting up approved share option schemes, profit sharing schemes and employee share ownership plans, where they are incurred on or after 1 April 1991.

From 1 January 1992, shares acquired under approved profit sharing and SAYE linked share option schemes may be transferred free of capital gains tax to a single company personal equity plan (PEP)—see page 440.

Limits on participation by close company members

A director or employee of a close company (see page 34) cannot participate in profit sharing or SAYE linked option schemes or a profit-related pay scheme if he and his associates own more than 25% of the ordinary share capital. The shareholding limit for non-SAYE linked share option schemes is a holding, with associates, of no more than 10% of the ordinary share capital. For employee share ownership plans there is a 5% limit (which applies to all companies, not just close companies). Apart from these limits, close companies may introduce appropriate schemes so long as the other conditions are satisfied.

Share options

Directors and employees granted rights to acquire shares (TA 1988, ss 135–137, 185, 187 and Sch 9)

Where a director or employee acquires shares in the employing company, or an associated company, by reason of a right to acquire them (an option), favourable tax treatment is given for approved SAYE linked share option schemes and for approved discretionary share option schemes (see below). Where the option does not arise under an approved scheme, an income tax charge arises on the difference between the open market value at the time of exercising the right and the cost of the shares, including any amount paid for the option. Similarly, where a right to acquire shares is assigned or released, an income tax charge arises on the consideration received less the cost of acquisition of the rights. An income tax charge also arises where an option holder realises a gain or benefit by allowing the option to lapse, or granting someone else an option over the shares.

Employees and directors are thus prevented from being indirectly remunerated without an appropriate tax charge by the allotment of shares for less than they are worth. The tax charge cannot be avoided by the right being granted or the shares allotted to another person.

For options granted before 6 April 1984, tax in excess of £250 payable as a result of exercising an option may be paid by equal annual instalments over five years. This saves the director or employee from having to sell some of the shares to satisfy the income tax liability. An election for payment by instalments must be made within sixty days after the end of the year of assessment for which the tax charge arises. The instalment facility is not available in respect of options granted on or after 6 April 1984.

The capital gains tax base cost of the shares is the open market value at the time of exercising the option.

Charge on granting a right to acquire shares (TA 1988, s 135(5))

If an option is capable of being exercised more than seven years after it is granted, a charge arises at the time the right is granted on the excess of the then market value of the option shares over the price which, under the option, has to be paid for the shares. The tax paid may, however, be deducted from any tax arising when the option is exercised.

SAYE linked share option schemes (TA 1988, ss 185, 187, Sch 9)

An exemption from the option charging provisions is given for approved savings-related share option schemes. No charge will arise on the difference between cost and market value when a share option is exercised, nor at the time it is granted, where the cost of the shares is paid out of the proceeds of a linked SAYE scheme. Contributions of between £10 and £250 per month (£150 before 1 September 1991) are paid under a SAYE contract with a building society, bank, or the Department of National Savings. The option will normally be able to be exercised after five or seven years, when the SAYE contract ends, but earlier exercise of the option is permitted if the employing company or part of its business in which the employee is employed is sold or otherwise leaves the group operating the scheme. If in these circumstances an employee exercises his option within three years of joining the scheme, however, any gain arising will be charged to tax.

The scheme enables an option to be granted now to acquire shares at today's price, the shares eventually being paid for by the proceeds of a linked SAYE scheme. The price at which the option may be exercised must not normally be less than 80% (90% for options granted before 27 July 1989) of the market value of the shares at the time the option is granted. The employee does not get tax relief for the SAYE contributions but when the shares are taken up there is no tax charge on the excess of the market value over the price paid. If the shares are not taken up, the employee retains the proceeds of the SAYE contract and any interest and bonuses received are tax-free.

Various conditions must be complied with and in particular the scheme must be available to all directors and employees with five years' full-time service, it must not stipulate a minimum monthly contribution higher than £10 and it must not have features that discourage eligible employees from participating. Companies may require scheme shares to be sold if an employee or director leaves the company thus helping family companies who wish to ensure that their control is not diluted, and scheme rights can be exchanged for equivalent rights in a company taking over the employer company.

The capital gains tax base cost of the shares is the price paid by the employee.

Discretionary share option schemes (TA 1988, ss 185, 187 and Sch 9)

For options granted under an approved discretionary share option scheme there is no tax charge when the option is granted, unless the price paid for the option plus the price at which the shares may be acquired is less than their current market value. In that event, tax will be charged on the difference (the discount) under Schedule E in the year the option is granted. If, however, the employer also has an approved SAYE linked share option scheme (see above) or an approved profit sharing scheme (see page 151), the price of the shares under the discretionary scheme may be set at a discount of up to 15% for options granted on or after 1 January 1992. There will also be no tax charge when the option is exercised, providing options under the scheme are exercised between three and ten years after they are granted, and not more frequently than once in three years. Tax will arise only at the time of disposal of the shares, when the total amount paid for the shares, including any discount charged to tax when the option was granted, will be brought into a capital gains tax computation. If options are exercised in breach of the stipulated time limits, they will be treated in the same way as unapproved options (see page 147).

If the disposal takes place at a time when the scheme is not an approved scheme, the income tax charges under TA 1988, ss 135, 136 (see page 147) or TA 1988, s 162 (where shares are issued partly paid – see below) may arise, but any discount that has already been charged to tax when the option was granted will be excluded.

For a scheme to be approved, various conditions must be complied with, including:

(a) The value (at the time of the grant) of shares on which a person holds options must not exceed the greater of £100,000 and four times his Schedule E earnings of the current or previous year (excluding benefits and after deducting superannuation contributions).
(b) The price to be paid for the shares must be fixed and must not be manifestly below their current market value (subject to what is said above about discretionary schemes running alongside approved all-employee schemes).
(c) The scheme must be restricted to full-time directors and employees, the definition of full-time being 25 hours a week for directors and 20 hours a week for employees.

The scheme may provide that participants must sell their scheme shares when their employment ends but the scheme rights can be exchanged for equivalent rights in a company taking over the employer company.

Share incentives

Issue of shares at an undervalue (TA 1988, s 19)

The general charging provisions of Schedule E are wide enough to catch any issue of shares to a director or employee at an undervalue where the benefit arises out of the employment. The difference between the then market value of the shares and the price paid by the employee or director is assessable as emoluments at the time of the issue of the shares (unless covered by the specific provisions dealt with above).

Issue of shares partly paid up (TA 1988, s 162)

If shares are issued at a price equal to the current market value, with the price being paid by agreed instalments, no charge will arise under the general charging provisions since full market value is being paid, and this will apply even though the market value has increased by the time the shares are paid for. Any growth in value of the shares is liable only to capital gains tax.

There is, however, a charge on directors and employees earning £8,500 per annum or more who do not pay the full price for shares immediately. They are regarded as having received an interest-free loan equal to the deferred instalments, and tax will be charged accordingly at the beneficial loans interest rate (see page xxiv). The loan will be regarded as being repaid as and when the instalments are paid. This charge will not apply if the interest would have qualified for tax relief if it had been paid, for example if the share acquisition is in a close company or employee-controlled company (see pages 12, 13).

Share incentive schemes (FA 1988, ss 77–89; F(No 2)A 1992, s 37)

Since the tax charge on shares issued at an undervalue depends upon the difference between the price paid and the then value of the shares, it follows that the tax charge may be reduced if the shares, or interests in them, are issued subject to restrictions, because the restrictions will depress the market value. A tax charge may arise in these circumstances, as described below.

The shares must be acquired as a result of a right given or opportunity offered to an individual as a director or employee of a company or an associated company. The charge does not apply where the shares are acquired as a result of an offer to the public.

Where shares or an interest in them are acquired after 25 October 1987, the person acquiring the shares is chargeable to income tax if, while he still has an interest in them, their value increases because of the creation or removal of restrictions or variation of rights relating to the shares or to other shares in the company.

For the charge to apply, the person concerned must have been a director or employee of the company or of an associated company within the seven years before the event causing the increase.

The charge does not apply if, at the time of the event causing the increase, the majority of the shares of the class concerned do not belong to directors or employees of the company or to an associated company or its directors or employees; or if the company is 'employee controlled' by reason of holdings of shares of that class.

There are also provisions for charging an increase in value of the shares of a company, called a dependent subsidiary, the principal business of which is with, and the performance of which effectively depends upon, other companies in the group.

With certain exceptions, the employee is also charged to tax on the value of any benefit received (a 'special benefit') that is not available to at least 90% of shareholders of the same class.

If tax is chargeable under the legislation which applied before 26 October 1987 (TA 1988, s 138), by reference to the market value of shares after 26 October 1987, the value on which the charge is based cannot be higher than the value at 26 October 1987. Apart from that, the new rules, other than those relating to dependent subsidiaries, apply equally to shares acquired before 26 October 1987.

The charge to income tax arises in the tax year in which the event or special benefit occurs.

Any amount charged to income tax under these provisions is part of the base cost of the shares for capital gains tax.

Approved profit sharing schemes (TA 1988, s 186 and Schs 9 and 10)

Favourable tax treatment is given to an approved profit sharing scheme under which a company appoints trustees and provides money for them to use to acquire shares in the company. The amount provided by the company is a tax deductible expense.

A director or employee is not charged to tax on shares allocated to him by the trustees under the scheme. He is regarded for capital gains tax purposes as being absolutely entitled to the shares even though they are still held by the trustees, and any dividends arising are regarded as his for income tax purposes.

There is a limit on the value of shares that can be allocated to any one employee in any tax year. For 1992/93 the limit is 10% of the employee's salary (excluding benefits and after deducting superannuation contributions) for 1992/93 or 1991/92, but subject to a minimum limit of £3,000 and a maximum of £8,000.

A scheme will not receive Revenue approval unless it is available on similar terms to all qualifying employees—broadly those with five years' full-time service—but it is recognised that different levels of share allocation may apply to individuals on different salary levels. It must be demonstrated that the scheme does not have characteristics which discourage some of those eligible from participating. Part-time employees or those with less than five years' full-time service may be included if the company wishes.

No income tax charge arises if the shares are transferred to the employee after five years. The shares must remain in the hands of the trustees for a minimum period which is generally two years, and an income tax charge arises if the shares are disposed of within five years, based on their market value when allocated to the employee or the sale proceeds if less. The charge is on the whole of that amount if the disposal is within four years and on 75% if it is in the fifth year, but the charge is reduced to 50% if the disposal occurs within the five years because the employee leaves as a result of injury, disability, redundancy, or reaching an age between 60 and 75 as specified by the scheme.

A similarly reducing tax charge will also arise if there is a capital receipt, as for example on a rights issue, within five years, but only if it exceeds a stipulated amount (broadly £20 per annum cumulatively up to a maximum £100).

Any amounts charged to income tax are not liable to national insurance.

The income tax charge has no effect on the capital gains tax base cost. Whether shares are disposed of within or after the five-year period the capital gains tax base cost is the market value at the time the shares were appropriated to the employee.

While such schemes appear attractive, there are drawbacks for unquoted companies in that the company cannot choose which employees may participate; there may not be a ready market for the shares if the employee wants to sell them; an immediate market valuation is not available; and the effect on established shareholders has to be considered.

A condition can, however, be imposed that employees must sell their shares when the employment ends.

Employee share ownership plans (FA 1989, ss 67–74 and Sch 5; FA 1990, ss 31–40)

Under provisions introduced in Finance Act 1989, companies are encouraged to set up trusts that will acquire shares in the company and distribute them to the employees. Revenue approval is not required. The company's payments to the trust will be tax deductible. All employees and directors who have been employed throughout a period specified in the trust deed (which must be between one year and five years) and who have worked 20 or more hours a week throughout that period (except someone who owns 5% or more of the company's ordinary share capital) must be included as beneficiaries. Distributions out of the trust must be on similar terms to all beneficiaries, but allowing for different distributions according to length of service and level of remuneration.

The trustees must use sums received for a qualifying purpose, principally to acquire the company's shares, within nine months of receipt, and must distribute the shares to employees within seven years of acquisition. If any of the conditions are breached, the trust will be charged to tax at 35% on the sums received by it on which tax relief has been given.

There are no special tax reliefs either for the trust or for the employees receiving shares out of it, but it may operate in conjunction with an approved profit sharing scheme trust (see page 151), in which case shares allocated within the approved profit sharing scheme conditions will not be charged to tax.

These provisions may be seen as an extension to the approved profit sharing scheme trusts, in order to give the trustees more flexibility than is permitted under the approved schemes.

One of the perceived disadvantages of the provisions—the charge to capital gains tax on a shareholder who sells his shares to the trust—was removed by Finance Act 1990. Subject to detailed and complex conditions (in particular the condition that the trust must have a 10% stake in the company either immediately or within 12 months of the sale), the shareholder may treat the gain as reducing the capital gains tax cost of replacement taxable assets acquired within six months of the sale or of the 10% condition being satisfied, if later.

Employers interested in establishing employee share ownership plans may submit draft deeds to the Revenue to see if the proposed trust will qualify.

Priority share allocations for employees (FA 1988, s 68)

When shares are offered to the public, a priority allocation is often made to employees and directors. Where there is no price advantage, a taxable benefit will not arise because of the right to shares in priority to other persons, so long as the shares that may be allocated do not exceed 10% of those being offered, all directors and employees entitled to an allocation are entitled on similar terms (albeit at different levels), and those entitled are not restricted wholly or mainly to persons who are directors or whose remuneration exceeds a particular level. This treatment still applies where the offer to employees is strictly not part of the public offer, as a result of the employees' offer being restricted to shares in one or more companies and the public offer being a package of shares in a wider range of companies.

Where employees get shares at a discount compared with the price paid by the public, the discount will be chargeable. The employee's base cost for capital gains tax will be the amount paid plus the amount of the discount that was charged to income tax.

Profit-related pay (TA 1988, ss 169–184 and Sch 8)

Part of an employee's pay is permitted to be tax-free where it is related to profits of the employer, and is paid under a scheme which has been registered with the Revenue. Those employed by the Crown or by local authorities are excluded.

The tax-free profit-related pay cannot exceed one-fifth of the total pay (which for this purpose excludes benefits in kind), with an overriding maximum of £4,000 per annum. Even though this amount is exempt from income tax it is chargeable to national insurance contributions. The maximum tax saving to a 40% taxpayer is £1,600.

The scheme must be registered with the Revenue by the employer or by the parent company in the case of a group scheme. The application must include a certificate from an independent accountant that the scheme complies with the conditions laid down by the legislation. Payments under the scheme cannot be made to an employee who with his associates owns more than 25% of the ordinary share capital of the company. Employees may be excluded if they work for less than 20 hours a week, or if they have not worked for the employer for a minimum period (which cannot exceed three years). The scheme must include at least 80% of employees in a particular employment unit (not counting those who are disqualified as indicated above). There are two methods for calculating the amount which is to be distributed to employees (the 'distributable pool') and the scheme must specify the method to be used. The scheme must provide similar terms for all participating employees, although payments may vary according to remuneration, length of service or similar factors. An independent accountant must submit a report to the Revenue after each profit period.

An employee cannot get tax relief on profit-related pay from more than one employment. The Revenue have power to cancel the registration of a scheme in the case of abuse and to recover income tax from the employer where relief has been given since the date of cancellation.

Tax points

- There is no clearance procedure under FA 1988, ss 77–89 (share incentive schemes) and since these provisions tax increases in the value of shares, as distinct from an advantage when they are purchased, it makes the schemes particularly vulnerable to uncertainty.

- Business expansion scheme relief is not available to directors and shareholders who take up shares in their employing company.

- In the case of unquoted companies, the value of shares has, when appropriate, to be agreed with the Revenue Shares Valuation Division.

- The time limit for an election to spread income tax charged on the exercise of a share option granted before 6 April 1984 is strictly applied by the Revenue, and care should therefore be taken to see that it is in their hands by 4 June after the end of the tax year in which the option is exercised.

- Group employees may participate in schemes through their parent company.

- Part-time directors and employees (as defined) may not participate in a discretionary share option scheme but they may be included in any of the other schemes if the scheme rules permit.

- Any income tax charged on an employee under an approved profit sharing scheme (see page 151) is deducted under the PAYE scheme. Where income tax is payable on an event under a share option or incentive scheme, the due date is 30 days after the date of the issue of the assessment (subject to any spreading which is available—see page 147).

- It is essential to file an income tax return promptly (and, at the latest, by 31 October following the end of the tax year) where a liability under share option and incentive schemes arises, since the Revenue may otherwise contend that a liability for interest on late paid income tax arises. Any return required from the employing company does not excuse the employee from showing the event on his personal income tax return.

- A profit-related pay scheme can apply to a business as a whole or to any identifiable part for which a separate account can be prepared and certified by an independent accountant.

- An approved share option or profit sharing scheme cannot apply to an unlisted subsidiary company unless the parent is a non-close listed company.

12
Directors of small and family companies

Directors and shareholders

In family companies, directors and shareholders are usually the same people, and they can benefit from the company in various ways, e.g.:

Payment of remuneration.
Provision of benefits.
Distribution of income through dividends.

The payment of remuneration and the provision of benefits will be allowed as a deduction in calculating the company's taxable profits. There will, however, in most instances be a liability for payment of employer's and employee's national insurance contributions in respect of the remuneration, although not on most benefits or on dividends.

Dividends are not an allowable deduction in calculating the company's profits, but the tax credits on dividends are set against the corporation tax payable (up to a limit of 25% of the company's taxable profits), even though the tax credit passed on to a shareholder covers his basic rate income tax. Where the 25% small companies corporation tax rate applies, the basic rate tax credit passed on to the shareholder effectively eliminates the corporation tax on distributed profits.

Dividends are unearned income in the hands of the shareholder. Remuneration and benefits are earned income. The main distinction is that only earned income is taken into account for pension purposes.

A combination of remuneration and dividends can sometimes be helpful, as shown in example 1 on page 158, but remember that if you do not have a company pension scheme, taking a low salary means that you can only pay very low personal pension contributions, and if you are in a company pension scheme, you need to watch the definition of final remuneration on which your pension will be based (see page 197). Profits of around the £28,800 figure used in example 1 are the amount which a married man with no other income can draw without paying higher rate tax. (For a further example, see page 215.) The figures in the example are still valid if £28,800 is drawn out of higher profits, up to the small companies rate limit of

£250,000. Where profits lie in the marginal small companies rate band, the tax saved on salary plus employer's national insurance contributions will be at 35%, compared with 25% advance corporation tax (ACT) saving on dividends, so that the employer's national insurance cost is marginally outweighed by the difference in tax rates saved. If profits exceed £1,250,000, so that the full rate of 33% is payable, the marginal advantage of salary is even smaller—see example 2 on page 159. If employee's national insurance contributions were payable, the cost of paying a dividend would still be lower.

A dividend may be tax-efficient even where there is not enough taxable profit in the year in which it is paid, if the company has not used up the maximum permitted ACT set-off in earlier years. This is because ACT paid on a dividend that cannot be set off against the company's corporation tax liability for the year can be carried back and set off against the liability for up to six earlier years, latest first, resulting in the repayment of an equivalent amount of corporation tax already paid for the earlier years. The dividend will thus have been paid at no tax cost to the company just as if it were paid from current profits, with the basic rate tax credit still having been passed on to the shareholder. See example 3 on page 161.

Retention of profits within the company or payment as remuneration or dividends

Retention of profits within the company will increase the net assets and hence the value of the shares if they are subsequently sold on the basis of underlying assets. Having already suffered corporation tax, the retained profits will thus swell the value of the shares for capital gains tax purposes. Reducing retentions through paying remuneration or dividends may therefore ultimately reduce the shareholders' chargeable gains, but this must be weighed against the immediate tax cost. A permissible contribution to a pension fund from which the director will benefit will often be a better alternative.

Effect on earlier years (TA 1988, s 393A)

A decision on whether to pay remuneration or leave profits to be charged to corporation tax should not be taken by reference to the current year in isolation. The payment may convert a trading profit into a trading loss, which, after being set against any non-trading profits of the current year, may be carried back against the total profits of the previous three years, latest first, so long as the trade was carried on in those years (the carry-back being restricted to a period equal in length to the loss period for accounting periods ended before 1 April 1991) (see chapter 26).

Looking into the future

If all current-year profits are used to pay remuneration, there will be nothing against which to carry back any later losses. The expected future performance (including any imminent expenditure on commercial buildings

Example 1

Company makes profit (before director's remuneration) of £28,800 in year to 31 March 1993. Director has available personal allowances of £5,165.

If profit is taken as	salary only £	salary and dividend £
Company's tax position is:		
Profits	28,800	28,800
Salary	(26,087)	(2,808)
Employer's national insurance	(2,713)	(129)
Taxable profits	—	25,863
Corporation tax at 25%		6,466
Cash dividend		19,397
ACT thereon (set against corporation tax liability)		6,466
		25,863
Director's tax position		
Salary	26,087	2,808
Dividend	—	25,863
		28,671
Personal allowances	(5,165)	(5,165)
Taxable income	20,922	23,506
Tax thereon (£2,000 @ 20%, rest @ 25%)	5,130	5,776
Tax credit on dividend		(6,466)
Tax refund		(690)
Disposable income:		
Salary	26,087	2,808
Employee's national insurance	(1,699)	(56)
Dividend	—	19,397
Tax/tax refund	(5,130)	690
	19,258	22,839
Saving through paying dividend		£3,581

The saving represents the reduction in national insurance contributions through paying dividends instead of salary. An extra saving of approximately £153 could be made by fixing the salary at £2,800, thus avoiding employer's and employee's national insurance. The right to short-term and possibly long-term national insurance benefits would, however, be affected (see page 169).

Example 2

Director who is already paying maximum national insurance contributions takes £24,000 from company either as bonus or as a dividend of £18,000 with ACT of £6,000, as follows:

Profit taken as	bonus	dividend	bonus	dividend
	£	£	£	£
Company's profits in year to				
31 March 1993	300,000	300,000	1,300,000	1,300,000
Bonus	(24,000)		(24,000)	
Employer's national insurance	(2,496)		(2,496)	
Taxable profits	273,504	300,000	1,273,504	1,300,000
Corporation tax @ 33%	90,256	99,000	420,256	429,000
Less: marginal relief				
1/50 ×				
(1,250,000 − 273,504)	(19,530)			
(1,250,000 − 300,000)		(19,000)		
	£70,726	80,000	£420,256	429,000
ACT on dividend to shareholder		(6,000)		(6,000)
		£74,000		£423,000

Director's income before tax is £24,000 either as bonus or dividend and since no employee's national insurance contributions are payable, the net of tax amount is also the same for either. The extra cost to the company of the dividend route is as follows:

	£	£
Extra corporation tax payable if dividend chosen		
£(74,000 − 70,726)	3,274	
£(423,000 − 420,256)		2,744
Reduced by the extra employer's national insurance contributions if bonus chosen	(2,496)	(2,496)
	£778	£248

This represents 3.24%/1.03% of £24,000, arrived at as follows:

Difference between marginal small companies rate/full rate and ACT rate	10.00%	8.00%
National insurance contributions payable 10.4%, net of: marginal small companies rate 35%	6.76%	
full rate 33%		6.97%
	3.24%	1.03%

in an enterprise zone) should therefore be taken into account in considering whether to reduce or eliminate profits for the current year.

Other circumstances of the directors

With the current tax-efficient opportunities for investment in commercial buildings in enterprise zones (see chapter 32) and business expansion scheme investments (see chapter 29), directors may be able to create substantial available allowances to set against personal income. These can be used to cover remuneration or dividends from a company, thus enabling it to be received in a tax-efficient way.

You should remember that whilst chargeable gains are now taxed at income tax rates, they remain capital gains and cannot be offset by enterprise zone and business expansion scheme investment. The withdrawal of funds through remuneration or dividends (which can be sheltered in this way) may therefore be preferable to later capital gains (which cannot).

Pensions (TA 1988, Part XIV, Chapters I–IV)

The company may have its own pension scheme, either through an insurance company or self-administered. Provided that the benefits under the scheme are within the limits laid down by the Revenue, the company's contributions are allowable in calculating its taxable profit, and are not taxable on the director.

If there is no such scheme, the director may pay premiums himself under a personal pension plan. Although the allowable premium is limited annually to a percentage of earnings depending upon age (see chapter 17), it is possible to include the earnings of the previous six years in the maximum premium calculation to the extent that they have not already been used to support a pension contribution. This may enable a large payment to be made in a single year and equivalent remuneration to be taken from the company without tax arising thereon. The premium payment might be funded by a loan-back facility arranged by or in conjunction with the insurance company. Since the income and gains of both company and personal pension funds are usually exempt from tax, paying pension contributions rather than taking salary and investing it privately will be a

Example 3

In 1992/93, husband and wife directors have available personal allowances of £5,165 and £3,445 respectively and no sources of income apart from the company.

In the year ended 31 March 1993 the company pays them remuneration of £3,000 each and a dividend of £15,000 each (paying advance corporation tax of £10,000 to the Revenue). Company's recent results after directors' remuneration are:

Year to 31 March 1991 Profit (no dividend paid) £25,000
Year to 31 March 1992 Profit (no dividend paid) £15,000
Year to 31 March 1993 Profit £20,000

Company's tax position:

Year to 31 March	1991	1992	1992
	£	£	£
Profits chargeable to corporation tax	25,000	15,000	20,000
Corporation tax @ 25%	6,250	3,750	5,000
ACT paid on dividends of £30,000	—	—	(10,000)
ACT carried back (and repaid)	(1,250)	(3,750)	5,000
Final corporation tax payable	£5,000	—	—

Directors' tax position in 1992/93:

	Husband	Wife
	£	£
Remuneration	3,000	3,000
Dividend (£15,000 + £5,000)	20,000	20,000
	23,000	23,000
Less: Personal allowances	(5,165)	(3,445)
Taxable income	£17,835	£19,555
Tax thereon: £2,000 @ 20%	400	400
Balance @ 25%	3,959	4,389
Tax credit on dividend	(5,000)	(5,000)
Tax credit repayable	£641	£211

The overall result is that the company has passed on to the directors in the form of tax credits £5,000 of the corporation tax which it paid for earlier years, as well as the £5,000 which it paid for 1993, the directors recovering £852 of the total tax credits of £10,000 and covering their tax liability on nearly £40,000 of taxable income with the remainder.

more tax-efficient method of saving for the future. With company schemes, the permissible benefits depend upon remuneration, so that restricting salary unduly may affect the available benefits. With personal pension schemes, the benefits depend only upon contributions (which will themselves have been limited by relevant earnings). For further details on pensions, see chapters 16 and 17.

Limits on allowable remuneration

Remuneration, like any other trading expense, must be incurred wholly and exclusively for the purposes of the trade (see chapter 20). If it is regarded as excessive in relation to the duties, part may not be allowed as a deduction in calculating company profits. This should be borne in mind when considering payments of remuneration, either by way of cash or as benefits in kind, to members of a director's or shareholder's family.

Employing a spouse and children in the family company may be useful, particularly if they are not otherwise using their personal allowance, but the amount may be questioned by the Revenue, who will want to be sure that the work done is of sufficient quantity and quality to justify the amount paid. If children are under sixteen you must also comply with the regulations as to permitted hours of work, which vary according to local bye-laws. Payments by a farmer to his very young children have been held to be 'pocket money' and disallowed in calculating the taxable profits of the farm.

Waiving an entitlement to remuneration (IHTA 1984, s 14; TA 1988, s 231(3A) – (3D))

There is no income tax on remuneration which is not received, so that an entitlement to remuneration can be waived to assist in a difficult period of trading, or because of a high personal tax rate. It is also specifically provided that no inheritance tax liability arises from such a waiver. The waiver might enable the company to pay higher remuneration to other directors or family members (provided as always that it is justifiable under the 'wholly and exclusively' rule) or to increase its profits available for dividends. But if the company is within the definition of a close investment-holding company (see page 34), repayment of the tax credit on a dividend may be restricted if it is considered by the Revenue to arise as a result of deliberate arrangements aimed at generating the tax refund, such as the waiver of dividends by those liable at the higher rate of tax in favour of young family members with unused personal allowances.

Benefits in kind provided by the company

Directors and employees with earnings of £8,500 or more per annum are charged to tax on the cash equivalent of benefits in kind. Directors are caught by these provisions even if they earn less than £8,500 unless they do not have a material interest in the company (a material interest being more than 5% of the ordinary share capital, including shares owned by close family and certain other people) *and* either work full-time or work for a charitable or non-profit-making body.

Benefits may take the form of the outright gift of an asset or of allowing the director/employee to use a company asset. The company is allowed to deduct the cost of providing benefits in calculating its taxable profit, subject to what is said on page 162. The charge on the director/employee is broadly the cost to the company, including VAT where appropriate (whether recovered or not, in the view of the Revenue), or, if the asset remains the company's property, the 'annual value' of its use. The detailed provisions for calculating the charge are in chapter 10.

Family companies are not required to distribute profits as dividends unless they wish to do so. It may be worthwhile retaining funds in the company to buy assets which the directors are able to use (albeit being charged to tax on the benefit arising) rather than the directors being provided with funds enabling them to purchase the assets personally. Most benefits do not attract national insurance contributions (see chapter 13 for exceptions). If, however, the expenditure has no relevance to the management or trade of the company, the Revenue would be justified in arguing that it relates to the directors personally, and would look to them to pay in an equivalent amount to the company.

Gifts of company assets to persons who are not directors or employees (IHTA 1984, s 94; TA 1988, s 418)

Gifts of company assets to directors and employees are covered by the benefits rules mentioned above and explained in detail in chapter 10. If an asset is given to a shareholder who is not a director or employee, its cost is treated as a distribution of profits, the appropriate amount of ACT being payable by the company as if it was a cash dividend and the total of the cost and the ACT being included in the shareholder's taxable income.

If a gift is made to someone who is neither a director/employee nor a shareholder nor connected with them, an apportionment of its value is made among the shareholders for inheritance tax purposes, the shareholders then being treated as having made personal transfers of the amount apportioned to them.

Loans from the company (TA 1988, ss 160, 161, 419–421; Revenue Statement of Practice SP 7/79)

Directors and employees earning £8,500 or more per annum who overdraw their current accounts with the company or who receive specific loans from the company, either interest-free or at a beneficial rate, are treated as having received remuneration equivalent to interest, on the amount overdrawn or lent, at the 'official rate' (see page 134) less any amount paid to the company towards the benefit they have received. This does not apply if the calculated interest amounts to £300 or less, nor if the interest on a specific loan from the company (not an overdrawn current account) would have been tax deductible if the director or employee had paid it. The main example of tax deductible interest used to be on loans up to £30,000 to buy the principal private residence (see chapter 2), but following the withdrawal of higher rate relief on mortgage interest, employees will be charged to tax at 15% on such loans to the extent that their income is above the basic rate limit (see page 134). Where a director or employee receives an advance for expenses necessarily incurred in performing his duties, the Revenue do not treat the advance as a loan, provided that

(a) the maximum amount advanced at any one time does not exceed £1,000,
(b) the advances are spent within six months, and
(c) the director or employee accounts to the company at regular intervals for the expenditure.

As well as the tax charge on the director or employee on interest-free or cheap loans, there are tax implications for the company if it is a close company in which the director or employee is a shareholder, and these provisions do not depend on whether any interest is charged. A close company is broadly one controlled by its directors or by five or fewer people. Loans and advances to shareholders (including shareholders who are directors or employees) give rise to a tax liability on the company, except for loans not exceeding £15,000 made to a full-time working director or employee who does not have a material interest (see page 163) in the company. The company has to pay tax at the ACT rate (currently 25/75ths) on the amount of the loan or overdrawn account balance, the tax paid being recoverable from the Revenue as and when the overdrawn amount or loan is repaid to the company. If the company does not account to the Revenue for the tax at the appropriate time, interest is payable at the rate applicable to overdue tax.

If a loan or overdrawing is written off by the company, the tax treatment is different for loans made by close companies to shareholders and for other loans.

If a loan by a close company to a shareholder is written off, the shareholder is liable to tax on the gross equivalent of the amount written off. Tax at the basic rate is treated as having been already accounted for by the company, so the shareholder will only have to pay tax if he is liable at the 40% rate, the amount payable being the excess of the higher rate tax over the basic rate, i.e. 15%.

If the write-off of a loan is not caught by the close company rules, and it has been obtained by reason of the borrower's employment, whether it is made to an employee who is within or outside the benefits charging rules, and whether or not it is at a rate of interest below the 'official rate', the director or employee is treated as having received an equivalent amount of remuneration at that time. (This does not apply to loans written off on death or to 'stop loss' arrangements on employee profit sharing schemes where the shares were acquired before 6 April 1976—see chapter 11.)

If a non-close company wrote off a loan made to someone who was not a director or employee, there would not usually be any tax consequences for the borrower whether he was a shareholder or not, but the company would not be able to claim a deduction for the write-off unless its business included lending money.

As well as the tax aspects, company law also imposes restrictions on directors' loans. Loans up to £5,000 are permitted. Generally, loans exceeding this amount are not permitted unless they fall within some very limited exceptions, one of which is a loan to enable a director properly to perform his duties, providing the loan is sanctioned by the company in general meeting (but for relevant companies, which broadly means public limited companies and members of groups that include public limited companies, such a loan cannot exceed £20,000). A relevant company which breaches the rules may be liable to both criminal penalties and civil remedies. If a company is not a relevant company, only civil remedies are available, enabling a company to avoid the contract and making the directors jointly and severally liable for any loss the company suffers as a result of the transaction. Family companies will usually not be relevant companies so that they will normally be exposed only to civil remedies.

Liabilities in connection with directors' remuneration

Remuneration is regarded as paid not only when it forms part of the payroll but also when it is credited to the director's current account with the company and the liability of the company to account for PAYE and national insurance arises at that time. The credit to the current account should therefore be made net of employee's tax and national insurance contributions. Drawings from the account can be made without any further liability once the PAYE and national insurance have been accounted for to the Revenue. If a company pays remuneration to a director and bears the PAYE itself, the amount that should have been borne by the director is treated as extra remuneration and taxable accordingly (TA 1988, s 164).

Where a director receives payments in advance or on account of future remuneration this has to be treated as pay for tax and national insurance purposes at the time of the advance, unless the advances are covered by a credit balance on the director's loan account or are on account of expenses as indicated above.

It used to be possible to reduce national insurance contributions by paying remuneration at uneven rates and irregular intervals, but this is now prevented by the method of calculating earnings limits. The detailed provisions are in chapter 13.

If employers fail to deduct and account for PAYE and national insurance contributions when due, they may incur penalties. Directors may also be personally liable to pay the tax on their remuneration if they knew of the failure to deduct tax.

Tax points

- Always look at the combined company/director/shareholder position in considering the most appropriate way of dealing with available profits, and consider past and future years as well as the current year.

- Make effective use of company or personal pension funds, which should grow faster than individual investments because of their tax exemption. Remember in the case of company pension funds that in calculating corporation tax, relief is only given in the accounting period when the pension premium is paid, so that it is not possible to reduce taxable profits of one year by making a payment in the next year and relating it back. It is therefore essential to anticipate the profit level if a pension contribution is envisaged as a way of reducing corporation tax for a particular accounting period.

- A similar timing point applies to dividends, in that ACT on a dividend paid say in August 1992, following a 30 June year end, will be due to be paid to the Revenue under the quarterly system by 14 October 1992, but it will be set against the corporation tax due on 1 April 1994 (for year to 30 June 1993) and not that due on 1 April 1993 (for year to 30 June 1992) (see page 30).

- The basic rate of tax on a dividend will usually be covered by the company's corporation tax. The recipient is liable only for the excess, if any, of higher rate tax over basic rate.

- When considering dividend payments, remember that dividends to minority shareholders will affect the valuation of their holdings.

- In considering the payment of a dividend instead of remuneration, remember that future entitlement under a pension scheme may be adversely affected by limiting the amount of remuneration.

- There is no upper limit on the amount of pay on which employers' national insurance contributions are payable, so that all extra salary will have an additional national insurance cost. Consider providing the director with benefits instead of extra pay. Benefits do not usually attract national insurance contributions, although the most common benefit, the company car with private petrol provided, is chargeable to employers' national insurance contributions from 6 April 1991.

- If you pay personal pension premiums rather than pay into a company scheme, remember that national insurance contributions are payable by reference to your pay before deducting those premiums. With a company scheme, there will be no national insurance contributions on the company's payments to the pension scheme, although both employer's and employee's national insurance contributions will be calculated on your pay before deducting your own contributions to the company scheme.

- See at the end of chapter 10 the tax point dealing with the provision of a company car to an employee who is a member of a director's family or household.

- Remuneration is regarded as paid when it is credited to an account with the company in the name of a director. The fact that it is not drawn by him but left to his credit in the company (in other words, available for drawing) does not prevent the appropriate tax and national insurance being payable at the time the remuneration is credited. The director's account should be credited only with the net amount after tax and national insurance. If the gross amount is credited, whether or not it is drawn out, and the company fails to account to the Revenue for the tax and national insurance, the director may be personally liable for the failure under the PAYE regulations.

- Where an employer has failed to deduct tax from employees' earnings and the Revenue have made a determination of the tax thought to be due (a Regulation 29 determination), interest is payable on the outstanding tax, from the fourteenth day after the end of the tax year to which the tax relates. Interest cannot, however, run from a date earlier than 19 April 1988.

  Where overdue PAYE is paid before a formal Regulation 29 determination is made, these interest provisions will not apply. (Inland Revenue press release 30 March 1988).

- If, at the end of 30 days after a Regulation 29 determination has been made, the tax has still not been paid, the Revenue may look to the employee for payment as well as to the company, providing the employee had been aware of the failure to operate PAYE on his remuneration.

- If, before a director is credited with additional remuneration, his current account with the company is overdrawn, the Revenue will usually contend that the date on which the additional remuneration can be regarded as credited is that on which the accounts are signed rather than the end of the accounting year for which the additional remuneration was paid. This can significantly affect the tax charge on the director in respect of beneficial interest (see page 134).

- Benefits in kind assessed to income tax on directors must be distinguished from personal commitments of a director which are paid for by a company. The latter, including any VAT, must be reimbursed to the company by the director or charged against money owed by the company to the director. They are neither allowable in calculating the company taxable profit nor assessable as income on the director. The company is accountable to the Revenue for basic rate income tax on any amount owing to the company by a director at the end of an accounting period. The tax is repayable to the company when the director repays his indebtedness to the company, but in the meantime interest is charged on it if it is not paid on time, and a possible penalty if it is not clearly disclosed.

13
National insurance contributions—employees and employers

Background

A large part of the cost of the social security system is funded from contributions made by people currently earning money either as employees or as self-employed persons. The legislation is in the Social Security Contributions and Benefits Act 1992 (SSCBA 1992). The level of a person's contribution and the regulations relating to its collection depend upon which 'class' of contribution is to be paid. The contribution rates are shown on page xxvii.

Employees and their employers pay Class 1 contributions which are earnings-related and are payable as a percentage of earnings. Payments made by employees are known as 'primary' contributions, those by employers as 'secondary' contributions. A new category of contributions, Class 1A, is payable annually from 1991/92 by employers (not employees) on the provision of cars and private fuel to P11D employees—see page 171. Class 1 and 1A national insurance contributions are collected through the PAYE system—for details, see chapter 10. The self-employed pay Class 2 and Class 4 contributions (see chapter 24).

Pensions

In general, in order to get a full basic pension, Class 1 contributions must be paid or credited equal to 52 times the lower earnings limit (see page 173) in at least nine in every ten years of your working life from 16 to 65 for a man or 60 for a woman, or you must have paid 52 Class 2 or Class 3 (voluntary) contributions for those years. You are credited with contributions when you are registered as unemployed, or unable to work through sickness or disability, or because you receive invalid care allowance for looking after someone who is disabled. If you are an unemployed man aged 60 to 64 you automatically get credits whether or not you are ill or on the unemployment register. Those who stay at home to look after children or sick or elderly people usually get Home Responsibilities Protection, which reduces the number of years needed to qualify for full pension. If you do not earn enough, either as an employee or in your self-employment, to pay enough Class 1 or 2 contributions, you may pay voluntary Class 3 contributions to help you to qualify for the retirement and widow's pension. You can check with your local DSS office to see whether your contribution record is not good enough to earn you a full pension. Late contributions can be paid for the previous six years (but sometimes at a higher rate). Married women paying reduced contributions (see page 173) cannot pay Class 3 contributions. They get a pension equal to 60% of the husband's basic pension when the husband is over 65 and the wife is over 60. The same applies to other married women who have not paid enough full rate contributions to earn a higher pension in their own right. A husband with a non-working wife under 60 gets an addition to his pension for her, unless she earns more than £43.10 a week. (This addition counts as his income, not hers.)

Widows usually get a full basic pension at 60, (subject to the contribution requirements), whether it is based on their own or their husband's contributions, unless in the latter case they were too young when their husband died or when their children grew up. But if they remarry before age 60, then unless they are claiming on their own contributions the pension will only be at 60% of the full amount and they will not get a pension until they are 60 and their new husband is 65. Remarriage after age 60 would not affect their entitlement to the full pension.

Those of pension age who are entitled to invalidity benefit or severe disablement allowance should usually not claim retirement pension, because retirement pension is taxable, whereas the other benefits are not.

Persons liable to pay Class 1 contributions (SSCBA 1992, ss 2, 6(1))

Unless specifically exempted (see below), all 'employed earners' and their employers must pay Class 1 contributions. An 'employed earner' is a person who is paid either as an employee under a contract of service or as the holder of an office with earnings chargeable to income tax under Schedule E (see chapter 10).

DSS leaflet NI 39 'National Insurance and contract of service' outlines various criteria which are taken into account in deciding whether a person is employed. For example, an employer exercises control over the work of an employee whereas a self-employed person is normally his own master. Also, whereas a self-employed person usually takes a degree of financial risk in attempting to make a profit, an employed person receives a wage in return for doing work which he is instructed to do.

Certain people are specifically brought within the liability to Class 1 contributions, including office and similar cleaners, most agency workers (including 'temps' but excluding outworkers), wives employed in their husbands' businesses and vice versa, ministers of religion paid chiefly by way of stipend or salary, and certain part-time lecturers and teachers.

Certain employees and their employers are exempted from payment of Class 1 contributions. These are

(a) people employed outside Great Britain and its Continental Shelf,

(b) people aged under 16,
(c) people whose earnings are below the weekly lower earnings limit (£54.00 for 1992/93),
(d) a wife employed by her husband for a non-business purpose and vice versa,
(e) people employed for a non-business purpose by a close relative in the home where they both live,
(f) returning and counting officers and people employed by them in connection with an election or referendum, and
(g) certain employees of international organisations and visiting armed forces.

Earnings (SSCBA 1992, ss 3, 4)

Class 1 contributions are calculated on gross pay, which is broadly the same as pay for income tax, but before deducting:

> Employees' pension contributions to occupational scheme or private scheme;
> Charitable gifts under payroll giving scheme;

and including:

> Profit-related pay (even if exempt from income tax) (see chapter 11);
> Reimbursed parking expenses, except for recorded business journeys.

Contributions are not normally payable on benefits in kind or on tips unless the employer decides how they are to be shared out and the money passes through the employer. There are, however, various traps that may cause benefits to be chargeable depending on the way they are provided, and the information in the Employers' Manual on National Insurance Contributions (NI 269 with April 1992 supplement) needs to be studied carefully. One item that needs particular care is the payment by the employer of a debt contracted by the employee, which counts as pay both for national insurance and for income tax. The NI guide states that liability arises if a director's bills are paid and the amount is transferred to his loan or current account. This is considered to be wrong if the director's account is in credit. But to avoid problems it is sensible for the director to draw from his loan account and pay his own bills.

Benefits in the form of gilt-edged securities, shares, debentures, units in unit trusts, futures, options, premium bonds or national savings certificates are specifically included in gross pay.

Cars and car fuel—Class 1A contributions (SSCBA 1992, s 10)

From 6 April 1991, the provision of cars and private fuel to employees has been subject to a new category of national insurance contributions, Class 1A, payable by employers at 10.4% (see pages xxviii, xxix). Employees' contributions are not, however, payable. The income tax car and fuel scales are used to determine the chargeable amount and the amount due is payable annually in arrear (see page 141), the 1992/93 payment being due by 19 June 1993 (or 19 July 1993 if quarterly payments are made). Records must be kept in order to substantiate business mileage above the 2,500 threshold, otherwise the 'insubstantial business mileage' rates will apply, and, similarly, a claim that business mileage is 18,000 or more must be supported by documentary evidence.

The position on private fuel provided before 6 April 1991 is broadly that there is no Class 1 liability if the fuel was supplied from an employer's pump, or if the employee had informed the garage that he was buying the fuel on behalf of his employer. Where an employer's garage account or petrol vouchers were used, the DSS will not pursue the payment in any event if an employer can show that he had relied on their past guidance. In any other circumstances, DSS claim that Class 1 contributions are due for both employer and employee on the full cost of fuel, except to the extent that business mileage has been logged, although this is arguable in some cases. Full details are in the April 1992 supplement of NI 269.

Contracted-out employees

Retirement and widows' pensions consist of two parts, a basic flat-rate pension, and an additional pension related to the level of the employee's earnings. The additional pension is paid under the State Earnings Related Pension Scheme (SERPS).

Employees who are members of occupational pension schemes which meet the requirements of the Occupational Pensions Board can be 'contracted-out' of the additional pension for retirement and part of the additional pension for widowhood by their employers. Contracted-out employees are still eligible for the basic pension from the state but obtain their additional pension from their employer's occupational pension scheme. To help meet the cost of setting up and running a separate pension scheme, contracted-out employees and their employers pay reduced rates of Class 1 contributions. The combined employer/employee contracting-out rebate is currently 5.8%, but it will be reduced to 4.8% from 6 April 1993.

Since 1 July 1988, employees have been able to enter into personal pension arrangements, to which their employers may or may not contribute (see chapter 17). Such employees are able to contract out of the State Earnings Related Pension Scheme (SERPS), and the contracting-out rebate will be paid by the DSS into the personal pension scheme. To encourage contracting out of SERPS, the rebate will be topped up by a bonus of 2% of earnings between the lower and upper earnings levels for up to six years, to April 1993. The 2% bonus will not be given to employees who have belonged to a contracted-out scheme within the previous two years (or who would have belonged to such a scheme had they not voluntarily left it). From 6 April 1993, the reduction of the contracting-out rebate and the withdrawal of the 2% bonus will be partly offset for those aged over 30 by the introduction of a new 1% bonus.

Contribution rates (SSCBA 1992, ss 1, 5, 8, 9)

National insurance rates for 1992/93 and 1991/92 are shown in the tables on page xxvii.

Employers' national insurance contributions are deductible in arriving at their taxable profits, so that the burden of employers' national insurance contributions is reduced by the tax saved on them. Tax on employees' earnings, on the other hand, is calculated on the gross pay before deducting national insurance contributions.

No national insurance contributions are payable by either employee or employer if weekly earnings are below the lower earnings limit (£54 for 1992/93). If weekly earnings exceed that amount, then for 1992/93, employees who are not contracted out pay 2% on the first £54 and 9% on the balance up to the upper earnings limit of £405 per week; their employers pay 4.6% if weekly earnings are less than £90, 6.6% if they are less than £135, 8.6% if they are less than £190 and 10.4% on all earnings of £190 per week and over, with no upper limit.

As far as employers' contributions are concerned, there is a disproportionate extra cost when an employee's earnings move from one rate band to another. For example, on earnings of £189 an employer's contributions are 8.6%, amounting to £16.25. On earnings of £190 the rate is 10.4%, giving contributions of £19.76, so that the extra £1 pay has cost an extra £3.51 contributions. (The employer's contributions are, however, tax deductible, so that the net of tax extra cost will be less.) There is a similar, though less significant, anomaly for an employee in that if wages rise from £53 to £54 per week, the additional £1 will cost national insurance contributions of £1.08.

Contributions for contracted-out employees are payable at the above rates, less a reduction on weekly earnings, for 1992/93, between £54 and £405 of 2% for the employee and 3.8% for the employer (to be reduced to 1.8% and 3% from 6 April 1993).

The reduced rate of employees' contributions for certain married women and widows is shown below.

Employee contributions

Reduced rate for certain married women and widows

Women who were married or widowed as at 6 April 1977 had a right to choose on or before 11 May 1977 to pay Class 1 contributions at a reduced rate. Entitlement to pay reduced rate contributions is evidenced by a certificate (Form CF 383) which must be handed over to the employer to enable him to deduct contributions at the correct rate.

If a married woman is self-employed, the election makes her exempt from paying Class 2 contributions, but not Class 4 contributions (see chapter 24).

The reduced rate for 1992/93, which is the same for both contracted-out and non-contracted-out employees, is 3.85% on earnings up to £405 per week.

A wife who pays reduced rate contributions is not eligible to receive contributory benefits, but she can claim retirement and widow's pension on the contribution record of her husband. The retirement pension a wife will get is 60% of the husband's basic pension if the husband is over 65 and the wife is over 60 (see page 170). She will not get any earnings-related pension. She is also entitled to receive statutory sick pay and statutory maternity pay.

The election to pay reduced rate contributions is effective until it is cancelled or revoked. A woman will lose the right to pay reduced rate contributions

(a) if she is divorced, in which case the right is lost immediately, or
(b) if she becomes widowed and is not entitled to widow's benefit, in which case the right is not lost until the end of the tax year in which the husband dies, or the end of the following tax year if he dies between 1 October and 5 April, or
(c) if she pays no reduced rate Class 1 contributions and has no earnings from self-employment for two consecutive tax years.

An election can be revoked in writing at any time and the revocation will, in most instances, take effect from the beginning of the following tax year. If the election is revoked, the wife will start earning a pension, including earnings-related pension, in her own right, and she will also be entitled to claim maternity allowance, unemployment benefit, sickness benefit and invalidity benefit.

Some women on low pay could pay lower contributions if they revoke their reduced rate election, as shown in example 1. But once the election is revoked, it cannot be revived, so if the earnings rise, the contributions will increase. Older women will often be no better off by revoking the election. Those who are considering revoking may get a pensions forecast from the DSS. They should get form BR19 from their local social security office.

Example 1

A married woman who has made a reduced rate election earns £60 a week.

Her weekly reduced rate contribution is £2.33. If she revoked the election, she would pay full rate contributions of £1.62 a week.

People over pensionable age

No contributions are payable by an employee who is over pension age (65 for a man, 60 for a woman), although the employer is still liable for secondary contributions where earnings reach the lower earnings limit, such contributions always being at non-contracted-out rates.

Employees who are not liable to pay contributions should apply for a certificate of age exception (form CF 384). This should be given to the employer as authority for Class 1 contributions not to be deducted from earnings.

More than one employment

Where a person has more than one employment, he is liable to pay primary Class 1 contributions in respect of each job. There is however a prescribed annual maximum contribution.

The maximum is based on 53 weeks' contributions. The amounts for 1992/93 are:

All employments non-contracted-out	All employments contracted-out	Reduced rate
£1,731.51	£1,359.45	£826.27

Where an employee has both contracted-out and non-contracted-out employments, the contracted-out contributions are converted to the non-contracted-out level to see whether the annual maximum has been exceeded.

If at the end of a tax year an employee's contributions have exceeded the prescribed maximum by a stipulated amount (£2.18 for 1992/93), a refund is available. An employee may obtain a refund by submitting form CF 28F together with evidence of excess payments, e.g. certificates of pay, tax and NIC (forms P60). Refunds of over £27.00 are made automatically, without the need for a claim.

To avoid having to pay contributions in all employments throughout the year and being refunded any excess after the end of the year, an employee may apply to defer some of his contributions. An application form for deferment of contributions can be found in DSS booklet NP 28—'More than one job?', and if deferment is granted, a certificate (form RD 950) will be sent to the employers concerned (except those paying the earnings upon which the maximum contributions are calculated) authorising them not to deduct the employee's contributions. All employers must, however, continue to pay employers' contributions.

As an alternative to applying for deferment of contributions, an employee may pay the maximum contributions in advance. Where this is done, all employers will be instructed not to deduct primary contributions.

To prevent abuse of the system, the following 'anti-avoidance' provisions have been included in the legislation:

(a) Where a person has more than one job with the same employer, earnings from those employments must be added together and contributions calculated on the total;
(b) Where a person has jobs with different employers who 'carry on business in association with each other', all earnings from 'associated'

employers must be added together for the purpose of calculating contributions.

These rules will not be enforced if it can be shown that to do so would be impracticable.

Income from self-employment

The position of the employee who also has income from self-employment is dealt with in chapter 24.

Company directors

Directors sometimes receive a salary under a service contract and also fees for holding the office of director. They are often paid in irregular amounts at irregular time intervals, for example a fixed monthly salary together with a bonus after the year end, once the results of the company are known. To ensure that this does not lead to manipulation of liability to pay national insurance contributions, directors in employment at the beginning of a tax year have an annual earnings period coinciding with the tax year. Those appointed during a tax year have an earnings period equal to the number of weeks from the date of appointment to the end of the tax year. No Class 1 contributions are due if the director's earnings are less than the annual lower earnings limit (1992/93 £2,808) or a pro-rata limit for directors appointed during a tax year (using the appropriate multiple of the weekly limit).

All earnings paid to a director during an earnings period must be included in that earnings period (irrespective of the period to which they relate). Earnings include fees, bonuses, salary, payments made in anticipation of future earnings, and payments made to a director which were earned while he was still an employee.

If a director resigns, all payments made to him between the date of resignation and the end of the tax year that relate to his period of directorship must be linked to his other 'directorship earnings' of that tax year. If any such earnings are paid in a later tax year, they are not added to any other earnings of the year in which payment is made. Instead, they are considered independently on an annual earnings basis, and Class 1 contributions accounted for accordingly.

Many directors have payments in anticipation of future earnings, e.g. a payment on account of a bonus to be declared when the company's results are known. Liability for Class 1 contributions arises when the payments are made (subject, of course, to the lower earnings limit). The advance bonus payments are added to all other earnings of the annual earnings period. When the bonus is voted (probably at the annual general meeting) the balance, if any, will become liable to Class 1 contributions in the tax year in which the annual general meeting is held. Once a bonus is voted for a past period, it is deemed to be paid whether it is placed in an account on which the director can draw or left in the company, unless exceptionally it is not placed at the director's disposal.

To the extent that a director makes drawings against a credit balance on his director's loan account, no Class 1 liability will arise as these drawings simply reduce the balance of the loan account. If the loan account has been built up from undrawn remuneration, the Class 1 liability will have arisen at the time the remuneration was credited to it.

Tax points

- If an employee has several employments, he can get back national insurance contributions in excess of the annual maximum. Refunds are not, however, available in respect of employers' contributions.

- If your wife or husband pays maximum contributions in a separate job and also does some work in the family business run by you, you cannot get back employers' national insurance on the earnings from the family business, so it may be more sensible to pay your spouse less than the weekly limit. Remember, however, that earnings of either of you as an *employee* of the family business must be justified if relief for tax is to be given in calculating the business profits.

- Except for company directors, who have an annual earnings period coinciding with the tax year, or for the remainder of the tax year in which they are appointed, national insurance does not work on a cumulative basis. If average earnings will not exceed the national insurance threshold, try to ensure that the actual earnings in any week do not do so, otherwise both employer and employee will be liable to pay contributions for that particular week even though on a cumulative basis the earnings threshold may not have been reached.

- The annual maximum contribution liability is based on 53 weeks' contributions, although there are rarely 53 pay days in a year. If you have more than one job and earn more than £405 a week from one of them, make sure you apply for deferment. You will then not have any more to pay at the year end, whereas if you wait for a refund, you will only get back any excess over 53 *weeks'* contributions. Even if you do not earn more than £405 a week from one job, applying for deferment where your *total* earnings exceed that amount is better than waiting for a refund after the year end.

- Since there is no upper limit to the earnings on which employers' contributions are payable, it may be cheaper for the remuneration package to include benefits in kind which, whilst taxable, do not presently attract a national insurance liability (apart from the exceptions dealt with in this chapter).

- Similarly, dividends paid to shareholders do not attract national insurance contributions. It may be appropriate for shareholders/directors to receive dividends rather than additional remuneration.

  This aspect must not, however, be looked at in isolation. Many others are important, e.g. the level of remuneration for company or personal pension purposes, and the effect of a dividend policy on other share-holders. See chapter 12 for illustrations.

- If you can justifiably pay remuneration to your wife or husband up to the limit of the available allowance, consider paying just below the national insurance threshold each week and a bonus to make the wages up to the required amount at the end of March. Employer's and employee's contributions will then only be payable for the week in which the bonus is paid, giving a significant national insurance saving. This will not apply if the wife/husband is a director with an annual earnings period. The effect on benefit entitlement should also be considered. The DSS might take action to block the saving, but not retrospectively.

- If you have been paying the reduced married woman's rate of contribution, watch the circumstances in which you have to revert to the full rate, for example when you get divorced (see page 174). If you under-pay, even by mistake, you will probably have to make up the difference. But you do not have to pay contributions at all from age 60.

- Remember that if you have not paid enough contributions for a year to be classed as a qualifying year, your State pension may be affected (see page 169).

- If an employer pays an employee's debt, it counts as pay for national insurance and for income tax. The DSS are currently examining the treatment of vouchers, to check whether they are used in circumstances where the employee has in fact contracted personally for something which is then settled by tendering the voucher. This will not be the case unless the contract is made before the voucher is handed over.

- For Class 1A contributions on cars and fuel, you need records to show that business miles exceed 2,500 or 18,000 as the case may be. This does not mean *all* business miles must be logged, only enough to show that the appropriate threshold has been reached.

- Records are needed to prove business use in other areas, such as for mileage allowances to those who use their own cars, and for contributions towards an employee's telephone bill.

- Where you were supplying private fuel to employees before 6 April 1991, you could be liable for up to six years' back contributions. Study the April 1992 supplement to NI 269 carefully and consider what evidence you can put forward to show that the contributions are not due.

14
Statutory sick pay and statutory maternity pay

Background

Statutory sick pay (SSP) was introduced by the Social Security and Housing Benefits Act 1982. Statutory maternity pay (SMP) was introduced by the Social Security Act 1986. The provisions on both SSP and SMP are now in the Social Security Contributions and Benefits Act 1992. Most employees are entitled to receive SSP from their employers for up to 28 weeks of sickness absence. SSP is paid at one of two flat rates, according to the employee's average weekly earnings. SMP is paid at two rates, the higher rate being dependent on the employee's earnings and the lower rate being a fixed amount. Both SSP and SMP count as pay for income tax and national insurance contributions. Employers can recover both the direct cost of SMP and an amount which broadly equals their 'secondary' national insurance contributions thereon (see chapter 13). This previously applied to SSP as well, but from 6 April 1991 employers can normally recover only 80% of SSP, and get nothing to compensate for their secondary national insurance contributions on the SSP (see page 184).

Employees entitled to receive SSP

The definition of an employee is the same as that of an 'employed earner' for Class 1 national insurance contributions (see chapter 13). Married women and widows paying reduced rate Class 1 contributions are therefore entitled to SSP.

All employers and employees must participate in the operation of SSP and neither party can opt out of the scheme. An employee is entitled to SSP for each job he has, so that if an individual is employed by two different employers he will be paid SSP by each employer when off work through illness.

An employee is entitled to SSP unless he/she falls into one of the excluded groups.

When an employee is being paid SSP he has no entitlement to state sickness benefit. Employees who are not entitled to SSP and employees who have exhausted their SSP entitlement may claim sickness, and later invalidity, benefit.

Employees excluded from SSP

Employees who, at the beginning of a 'period of incapacity for work' (see below), fall into one of the following categories are excluded from entitlement to SSP.

(a) People over state pensionable age (men 65, women 60).
(b) Those who have claimed certain state benefits within the 57 days before falling ill. The benefits concerned are:
  (i) sickness benefit;
  (ii) invalidity benefit or severe disablement allowance;
  (iii) maternity allowance;
  (iv) unemployment benefit, where, prior to claiming, the claimant was receiving either of the benefits in (ii).
An employee who has received one of these benefits will receive a letter from the DSS (known as a 'linking letter') notifying the employer of the period of exclusion.
(c) Those whose average weekly earnings are below the lower earnings limit for national insurance contributions (£54 for 1992/93—see chapter 13).
(d) A person who has not begun work under his contract.
(e) Those who become ill during a stoppage of work at their place of employment during a trade dispute, unless the employee can prove that he is not participating in, or directly interested in, the dispute.
(f) A pregnant woman during her 'disqualifying period' of eighteen weeks beginning between eleven and six weeks before the expected week of confinement.
(g) Those who have received 28 weeks SSP from their previous employer(s). This further exclusion does not prevent an employee receiving SSP if he should fall ill more than eight weeks after the end of the previous period of incapacity.
(h) Those who fall ill while working outside the EC.
(j) Those who fall ill while in prison or in legal custody.
(k) Those contracted to work for a period not exceeding three months (e.g. seasonal workers). If, however, an employee works on beyond the three months (even though the contract is not formally extended) he will be entitled to SSP thereafter. Moreover, if an employee starts work under a new contract within eight weeks of an earlier contract with the same employer, and the contracts together produce a contract of thirteen or more weeks, the employee will be entitled to SSP.

Where an employer receives notification of illness from an employee who falls into an 'excluded' category, he must issue the employee with a change-over form SSP 1. Failure to issue a change-over form within seven days of the notification of the illness is a criminal offence.

Qualifying conditions for SSP

For SSP to be payable two qualifying conditions must be met:

(i) there must be a 'period of incapacity for work' ('PIW'); and
(ii) there must be one or more 'qualifying days'.

Incapacity for work

A PIW is a period of four or more consecutive days of incapacity for work, counting rest days and holidays as well as normal working days. A person may be deemed incapable of work on the advice of a doctor or medical officer of health (e.g. where a pregnant woman is advised to stay at home during an outbreak of German measles at her place of work), but a day counts towards a PIW only if the employee is, or is deemed to be, 'incapable by reason of specific disease or bodily or mental disablement of doing work which he/she can reasonably be expected to do under the contract of employment'. The incapacity must exist throughout the day, nightshift workers falling ill during a shift being treated as working only on the day in which the shift began.

If two PIWs are separated by 56 days or less, they are treated as one single PIW (called a linked PIW). See example 1.

Example 1

An employee is incapable of work through illness from Thursday 28 May 1992 to Monday 1 June 1992 inclusive and from Sunday 19 July 1992 to Thursday 10 September 1992 inclusive.

The two PIWs are separated by 47 days and are therefore treated as a linked PIW.

Tables to help employers work out whether PIWs link are included in the SSP Tables issued by the DSS.

Qualifying days

SSP is payable only in respect of 'qualifying days'. These are days of the week agreed between the employer and employee and will normally be those days on which the employee is required to work. Employer and employee may, however, come to other arrangements if they wish but qualifying days cannot be defined by reference to the days when the employee is sick. There is an overriding rule that there must be at least one qualifying day each week even if the employee is not required to work during that week.

SSP is not payable for the first three qualifying days in any PIW not linked to an earlier PIW. These are 'waiting days'. See example 2.

Example 2

An employee with qualifying days Monday to Friday each week, who had not been ill during November 1992, was ill on the days ringed in December.

M	T	W	Th	F	Sa	Su
	1	2	③	④	⑤	⑥
7	8	9	10	11	12	13
14	15	16	17	18	19	20
㉑	㉒	㉓	㉔	㉕	26	㉗
㉘	㉙	㉚	31			

There are three PIWs, from the 3rd to the 6th, from the 21st to the 25th, and from the 27th to the 30th.

In the first, there are two qualifying days which count as waiting days, and no SSP is payable.

In the second, which begins not more than 56 days after the end of the first and is therefore linked with it, the 21st is the third waiting day and SSP is payable for the other four qualifying days.

The third begins not more than 56 days after the end of the second and is therefore linked with it. As there are three waiting days in the linked PIWs, SSP is payable for each of the three qualifying days in the third PIW.

Amount of SSP

Average earnings

SSP is payable on a daily basis at a rate which depends on the employee's average weekly earnings. 'Average earnings' are gross earnings (including bonuses and overtime) paid in the eight weeks immediately before the period of illness. Where an employee is paid monthly, the weekly rate is computed by adding together the two salary payments prior to the illness, multiplying the result by six and dividing the total by 52. There are special rules where an employee is paid at irregular intervals.

Rates

The weekly earnings bands and applicable rates of SSP from 6 April 1992 are as follows.

Average weekly earnings	Standard £190.00 and over	Lower £54.00–£189.99
SSP weekly rate	£52.50	£45.30

The daily rate of SSP is the appropriate weekly rate divided by the number of qualifying days in the week (e.g. an employee who has five qualifying days in a week and who has average weekly earnings of £190 will receive SSP at a daily rate of £10.50 (£52.50 ÷ 5)).

Although there are no rules about when SSP must be paid out, it would usually be paid on the employee's normal pay day.

Wages paid to an employee can be offset against any SSP due for the same day. If the wages are less than the SSP due, the employer must make up the payment to the appropriate rate of SSP.

When SSP ends

SSP ends with whichever of the following first occurs:

(a) the period of incapacity ends and the employee returns to work;
(b) the employee reaches his maximum entitlement to SSP;
(c) the employee's linked PIW has run for three years (which could only happen in exceptional circumstances where there were a large number of very short, four-day illnesses);
(d) the employee's contract of employment ends;
(e) the employee goes abroad outside the EC;
(f) the employee is detained in legal custody;
(g) a pregnant woman employee starts her 'disqualifying period' (see above).

The maximum period for which the employer is liable to pay SSP is normally 28 weeks. Where, however, a new employee commences a PIW within eight weeks of the day when a PIW with a previous employer ended, the weeks of SSP shown on the leaver's statement provided by the previous employer (see below) are taken into account to determine the new employer's maximum SSP liability. The previous period of sickness does not, however, affect the new employer's calculations in any other way and is not treated as a linked PIW.

Where entitlement to SSP ends while the employee is still sick, the employee will be able to claim sickness benefit. To facilitate the change-over, the employer must issue change-over form SSP 1 to the employee at the beginning of the 23rd week of SSP (or, if sooner, two weeks before the employee's entitlement to SSP is likely to or will end). If the employee's entitlement ends unexpectedly (e.g. through being taken into legal custody), the change-over form must be issued immediately. It is a criminal offence not to issue the form within seven days of the required date.

Leaver's statements

If an employee has a PIW which ends not more than 56 days before his employment ceases, and SSP was payable for one week or more, a leaver's statement SSP 1(L) must be issued showing the number of weeks' SSP payable (rounded to whole weeks, counting more than three odd days of payment as a week, and ignoring three odd days or less). The statement must normally be issued not later than the seventh calendar day after the day the employment ceases. It is a criminal offence not to comply with the time limit.

Notification and evidence for SSP

The payment of SSP is triggered by the employee notifying his employer that he is unfit for work. An employer can draw up his own procedure for notification subject to the following limitations:

(a) reasonable steps must be taken to notify employees of the procedures;
(b) it is not legal to insist that notification
  (i) is made by the employee in person, or
  (ii) is made by a particular time of day, or
  (iii) is made more than once weekly for the same illness, or
  (iv) is made on a document provided by the employer or by way of a medical certificate, or
  (v) is given earlier than the first qualifying day; and
(c) where the employee is a new employee with a leaving statement from his former employer, the statement must be accepted if it is produced not later than the seventh day after his first qualifying day of sickness.

If no notification procedures have been drawn up, the employee should inform his employer in writing by the seventh day after his first qualifying day of absence. If an employee fails to notify within the laid-down time limits an employer may withhold SSP.

Having been notified by an employee of his illness, the employer must satisfy himself that the illness is genuine before paying SSP. The DSS anticipates that employers will obtain 'self-certificates' for the first week of illness and medical notes for longer absences.

An employer may withhold SSP when notification is late, and he may refuse to pay SSP if he feels that the employee is not in fact sick. In both these instances the employer, if required by the employee, must provide written reasons for withholding or refusing to pay SSP. An employee who disagrees with his employer's actions has the right to appeal for an official decision.

Recovery of SSP by employer

Employers used to be able to recover the full amount of SSP plus compensation for their national insurance contributions on the SSP, which gave a recovery rate for 1990/91 of 107%. From 6 April 1991, they can only recover 80% unless they qualify for Small Employers' Relief at 100%, and the 100% recovery will even then only be available on SSP for days of sickness after the first six weeks in a period of incapacity (but from 6 April 1992 the six-week period can straddle two tax years). The Small Employers' Relief is available for days of sickness in 1992/93 if the total employers' and employees' national insurance contributions for 1991/92 were £16,000 or less (£15,000 for the previous year).

> **Example 3**
>
> Employee fell sick on Friday 19 February 1993 and was still sick on and after Friday 2 April 1993 (i.e. six weeks later), so 100% recovery applies from that date if the employer qualifies. The relevant tax year's contributions for Small Employers' Relief are those paid for 1991/92 (the last complete tax year before 2 April 1993). If the sickness had commenced on Tuesday 23 February 1993 and lasted beyond Tuesday 6 April 1993, the relevant tax year would be 1992/93.

SSP is recovered from amounts due to be paid over to the Collector of Taxes in respect of Class 1 national insurance contributions. If the total paid exceeds contributions due, the excess can be deducted from PAYE payable to the Collector, and if it exceeds both national insurance and PAYE payable, the employer can either carry the excess forward or apply to the Collector for a refund.

Employees entitled to SMP

Statutory maternity pay (SMP) was introduced on 6 April 1987. Self-employed and unemployed women, and employed women who cannot get SMP, may claim maternity allowance from the DSS. SMP is usually paid for 18 weeks, even if the employee is not returning after the baby has been born. Married women paying reduced national insurance contributions, and widows getting a state widow's benefit, are entitled to SMP if they satisfy the qualifying conditions. SSP and SMP cannot be paid at the same time, and SSP must cease on the last day before the Maternity Pay Period (see below) starts, even if for some reason the employee is not entitled to SMP.

Qualifying conditions for SMP

To qualify for SMP an employee must have been employed for at least 26 weeks, including the 15th week before the baby is due. The 15th week is called the qualifying week. The employee's average weekly earnings in the eight weeks ending with the qualifying week must be not less than the lower earnings limit for national insurance contributions (currently £54). The employee must still be pregnant at the 11th week before the expected date of birth. There are special rules for premature births. If an employee satisfies the qualifying rules with more than one employer she can receive SMP from each employer.

Payment of SMP

SMP is payable for a maximum of 18 weeks, called the Maternity Pay Period (MPP), and the employee has some flexibility as to when it starts. It cannot commence earlier than the 11th week before the baby is due, and it will only run for a maximum of 18 weeks from the 6th week before the baby is due, so the employee must have stopped work by that 6th week to get the full 18 weeks. SMP will cease if the employee is taken into legal custody, or goes abroad outside the EC, or starts work for another employer after the baby is born. SMP is not payable for any week in which the employee is at work.

Employees excluded from SMP

An employee is not entitled to SMP if:

(a) she is not employed during the qualifying week;
(b) she has not been continuously employed for 26 weeks;
(c) the earnings rule is not satisfied;
(d) she has not given notice at an acceptable time of the date she is stopping work;
(e) medical evidence of her expected confinement date is not provided;
(f) the employee is abroad outside the EC at any time in the first week of her MPP;
(g) an employee is in legal custody at any time in the first week of her MPP.

If an employee is not entitled to SMP at the start of the MPP, she will not be entitled to it at all.

An employee who is not entitled to SMP must be given form SMP1 within seven days of the decision not to pay it, together with any maternity certificate she has provided. These forms will need to be produced to her social security office if she claims maternity allowance.

Amount of SMP

There are two rates of SMP. The higher rate is 9/10ths of the employee's average weekly earnings, and is payable for the first six weeks that SMP is due. For the remaining weeks, SMP is paid at the lower rate (£46.30 for 1992/93). The higher rate is only payable if the employee has been employed for at least 16 hours per week for a period of two years up to and including the qualifying week (the 15th week before expected confinement) or for at least eight hours per week for a period of five years up to and including the qualifying week. If neither condition is satisfied, the employee gets the lower rate throughout the MPP.

Notification and evidence for SMP

To get SMP an employee must give 21 days' notice of maternity absence in a manner prescribed by the employer, and must produce evidence of her expected week of confinement, normally on a maternity certificate form Mat B1 issued by a doctor or midwife.

Recovery of SMP by employer

Employers are able to recover the gross amount of SMP paid in any month from amounts due to be paid over to the Collector of Taxes in respect of

Class 1 national insurance contributions. They can also deduct an extra amount to compensate for the secondary class 1 contributions (see chapter 13) paid by the employer on SMP. For 1992/93 the compensation is calculated as 4½% of the total SMP paid. If the total paid, plus the compensation, exceeds contributions due, the excess can be deducted from PAYE payable to the Collector; and if it exceeds both national insurance and PAYE payable, the employer can either carry the excess forward or apply to the Collector for a refund.

Employer's records

Employer's records are particularly important, as the information required to be kept may have to be made available to DSS inspectors. The form the records take is up to the employer, but the following must be kept:

For SSP

(a) records of dates of employees' PIWs;
(b) records of qualifying days in each PIW;
(c) records of days within each PIW for which SSP was not paid with reasons (including 'excluded categories', see page 180);
(d) any leaver's statements from new employees whom the employer did not exclude from SSP;
(e) copies of leaver's statements issued.

For SMP

(a) records of dates of maternity absence;
(b) records of weeks for which SMP not paid, with details;
(c) maternity certificates (forms Mat B1) or other medical evidence, and copies of certificates returned to employees, for example when liability has ended.

For both SSP and SMP

Records must also be kept of the monthly SSP and SMP paid, and the details should be included on the end of year returns of pay, tax and national insurance.

Records must be kept for a minimum of three years after the end of the tax year to which they relate.

In addition to the records outlined above, the DSS recommends that the following are also retained for further reference:

(i) medical notes and 'self-certificates' relating to PIWs;
(ii) an outline of the employer's SSP and SMP rules;
(iii) a record of when employees report absence through sickness or notify maternity absences;
(iv) a record of all correspondence concerning appeals etc., with copies of all decisions by Social Security.

15
Golden handcuffs and golden handshakes

A 'golden handcuff' or 'golden hello' is the popular term for a lump sum payment received on taking up an employment, and a 'golden handshake' or 'golden goodbye' the term for a lump sum payment received when you leave an employment.

Lump sum payments on taking up employment (TA 1988, s 313)

Where a lump sum payment is made to a prospective employee, it will be treated as remuneration for future services unless it represents compensation for some right or asset given up on taking up the employment. It is difficult to show that a payment does represent compensation, and professional advice should be sought if you think a payment you are about to receive is in this category.

Sometimes a lump sum is paid in return for your agreeing to restrict your conduct or activities in some way, for example agreeing not to leave to join a competitor within a certain period of time. Any such special payments are treated as pay in the normal way, both for tax and for national insurance.

Lump sum termination payments (TA 1988, ss 90, 148, 188, 579, 580, 596A, 612 and Sch 11)

Lump sum termination payments are taxable under special rules (see page 189), unless they are already taxable under Schedule E.

Such payments may arise in two different ways, as compensation for breach of the contract of employment or as ex gratia payments by employers. A payment will be taxable as earnings under Schedule E in the normal way if it is a payment for services rendered.

A termination payment will generally be regarded as for services rendered only where it was specifically provided for in the contract of employment, or where the contract was made under an expectation that it would be received.

In the case of an ex gratia payment, however, since there is no obligation on the employer to make the payment, it will be more difficult to demonstrate to the Revenue that it was made in respect of the termination of employment rather than for services rendered. When employment is terminated by the employee's retirement or death (other than as the result of an accident), the Revenue now consider that ex gratia payments are fully taxable under Schedule E as benefits under an unapproved 'retirement benefits scheme'. This will not apply if the employer gets tax approval for the payments, which will then become 'relevant benefits from an approved scheme', but approval will be subject to the normal rules limiting the maximum lump sum payable, and will not be given if the ex gratia sum is in addition to other lump sum entitlements, except any payable only on death in service. Alternatively, approval need not be sought if the lump sum is the only potential lump sum payable and does not exceed one-twelfth of the pensions earnings cap figure for the year of payment (£75,000 for 1992/93, giving a limit for that year of £6,250). (Revenue Statement of Practice SP 13/91).

For either compensation or ex gratia payments, the following circumstances may give rise to further complication:

(i) Where the employee is also a shareholder, it may be difficult to demonstrate that the payment is not a distribution on which the company would have to pay advance corporation tax, with no deduction being given for the payment in calculating the employer's trading profit (see chapter 3).

(ii) Where the payment is made at the same time as a change in voting control, a clear distinction between the payment and the share transactions must be demonstrated if the payment is not to be regarded as part and parcel of the capital transaction.

(iii) If the employee continues with the employer in a new capacity, either as an employee or perhaps under a consultancy agreement, it becomes that much harder to demonstrate that the payment was not in respect of services rendered or to be rendered in the future.

Taxation of the lump sum termination payment

Provided that the payment is not caught either as taxable earnings, or as a distribution, or as part of a capital transaction, it will be taxed according to the special rules for termination payments. Under these, the first £30,000 is exempt and the balance is taxable as remuneration in the normal way.

Statutory redundancy payments, whilst not themselves taxable, are included within the first £30,000. Most payments in lieu of notice will be covered by the first £30,000 and thus not charged to tax unless, exceptionally, they are taxable as earnings under Schedule E in the normal way.

Exemptions

Some payments are completely exempt from tax, for example those on death in service (subject to what is said above) or in respect of disability, or where the service has been predominantly abroad. There is partial exemption for shorter periods of work abroad.

Lump sums received under approved pension schemes are exempt. They may be boosted by agreed special contributions from the employer to the fund prior to the termination of employment so long as the permitted maximum lump sum is not exceeded (see chapter 16). In view of the Revenue's new view on ex gratia payments (see page 189), this route provides an alternative where there is an approved pension scheme.

The £30,000 is taken into account after allowing for any other available exemptions.

Application of PAYE

The employer must deduct and account for PAYE on the excess of chargeable termination payments over £30,000 and also on ex gratia sums on retirement or death for which approval has not yet been granted (tax being refunded as and when approval is received).

Tax position of the employer (TA 1988, s 90)

In deducting any expense to arrive at the employer's profits, it must be shown that the expense was wholly and exclusively for the purposes of the trade. Apart from statutory redundancy payments, which are specifically allowable, there is no special rule for termination payments, but it will usually be easier to demonstrate that they meet the 'wholly and exclusively' requirement when they are compensation rather than ex gratia payments, and when the trade is continuing rather than when it is not.

Where a trade is permanently discontinued, it is specifically provided that an additional payment up to three times any amount paid under the statutory redundancy pay provisions is allowable as a deduction in computing the employer's profits, any payments in excess of this amount being disallowed. Any rebates received under the statutory redundancy scheme must be brought into account to reduce the cost to the employer. (Rebates are now given only to employers with less than ten employees.)

It may be particularly difficult for the employer to obtain a deduction where the payment is ex gratia and is associated with a sale of the shares or a change in voting control, or where it is an abnormally high payment to a director with a material interest in the company.

National insurance position

The national insurance position is essentially the same as that for income tax, i.e. if the employee has a contractual right to the payment, or there is an expectation that the payment will be made, it is liable to national insurance contributions as earnings from the employment. Otherwise, contributions are not payable.

Expenses incurred in obtaining a lump sum payment

Some employees may incur expenses, for example fees to advisers, in obtaining a lump sum payment. These will not reduce the lump sum payment for tax purposes as they will not have been wholly, exclusively and necessarily incurred in the performance of the duties of the employment.

Tax points

- An ex gratia payment to a director or shareholder of a close company is especially vulnerable to Revenue attack, on either or both of the following grounds:

  (a) it is not a deductible trading expense.
  (b) it is a distribution of profits.

- If an ex gratia payment by a close company is not allowed in calculating profits, the Revenue may contend that each shareholder has made a proportionate transfer of value for inheritance tax. There is a specific exclusion where the payment is allowed in computing profits.

- Ex gratia payments may be taxed as non-exempt 'retirement benefits'—see page 189.

- If an employee who receives a severance payment is allowed to keep a company car as part of the package, it may be regarded as a reward for past services, so that the market value of the car would be chargeable in full and not treated as part of the exempt £30,000. It is better to increase the lump sum and give the employee the opportunity to purchase the car at market value. If the lump sum was taxable as an unapproved retirement benefit (see page 189), the value of the car would similarly be taxable.

- Unless you obtain new sources of income to replace your salary, the tax cost of a termination payment in excess of £30,000 may be lower if the termination occurs shortly after 6 April rather than before, because all or part of the payment may fall within the 20%/25% rate bands, whereas it might have attracted 40% tax if it was received in addition to a full year's salary.

- It is essential that proper documentation and board minutes are available so that the nature of payments can be demonstrated to the Revenue.

- The tax reliefs for lump sum payments are only available to *employees* taxed under Schedule E and not to those employed under a *contract for services*, whose earnings are charged under Schedule D, Case I or II (see page 222). If, exceptionally, Schedule E earnings are included by agreement with the Revenue in the calculation of self-employed profits, e.g. directors' fees where the directorship is held in a professional capacity and the fees are included as income of the professional practice, this in itself will not prevent a lump sum qualifying for the reliefs outlined in this chapter.

- The chargeable part of a termination payment does not count as relevant earnings for the purpose of calculating maximum contributions to a personal pension plan taken out on or after 1 July 1988. (See chapter 17.) It is included for retirement annuity contracts made before that date.

- A termination payment may affect the former employee's entitlement to social security benefits if he is then unemployed, but the employee will be entitled to unemployment credits for the period covered by the compensation payment so that his national insurance contribution record is not affected.

16
Occupational pension schemes

Background

The Government has for many years recognised that the retirement benefits provided by the state scheme are inadequate, and whilst itself having provided an additional earnings-related pension (SERPS), it has also encouraged the provision of benefits through employers' schemes by generous tax treatment. Government support for employers' schemes continues, but there has been a feeling that the beneficial tax treatment has in some instances been misused, and although there is now greater flexibility in the making of pensions arrangements, there has also been a tightening of the rules relating to occupational schemes in order to stem the misuse which has occurred.

Where an employer's scheme provides at least equivalent benefits to the earnings-related state scheme, employees may be contracted out of the earnings-related element of the state scheme, thus paying lower contributions to it. From 6 April 1988, a pension scheme has been able to contract out of SERPS by guaranteeing minimum contributions to employees' pensions (contracted-out money purchase schemes—COMPS) rather than having to guarantee the benefits on retirement. Contracted-out employees receive their basic pension from the state and the additional benefits from their employer's scheme. A special contracting-out rebate of 2% of earnings between the lower and upper earnings levels will be paid by the DSS up to 5 April 1993 to occupational schemes set up between 1 January 1986 and 5 April 1993. The combined employer/employee reduction in contributions for contracted-out employees, excluding the 2% bonus, is currently 5.8%, but it will be 4.8% from 6 April 1993.

Many employers, particularly family companies, none the less remain contracted in to the state scheme and provide their own pension scheme in addition. The employee then gets full benefits under the state scheme (and pays full contributions) plus the additional benefits provided by his employer's scheme. Family companies have the same facility as others for establishing schemes, but there are tighter rules on the calculation of maximum possible benefits where the employee is a shareholder holding 20% or more of the share capital, and of course the benefits are themselves limited by what has been paid into the fund. If a company is an investment company, the scheme must comply with the rules for *automatic* approval (see below) if it is to include 20% directors or directors who are members of a family who control more than 50% of the company's shares.

Employees in a contracted-in scheme are able to contract out of SERPS independently while remaining in their employer's scheme, either by making a free-standing additional voluntary contribution (see page 196) or through a separate personal pension plan (see page 208).

Membership of employers' schemes

From 6 April 1988, employees cannot be compelled to be members of their employers' schemes, unless the schemes are non-contributory and provide only death benefits. Employees are able to take out personal pension plans instead (see chapter 17) or rely on the state pension scheme. Pension rights from an existing occupational scheme may be transferred to a personal pension plan, but if an employee remains in the employment, benefits accrued before 6 April 1988 cannot be transferred unless the scheme permits. It will also normally be possible to transfer back from a personal pension plan to an employer's scheme if the scheme agrees.

Revenue approval for employers' schemes (TA 1988, ss 590–612; SI 1992/246)

In order to obtain Revenue approval, the employer must contribute to the scheme but the employee need not. (See, however, the rules regarding pension scheme surpluses on page 200.)

A pension scheme gains automatic Revenue approval if it conforms precisely to the statutory conditions. The Revenue may, however, approve a scheme which does not precisely conform and many schemes receive this discretionary approval under which greater benefits can be paid (but of course at a higher cost in contributions). The Revenue issue Practice Notes on the manner in which they exercise their discretion, and specialist pensions advisers are able to structure schemes so that they will receive the approval of the Pension Schemes Office (PSO). Schemes may be either 'defined benefit' schemes, under which the benefits depend on final salary, or 'defined contribution' (money purchase) schemes, under which the contributions are fixed and the benefits depend on those contributions and on the investment performance of the scheme. Two forms of simplified 'off-the-peg' schemes that qualify for immediate approval, one based on final salary and the other a money purchase scheme, are available to help employers who would not normally provide employees with pension arrangements. These schemes may not include directors of family companies who control 20% or more of the voting rights. The Revenue has issued standard documentation for these two schemes.

New regulations came into force on 9 March 1992 limiting a fund's investment in employer-related investments to 5% of the current market value of the fund (except for small self-administered schemes—see page 200). Self-investments already held at that date can be retained indefinitely, except loans and securities, which cannot be retained beyond 8 March 1994 (8 March 1997 for second-tier market investments).

Taxation advantages of Revenue approval

(a) The employer's contributions are deductible in calculating business profits.
(b) The employer's contributions are not treated as a benefit in kind to the employee.
(c) An employee's own contributions are deductible in calculating his taxable earnings (although they are not deductible in calculating national insurance contributions).
(d) A tax-free lump sum can be paid from the scheme to the employee on retirement.
(e) Provision can be made for a lump sum to be paid on an employee's death in service, which is usually free of taxation (see page 198).
(f) The income of the fund is not liable to income tax and the capital gains are not liable to capital gains tax.

Retirement age

Normal retirement age may be any age between 60 and 75. (For schemes approved before 25 July 1991, the normal retirement age is 55 for women and 60 for men, with an upper limit for both of 70.) Early retirement may be allowed from age 50 and is also permitted for incapacity.

Maximum contributions

Except for the new 'off-the-peg' simplified schemes (see above), few pension schemes are money purchase schemes. The maximum combined contributions of employer and employee to an off-the-peg money purchase scheme are 17½% of the employee's earnings, of which the employer must contribute some and the employee cannot contribute more than 15%. For other money purchase schemes, contributions to produce the maximum permitted benefits on retirement may currently be calculated on a level premium basis, thus enabling a substantial fund to be built up at an early stage. The Revenue is, however, considering moving to a percentage of salary basis.

For final salary schemes, there is no specific upper limit on the amount that an employer may contribute, subject only to the requirement that the benefits provided as a result are within the permitted levels and the contributions are not excessive in relation to those benefits. Regulations were, however, introduced in 1987 to prevent schemes being overfunded (see page 200).

If an employee joins a scheme late, it is possible to make contributions of several times the employee's current remuneration in order to fund the maximum benefits. Inflation-proofing may be provided for. Special irregular contributions may be made by the employer in addition to the normal annual contributions. Such irregular contributions may, if they are very large, have to be spread forward over a maximum of four years in calculating the employer's taxable profits, rather than all the relief being given in the year of payment.

Whilst it is not necessary for an employee to be required to contribute to a scheme, where he does so the contributions (including any additional or special contributions to obtain additional benefits) must not exceed 15% of his remuneration. For new schemes set up on or after 14 March 1989 and for those joining existing schemes on or after 1 June 1989, there is a limit (referred to as the earnings cap) on the earnings on which contributions may be paid. This limit is increased annually in line with increases in the Retail Prices Index (note — not in line with increases in average earnings). For 1992/93 the limit is £75,000.

Additional voluntary contributions (AVCs)

The benefits available to an employee depend on the funds available in the employer's scheme. An employee wishing to increase his potential pension may pay additional voluntary contributions (AVCs) to the employer's scheme, or to a scheme of his choice (free-standing AVCs). Free-standing AVCs are paid net of basic rate tax and the Revenue pays the tax to the pension scheme. Any AVCs paid must not take the employee's total contributions to more than 15% of his salary (the salary being subject to the £75,000 limit previously mentioned for new schemes and new entrants to existing schemes). No part of the additional benefits earned may be taken as a tax-free lump sum, except for AVCs to an employer's scheme under a contract to purchase added years which will produce a precise level of pension and lump sum benefit and AVCs that are paid under arrangements made before 8 April 1987.

A free-standing AVC may be used to enable an employee to contract out of SERPS individually, even though his employer's scheme is contracted in. The AVC will be boosted by the DSS contracting out rebate, currently amounting to 5.8% (2% employee's contribution, 3.8% employer's contribution) of earnings between the national insurance lower and upper earnings levels, plus an additional 2% of those earnings. (Lower rebates will apply from 6 April 1993—see page 193.) The employee does not, however, get the benefit of an addition for tax relief on the payment by the DSS in respect of his 2% share of the contracting-out rebate. If an employee wishes to contract out of SERPS while remaining in his employer's scheme, it is therefore more sensible to do so by means of a personal pension plan, where the DSS 2% boost is grossed up for tax relief (see page 208).

Maximum benefits for employees

Basis for calculating maximum benefits

For off-the-peg money purchase schemes, there is no restriction on the benefits, since the restriction is made in the amount contributed. For other schemes, maximum benefits are measured in terms of 'final pensionable remuneration'. Final pensionable remuneration is the greater of the remuneration in any one of the five years before retirement (with averaging for fluctuating payments) or the average of total remuneration for any period of three or more consecutive years ended in the last ten years before normal retirement date. Remuneration includes taxable benefits in kind, but for those retiring on or after 17 March 1987 it does not include taxable amounts under share option or incentive schemes or lump sum termination payments.

Unless the 'final remuneration' is that of the twelve months ending with normal retirement date, each year's remuneration included in the calculation may be 'dynamised', i.e. increased in proportion to the increase in the Retail Prices Index for the period from the end of the year up to normal retirement date.

A director who, together with his defined family and trustees, has controlled 20% or more of the employing company's voting rights at any time in the last ten years cannot use a 'best of the last five years' final remuneration calculation and must instead use the three consecutive year averaging of earnings, but the increases from indexing may be taken into account. This averaging provision also applies with effect from 6 April 1987 to employees whose 'final pensionable remuneration' would otherwise exceed £100,000. Those who retired before 6 April 1991 could, however, use their 1986/87 remuneration instead if it gave a higher figure.

For new schemes set up on or after 14 March 1989, and those joining existing schemes on or after 1 June 1989, there is an index-linked ceiling, £75,000 from 6 April 1992, on final remuneration taken into account for calculating benefits.

Maximum pension

The maximum pension payable under final salary schemes is 2/3rds final remuneration, at the rate of 1/30th for each year's service up to 20 years. For members of an existing scheme at 16 March 1987, the maximum can apply after 10 years' service. Inflation-proofing may be provided for within the funding of the scheme. Under provisions in the Social Security Act 1990, pension rights built up from a date to be fixed must be inflation-proofed in line with the Retail Prices Index, up to a limit of 5% per annum. (See also page 200 under Pension scheme surpluses.) The introduction of inflation-proofing has been delayed pending a decision on equalising pension ages for men and women. Part of the pension may be commuted for a lump sum (see below).

Pensions from other schemes

Benefits at the 1/30th per year rate (or accelerated rate for members of pre-16 March 1987 schemes) may usually be provided in addition to any pension benefits from previous occupations or self-employment pension plans, providing the combined benefits do not exceed 2/3rds of final remuneration.

Lump sums

Part of the maximum available benefits may be commuted to a lump sum. The maximum lump sum is normally 3/80ths final remuneration for each year of service up to 40, giving a maximum of 1½ times final remuneration, but this may be varied or restricted depending on when the employee joined the scheme.

For those joining schemes after 16 March 1987 but before 14 March 1989 (1 June 1989 for schemes in existence at 14 March 1989), there is an overall limit of £150,000.

For schemes set up on or after 14 March 1989 and those who join existing schemes on or after 1 June 1989, the lump sum cannot exceed 1½ times the 'earnings cap' figure of £75,000 (index-linked), giving a maximum lump sum of £112,500 using current figures. There is also an alternative to the 3/80ths calculation. If it gives a higher figure, the lump sum is calculated as two and a quarter times the amount of the pension before commutation. This enables late entrants to get the maximum lump sum as well as maximum pension in appropriate circumstances—see example 1.

Example 1

An employee retires after 25 years service, his final remuneration being £80,000.

If his pension entitlement is based on the rules applicable from 14 March 1989, the maximum pension is 2/3rds × £75,000 (since he has completed 20 years' service) = £50,000.

The maximum lump sum is the greater of:

3/80 × £75,000 × 25	£70,313
2¼ × £50,000	£112,500

The maximum lump sum is therefore £112,500.

In calculating the maximum lump sum payment, lump sums from earlier employments must be taken into account. If dynamised final remuneration is used to calculate the pension, it may also be used to calculate the lump sum. If a lump sum is to be taken, the maximum pension of 2/3rds final remuneration must be reduced.

Provision for dependants

Provision for dependants may be made both in respect of death in service and for death after retirement. Inflation increases may be provided for in both cases. A pension to a surviving spouse may continue for the spouse's lifetime, but children's pensions must cease when they reach age 18 or cease full-time education.

Death in service

When an employee dies in service, a lump sum not exceeding four times final remuneration (which is defined in a more generous way than for other benefits) may normally be paid without attracting inheritance tax. In addition, the employee's own contributions to the pension scheme may be repaid with interest. The pension scheme trustees usually have discretion as to who receives the death in service lump sum, but they generally act in accordance with the employee's known wishes. There may be an inheritance tax problem where the death benefit is to be held in trust for the employee's dependants, because if the employee dies in service after the earliest age at which he could have retired, the capital value of the pension he could have taken immediately before death may be taken into account for inheritance tax. The Revenue have, however, stated that this will not apply in genuine cases of deferred retirement, and will only apply where there is evidence that the intention of deferring benefits was to increase the estate of someone else.

Pensions may also be paid to the surviving spouse and/or dependants. The pension paid to any one person cannot exceed two thirds of the maximum pension the employee could have received if he had retired on incapacity grounds at the date of death (with potential service up to normal retirement age being taken into account). The total pensions to spouse and dependants cannot exceed the total incapacity pension the employee could have received.

Death after retirement

Provision may be made for an employee's pension to continue for a set period after retirement despite his earlier death. Separate pensions for spouse and dependants can also be provided, subject to the individual pensions not exceeding two-thirds of the maximum pension that could have been approved for the employee and the total pensions not exceeding the whole of that maximum. Lump sum benefits will not normally be permitted.

Unapproved pension schemes

Before the Finance Act 1989, it was not possible for an employer to have both an approved pension scheme and an unapproved pension scheme if the combined benefits exceeded those permitted for approved schemes, even though no tax advantages were derived from the unapproved scheme. From 27 July 1989, it has been possible to set up such 'top-up' schemes. But since they do not carry any tax advantages, it seems likely that most employees would prefer increased salary so that they could invest it or not as they wished.

Changing employment

When you change employment, then providing you have accrued benefits for at least two years, you may either have a preserved pension which will become payable on retirement, or a transfer payment to a new scheme (if the scheme will accept it) or to an insurance company or to a personal pension plan. Where there is a preserved pension, then for service from 1 January 1985 onwards, the pension must be increased each year in line with the increase in retail prices (or by 5% if less). For contracted-out schemes, the employer must ensure that the pension must at least equal the guaranteed minimum pension under the State scheme.

Refunds of contributions are not usually available except for contributions made before April 1975 or for periods of employment of less than two years, but where they are made tax is deducted at the rate of 20%.

Pension scheme surpluses (TA 1988, ss 601–603 and Sch 22)

Regulations came into force on 7 April 1987 concerning pension scheme surpluses. A fund is in surplus where an objective actuarial valuation, in accordance with guidelines specified by the Government Actuary, shows that the projected value of the scheme's assets is more than 5% higher than the projected cost of paying pension benefits to members. The trustees are required to reduce the surplus at least to the 5% level by any combination of:

 (i) increases in pension benefits (within the permissible limits);
 (ii) a reduction or suspension of contributions by the employer and/or employees for up to five years; and
(iii) a refund to the employer.

If a refund is made, it cannot reduce the surplus to *below* 5%. The trustees are required to deduct 40% tax at source from any refund they make to the employer and pay it over to the Revenue within 14 days. Interest is charged for late payment. In no circumstances can a company obtain a repayment of the 40% tax because of trading losses or other available reliefs.

Under new provisions in the Social Security Act 1990, effective from a date which has not yet been fixed, scheme surpluses must first be used under heading (i) to provide inflation proofing up to a 5% limit for pension rights already accrued, including pensions already in payment. Action under headings (ii) and (iii) (contribution holiday or refunds) cannot be taken unless the scheme has been inflation-linked to the required level.

Self-administered pension schemes (SI 1991/1614)

A self-administered pension scheme is one where the contributions remain under the control of trustees appointed by the company, as distinct from being paid to a life assurance company. While it gives maximum flexibility in managing a fund, the pension scheme trustees must invest in the best interests of the members in order to provide their pension benefits. It is possible to have what are often called hybrid schemes where the funds are partly managed by a life assurance company. The fund will also usually hold life assurance cover on the scheme members so that its funds are not unacceptably diminished by the premature death of a member.

A self-administered scheme may borrow up to an amount which is the equivalent of three times the normal annual contribution which it receives from the company plus 45% of the scheme assets. This could be helpful in boosting its funds for, say, the purchase of premises for use by the company. The borrowing is paid off by future annual contributions from the company, and in the meantime the interest cost is covered by the rent charged by the pension fund to the company.

Loans to pension scheme members or their families are forbidden, but loans to the company itself, or to buy shares in it, or the purchase by the trustees and leaseback of the company's premises, may be permitted (subject to certain restrictions), providing the scheme has less than 12 members, each of whom is a trustee, and each of whom gave written agreement in advance to the proposed investment.

Specialist advice is essential for such schemes.

Tax points

- Contributions by employers to approved pension schemes are one of the few non-taxable benefits for employees earning £8,500 per annum or more and directors, so generous funding of a scheme within the permitted limits is particularly beneficial to them.

- A family company can have a pension scheme for its controlling directors. The contribution limits are less restrictive than those for personal pension plans.

- A family company may be able to eliminate taxable trading profits by contributions to an approved scheme, and perhaps create a trading loss for carry-back. But watch the provisions mentioned on page 195 for the spreading forward of contributions for relief purposes.

- Younger people should remember that once AVCs have been paid into a scheme, they cannot be recovered—you will not benefit from them until you retire.

- If you are young and highly mobile, a personal pension plan may be preferable to an employer's scheme because you will be able to take it with you from job to job, whereas there may be problems transferring a fund from one occupational scheme to another. But there is the disadvantage that your employer is unlikely to contribute to the personal plan, and also the higher administration charges involved.

- If someone deliberately fails to exercise a right in order for someone else or a discretionary trust to benefit, this counts as a transfer for inheritance tax at the latest time the right could be exercised. The value of the transfer is the value of the rights not taken up. This rule may catch some death in service lump sums under pension schemes if the death benefit was held in trust for the family and the employee had deliberately deferred retirement so that the family could benefit. See page 199.

- Where a pension is paid direct to a child, the child's personal allowance will be available to reduce the tax payable, making this more tax efficient than if the whole pension were paid to the surviving parent who then maintained the child, but the possible effect on other benefits available to the child, e.g. grant aid, must not be forgotten.

- Although benefits in kind may be reckoned in remuneration for calculating maximum pension benefits, dividends received from family companies by working directors may not. This needs to be taken into account in considering whether remuneration or dividends should be paid.

- In the case of a self-administered scheme, the Revenue will not approve the use of fund monies to acquire residential premises or to buy assets from scheme members, nor may the trustees sell assets to scheme members.

- Early retirement is available in many occupations. Those who retire before state pension age (65 for a man and 60 for a woman) may need to pay voluntary national insurance contributions to ensure that they get a full basic pension under the state scheme (see page 169). But providing they are registered as unemployed and available for work, contributions will be credited, and unemployed men over 60 are automatically credited with contributions without the need to be registered.

- If you are over 55, unemployment benefit is reduced to the extent that your occupational pension (or personal pension) exceeds £35 a week.

17
Providing your own pension

Background (TA 1988, ss 618–626 (old schemes), 630–655 (new schemes))

Since 1956, the self-employed and employees not in an employer's pension scheme have been able to get tax relief on premiums under a retirement annuity contract to provide their own pension (in addition to earning the state pension by paying national insurance contributions).

With effect from 1 July 1988, a new type of personal pension scheme was introduced. Those with continuing retirement annuity contracts still receive tax relief under the previous legislation. Most of the rules for old and new schemes are the same, but new schemes must make provision for transfers on change of employment/self-employment. Other differences are indicated later in the chapter.

From 11 October 1989, personal pension schemes may allow members to direct where their funds are to be invested, subject to various restrictions to ensure that the scheme still meets the conditions necessary for tax approval.

Qualifying individuals

Those who are self-employed, or who are not members of an employer's pension scheme, may contribute to a personal fund for themselves by paying premiums within stipulated limits to one or more pension providers, the premiums being accumulated in a fund free of income tax and capital gains tax. A person who has both pensionable and non-pensionable earnings may pay premiums in respect of the non-pensionable earnings, and husband and wife who each have non-pensionable earnings may make separate pension provision in this way.

For old schemes, the premiums have to be paid to an insurance company, but the pension provider under the new schemes can be a life assurance company, friendly society, bank, building society or unit trust. Under old and new schemes, the retirement benefits themselves are purchased from an authorised insurance company with the fund monies at retirement, and the 'best buy' available at that time can be selected.

It was not possible under the old rules for someone to be in both an occupational scheme and a personal scheme in respect of the same earnings. This also applies to the new pension plans, except where an employee uses a personal pension plan to contract out of the State Earnings Related Pension Scheme (SERPS) (see page 208).

Permissible benefits

The retirement benefits must commence not later than age 75 nor earlier than age 50 (60 for old schemes), except in cases of ill health or where the occupation is one in which earlier retirement is customary, for example entertainers and athletes, in which cases the Revenue may approve a scheme with an earlier retirement date.

At retirement a tax-free lump sum is permitted. For new schemes, the lump sum may not exceed one quarter of the fund. There is no overall maximum, but the index-linked limit for net relevant earnings (currently £75,000—see below) on which premiums can be based will itself limit the size of the pension fund. For old schemes, the maximum is three times the remaining annual pension, subject to an upper limit of £150,000 for old scheme contracts made between 17 March 1987 and 30 June 1988 inclusive.

It is possible for payment of the pension to be guaranteed for up to ten years even if the taxpayer dies within that time. Should death occur before retirement, the contributions are refunded, with or without interest and bonuses. The refund may be to the personal representatives or to any other person. Alternatively, the contract may provide for the death benefits to be held in trust, with the monies payable at the trustees' discretion. If paid to the personal representatives, the sum refunded will form part of the estate for inheritance tax purposes, but tax will not be payable to the extent that the estate is left to the surviving spouse. Inheritance tax will also usually be avoided where the proceeds are held in trust, but where someone works on past the earliest pension age under the policy with the deliberate intention of benefiting someone else, a charge to inheritance tax may arise as with an occupational scheme (see page 199).

Allowable contributions

Contribution limits are fixed by reference to 'net relevant earnings'. For a self-employed person, this means his tax adjusted profits, after deducting capital allowances, losses and any excess of business charges (such as his share of an annuity paid by a partnership to a retired partner) over general investment income. For an employee, net relevant earnings are his non-pensionable earnings, including benefits, but after deducting expenses allowable against those earnings. In line with the change for occupational schemes, an employee's relevant earnings under the new scheme exclude earnings under share option and incentive schemes and lump sum termination payments. An overall limit applies to net relevant earnings under the new scheme, the limit being £75,000 for 1992/93, in line with the new limit for occupational pensions. This figure is increased annually in line with inflation.

The maximum contributions which may be allowed as a deduction from relevant earnings in any one tax year for someone aged 35 or under (new schemes), or 50 or under (old schemes) are 17½% of the net relevant earnings, plus any unused relief for the previous six years. The percentage limit is increased for taxpayers over 36 (new schemes), 51 (old schemes) at the beginning of the tax year, as follows:

New schemes

	%
age 36 to 45	20
46 to 50	25
51 to 55	30
56 to 60	35
61 and over	40

Old schemes

	%
age 51 to 55	20
56 to 60	22½
61 and over	27½

Where someone has pension contracts both under the old and new schemes, the premium limits under the new scheme are reduced by any premium payments under the old scheme. For someone aged 53, for example, with net relevant earnings of £20,000, the maximum premiums under old scheme contracts would be 20%, i.e. £4,000, and if premiums of that amount were paid, the amount available for new scheme contracts would be reduced from £6,000 (i.e. 30% of £20,000) to £2,000.

The different age limits for new scheme and old scheme payments, and the fact that new scheme payments are subject to the earnings cap whereas old scheme payments are not, makes the calculation of maximum available premiums tricky in some cases. To work out the maximum personal pension contributions payable, add unused new scheme relief brought forward to the new scheme limit for the year and deduct any retirement annuity premiums paid. The unused new scheme relief carried forward is then the balance remaining after deducting the personal pension contributions paid. To work out the unused relief carried forward for retirement annuity premiums, any new scheme payments in the year are deducted. See example 1.

The opportunity of using unused past relief can substantially reduce or even eliminate the net relevant earnings for the tax year, but, as indicated in example 2, it is not necessary to utilise all the unused past relief in one year. Any contribution made uses up first the available relief for the current year, then any unused relief for the previous six years, earliest first.

Example 1

Man aged 53, with a personal pension contribution limit for 1992/
93 of 30% of £75,000 and a retirement annuity premium limit of
20% of £120,000 is in the following position:

Max PPC	Less RAP paid	Available	PPC paid	Unused relief c/fwd
£	£	£	£	£
22,500	10,000	12,500	6,500	6,000

Max RAP	Paid	PPC paid	Unused relief c/fwd
£	£	£	£
24,000	10,000	6,500	7,500

If the limits and earnings remained unchanged for 1993/94 (they
would not, in fact, because they are index-linked), the maximum
PPC for that year would be £22,500 + £6,000 b/fwd = £28,500,
reduced by any RAP paid, and the maximum RAP would be
£24,000 + £7,500 = £31,500.

Example 2

				£
Net relevant earnings in 1992/93				15,000
17½% thereof			2,625	

Unused relief for earlier years:

	Appropriate percentage of net relevant earnings, say	Less contributions already relieved for that year, say		
1991/92	3,500	2,000	1,500	
1990/91	2,500	2,200	300	
1989/90	2,900	1,700	1,200	
1988/89	3,000	1,000	2,000	
1987/88	2,000	500	1,500	
1986/87	2,200	1,400	800	
Maximum relief available for year 1992/93				9,925

The minimum contribution required for 1992/93 in order to avoid
wasting any unused relief would have to be:

	£
17½% of £15,000 (relevant earnings for 1992/93)	2,625
Unused relief for 1986/87	800
	£3,425

The unused relief for 1987/88 to 1991/92 inclusive would then be
available to increase the funding limit for 1993/94.

Employees making new scheme arrangements may elect to contract out of State Earnings Related Pension Scheme (SERPS), still, however, contributing for a basic retirement pension. See below. It is also possible for an employee in a contracted-in pension scheme to remain in the scheme but contract out of SERPS independently through a personal pension plan. See page 208.

Under the new scheme, an employer can contribute to the personal pension scheme of an employee, but the maximum contribution levels (17½% or higher) cover the combined contributions (but not those by the DSS—see below).

Backdating of contributions to earlier years

A contribution made in one tax year may, by election before 6 July following the end of that tax year, be treated for all purposes as a payment in the previous tax year (or, if there were no net relevant earnings in the previous year, as a payment made two years earlier). Thus in example 2, the contribution of £3,425 could have been paid wholly or partly in 1993/94 and by election treated as relating to 1992/93. This gives a breathing space to establish what the maximum allowable contribution is for a particular year, and also to provide the cash resources to make the payment. It is a useful provision since it is not possible to carry forward an excess of contributions, over the allowable limit, for relief in a later year. Indeed, under the new scheme, any excess contributions have to be refunded.

Contracting out of the State Earnings Related Pension Scheme (SERPS) by employees not in an employer's scheme

From 1 July 1988, such employees may contract out of SERPS by taking out an appropriate personal pension plan (i.e. one that satisfies conditions laid down in the Social Security Act 1986). The premium under the plan will be paid net of basic rate tax and the Inland Revenue will pay the tax into the plan. The employee and his employer will continue to pay full national insurance contributions, but the DSS will pay into the plan the contracting-out rebate (currently 5.8% of earnings between lower and upper levels), plus an incentive payment of a further 2% of those earnings. The 2% incentive payment is not, however, available to an employee who was in a contracted-out scheme for the two years immediately before the personal plan is taken out (or would have been but for his having left such a scheme voluntarily). Since personal pension plans qualify for tax relief whereas national insurance contributions do not, the DSS will also pay in tax relief on the gross equivalent of the employee's 2% share of the 5.8% rebate. See example 3.

The 2% incentive payment will be paid until 5 April 1993. Plans taken out before 6 April 1989 could be backdated to 6 April 1987, giving a maximum of six years for the incentive payments. The combined employer/employee contracting-out rebate is to be reduced to 4.8% from 6 April 1993. The withdrawal of the 2% incentive will be partly offset from that date for those over 30 by an extra rebate of 1%.

Example 3

Employee in non-pensionable employment who earns £250 a week contracts out of SERPS by contributing £12 a week to an appropriate personal pension plan.

Earnings on which contracting-out rebate is paid are £250 less £54 lower earnings level, i.e. £196.

Weekly investment in plan is as follows:

	£
Employee pays £12 less 25% tax (£3)	9.00
Inland Revenue pays in the tax relief of	3.00
DSS pays:	
Contracting-out rebate	
Employer's contribution 3.8% × £196	7.45
Employee's contribution 2% × £196	3.92
Tax relief on gross equivalent of employee's contribution (£3.92 × 100/75 @ 25%)	1.31
Incentive payment 2% × £196 (up to 5 April 1993)	3.92
	£28.60

The part of the pension funded by the DSS payment can only be paid from age 65 (60 for women), it cannot be commuted for a lump sum and it must include provision for index-linking and for widows'/widowers' pensions.

Contracting out of SERPS and remaining in an employer's scheme

An employee who is in an occupational scheme that is contracted in to SERPS may remain in the employer's scheme but opt out of SERPS by means of an individual personal pension plan. The way that this is done is that the employee and employer continue to pay full national insurance contributions, and the payment into the personal pension plan is made solely by the DSS, who contribute the same amount as indicated in example 3 for employees not in a pension scheme, i.e. currently 7.8% of the employee's earnings between the lower and upper earnings levels plus tax relief on the employee's share of the contracting-out rebate.

Funding the contributions

Two often expressed objections to personal pension provision are, first, the cost and, second, the fact that you cannot use the fund until retirement. Although it is not possible for a lender to take a charge on a personal pension fund, several pension providers have arrangements under which a lender will make an appropriate advance to a taxpayer with a sufficiently large accumulated fund, or who is paying regular contributions to a fund, usually in the latter case based on a multiple of recurrent contributions and the age of the taxpayer. The terms of the advance are usually that interest is payable year by year but capital repayments are taken from the eventual tax-free lump sum on retirement. Whether security for the borrowing is required often depends upon the trade or profession carried on by the taxpayer.

The loan could itself be used to fund contributions to the scheme, so that in example 2 (on page 206) a substantial part of the £9,925 maximum contribution might be funded from a loan made in conjunction with the pension scheme contribution arrangements.

Tax relief on the interest paid will be available if the borrowing is for a qualifying purpose, such as the acquisition of a main residence (limited to basic rate relief), a business property or a partnership share (see chapter 2), but not otherwise. There will thus not be any relief in the case of a loan used to pay pension scheme contributions.

Term assurance and pensions for dependants (TA 1988, ss 621, 636, 637)

The return of contributions on death prior to retirement is in itself a form of lump sum provision. The amount refunded is the gross contributions, usually with reasonable interest, whereas the cost to the payer was net of tax relief, so that a cash profit automatically arises. Clearly, the longer the contributions have been paid the greater the capital sum on death before retirement or lump sum following retirement.

To cover the possibility that death might occur before a reasonable sum has been built up, the taxpayer may also pay a premium to provide a lump sum on death before age 75. Such a policy may be written in trust, which has the advantage of making the sum quickly available instead of waiting for a grant of representation, and also avoids the sum assured swelling the estate for inheritance tax. Relief for premiums paid is given at the payer's top tax rate, thus giving opportunity for life cover with tax relief, even though tax relief is not now available on ordinary life assurance policies taken out after 13 March 1984.

Alternatively or additionally, a premium may be paid to provide a pension for dependants.

The allowable premiums for the term assurance (and/or dependants' pensions for old schemes) are subject to a limit of 5% of net relevant earnings, the 5% being part of, and not additional to, the 17½% (or higher because of age) limit (see above).

Way in which relief is given

Old scheme relief is given to the self-employed by deduction in the tax assessment and to employees by coding adjustment.

The way in which new scheme relief is given depends on whether the pension plan is taken out by a self-employed person or by an employee. Premiums paid by the self-employed are paid in full and tax relief is given in the assessment on the self-employed earnings. Premiums paid by employees are paid net of basic rate tax, and relief at the higher rate, where relevant, is given by coding adjustment. Where an employee contracts out of SERPS, however, there is no higher rate relief on the part of the DSS contribution that relates to the employee's contracting-out rebate.

Where basic rate tax is deducted at source by an employee, the relief is retained whether the employee is a taxpayer or not. This could give the opportunity for an employee with relatively low non-pensionable earnings to get tax relief on a substantial premium in one year, even though earnings were largely covered by the personal allowance.

Example 4

A married woman aged 40 has unused relief brought forward of £3,000. Her only income was a salary of £5,000 in 1992/93, giving an allowable premium for that year of £1,000. If she paid the maximum allowable premium of £4,000 gross, £3,000 net, the position would be:

	£
Salary	5,000
Personal pension premium paid	(4,000)
Personal allowance	(3,445)
Taxable income	Nil

Amount invested in pension fund is £4,000 at a net cost of £3,000.

Had she been self-employed, the maximum tax-efficient premium would have been £1,555 (i.e. £5,000–£3,445).

Late assessments and investigation settlements (TA 1988, ss 625, 642; Revenue Statement of Practice SP 9/91)

Assessments are sometimes made more than six years after the tax year to which they relate, usually owing to the fraudulent or negligent conduct of the taxpayer (see chapter 9). Where an assessment becomes final and conclusive more than six years after the tax year to which it relates, a taxpayer may utilise any unused relief created by the assessment to cover a contribution made in excess of the 17½% (or higher because of age) limit (see above) for the year of payment, provided that he both makes the contribution and makes an election within six months after the assessment becomes final and conclusive. Relief is then given against the earnings of the year of payment. (Only the contribution related to the unused relief need be made within the six-month period. The contribution under the normal rules could be made in the following year and carried back.)

Strictly, this relief is only available where assessments are formally determined, but the Revenue will usually allow it where an investigation settlement is concluded in the more usual way by their acceptance of an offer in respect of tax, interest and penalties rather than by the formal determination of assessments.

Tax points

- Contributions to personal pension plans attract tax relief at your top rate making them a highly efficient means of providing for the future.

- Consider replacing life cover with tax-efficient term assurance under the personal pension scheme rules. But remember that a term assurance can only provide a lump sum on death before age 75, not on surviving to a certain age as with an endowment policy.

- Also bear in mind that life assurance contracts taken out before 14 March 1984 will probably still entitle you to 12½% income tax relief on the premium payments, so it may be more appropriate to surrender later policies.

- An inheritance or unexpected windfall may be used to fund an exceptional personal pension scheme contribution supported by current earnings and unused past relief.

- Even though non-pensionable earnings have been eliminated by personal allowances, they still qualify as relevant earnings for the calculation of relief. Thus a working wife may have paid very little tax on modest earnings because of the wife's earned income relief or personal allowance, but those earnings can nonetheless create unused relief to support a pension contribution in a later year when her earnings have increased enough for the set-off to be beneficial. Also, if she is an employee, she can get tax relief on a premium even though all or part of her salary is covered by her personal allowances.

- Where someone who is UK resident has non-pensionable earnings abroad that escape tax because of the 100% deduction for long absences (see page 460), those earnings also create unused relief that can be used to cover a pension premium in the following six years.

- There are special rules for doctors and dentists, who, despite having to pay pension contributions under the National Health Service Acts, can also make personal pension scheme contributions along the lines of this chapter, subject to certain modifications because of the NHS pension contributions. The calculation rules are complicated and should be considered very carefully in deciding to what extent relief is available.

- Some building societies and other lenders will permit the borrower to pay only interest during the period of a loan, with an undertaking that the loan itself will be repaid from the tax-free lump sum on retirement.

- If, after retiring from a pensionable employment, you then have earnings from a non-pensionable employment, you may make further pension provision by paying contributions under a personal pension scheme.

- If a person works on after the earliest permitted retirement age under a pension contract and dies before drawing the pension, the value of the pension rights immediately before his death may be taken into account for inheritance tax—on the same grounds as those indicated on page 201 for employees in occupational schemes.

- Trading losses set off against other income (see chapter 25) must even so be taken into account in calculating unused relief by reducing the next available profits from the trade.

- If you retire early and register as unemployed, unemployment benefit is reduced to the extent that a personal pension or occupational pension exceeds £35 a week if you are over 55.

- Old scheme retirement annuity premiums may be fixed or variable. The Revenue have announced that they will give provisional relief against business profits for variable as well as fixed premiums without proof of payment, tax being not assessed or postponed accordingly. If the premium is not in fact paid, interest will arise on the tax that should have been paid.

18
Sole trader, partnership or company?

Non-tax considerations

When you start a new business the alternatives are to become a sole trader, to form a partnership with others or to form a limited liability company. A sole trader or partner is liable for the debts of the business to the full extent of his personal assets, and can in the extreme be made bankrupt. A company shareholder's liability is normally limited to the amount, if any, unpaid on his shares. Protection of private assets is usually one of the main reasons for commencing a new venture in the form of a company. However, lenders and landlords frequently require directors to give a personal guarantee in respect of the company's obligation, which reduces significantly the benefit of limited liability. There are also major compliance requirements for a company under the Companies Acts, including the need to prepare and publish audited accounts, which must be sent promptly to the Companies Registry (see page 117).

The general commercial and family considerations must be weighed alongside the comparative tax positions when choosing what form the business is to take.

Comparative income tax and national insurance position for the unincorporated trader and the company director

As a sole trader or partner, you will pay income tax at 40% on all your income (after personal allowances) in excess of £23,700, whether you leave the profits in the business or withdraw them. This threshold is available to each of a husband and wife partnership. If you are a controlling director/shareholder you can decide how much profit to take in the form of remuneration or dividends (on which you will pay income tax) and how much to leave to be taxed at corporation tax rates. (Your remuneration need not be withdrawn from the company, it can be left to your credit on loan account. The important point is whether more tax will be paid overall if it is treated as your personal income rather than as company profit.) The corporation tax rate on profits up to £250,000 is 25% (see page 26 for further details). Once profits reach a certain level, therefore, it is better from the immediate tax point of view to operate as a company, to take advantage of the lower company tax rates.

But you also need to look at the national insurance position. A sole trader or partner pays class 2 national insurance contributions of £5.35 a week, amounting to £278 in 1992/93, and class 4 contributions of 6.3% on profits between £6,120 and £21,060, giving a maximum class 4 liability for 1992/93 of £941. The maximum total class 2 and class 4 contributions for 1992/93 are therefore £1,219. However, half of the total class 4 contributions may be deducted in arriving at taxable income, thus saving tax at your marginal rate on that amount (the maximum net of tax contributions for a basic rate taxpayer being around £1,100). In a husband and wife partnership both have to pay class 4 national insurance contributions. They also both have to pay class 2 contributions unless the wife elected not to do so on or before 11 May 1977 and holds a certificate of exemption. The national insurance contributions on remuneration drawn from a company depend on the earnings (see page 173). The employee's contribution is 2% on the first £54 of weekly earnings and 9% on the next £351 up to the upper earnings limit of £405 per week. The employer's contribution is 10.4% on all earnings if they are £190 per week or more. If remuneration of £21,060 is taken (i.e. the upper limit for employee's contributions, £405 × 52), the combined employer's and employee's contributions in 1992/93 would be £3,889. The employer's share (£2,190) is, however, allowable as a deduction in calculating the profits of the company which are liable to corporation tax (reducing the figure to around £3,340 with corporation tax at 25%). In broad terms, the extra national insurance cost of operating through a company at that profit level is therefore around £2,200.

Three other points should be borne in mind. Some benefits, in particular unemployment benefit and earnings-related retirement pension, are not available to the self-employed. Earnings as a director or employee are required to be 'wholly and exclusively for the purposes of the trade', so particularly where a wife or husband does not work full-time in a business, the earnings may be challenged by the Revenue as excessive. There is no such requirement for a wife or husband who is an active partner, albeit working less than full-time, although artificial arrangements will not work (see page 275). Capital gains tax retirement relief on a company shareholding is only available to full-time working directors. Part-time directors do not qualify (see page 50). Again, there are no such restrictions where a partner working less than full-time disposes of all or part of his partnership interest.

The profit level at which the retentions after tax and national insurance will be less operating through a company than as a sole trader or partner is not a static figure but one which will vary according to how much remuneration is drawn from the company. Example 1 shows that if a married man draws a salary of £28,865 from a company to leave him with taxable income equal to the basic rate band of £23,700, the profit level at which the company format equates with that of an individual trader is £48,328. The turning point would be at a lower profit level on a salary of less than £28,865 and a higher

Example 1

Business profits before tax and national insurance are £48,328. A sole trader is liable to income tax on the full amount. If a company director drew a salary of £28,865 in equal monthly amounts during 1992/93 (which after married man's allowances totalling £5,165 leaves income of £23,700 to use the lower and basic rate tax bands), the comparative position is:

		Trader	Company director
Profits/remuneration		48,328	28,865
Personal allowances	5,165		5,165
½ class 4 NI	471	5,636	
Taxable income		42,692	23,700
Tax thereon: On 2,000 @ 20%	400		400
21,700 @ 25%			5,425
18,992 @ 40%	7,597		
42,692			
		13,422	5,825
Class 2 NI (flat rate)		278	Employee's NI
Class 4 NI (maximum)		941	(maximum) 1,699
Total personal tax and NI		14,641	7,524

Company's tax and NI:

Profits	48,328	
Less: Director's remuneration	(28,865)	
Company's NI thereon	(3,002)	3,002
Taxable profits	16,461	
Tax thereon @ 25%	(4,115)	4,115
	12,346	
Total tax and NI liabilities	£14,641	£14,641
Drawn or undrawn profits	33,687	33,687
	£48,328	£48,328

Each extra £1 of profit would cost the sole trader 40p in tax and the company 25p.

Possible further tax liabilities if company retentions of £12,346 are paid out:
   If distributed as dividends, maximum of
      (40–25)% on £16,461 (basic rate tax being imputed
      from company's corporation tax)   £2,469
   If taxed as capital gains, 40% on £12,346   £4,938

level on a salary above £28,865 (and would in any event be nearly double for a husband/wife partnership). There could, however, be further tax liabilities on the company retentions at a later date, but these may never materialise, through changes in tax rates, exemptions etc., and in the meantime cash will have been conserved in the company.

Timing of tax payments (TA 1988, ss 5, 10, 60)

Individuals (including partners) are normally assessed to tax on the basis of the profits earned in the accounts year ending in the previous tax year, but at the rates in force during the tax year itself. The tax is generally payable in two equal instalments on 1 January in the tax year and on 1 July following. Depending on the choice of accounting date, there can be a gap of anything from nine to nearly twenty-one months between earning the profits and paying the first instalment.

Companies, on the other hand, are charged to corporation tax at the rate in force during the accounting period when the profits are earned, and they are required to pay the tax nine months after the end of the accounting period, except where assessments are issued late, in which case the due date is 30 days after the issue of the assessment. Furthermore, director's remuneration will be subject to tax and national insurance under the PAYE scheme immediately it is paid or credited to the director's current account.

Unincorporated businesses thus have considerable cash flow advantages. They may also benefit from lower tax rates and thresholds in the year of assessment compared with those in force when the profits were earned, although tax rates can of course go up as well as down.

Effect of basis period rules for individuals (TA 1988, ss 61–63)

The profits of an unincorporated business are assessed to tax more than once in the opening years of a new business, with a corresponding drop out of profits for an equivalent time when the trade ceases. The possible advantages to the taxpayer are dealt with in chapter 21.

No such planning opportunities are available to a company, whose profits are taxed once and once only.

Losses (TA 1988, ss 380–385, 393, 574–576; FA 1991, s 72; TCGA 1992, s 253)

If a new business is expected to make losses in its early years, it is essential to bear in mind the different loss reliefs available to individuals and to companies. (These are dealt with more fully in chapters 25 and 26.)

Reliefs available to individuals in respect of trading losses in a new business are generous. Losses incurred in any of the first four tax years of a new business may be carried back to set against *any* income of the previous three tax years, earliest first, and a tax repayment obtained, enhanced by a tax-free repayment supplement. For losses in later years (or instead of a carry-back claim for opening year losses) a claim may be made to set them against the total income of the tax year in which the loss is sustained or the next following year, resulting in the discharge or repayment of tax. The losses may be boosted, or indeed created, by capital allowances. From 6 April 1991, trading losses may be set against capital gains in some circumstances. Unrelieved trading losses may always be carried forward to set against future trading profits of the same trade. Married couples used to be able to avoid wasting personal allowances by restricting claims to the lossmaker's income, but with the introduction of independent taxation of husband and wife from 6 April 1990, it is no longer possible for a husband to set his losses for the tax year 1990/91 onwards against his wife's income or vice versa.

If trading losses are sustained in a new company, they may only be set against any current profits of the company, such as bank interest or chargeable gains, or carried forward against the company's later trading profits. Trading losses of an established company may be set against the profits from other sources, if any, in the same accounting year, then against the total profits of the previous three years, with any balance being carried forward against trading profits. The extended carry-back period makes the trading loss relief available to an established company more generous than that available to established unincorporated businesses.

Funds introduced to a limited company to support losses, either as share capital or on loan, do not qualify for any immediate relief (but see pages 12 and 13 as regards relief for interest payable on any borrowing to enable the funds to be introduced). There are two relieving measures for shares and loans, but they are only available when shares are disposed of or when money lent becomes irrecoverable. The provisions are as follows:

(a) An individual can set a capital loss on the disposal of shares that he had subscribed for in an unquoted trading company against any of his income in the same way as a trading loss, as an alternative to being set against capital gains.
(b) The loss of money loaned to the company (or paid to cover a bank guarantee) may be deducted against the lender's capital gains.

To get the first relief, you need to dispose of the shares, or they need to have become virtually worthless, probably because the business has failed. The second relief is also only likely to be available because the company is in financial difficulties. The distinction between the shares relief being given against income and the loan relief only against capital gains is important, because relief against income gives more flexibility and the opportunity for early relief. With income and capital gains tax rates now being the same, consideration of the tax rate at which the loss is relieved is of less significance.

These two relieving measures are available both to working directors and to others providing funds to a company.

Pensions

If you are self-employed, you are entitled to relief at your top rate of tax on premiums paid to provide a pension when you retire. The maximum allowable premium is presently between 17½% and 40% of your profits (subject to a £75,000 ceiling for 1992/93 – see page 204), depending on your age. If the maximum premium is not paid in any year, the unused relief may be carried forward to support premium payments for the next six years. Company directors/employees in non-pensionable employment can also take advantage of these provisions, but it is often preferable for a family company to operate its own pension scheme.

Company pension schemes are less restrictive in that the only limit on the company's contributions is that the retirement benefits provided must not exceed certain limits and the scheme must not be overfunded. The company scheme can be contributory or non-contributory, the company's contributions being deductible in arriving at the company's taxable profits and the individual's contributions, if any, being allowed against his earnings from the company (although not deducted from pay in calculating employers' and employees' national insurance contributions).

For details on company and personal pension schemes, see chapters 16 and 17.

Capital gains (TCGA 1992, ss 163–165 and Sch 6)

Where chargeable gains are realised which cannot be eliminated by available reliefs, the first £5,800 of the total gains in 1992/93 are exempt from tax for individuals (£5,800 each for husband and wife), tax being charged at the appropriate income tax rate of 20%/25%/40% on the remainder. Companies are not entitled to any exemption and pay corporation tax on the full amount. The rate of tax on the company's gains for the year to 31 March 1993 is therefore either the small companies rate of 25%, the full rate of 33% or the marginal rate of 35% if profits lie between £250,000 and £1,250,000. ACT on dividends may, however, be set against the corporation tax on capital gains. This means that the effect of gains being realised within a company depends on the company's tax rate and the way in which the gains are passed to the shareholder. The possible effect if the gains are passed on as a dividend is shown in example 2. If the gains are retained within the company until the shareholder disposes of his shares or the company goes into liquidation, the shareholder will be liable to capital gains tax on the increase in value of his shareholding, and since the gain will have borne corporation tax when it was made this would effectively give a double tax charge. Reliefs may, however, be available at the time the shares are disposed of (see below).

Whether or not a business is incorporated, the increase in the value of its chargeable assets may lead to chargeable gains in the future, but in the case of a company this applies more so where assets are swelled by profit retentions. Death is an effective, albeit unwelcome, way of escaping capital gains tax liabilities. Legatees effectively take over the assets at their market value at the date of death and thus get a tax-free uplift in base cost where values have risen.

Example 2

Company makes a gain of £10,000 in year to 31 March 1993, which is passed on to shareholders as a dividend.

	Rate of tax on profits		
	25%	33%	Marginal rate of 35%
	£	£	£
Company gain	10,000	10,000	10,000
Corporation tax	(2,500)	(3,300)	(3,500)
Leaving for cash dividend	7,500	6,700	6,500
Tax credit on dividend at 25/75ths	2,500	2,233	2,167
Shareholder's income	10,000	8,933	8,667
Maximum income tax @ 40%	4,000	3,573	3,467
Leaving shareholder with net cash of	£6,000	£5,360	£5,200
Combined company and personal tax	£4,000	£4,640	£4,800
i.e.	40%	46.4%	48%

The total tax on the gain could therefore be anything from Nil (if the company is liable to tax at small companies rate and shareholder is entitled to refund of tax credit because of available personal reliefs) to 48%.

Less drastically, two important reliefs lessen the capital gains tax impact, and both reliefs are available to sole traders, partners and company shareholders who are full-time working directors.

Subject to certain restrictions, gains on the disposal of a business, or of an interest in a business, or of shares in your family trading company are exempt up to a maximum of £150,000, with 50% exemption on gains between £150,000 and £600,000, if you are over 55 (or if you are forced to retire before age 55 through ill health). A family company is one in which your personal shareholding is at least 25%, or in which your family hold more than 50%, your own shareholding being at least 5%.

If you make gifts of chargeable business assets, the gifts are treated as disposals at open market value, which may give rise to chargeable gains.

Tax on the gains may, however, be deferred by a joint election by you and the donee, so that the donee effectively takes over your base cost. For those entitled to retirement relief, the gifts relief may be used to cover gains in excess of that relief.

See chapter 4 for a fuller treatment of these provisions.

Inheritance tax (IHTA 1984, ss 103–114)

There is usually no inheritance tax to pay on gifts in lifetime or on death of all or part of your business, whether you operate as an individual or through a company. For transfers on and after 10 March 1992, business property relief is available at the rate of 100% on transfers of all or part of an individual's business and on transfers out of unquoted shareholdings of more than 25% (providing any lifetime gifts of such property, or qualifying replacement property, are still retained by the donee when the donor dies). Shares on the Unlisted Securities Market count as unquoted shares. For details, see chapter 5.

If you want to pass on your business gradually to other members of the family, the company format has the edge in terms of flexibility, since it is easier to transfer shares than to transfer a part of an unincorporated business. You should, however, bear in mind that if your own shareholding, together with that of your spouse, falls to 25% or less, any subsequent transfers which prove to be chargeable will only qualify for business property relief of 50%.

Raising finance (TA 1988, ss 289–312)

The business expansion scheme currently gives a company an advantage over an unincorporated business in attracting funds from outside investors. Some types of business are excluded, such as leasing and financial services and there is generally a limit of £750,000 on the amount which can be raised in a tax year or a period of six months spanning two tax years. There are also restrictions for companies with a high asset backing in land and buildings, and where assets are held primarily for investment purposes rather than for trading. Where applicable, the scheme offers relief from income tax for investment by individuals in new ordinary share capital of an unquoted trading company. The maximum amount for which an individual can obtain relief in this way in a tax year is £40,000 (£40,000 each for husband and wife), some of which can be carried back from the next tax year. The company need not be a new company. There is a minimum investment of £500 in any one company, but this limit does not apply when the investment is made through a Revenue approved investment fund. The scheme is being withdrawn on 31 December 1993. The detailed rules are in chapter 29.

Tax points

- Don't let the tax tail wag the commercial dog. Consider *all* aspects of alternative business forms.

- If profits are at or above the £50,000 level, operating through a company will reduce the tax rate on retained profits up to £250,000 from the top income tax rate of 40% to the corporation tax rate of 25%. There are long-term factors to consider, but these will probably be outweighed by the short-term advantage.

- Unincorporated businesses can have significant cash flow advantages over companies when it comes to the due date of paying tax.

- A slow start is particularly advantageous to an unincorporated business because of the multiple assessment of the early profits. A transfer to a company when the business has prospered can be timed to maximise the benefit of the corresponding profits that escape tax.

- The loss rules for individuals, particularly the three year carry-back of new business losses, make an unincorporated start an attractive proposition where there is heavy initial expenditure, particularly on revenue items but also on capital items which attract tax allowances. The business can later be converted to a company if appropriate.

- A company with growth potential may currently attract funds from investors because of the tax advantages to them of the business expansion scheme.

- To get income tax relief on a capital loss where shares are disposed of in an unquoted trading company, the shares must have been issued *to you* by the company. Shares acquired by transfer from a previous shareholder do not qualify.

- The possible double tax charge where a company first sells chargeable assets, thus increasing the value of its shares, can be avoided by shareholder/directors retaining personal ownership of assets such as freeholds or leaseholds and allowing the company to use them. See chapter 27 for the effect of charging rent.

- Although chargeable gains are now taxed at income tax rates, they are none the less still chargeable gains. Thus, business expansion scheme relief and allowances for buildings in enterprise zones cannot be set off against them. But a dividend from a company, even if payable out of a capital profit, counts as income in the hands of the shareholder, and these reliefs would then be available for set-off, with an appropriate repayment of the tax credit attaching to the dividend.

- The way self-employed profits are charged to tax is under review and may be changed, although probably not for some time. The changes could take away some of the advantages of the self-employed format. There are currently no proposals to alter the national insurance treatment.

19
Starting up a new small or part-time business

Is it a self-employment?

It is important to establish at the outset whether your activities amount to self-employment or whether the income should be assessed as that of an employee, or as income from neither self-employment nor employment, but as a casual receipt assessable under the 'any other income' provisions (for example writing the occasional article, but not often enough to be regarded as an author), or indeed whether the activity is taxable at all.

The distinction between employment and self-employment is important principally in deciding whether tax and employees' national insurance should be deducted from payments (and employers' national insurance paid), what expenses may be deducted from the income in calculating the tax liability, and whether the recipient should register for VAT.

The main distinction between employment and self-employment used to be whether the contract was a contract of service chargeable under Schedule E or a contract for services entitling you to payment against your invoice or fee note, chargeable under Schedule D, Case I or II. But the decision is now not so clear-cut, and many factors other than the form of the contract are taken into account. Factors pointing to employment are that you work wholly or mainly for one business, you need to carry out the work in person, you have to take orders as to how and when to do it, to work where those providing the work tell you to, and to work set hours at an hourly, weekly or monthly rate, and you get paid for overtime, sickness and holidays. Factors pointing to self-employment are that you risk your own capital and bear any losses arising, you control whether, how, when and where you do the work, provide your own equipment, are free to employ others to do the work and are required to bear the cost of correcting anything that goes wrong. None of these factors is conclusive and all the circumstances have to be taken into account. The decision affects your status both for income tax and national insurance, and a decision taken by one department will be accepted by the other. The tax/national insurance treatment is not, however, conclusive for VAT.

You can challenge a ruling by the Revenue, the DSS or Customs that you are an employee, and some taxpayers have recently had some success, but it could be costly and time consuming. The Revenue have recently targeted the theatrical profession for particular scrutiny. From 6 April 1990, entertainers on standard Equity contracts will be treated as employees, unless they joined the profession before 6 April 1987 and comply with various conditions, in which case they may continue to be taxed as self-employed. Agents' fees (including VAT) paid by entertainers are, however, specifically allowed as a deduction from employment earnings from 6 April 1990 (subject to an overall maximum deduction in any tax year of 17½% of the employee's earnings) (TA 1988, s 201A). For VAT, particular care is needed with licensing and franchise arrangements, and even if someone is regarded as self-employed, they may be treated as the agent of the licensor/franchisor, so that the VAT liability is decided by reference to the licensor's/franchisor's VAT status. In two recent cases involving driving instructors, the instructors in one were held to be agents (even though accepted as self-employed by the Revenue and DSS), while the others were held to be self-employed principals. And in two hairdressing cases, one group of stylists working under a franchise arrangement were treated as self-employed principals, whereas the others were held to be agents of the salon owner.

Many businesses which use part-time assistance are justifiably wary of paying fees in full, since they could be held liable for the PAYE and national insurance they should have deducted if someone is later held to be an employee. Some businesses will, however, accept an assurance from a tax office or accountant that the income is included in self-employed accounts of the recipient and that the payment should not be taxed under PAYE.

Someone who occasionally buys and sells may contend that his activities do not amount to a trade but remain a hobby, a collector's activity or an investment (albeit profitable) such as collecting and restoring antique furniture, sometimes selling the occasional piece at a profit. It is important to establish that the Revenue agree with this contention and not to leave it until they make a challenge, otherwise you could be faced with interest and penalties for non-disclosure. It may be the Revenue rather than the taxpayer who take the view that an activity is a hobby, particularly where there are losses, because to accept that it is a commercial activity would open the way for loss reliefs against other income. Each case depends on the facts, with appropriate rights of appeal if the Revenue do not see it in the same way as the taxpayer.

Where a self-employment has been established, the following points should be borne in mind.

Computation of taxable profits

The detailed rules for calculating profits are in chapter 20. Chapter 22 deals with capital allowances for the purchase of buildings, equipment etc. A newly established business is often run from your home, perhaps using your existing car for any business travelling that is required. You can claim for the business proportion of car expenses, and also the business proportion of capital allowances on the value of the car when you started using it for business. You can also claim a deduction for business calls made from your home telephone. Where the business is conducted from your home, expenses of part of the home can be allowed against taxable profits if they are wholly and exclusively for the trade, so that a fixed proportion of, for example, the light and heat can be charged on the basis of the parts of the residence which are used only for the business, such as a study/office, surgery, workshop etc. But to do that implies that this proportion is not used as your home. You will therefore be liable to pay business rates on that part of the property, as well as paying the personal poll tax by reason of the rest of the property being your only or main home. The rates will be allowable against your profits. Business rates will not be charged if the business use does not materially detract from the domestic use, but you need to be able to show that the business use does not stop you continuing to use that part of the property for domestic purposes. Claiming a deduction for such expenses as light and heat might weaken your contention that there is no clear division between the business and private use. It is not possible to claim a deduction against profits for any part of the personal poll tax, because it is not a business expense.

If part of your property is treated as non-domestic, it will be outside the capital gains tax owner-occupier exemption. Any gain need not be charged to tax immediately if you sell the property and continue the business from a new residence, because a claim could be made for the gain to be regarded as reducing the cost for capital gains tax of the business part of the new residence (see page 48), although it would not be necessary to make that claim if the chargeable gain was covered by the annual capital gains tax exemption (see example 1).

Yet another possibility if you dispose of the property when you retire is retirement relief (see page 49).

Example 1

House bought April 1984 for £60,000, sold 10 April 1992 for £140,000, indexation allowance £33,960.
Used to April 1988 wholly as residence
     then 1/6th for self-employment
     for remainder of period

Total gain (140,000 − (60,000 + 33,960))   £46,040

Chargeable gain:
     Business use 1/6th for 4 years out
     of 8, $1/6 \times 4/8 \times £46,040$ £3,837

Covered by annual exemption of £5,800 unless already used.

Where the business is carried on from your home, but no part is used wholly and exclusively for the business, your capital gains tax owner-occupier exemption will not be affected, but it could be more difficult to establish a deduction for business expenses.

Employing staff (FA 1989, s 43)

If you employ staff in the business, you will need to operate the PAYE scheme (see chapter 10). The Revenue will supply you with all the necessary documentation. It is important to make sure that PAYE is operated properly, particularly where you take on casual or part-time employees. Even if you pay someone less than the tax and national insurance threshold, you must still deduct tax if they have significant other earnings. Form P46 must be completed for any employee who does not produce form P45 (employee's leaving certificate). In a new small business, the first employees are very often members of the family. If you employ members of your family, the salary payments must be both justified and paid. The Revenue will, for example, resist a contention that an amount drawn for housekeeping or personal use includes family wages, and will also be better able to challenge the validity of the expense if it is left as an amount owing rather than having actually been paid. Payments of wages must in any case be made within nine months of the end of the accounting period if they are to be allowed for tax against the profits of that period rather than a later period.

If family wages can be justified for the work done, they enable personal allowances to be used if not already covered by other income. Although the amount of the single person's allowance is £3,445, there will still be a cost unless the wages are kept below the national insurance level of £2,808 (see example 2).

Paying a wife below the national insurance threshold does mean that she is not building up any state pension entitlement in her own right, nor can she claim contributory benefits, but she will get a pension based on her husband's contributions when he is 65 and she is 60 (see page 170).

How are profits charged to tax?

Tax is payable in two equal instalments on 1 January in the tax year and 1 July following.

Since the first profits form the basis of several assessments (see page 239), a part-time start may help to reduce the tax burden so long as the transition from the part-time activity to full-time self-employment cannot be argued by the Revenue as the start of an entirely new trade.

Loss relief

If losses are incurred in the first four tax years of a new business, they may be carried back and treated as reducing any income of the previous three tax

Example 2

If a husband pays his wife a wage of £2,800 in 1992/93, it will reduce his profit for tax, his wife will pay no tax providing she has no other income, and neither he nor she will pay any national insurance contributions thereon. If he pays her an extra £645, making a wage of £3,445, he will save tax on the £645 against his profit and the wife will still pay no tax on it, but there will be a cost of paying it, as follows:

Employee's contributions:
2% of £2,808	56	
9% of £637	57	113

Employer's contributions 4.6%	158	
Less tax relief for expense against husband's profit, say 25%	40	118

Total national insurance cost	231
Offset by tax relief on extra wage of £645 against his profit, at say 25% (ignoring any possible saving in class 4 national insurance)	(161)
Net cost of paying extra £645	£70

years, earliest first, or set off against any other income and (from 6 April 1991) chargeable gains of the tax year of the loss or of the following year. Capital allowances may be taken into account in the loss claims.

See chapter 25 for details of the claims.

Pension provision

Earnings from a small business can support a personal pension premium, both in respect of the self-employed earnings and for the family employees. It does not matter that the self-employed taxpayer or family employee is also in separate pensionable employment. If you do not pay premiums out of early profits because you want to use the profits to build up the business, or for any other reason, the earnings will enable you to make a larger premium payment within the next six years, even if you paid no tax on the earnings when they were earned, because they were covered by allowances. See chapter 17 for details.

VAT registration

You need to register for VAT at the end of any month if your turnover in the previous twelve months exceeded £36,600. You are required to notify

Customs and Excise and you will then be registered unless you can show that your turnover will not exceed £35,100 in the coming twelve months. If you expect your turnover in the next *30 days* to exceed £36,600, you must register immediately. You need to watch these limits carefully because there are severe penalties for not complying with the rules. Even if your turnover is below the limit you may wish to register voluntarily in order to recover VAT input tax on your purchases. But this will not be to your advantage unless most of your customers are themselves VAT registered (see chapter 7).

National insurance

A self-employed person pays class 2 contributions, of £5.35 a week, and also class 4 contributions, at 6.3% on profits between £6,120 and £21,060 in the tax year 1992/93. The detailed provisions are in chapter 24. Note particularly the provisions for deferring contributions if you are both employed and self-employed. Neither deferment nor a refund affect the liability of the employer to pay employers' contributions.

If your self-employed earnings were below £2,900 in 1991/92 and your circumstances have not materially changed, or are expected to be below £3,030 in 1992/93, you can apply for a certificate of exception from Class 2 contributions (see chapter 24). But you need to consider the effect of not paying on your benefit entitlement, particularly retirement pension, and you may think it best to pay Class 2 contributions even though your earnings are small. Class 2 contributions may be refunded in some circumstances where the small earnings exception would have applied if claimed—see chapter 24.

Occasional earnings not treated as from self-employment

If you are not treated as self-employed, occasional earnings are taxed under Schedule D, Case VI according to the amount earned in the year itself, with a deduction for justifiable expenses. The tax is due on 1 January in the tax year. If you are also an employee, the Revenue will sometimes, for convenience, offset small amounts of occasional earnings against your tax allowances when arriving at your PAYE code number.

Any losses can technically be set off against any income from other sources charged under Case VI, but it is unlikely that there will be any, in which case the losses are carried forward to reduce any future Case VI profits.

Tax points

● Do not forget to show the self-employment on your tax return or delay in advising the Revenue and submitting accounts, otherwise interest for late payment of tax, and sometimes penalties for negligence, may arise. If your turnover is below £15,000 you can send in a simple three-line account—see page 107.

- Similarly, wages paid to your wife from your self-employment should be shown on her tax return.

- When starting a new self-employment, remember that the profits of the first trading period will form the basis of several assessments, so that establishing a sound business base rather than pursuing maximum available profits will reduce the tax bills for the first few years. These rules are currently under review, so the advantage may not be available to future new businesses.

- If early earnings are small and covered by allowances, they can still create unused relief for personal pension premium purposes, enabling you to pay a larger premium later on when you can afford to do so (see chapter 17). The same applies to small earnings of a spouse.

- Disabled people and people who have been on the unemployment register for six weeks or more, or on certain Government training schemes, may be entitled to a cash allowance called the Enterprise Allowance if they become self-employed, subject to criteria established by Training and Enterprise Councils. The weekly allowance is between £20 and £90 for between 26 and 66 weeks, depending on the potential the business is considered to have. To prevent the allowance being taxed more than once because of the opening year rules, it is taxed separately from the profit. It still counts as trading income for Class 4 national insurance contributions and personal pension premiums.

- The time limits for lodging DSS applications for deferral and exception from national insurance contributions are important, and applications have to be renewed each year. There could also be a cost of making late payments, either in lost or delayed benefits, or increased contributions. Class 2 repayments are now available to some people with small earnings, but again only if claimed within the time limit.

- A useful test on the self-employed status is whether there is a risk of loss as well as gain, normally implying self-employment; and whether you have to carry out corrective work without payment.

- The Inland Revenue and DSS each have one nominated officer at each office who is responsible for queries and decisions about employment status. A written decision made after investigation by one department will be accepted by the other so long as all the facts have been accurately and fully given and the circumstances remain the same.

- Do not forget to register for VAT if appropriate. You need to check at the end of every *month* to make sure that the annual turnover limit has not been exceeded. See chapter 7.

20
How are business profits calculated?

Background (TA 1988, ss 18, 832)

Trading profits are charged to tax under Schedule D, Case I. Profits from carrying on a profession or vocation are charged under Schedule D, Case II. The same rules are, however, used to calculate profits under both headings. It is usually obvious that a trade is being carried on, but the charge under Case I is extended beyond what would normally be regarded as trading. Trade is defined as including 'every trade, manufacture, adventure or concern in the nature of trade'. The definition is thus wide enough to cover occasional transactions and those to which an investment motive cannot be attributed.

Important indicators of possible trading, when there is any doubt, are the nature of the asset itself (whether it is income producing, or something you get enjoyment from owning, which will indicate investment rather than trading), your reason for acquiring it, how long you owned it, whether you worked on it to make it more saleable, your reason for selling and how often such transactions were undertaken.

General rules for computing profits (TA 1988, s 74)

Whether the business is that of an individual trader, a partnership or a company, profits are calculated according to normal commercial accounting rules unless those rules conflict with the Taxes Acts as interpreted by the courts. The two most important rules for expenses are firstly that they must be wholly and exclusively for the purposes of the trade, and secondly, that they must be of a revenue, and not capital, nature.

'Wholly and exclusively'

You cannot claim a deduction for an expense that is for both business and private purposes, such as the rental for a telephone that you use both for business and private calls, but part of a mixed expense may be wholly and exclusively for the purposes of the trade and thus be a valid deduction in calculating profits, such as the charges for the business telephone calls.

229

Some of the miles travelled in a car are wholly and exclusively for business, others are purely for private purposes, and others again may be partly both. No part of a business trip combined with a holiday satisfies the rule, even though the business derives benefit from the trip, but a conference fee within that trip might qualify. See example 1. The same applies to mixed business and living accommodation, where again it may be possible accurately to separate the business and private areas. Where expenditure is for the sole purpose of the business, any incidental private benefit would be ignored. So that if, for example, a trader went away to a two-day business conference, and went to the theatre in the evening, this would not invalidate the business purpose of the conference trip, unless the whole trip had been planned for mixed business/private purposes.

The Revenue might sometimes allow concessional relief for a part of mixed expenses but they are under no obligation to do so.

Example 1

A trader's recorded mileage in a twelve-month period of account was as follows:

Purely business journeys		5,000
Purely private journeys	4,000	
Home to business	2,000	
Journeys for combined business/private purposes	1,000	

		7,000

		12,000

Allowable business proportion is 5/12ths.

Where an employer incurs expenses that benefit employees or directors, the usual treatment is that the expenses are allowed in calculating the taxable profits of the employer, but are charged to tax on the employee or director (see chapter 10). Sometimes, directors' fees, wages paid or the cost of benefits provided to members of the family who do not work full-time may not be allowed in full if the payment is considered excessive in relation to the work done. It is also particularly important where a business employs family members that the wages payment is properly made (see page 225).

In the case of family and similar companies, a distinction must be drawn between company expenditure which benefits a shareholder who is a director and the payment by the company of the personal debts of the shareholder/director, for example school fees, private entertaining, or expenses of a private residence. Unless the amount has been treated as a payment of salary, the shareholder/director must reimburse the company for such payments and they are neither allowable business expenses nor assessable as benefits on the shareholder/director.

Capital or revenue

Revenue expenditure is an allowable expense against your profit (unless specifically prohibited).

A capital expense cannot be deducted in calculating profits, although many items of capital expenditure may attract capital allowances (see chapter 22). The usual definition of a capital expense is one made 'not only once and for all, but with a view to bringing into existence an asset or an advantage for the enduring benefit of the trade'. One person's stock in trade will be another person's fixed assets. Your business premises are clearly a capital item, but if you build and sell factories, they will be trading stock and the cost will be taken into account in calculating your profit. Cars used by you and your employees will be capital items, but cars held for sale by a motor dealer will be trading stock. Normally, repair expenditure is revenue expenditure and is allowable, but if you buy a capital asset that cannot be used in your business until it is renovated, the cost of renovating it is part of the capital cost. The distinction is often hard to draw, and has led to many disputes between the taxpayer and the Revenue which have had to be settled by the courts.

Similar considerations apply in deciding whether a particular item is income chargeable under Schedule D, Case I or II or a capital profit.

Allowable and non-allowable expenses (TA 1988, ss 77, 87, 577)

The principles outlined above provide a broad guide to what expenses are allowed. Some specific examples are given in the table on page 234, including items specifically allowed or disallowed by the Taxes Acts.

Payment of remuneration (FA 1989, s 43)

Directors' and employees' pay may only be taken into account as an expense of the accounting period to which it relates if it is paid within nine months after the end of the period. Otherwise it may only be deducted in the accounting period in which it is paid.

Interest paid (TA 1988, ss 74(a), 338, 349, 360, 362, 363, 787)

Interest paid on business borrowings must be wholly and exclusively for the purposes of the business. Companies normally pay interest net of income tax, except for bank interest, which is paid in full and deducted as a trading expense. Interest paid net of tax by companies is deducted as a charge against their total profits (see page 24). Individuals normally pay interest in full and deduct it as a trading expense. Partners may obtain tax relief by way of a deduction from their total income for interest on a loan used for advancing money to a partnership (see pages 12 and 269). A similar provision applies to those who introduce funds into their family company (see page 12).

Now that MIRAS interest saves only basic rate tax, and is in any event not available on a loan above £30,000, individuals should consider business borrowings instead. This must not lead to a proprietor's capital/current account with the business becoming overdrawn, because interest paid on business borrowings that had enabled the drawings to be made would breach the 'wholly and exclusively' rule. You cannot treat an increase in your capital account as a result of asset revaluations as being available to cover drawings. You must also ensure that you do not make capital withdrawals *after* making loans to the business (but you could withdraw your capital and *replace* it with a loan).

There are some anti-avoidance provisions affecting both individuals and companies, and professional advice is essential.

Lease of cars (CAA 1990, s 35(2)–(4); F(No 2)A 1992, s 71)

If you buy a car costing more than £12,000 (£8,000 for expenditure under a contract entered into before 11 March 1992), capital allowances are restricted (see page 253), but the full cost will be allowed to you eventually (unless you use it partly for private purposes).

If instead you lease a car with a retail price when new of more than £12,000, part of the leasing cost is disallowed, so that you do not get tax relief at all for that part. You can only deduct from profit the proportion of the total hire charge that £12,000 plus one half of the excess of the retail price over £12,000 bears to the retail price.

Example 2

Car with retail value of £30,000 leased on 1 May 1992 for £9,000 a year.

Allowable hire charge:

$$9,000 \times \frac{12,000 + (\frac{1}{2} \text{ of } 18,000)}{30,000} = £6,300.$$

No tax relief is available for the remaining £2,700.

Finance leases

Although for accounting purposes an asset you acquire under a finance lease is treated as owned by you, it is in law owned by the lessor so the lease rental payments are a revenue expense allowable against your profit. The Revenue have issued a Statement of Practice (SP 3/91) giving their view as to how lease rentals are to be spread over the term of the lease for tax purposes. The date of payment is not the decisive factor and all relevant circumstances must be taken into account.

Goods for own use

A retail sole trader or partnership must include in sales the retail value of goods taken from stock for own use (the wholesale price being used for a wholesaler). Services are valued at cost, so no notional profit has to be included for services provided free of charge to, say, a relative. Where business is carried on through a limited company, the directors are charged on goods taken for their own use under the benefits rules (see chapter 10) and the cost will not be disallowed to the company, unless some of the directors' total remuneration including benefits is considered not to be wholly and exclusively for the trade (see page 162).

Stock and work in progress—valuation (TA 1988, ss 100–102)

Stock is valued at the lower of cost or realisable value, opening and closing stock being brought into the accounts in determining profit. Work in progress is similarly brought into account, and may be valued on any one of three bases, provided that the chosen base is used consistently:

(a) Cost including production overheads.
(b) Cost plus all overheads.
(c) Cost plus overheads plus profit contribution.

The value of a proprietor's or working partner's own time is not a contributory part of cost but effectively represents profit, so this element need not be included in a work in progress valuation.

When a trade ceases, stock is valued at the price received if sold to a UK trader, and otherwise, for example if taken by a trader for his personal use, at open market value.

Value added tax

If you are registered for VAT, VAT will not normally be taken into account either as part of your receipts or part of your expenses. You will effectively be collecting VAT for Customs and Excise on your supplies of goods and services and recouping any VAT that anyone has charged you. VAT on business entertaining expenditure and cars cannot, however, be recovered from Customs. (From 1 August 1992, there is an exception for private taxi firms, self-drive hire firms and driving schools, who will be able to recover input tax on the cars used in the business.) The VAT on entertaining cannot be recovered against your profit either, because business entertaining is specifically disallowed. But disallowed VAT on cars forms part of the cost for capital allowances (see chapter 22). Private petrol is subject to a VAT scale charge (see page 86). The VAT accounted for to Customs on the petrol may be included as part of the travelling expenses allowed against your profit, except any relating to private use by a sole trader or partner, which will be disallowed along with the private expenditure itself (see page 230).

If you are not registered for VAT, any VAT you have suffered (other than on business entertaining expenses, which are wholly disallowed) will form part of your expenditure. It will either be part of the cost of a capital item and may qualify for capital allowances or it will be an expense in arriving at your profit. The same applies where although you are registered for VAT, some of the supplies you make are exempt from VAT. You may then not be able

EXAMPLES OF ALLOWABLE AND NON-ALLOWABLE EXPENDITURE

Allowable	*Not allowable*
Wages and directors' fees	Drawings on account of profits by
Employer's national insurance	a sole proprietor or partners
contributions on employees'	Profit shares in the form of interest
wages, cars and fuel	on partners' capital
Rent of business premises	Self-employed national insurance
Business rates	contributions (but see
Repairs	chapter 24)
Premium for grant of lease	Cost of improvements, extensions,
for 50 years or less,	additions to premises and
but limited to the amount	equipment
assessed on the landlord as	Depreciation (capital allowances
extra rent (see chapter 32),	are available on certain assets—
spread over the term of the	see chapter 22)
lease	Expenses of private living
Interest on business borrowings	accommodation (unless assessable
Cost of raising loan finance	on directors or employees as a
(excluding stamp duty), for	benefit in kind)
example debentures (not	Legal expenses on forming a
share capital)	company, drawing up
Advertising	partnership agreement,
Business travel	acquiring assets such as leases
Bad debts written off and	Fines and legal expenses connected
provision for specific bad	therewith
debts	Business entertaining expenses
Legal expenses on debt	including the VAT thereon
recovery, trade disputes,	(except on a reasonable scale
defending trade rights,	when entertaining staff)
employees' service	Gifts to customers, except gifts
agreements and, by	with a conspicuous advertisement
concession, renewing a short	that cost not more than £10 per
lease (i.e. 50 years or less)	person per year
Contributions to local enterprise	Charitable subscriptions and
agencies (who promote local	donations, unless exceptionally
enterprise, particularly the	the donation satisfies the wholly
development of small	and exclusively rule (but see
businesses)	chapter 43 re allowance of
Contributions to training and	company donations as charges
enterprise councils (private	on income)
companies mainly concerned	Donations to political parties
with government training	Taxation (but see opposite column
programmes)	as regards VAT)
Gifts to educational	
establishments of equipment	
manufactured, sold or	
used in the donor's trade	
Non-recoverable VAT relating	
to allowable expenses, for	
example where turnover is	
below VAT threshold, or	
relating to private petrol for	
employees	

to recover all your input tax from Customs, and the non-deductible amount will be taken into account as part of your expenditure for income tax or corporation tax.

National insurance

The national insurance contributions you pay on your employees' wages, and the new national insurance contributions you pay on the provision of cars and private petrol to staff, are allowable against your profit. No part of a sole trader's or partner's own Class 2 and Class 4 contributions is directly allowed against profit, but half of the Class 4 contributions is allowed as a general deduction from the total income from all sources.

Non-trading income and capital profits

Any non-trading income of sole traders and partners included in the business accounts is not part of the profits assessable under Schedule D, Case I. The precise nature of the income will determine under what head it is chargeable, for example untaxed interest under Schedule D, Case III and rent from unfurnished lettings under Schedule A. In the case of a partnership, such income will usually be included in the accounts for the purposes of division between the partners, but it will have to be excluded from the trading assessment, and appropriate assessments made under other Schedules or Cases. These will be charged separately on each partner since the principle of joint assessment only applies to partnership trading profits and not to other income or to capital gains (see chapter 23).

A company's non-trading income is also excluded from the Case I trading profit, but the company is charged to tax in a single assessment on all its sources of income plus its chargeable gains, as indicated in chapter 21.

Capital profits of sole traders and partners are liable to capital gains tax, subject to any available reliefs and to the annual exemption. See chapter 4.

Tax points

● Try to avoid mixing business and private expenditure. Make sure you do not cloud a genuine business expense with a private element.

● If you are a retailer, use your business connections to make private purchases at lower cost, rather than taking goods out of your own stock and suffering tax on a figure equivalent to the profit you would have made if you had sold them to a customer.

● Since any expense for the benefit of staff is normally allowable in computing profits, it will usually be cheaper because of the saving in national insurance contributions to provide acceptable benefits than to pay higher salaries. The employee may be taxable on the benefits but not always at the full value, and sometimes not at all (see chapter 10).

- If a deduction is claimed that is not commercially justifiable, it could lead to interest being levied on tax underpaid as a result, and possibly a penalty as well. This is very important when considering the 'wholly and exclusively' business element of a mixed expense, such as accommodation and motor expenses. An inaccurate claim and/or providing insufficient information to the Revenue can be costly in the long run.

- Wages payments to a wife must not only be commercially justifiable for her participation in the business but must be properly made and recorded in the business books. The Revenue will usually challenge the charge if it has not been separately paid, but has instead been regarded as included in the amount drawn by the husband or for housekeeping, with an accounting entry being made to create the wages charge.

- Similar considerations apply where mature children are able genuinely to participate in the business, for example in farming, retail and wholesale trades.

- Remember that wages paid after the end of an accounting period must be paid within nine months if they are to be deducted from the profits of that period, otherwise they will be deducted from profits in the period of payment.

- Although expenses, incurred by a company, from which a director or employee derives a personal benefit are allowable in computing trading profit and assessable on the director or employee, this treatment does not generally extend to private expenditure of a director or employee which is borne by the company where the director or employee is a shareholder. In such cases the Revenue would usually regard the director or employee as accountable to the company for that expenditure, and until he has accounted for it the company would be charged to income tax at the basic rate on the grossed-up equivalent of the expenditure (TA 1988, s 419), with the director or employee being taxed as having received a taxable benefit equal to interest calculated at the official rate (see page 134) whilst the amount is outstanding.

- Business rates will be deductible in calculating trading profits, but not any part of the poll tax. Those traders who under the old system had part of the rates allowed in calculating business income must be careful that the change in the rating system is properly reflected in their profit computation.

21
How are business profits charged to tax?

Companies (TA 1988, ss 8–12 and Sch 30)

Although taxable business profits for individuals and companies are broadly computed in the same way, the assessment of company profits is much more straightforward. A company's trading profits are assessed along with any other profits the company has, such as interest, rents and chargeable gains, by reference to chargeable accounting periods (see page 24). A chargeable accounting period can be as short as the company wishes but cannot exceed twelve months. If a company makes up an account for say fifteen-months it is split into two chargeable accounting periods for tax purposes, the first of twelve months and the second of three months. Capital allowances are then deducted in arriving at the trading profits. The capital allowances are not calculated for the fifteen-month period and divided pro rata. They are calculated for the separate periods of twelve and three months according to the events of those periods.

Example 1

A company makes trading profits of £150,000 in the 15 months to 30 September 1992. The profits will be included in assessments as follows:

	12 months to 30.6.92 £	3 months to 30.9.92 £
12/15, 3/15	120,000	30,000
Less capital allowances (say)	10,000	8,000
	£110,000	£22,000

The due date for payment of corporation tax is nine months after the end of the chargeable accounting period, i.e. 1 April 1993 for the twelve-month account and 1 July 1993 for the three-month account in example 1, or

30 days after the assessment is raised if later. Companies in existence before April 1965, when corporation tax was introduced, used to retain the same time interval between the end of an accounting period and the payment date as they had for income tax, which in some cases could be as long as 20 months. The payment interval for all companies has, however, now been reduced to nine months, over a three-year transitional period beginning with the company's first accounting period starting after 16 March 1987.

Many companies currently take much longer than nine months to pay their tax by delaying sending in their accounts. Starting with a company's first account ending after 30 September 1993, a new system called 'Pay and File' will come into effect, under which companies will pay tax, estimated if necessary, nine months after the end of the account, or be charged interest on any underpayment, and must file returns and accounts within twelve months from the end of the account, or face penalties for late filing. For details, see page 29.

Individuals

Normal basis of assessment (TA 1988, s 60)

For the self-employed person or those in partnership, income tax on trading profits is payable in equal instalments on 1 January within the tax year and 1 July following it, or 30 days after the assessment is raised if later. Thus the tax for 1992/93 is payable in equal instalments on 1 January and 1 July 1993.

An individual (or partnership) is free to choose the annual date to which accounts are made up and it is usual, but not compulsory, for accounts to be made up to a calendar month end. The assessment to tax for an established business is usually based on the trading profits of the accounting year which ended in the previous income tax year. The 1992/93 assessment for an established trader would therefore be based on the result of his accounting period of twelve months ended in the previous tax year 1991/92, i.e. between 6 April 1991 and 5 April 1992, for example:

> Year ended 30 April 1991
> Year ended 31 May 1991
> Year ended 30 November 1991
> Year ended 31 March 1992

The earlier the accounting date in the tax year the greater the time interval between earning the profits and paying the tax on them (see example 2).

An established trader or partnership may wish to alter the interval by changing the previously adopted accounting date (see page 243).

Assessment in early years (TA 1988, ss 61 and 62)

Since there are no previous year's accounts for a new business, a special basis of assessment is used in the early years. The assessment for the tax year in which a business starts is based on the profit from the date of commencement to the following 5 April. If necessary, profits are

Example 2

	Due date of payment of tax for 1992/93	Interval between end of accounting year and payment date
Year ended 30.4.91	1.1.93	20 months
	1.7.93	26 months
Year ended 31.10.91	1.1.93	14 months
	1.7.93	20 months
Year ended 31.3.92	1.1.93	9 months
	1.7.93	15 months

apportioned on a time basis. The second tax year's assessment is based on the profits of the first twelve months' trading and assessments thereafter are normally based on the profits of the accounting year ended in the previous tax year.

Example 3

Trade commenced on 1 January 1991. Profits are £3,650 for the year ended 31 December 1991 and £12,000 for the year ended 31 December 1992.

Year of Assessment	Basis period	Assessment £
1990/91	1.1.91–5.4.91 95/365ths × £3,650	950
1991/92	1.1.91–31.12.91	3,650
1992/93	1.1.91–31.12.91	3,650
1993/94	1.1.92–31.12.92	12,000

When the first accounts are prepared for a period other than twelve months, it may not be possible to base the assessment of the third tax year on the profits of twelve months ended on the chosen accounting date in the previous tax year. In these circumstances, the assessment for the third tax year is again based on the profit of the first twelve months' trading.

Significant tax advantages may sometimes be obtained by careful choice of the date to which accounts are to be made up and the length of the first account. Professional advice is essential.

Regardless of the dates to which accounts are made up, some profits are used more than once in establishing the assessments for the early years. In example 3 the first year's profits formed the basis of assessment for 27 tax months (3 months in 1990/91 and the whole of 1991/92 and 1992/93). This overlap is balanced by profits for an equivalent time escaping assessment when an established trade ceases (see page 241). If profits are increasing year by year, the opening year rules and subsequent previous year basis of assessment work in the taxpayer's favour, because the assessable profits will be less than the profits currently being earned. The trader in example 3 is being taxed on £3,650 in 1992/93, although his profits for the year to 31 December 1992 are £12,000. But if profits fall, the multiple assessment of the initial higher profits could cause hardship. The taxpayer is able to claim within six years after the end of the third tax year to have the assessments for both the second and third tax years (not just one of them) based on the actual profits made in those tax years rather than on the profits of the earlier period. This means that later, lower profits will be multiple-assessed instead of the earlier, high ones. See example 4.

Different rules apply if the business is new because of a change of partners. These are dealt with in chapter 23.

Capital allowances in early years (CAA 1990, s 160)

Where expenditure qualifies for capital allowances, they normally commence in the tax year based on the accounting year in which the expenditure is incurred.

Example 4 (all calculations taken to the nearest month for simplicity)

Trade commenced on 1 January 1991. Profits of the 4 months to 30 April 1991 are £1,000, those of the year to 30 April 1992 are £15,000 and those for the year to 30 April 1993 are £2,400.

The assessment for the first year, 1990/91, is based on the profit from 1.1.91 to 5.4.91, i.e. three quarters of £1,000 = £750.

Assessments for the **second** and **third** tax years are as follows:

Year of assessment	Basis period			Assessments

Normal basis

			£	£
1991/92	1.1.91–30.4.91	£1,000	1,000	
	1.5.91–31.12.91	8/12 × £15,000	10,000	
				11,000
1992/93	1.1.91–31.12.91			
	(As for 1991/92)			11,000
				£22,000

example 4 continued opposite

example 4 continued

With taxpayer's claim to be taxed on actual profits

			£	£
1991/92	6.4.91–30.4.91	1/4 × £1,000	250	
	1.5.91–5.4.92	11/12 × £15,000	13,750	
				14,000
1992/93	6.4.92–30.4.92	1/12 × £15,000	1,250	
	1.5.92–5.4.93	11/12 × £2,400	2,200	
				3,450
				£17,450

Clearly it is in the taxpayer's interest to have the 1991/92 and 1992/93 assessments based on the profits actually earned in those tax years.

The normal rules will apply to later assessments, as follows:

		£
1993/94	1.5.91–30.4.92	15,000
1994/95	1.5.92–30.4.93	2,400

Since the early accounting periods of a new trade form the basis of assessment for more than one tax year, expenditure incurred in an accounting period is taken into account for capital allowances in the first of those tax years only (see chapter 22).

Assessment on cessation of trade (TA 1988, s 63)

The taxing of profits more than once in the opening years is compensated by the rules for assessment when a business ceases. The final assessment is based on the profit from the beginning of the tax year (i.e. 6 April) in which the business ceases to the date of cessation, and replaces the assessment based on the 12 months account ended in the previous tax year. This means that some profits are never assessed at all. However, just as the taxpayer can choose which profits are used more than once for assessment at the start of the business, so the Revenue has the right to decide which profits escape assessment when the business ceases. The assessments for the two tax years before the final tax year may, at the option of the Revenue, be revised to the profits actually made in those tax years instead of the profits of the accounts ended in the previous tax years. As with the taxpayer's claim in the opening years, this revision must be made for both tax years or for neither.

See example 5.

Example 5

A trader who has prepared accounts to 30 April for many years ceases to trade on 31 August 1992, the recent and final profits having been:

		£
Year ended	30.4.89	24,000
	30.4.90	30,000
	30.4.91	36,000
	30.4.92	48,000
Four months to	31.8.92	15,000

Assessments for the last three tax years are as follows:

Year of assessment	Basis period		£	Assessments £
1992/93	6.4.92–30.4.92	1/12 × £48,000		4,000
	1.5.92–31.8.92			15,000
				£19,000

and either
Normal preceding year basis

1991/92	1.5.89–30.4.90	30,000
1990/91	1.5.88–30.4.89	24,000
		£54,000

or
Revenue's revised actual basis

1991/92	6.4.91–30.4.91	1/12 × £36,000	3,000	
	1.5.91–5.4.92	11/12 × £48,000	44,000	
				47,000
1990/91	6.4.90–30.4.90	1/12 × £30,000	2,500	
	1.5.90–5.4.91	11/12 × £36,000	33,000	
				35,500
				£82,500

Although following revision by the Revenue the total assessments for 1990/91 and 1991/92 will be increased by £28,500 (from £54,000 to £82,500), the profits of the 23 months from 1 May 1988 to 5 April 1990, amounting to £51,500, will not be assessed at all.

Choice of cessation date

A significant tax advantage can sometimes be obtained where a choice of cessation date is possible. There is a cessation for tax purposes:

When trading comes to an end.
When a trader dies (although, by concession, assessments can continue to be made on a previous year basis if the trade is continued by the spouse).
When partners change in a partnership (although the partners may choose to have assessments continue on a previous year basis, see chapter 23).
When a trader or partnership transfers its trade to a company (see chapter 27).

It will normally be advantageous to delay the cessation until a later tax year if profits are rising, since the profits that escape tax will be later higher profits, and to cease in an earlier tax year if profits are falling, since the later the cessation the smaller the escaping profits.

Capital allowances in closing years (CAA 1990, s 160)

For capital allowances purposes, expenditure in the period for which profits escape tax on cessation is regarded as incurred in the next period unless that is the last tax year, in which case it is regarded as incurred in the previous period. This ensures that no qualifying capital expenditure or sales are omitted. See example 6.

In the final tax year, the disposal of the assets on which allowances have been claimed has to be taken into account (see chapter 22).

Example 6

	Normal basis	Revenue's revised basis
In example 5 the 'profits gap' was	1.5.90–5.4.92	1.5.88–5.4.90
It is added to the basis period for	1991/92	1990/91
Which then covers capital		
expenditure and sales from	1.5.89–5.4.92	1.5.88–5.4.91

Change of accounting date (TA 1988, s 60)

A change of accounting date by a trader or a partnership will have the effect of profits escaping assessment or being assessed more than once at that time, with a corresponding adjustment to the length of the period for which profits escape tax when the trade ceases. This can provide an opportunity to reduce assessments overall as long as the change is commercially justifiable. The detailed provisions are beyond the scope of this book, but broadly the Revenue practice is to use a period of twelve months based on the new accounting date as the basis of the next year's assessment and to adjust the previous year's assessment according to recent average profits, unless the adjustment would be insignificant.

Partnership

Although the rules for assessing an entirely new or continuing partnership are the same as those for individual traders, there are some special points to be considered about the way assessments are divided between partners, what happens on a change of partners and the treatment of losses and capital gains. These are dealt with in chapter 23.

Pre-trading expenditure (TA 1988, s 401)

Some expenditure, for example rent and rates, may be incurred before trading actually starts. So long as it is a normal trading expense and is incurred not more than five years before the trade starts, it may be treated by individual traders and partnerships as a separate loss of the first tax year of trading and loss relief may be claimed for it. The types of loss relief available are dealt with in chapter 25. Where the expenditure is incurred by a company it may be treated as an expense of the first trading period. The different treatment for individuals ensures that they do not get the benefit of deducting the expense several times over because of the assessment rules for the opening years (see page 239).

Post cessation receipts (TA 1988, ss 103–110)

Income may arise after a business has ceased which has not been included in the final accounts. This may be because of the nature of the business and is particularly relevant for barristers because their accounts are traditionally prepared on the basis of cash received rather than on earnings. Whatever the reason, the income is assessed under Schedule D, Case VI in the tax year when it is received, unless it is received within six years after cessation, when the taxpayer can elect to have it assessed in the tax year when trading ceased. The election must be made within two years after the end of the tax year in which the income was received.

Tax points

- The way the self-employed are taxed is currently under review, and the 'previous year basis of assessment' is a specific target for reform. Although the aim is stated to be simplification, an inevitable result will be the loss of the tax planning opportunities now available. Any change is, however, probably some years away, so that significant savings can still be made in the short term.

- Choosing an accounting date early in the tax year not only gives more time for planning the funding of tax payments but also maximises the profits which escape assessment when the business ceases.

- Where possible, plan your expenses in the opening years to maximise the benefit of the opening year rules. Expenses are effectively relieved as many times as the profits are assessed.

- Consider leasing plant (particularly cars) instead of buying, so that the early leasing charges reduce the assessments of several tax years. (Capital allowances reduce them once only.) An additional consideration is that VAT can be reclaimed on the leasing payments, whereas VAT on the cost of a purchased car cannot. But see page 232 re leased cars costing £12,000 or more.

- If possible, postpone cessation of a trade to a date after the next 5 April if profits are rising, but cease before that date if profits are falling. The maximum possible profits will then escape assessment.

- This chapter contains two examples of claims which are available to taxpayers. There is always a time limit involved, which depends on the type of claim being made. The legislation should be checked for the time limit whenever a claim is available. There is a general six-year time limit where no other time limit is specified.

- In example 3, the tax for 1990/91 (due 1.1.91 and 1.7.91) and the first instalment for 1991/92 (due 1.1.92) will be due before the first accounts to 31.12.91, on which the tax is based, are available. The same may apply to the second instalment of tax for 1991/92 (due 1.7.92) and so on. In such cases, you should not delay informing the Revenue that you have started to trade. They will issue estimated assessments (see chapter 9) and amend them later when the accounts are available. If the Revenue are not told until you send in the first accounts, they may seek to charge interest on overdue tax and penalties because of your earlier failure to notify them.

22
Capital allowances

Background

Capital expenditure is not allowable in calculating income profits, but relief is given on certain capital expenditure by means of allowances when the expenditure is incurred and / or over the later years of the ownership of the assets.

The law on capital allowances is in the Capital Allowances Act 1990 as amended by later Finance Acts. References in this chapter are to the 1990 Act unless otherwise stated.

The most important allowances available to companies, sole traders and partnerships are those in respect of expenditure on:

Plant and machinery
Industrial buildings
Agricultural buildings
Hotels
Buildings in enterprise zones, other than dwelling houses
Patents
Know-how
Scientific research
Mineral extraction

Dwellings let under the assured tenancy scheme qualify for relief, broadly on expenditure incurred before 15 March 1988 or under a contract entered into before that date.

Plant and machinery allowances are also available to employees who have to provide plant and machinery for use in their employment, and to those letting property in respect of landlord's fixtures, fittings etc. The most common example of qualifying expenditure by an employee is that on provision of a car, but another might be a musical instrument purchased by an employee of an orchestra. A landlord of let property may obtain relief on such items as lifts. Industrial and agricultural buildings allowances are also available to landlords when qualifying buildings are let.

If an asset is used partly for private purposes, only the appropriate business fraction is allowed against the assessable income.

The following capital allowances are dealt with in more detail in other chapters:

Agricultural buildings—chapter 31
Dwellings let under the assured tenancy scheme—chapter 32

Expenditure qualifying for relief (ss 11, 60, 153, 154)

Capital allowances are available to the person incurring the expenditure, and if the expenditure is funded by means of a loan or bank overdraft the allowances can still be claimed in the usual way. Interest on such funding is, however, allowed as a business expense and not as part of the cost of the asset. Where an industrial building is let at a premium on a long lease (more than 50 years), the landlord and tenant may elect for the premium to be treated as the purchase price for the building, so that industrial buildings allowances may be claimed by the tenant. A tenant who incurs capital expenditure on a qualifying building is entitled to allowances on that expenditure.

When an asset is purchased under a hire-purchase agreement, the expenditure is regarded as incurred as soon as the asset comes into use, even though ownership does not strictly pass until the option to purchase payment is made. The hire-purchase charges are not part of the cost but are allowed as a business expense spread over the term of the agreement.

Where assets are acquired on a finance lease, then although for accounting purposes they are treated as owned by the lessee, they belong in law to the lessor and it is the lessor who gets the capital allowances. See page 232 for the treatment of the lease payments.

Subsidies or contributions from third parties must in general be deducted from the allowable cost. Regional development grants, however, are specifically excluded from this requirement and do not have to be deducted.

Any contribution for trading purposes towards another person's eligible expenditure which restricts the allowances available to the recipient will be treated as expenditure by the contributor, even though strictly he does not have an interest in the asset.

Where value added tax has been paid and cannot be recovered, for example on motor cars or, in the case of other asset purchases, because of the partial exemption rules or because the trader is not VAT registered, it forms part of the allowable expenditure for capital allowances. Provisions have been introduced to adjust capital allowances computations where input VAT is later adjusted on land and computers under the capital goods scheme (see page 260).

Basis periods (ss 140, 141, 144, 145, 160)

Allowances are first given by reference to the expenditure incurred in a basis period. For a company this is its chargeable accounting period, so that where a period of account exceeds twelve months, it is split into a twelve-month period or periods and the remainder, and relief for capital expenditure is first given according to the chargeable period in which the expenditure is incurred.

For employees and landlords the basis period is the income tax year itself.

For traders and partnerships the basis period is the accounting period on which the assessment is based. Thus expenditure incurred by an established businessman in his year ended 31 December 1991 would first qualify for relief in 1992/93, when the profits of the year to 31 December 1991 are assessed.

Because of the income tax rules for assessments in the opening and closing years and on changes of accounting date, some trading periods may be taken into account for more than one assessment and other periods may escape assessment (see chapter 21). Where expenditure is incurred in the basis period for more than one assessment, it is regarded as being incurred in the first period. Where it does not come within any basis period, it is regarded as incurred in the next period, unless the next period is the last tax year of the business, in which case it is regarded as being incurred in the previous period.

Date expenditure is incurred (s 159)

This is generally the date on which the obligation to pay becomes unconditional, but if any part of the payment is not due until more than three months after that date, that part of the expenditure is regarded as incurred on the due date of payment. The due date of payment is also substituted where the unconditional obligation to pay is earlier than normal commercial usage and the sole or main benefit of that would be for allowances to become available in an earlier chargeable period. It sometimes happens that, under large construction contracts, ownership of an asset passes, and the obligation to pay subsequently becomes unconditional, e.g. on presentation of an architect's certificate. Where, in those circumstances, ownership passes in one basis period, but the obligation becomes unconditional in the first month of the next, the obligation is regarded as having arisen in the earlier period.

Way in which allowances are given (ss 24, 140, 141, 144, 145)

Allowances for sole traders and partners are available against the trading profits for the relevant tax years, enabling loss relief to be claimed if they turn what would otherwise be a profit into a loss (see chapter 25).

Allowances for a trading company are deducted in computing trading profit, and as with the unincorporated trader, might turn a profit into a loss, for which the usual relief for company trading losses could be claimed (see chapter 26).

Allowances claimed by individual or corporate investors are given first against rent income. A claim may be made, within two years after the end of the tax year or company accounting period, to set any excess against other income in the case of the individual, or against other profits in the case of a company. For the individual investor, the excess allowance will be set against any other rent income of the same tax year and then any other income of that tax year or of the following tax year. See example 6 on page 259. A corporate investor is allowed relief against the total profits (including capital gains) first of the same accounting period and then of the previous accounting period.

For both individuals and companies, allowances not given by set-off against other income can be carried forward, against future trading income of traders, and against future rent income of investors.

Allowances for companies are given automatically, whereas individuals must make a specific claim for them.

Some allowances need not be taken in full, e.g. writing-down allowances on plant and machinery and initial allowances (when available) on industrial buildings. This may enable you to make better use of other available reliefs and allowances (see Tax points at the end of this chapter).

Balancing allowances and charges (ss 4, 5, 24)

When an asset is sold, the proceeds are in most cases compared with the expenditure, if any, for which allowances have not yet been given and a 'balancing allowance' given for any deficiency. If the proceeds exceed the unrelieved expenditure, the excess is included in taxable income by means of a 'balancing charge'. If the proceeds exceed the original cost, however, the excess over cost is dealt with under the capital gains tax rules (see page 254), except for sales of know-how (see page 262).

For plant and machinery, balancing allowances and charges are normally dealt with on a 'pool' basis except for assets which are expected to be sold within five years (see page 251).

Connected persons etc. (ss 26, 77, 78, 152, 157, 158)

If an asset is withdrawn from a business for personal use or sold to a connected person for use other than in a business, the amount to be included as sales proceeds is broadly the open market value. (The definition of 'connected person' is broadly the same as that for capital gains tax—see page 51—although it is slightly wider.)

On a sale of plant and machinery between connected persons, open market value is not used for the seller if the buyer's expenditure is taken into account for capital allowances (so that, for example, inter-group transfers are taken into account at the price paid). On a sale of assets other than plant and machinery, open market value will apply unless a joint claim is made by seller and buyer, within two years after the transfer, for the transfer to be treated as made at written-down value.

Where the sale of an asset takes place at the time when the business itself is sold, the assets are treated as being sold at open market value. But the seller and buyer may make a joint election, within two years from the date of the sale, for the transfer to be treated as made at the tax written-down value, so there will be no balancing adjustment on the seller and the buyer will take over the allowances from that point. The most common example of the application of these rules is when a business is transferred to a company (see page 307).

Plant and machinery

The treatment of capital expenditure on plant and machinery is a very complex area, particularly in relation to assets which are leased out, the following being an outline of the position.

What is plant and machinery?

Plant and machinery is not defined, and although 'machinery' is generally well understood, the question of what is and is not 'plant' has come before the courts many times. The main problem lies in distinguishing the 'apparatus' *with* which a business is carried on from the 'setting' *in* which it is carried on. Items forming part of the setting do not attract relief unless they do so as part of the building itself and not as plant, for example where it is an industrial building, or unless the business is one in which atmosphere, or ambience, is important, but, even so, allowances for plant will not be available on expenditure which becomes part of the premises, such as shop fronts, flooring and suspended ceilings. (Although initial expenditure on a shopfront is disallowed, the cost of a subsequent replacement will be allowed as a revenue expense against the profit, but excluding any improvement element.) Lifts and central heating systems are treated as plant, while basic electricity and plumbing systems are not. Specific lighting to create atmosphere in a hotel and special lighting in fast food restaurants have been held to be plant. A tenant who incurs expenditure on items that become landlord's fixtures can nonetheless claim allowances—see page 362.

Expenditure on computer hardware is capital expenditure on plant and machinery. Allowances will usually be claimed under the 'short-life assets' rules (see page 251). Where software is bought in conjunction with the hardware and has a life of two years or more, the Revenue view is that it should be treated as part of the capital cost. Where software is bought separately, the treatment will depend on whether it is considered to be capital expenditure, in which case again short-life asset treatment will probably be appropriate, or whether the rate of technological change in relation to the software is such that it can properly be regarded as revenue expenditure and charged in full against the profit. Where payment is made for a licence to use software, regular payments will usually be a normal expense against profit. Most purchased software packages carry with them a lifetime licence for a particular user or users, so that strictly the expenditure is capital expenditure on an intangible asset rather than on plant and machinery. It has now been provided that for expenditure incurred on or after 10 March 1992, capital expenditure on licensed software and electronically transmitted software qualifies for plant and machinery allowances.

Certain items that are not plant are specifically allowable as such, for example expenditure by traders on fire safety, heat insulation in industrial buildings, and expenditure on safety at sports grounds.

Allowances available (s 24)

The allowances available are writing-down allowances of 25% per annum on the reducing balance method.

In the first year of business for individuals and partnerships, the 25% writing-down allowance is reduced according to the length of the basis period, and it is also reduced proportionately for companies in respect of accounting periods of less than twelve months.

Pooling expenditure (s 25)

All qualifying expenditure on plant and machinery is included in a single 'pool' except for the following:

At the taxpayer's option, acquisitions on or after 1 April 1986 which are expected to be disposed of within five years ('short-life assets').

Any asset with part private use by a sole trader or partner.

Assets for foreign leasing.

Any 'car' costing over £12,000 (£8,000 for cars bought before 11 March 1992).

Any other 'cars'—defined as all other motor vehicles except those primarily suited for carrying goods, those not commonly used as private vehicles and unsuitable to be so used, those let on a short lease (i.e. where the car is normally hired to the same person for less than 30 consecutive days and for less than 90 days in any twelve months), and those let to someone receiving mobility allowance.

Cars under the last heading are kept in a separate 'pool'—see page 253. Plant and machinery that is to be leased out used to be included in this separate pool as well, and pool balances will include unallowed expenditure on such assets, but assets for leasing now go into the main pool *unless* they are for foreign leasing.

The writing-down allowance at the rate of 25% per annum (reducing balance method) is calculated on the unrelieved expenditure brought forward from the previous period, plus expenditure in the period, less any sales proceeds (up to, but not exceeding, the original cost—see page 254). If the proceeds exceed the pool balance, a balancing charge is made.

A balancing allowance will not arise on the main pool, except on a cessation of trade where the total sales proceeds are less than the pool balance.

De-pooling of short-life assets (ss 37, 38)

Some assets have a very short life and depreciate very quickly. The normal pooling system does not give relief for such assets over their life span. For

Example 1

A trader has the following transactions in plant in the years ended
31 December 1990 and 1991:

		£
June 1990	Proceeds of sales	3,000
November 1990	Purchase from associated business	1,000
January 1991	Proceeds of sales	8,500
February 1991	Arm's length purchase	10,000

The pool balance brought forward at 1 January 1990 is £8,000.

The allowances are calculated as follows:

1991/92 (based on year to 31 December 1990)

Pool value brought forward	8,000
Additions (dealt with as a sale in the computations of the associated business)	1,000
	9,000
Less sales proceeds	(3,000)
	6,000
Writing-down allowance 25% (reduces taxable profit)	(1,500)
	4,500

1992/93 (based on year to 31 December 1991)

Additions	10,000
	14,500
Sales proceeds	(8,500)
	6,000
Writing-down allowance 25% (reduces taxable profit)	1,500
Balance carried forward	£4,500

The balance carried forward attracts a 25% writing-down allowance
in 1993/94 and later years, on the reducing balance method.

items of machinery or plant acquired on or after 1 April 1986, an election
may be made to have the capital allowances calculated separately. A
balancing allowance or charge will then arise if the asset is disposed of
within five years. If the asset is still held at the end of the five-year period,
the tax written-down value will be transferred into the main pool. This

provision does not apply to cars and any other assets which would not in any event have been included in the main pool of expenditure. The election for this treatment is irrevocable, and must be made within two years after the end of the accounting period in which the expenditure is incurred. The Inland Revenue have issued guidelines (Statement of Practice SP 1/86) on practical aspects of these rules, including provisions for grouping classes of assets where individual treatment is impossible or impracticable.

Assets with part private use (s 79)

Any asset that is privately used by the sole proprietor or by a partner in a business is dealt with separately. This does not apply to assets used by directors of family companies. The use of company assets for private purposes by directors or employees does not affect the company's capital allowances position, but results in a benefits charge on the director/employee (see chapter 10).

Allowances and charges on privately-used assets are calculated in the normal way, but the available allowance or charge is restricted to the business proportion.

There is no 'pooling' of privately used assets. A separate calculation is made for each asset which is so used, and an individual balancing adjustment is made when it is disposed of.

Cars costing more than £12,000 (ss 34–36; F(No 2)A 1992, s 71)

Each car that costs more than £12,000 (£8,000 for cars bought before 11 March 1992) is dealt with separately, and the available writing-down allowance is £3,000 (£2,000 for pre-11 March 1992 purchases) per annum or 25% of the unrelieved balance, whichever is less. If such a car is used privately by a sole trader or partner the available amount is further restricted by the private proportion. When the car is sold a balancing allowance or charge arises. See page 232 for the treatment of a car with a value of more than £12,000 that you lease instead of buy.

Car pools (ss 39–50)

Any car costing over £12,000 and/or with part private use is dealt with in a separate individual pool.

All other cars are dealt with in the car pool. This pool also includes any unrelieved balance of expenditure incurred before 1 April 1986 on assets for UK leasing, but new expenditure on or after that date on assets for leasing is included in the main pool. The expenditure on the car pool qualifies for writing-down allowances of 25%. Sales proceeds are deducted before the writing-down allowance is calculated, and a balancing charge is made if the sales proceeds exceed the pool balance. If all the items in the car pool are disposed of, a balancing allowance or charge arises. The car pool will then be reopened as and when a further car is acquired.

Films (s 68; F(No 2)A 1992, ss 41–43, 69)

Expenditure on the production and acquisition of films is treated as revenue expenditure and not capital expenditure, with the cost being written off over the income-producing life of the film. This does not apply to qualifying EC films in respect of pre-production expenditure incurred, and production expenditure on films completed, on or after 10 March 1992. For such qualifying films, pre-production expenditure up to 20% of the total budgeted expenditure, and abortive expenditure, may be written off as it is incurred, and production expenditure may be written off at a flat rate of 33⅓% a year from completion of the film. The 33⅓% relief also applies to expenditure on acquiring qualifying EC films. An alternative treatment may be claimed for qualifying EC films, under which writing-down allowances may be claimed under the normal plant and machinery rules instead, but this would give lower allowances.

Assets for foreign leasing (s 42)

Assets leased to non-UK residents who do not use them for a UK trade are kept in a separate pool, normally attracting writing-down allowances at 10%, balancing charges where the sales proceeds exceed the tax written-down value, and a balancing allowance where the tax written-down value exceeds the proceeds on a cessation of trade. In some circumstances, no allowances at all are available.

Effect of capital allowances on capital gains computation (TCGA 1992, ss 41, 55 (3))

Capital allowances are not deducted from the cost of an asset in computing a gain, but are taken into account in computing a loss. There will only be a gain if an asset is sold for more than cost, and in that event any capital allowances given will be withdrawn by the cost being taken out of the capital allowances computation (except for certain agricultural buildings allowances—see chapter 31) and will not therefore affect the computation of either a gain or a loss. See example 2.

Example 2

Machine bought for £5,800 is sold two years later for £6,200. Indexation allowance say £980.

Disposal proceeds in plant pool will be restricted to £5,800, effectively withdrawing capital allowances given.

	£
Sale proceeds	6,200
Cost	(5,800)
Indexation allowance	(980)
Allowable capital loss	£580

Example 3

Moveable plant cost £5,900 in September 1987 and is sold in May 1992 for £5,000. The difference of £900 between purchase and sale price is reflected in the allowances given in the capital allowances computation. The allowable loss for capital gains tax purposes, taking into account indexation allowance at 36%, is:

	£	£
Proceeds treated as		6,000
Cost	5,900	
Less taken into account for capital allowances	900	
		5,000
		1,000
Indexation allowance at 36% on £5,000		(1,800)
Allowable capital loss		£(800)

For plant and machinery that is moveable rather than fixed, there is no chargeable gain if it is sold for £6,000 or less. Where the proceeds exceed £6,000, the chargeable gain cannot exceed 5/3rds of the excess of the proceeds over £6,000 (see page 445). Allowable capital losses can be created on moveable plant and machinery whether it is sold for more or less than £6,000, but in computing the allowable loss, an item sold for less than £6,000 is treated as sold for £6,000. Even so, the indexation allowance can create an allowable loss (see example 3).

If plant and machinery is fixed rather than moveable, there are no special rules restricting capital losses and there is no capital gains tax exemption for gains, but gains may be deferred if the item is replaced (see page 48).

Where the asset was acquired before 31 March 1982, the capital allowances are deducted from the 31 March 1982 value when making calculations using that value. Plant and machinery is not covered by a general 31 March 1982 rebasing election (see page 41) so gains and losses have to be computed both under the old rules and the new. See example 4 on page 256.

Industrial buildings

Definition (s 18)

Industrial buildings are broadly those in use for the purpose of qualifying trades, the most common of which are manufacturing or processing goods or materials. Buildings used to store goods and materials before and after manufacture or processing are included. Offices, shops, hotels and whole-sale warehouses are excluded from the definition, but hotels qualify for allowances under a separate heading (see page 260). Where part of a

---

Example 4

Plant cost £12,000 in September 1980 and is sold in April 1992 for £8,000. The value of the plant at 31 March 1982 was £11,000. Indexation allowance from March 1982 is 74.7%.

	Old scheme		New scheme	
	£	£	£	£
Proceeds		8,000		8,000
Cost/31 March 1982 value	12,000		11,000	
Less capital allowances	4,000	(8,000)	4,000	(7,000)
		—		1,000
Indexation allowance at 74.7% on £8,000 (being higher than 31 March 1982 value after deducting capital allowances)		(5,976)		(5,976)
		(5,976)		(4,976)

Allowable capital loss is lower of the two, i.e. £4,976

---

building is outside the definition (for example offices in a factory), the whole building qualifies for relief providing the expenditure on the non-industrial part does not exceed 25% of the total cost (10% for expenditure incurred before 16 March 1983). This applies only where the non-industrial part is housed within the same building, not where it is a separate entity. Where a building is in an enterprise zone, there is no restriction on the use to which it may be put, except that a private dwelling does not qualify, and much more generous allowances are available (see page 260).

Allowances for new buildings and additional capital expenditure on existing buildings (ss 3–5, 8, 10, 12, 13, 15, 21)

Relief is given on the cost of construction and no relief is available for the cost of the land, although site preparation works qualify. Where a building is bought from the builder, allowances are available on the amount paid. Where additional capital expenditure is incurred on an existing building, the additional expenditure qualifies for relief as if it were a separate building. This provision enables a tenant to get relief on any capital expenditure he incurs on the building, and it is specifically provided that any repair expenditure disallowed as a business expense is treated as qualifying capital expenditure. Furthermore, expenditure on items that become part of the building does not qualify for plant and machinery allowances and counts instead as part of the building expenditure—see page 250.

The allowances available used to be an initial allowance on construction expenditure incurred in the basis period, and annual writing-down allowances for any basis period at the end of which the building was in qualifying use, until the expenditure was fully relieved. Initial allowances were generally withdrawn for expenditure incurred after 31 March 1986, except for buildings in enterprise zones (see page 260).

For industrial buildings not in enterprise zones, the only allowances now available for new buildings and additional capital expenditure on existing buildings are writing-down allowances at the rate of 4% of the construction cost per annum, which are given until the cost has been fully written off. (Writing-down allowances are at the rate of 2% per annum on capital expenditure incurred before 6 November 1962, such buildings having a tax life of 50 years. The allowances were introduced in 1946/47 for existing as well as new buildings, available for the remainder of an existing building's 50-year life.) The rates of initial allowance from 11 March 1981 until their withdrawal were as follows:

Date expenditure incurred	Rate
11 March 1981 to 13 March 1984	75%
14 March 1984 to 31 March 1985	50%
1 April 1985 to 31 March 1986	25%
1 April 1986 onwards	Nil

The allowances were at various rates for earlier years, having commenced on 6 April 1944.

If a building is sold before the expenditure has been fully relieved, there is a balancing adjustment between the seller and the buyer, and the buyer is entitled to writing-down allowances over the remainder of the building's tax life (see below).

Sale of the building (ss 4, 5, 15)

This will involve a balancing adjustment on the vendor (unless the building is sold after the end of its tax life—see below) and a possible claim for relief by the purchaser.

Whilst there are rules to deal with periods of non-industrial use, the basic adjustment is to amend the vendor's relief to the cost of having owned the building, a balancing charge normally being made to withdraw excess allowances or a balancing allowance being given to make up any shortfall.

If the building is used for a qualifying trade, the purchaser gets relief on the part of the original building cost remaining unrelieved after the balancing adjustment on the seller. This amount is relieved by way of equal annual allowances over the remainder of the 'tax life' of the building. No matter how much the purchaser pays for the building, the maximum amount on which he can claim relief is the original building cost, which may have been incurred many years earlier and bear little relation to current prices. No relief is available for the cost of the land whether relating to new or used buildings. The tax life of industrial buildings is 25 years for expenditure on or after 6 November 1962 and 50 years for expenditure before that date. See

Example 5

The construction costs of an industrial building in December 1985 were £100,000, the land cost being £25,000. Initial allowance of £25,000 and annual allowances of £4,000 for seven years, totalling £53,000, have been claimed.

The building (including £40,000 for the land) is sold in November 1992 for

(a) £74,000   (b) £120,000   (c) £200,000

The vendor's position is

	(a) £	(b) £	(c) £
Sale proceeds	74,000	120,000	200,000
Land included	40,000	40,000	40,000
Building proceeds	34,000	80,000	160,000
Building cost	100,000	100,000	100,000
Cost of owning building	66,000	20,000	Nil
Allowances already given	53,000	53,000	53,000
Balancing allowance/(charge)	£13,000	£(33,000)	£(53,000)

In the case of (c) there would also be a chargeable gain:

Proceeds (land and buildings)	200,000
Cost (land and buildings)	125,000
Chargeable gain (before indexation allowance)	£75,000

The purchaser would get reliefs as follows.

	(a) £	(b) £	(c) £
Cost to him (building only)	£34,000	£80,000	£160,000
Restrict to original cost if less than purchase price			£100,000
Annual allowance 1/18th*	£1,889	£4,444	£5,556

(*18 years of 25-year life remaining, ignoring fractions of year for illustration.)

If the building had been built in June 1966, there would have been no balancing adjustment for the seller and no allowances to the buyer, because it would be over 25 years old. The capital allowances given would not be deducted from the cost to calculate the capital gain.

Example 6

In February 1992, i.e. in the tax year 1991/92, a married man purchased a workshop in an enterprise zone from a developer for
£72,000 (including land £6,000), the first letting taking place in the
following tax year, i.e. 1992/93. He had rent income from another
property of £9,800 in 1991/92 and he had other income of £40,000.
His total income in 1992/93 was £60,000 and is expected to continue
at that level. He could claim industrial buildings allowances as
follows.

Available initial allowance   100% × £66,000 but take 21,000
which can be utilised as follows:

Against rent income of 1991/92	9,800
	11,200
Then against other income of 1991/92	40,000
Leaving taxable income (just above basic rate threshold after personal allowances) of	£28,800

The unrelieved expenditure is £45,000 (£66,000–£21,000) and this is
relieved as follows:

1992/93 (25% × £66,000)	16,500
1993/94 (25% × £66,000)	16,500
1994/95 (the remainder)	12,000
	£45,000

If he wanted to eliminate his taxable income in 1991/92 he could
instead claim initial allowance of £44,785 for that year and then
claim relief as follows.

	1991/92	1992/93	1993/4
Total income	49,800	60,000	60,000
Initial allowance	44,785		
Writing-down allowance		16,500	4,715
Leaving taxable income (before personal allowances) of	£5,015	£43,500	£55,285

This would save basic rate tax in 1991/92 at the expense of
additional higher rate tax in 1993/94 and 1994/95.

example 5 on page 258. If a building's tax life has already expired, there is no balancing adjustment for the seller and the purchaser cannot claim any allowances at all.

Where plant and machinery is purchased with a building, the purchase price needs to be apportioned and plant and machinery allowances can then be claimed on the appropriate part of the purchase price. There is no restriction of plant and machinery allowances to the original cost of the items.

Interaction with VAT capital goods scheme (s 159A; FA 1991, Sch 14)

Input tax adjustments under the VAT capital goods scheme (see page 88) are reflected in capital allowances computations. Changes to VAT paid in respect of an industrial building will be added to or deducted from the unrelieved expenditure on the building and writing-down allowances re-calculated over the remainder of the building's tax life. Similarly, adjustments for VAT on computers will be made in the plant and machinery pool or short-life asset computation in the period in which the VAT adjustment is made.

Hotels (ss 7, 19)

Relief is available for construction costs in respect of a qualifying hotel or hotel extension. The hotel or extension must be of a permanent nature, be open for at least four months between April and October, and when open must have at least ten letting bedrooms offering sleeping accommodation. It must provide services of breakfast, evening meal, making beds and cleaning rooms. The relief works in the same way as that for industrial buildings (see above). The annual writing-down allowance is 4% of cost. If the hotel is in an enterprise zone, it qualifies for the allowances described below, with no restriction on months of opening or number of bedrooms etc.

Buildings in enterprise zones (ss 1, 6, 10A, 10B, 17A; F(No 2)A 1992, s 70 and Sch 13)

When an area has been designated as an Enterprise Zone by the Secretary of State, expenditure incurred or contracted for within ten years after the creation of the zone on any buildings other than dwelling houses qualifies for an initial allowance of 100%, or whatever lower amount is claimed. (If part of a building was used as a dwelling, the whole expenditure would still qualify, providing the expenditure on that part did not exceed 25% of the total building cost.) Any expenditure on which initial allowance is not claimed qualifies for writing-down allowances of 25% of cost (straight line method) until it is written off in full. See example 6 on page 259. Where fixed plant or machinery is an integral part of the building, it can be treated as part of the building for the purposes of claiming enterprise zone allowances. Balancing allowances or charges apply on the disposal of buildings in enterprise zones using the same rules as for industrial buildings (see page 257), and treating the life of the building as being 25 years.

Purchase within two years after first use

For enterprise zone buildings first used on or after 16 December 1991, someone who buys such a building within two years after it is first used is treated as if he had bought an unused building, so that he can claim the 100% initial allowance or 25% writing-down allowance as indicated above. As far as any subsequent second-hand purchaser is concerned, the position is the same as for purchasers outside the first two years (see below), but the 25-year life of the building dates from the date of first use by the person who purchased within the first two years of use.

Purchase more than two years after first use

Where the first disposal of an enterprise zone building occurs more than two years after it is first used, the purchaser cannot claim the 100% or 25% enterprise zone allowances. He gets writing-down allowances only, normally on the lower of the price paid by him and the original construction cost. The writing-down allowance is calculated by spreading the unrelieved expenditure over the balance of the building's 25-year life which is unexpired at the date of purchase. Where, however, a building is transferred between connected persons (say husband and wife), they may make a claim to treat the transfer as being at written-down value (see page 249), so that the benefit to the vendor of the higher enterprise zone building allowances is not lost as a result of the transfer.

Limits on enterprise zone allowances

Where part of the expenditure on a building was incurred neither within the ten-year life of the enterprise zone, nor under a contract entered into within the ten-year period, that part of the expenditure qualifies only for the normal level of buildings allowances (i.e. for industrial buildings or hotels), or not at all if it is a non-qualifying building.

Enterprise zone allowances cannot be claimed on expenditure incurred more than 20 years after the site was included in the enterprise zone, no matter when the contract was entered into.

Way in which allowances are given

Enterprise zone allowances may be claimed both by traders and investors. The treatment is dealt with on page 248.

Patents (TA 1988, ss 520–522, 524, 528)

Expenditure incurred in devising and patenting an invention (or an abortive attempt to do so) is allowable as a business expense. Where, however, patent rights are purchased, writing-down allowances at 25% on the reducing balance method are available, with all expenditure on patent rights after 31 March 1986 being pooled.

Balancing charges arise in the usual way, and a balancing allowance will be given on any unallowed expenditure, if the last of the rights come to an end without subsequently being revived or on the permanent discontinuance of the trade.

Expenditure before 1 April 1986 was relieved by way of capital allowances in equal annual instalments over seventeen years, or over the period for which the rights were acquired, whichever was less. So if accounts were made up to 31 March and patent rights with twelve years to run were purchased for £1,800 in January 1986, allowances of £150 p.a. are given for twelve years, commencing in 1986/87 in the case of an individual or in the accounting period ended 31 March 1986 for a company.

Although a balancing charge can never exceed the allowances given, there are specific provisions to charge a capital profit on patent rights as income rather than as a capital gain. The profit is not dealt with as part of the business profits but is charged to income tax under Schedule D, Case VI over six years in equal instalments, commencing with the tax year of receipt, unless the taxpayer elects to have the whole sum charged in the year of receipt.

Patents allowances granted to non-traders can only be set against income from the patent rights and not against any other income.

Know-how (TA 1988, ss 530–533)

'Know-how' is defined as any industrial information or techniques which are likely to assist in a manufacturing process, or the working of a mine, or the carrying out of agricultural, forestry or fishing operations.

Before 1 April 1986, capital expenditure on its acquisition for use in a trade was allowed by way of a writing-down allowance in equal instalments over six years. This system is replaced for expenditure on or after 1 April 1986 by an annual writing-down allowance of 25% on the reducing balance method. Any additional expenditure is added to the unrelieved balance and any sale proceeds are deducted from it before calculating the writing-down allowance. If the sale proceeds exceed the tax written-down value, a balancing charge is made and this is not restricted to the allowances given, so that the balancing charge will include any excess of the proceeds over the original cost. For sales where the expenditure was incurred on or before 31 March 1986, the proceeds are treated as a trading receipt.

If know-how is sold as part of a business, the payment is regarded as being for goodwill, unless both seller and buyer elect within two years of the disposal for it to be treated as a sale of know-how.

If the trade ceases during the writing-down period but the know-how is not sold, relief for the unallowed expenditure is given by way of a balancing allowance.

Scientific research (ss 136–139)

Capital expenditure for the purposes of scientific research is allowed in full, when incurred, in taxing trading income. Expenditure on land and dwelling houses does not generally qualify for relief.

Proceeds of sale or compensation payments on destruction (not exceeding the allowance given) are treated as a trading receipt, with open market value sometimes being substituted for those proceeds.

If the sale takes place in the same basis period as the expenditure is incurred, any deficiency between the cost of expenditure and the proceeds is allowed as a deduction.

Mineral extraction (ss 98–121)

Expenditure on mineral extraction before 1 April 1986 was relieved by initial allowances and by writing-down allowances based on future estimated output.

The system changed for expenditure after 31 March 1986, any unallowed capital expenditure under the old system being treated as qualifying expenditure incurred on 1 April 1986. Writing-down allowances are available on a reducing balance basis on:

	Rate
Pre-trading expenditure	10%
Acquisition of a mineral asset (mineral deposits, land comprising mineral deposits etc.)	10%
Other qualifying expenditure	25%

A balancing charge will be made if sales proceeds exceed tax written-down value. A balancing allowance will be given in the chargeable period when the mineral extraction trade ceases, or when particular mineral deposits cease to be worked, and in the case of pre-trading expenditure, when trading commences or exploration is abandoned before then.

Tax points

- A specific claim for capital allowances must be made by individuals and partnerships, so it is important to ensure that the appropriate entry is made on the tax return and supported by computations.

- If claiming the maximum allowances means wasting personal allowances, you can reduce your claim for certain allowances—see page 249. You will then get writing-down allowances on an increased amount in future years.

- Alternatively you can use capital allowances to turn a trading profit into a loss which you can relieve against other income (see chapter 25).

- Companies will benefit by not taking allowances, where they want to leave profits high enough to take advantage of reliefs which are only available in the current period, such as group relief for losses or double tax relief. The amount on which writing-down allowances can be claimed in later years is increased accordingly.

- Allowances available on capital expenditure incurred on commencing trading on your own or in partnership may contribute to a trading loss, which may be carried back against the income of earlier years (see chapter 25).

- Whereas you only get 25% writing-down allowance when you buy cars, if you lease a car instead, you can set the whole of the leasing charge against your profit, subject to disallowance of any private element and the restriction on the allowable hire charge where the car cost the leasing company more than £12,000—see page 232.

- When you buy or sell a group of assets, such as goodwill, plant and machinery and trade premises, some will be subject to capital allowances at different rates and some will not qualify for allowances at all. It is essential that the price apportionment is realistic and is agreed with the other party at the time of purchase or sale in order to avoid complications when you submit the tax computations.

- If there is doubt as to whether a contract for the purchase of plant or machinery is a hire-purchase contract or a leasing contract, it is advisable to check with the finance company as to the nature of the payments to them to ensure the correct treatment in tax computations.

- Writing-down allowances at 25% on the reducing balance method will write off about 90% of the expenditure in eight years. The option to keep short-life assets out of the plant and machinery pool enables you to shorten this time to five years or less if the assets are sold or scrapped within that period.

- The election to continue the capital allowances computation of the vendor of a business, where the successors are connected persons, has to be made within two years after the date of succession. Do not forget the time limit.

- Plan the expenditure on any non-qualifying parts of a new industrial building (for example, offices) to ensure, if possible, that it does not exceed the allowable 25% for non-qualifying expenditure.

- Since the purchase of land does not qualify for industrial buildings allowances, more tax-efficient use of capital expenditure can be achieved by constructing on leasehold land.

- An intending investor, who considers the cost of a qualifying building in an enterprise zone is too high for him, may participate on a co-ownership basis, sharing the allowances in proportion to the cost borne, or through an enterprise zone property trust.

- The allowances for buildings in enterprise zones are available for *any* commercial buildings and not just industrial buildings—see page 260.

23
Partnerships

Assessment (TA 1988, ss 60–63, 111; TCGA 1992, s 59)

An assessment on the trading profits of a partnership is made jointly in respect of all the partners. The assessment is normally calculated in the same way as an assessment on any self-employed person (see chapter 21). Thus the profits of an established partnership for the year ended 31 August 1991 will be assessed in 1992/93.

One assessment is made in the partnership name, any partner being liable for the whole of the tax if it is not paid. The liability of one of the partners, or of any group of partners, can never be separated from that of the other partners.

There is no joint assessment on non-trading income or on capital gains of the partnership. Here, each partner is assessed on his share, and there is no recourse against the others if he does not pay. Thus an assessment on each partner will be made in respect of his share of interest received, or of rent where there is co-ownership of land.

Division of assessments (TA 1988, s 277)

To arrive at each partner's income for tax purposes, profits assessable in a tax year are divided amongst the partners in the way they have agreed to share profits for that tax year under the partnership agreement. This division may not be in the same proportions as those used to divide the profits on which the assessment is based. See example 1.

Example 1

A, B and C, who have been in business for many years, share profits equally in the year ended 30 November 1991. The profit is £60,000, each taking a £20,000 share. By 6 April 1992 they have amended the profit-sharing ratio to 2:1:1.

The 1992/93 assessment is divided as follows:
A £30,000   B £15,000   C £15,000.

Sometimes, the profit-sharing arrangement may not be a straight split but may provide for interest on partners' capital, partnership salaries or perhaps a system of slices by which profits are disproportionately divided. The division for tax purposes takes into account any variation of profit-sharing arrangements during a tax year. See example 2.

Example 2

The profit of X, Y and Z for the year ended 30 June 1991 is £40,000, shared in the ratio 3:1:1, so that X has £24,000, and Y and Z £8,000 each.

They continue sharing in this way until 5 October 1992, when the arrangements are changed to give interest on partnership capital amounting to £4,000, £1,000 and £700 per annum respectively, annual partnership salaries of £7,500, £12,000 and £10,000 respectively, with the balance being shared equally.

The division of the tax assessment for 1992/93 is:

	Total	X	Y	Z
Profit from 6.4.92 to 5.10.92 (½ of that of year to 30.6.91)	20,000			
Split 3:1:1		12,000	4,000	4,000
Profit from 6.10.92 to 5.4.93 (½ of that of year to 30.6.91)	20,000			
Interest on capital (6 months)	(2,850)	2,000	500	350
Partnership salaries (6 months)	(14,750)	3,750	6,000	5,000
Balance remaining (split equally)	2,400	800	800	800
Division for tax purposes	40,000	18,550	11,300	10,150
Whereas accounts profit was divided	40,000	24,000	8,000	8,000

Change of partners (TA 1988, s 61, 62, 113)

If all the old partners sell out to new partners, then clearly the old trade has ceased for tax purposes. But there is a cessation of trade for tax purposes whenever a new partner is introduced or an existing partner leaves the partnership. If, however, there is at least one continuing partner, and all those who were partners before and after the change elect in writing to the Revenue within two years after the date of the change, assessments will continue on the normal previous year basis.

Since, in calculating the tax payable by a partnership, an assessment is divided between the partners in the way in which they share profits in the year of assessment, it follows that where a continuation election is made on a change of partners, the tax assessment will be divided between different persons from those who actually shared the profits. See example 3.

Example 3

Profits in the year ended 30 June 1991 £30,000, and in the year ended 30 June 1992 £45,000, were divided equally between the then partners A and B.

C is admitted as a partner on 1 July 1992. A, B and C share profits equally thereafter.

All three partners sign and submit to the Revenue an election for continuity within two years after 1 July 1992.

Assessments and their division, leading to the calculation of tax payable, become:

	Total	A	B	C
1992/93 £30,000 (profits of year to 30.6.91)				
To 30 June 1992, say 3 months	7,500	3,750	3,750	—
1 July 1992 to 5 April 1993, say 9 months	22,500	7,500	7,500	7,500
	30,000	11,250	11,250	7,500
1993/94 £45,000 (profits of year to 30.6.92)	45,000	15,000	15,000	15,000

C is charged to tax on a share of the profits of £30,000 to 30 June 1991 and £45,000 to 30 June 1992 even though he did not actually share in those profits.

The partners cannot alter the statutory rules for dividing the taxable profit, and the *total* tax payable as a result of the statutory division will depend on each partner's personal circumstances. They could, however, agree to bear the calculated tax charge in a different way, so that for example C in example 3 did not bear any of the tax, not having received any of the profit. This will not normally be done in an established partnership, since C will after all have received partnership income from 1 July 1992 onwards, and it is from this date that he is being included in the division of the assessment and paying tax on his share. He will get a compensating benefit when he leaves the partnership, either because a continuation election is made and some of the profit in which he has shared is assessed on those remaining in the business in a later tax year or years or because the closing year rules apply when he leaves, the firm having either not made the continuation election or closed down completely. The tax charge for the final tax year is then based on the profits actually made in that year, with the Revenue having the option to assess the two years before the last on the basis of the profits actually earned in those two years. Some profits will, however, escape assessment as indicated in chapter 21, compensating in terms of time for those assessed more than once at the beginning but the amounts not being in any way related.

The tax position for the new firm where a continuation election could have been but was not made depends on the nature of the change. If the change is from sole trader to partnership or vice versa, the normal opening year rules apply (see page 238). If there is more than one individual in both the old and new firms, then the assessments for the first four tax years on the new partnership are based on the actual profits made. The partnership can elect for the assessments of the fifth and sixth tax years to be based on the actual profits made in those years (instead of the election applying in the second and third tax years as is the case when the normal new business rules apply). This election must be made within six years after the end of the sixth year of assessment in the new partnership. These special rules for multi-partner firms were introduced to counter widespread tax avoidance through mani-pulation of the normal opening and closing year rules.

Capital allowances (CAA 1990, ss 77, 152)

Where a continuation election is made on a change of partners, capital allow-ances are computed as if no change had taken place. If the continuation election is not made, allowances are computed as if the assets had been disposed of and reacquired at market value, but, for plant and machinery, the partners may elect within two years of the change for a deemed disposal value equal to the written-down value brought forward by the old firm, so that there will be no balancing adjustment, but the old firm will get no allowance in the tax year of transfer.

Work in progress (TA 1988, s 104(4); Revenue Statement of Practice SP 3/90)

Profit is affected by the amount of work in progress at the start and end of an accounting period. The Revenue will accept that the accounts of established professional practices can be prepared without including work in progress, so that an increase or decrease in work in progress over the accounting period does not affect the profit. If it is then decided that work in progress should in future be included, tax is payable on the amount that is introduced into the accounts. If, on the other hand, work in progress is currently taken into account and you wish to exclude it, tax will have been paid on its value up till then and tax will again be paid when the work is invoiced. There is no relief for the double charge.

Where work in progress is included, there is a choice as to whether it is valued at cost including production overhead, cost plus all overhead, or cost plus overhead plus profit. A change in the way in which work in progress is valued will affect the profit figure, and while the tax arising will usually be dealt with in one year only, the Revenue may seek to spread the effect over a number of past years if insufficient regard had in the past been paid to the valuation under whichever of the three valid methods had been used.

Changes both in the way work in progress is valued and in the way it is accounted for are often made in the interests of consistency when two firms amalgamate. This is a complex area, on which professional advice is essential.

Introducing funds to a partnership (TA 1988, ss 362, 363)

If a partner who is not a limited partner borrows to introduce funds to a partnership, either as capital or on loan, interest on the borrowing is allowable at his top tax rate. If, however, a partner then withdraws all or part of his capital, the introduced funds will be treated as repaid accordingly, restricting or eliminating the amount on which interest relief is available. This provision does not apply if the partner withdraws his capital *before* introducing new funds. The partnership would, however, need to be able to bridge the gap between the withdrawal of the existing funds and the introduction of the new. See page 232.

Consultancy

An outgoing partner may perform consultancy services for the partnership. He will be taxed on the income either under Schedule E, if the services are provided under a contract of service, or under Schedule D, Case I or II, if performed under a contract for services (see page 222). The payments will be an allowable deduction in calculating the taxable profits of the partnership so long as they satisfy the 'wholly and exclusively' rule (see chapter 20).

Trading losses (TA 1988, ss 380–390)

Chapter 25 deals with the calculation of the available loss reliefs and ways in which relief may be given. Relief for partnership trading losses may be claimed by each partner quite independently of the others. Thus one partner may decide to carry forward his share of the loss, another to set his against other income of the same tax year, another to set it against any income of the next tax year, another to carry back against the income of previous years in the early years of his being a partner, and so on.

Where there have been changes in profit-sharing arrangements, the ability of partners to make different loss claims can result in the total relief available being greater than the actual loss, because a claim under TA 1988, s 380, against other income of the tax year of loss and the following year, requires losses to be split according to the sharing arrangements of the tax year itself, while carrying forward a loss under TA 1988, s 385 requires a split on the accounts year basis.

The carry-back loss rules for the first four years of a new trade only apply to a new partner, not to the continuing partners, whether or not the change of partnership has been treated as a cessation and restart. There is an anti-avoidance provision blocking carry-back claims by a new partner if he is joining his spouse in a continuing business.

Partnership assets (TCGA 1992, ss 59, 286; Revenue Statements of Practice D12 (17/1/75), SP 1/79 and SP 1/89)

When partners join or leave a partnership, this will usually involve a change in the persons who are entitled to share in the partnership assets. There is no capital gains tax consequence if an incoming partner introduces cash which is credited to his capital account. Nor is there normally any capital gains tax consequence when an outgoing partner withdraws his capital account. In the first instance, an incoming partner is paying in a sum which remains to his credit in his capital account, whilst in the second instance, an outgoing partner is only withdrawing what belongs to him.

If, however, before an outgoing partner withdraws his capital account, that capital account has been credited with a surplus on revaluation of partnership assets (e.g. premises or goodwill), his leaving the partnership will give rise to a realised capital gain in respect of the excess on revaluation, and to that extent his withdrawal of capital is chargeable to capital gains tax.

This charge will arise not only on a person ceasing to be a partner, but whenever a partner's capital account includes a revaluation of chargeable assets and his entitlement to share in the assets is reduced. He is treated as having disposed of a proportion of the chargeable assets equivalent to the drop in his entitlement. The change will usually correspond with that in the profit-sharing ratio, except where income and capital profits are shared differently, when the capital ratio will apply.

A payment by an incoming partner to the existing partners for a share in the chargeable assets such as goodwill or premises will constitute a disposal by the existing partners for capital gains tax, and a cost for capital gains tax to the incoming partner. The same applies where cash passes on a variation of profit-sharing arrangements without a change in partners. It makes no difference whether the cash is left in the partnership (by a credit to the capital account of those disposing) or is withdrawn by them, or indeed is dealt with outside the partnership itself. The test is whether a partner receives consideration for reducing his share in the partnership. Conversely, if he does not receive consideration, whilst there is still a disposal in the sense that his partnership share is less than it was, then, unless the partners have a family connection, the market value of the assets is not substituted for the purpose of calculating and charging the gain that could have been made, and thus no chargeable gain arises.

See example 4.

Annuities to outgoing partners (TA 1988, s 628 and Revenue Statements of Practice D12 (17/1/75) and SP 1/79)

An outgoing partner may be paid an annuity by the continuing partners when he retires. He will not be subject to capital gains tax on the capitalised value of the annuity so long as the annuity is regarded as reasonable recognition for past services to the partnership. The average of the partner's best

Example 4

X and Y are in partnership. Z is admitted as an equal partner, introducing £45,000 as capital which is credited to his capital account. The £45,000 is neither a capital gains tax base cost for Z nor a disposal by X and Y. The partnership assets include premises worth £180,000, which cost £63,000 when acquired in 1983.

Consider the following alternatives:

(1) Before Z's admission, X and Y revalue the premises up to £180,000 by crediting each of their capital accounts with £58,500.

On Z's admission they each make a chargeable gain of:

		£
Value of premises reflected in their capital account (½ each)		90,000
Share of premises retained after Z's admission (⅓ each)		60,000
Disposal proceeds		30,000
Less cost:		
Cost was ½ each × £63,000	31,500	
Cost is now ⅓ each × £63,000	21,000	
Cost of part disposed of		10,500
Gain (subject to any available indexation allowance)		£19,500

The cost of Z's share in the premises is £60,000 (⅓ × £180,000), equivalent to the disposal proceeds of X and Y.

(2) The premises are not revalued on the admission of Z.

There is then no deemed gain by X and Y, and the cost for capital gains tax purposes for each of X and Y is ⅓ × £63,000 = £21,000. Z's cost will be £21,000 plus indexation allowance to date. On future disposals, X and Y will get indexation allowance from 1983 and Z from the date he acquired his share.

(3) Z privately pays £60,000 (£30,000 each) to X and Y, for a ⅓rd share in the partnership premises.

X and Y are treated as receiving £30,000 each as in (1).

The capital gains cost for future disposals in the case of (1) and (3) is:

	X	Y	Z
Original cost	31,500	31,500	—
On introduction of Z	(10,500)	(10,500)	21,000
Gains on which X and Y are assessable (subject to indexation)			39,000
	21,000	21,000	60,000

On future disposals, X and Y will each get indexation allowance on £21,000 from 1983 and Z on £60,000 from the date he acquired his share.

three years' assessable profit shares out of the last seven is calculated. The annuity is considered reasonable if it does not exceed the fraction of that average amount obtained from the following table:

Years of service	Fraction
1-5	1/60 per year
6	8/60
7	16/60
8	24/60
9	32/60
10	2/3

The annuity is a charge against the income of the paying partners. They will deduct basic rate income tax when making the payment and claim relief at the higher rate where appropriate by an adjustment in the partnership or personal assessments.

Capital gains tax

Retirement relief (TCGA 1992, s 163, Sch 6)

The relief on gains up to £150,000 and on one half of the gains between £150,000 and £600,000 (gains up to £125,000 exempt with 50% relief up to £500,000 for disposals before 19 March 1991) applies to the disposal of a partnership share or of business assets owned personally by a partner and used in the business of the partnership. He must be 55 years of age or over (60 for disposals before 19 March 1991), or be retiring before age 55 through ill health. Husband and wife partners can each get the relief if the conditions are satisfied. To qualify for the maximum relief there must be ten years qualifying trading. If there are less than ten qualifying years but at least one, the available relief is reduced according to the number of qualifying years (see example 6 on page 50).

A mere sale of assets by the partnership when a partner is eligible for the relief will not entitle that partner to the relief on his share of the gain. There must be a reduction of his interest in the partnership.

Where an asset is owned personally by a partner, retirement relief is restricted if the partnership pays rent, and if a full market rent is charged for any part of the ten-year qualifying period relief is lost for that part of the period. The Revenue take the view that if, instead of rent, it had been agreed to pay the partner an appropriate amount by way of a first slice of profits, the retirement relief is still restricted.

Replacement of business assets (TCGA 1972, ss 152–157)

Rollover relief for the replacement of business assets (see page 48) is available where an asset owned personally by a partner and used in the partnership is disposed of and replaced. This is not affected by the payment of rent by the partnership.

Death of a partner

Where a partner dies in service:

(a) any election which is made for continuity of assessments must be signed by his personal representatives, otherwise a cessation of the partnership cannot be avoided.
(b) any gains arising on the disposal of his share in partnership assets by reason of the death are exempt, like gains on any other chargeable asset held at death.
(c) the annuity referred to earlier may be paid to his widow or dependants.

Inheritance tax

The interest of a deceased partner in the partnership (including his capital account) ranks as relevant business property for the 100% business property relief unless the surviving partners are obliged to acquire his share, in which case it is regarded as an entitlement under a contract for sale and not therefore eligible for relief. Relief is not lost where there is an option, as opposed to an obligation, for the share to be acquired by the surviving partners.

Although the option to pay tax by ten annual instalments applies to the transfer of a partnership share, the introduction of the 100% relief has made the instalment option irrelevant for such transfers. The instalment option is still relevant for transfers of land owned by an individual partner and used in the business, the rate of business property relief for such land being 50% (see chapter 5). Interest is, however, charged on the full amount of tax outstanding rather than just on overdue instalments.

Value added tax

Customs and Excise need to be notified of a change of partner within 30 days, but not of a change in profit-sharing arrangements. The registration number will normally continue. A retiring partner remains liable for VAT due from the partnership until the date on which Customs are notified of his retirement.

National insurance

For the national insurance position of partnerships, see page 281.

Stamp duty

There is no stamp duty on a partnership agreement. When a partnership is dissolved, the division of assets on the dissolution attracts only a 50p stamp as a conveyance or transfer other than on sale.

Stamp duty arises on a document evidencing a payment by one person to another for a share in the partnership (but not where an incoming partner merely introduces capital to his own capital or current account), and also when the partnership transactions involve documents requiring to be stamped, for example in respect of land transactions. Stamp duty on all transactions other than those relating to land and buildings is shortly to be abolished (see chapter 6).

Business rates

Transitional relief for business rates (see page 103) is not now lost on a change of partners whether or not someone who on 31 March 1990 was a sole or joint owner of the property now occupied by the new firm remains a partner.

Miscellaneous

A *salaried partner* is not the same as a partner who is allocated a salary as part of the profit-sharing arrangement. Senior employees are often described as partners in professional firms. They remain liable to income tax under Schedule E as employees, receiving a salary for the duties of their employment.

The share of a *sleeping partner* ranks as unearned income and cannot therefore support a pension premium.

A *company* may be a partner with individuals. In this case the profit share of the company for the relevant accounting period is liable to corporation tax, whilst the share applicable to the partners who are individuals is assessed to income tax on the normal previous year basis. This does not, however, apply to capital allowances. Capital allowances are computed for the accounting period and the shares of the individuals are apportioned to the tax years comprised in that period.

A partnership may include a *limited partner* under the Limited Partnership Act 1907, whose liability is limited to the amount of the partner's agreed capital contribution. The limited partner, who may be either an individual or a company, cannot take part in the management of the partnership. If the profit share of a limited partner ranks as unearned income, it cannot be used to support a pension premium. Certain reliefs available to a limited partner cannot exceed the amount of the partner's agreed capital contribution plus undrawn profits. The reliefs concerned are reliefs for trading losses (including capital allowances) against income other than trading income (see pages 286 and 296), interest paid in connection with the trade by an individual, trade charges on income paid by a company, and certain capital allowances in connection with the trade for which relief is given by discharge or repayment of tax (such as some buildings allowances).

Husband and wife partnerships. The national insurance cost of employing a wife is usually greater than if she were a partner with the husband. Moreover, if she is a partner, capital gains tax retirement relief will apply to the disposal of her share as well as his. But this must be weighed against her taking on the legal liability associated with partnership. Taking a wife into partnership may be regarded as an appropriate way of getting the best out of independent taxation, but it must be genuine, with the wife's share being appropriate to her contribution to the business, otherwise there is the risk of the partnership arrangement being treated as a settlement by the husband, in which case the income would remain his.

Partnership itself, and matters arising, need not be governed by *formal written agreement*. In the absence of such agreement, sometimes indeed despite it, the Revenue will require other evidence of partnership, for example the name of, and operating arrangements for, bank accounts, VAT registration, names on stationery, contracts, licences etc.

The overseas aspect of partnerships is dealt with in chapter 41.

Tax points

- Failure to make a continuation election can be costly as well as inconvenient, particularly if the actual basis of assessment has to apply for the first four years following the change, with later, perhaps higher, profits then forming the basis for more than one assessment. To avoid the risk of a partner not being prepared to sign an election, include a clause in the partnership agreement requiring an incoming or outgoing partner to sign one if asked to do so by the other partners, giving each partner power of attorney for the others under the partnership deed.

- An election for continuity is not, however, always advantageous, and a comparison of the alternatives should be made in respect of the old and new partnerships taken together.

  An agreement between the partners that a disadvantaged partner is compensated for any extra tax suffered is always possible and may persuade an otherwise dissenting partner to join in the election.

- An election for assessments to continue on a preceding year basis can be made so long as there is one individual engaged in carrying on the business both before and after the change. It can, therefore, apply where a sole proprietor is joined by a person or persons in partnership, or where a sole proprietor is left following the departure of one or more persons who were in partnership with him. In those circumstances, the normal new business assessment rules apply if an election for continuity of assessments is not made. The special rules set out on page 268 only apply where there was a partnership before *and* after the change.

- Calculate annuities to retiring partners within the allowable capital gains tax limits, leaving them taxable only as income in the hands of the recipient and allowable for income tax to the payers. An inflationary increase to an annuity which is initially within the allowable limits will not affect the capital gains exemption.

- Because of the previous year basis, tax is usually payable some time after the profits are earned. It is sensible to set aside sufficient funds to pay the liability on trading profits on 1 January and 1 July yearly, retaining an appropriate part from each partner's profit share for this purpose.

- To get maximum retirement relief, you do not need to have owned the business assets for ten years, only your interest in the business. If husband and wife intend to retire at the same time but one will be too young to claim any retirement relief, and the other will not use the maximum relief available, an interest in partnership assets may be transferred by the younger to the elder before they put the business up for sale.

- In the opening years of an entirely new business, consider whether it is appropriate to employ an intended partner before his admission to the partnership. Profits which form the basis of assessment for more than one tax year will then be reduced by deductions for his salary and for employers' national insurance contributions. The national insurance cost of an employee compared with a partner will need to be taken into account.

- If you have the choice of borrowing to buy your home and borrowing to introduce funds to a partnership, (other than as a limited partner), the partnership borrowing will save you tax at your highest rate, whereas the home loan will now only save you basic rate tax.

- If one spouse takes the other into partnership, it should not be forgotten that a Class 2 national insurance liability arises on the second spouse as a self-employed person. It can be costly to remember this only after the partnership has traded for some time.

- Where partners sell partnership assets (e.g. land) to raise funds to pay out a retiring partner, a capital gain may arise. The partners may, however, be able to claim to roll over the gain against their acquisition of the outgoing partner's share of the remaining business assets of the partnership.

- A merger of two or more firms is strictly a cessation of each firm and the commencement of one new firm. The converse applies where one firm splits into two or more new firms. In both cases it may not be clear whether a continuation election may be made, and whether the special partnership opening year rules apply if it is not. The Revenue have issued a Statement of Practice (SP 9/86) explaining their view and the area is one where professional advice and consultation with the the Revenue is essential.

- Income and capital profit-sharing ratios need not always be the same. Established partners can retain the whole of the future increase in value of partnership premises, to the exclusion of incoming partners, by excluding the incoming partners from the capital profit-sharing ratio.

Any running expenses of those premises, including interest on borrowing, remain allowable in calculating trading profit, which is divided in the income sharing ratio.

24
National insurance contributions for the self-employed

Background

A self-employed person over the age of 16 must, unless specifically exempted, pay both Class 2 and Class 4 contributions. Class 2 contributions are payable weekly at a flat rate and entitle the contributor to most contributory benefits, but not unemployment benefit, earnings-related supplement to retirement pension, invalidity pension and widow's benefit. Class 4 contributions are payable at a fixed percentage on profits chargeable to income tax under Schedule D, Case I or II (see chapter 21). They carry no entitlement to benefits of any kind. The legislation is in the Social Security Contributions and Benefits Act 1992 (SSCBA 1992).

Class 2 contributions

Payment (SSCBA 1992, s 11)

Class 2 contributions are payable weekly and can be made by either:

(a) purchasing a special stamp from Post Offices which is then stuck on a contribution card; or

(b) making a transfer by direct debit out of a bank or National Giro account.

The weekly rates for 1991/92 and 1992/93 are:

1991/92	£5.15
1992/93	£5.35

If Class 2 contributions are paid late, they may affect your entitlement to benefits. If they are paid after the end of the tax year following the one in which they were due, they normally have to be paid at the highest rate applicable between the due date and the payment date.

Exempt persons

Class 2 contributions are payable by 'self-employed earners', which means those who are 'gainfully employed' other than as employees. The Class 2 net is wider than Class 4, because it includes a 'business', whereas Class 4 only covers a trade, profession or vocation.

The following people are, however, not liable to pay Class 2 contributions:

(a) men and women over state pension age (men 65, women 60);
(b) someone working outside Great Britain throughout any contribution week;
(c) married women who chose on or before 11 May 1977 to pay reduced rate Class 1 contributions or to pay no Class 2 contributions (provided that this election has not been automatically revoked by divorce or possibly revoked by widowhood—see page 282);
(d) someone with small earnings who obtains a certificate of exception (see below);
(e) someone who is not 'ordinarily' self-employed (see below);
(f) someone who, for a full week, is
  (i) incapable of work, or
  (ii) in legal custody or prison, or
  (iii) receiving sickness, invalidity or injury benefit or maternity allowance; and
(g) someone who, for any day in a particular week, receives unemployability supplement or invalid care allowance.

In the case of (f) and (g), the exemption is applicable only to the particular week concerned.

Small earnings

You may apply for a certificate of exception for a tax year if you can show that:

(i) your net earnings for that tax year are expected to be less than a specified limit; or
(ii) your net earnings for the previous tax year were less than the limit specified for that year and that circumstances have not materially altered.

In this context 'net earnings' are earnings shown in the profit and loss account as opposed to taxable earnings. Enterprise allowance is not included. Where an accounting period overlaps 5 April earnings are strictly apportioned on a time basis between tax years but in considering (ii) above, the DSS will normally take the accounts year ended in the previous tax year.

The small earnings exception limits are

1990/91	£2,600
1991/92	£2,900
1992/93	£3,030

Certificates of exception must be renewed each tax year and can be applied for on form CF 10 which is contained in DSS leaflet NI 27A—'People with small earnings from self-employment'. Exception from payment cannot apply from a date earlier than 13 weeks before the date of the application.

Not paying contributions will affect your retirement pension (see page 169) and other contributory benefits. You need not apply for a certificate of exception if you don't want to, in which event self-employed contributions will be payable unless you are not 'ordinarily' self-employed—see below.

If you paid contributions (after 6 April 1988) but could have claimed exception, you may apply for a refund. Refund claims must be submitted by 31 December after the end of the relevant tax year. Where repayments are concerned, the earnings will be calculated strictly over the tax year, which means claims may have to be made before the earnings have been accurately calculated.

Persons not 'ordinarily' self-employed

When someone applies to pay Class 2 contributions he may be informed by the DSS that they consider that he is not ordinarily self-employed and that there is therefore no liability to such contributions. There is no statutory definition of 'not ordinarily self-employed' but the example quoted by the DSS in leaflet NI 27A is of a person employed in a regular job whose earnings from spare-time self-employment are not expected to exceed £800 in a tax year.

If you are in this category, you do not have to apply for a certificate of exception. You would be eligible for relief under the small earnings rule anyway, but this lower limit avoids the need to apply for a certificate.

More than one self-employment

People who are self-employed have to pay only one Class 2 contribution per week no matter how many self-employed jobs they may have. In deciding whether you are entitled to a certificate of exception on the grounds of small earnings, self-employed earnings from all sources are added together.

Class 4 contributions

Payment (SSCBA 1992, ss 15–17)

Class 4 contributions are payable at a percentage rate on profits chargeable to income tax under Schedule D, Case I or II which fall between specified upper and lower limits.

Contribution rates and limits for 1991/92 and 1992/93 are:

Year	Rate	On profits	Maximum
1991/92	6.3%	Between £5,900 and £20,280	£906
1992/93	6.3%	Between £6,120 and £21,060	£941

If you have more than one self-employment, all the profits are added together when calculating your Class 4 liability.

In general, 'profits' are computed in the same way for Class 4 contributions as for income tax but certain special rules apply, for example losses allowed under TA 1988, ss 380, 383 (see chapter 25) against non-trading income and capital gains for tax purposes are set only against trading income for national insurance, and may thus be carried forward against future profits for calculating Class 4 contributions. Class 4 contributions are calculated and collected by the Inland Revenue together with income tax payable under Schedule D, Case I or II; the contributions are therefore payable at the same time as the income tax liability on the relevant profits, usually in equal instalments on 1 January in the tax year and on the following 1 July.

One half of the Class 4 contributions is deductible from total income in calculating your income tax liability. This deduction is made in the Schedule D, Case I or II assessment.

Exempt persons

The following people are not liable to pay Class 4 contributions:

(a) men and women over state pension age (men 65, women 60);
(b) individuals who are not resident in the UK for income tax purposes;
(c) trustees and executors who are chargeable to income tax on income which they receive on behalf of other people (e.g. incapacitated persons);
(d) 'sleeping partners' who supply capital and take a share of the profits but take no active part in running the business;
(e) divers and diving supervisors working in connection with exploration and exploitation activities on the Continental shelf or in UK territorial waters;
(f) someone who is under 16 on 6 April in a particular tax year and holds a certificate of exception for that year. Application for an exception certificate should be made on form RD 901; application need only be made once as any certificate granted will cover all the relevant tax years; and
(g) someone who is not 'ordinarily' self-employed (see under Class 2 above).

Late payment of contributions

Although Class 4 contributions are collected along with Schedule D, Case I or II income tax, they do not currently attract interest if paid late, except in cases of fraudulent or negligent conduct, where the same interest and penalty provisions apply as for unpaid income tax (see page 120).

Partnerships (including husband and wife partners)

Each partner is liable to both Class 2 and Class 4 contributions, the Class 4 profit limits applying to each partner's profit share.

When computing the Class 4 liability of partnerships, including husband/wife partnerships, the Revenue will add the separate liabilities together and collect the total liability from the partnership, together with the income tax liability arising under Schedule D. Where a partner carries on a further trade or trades, the profits of all such businesses are considered together when calculating his overall Class 4 liability. Class 4 contributions are payable only up to the upper earnings limit regardless of how many businesses are involved.

Married women

If you were married or widowed before 6 April 1977, you could elect on or before 11 May 1977 not to pay full national insurance contributions. If you have made the election, you pay Class 1 contributions as an employee at a reduced rate, and you do not have to pay Class 2 self-employed contributions. You do, however, have to pay Class 4 contributions in the normal way.

You lose the right to pay no Class 2 and reduced rate Class 1 contributions in some circumstances. For details, and further points on the reduced rate election, see pages 173 and 174.

Self-employed and employed in the same tax year

If you are both self-employed and an employee, you are liable to pay Class 1, 2 and 4 contributions, and if you have more than one employment you will be liable to Class 1 contributions in each employment. There are, however, two separate maximum figures above which contributions will be refunded.

The Class 4 maximum is worked out by taking 53 Class 2 contributions plus the maximum Class 4 contributions, and is £1,225 for 1992/93. If your total contributions under Classes 1, 2 and 4 exceed this amount, you may claim a refund of the excess up to the amount of Class 4 contributions paid.

The overall maximum for all contributions is based on 53 times the maximum weekly Class 1 contribution, and is £1,731 for 1992/93. If your total contributions exceed this amount by £2.18 or more, the excess will be refunded.

Where you expect your contributions to exceed the maximum, you should apply to defer payment of Class 4, 2 or 1 contributions as appropriate (in that order).

Application for deferment of Class 4 and 2 contributions must be made on form CF 359, which is part of leaflet NP 18 'Class 4 NI Contributions'. Where deferment is granted, responsibility for the computation and collection of Class 4 contributions is transferred from the Inland Revenue to the DSS. Application for deferment of Class 1 contributions should be made on form CF 379 (part of leaflet NP 28 'More than one job').

If you feel you have overpaid contributions you may apply to the DSS for a refund. This could happen, for example, if you have several businesses and the profits of those businesses have been totalled incorrectly in arriving at your overall Class 4 liability, or if you have paid Class 1 contributions that have not been taken into account in calculating your Class 4 liability.

Tax points

- If you pay Class 2 contributions by direct debit, make sure you notify the DSS of any weeks for which a contribution is not due, for example when you are receiving sickness benefit or working abroad, so that an adjustment can be made.

- If you are both employed and self-employed, make sure you claim deferment if you are eligible. This is better than waiting till after the year end for a refund. As well as the cash flow benefit, there is another advantage if your employed earnings exceed £405 per week. If you apply for deferment on the self-employed earnings, you will have no liability at the year end because you are already paying maximum contributions. If instead you pay employed and self-employed contributions, the amount refunded is any excess over the stipulated maximum, which is based on 53 weeks' contributions. Weekly paid employees rarely have 53 pay days in a tax year, and monthly paid employees always have the equivalent of 52 weeks' contributions, so that any refund is reduced by the extra week's contribution.

- If you have applied for deferment of Class 4 contributions, make sure that tax relief is given against your income for half of any Class 4 contributions that you do eventually pay.

- If you are a married couple who both work in the business, consider whether it is better for the wife to be a partner or employee. Whilst the national insurance aspect cannot be considered in isolation, it would usually be better for her to be an employee if she earns less than £54.00 a week and to be a partner if she earns more.

- Remember that trading losses set off against non-trading income for income tax purposes are carried forward against trading profits for Class 4 contributions purposes. You will need to claim this relief from the DSS. It will not usually be given by the inspector of taxes.

- Self-employed contributions are due immediately the self-employment commences. The DSS should be asked for an application form. A small earnings exception may be asked for at the same time if the early profits are anticipated to be minimal.

- Do not delay making payment of contributions. Class 2 contributions paid more than one year after the end of the contribution year in which they were due are payable at a higher rate.

- If you take your wife or husband into partnership do not forget that a liability to Class 2 contributions will almost certainly arise. The arrears will have to be paid later if this is overlooked.

- If you are a married woman who has elected not to pay Class 2 contributions, watch the circumstances in which contributions become payable, for example following widowhood or divorce.

25
Trading losses: sole traders and partners

Calculation of loss

The rules for calculating the trading loss of an accounting period are the same as those for calculating profits (see chapter 20). There are, however, special rules as to the way in which relief is given for the loss, and, in particular, in calculating what part of the loss of an accounting period is available for relief in the opening years of a new business. Where a loss occurs in a partnership, each partner may choose what loss claim(s) to make for his share of the loss quite independently from how the other partners relieve their loss shares (see page 269).

Loss reliefs available

There are various alternative ways in which relief for trading losses may be claimed:

Carry forward against later profits of same trade (TA 1988, s 385).
Set against general income of current tax year then, from 1991/92 onwards, against capital gains of that year. Similar claims may be made in the following tax year (if the same trade is still carried on by the taxpayer) (TA 1988, s 380 and FA 1991, s 72).
In a new trade, carry back against general income of previous three tax years (TA 1988, s 381).
When a loss occurs on ceasing to trade, carry back against trading income of previous three tax years (TA 1988, ss 388, 389).

Assessments (TA 1988, s 60)

The first thing a trading loss does is to fix the assessment based on the accounting period at Nil. See example 1. However, this does not give relief for the loss.

Loss carried forward (TA 1988, s 385)

The most straightforward way of obtaining relief for a loss is by carrying it forward to reduce later income of the same trade, so that in example 1 the loss of £7,000 would reduce the 1993/94 assessment to £3,000. The carry-forward

---

Example 1

The results of a sole trader or the shares of a partner are as follows:
Year ended 31 December 1990 Profit £10,000
                         1991 Loss (£7,000)
                         1992 Profit £10,000
Assessments based thereon:
1991/92   £10,000
1992/93   Nil
1993/94   £10,000

---

is only against profits of the *same* trade, so that a change in activity will cause relief to be denied.

There are obvious disadvantages in carrying forward a loss. The trade may cease, or its nature change, before the loss is fully relieved. The relief is against the first available profits and the size of those profits may leave insufficient income to utilise the taxpayer's personal allowances, so that if the taxpayer in example 1 had personal allowances in 1993/94 of £5,165 and no other income, allowances of £2,165 would be wasted.

It is not possible to set off only £4,835 of the losses brought forward and leave £5,165 taxable profit to be covered by personal allowances. There is also a considerable delay before the loss results in a cash saving by reducing or eliminating a tax bill. If the loss in example 1 of the year to 31 December 1991 was carried forward, it would reduce the 1993/94 tax bill, which is payable in equal instalments on 1 January 1994 and 1 July 1994, so that relief in cash terms is delayed for at least two years.

Loss set against other income and gains (TA 1988, s 380; FA 1991, s 72)

Relief may be obtained more quickly by setting off the loss against any other income of the tax year in which the loss is incurred or of the next tax year, or, if the loss is large enough, of both tax years. This claim, however, cannot be made for losses incurred in 'hobby' trades as distinct from commercial activities. The set-off is also specifically prohibited for the sixth year of a consecutive run of farming and market gardening losses (reckoned before capital allowances) (TA 1988, s 397).

Strictly, a loss for set-off against other income should be calculated by reference to an income tax year, arrived at by splitting accounts, so that in example 1 the position for the income tax year 1990/91 would be:

¾ × £10,000	7,500
¼ × (£7,000)	(1,750)
Surplus	£5,750 (so no loss claim)

and for the income tax year 1991/92:

¾ × (£7,000)	(5,250)
¼ × £10,000	2,500
Loss	£(2,750)

It is important to remember that these calculations are not concerned with assessments. Those have been calculated at example 1. These calculations are of the loss for which relief may be claimed.

Since the accounting loss incurred was £7,000 and only £2,750 would be relieved by reference to the loss actually incurred in the income tax year 1991/92, the balance of the loss, i.e. £4,250, would be carried forward. However, the Revenue will in practice usually accept that the loss of an income tax year may be treated as being the loss of the accounting year ended within it, so that the loss of £7,000 in the accounting year ended 31 December 1991 may be regarded as the loss of the income tax year 1991/92. As well as being more straightforward than splitting accounts, the Revenue concession usually operates in the taxpayer's favour, giving an immediate loss claim of £7,000 in example 1 rather than £2,750 now and £4,250 carried forward. The Revenue will not follow this practice in the first three years of assessment of a new business, nor in the last year of assessment. In those years, the loss of the income tax year itself must be calculated by splitting the accounts. But otherwise their practice is normally followed. Sometimes the strict basis would benefit the taxpayer. In example 1, if the figures had related to accounts to 30 April instead of 31 December, there would be a loss on the strict basis one year earlier than the concessionary basis, i.e. in the tax year 1990/91 instead of 1991/92, as follows:

1/12 × £10,000	833
11/12 × (£7,000)	(6,417)
Loss available for relief	£(5,584)

The balance of the loss of (7,000 − 5,584 =) £1,416 would be carried forward. The benefit of claiming loss relief a year earlier would need to be weighed against the smaller loss available to set against current income compared with £7,000 on the concessionary basis.

Having ascertained the loss, relief is available against assessable income of the tax year of the loss, or of the following tax year (providing the trade is still carried on at some time in that year), or, if the loss is large enough, of both years. Claims may thus be made in example 1 for 1991/92 (the tax year of loss) and/or for 1992/93.

The assessable income against which relief is given is all income from whatever source and not just the income from the trade. (Indeed, there will usually be no income from the trade itself in the second year of claim because the assessment for that year is based on the result of the previous period, in which the loss was incurred.) It is not permissible to restrict the set-off to just part of the income, and as with the carry-forward loss claim, the loss set-off must be made *before* deducting personal allowances, so that in some cases they may be wasted.

If the trade is the only source of income, the effect of the claim against current income will be to set the loss against the previous year's assessable profits. Thus, using the figures in example 1 and assuming no other sources of income, the assessments will be:

1991/92 (based on profit of year to 31 December 1990)	10,000	
Less loss claim under Section 380	(7,000)	
		£3,000
1992/93 (based on result of year to 31 December 1991)		Nil
1993/94 (based on profit of year to 31 December 1992)		£10,000

A loss claim would not be possible in 1992/93 because there is no income for that tax year.

For married couples who both have income, the choice of how to claim relief was much wider for years before 1990/91, because it was possible, in either or both of the year of loss and the following year, either to include the spouse's income in the claim or to exclude it. The loss was thus set either against the lossmaker's income, earned before unearned, followed by the spouse's income in the same order, or just against the lossmaker's income. This gave added flexibility and a better chance of using the personal allowances. This flexibility is no longer available from 6 April 1990, when independent taxation of husband and wife came into effect, because a husband's loss cannot be set against his wife's income or vice versa. If a husband's income is too low to use his married couple's allowance, however, the unused amount may be transferred to his wife (but not any unused personal allowance, other than under the transitional provisions—see page 15).

Extending Section 380 claim to capital gains (FA 1991, s 72)

For losses incurred in 1991/92 onwards, a Section 380 claim may be extended to include set-off against capital gains, in either or both of the tax year of loss and the following year, providing the trade is still carried on in that year. The claim against income of the year must be made first (personal allowances therefore being wasted, except where married couple's allowance is transferred to a wife) and the loss available to set against capital gains is also reduced by any other loss relief claimed, for example under Section 380 in the following year or by carry-back under Section 381 in a new business. The amount of capital gains available to relieve the trading loss is the amount of the capital gains less any capital losses of the relevant year less unrelieved capital losses brought forward from earlier years. Having identified the amount *available* for relief in this way, that amount is then treated as an allowable loss of the relevant year and is therefore given *in priority to* brought forward capital losses. The claim may mean wasting all or part of the annual exemption. See example 2. Where there are capital losses brought forward that already reduce gains to the exempt level, the trading loss claim would give no immediate tax saving and it would be a question of whether it would be preferable to have unrelieved trading losses carried forward or unrelieved capital losses carried forward. See example 3.

Example 2

Trader makes loss of £15,000 in year to 31 December 1992, and claims Section 380 relief for 1992/93 against his total income for that year of £10,000 (being trading profits for year to 31 December 1991 of £7,000 plus other income £3,000), and against his capital gains. His gains and losses of the year were £12,000 and £2,000 respectively.

The Section 380 claim against income covers £10,000 of the loss, and wastes personal allowances (although if he is married, the married couple's allowance may be transferred to his wife).

The claim against the net capital gains of £10,000 covers the remaining £5,000 loss, with the balance of gains of £5,000 covered by the annual exemption, but with £800 of the annual exemption wasted.

Example 3

Facts as in example 2, but there are capital losses brought forward of £5,500.

If relief for the trading loss is claimed against capital gains, the gains available are £10,000 less £5,500 = £4,500, leaving £500 trading loss to be carried forward. The gains of the year of £10,000 are reduced by trading losses of £4,500 to £5,500, which will be covered by the annual exemption, and the brought forward capital losses of £5,500 will still be carried forward.

If the claim against gains had not been made, the gains of £10,000 would be reduced by £4,200 of the capital losses brought forward, leaving gains of £5,800 covered by the annual exemption and unrelieved capital losses carried forward of £1,300, in addition to unrelieved trading losses carried forward of £5,000.

New trades—carry-back of losses (TA 1988, s 381)

Where a loss occurs in any of the first four years of assessment of a new sole trade, or of a new partner's membership of a partnership, relief is permitted against that person's general income of the three previous tax years, earliest first. See example 4 on page 290. There is no set-off against capital gains. As with Section 380 (see page 286), this carry-back claim cannot be made unless the trade is carried on on a commercial basis.

Where a loss is large enough, a claim under Section 380 may be preceded or followed by a Section 381 claim. The set-off rules as regards earned and unearned income and restricting a claim to the lossmaker's income or extending it to the income of the spouse that applied to Section 380 claims up to 5 April 1990 as indicated on page 288 also applied to Section 381 claims, and are still relevant where a loss is carried back to 1989/90 or earlier. A loss sustained in 1992/93 for which Section 381 relief was claimed would, for example, be set first against the income of 1989/90, then 1990/91, then 1991/92, and a spouse's income in the first of those years could be included in the claim.

Example 4

Trade started 1 August 1990.
Year ended 31 July 1991   Loss   (£10,800)
Year ended 31 July 1992   Profit   £2,400
There will be Nil assessments for 1990/91, 1991/92 and 1992/93 (see chapter 21), so, unless there are other sources of income, there would be no loss claims at all under Section 380, nor under Section 385 until 1993/94.

For the first three years of assessment, loss claims under Sections 380 and 381 must be calculated on the basis of the loss in the tax year itself, not in the accounting year ended within it.

The losses on this basis are:

	1990/91	1991/92
8/12 × (£10,800)	(£7,200)	—
4/12 × (£10,800)		(3,600)
8/12 × £2,400		1,600
		(£2,000)

Relief is available by carry back against general income of:		
First	1987/88	1988/89
Then	1988/89	1989/90
Then	1989/90	1990/91

There would be a loss of £1,600 not covered by the carry-back claims and this would be carried forward under Section 385 to set against later trading profits. If the losses of £7,200 and £2,000 were not fully relieved under the carry-back claims, any balance remaining would also be carried forward.

If there were also losses in 1992/93 and 1993/94 (making with 1990/91 and 1991/92 the first four years of assessment) relief for those losses would be available as follows:

For losses incurred in	1992/93	1993/94
Relief would be available by carry back against general income of:		
First	1989/90	1990/91
Then	1990/91	1991/92
Then	1991/92	1992/93

Capital allowances (TA 1988, s 383)

Where there are losses or where capital allowances exceed profits, unused capital allowances relating to the loss period may be carried forward to set against later trading profits or used to increase Section 380 and/or Section 381 loss claims. The choice of including or excluding capital allowances again gives flexibility in arriving at the best loss claim bearing in mind available personal allowances. Even more flexibility is available for writing-down allowances on plant and machinery, because the capital allowances claim itself can be reduced to whatever amount is required (see pages 249 and 263).

Pre-trading expenditure (TA 1988, s 401)

Where expenditure is incurred within five years before a trade commences and it would have been allowable as a trading expense if incurred afterwards (see chapter 20 for allowable and non-allowable expenses), it may be treated as a loss of the first tax year and relief claimed under Sections 380, 381 or 385. This would cover, for example, rent paid on business premises before starting to trade.

Losses of limited partners (TA 1988, ss 117 and 118)

Some partnerships have 'limited partners', whose liability for partnership debts is limited to a fixed capital contribution. These limited partners may be either individuals or companies. A loss claim by such partners in any year against income other than from the trade cannot exceed the total of the limited partner's fixed capital contribution plus undrawn profits at the end of that year. The loss claims referred to are those under Sections 380 and 381 for individuals, and under TA 1988, s 393A(1) or the group relief provisions for companies (see pages 296 and 301).

There is no restriction on the right of limited partners to carry forward their unused losses against later profits from the same trade.

Loss on cessation of trade (terminal loss) (TA 1988, ss 388 and 389)

Losses arising when a trade ceases clearly cannot be carried forward against future profits of the same trade. A Section 380 claim may be made to set such a loss against current general income, if there is any. Alternatively, or if the loss is large enough, additionally, a claim may be made to set the loss of the last twelve months of trading (called a terminal loss), or the balance of such a loss after Section 380 relief, against the *trading* income (after capital allowances) of the three tax years prior to that in which the trade ceases, *latest* first. If there are unrelieved capital allowances for that twelve months, they may be included in the claim. See example 5.

By extra-statutory concession B19, where an industrial building, qualifying hotel or enterprise building is sold after the cessation of a trade and a balancing charge arises, unrelieved trading losses may be carried forward to set against the balancing charge.

Example 5

Trade ceases 30 September 1992.
Previous accounts have been to 31 December, recent results and
assessments thereon (see chapter 21) being:
Period to 30 Sept. 1992   Loss (£9,000) 1992/93 assessment Nil
Year to 31 December 1991 Profit £2,400 Escapes assessment
Year to 31 December 1990 Profit £1,000 Assessed in 1991/92
Year to 31 December 1989 Profit £5,000 Assessed in 1990/91
Year to 31 December 1988 Profit £7,000 Assessed in 1989/90

Terminal loss:
1 October 1991 to 5 April 1992
   First three months   Profit   600
   Next three months   Loss   (3,000)
                                    ———   (2,400)
   6 April 1992 to 30 September 1992   (6,000)
                                                  ———
                                                 (£8,400)
                                                  ———

This may be carried back against trading assessments for:
1991/92   £1,000
1990/91   £5,000
1989/90   £7,000, reducing it to
                                     £4,600

Alternatively a Section 380 claim may be made to set the 1992/93
loss of £6,000 against any income or chargeable gains of that year—
which could arise through balancing charges on the disposal of
assets on which capital allowances have been claimed and through
chargeable gains on the sale of business assets, in addition to any
regular sources. If loss relief were obtained in that way, only the
balance of the terminal loss of £2,400 would be the subject of a
terminal loss claim. It may, however, be preferable to leave other
income to cover personal allowances in 1992/93 and claim terminal
loss relief on the full amount as illustrated.

Time limits for claims

TA 1988, s 380	Set-off against income and gains of same tax year or following year	Within two years after the end of the year of assessment to which the claim relates
TA 1988, s 381	Set off new business losses against income for three previous tax years, taking earlier before later years	Within two years after the end of the year of assessment in which the loss is sustained

| TA 1988, s 385 | Carry forward against future profits of same trade | Within six years after the end of the year of assessment to which the claim relates |
| TA 1988, ss 388, 389 | Carry back of terminal losses | Normal six-year time limit since no other time limit specified |

Formal claims for relief must be made within these time limits, except for Section 385, where the Revenue will accept a computation indicating that the loss is being carried forward.

Repayment supplement (TA 1988, s 824)

A loss claim will either prevent tax being payable or cause tax already paid to be repaid. A tax-free repayment supplement is paid to individuals receiving a repayment more than one year after the end of the tax year to which it relates. The supplement runs from the end of the tax year following that for which the repayment is made (or from the end of the tax year in which the tax was paid, if later) to the end of the tax month in which the repayment is made. The rate of interest changes from time to time (see page xxiv). The supplement applies to all loss claims but is particularly beneficial in relation to carry-back claims on new business losses.

National insurance

Losses reduce your profit for Class 4 national insurance as well as for income tax. If you claim income tax relief for your loss against non-trading income or against capital gains, you can still set the loss against future trading income for Class 4 national insurance purposes.

Example 6

Using the figures in Example 2 on page 289, the trader has set £3,000 of his loss against unearned income and £5,000 against capital gains in 1992/93.

If his profits for the year to 31 December 1993 were £9,000, they would be reduced by £8,000 for Class 4 national insurance purposes, so that no Class 4 contributions would be payable in 1994/95.

Where a loss claim results in Class 4 contributions being refunded, the refund does not attract any repayment supplement.

Tax points

- The earliest relief is not always the best. The key questions are how much tax will you save, when will you save it and how much tax-free repayment supplement will be received. Watch the effect of changes in tax rates and allowances in the various years.

- Claiming carry-back relief under Section 381, instead of current year relief under Section 380, for a first year loss leaves other income of that year available for a possible carry-back claim under Section 381 for a loss in later years.

- The tax-free repayment supplement on loss claims under Section 381 can substantially boost the repayment. The supplement on claims under Section 380 is likely to be much less.

- Loss relief against general income is restricted to those losses incurred in a demonstrably commercial trade and this may be difficult to prove. This is particularly so in the case of a new trade, so that a viable business plan is often essential to support a carry-back claim under Section 381.

- A loss carried back under Section 381, in preference to a current or next year claim under Section 380, must be fully relieved under Section 381 before the balance of available losses can be relieved under Section 380. It is not possible to carry back sufficient of the loss to relieve income of the third year back and then not to proceed against the income of the second year back and then the first. The carry-back facility must be exhausted if claimed at all, before a current or next year loss claim is made in respect of the balance remaining unrelieved.

  If there is a loss in the next year of trading this forms an entirely new claim. Relief can be claimed under Section 380 in preference to Section 381, but if a Section 381 claim is embarked upon first, the same remarks as above apply, so that the carry-back facility must be exhausted in respect of that particular loss before the balance can be relieved under Section 380.

- If a loss is large enough, claims for relief under Section 380 may be made both for the tax year of loss and the following tax year. Normally the loss would be set against the first year's income before the second. The Revenue have stated that a taxpayer may make the second year's claim before the first, or make both claims together and stipulate that the loss is to be relieved against the second year's income before the first. This may or may not be beneficial depending on the total income and available allowances of each year.

- Before the introduction of independent taxation of husband and wife from 6 April 1990, married couples had more flexibility with loss claims, because a loss could be set off against just the lossmaker's income or against the joint incomes, whichever gave the best tax result. This only applies to loss claims up to 1989/90. But if a new business loss in or after 1990/91 is carried back to 1989/90 or earlier years, the claim may still include or exclude the spouse's income for any years before 1990/91.

- If including capital allowances in a loss claim means wasting personal allowances, the capital allowances can be left out altogether, or the claim for writing-down allowances on plant and machinery can be reduced to an appropriate level, so that the total allowances added to the loss claim are less.

- It is not always possible to agree the amount of a loss claim under the current year set-off and carry-back rules before the two-year time limit for claiming runs out. The Revenue will usually accept an unquantified claim, with the figures being agreed later, but they should be asked to confirm that they will do so, since the Sections specifically refer to 'the amount of the loss'.

26
Trading losses: companies

Loss reliefs available

As for individuals and partnerships (see chapter 25), trading losses of companies are calculated in the same way as profits, but the company's losses already include any capital allowances which have been claimed, whereas for individuals and partnerships, capital allowances may be included in or excluded from a loss claim. The following alternatives are available for relief of the loss:

Set-off against current profits (TA 1988, s 393A(1)).
Carry-back against earlier profits (TA 1988, s 393A(1)(2)).
Carry-forward against future trading profits (TA 1988, s 393(1)).
Set-off against franked investment income (TA 1988, s 242).
Group relief (TA 1988, s 402).
When a loss occurs on ceasing to trade before 1 April 1991, carry-back against earlier trading profits (TA 1988, s 394).

Set-off against current profits (TA 1988, s 393A(1))

A trading loss of a company, which includes its capital allowances, can be set against any profits of the same chargeable accounting period, thus reducing or eliminating the corporation tax thereon. Profits for this purpose include not only all sources of income (other than UK dividends) but also capital gains (see page 24).

Carry-back against previous profits and carry-forward (TA 1988, ss 393(1), 393A(1)(2))

When a trading loss has been set against all profits of the current period, any balance may be carried back and set against the profits of the previous three years, latest first, so long as the trade was carried on in the earlier period. This applies to losses in accounting periods ended on or after 1 April 1991. For trading losses in accounting periods ended before that date, the carry-back was restricted to a period of time equal to the accounting period of loss.

As with the claim against current profits, the set-off in the carry-back period is not limited to trading profits and may be made against profits of any description.

Any loss not relieved against current or previous profits may be carried forward for set-off against future trading profits of the same trade, without time limit on its use (see example 1).

Example 1

In its year to 31 March 1992 a company made a trading loss of £70,000. It has no franked investment income and no associated companies. Its other results and loss claims arising are:

	Year ended 30.9.89 £	Year ended 30.9.90 £	6 mths to 31.3.91 £	Year ended 31.3.92 £	Loss and Loss claims £
Trading profits	20,000	16,000	12,000	—	(70,000)
Investment income	4,000	7,000	8,000	6,000	
Capital gains	—	5,000	3,000	1,500	
Total profits	24,000	28,000	23,000	7,500	
Loss set-off:					
Against profits of same period				(7,500)	7,500
Against previous profits for up to 36 months:					
6 mths to 31.3.91			(23,000)		23,000
yr to 30.9.90		(28,000)			28,000
yr to 30.9.89	(11,500)				11,500
Profits remaining in charge	£12,500	—	—	—	

If the loss had not been fully relieved, it could have been set against 6/12 of the profits of the year to 30 September 1988.

Had all the figures related to one year earlier, the loss could only have been relieved against the following profits:

	£
Same year (to 31.3.91)	7,500
6 mths to 31.3.90	23,000
6/12 × year to 30.9.89	14,000
Carried forward against *trading* profits of future years	25,500

Claims to set off losses against current and previous profits of any description are only permitted if the company carries on business on a commercial basis with a view to the realisation of profit. There is no commercial basis restriction for carrying losses forward, since the permitted set-off is only against trading profits of that same trade.

Charges on income (TA 1988, ss 393(9), 393A(7)(8))

A company pays charges such as loan interest (other than to a bank), patent royalties and charity covenants net of basic rate income tax, and accounts to the Revenue for the income tax deducted. (Bank interest in respect of its trade on the other hand is paid in full and is deducted as a normal trading expense.)

Charges may be deducted not just from trading profits but from total profits, including capital gains. If, however, the charges are not paid wholly and exclusively for the purposes of the trade (for example, charity covenants), they qualify for tax relief only if the company has sufficient profits to cover them in the accounting period in which they are paid. Where there are current trading losses, the losses are set off in priority to both trade and non-trade charges (except for terminal losses – see below). If as a result there are unrelieved trade charges, they may be *carried forward* (*but not carried back*) as a trading loss. Excess charges, whether trade charges or non-trade charges, may never be carried back against previous profits except in relation to terminal losses, where the rules permit unrelieved trade charges to be included (see below).

Where losses are carried back, they are set against total profits *after* deducting trade charges but *before* deducting non-trade charges (except for losses in accounting periods ended before 1 April 1991, which are set off in priority to both trade and non-trade charges, any unrelieved trade charges arising then being carried forward as a trading loss).

Terminal losses (TA 1988, ss 393A(1)(7), 394)

It is clearly not possible to carry losses forward when a trade ceases (although concession B19 outlined on page 291 enabling trading losses to be set against balancing charges when buildings are sold after the trade has ceased also applies to companies). Special rules therefore applied for accounting periods ended before 1 April 1991 in relation to a loss in the last 12 months trading (called a terminal loss). These special rules no longer apply for accounting periods ended on or after 1 April 1991, because more generous carry-back provisions are now available for trading losses in general (see page 296). There is, however, still one specific provision relating to the accounting period in which a trade ceases. Any unrelieved trade charges of that accounting period may be treated as part of the loss that may be carried back.

Losses in accounting periods ended before 1 April 1991

Before a pre-1 April 1991 terminal loss claim is made, any available current set-off and carry-back claims under TA 1988, s 393 (the carry-back being restricted to a period equal in length to the loss period) must be made first.

After all such loss claims have been made, any remaining losses of the last twelve months may be carried back against the *trading* profits (not other income or chargeable gains) of the three years immediately before the last year, being set against profits of later periods before earlier periods. Any unrelieved trade charges of the last twelve months are included in the terminal loss.

Terminal loss relief does not displace relief for trade charges, so if the trading profits of the period to which losses are carried back have been used to cover trade charges, terminal loss relief is given on the balance of trading profit remaining.

Effect of carry-back of losses on tax paid and ACT set-off (TA 1988, s 825)

Loss relief may be obtained at one of three possible corporation tax rates: at the small companies rate if the loss set-off is against profits charged at that rate; at the full corporation tax rate if the set-off is against profits in excess of the upper limit for marginal small companies relief; and at a higher marginal rate on profits between the small companies rate marginal relief upper and lower limits. For the years to 31 March 1992 and 1993, the rates are 25%, 33% and 35% respectively. Higher rates applied for earlier years. See page xxv for detailed figures and rates for recent years.

Carry-back loss claims will result in corporation tax already paid being repaid, or in tax otherwise due not having to be paid, and the new three-year carry-back period enables repayments to be made at earlier higher tax rates where appropriate. The carry-back will also affect the calculation of the maximum advance corporation tax set-off which may be made, so that if ACT has either been paid in that period or carried back or forward to it, the loss claim may require the ACT set-off to be adjusted, and surplus ACT may arise as a result. See example 2.

For the treatment of surplus ACT, see page 32. Where surplus ACT arises as a result of a loss claim, the time limit for a claim to carry back the surplus ACT is still two years from the end of the accounting period in which the surplus arose, so it will often not be possible to make the claim in time and the surplus ACT may have to be carried forward. But a provisional claim to carry back surplus ACT may be made after the end of the accounting period of loss, but within the time limit, even if the amount of the loss and surplus ACT have not been quantified at that time. Such a provisional claim could not, however, cover surplus ACT that arose as a result of events outside the time limit. If in example 1, the result of carrying back the loss of the year to 31 March 1992 was that surplus ACT then arose in the year to 30 September 1989, the surplus ACT could not have been carried back from that year, because the time limit for the ACT carry-back claim would be 30 September

Example 2

A company has the following results.

Year ended 31 March	1992	1993
	£	£
Trading profit (loss)	20,000	(12,000)
Investment income	3,000	3,000
Chargeable gains	4,000	2,000
Total profits	27,000	5,000
ACT maximum set-off before loss relief:		
25% × profits of £27,000	6,750	—
25% × profits of £5,000	—	1,250
If loss relief under TA 1988, s 393A(1) is claimed:		
Profits	27,000	5,000
Less loss	(7,000)	(5,000)
Total profits	20,000	—
ACT maximum set-off following loss relief:		
25% × £20,000/Nil	5,000	—

Any tax repayment resulting from the carry-back loss claim will attract repayment supplement from 6 January 1994 (one year after the 1 January 1993 payment date for corporation tax for the year to 31 March 1992).

Assuming a dividend was paid in the year to 31 March 1993, any repayment relating to the carry-back of the ACT on that dividend would attract repayment supplement only from 6 January 1995 (one year after the corporation tax payment date for the year in which the dividend was paid). If the loss had been larger and had been carried back to accounting periods earlier than the year to 31 March 1992, repayment supplement would apply to the repayment for that part of the loss from the same date as the ACT date, i.e. 6 January 1995.

1991, at which time the loss available for carry-back had not occurred. The Revenue have stated, however, that where surplus ACT arising from a loss claim is carried forward, it is treated as part of the ACT of the year to which it has been carried, so that in the example, surplus ACT of the year to 30 September 1989 could be carried forward to 30 September 1990 and treated as paid in that year. A claim to carry back surplus ACT for up to six years from that year would then be in time if made by 30 September 1992.

Carried back ACT, is treated for repayment supplement purposes as ACT for the year in which the related dividend was actually paid rather than for the year to which the ACT has been carried back, so that it will usually attract tax-free repayment supplement only from twelve months after the due date of payment of corporation tax for that later period. The same applies to current and carried back losses, i.e. a repayment is treated as relating to the *loss* period, except that a repayment relating to an accounting period falling *wholly* in the twelve months before the loss period is treated as relating to that accounting period. The rates of repayment supplement are set out at page xxiv.

Loss relief against dividends from other UK companies (franked investment income) (TA 1988, s 242)

Although franked investment income (i.e. dividends from United Kingdom companies, including the attached tax credits) is not chargeable to corporation tax, it nonetheless forms part of the fund of corporate profit. When all other loss reliefs are exhausted, it is possible to set any remaining losses against such dividend income (unless it has itself been used to make a dividend payment), thus obtaining a refund of the dividend tax credits, rather than carry forward the loss to set against future trading profits. The accounting periods in respect of which such a claim may be made are the same as for normal current and carry-back loss claims, i.e. the current period and the previous three years. The relief obtained is, however, only at the basic rate of income tax, which, unless the small companies rate of corporation tax applies, will be less than the corporation tax rate.

Such a claim is subject to adjustment in a later year if the company pays dividends in excess of dividends which it receives. The adjustment is rather complex, but it effectively means that the company gives back to the Revenue the tax credit originally refunded and obtains relief for the trading loss at the corporation tax rate then applicable to its trading profits.

Group relief for losses (TA 1988, ss 402–413)

In a group consisting of a holding company and its 75% subsidiaries, trading losses may be surrendered from one company to one or more other companies within the group, provided that all the companies are resident in the UK. The accounting period of the loss-making company must correspond with that of the claimant company. This will not pose any difficulty when accounts within the group are prepared to the same date, but where accounts are prepared to different dates, part of the loss period will correspond with part of one accounting period of the claimant company and the remainder with part of the next accounting period. The loss available for relief and the profits against which it may be set must be apportioned accordingly. Relief is also proportionately restricted if the parent/subsidiary relationship does not exist throughout the accounting period, usually on a time basis, but by reference to what is just and reasonable where a time basis would give an unreasonable result.

The set-off rules are quite flexible, and broadly the loss-making company may surrender any part of its trading loss, up to a maximum of the available total profits of the claimant company or companies for the corresponding period. The profits of the claimant company available for relief are profits

---

Example 3

Company A has been the wholly owned subsidiary of Company B for many years. (Small companies rate marginal relief limits are therefore reduced for each company to £100,000 and £500,000 for the year to 31 March 1991 and £125,000 and £625,000 for the years to 31 March 1992 and 1993.) Both companies prepare accounts to 31 March, and for the year to 31 March 1992, results are as follows:

Company A has a trading loss of	£80,000
and other profits of	£10,000
Company B has total profits of	£180,000

In the year to 31 March 1991, Company A had total profits of £120,000. Company A's profits for the year to 31 March 1993 will be below £125,000.

Company A may claim its own available loss reliefs and not surrender any part of the loss to Company B; or it may surrender the full £80,000 and pay tax on its own profits of £120,000 in 1991 and £10,000 in 1992; or it may surrender any other amount up to £80,000, as the companies wish, and claim its own loss reliefs on the balance.

Rates of tax available:	On Company A's profits	On Company B's profits
Year to 31 March 1992	25% on £10,000	35% on £55,000
		25% on £125,000
Year to 31 March 1991	36¼% on £20,000	No relief
	25% on £100,000	available
Year to 31 March 1993	25%	

Clearly, the loss will not be carried forward, since more tax can be saved under the other claims. Company A should surrender £55,000 of the loss to Company B, obtaining relief thereon at 35%. Relief for the remaining £25,000 should be claimed against Company A's own profits, giving relief on £10,000 at 25% in the year to 31 March 1992 and £15,000 at 36¼% in the year to 31 March 1991.

---

from all sources, including capital gains, but *after* deducting charges on income.

Relief for surrendered losses is not, however, available against the dividend income of a claimant company.

A significant factor in deciding the optimum loss claim is the rate of tax saving. Other things being equal, it will be best to surrender the loss against profits being charged at the small companies marginal rate (or indeed not to surrender it at all if the company's own profits are charged at that rate). The rules enable the loss to be divided among several group companies in order to obtain the maximum loss relief. See example 3.

Where a loss would otherwise be unrelieved, it might be appropriate for a profit company in a group to disclaim some of the writing-down allowances on its plant and machinery, to give it a higher profit against which to make a group relief claim (see pages 249 and 263). The profit company would then have a higher pool balance carried forward on which to claim capital allowances in the future, whereas if it has insufficient current profit to cover the loss available for surrender, that part of the loss cannot be surrendered.

The group relief provisions are also available in certain circumstances to a consortium of companies that owns at least 75% of the ordinary share capital of a trading company or of a holding company with 90% trading subsidiaries, with the consortium members each owning at least 5% of that ordinary share capital. Losses in proportion to the consortium member's shareholding in the consortium-owned company can be surrendered both from the trading companies to the consortium companies and from the consortium companies to the trading companies.

Time limits for claims

TA 1988, s 393A	Set off against profits of same accounting period and previous accounting periods	Within two years after the end of the accounting period of loss or such further period as the Board allow
TA 1988, s 393(1)	Carry forward against later trading profits from same trade	Within six years after the end of the accounting period of loss
TA 1988, s 242	Set trading loss against an excess of dividends received over those paid (surplus franked investment income)	Within two years after the end of the accounting period of loss or such further period as the Board allow
TA 1988, s 402	Group loss relief	Within two years after the end of the accounting period of loss

| TA 1988, s 394 | Three-year carry-back of terminal loss in account ended before 1 April 1991 | Within six years after cessation of trade |

Anti-avoidance provisions

There are provisions to inhibit the purchase of tax-loss companies, which prevent losses (and surplus ACT) incurred before a change of ownership being carried forward if either:

(a) within a period of three years there is both a major change in the nature or conduct of a trade carried on by a company and a change in its ownership; or

(b) after the scale of activities in a trade carried on by a company has become negligible and before any considerable revival, there is a change in ownership. (TA 1988, ss 245, 768).

For changes of ownership on or after 14 June 1991, similar provisions have now been introduced (in Section 768A) to prevent losses in an accounting period *after* the change of ownership from being carried back to an accounting period *before* the change. The Revenue have issued Statement of Practice SP 10/91 giving their views on the meaning of a 'major change in the nature or conduct of a trade'.

Where one company transfers a trade to another and a 75% interest in the first and second companies is owned by the same persons, the trade is treated for certain purposes as continuing. Thus the accumulated trading losses incurred by the first company are available for relief against future profits of the trade in the hands of the successor company. The loss relief available for carry forward into the successor company is restricted if it does not take over the predecessor company's unpaid liabilities (TA 1988, ss 343, 344).

The 75% link for group relief purposes (see above) is defined very much more restrictively than simply 75% of ordinary share capital, to prevent companies taking advantage of the provisions by means of an artificial group relationship (TA 1988, s 413 and Sch 18).

Group relief is not available for a part of an accounting period in which arrangements exist whereby the loss-making company could cease to be a member of the group (TA 1988, s 410).

Pay and File (FA 1990, ss 100–102 & Schs 15, 16)

The current rules for claiming capital allowances and group relief often give problems because of the time limits for claims, and uncertainty as to the extent to which claims may be revised. For accounts ending after 30 September 1993 a new system of handling corporation tax assessment and collection is to be introduced, called Pay and File (see page 29). At the same time, the procedure for making claims to capital allowances and group relief is to be simplified. Companies will be able to make, vary and withdraw claims to capital allowances and group relief up to the later of two years after the end of their accounting period and the date that the profits and losses for the period are determined, but not normally beyond six years after the end of the period. Each group company will make its own individual return initially, but groups will be able to make a single amending return where the original claims are to be varied.

Tax points

● When considering loss claims, always look at the amount of tax saved. For the year ended 31 March 1990, set-off of losses may save tax at 35% if profits are charged at the full rate, 37½% where the set-off is within the marginal small companies tranche of profits, or only 25% if profits are charged at the small companies rate. The rates for the year to 31 March 1991 are 34%, 36¼% and 25%, and for the years to 31 March 1992 and 1993, 33%, 35% and 25%.

● Interest paid to a bank in respect of borrowing for the purposes of the trade is a trading expense and can thus form part of a trading loss for carry-back. Interest paid to other lenders is a charge on income, and unrelieved charges can only be carried forward (except in relation to the accounting period in which a trade ceases). Bear this in mind if you have a choice between borrowing from a bank and borrowing elsewhere on equivalent terms. In some trades where a supplier to tied customers customarily makes loans to customers, notably motor fuel and licensed premises, it is sometimes possible to structure the loan arrangements so that the borrowing is from a bank, supported by a guarantee from the supplier, who also contributes to the cost of the interest.

● Remember that group relief for losses is not available if there is less than a 75% link holding/subsidiary relationship.

● If two or more companies are controlled by the same individual(s), group relief is not available.

● Watch the anti-avoidance provisions on group relief. An arrangement made part-way through an accounting period to sell a loss-making subsidiary will prevent group relief being claimed for the remainder of the accounting period even though the parent/subsidiary relationship exists throughout.

● Exceptional revenue expenditure, such as extraordinary repairs, or establishing or boosting a company pension scheme within permissible limits, may result in a normally profitable trade incurring a loss. When a company is planning such expenditure or considering when, or indeed whether, it should be incurred, the carry-back of losses against profits of the previous three years, resulting in tax not having to be paid, or being repaid, is an influential consideration.

- Tax repaid as a result of the new three-year loss carry-back period will only attract interest from 21 months after the end of the loss period, except for the repayment relating to the accounting period immediately before the loss period, which will carry interest from 21 months after the end of that earlier period.

27
Transfer of business to limited company

Choice of date

When the trade of an individual or partnership is transferred to a company the trade is treated as having ceased for income tax purposes, so that the closing year rules dealt with on page 241 will apply. The Revenue will have the option of taxing the profits of the two tax years before the last on an actual rather than a preceding year basis, but some profits will still escape assessment, provided that the trade has been carried on long enough for the early profits to have been assessed more than once.

The transfer date will determine what profits escape assessment, so it is important to make an appropriate choice. If profits are rising it will generally be better to transfer after the end of a tax year rather than before (see page 243) and rising profits may make it advisable to delay the transfer even longer, so that two high years drop out of assessment.

Capital allowances (CAA 1990, ss 77, 78, 152, 157, 158)

Normally the cessation of trade would involve a balancing allowance or charge on the disposal to the company of plant and equipment and, where relevant, industrial buildings.

The sole trader or partners and the company may usually, however, jointly elect within two years after the transfer date for the assets to be treated as transferred at the tax written-down value. If the election is not made, the transfer is deemed to be at market value, with a resulting balancing allowance or charge on the sole or partnership trade, and the company getting writing-down allowances on its acquisition cost.

Unused trading losses (TA 1988, s 386)

If there are unused trading losses, these cannot be carried forward to a company as such, but they may be relieved against income received by the trader or partners from the company, either in the form of directors' fees or dividends, so long as the business is exchanged for shares and the shares are still retained at the time of the loss set-off. Other available loss claims may be made first, e.g. under TA 1988, s 380 against income of the year of loss, or terminal loss relief for a loss of the last twelve months against the trading income of the previous three years (see chapter 25), and the relief against income from the company would then be available on the balance of unrelieved losses.

Capital gains tax (TCGA 1992, ss 17, 18, 286)

When the transfer takes place, the general rule is that assets chargeable to capital gains tax will be deemed to have been disposed of to the company at their open market value. Current assets are not chargeable assets, and moveable plant and machinery, although chargeable unless valued at £6,000 or less, will not normally be valued at more than cost, so the most likely assets on which a liability may arise are freehold or leasehold premises, fixed plant and machinery and goodwill.

Example 1

The net assets of a trader at the time of incorporation of his business were:

	£
Freehold premises at market valuation	204,000
Goodwill at valuation	120,000
Plant and equipment (cost £320,000)	140,000
Net current assets other than cash	256,000
Cash and bank balances	80,000
	£800,000

The premises had been acquired for £120,000 and the trade newly commenced after 31 March 1982. Assume indexation allowance to date of transfer to be £32,000 on the premises.

The potential chargeable gains on incorporation are:

			£
Freehold premises—market value		204,000	
Less: Cost	120,000		
Indexation allowance	32,000	152,000	52,000
Goodwill		120,000	
Less: Cost	Nil		
Indexation allowance	Nil	—	120,000
			£172,000

The gain on the premises can be avoided by the trader retaining ownership, but that on the goodwill cannot, unless it is possible to retain it while licensing the company to use it.

An obvious way of avoiding the charge on premises is for the proprietor or partners to retain ownership and to allow the company to use them either at a rent or free of charge. This will also save the stamp duty that would have been incurred on the transfer. Further stamp duty can be saved if the business debts are collected by the proprietor/partners instead of being transferred to the company.

The only way of not transferring the goodwill is if the sole trader/partners continue to own it whilst licensing the company to carry on the trade, but unless this is commercially practicable and sensible, the goodwill will automatically be transferred with the trade. The valuation of goodwill depends not only on the size of the profits but also on the extent to which the profits depend on the skills of the proprietor or partners, the nature of the trade and many other factors.

Any gain arising may be covered by reliefs, such as the annual exemption or possibly retirement relief if the sole trader or partners are over 55 or retire through ill-health. Otherwise the capital gains tax effect must be considered. See example 1 on page 308.

There are two alternatives for reducing or eliminating an immediate capital gains tax charge. One is the rollover relief of TCGA 1992, s 162, which requires *all* the assets (except cash) to be transferred to the company, and defers gains only to the extent that the consideration is received in the form of shares in the company. The other is a combination of retaining some assets in personal ownership and using the business gifts relief of TCGA 1992, s 165 (outlined on page 52) to defer the gains on other chargeable assets (notably goodwill), the company then being treated as acquiring those assets at market value less the gains. Any consideration received from the company need not be shares and a credit may be made to a director's loan account or cash taken instead.

Capital gains rollover relief on transfer (TCGA 1992, s 162)

If relief under section 162 were claimed in example 1, all assets other than the £80,000 cash would have to be transferred.

The relief is given automatically without the need for a claim. The chargeable gains arising on the disposal of the business are calculated and they are treated as reducing the tax cost of the shares received in exchange for the business. The lower base cost for the shares will of course increase the potential capital gains tax liability in the future, but further reliefs may be available at the time the shares are disposed of, for example retirement or gifts relief, or total exemption if the shares are still held at death. See example 2.

The difference between the £700,000 par value of the shares and the £720,000 assets value in example 2 represents a share premium. It is almost inevitable that the par value will not correspond with the asset values since those values cannot be precisely determined before the transfer date.

If the transfer is made only partly for shares, and partly for cash or credit to a director's loan account, then only proportionate relief is given. See example 3.

Example 2

In consideration of the transfer of the trade in example 1, the trader receives 700,000 shares of £1 each, fully paid, in the new company, transferring all assets except the cash of £80,000.

The base cost of the shares will be:

700,000 shares	(£800,000 assets − £80,000 cash)	720,000
Less gains otherwise arising on premises and goodwill		172,000
Cost of 700,000 shares for capital gains tax purposes		£548,000

Example 3

Suppose the consideration of £720,000 in example 2 was satisfied as to £480,000 shares and £240,000 cash. Only two-thirds of the chargeable gains can be deducted from the base cost of the shares.

		Shares	Cash
Consideration		480,000	240,000
Gains	£172,000	114,667	£57,333
Cost of shares for capital gains tax purposes	£365,333		

The £57,333 is assessable to capital gains tax (subject to any available exemptions and reliefs).

Obtaining the maximum deferral of gains under TCGA 1992, s 162 therefore requires the consideration for the shares to be locked in as share capital. If the consideration is provided through leaving money on director's loan account, tax will not be deferred, but the money can later be withdrawn at no personal tax cost.

See page 42 for the treatment of disposals after 5 April 1988 that are affected by deferred gains on assets acquired before 31 March 1982.

Gifts of business assets (TCGA 1992, s 165)

If the premises were retained in personal ownership, saving capital gains tax and stamp duty, and further stamp duty was saved by not transferring debtors, this would leave the gain on the goodwill to be considered. The business gifts relief enables the whole of the gain on goodwill to be deferred providing any consideration received does not exceed the capital gains tax base cost of the goodwill. In example 1, that cost was nil, so that the full gain on the goodwill could only be deferred if nothing was charged for it.

Goodwill will have a capital gains tax cost either if it was purchased or if it had a value at 31 March 1982.

The disadvantage of charging consideration equal to the capital gains tax base cost is that the transferor is only credited in the accounts of the company with that amount (before reckoning indexation allowance), not with the market value at the time of transfer, and that lower value (plus any available indexation allowance up to that time) will be the company's acquisition cost on which future indexation allowance will be calculated.

The chargeable asset could be transferred at a figure in excess of capital gains tax base cost, but less than market value, available exemptions being set off against the gains arising. This has the advantage of more cash being received on the transfer or a higher credit to the director's account, and in either case a higher base value for the asset in company ownership. The business assets gifts relief eliminates the chargeable gain on the difference between market value and the value used for the transfer.

Retirement relief (TCGA 1992 ss 163, 164 and Sch 6)

Retirement relief is available both to sole traders and partners and to full-time working directors in a family company (see page 49) and for the purpose of the ten-year qualifying period, the periods of operating the unincorporated and incorporated businesses are taken together.

If husband and wife partners incorporate their business, however, and one of them then works only part-time in the business, he/she will lose the entitlement to retirement relief. The same could happen where several partners who are not members of the same family incorporate their business, because the minimum share ownership for retirement relief, if there are no family holdings, is 25%.

Stamp duty

Stamp duty is a fixed or ad valorem charge on instruments, and if there is no instrument no duty is normally payable.

Stock and plant can be transferred to the company by delivery, so no stamp duty will be payable, and the company can either pay cash or credit the director's loan account.

Stamp duty will arise on the agreement for the transfer of the trade to the company according to the amount of the consideration. As already indicated, the stamp duty can be reduced by not transferring premises to the company and by the sole trader or partners collecting the debts instead of assigning them.

From some time in 1993, stamp duty other than on land and buildings is to be abolished, so it will then only be relevant to the business premises.

Value added tax (VATA 1983, s 33; SI 1981/1741, para 12 as amended by SI 1991/2503; SI 1985/886, para 4)

On the transfer of a business to a company, VAT will not normally arise on the assets transferred and the company will take over the VAT position of the transferor as regards deductible input tax and liability to account for output tax (see page 89). From 1 December 1991, the VAT-free treatment does not apply to transfers of land and buildings on which the transferor has opted to tax (see page 368), or of commercial buildings that are either unfinished or less than three years old, unless the transferee gives written notification before the transfer that he has opted to tax. Otherwise, VAT must be charged. A claim may be made by the trader or partners and the company for the existing VAT registration number to be transferred to the company. It is advisable to contact the appropriate VAT office in good time to obtain the necessary forms and ensure that the various requirements are complied with.

Inheritance tax

There will not usually be any direct inheritance tax implications on the incorporation of a business, but two situations need watching.

The first is the effect on the rate of business property relief subsequently available where partners form a company. The 100% relief available in respect of the interest of a partner in a partnership is reduced to 50% for any partner whose share allocation after taking into account related property holdings does not exceed a 25% interest in the company.

As regards assets such as premises used in the company but owned personally, while business property relief at the rate of 50% is available to a partner, it is available only to a controlling shareholder, and no relief is available at all for such assets owned by minority shareholders. Shares of husband and wife are related property and the available rate of relief is determined by their joint holdings.

The second situation arises out of the use of the capital gains provisions for gifts of business assets to the company (TCGA 1992, s 165). Such gifts will not be potentially exempt for inheritance tax since they are not to an individual or qualifying trust fund. They may be covered by the 100% business property relief, but if not the amount of the transfer of value is the reduction in the estate of the donor. In measuring that reduction, the value of the shares acquired in the company (enhanced by the gifted assets) will be taken into account. The result may be that there is no transfer of value. If there is a transfer of value, no tax may be payable, because of annual exemptions and the nil rate threshold. If tax is payable, the instalment option may apply if the company as donee pays the tax.

See chapter 5 for further information on inheritance tax.

National insurance

If a sole trader or partner becomes a director and/or employee in the company, national insurance contributions are payable by both the employer and the employee, and the burden is significantly higher than the maximum self-employed contributions under Classes 2 and 4. See chapter 18 for further details.

Business rates

Although the incorporation of a business means a change of occupier for rating purposes, any transitional relief to which the unincorporated business was entitled is now available to the company (see page 104).

Tax points

- Choose the transfer date with care to maximise the profits that escape income tax. With steadily rising profits this means after 5 April rather than before.

- Where you want to claim relief under TCGA 1992, s 162 on the transfer of a business, minimise the amount locked up in share capital by not transferring cash. If the cash is needed to assist the liquidity of the company, it can always be introduced on director's loan account.

- Rollover relief on the replacement of business assets (see page 48) can still be claimed on premises owned personally and used in the owner's family company—see page 49. A family company is one in which the individual owns at least 25% of the voting rights, or he and his family own more than 50% with his own share at least 5%.

- The payment of rent by the company for property owned personally by the former sole trader or partners will affect their entitlement to retirement relief for capital gains tax—see page 51. It will not, however, affect business property relief for inheritance tax.

- You cannot get the best of all worlds on incorporation of a business. Maximising the capital gains deferral can only be done at extra cost in terms of stamp duty and with the disadvantage of locking funds into share capital. Retaining some assets and using gifts relief on those that are transferred saves stamp duty and enables funding of the company to be done through loans which you make to it, but your director's account is credited with a lower figure in respect of the gifted assets and that value becomes the company's base value for capital gains. This could also significantly reduce the indexation allowance when the company disposes of the assets.

- When considering how much of the consideration for the transfer of the business should be locked in as share capital, do not forget that funds may need to be drawn for the payment of taxation relating to the former sole trade or partnership. Unless the potential tax has been included in the last sole trade or partnership accounts as a liability, or there are sufficient funds on directors' loan account, it will not be possible to withdraw the required funds from the company without incurring a further tax liability on remuneration or dividends.

- It may be possible to reduce the problems of locking in share capital by using redeemable shares, which can be redeemed gradually as and when the company has funds and possibly using the annual capital gains exemption to avoid a tax charge on the shareholder. There are, however, anti-avoidance provisions, and also a clearance procedure, and professional advice is essential.

- It is sometimes worth considering transferring chargeable assets, such as goodwill, at their full value, with a corresponding credit to your director's account. This will increase the capital gains tax payable at the time, but will provide a higher facility to draw off the director's loan account at no future personal tax cost. This is particularly relevant where the chargeable gains would in any event be covered by retirement relief, which may otherwise be lost because of your later reduced activity or size of shareholding.

- Retaining business premises in personal ownership, while avoiding a capital gains tax charge, may mean that, because of an insufficient shareholding, inheritance tax business property relief is denied even though the company is using the premises for its trade.

28
Selling the family company

Background

There are two ways in which the family company may be sold—selling the shares or selling the assets and liquidating the company, and the most difficult aspect of the sale negotiations is usually reconciling the interests of the vendors and the purchasers.

The vendors will often prefer to sell the shares rather than the assets to avoid the double capital gains tax charge which will arise on the assets sale and on the distribution to the shareholders if the company is wound up. The purchaser may prefer to buy assets in order to be able to claim capital allowances on purchases of equipment, plant and qualifying buildings, and because buying assets is frequently more straightforward, involving less legal formalities than a share purchase, with consequently lower costs. On the other hand, stamp duty on share transactions is to be abolished some time in 1993, whereas stamp duty will still be charged on the acquisition of property, so the share purchase may become more attractive from that point of view. Yet again, the vendors may intend staying in business, so that a sale of assets, with the company then acquiring replacement assets, may give an opportunity for rollover relief, which is denied if shares are sold and new assets or shares in another company purchased with the cash received.

A share purchaser will take over any latent liabilities and obligations of the company. The purchaser will clearly require indemnities and warranties from the vendors, but the vendors will want to limit these as much as possible, and in any event the purchaser would have the inconvenience of enforcing them or perhaps be unable to do so if the vendor had insufficient funds or was not able to be contacted.

The outcome will depend on the future intentions of the vendor, the relative bargaining strength of each party and the adjustments each agrees to in order to resolve points of difference.

Selling shares or assets

Part of the sale consideration may relate not to tangible assets but to the growth prospects or the entrepreneurial flair of those involved with the company, and where goodwill is a substantial factor, the valuation placed on it will be an important part of the negotiations, providing flexibility in agreeing a price.

The tax cost of selling the shares can be significantly less than that of selling the assets followed by a liquidation. See example 1 for a straight comparison of a share sale and an assets sale based on the same values. So long as the ACT can be set off, the disadvantage could be mitigated, but not eliminated, by the company paying a dividend equivalent to the profit less tax on the sale of its assets, and then distributing the remainder of its funds upon liquidation. See example 2. Knowing the tax advantage of the share sale to the vendor, coupled with the potential tax liability if the company in its new ownership sells its premises and goodwill, the purchaser may well seek a reduction in price if this route is to be followed.

Example 1

Company was formed in 1984 and 1,000 £1 shares were issued at par. Balance sheet of company immediately prior to intended sale was:

	£		£
Share capital	1,000	Net current assets	50,000
Accumulated profits	99,000	Premises at cost	50,000
	£100,000		£100,000

A sale is now proposed on the basis of the goodwill and premises being worth £350,000.

If the shares are sold:

Assets per balance sheet		100,000
Increase in value of premises and goodwill		
(350,000 – 50,000)		300,000
Sale proceeds for shares		400,000
Cost	1,000	
Indexation allowance, say	520	1,520
Chargeable gain		£398,480
Capital gains tax @ 40% (ignoring any set-offs and exemptions and assuming that the shareholders' lower rate bands have been fully utilised)		£159,392

If assets are sold and company is liquidated:

Assets per balance sheet		100,000
Increase in value of premises and goodwill	300,000	
Less provision for corporation tax on sale		
(£300,000 less, say £26,000 for		
indexation on cost of premises)		
Gain £274,000 @ say 33%	90,420	209,580

Amount distributed to shareholders on liquidation		
(ignoring liquidation costs)		309,580
Cost of shares	1,000	
Indexation allowance, say	520	1,520
Chargeable gain		£308,060

Capital gains tax @ 40% (ignoring any set-offs and exemptions and assuming that the lower rate bands have been fully utilised)	£123,224

Amounts received by shareholders:

	Proceeds	Capital gains tax	Net
On sale of shares	400,000	159,392	240,608
On liquidation	309,580	123,224	186,356
Extra cost of liquidation route			£54,252

Example 2

	£
Assets on balance sheet per example 1 are £100,000.	
Profit after tax on sale of assets	209,580
Dividend	(209,580)

ACT of £69,860 on dividend is set off against the liability of £90,420 on sale of the assets.

Distribution on liquidation	100,000
Indexed cost of shares	1,520
Chargeable gain	£98,480

example 2 continued overleaf

example 2 continued

Capital gains tax @ 40%   £39,392

Received by shareholders:

Dividend	209,580	
Less higher rate tax on		
(209,580 + 69,860 =)		
£279,440 @ (40% − 25%)	41,916	167,664
On liquidation	100,000	
Less capital gains tax	39,392	60,608
		£228,272

Comparison of amounts received by shareholders in example 1 and in this example:

	Share sale	Asset sale/ liquidation	Asset sale/ dividend/ liquidation
	£	£	£
Value of assets	400,000	400,000	400,000
Corporation tax		(90,420)	(90,420)*
Shareholders' higher rate tax			(41,916)
Shareholders' capital gains tax	(159,392)	(123,224)	(39,392)
	£240,608	£186,356	£228,272

* Comprising ACT £69,860 and mainstream tax £20,560.

Where the company was established before 31 March 1982, the value of its chargeable assets and of the shares at that date may be substituted for cost, and indexation also calculated on that value, if it reduces the gains or if an election has been made to use 31 March 1982 value for all assets. Whilst the chargeable gains may be correspondingly less, the same principles apply.

Other factors

The disadvantages of selling assets may be mitigated if the company has current (as distinct from brought-forward) trading losses which may be set off against the gains on the assets.

If it is intended that the company shall continue trading in some new venture rather than be wound up, it may be possible to roll over or hold over the gains by the purchase of new assets. Alternatively, if the new trade commences before the old trade ceases, trading losses may arise in that new trade against which the gains may be set under the normal rules for set-off of trading losses.

Paying a dividend out of accumulated profits

Advance corporation tax on dividends can be set off against corporation tax on any profits, including capital gains, and if the maximum ACT set-off has not been made by the company in the previous six years, then to the extent that a dividend could be paid without creating unrelieved ACT, the net amount received by the vendor could be increased. See example 3. The overall effect of paying dividends would, however, need to be considered very carefully.

Example 3

If in examples 1 and 2 the accumulated profits of £99,000 were distributed as a dividend, and the ACT of £33,000 was fully recoverable against corporation tax liabilities of earlier years, the after tax benefit to the shareholders would in either case be:

	£
Higher rate tax on (99,000 + 33,000 =)	
£132,000 @ (40% − 25%)	£19,800
Compared with capital gains tax @ 40%	
on additional share proceeds of £99,000	39,600
	£19,800

Capital gains tax retirement relief

Shareholders over age 55 who are full-time directors owning 25% of the shares on their own, or 5% themselves within a family holding of more than 50%, will be entitled to complete exemption on chargeable gains up to a maximum £150,000 and on a maximum of one half of the gains between £150,000 and £600,000 (see page 49). The gain on which relief is given is restricted to the business assets proportion of the gain on the shares, and is thus restricted to the extent that the company's assets include shares in other companies or other investments, but on a disposal of shares in the holding company of a family trading group, it is the group's assets that are taken into account and holdings of shares in other group companies are ignored.

There is no difference in the relief available to a shareholder on a sale of shares and a return of monies through a liquidation. Retirement relief is available in both cases on the business assets proportion of the shareholder's gain. The return of funds to the shareholder on a liquidation will still be less because of the corporation tax paid by the company on the sale of assets. A shareholder whose retirement relief would eliminate his gains would, however, prefer to receive funds on a liquidation rather than an income dividend. There may be a problem in reconciling the best interests of different shareholders where not all of them are entitled to retirement relief. Retirement relief is not available to the company itself, irrespective of the age of the shareholders, as distinct from its being available to each shareholder depending upon age, participation in the company and the length of time for which the shares have been held.

If the controlling shareholders personally own the premises from which the company's business is carried on, retirement relief is given on any gain arising where the premises are disposed of in conjunction with a share disposal or a return of monies to the shareholders on a liquidation. The relief is, however, restricted if the company pays rent, and if the rent is the full market rent, no relief is available.

Payments in compensation for loss of office

Compensation and ex gratia payments are dealt with in detail in chapter 15. They may be challenged by the Revenue as not being 'wholly and exclusively for the purposes of the trade', and the company must be able to demonstrate that any payments are wholly unassociated with a sale of the shares and moreover are not a distribution of profits to a shareholder. Ex gratia payments may also now be challenged as being benefits under an unapproved retirement benefits scheme (see page 189). If all the hurdles can be surmounted, then in addition to £30,000 being exempt from income tax, the termination payment will reduce not only the corporation taxable profits prior to sale of the shares, but also the value of the net assets supporting the consideration for the shares, and thus the share sale proceeds.

Payments into a pension scheme

Prior to selling the shares, the cash resources of the company, and thus, effectively, the eventual sale proceeds, may also be reduced by an appropriate pension scheme contribution, the benefits of which may be taken partly as a tax-free lump sum and partly as a pension. Again, the trading profits prior to the sale are reduced, with a corresponding saving in corporation tax. This is of course only acceptable if the levels of contributions and benefits payable are within the stipulated limits. Company pension schemes are dealt with in chapter 16.

Selling on the basis of receiving shares in the purchasing company (TCGA 1992, ss 126–140, 163, 164 and Sch 6)

Where, as consideration for the sale of their shares, the vending shareholders receive shares in the company making the acquisition, then each vending shareholder is normally treated as not having made a disposal of the 'old shares', but as having acquired the 'new shares' for the same amount and on the same date as the 'old shares'.

Where the consideration is part shares/part cash, that part received in cash is liable to capital gains tax, whilst the 'new shares' again stand in the shoes of the old. See example 4.

Example 4

Shares cost £1,000. As a result of an acquisition of the entire share capital by another company, the shareholder receives cash of £4,000 and shares in the acquiring company valued at £6,000. The capital gains position is:

		Cash £	Shares £
Cost of £1,000, divided in proportion to the proceeds		400	600
Proceeds:			
Cash	4,000	4,000	
New shares	6,000		
Total consideration	10,000		
Chargeable gain (subject to indexation allowance)		£3,600	
Cost of 'new shares'			£600

Where part of the consideration depends upon future performance, say the issue of further shares or securities if a profit target is met, the value of the right to receive further cash or shares is itself part of the disposal proceeds at the time the original shares are sold, and it is not strictly covered by the rules allowing the new shares to stand in the shoes of the old. By concession D27, the Revenue will allow the taxpayer to claim that the later shares or securities are part of the original transaction so that any capital gains are rolled over until the shares or securities are sold. The concession does not apply if the future consideration is cash. In that event, the whole of the right to future consideration is liable to capital gains tax at the time of the sale, with a further liability on the difference between that value and the consideration itself when it is received.

Where the vendor is entitled to retirement relief, he can claim that the provisions treating the new shares as standing in the shoes of the old do not apply, so that he can realise gains to use the retirement relief. He cannot, however, do this for only some of the shares, so he may be left with an immediate capital gains tax bill on any balance of gains over the retirement relief available.

Stamp duty

Stamp duty will normally be payable on the consideration whether the sale is of assets or shares. The rate of duty payable on the sale of shares is ½%. The duty on assets would normally be at 1%. From a date in 1993, however, the stamp duty on share transactions and all other transactions except those relating to land and buildings is to be abolished.

Stamp duty on the sale of assets can only be reduced to the extent that assets may pass by delivery, such as plant and machinery, or where the vendor company does not assign its debtors but appoints the purchaser as its agent to collect the debts.

Value added tax (VATA 1983, s 47, Sch 6 Group 5 and Sch 6A.2–4; SI 1981/1741; SI 1985/886 Part V as amended by SI 1987/510)

Where the family company is sold by means of a share sale, the sale does not attract value added tax because the shares are not sold in the course of business but by an individual as an investment.

Where all or part of the business is sold as a going concern by one taxable person to another, no value added tax is charged by the vendor and the purchaser has no input tax to reclaim on the amount paid (subject to the exception stated on page 312 for land and buildings). The going concern treatment only applies, however, where the assets acquired are such that they represent a business which is capable of independent operation.

Where the 'going concern' concept does not apply, value added tax must be charged on all taxable supplies, and any related input tax suffered by the seller will be recoverable. Taxable supplies will include goodwill, stock, plant and machinery, and motor vehicles (except that cars will only be chargeable to the extent, if any, that the disposal proceeds exceed original cost). Business premises on which the seller has exercised his option to tax will also be included, and the seller can therefore recover any VAT relating to the costs of sale, for example on legal and professional fees. The disposal of book debts, and of business premises over three years old on which the option to tax has not been taken, is an exempt supply and does not attract VAT. For partially exempt businesses there are some complex rules as to how the sale of the business is treated.

It is important to ensure that the purchase agreement provides for the addition of value added tax and that the purchase consideration is allocated over the various assets acquired. If value added tax is not mentioned in the purchase agreement, the price is deemed to be VAT inclusive.

Tax points

- When a company ceases to trade, this denotes the end of a chargeable accounting period, and if there are current trading losses these cannot be relieved against chargeable gains arising after the cessation. But gains are deemed to be made on the contract date, not on completion, so if the company enters into the contract while it is still trading, the right to set off current trading losses against chargeable gains in that trading period will be preserved.

- ACT must be paid in a 'chargeable accounting period' in order for a company to be able to set it off against earlier corporation tax liabilities. If a dividend is paid after a trade has ceased, make sure that the company still has some chargeable income, such as interest on bank deposits.

- Compensation for loss of office and ex gratia payments upon cessation of employment can only be expected to escape Revenue challenge if they are genuine payments for breach of contract or reasonable ex gratia amounts bearing in mind years of service etc. and even so, ex gratia payments may not qualify for the £30,000 exemption (see chapter 15).

- When selling shares in a family company with significant retained profits, the Revenue may argue that the increased share value as a result of the retained profits represents not a capital gain but sums that should have been paid out as income, and that they are chargeable as such. Whilst the rate of capital gains tax is now the same as that for income tax, retirement relief will only be available against a capital gain. You should therefore ensure that Revenue clearance is obtained for the proposed sale. On the other hand, income can be sheltered by investment via the business expansion scheme (until the end of 1993) or in an enterprise zone building, whereas a chargeable gain cannot.

- When buying the shares in a company, you should look particularly for any potential capital gains liabilities which will be inherited, such as the crystallisation after ten years of gains on depreciating business assets which have been held over because the company acquired new qualifying assets, or, if the company you are purchasing is leaving a group, the crystallisation of gains on assets acquired by it from another group company within the previous six years. Moreover, the accounts value of the company assets may be greater than the tax value because earlier gains have been deducted under the rollover relief provisions from the tax cost of the assets now held. Thus a chargeable gain may arise on the company even though the item is sold for no more than it is shown as costing in the accounts.

- If you buy a company with unused trading losses or surplus advance corporation tax, you will not be able to use them when you restore the company to profitability if the change of ownership takes place within a period of three years during which there is also a major change in the nature or conduct of the business. There is also a restriction on availability of trading losses where the company being acquired has succeeded to the trade of another company without taking over that other company's liabilities (see page 304).

- The capital gains retirement relief is available to sole traders, partners and qualifying shareholders. It is not available to reduce gains that a company makes on a sale of chargeable assets prior to liquidation of the company.

- The share capital in a family company is sometimes sold on the basis that the family shareholders receive shares in the purchaser company in exchange. In these circumstances, the new shares take the place of the old shares in the personal capital gains tax position of the vendor shareholders, and no capital gains tax is payable at that time. A proportionate part of the gain is chargeable where the purchase consideration is part cash/part new shares. If you are eligible for retirement relief, try to ensure that sufficient cash is received to use the retirement relief available. Alternatively, you can claim for the gain on the shares not to be rolled over, but this may leave you with an immediately chargeable gain if the retirement relief does not fully cover it.

- The purchase consideration may partly depend on the company's future profit performance, sometimes referred to as an 'earn out', and when it is received it may be partly in cash and partly in the form of shares in the purchasing company. The capital gains tax position is complicated and professional advisers have to look very carefully at this aspect, if possible obtaining the views of the Revenue when they apply for clearance on the share sale.

- To get the maximum retirement relief, you need to have been in business either as a sole trader, partner or full-time director of a family company for a total of ten years. Although the disposal date for capital gains tax is the date of the contract, you are allowed to count the period up to completion as part of the ten-year period if the business activities continue up to the completion date.

- Because there are so many pitfalls and problems when selling or buying a family company, it is essential to get expert professional advice.

29
Encouraging business efficiency

Background

The Government has introduced various measures to encourage investment in new and expanding companies and to enable companies that have become unwieldy to split into smaller units without adverse tax consequences. Provisions have also been introduced to enable a company to purchase its own shares, which makes it possible to resolve conflicts within a company by buying out disaffected shareholders, and also makes investment under the government schemes more attractive through enabling the investor to withdraw his funds after the appropriate period.

Although the aims are reasonable, the provisions that have been introduced are for the most part extremely complex and regarded by some as unnecessarily restrictive. This chapter gives only an outline of the provisions, professional advice being essential.

Business expansion scheme (TA 1988, ss 289–312; F(No 2)A 1992, ss 38–40)

The business expansion scheme was brought in from 6 April 1983 to replace the business start-up scheme introduced in 1981/82. It was to have ceased on 5 April 1987, was then extended indefinitely, but will now finally cease at the end of December 1993, and will apply only to shares issued before that time. Those who are attracted to this form of investment are unlikely to require immediate income by way of dividends, and the hope is that the company can by this means both reduce the cost of funding through lower bank or loan interest and also draw on the experience of successful business people.

Relief is given for investment by a 'qualifying individual' in 'eligible shares' in a 'qualifying company' carrying on or intending to carry on a 'qualifying trade' or 'qualifying activities'.

The relief will not be allowed unless and until the company has traded for four months (except where there is a bona fide winding-up in that period). If the company is not carrying on the trade when the shares are issued, it must begin to do so within two years after the issue of the shares, otherwise again no relief is allowed.

The relief must be claimed within two years after the end of the tax year in which the shares are issued, or, if later, within two years after the end of the first four months' trading. Claims must be accompanied by a certificate from the company, issued on the authority of an inspector of taxes, stating that the relevant conditions have been satisfied. Instead of investing directly, a taxpayer may invest through an investment fund (and thus spread his investment over several companies if he wishes), in which case the certificate is issued by the fund managers. Some funds are approved by the Revenue, which gives them certain advantages (see 'Amount of relief' below).

If any of the requirements for a 'qualifying individual' or 'qualifying company' are breached during a 'relevant period' (broadly, in the five or three years respectively after the issue of the shares), the relief will be withdrawn.

Limitation on the raising of funds under the business expansion scheme

There is a limit of £750,000 (£500,000 for shares issued before 1 May 1990) on the amount which any company can raise in one tax year or within six months of an earlier issue in a previous tax year. There is an exception for ship operating or chartering companies and those raising money for the provision and maintenance of dwelling-houses on assured tenancies. The limit in these cases is £5 million instead of £750,000.

Borrowing the money to subscribe for the new shares (TA 1988, s 360)

Relief for interest on a loan to buy the shares was previously available if the investor acquired 5% or more of the issued ordinary share capital, and the company was a close company (broadly, one owned by five or fewer people or by its directors). Relief for interest paid is not available for business expansion scheme shares issued on or after 14 March 1989.

Amount of relief

The maximum amount on which an individual can claim relief in any tax year is £40,000, this limit being available to each of husband and wife. Relief is given in the tax year when the shares are purchased, but one half of the amount subscribed before 6 October in any tax year can be carried back for relief in the previous tax year, up to a maximum carry-back of £5,000. The claim for carry-back must be made at the same time as the claim for relief, and the carry-back cannot increase the relief for a tax year to more than £40,000. The minimum subscription by an individual to one company is £500 except where the investment is made through an approved investment fund. Approved investment funds have another advantage over unapproved funds in that relief is normally given in the tax year in which the fund closes rather than that in which the funds are invested by the fund managers, which may give the relief a year earlier. The relief reduces taxable income and thus saves tax at the payer's highest rate. It may be given through the PAYE system.

Eligible shares

New ordinary shares carrying no present or future preferential right to dividends or assets or redemption for five years from the date of issue are eligible for relief. There is no overall restriction on the proportion of shares in a company on which relief may be given, although there are limits on individual holdings.

Qualifying individual

The individual must be resident and ordinarily resident in the UK, or a Crown employee serving overseas, when the shares are issued and must not be 'connected with' the company (as specifically defined) at any time in the period beginning on the date of incorporation of the company (or if later two years before the shares were issued) and ending five years after the shares were issued.

Broadly, an individual is connected if he or an associate is an employee or paid director of the company or of a partner of the company, or is a partner of the company; if he has or is entitled to acquire more than 30% of the capital, including loan capital (but excluding bank overdrafts), or voting power; if he would be entitled to more than 30% of the assets in a winding-up; or if he has effective control of the company. 'Associate' includes close family (but not brothers and sisters), partners and trustees of any settlement through which the individual has an interest in the company's shares.

Joint holdings are permitted.

The intention of the legislation is to attract investors not dependent on the business. Although they cannot be paid as employees, directors or partners, they may act as advisers, or receive professional fees in appropriate cases, and reasonable expenses may also be paid. At the end of the five-year period, the investor may become a working director or employee.

Qualifying company

The company must be incorporated in the UK and must satisfy the following conditions throughout the three years following the date of issue of the shares qualifying for relief, or the three years from the start of trading if later:

It must not be quoted on the stock exchange or unlisted securities market.

It must be UK-resident.

It must be a UK trading company and/or the holding company of a group of qualifying subsidiaries. It may not be an investment company, but there is nothing to stop a trading company owning land and buildings for use in its trade so long as the value of the land and buildings less liabilities secured thereon or of a long term nature does not, in the period of three years after the issue of the shares (or from the start of trading, if later), exceed 50% of the net assets of the company. This restriction does not apply unless the company raises more than £50,000 in a twelve-month period, and then applies only to the excess over £50,000. Neither does the restriction apply to companies carrying on 'qualifying activities' (see below).

All issued shares must be fully paid, but all shares need not be of the same class.

It must not be a subsidiary. Its own subsidiaries must normally be at least 90% owned. The subsidiaries may be resident or incorporated overseas provided that the trading activities of the group as a whole are carried on wholly or mainly in the UK.

Relief will not be withdrawn as a result of a bona fide winding-up during the three-year period. If, however, the company should cease to trade without going into liquidation shortly afterwards, it would cease to qualify and investors would then lose the BES relief. (The appointment of an Administrative Receiver is not the same as going into liquidation.) In these circumstances, shareholders may be able to claim that the shares have become of negligible value (see page 53) and then to claim relief for the capital loss against income (see page 436).

Qualifying trade

A qualifying trade is one conducted on a commercial basis with a view to the realisation of profits, but excluding finance, leasing (except certain ship chartering), holding commodities as investments (e.g. fine wines and antiques), legal and accountancy services and those excluded because of high asset backing in land and buildings (see above). Farming and property development are not specifically excluded, but must comply with the land and buildings rule.

Qualifying activities

These consist of the provision and maintenance of certain dwelling-houses which the company lets, or intends to let, on assured tenancies (other than short-term tenancies) under the Housing Act 1988. The general business expansion scheme provisions are modified for companies carrying on qualifying activities, and for their investors. For shares issued on or after 10 March 1992, the conditions have been amended to facilitate mortgage rescue schemes under which property is let to former owner-occupiers.

Withdrawal of relief

The shares must be held for a minimum of five years, otherwise the relief is withdrawn completely if the disposal is not at arm's length and is reduced by the amount received for an arm's length bargain. Relief is also withdrawn if the individual receives value from the company within that time. 'Value' is exhaustively defined and includes the repayment of loans that had been made to the company before the shares were subscribed for, provision of benefits, and purchase of assets for less than market value.

An amount received in respect of an option to sell BES shares will cause the loss of an appropriate amount of relief, but an arrangement to sell them (say to the controlling shareholders) after the qualifying five-year period will not.

Capital gains

For shares issued after 18 March 1986, there is no capital gains tax when the shares are disposed of so long as they are qualifying shares throughout the period of ownership. The relief thus provides a useful source of finance for companies and an efficient means of investment for shareholders. See example 1.

Example 1

For higher rate taxpayers, an investment under the business expansion scheme can show a significant growth over the five-year minimum period of ownership even if there is little or no increase in the value of the shares by the end of the period, viz:

	£
Cost of shares say	10,000
Tax relief at 40%	4,000
Net cost	6,000
Sale (or redemption by company) after five years (say)	10,500
Surplus (not subject to CGT) on £6,000 net cost	£4,500

The surplus will, of course, be reduced by any costs of share acquisition or disposal and by any charges made by scheme managers when investment is made through an investment fund.

Where an individual owns shares in a company, some of which have qualified for relief and some not, disposals are identified first with shares on which business start-up relief was given, then with shares on which business expansion relief was given, then with any other shares.

Anti-avoidance provisions

An individual is not entitled to relief if at the time when the shares are issued, or, if later, the date on which the company begins to trade, he is one of a group of persons who control the company or own an interest amounting to more than a half-share in the trade carried on by the company; and he, or a group of persons of which he is one, control another company or possess an interest amounting to more than a half-share in another trade; and the two trades, or a substantial part of them, deal with similar goods or services and serve substantially the same or similar outlets or markets.

Relief is restricted where the company, during the period commencing with its incorporation (or two years before the shares are issued, if later) and ending five years after the shares are issued, repays or redeems any of its share capital which belongs to other members.

Relief is also restricted where an individual has repaid to him a loan which he has made to the company, and then subscribes for shares in the company.

Withdrawal of investment after relevant period

Potential investors may see a disadvantage in their being locked in as minority shareholders. The company may, however, build up reserves by retaining profits, and use the reserves to purchase its own shares after the five-year period, using the rules described below.

Purchase by company of its own shares (TA 1988, ss 219–229)

Where an unquoted trading company or the unquoted holding company of a trading group buys back its own shares (or redeems them or makes a payment for them in a reduction of capital) in order to benefit a trade, the transaction is not treated as a distribution, and thus liable to income tax in the hands of the vending shareholder, with the company being liable for advance corporation tax, but as a disposal on which the vending shareholder is liable to capital gains tax. This does not apply if there is an arrangement the main purpose of which is to get undistributed profits into the hands of the shareholders without incurring the tax liabilities on a distribution.

The main requirements are that the shareholder must be UK-resident, he must normally have owned the shares for at least five years, and he must either dispose of his entire holding or the holding must be 'substantially reduced'.

A company may apply to the Revenue for a clearance that the proposed purchase will not be treated as a distribution.

Any legal costs and other expenditure incurred by a company in purchasing its own shares will not be allowable against the company's profits.

Management buyouts

The provisions enabling a company to purchase its own shares could assist a management buyout team to acquire the company for which they work, in that only shares remaining after those bought in by the company need then be acquired by them.

If only part of a trade is to be acquired, the existing company could transfer the requisite assets into a subsidiary company using the reconstruction provisions of TA 1988, s 343, the buyout team then buying the shares in the subsidiary.

Alternatively, if the buyout team form an entirely new company and purchase assets from their employing company, capital allowances will be available where appropriate and the new company may be able to raise some of the funds it needs through the business expansion scheme.

Demergers (TA 1988, ss 213–218)

The aim of the demerger legislation, according to the then Chancellor in 1980, was to enable businesses grouped inefficiently under a single company umbrella to be run more dynamically and effectively by being demerged and allowed to pursue their separate ways under independent management. Various tax obstacles to such a course were accordingly removed. The detailed provisions are very complex, the following being an outline.

A company is not treated as having made a distribution for corporation tax purposes (and the members are not treated as having received income) where the company transfers to its members the shares of a 75% subsidiary, or transfers a trade to a new company in exchange for that new company issuing shares to some or all of the transferor company's shareholders.

In order for these provisions to apply, all the companies must be UK-resident trading companies, the transfer must be made to benefit some or all of the trading activities, and the transfer must not be made for tax avoidance reasons.

The distribution by the holding company of shares in subsidiaries to its members is also not treated as a capital distribution for capital gains tax purposes, and the capital gains charge when a company leaves a group on assets acquired within the previous six years from other group companies does not apply.

There are detailed anti-avoidance provisions, and there is also provision to apply for Revenue clearance of proposed transactions.

Enterprise zones

Certain areas in which the government particularly wants to encourage investment have been designated as enterprise zones. Those who set up business within an enterprise zone get certain advantages for a limited number of years, such as not paying business rates and entitlement to 100% relief for expenditure on buildings for use in the trade. The relief for expenditure on buildings is also available to landlords and is dealt with in chapter 22. If you are considering setting up business in an enterprise zone, make appropriate comparisons to ensure that the cost of buying or leasing land is not higher because of tax relief on construction expenditure and the other known advantages of operating from a designated area.

Other measures to stimulate business enterprise (TA 1988, ss 79, 79A)

Businesses may claim a deduction from their profits for contributions they make to Local Enterprise Agencies (from 1 April 1982) and Training and Enterprise Councils and Scottish local enterprise companies (from 1 April 1990) up to 31 March 1995.

Local Enterprise Agencies are bodies approved by the Secretary of State that promote local industrial and commercial activity and enterprise, particularly in forming and developing small businesses. Training and Enterprise Councils are private companies whose directors are mainly local businessmen. They work under contract to the Department of Employment's Training Agency and are mainly concerned with Government training programmes. Scottish local enterprise companies are similar to Training and Enterprise Councils but cover economic development and environmental functions as well as training.

Tax points

- The anti-avoidance rules in relation to most of the provisions dealt with in this chapter are too extensive to deal with in detail, but should be looked at carefully by interested companies and investors.

- Business expansion scheme relief may be denied in circumstances where there seems to be no valid reason for doing so. For example, if while arrangements for the issue of share capital are being made, an investor temporarily lends money to the company, he will be regarded as having 'received value' when it is repaid, thus denying him relief on the shares.

- Although qualifying companies or fund managers will issue certificates to individuals investing under the business expansion scheme, each individual must make a specific claim to his own tax district within the time limit indicated on page 326.

- Stamp duty at 0.5% is currently payable on the purchase by a company of its own shares, and on demergers. Stamp duty on share transactions is, however, to be abolished from some time in 1993.

- The Revenue will not usually give a clearance under the demerger provisions where companies in the same ownership are first merged and then demerged so that each company ends up in the ownership of independent people.

30
Your family home

General

The tax system encourages you to own your own home by exempting any capital gain when you sell it and by giving relief at 25% (higher rate relief no longer being available from 6 April 1991) for interest paid on loans up to a maximum of £30,000 to buy it. The £30,000 is a joint limit for husband and wife. For loans after 31 July 1988 to unmarried home sharers, it applies to the property and not each individual borrower. Where there is more than one loan, relief is given on the earliest loans first, and when the total qualifying loans exceed £30,000 no relief is given on the excess. Relief is not available on home improvement loans. If, however, you obtained such a loan before 6 April 1988, you continue to get relief so long as the borrowing falls within the £30,000 overall limit. You will lose this relief if you remortgage the property. You will get relief on borrowing to cover repairs only if they are needed to put a newly acquired property into proper condition.

If the loan is not used for a qualifying purpose, then even if it is from a building society and secured on the house, it will not qualify for relief.

Relief from capital gains tax and for income tax on interest payments is extended in some cases to properties intended to be occupied in the future, and for those already occupied by a dependent relative at 5 April 1988 (see page 334). Interest and capital gains relief is also sometimes available on existing loans in respect of a property occupied at 5 April 1988 by a former or separated spouse—see chapter 33. The £30,000 interest relief limit is an umbrella figure, however, that must cover all qualifying loans to one borrower, and in all cases relief is now restricted to the 25% rate of tax (except for certain bridging loans—see page 341).

Buying a house and not moving in immediately (TA 1988, s 355)

If you do not move into your house immediately, you still get tax relief on interest on a loan to buy it providing you move in within twelve months from the making of the loan. (See also page 340 re job-related accommodation and page 341 re bridging loans.)

For capital gains purposes, the Revenue practice is not to treat any non-occupation in the first twelve months as affecting your exemption if you do not move in because you are altering or redecorating the property, or because you remain in your old home while you are selling it.

Empty property may attract the standard community charge, but newly built or structurally altered property is not subject to the charge for up to six months after the work is substantially completed, and there is no charge on any unfurnished property for up to six months.

Dwelling occupied by a dependent relative (TA 1988, s 355(1)(a); FA 1988, s 44; TCGA 1992, s 226)

If on 5 April 1988 you owned a property that was occupied rent-free and without any other consideration by a dependent relative, the property is exempt from capital gains tax when you dispose of it. Relief is also available for interest on borrowing to buy the property (and on borrowing for any other property similarly occupied) so long as your total qualifying loans are within the £30,000 borrowing ceiling.

Relief for interest will not continue if there is a change of occupant after 5 April 1988 even if the new occupant is also a dependent relative. The same applies to the capital gains tax exemption, but the period which did qualify for relief is taken into account in calculating any chargeable gain, on a time apportioned basis.

'Dependent relative' is defined as your own or your spouse's widowed mother, or any other relative unable to look after themselves because of old age or infirmity. There is no income restriction.

See page 391 for a tax-effective way of providing a home for a dependent relative now.

If part of your home is let (TCGA 1992, s 223(4); F(No 2)A 1992, s 59 and Sch 10)

A new relief ('rent a room relief') has been introduced from 6 April 1992 for owner-occupiers and tenants who let furnished rooms in their homes. The relief applies both where the rent comes under the furnished lettings rules of Schedule D, Case VI (see page 364) and where substantial services are also provided so that the rent is charged as trading income (traders being normally charged on the previous year's income—see chapter 21). No tax will be payable if the gross rents for the tax year, before deducting expenses, do not exceed £3,250. If the letting is by a couple, the relief is £1,625 each. You can claim for the relief not to apply for a particular year, for example if your expenses exceed your rent and you want to claim relief for a loss. If your rent exceeds £3,250, you can choose to pay tax either on the excess over £3,250 or on the rent less expenses under the normal rules described below. If you want to pay on the excess over £3,250 you must make a claim within one year after the end of the relevant tax year, and that basis will then apply until you withdraw your claim.

If the 'rent a room' relief does not apply, the income from letting is chargeable to income tax after setting off appropriate expenses. It is normally treated as unearned income, but if the letting qualifies as furnished holiday accommodation (see page 366), the income is treated as trading income, and can therefore support a self-employed pension premium (see chapter 17).

As far as the capital gains exemption is concerned, there is no loss of relief if the letting takes the form of boarders who effectively live as part of the family. Where, however, the letting extends beyond this, the appropriate fraction of the gain on disposal is chargeable but there is an exemption of the smaller of £40,000 and an amount equal to the exempt gain on the owner-occupied part. See example 1.

Example 1

The gain on the sale of a dwelling in 1992/93 is £80,000. The agreed proportion applicable to the let part is £48,000, the exempt gain being £32,000.

The £48,000 gain on the let part is reduced by the lower of

(a) £40,000 and
(b) an amount equal to the exempt gain, i.e. £32,000.

Therefore a further £32,000 is exempt and £16,000 is chargeable (but the £5,800 annual exemption will reduce the gain still further if not already used).

Where a married couple jointly let part of the home, each is entitled to the residential lettings exemption of up to £40,000.

The exemption is not available if the let part of the property is effectively a separate dwelling, such as a self-contained flat with its own access. But where part of the home is let, without substantial structural alterations, it will qualify, even if it has separate facilities.

The Revenue have taken the view that the residential lettings exemption is only available where the letting has some degree of permanence, but they have just lost a case on the point in the Court of Appeal, where it was decided that the exemption was available to the owners of a small private hotel who occupied the whole of the property during the winter months, with one or two guests, but moved to an annexe during the summer. The Revenue are appealing against this decision. The exemption can be claimed only if the property qualifies as your capital gains tax exempt residence for at least part of your period of ownership, so it cannot be claimed on a property which, although you live in it sometimes, has never been your only or main residence for capital gains tax purposes. Subject to that, it can be claimed where all of the property has been let for part of your period of ownership, or part of the property has been let for all or part of your period of ownership.

The position of furnished holiday lettings (see page 365) is not clear. Gains on such property are specifically eligible for rollover relief when the property is sold and replaced, but providing you comply with the rules outlined above, it would seem that the residential lettings exemption could apply instead. To continue to get the other benefits of the furnished holiday lettings provisions, you would have to make sure that you complied with the rules for such lettings (in particular ensuring that neither you nor anyone else normally occupied the accommodation for a continuous period of more than 31 days for at least seven months of the year).

Poll tax and business rates

If the let part of your property is let as self-contained living accommodation and occupied by long-term tenants, it will be their only or main home and they will pay personal poll tax. But for any period when it is not anyone's only or main home, for example when it is untenanted, you will be liable to the standard community charge on it, which will often be double the amount of the normal poll tax (subject to certain exemptions, for example unfurnished property for up to six months—see page 98). If the let part is let as short-term living accommodation, and is therefore no-one's only or main home, the standard charge will apply unless it is available for short-term letting for 140 days or more in a year (for example self-catering holiday accommodation), in which case you will pay business rates instead of the standard charge. If you offer bed and breakfast facilities in your own home, there are no poll tax implications, and you will not be liable to business rates providing you do not offer accommodation for more than six people, you live in the house at the same time and the house is still mainly used as your home. If part of your home is let for business purposes rather than as living accommodation, business rates will be payable.

Any standard charge or business rates paid will be deducted from the rent in arriving at your taxable letting income.

How relief is given for allowable interest (TA 1988, ss 353–358, 366–379)

Most loans for home buying are now covered by the Mortgage Interest Relief At Source (MIRAS) scheme, which applies to the first £30,000 of qualifying loans, but some lenders are not authorised to operate the scheme.

If the loan falls within the MIRAS scheme, you deduct basic rate income tax when paying the interest. From 6 April 1991, higher rate relief is not available, so that no further relief is due.

For loans above £30,000 made after 5 April 1987, MIRAS applies to the first £30,000 and the interest on the balance above £30,000 is paid in full. Lenders do not have to include loans above £30,000 made on or before 5 April 1987 in the MIRAS scheme, although they may do so if they wish. In any event, an increase above the £30,000 limit of up to £1,000 due solely to the addition of unpaid interest is ignored and the loan remains within the MIRAS scheme. When the balance on a loan falls below the £30,000 limit, the interest is brought within the MIRAS scheme from the beginning of the following tax year if MIRAS is not already in operation on the allowable part of the loan.

For loans outside MIRAS, basic rate relief has to be claimed, and is given by a coding adjustment or in an assessment. A certificate of interest paid, supplied by the lender, is essential in these cases.

MIRAS is not available if more than one-third of your home is let or used for business purposes, so that the interest in those circumstances would be paid gross. You would claim relief for the private proportion against your general income and the balance against the business profit or letting income as the case may be. If you are a higher rate taxpayer you should claim the deduction for the appropriate part of the interest against rents or business profits in any event, because MIRAS relief is now restricted to the basic rate of tax from 6 April 1991.

Non-taxpayers and those liable to tax at only 20% benefit from the MIRAS scheme because they are allowed to retain the 25% tax deducted, even though they would not otherwise be entitled to tax relief at that rate.

If you are married and buying your home in joint names, interest is regarded as being paid equally. This may not be best from a tax point of view, for example if the loan is outside MIRAS and one of you is a taxpayer and the other is not, or where income would otherwise be above the age allowance limit (see example 2). You can elect (on form 15(1990) available from the tax office) to have the interest split in any way you want. The

---

Example 2

In 1992/93, a man aged 65 and his wife aged 60 have income, before MIRAS interest, of £16,000 and £10,000 respectively. Their joint MIRAS interest is £1,000. The wife's tax position is not affected by the MIRAS interest. The husband's position is as follows:

	Interest split equally		Interest to husband	
	£	£	£	£
Income		16,000		16,000
Age allowances	6,665		6,665	
Less half of excess income (after MIRAS) over £14,200:				
Half of £(15,500 − 14,200)	650			
Half of £(15,000 − 14,200)			400	
		6,015		6,265
Taxable income		£9,985		£9,735

Tax: £2,000 @ 20%   400   400
      £7,985/7,735 @ 25%   1,996   1,934
                                    ——— £2,396   ——— £2,334

Extra saving if all mortgage interest claimed by husband is £62, which is an extra 12½% on the £500 transferred from the wife, making, with the 25% already retained under MIRAS, a total saving of 37½% (i.e. the rate of tax payable on any income above the age allowance limit—see page 390).

election must be made by twelve months from the end of the tax year to which it applies, for example by 5 April 1994 for 1992/93. You can vary your election or withdraw it (on form 15-1(1990)), if you wish. The main reason for making the election was to save more tax at the higher rate but this is no longer relevant.

Interest relief—unmarried home sharers (TA 1988, ss 356A–356D)

For loans made before 1 August 1988, unmarried home sharers could each claim interest relief on a loan of up to £30,000, and can continue to do so providing the loan is still outstanding.

For later loans, the £30,000 limit applies to the property and not to each borrower. This also applies to replacement loans. The £30,000 limit is divided between the borrowers in equal shares. Relief cannot be given to one borrower for interest paid by another. It is, however, possible for a borrower who does not fully use his or her share of the limit to transfer it to another sharer. See example 3.

Example 3

Three unmarried sharers borrow the following sums for an equal share in a residence:

A   £25,000
B   £9,000
C   £4,000

The balance of the £10,000 qualifying loan limit to which each of B and C is entitled, but which they have not fully used, can be transferred to A, giving relief for the borrowing as follows:

A (£10,000 + £1,000 + £6,000)   £17,000
B (£10,000 − £1,000 to A)   £9,000
C (£10,000 − £6,000 to A)   £4,000

Interest relief given for borrowing of   £30,000

Ways of funding a mortgage

There are many different ways of arranging the borrowing to buy your house. You can have a conventional repayment mortgage, where you repay both capital and interest over the period of the mortgage. You can have an endowment mortgage, under which you pay only interest on the borrowing, and pay endowment insurance premiums to produce a lump sum to repay the capital. The profit element in the lump sum is tax-free (see page 452). Another option is a mortgage linked to a Personal Equity Plan (PEP) (personal equity plans are explained on page 440). This is similar to an endowment mortgage, but it has extra tax advantages, although on the other hand it carries more risk. Interest is paid on the loan, and a further monthly payment is made, but it is invested in equities and/or unit trusts through the PEP. Dividends and capital gains on the investments are free of tax. To cover the early years when the fund is small, you have to take out temporary life assurance for the amount borrowed, but this is relatively cheap. PEP mortgages are more flexible than endowment mortgages.

The most tax effective choice of all for those who are able to contribute to personal pension plans (see chapter 17) is a pension mortgage. Some lenders will also lend on the basis of a company pension scheme. Again, interest is paid on the amount borrowed, and temporary life assurance is taken out to cover the borrowing, but the capital is repaid out of the lump sum entitlement from the pension fund. Tax relief on the contributions to the pension fund is obtained at the payer's highest tax rate, as well as the fund itself being free of tax. You should remember, however, that you are using part or all of the lump sum that was really intended to support you in retirement.

To help those who have difficulty meeting early high repayments, there are various deferred interest or 'low start' mortgages on offer, and they are usually structured in such a way that MIRAS relief is still obtained on the interest that is paid. Less interest at the beginning does of course mean more interest later on, but you may then be in a better financial position.

You need to think carefully about the different choices available, and consider the advantages and disadvantages of each.

More than one home (TA 1988, s 355(1)(a); TCGA 1992, s 222(5)(6))

You may elect within two years of acquiring a second home which of the two is to be the exempt home for capital gains tax. If you do not do so, the Revenue will decide, but you have a right of appeal. Provided that both houses have been your main residence for capital gains tax at some time, the last three years of ownership of both will in any event be counted as owner-occupied in calculating the exempt gain. The final exempt period was two years for disposals before 19 March 1991, and may be changed back to two years by statutory instrument if the housing market improves.

For mortgage interest relief, it is a question of fact which is your main residence. In the event of a dispute between you and the Revenue, it would be decided on appeal by the Appeal Commissioners.

The qualifying residence for interest relief need not be the one to which the capital gains exemption applies. In both cases, however, it is necessary for the house to be or have been your residence, and a pure investment property could not qualify.

For poll tax, you pay the standard charge (probably at double the personal poll tax) on a property which is no-one's only or main home. The question of which of two or more homes is your only or main home for the poll tax is a question of fact, decided in the first place by the community charge registration officer, but you may appeal against his decision. In some circumstances, one of the properties might be the main home of one spouse and the other property the main home of the other, in which case the standard charge would not be paid on either. This could apply, for example, if a wife lived at a house in the country and her husband at a house in town, going to the other house at weekends etc. But the length of time spent at the property would not necessarily be the deciding factor and all relevant circumstances would be taken into account. If the second home was a holiday property available for short-term letting for 140 days or more in a year, it would be liable to business rates rather than the standard charge.

If your second home is a caravan, it will not be liable to the standard charge. The site owner where the caravan is kept will pay business rates, which will be included in his charge to you. Touring caravans kept at your home when you are not touring will not be subject to the standard charge.

Job-related accommodation (TA 1988, s 356; TCGA 1992, s 222(8))

If you live in accommodation related to your employment, for example as a hotel manager or minister of religion, or to your self-employment, for example as the tenant of licensed premises, you may wish to acquire a residence for your future occupation. Interest paid on borrowing for its acquisition is allowable at 25% (up to the statutory limit), and the house qualifies for capital gains tax exemption, even though you do not live there.

Unless the house is someone's only or main home (for example if you let it long-term), you will pay the standard community charge on it, as well as being liable to the personal poll tax in the area where you live, but if the property is unoccupied the maximum standard community charge will be half of the personal poll tax.

Periods of absence (TCGA 1992, s 223)

Provided that a house has at some time been your only or main residence, the last three years of ownership (two years for disposals before 19 March 1991) are always exempt from capital gains tax, whether you are living there or not. Other periods of absence also qualify for exemption provided that the house was your only or main residence at some time both before and after the period of absence, and that no other residence qualifies for relief during the absence. Those periods are any or all of the following:

(a) three years for any reason whatsoever (not necessarily a consecutive period of three years);
(b) up to four years where the duties of a United Kingdom employment require you to live elsewhere; and
(c) any period of absence abroad where the duties of employment require you to live abroad.

If those periods are exceeded, only the excess is counted as a period of non-residence. If you have to move to another place of employment, so that it is not possible to have a period of residence immediately after an absence, that condition is waived.

You can thus have long periods of absence without losing any part of the capital gains tax exemption.

Periods of absence before 31 March 1982 are ignored in calculating the chargeable gain, which depends on the proportion of residence/deemed residence to total period of ownership after 30 March 1982.

For interest relief purposes, the Revenue, by concession, similarly disregard temporary absences of up to one year, or up to four years where required by your employment (or any longer period in the case of certain civil servants posted overseas). If the property is let, a loan of up to £30,000 may remain within the MIRAS arrangements providing the agreement of the tax office is obtained. This also applies to a loan above £30,000, unless the net rent will exceed the interest on £30,000. In that event, the taxpayer will be better off outside MIRAS because interest on the whole loan, rather than on the first £30,000, may be set against the rent. Where the net rent will sometimes be below the interest on £30,000 and sometimes above it, the Revenue will allow relief on the first £30,000 to be given through MIRAS and the balance as a deduction against the net rent. Higher rate taxpayers should claim relief for all the interest against rents no matter what the amount of the loan is because MIRAS relief is only at the basic rate from 6 April 1991.

There are no special poll tax provisions about permitted absences, other than the exemptions listed on page 97 for personal poll tax and page 98 for the standard community charge, although local authorities have drawn up some special rules for dealing with service personnel and merchant seamen. If a house is no-one's only or main home, the standard charge will usually be payable.

Bridging loans (TA 1988, s 354(5)(6); FA 1991, s 27(3)–(5); TCGA 1992, s 223)

Owning two houses at the same time is usually covered for capital gains tax purposes by the exemption of the last three years of ownership. For interest relief purposes, a separate £30,000 limit applies to a bridging loan for a statutory period of one year, generally extended to two years by Revenue concession. Bridging loan interest is normally paid gross and tax relief is obtained through a coding adjustment or in an assessment, the claim being supported by a certificate of interest paid. Where a bridging loan was made before 6 April 1991 (or in pursuance of a binding contract to buy a property, evidenced by a written offer of the loan from the lender, both made before 6 April 1991), higher rate relief will continue to be given on the original loan (not on the bridging loan) for the permitted period.

Where two people who are buying houses on mortgage get married and either sell both houses and buy a third, or go to live in one of the houses and sell the other, the bridging loan treatment does not strictly apply but is given by Revenue concession.

Employees earning £8,500 per annum or more and company directors are charged to tax on benefits received in respect of their employment (see page 131). If you are in this category, a special concessionary treatment (concession A5) applies if you have to move house as a result of changing your job. It is not known whether the Revenue will seek to make any change to this concession now that higher rate relief is no longer available on home loan interest. The concession provides that the reimbursement by your employer of the interest on a bridging loan (net of tax relief), or the provision by your employer of a bridging loan in excess of £30,000, which would otherwise be caught by the 'cheap loans' provisions (see page 134), is not chargeable to tax. This only applies to a loan that is used to pay off the loan on the old property, or to fund the purchase of a new property, or to meet incidental expenses such as legal fees. The loan must not be outstanding for longer than twelve months (or such longer period as the Revenue may allow). The concession is restricted to a loan not exceeding the value of the old property. If, however, your employers lend you a sum that does exceed the value of your old house, the part of the loan up to the value of the old house is ignored in deciding whether the balance of the loan is caught by the 'cheap loans' rules. If, for example, you owned a house worth £60,000 on which there was no mortgage, and you bought a house for £100,000 with a building society mortgage of £25,000 and an interest-free loan of £75,000 from your employer, £60,000 of the employer's loan would be covered by the bridging loan concession (unless the concession is amended). Of the remaining £15,000, £5,000 would be within the allowable £30,000 limit, so that it would not attract a tax charge unless the employee/director was a higher rate taxpayer, in which case interest at the official rate on the £5,000 would be charged to tax at 15%. (The same would apply to the interest on the £25,000 building society mortgage.) Interest at the official rate on the remaining £10,000 of the employer's loan would be charged at the employee/director's highest tax rate.

As far as poll tax is concerned, the same points apply as stated on page 341 for 'Periods of absence'.

Part use for business purposes (TCGA 1992, s 224)

Interest on that part of any borrowing attributable to the use of part of your home exclusively for business is allowed as a business expense, and the

£30,000 limit then applies to the remainder of the loan. MIRAS relief can still be given on such a loan providing the business use is not more than one-third. The authorisation of your tax office must be obtained.

You will pay business rates on the business part of the property (allowable against your profits for tax). Where part of the property is used for both business and domestic purposes, and the business use does not prevent the continued domestic use, such as a study where you do some work and your children do their homework, business rates will not be payable.

As far as capital gains tax is concerned, the private residence exemption is not available on any part of your property that is used exclusively for business purposes. Where a replacement property is acquired that is similarly used partly for business, rollover relief may be available to defer the gain (see page 48) and if you eventually dispose of the property when you retire, the gain may be covered by retirement relief (see page 49).

When a claim for Schedule E expenses has included part of the expenses of the residence (TCGA 1992, s 158(1)(c); SP 5/86)

Expenses are sometimes allowed concessionally within a Schedule E claim where there is some use of the residence in connection with your employment. Where such an allowance is not based on any specific proportion of the house being so used, the Inspector may well not seek to assess any part of any gain on eventual sale of the house. The position is not, however, free from doubt, and where a Schedule E expenses claim is being made, the possible effect on the dwelling house exemption should be carefully considered. A claim for rollover relief (see page 48) is possible where the employer does not make any payment or give other consideration for his use of the property nor otherwise occupy it under a lease or tenancy.

Selling to make a profit, including selling off part of the garden

The capital gains tax exemption for a principal private residence does not apply if you acquired the property with the intention of reselling at a profit, and if after acquiring a property you incur expenditure wholly or partly to make a gain on sale, an appropriate part of the gain will not be exempt (TCGA 1992, s 224).

The capital gains exemption extends to grounds not exceeding half a hectare (approximately 1¼ acres), or such larger area as is appropriate to the size and character of the house. If you sell some of the land, perhaps for building plots, the sale is covered by the exemption so long as the land is sold before the house and immediately surrounding grounds. The Revenue have stated that expenditure to get planning permission does not affect the exemption.

In exceptional circumstances, the Revenue may assert that selling part of the garden, or frequent buying and selling of properties, amounts to a trade, resulting not only in the loss of the capital gains tax exemption but also in the taxation of the profits as income.

Tax points

- Now that tax relief on home loans is restricted to 25%, consider whether you could pay for the home in full and borrow for other tax allowable purposes on which relief at your top tax rate is still available. For other allowable interest, see pages 12 and 13. See also page 231.

- If you acquire a second house, consider carefully which is your main residence for mortgage interest and poll tax purposes and which you wish to treat as your capital gains tax exempt residence, remembering that the last three years of ownership of a house which at some time has been your main residence for capital gains tax can in any event be counted as years of owner-occupation in the capital gains tax calculation.

- If you are living in job-related accommodation, be certain to tell the Revenue about the acquisition of a dwelling for your own occupation, thus avoiding any doubt that you regard it as your main residence for capital gains tax, and for claiming relief for interest paid on borrowing for its purchase.

- When considering the business proportion of mixed premises for the purpose of claiming relief for expenses, bear in mind the possibility of capital gains tax when the premises are sold.

- If you take in a lodger under the new 'rent a room' provisions, make sure you tell your contents insurer. Even so, you will probably be covered for theft only if it is by breaking and entering.

- The maximum £40,000 capital gains tax exemption for letting of the family home (£40,000 each if jointly let by husband and wife) applies where it is wholly let for residential occupation for part of the period of ownership, or partly let for residential occupation sometime during the period of ownership. Because of the residential requirement, it could not exempt that part of a gain which was chargeable because part of the accommodation was used by the family company for trading purposes.

- The Revenue regard a bridging loan as bridging an unavoidable gap between money being laid out for the purchase of a new property and the proceeds of the old property being received. Relief for interest on the bridging loan will therefore be restricted where the loan exceeds the expected proceeds of the old property. The loan must be used to pay off the mortgage on the old property, fund the purchase of the new, or meet the immediately related incidental expenditure such as legal and survey fees.

- Where a house has separate buildings to accommodate staff, they may count for the capital gains exemption if they are 'closely adjacent' to the main property, but not if they are so far away that the house and buildings cannot really be regarded as a single dwelling.

- Now that relief has been withdrawn for new loans after 5 April 1988 for the purchase of a dwelling for occupation by a former/separated spouse or a dependent relative, consider jointly owning the property with the occupant, with the occupant paying the interest.

- Relief is no longer due for new home improvement loans. When buying a new house, it will therefore pay to maximise the borrowing for the purchase, within the £30,000 limit, rather than borrow less at the outset and then have to top it up with home improvement loans, the interest on which does not qualify for tax relief.

- If you remortgage your home, you will get tax relief only on an amount equal to your previous qualifying loan, even if it was below £30,000. Any additional borrowing will not qualify for tax relief unless it is for a qualifying purpose—see pages 12, 13; and if any part of the earlier loan was for home improvements, you will lose your tax relief on that part of the replacement loan.

- Under independent taxation of husband and wife, each has a separate annual capital gains tax exemption and the use of the 20% and 25% rate bands, so far as not utilised against income, to restrict the tax charge on gains. Joint ownership of a second home might therefore reduce the capital gains tax on an eventual sale.

- If you are selling off part of your garden, make sure it is sold before the house and immediately adjoining land.

- If you have converted part of your home into a self-contained flat for letting, you will be liable to pay the standard community charge (usually at double the personal poll tax) if it is untenanted, except for the first six months if it is unfurnished.

- As a bed and breakfast provider you will not pay business rates providing you do not offer accommodation for more than six people, you still live there as well and the property's main use is still as your home.

31
A country life: farms and woodlands

Farming and market gardening profits

The profits of farmers and market gardeners are calculated in the same way as are those of other businesses, but some special rules apply.

It is common in farming for members of the family to be employed on the farm. As with all businesses, expenses must be 'wholly and exclusively for the purposes of the trade', and there has been a court decision that a farmer's wages to his young children were pocket money and were therefore neither allowable as an expense in calculating farm trading profits nor to be treated as the children's income to enable their personal allowances to be used. The fact that the children were below legal employment age was taken into account, although it was not conclusive.

Farming as a single trade (TA 1988, s 53)

All farming carried on by one farmer is treated as a single trade, so that several holdings are treated as a single business and a move from one farm to another will not be treated as the cessation of one business and the commencement of another.

Loss relief (TA 1988, ss 380–383, 385, 388, 389, 397)

The usual reliefs for losses in early and later years and on cessation of trading are available to farming businesses and the usual restriction applies to prevent losses being set against other income if the business is not operated on a commercial basis (see chapter 25). In addition, a loss in the sixth tax year of a consecutive run of farming and market gardening losses (calculated before capital allowances) cannot be relieved other than by carry-forward against later profits of the same trade. The same applies to a loss in a company accounting period following a similar five-year run of losses (before capital allowances). The restriction does not apply if a competent farmer or market gardener could not have expected a profit until after the six-year loss period. If losses are required to be carried forward, any related capital allowances are similarly treated. Once one year shows a profit, another six-year period then applies to later losses.

Averaging (TA 1988, s 96)

The results of an individual farmer or market gardener or of a farming or market gardening partnership may be averaged over two tax years if the profit of one year (before capital allowances) is less than 7/10ths of the profit of the other year, with marginal relief if it is more than 7/10ths but less than 3/4. A claim for averaging must be made within two years after the end of the second tax year. Averaging may not be claimed by farming companies.

If profits are averaged, the average figure is then used as the result of the second year and it may again be averaged with the result of the third year and so on. Losses are counted as nil profits in the averaging calculation, with relief for the loss being available separately.

An averaging claim cannot be made in the first or last year of trading.

Averaging enables farmers to lessen the effect of high tax rates on a successful year when preceded or followed by a bad year. See example 1.

Example 1

Farmer's profits for years ended 31 December 1989 and 1990 are £40,000 and £20,000 respectively, and in the year to 31 December 1991 he makes a loss of £7,000.

Assessments may variously be as follows:

	No averaging	Averaging 1990/91 and 1991/92 only	All three years averaged
	£	£	£
1990/91	40,000	30,000	30,000
1991/92	20,000	30,000	15,000
1992/93	–	–	15,000

The loss of £7,000 is available for relief whether or not averaging is claimed.

Since the figures are averaged before capital allowances, the benefit is sometimes reduced after capital allowances are taken into account, so it may be more effective for tax purposes not to claim plant and machinery capital allowances, or to claim a reduced amount, thus increasing the written-down value to attract writing-down allowances in later years. See example 2.

Herd basis (TA 1988, s 97 and Sch 5)

Farm animals and other livestock are normally treated as trading stock. A production herd may, however, effectively be treated as a capital asset if an election is made for the herd basis. The election is irrevocable. The time limit for making the election is two years from the end of the first relevant year of

---

Example 2

Say the farmer in example 1 had a written-down value brought forward on the plant and machinery pool at 1 January 1989 of £30,000. Assume he was a married man with no other income, and that averaging was claimed for all three years in example 1.

The loss of the year to 31 December 1991 may be treated as a loss of 1991/92, thus reducing the income of that year to £8,000, i.e. £2,985 more than the married man's allowances. The capital allowances computation could be as follows.

	£
Written-down value brought forward at 1.1.89	30,000
1990/91 (based on year to 31.12.89)	
Writing-down allowance (25%)	(7,500)
	22,500
1991/92 Writing-down allowance (claim limited to)	(2,985)
Written-down value carried forward	£19,515

The optimum capital allowance claim for 1992/93 cannot be calculated until it is known whether the 1992/93 averaged result of £15,000 is itself to be averaged with 1993/94.

---

assessment or company accounting period, but a change in the partners in a farming partnership (whether or not there is an election for the continuation of assessments) may enable the election to be made even where the farming business has been carried on for several years. There are, however, anti-avoidance provisions to prevent the change being used solely or mainly for the purposes of obtaining a benefit resulting from the right to make an election or flowing from the election.

A production herd is a group of living animals or other livestock kept for obtaining products such as milk, wool etc. or their young.

The effect of the election is that the initial purchase of the herd and any subsequent purchases that increase the herd attract no tax relief, but a renewals basis effectively applies where animals are replaced, so that the cost of the replacement is charged as an expense and the sale proceeds are brought in as a trading receipt. If the whole or a substantial part of the herd is sold and not replaced, no part of the proceeds is charged as income since it represents the sale of a capital asset, and capital gains tax does not arise since the animals are wasting assets on which capital allowances are not available and are therefore exempt (see chapter 4).

Compensation for compulsory slaughter

By concession, where compensation is paid for compulsorily slaughtered stock to which the herd basis does not apply, the compensation may be left

ut of account in the year of receipt and brought in over the next three years
in equal instalments.

Farm plant and machinery

Capital allowances on farm plant and machinery are available in the usual
way (see chapter 22).

Agricultural buildings allowances (TA 1988, s 393A(5); CAA 1990, ss 122–133)

The owners or tenants of agricultural land may claim agricultural buildings
allowances on the cost of construction of buildings, fences, roads and on the
installation of services, including up to one-third of the cost of a farmhouse
(see page 352). Any grants received are deducted from the allowable cost.

Expenditure incurred before 1 April 1986

The allowances available for expenditure incurred before 1 April 1986
(extended to 1 April 1987 for sums paid under a contract entered into before
14 March 1984) are an initial allowance of 20% and writing-down allowances
of 10% of cost per annum, commencing in the first year, so that a maximum
of 30% was available in that year with 10% available for each of the next
seven years. The initial allowance did not have to be claimed in full, however, so that the maximum writing-down period is ten years.

The allowances for individuals normally commenced in the tax year following the year ended 31 March in which the expenditure was incurred, but a
farmer could arrange with the Revenue to use his normal accounting period
instead of the year ended 31 March. The allowances for a company commenced in the accounting period in which the expenditure was incurred.

The allowances, both for those carrying on a trade and for agricultural
landlords, are given primarily against agricultural income, such as farming
profits or farm rents. For individuals, any excess allowances may be set
against other income of the same tax year and/or the next tax year. For
companies, the excess may be set against other profits of any description
(including capital gains) of the same accounting period, then against the
profits of the previous accounting period. Additionally, a trading company
may then claim to treat any unrelieved allowances as part of a trading loss to
be carried back for up to three years under TA 1988, s 393A (see page 296).
For both individuals and companies, if any balance still remains it will be
carried forward against agricultural income.

There is no clawback of allowances when a building is sold for more than its
tax written-down value, nor any balancing allowance if sold for less than
written-down value. The purchaser continues the vendor's computation,
and the price he pays is irrelevant. He will get no allowances at all if the cost
has already been fully relieved to the vendor, since the allowances are only
given by reference to the original expenditure.

Where a building is sold for more than cost, the full cost will be taken into account in the capital gains computation even though capital allowances have been given on part of it.

Expenditure incurred on or after 1 April 1986

For expenditure incurred on or after 1 April 1986, there is a 4% annual writing-down allowance over 25 years. The allowances for sole traders and farming partnerships commence in the tax year following the accounts year in which the expenditure is incurred. For non-trading agricultural landlords they commence in the tax year in which the expenditure is incurred. For both trading and non-trading companies the allowances commence in the accounting period in which the expenditure is incurred.

A balancing allowance or charge is made when agricultural buildings or works are disposed of or scrapped, but only if the seller and purchaser, if there is a sale, or the owner, if there is no sale, makes an election not more than two years after the end of the year of assessment or company accounting period, as the case may be. The purchaser then gets allowances for the remainder of the 25-year period, normally on what he pays or on what the first user paid, whichever is the less.

If the election is not made, the seller gets a final writing-down allowance which is proportionate to the length of the part of his basis period up to the date of sale, and the buyer gets the remaining allowances, with his first writing-down allowance depending on the part of his basis period that occurs after the date of sale. Where the basis periods differ there may sometimes be an unallowed balance at the end of the 25-year period, which is added to the allowance of the final year.

In the case of a farming trade, the allowances are given against the trading profits. For agricultural landlords (either individuals or companies), the treatment of the allowances, including the rules relating to excess allowances, is the same as that stated for pre-1 April 1986 expenditure (see page 349).

The different treatment of capital allowances for expenditure on or after 1 April 1986 makes no difference to the computation of a capital gain, the cost of the building still being deductible in full, despite any allowances that have been given against income.

It does, however, affect the use of the agricultural buildings allowances themselves where there are brought forward farming losses, because the allowances for expenditure before 1 April 1986 are set first against agricultural income, which would include the farming profit net of brought forward losses, and then against other income. For expenditure on and after 1 April 1986, the allowances are given against the trading profits, and the rules require them to be set off before brought forward losses, so that the farmer could be left with unrelieved losses to carry forward rather than excess agricultural buildings allowances that he could set against his other income.

The fact that the allowances under the new provisions form part of a company's trading loss, or may be included in an individual's trading loss, means that the full range of relief available for trading losses is available, including for an individual the right, from 6 April 1991, to set a trading loss against capital gains (see chapter 25) and for a company the right to carry back for three years losses in an accounting period ending on or after 1 April 1991 (see chapter 26). The provisions for an individual to set a trading loss against capital gains do not apply to agricultural buildings allowances on expenditure incurred before 1 April 1986, but the allowances can be included in a company carry-back claim (see page 349).

Agricultural landlords (TA 1988, s 53; CAA 1990, ss 122–133)

The basis of taxation of income from letting agricultural land is as for any investment property (see chapter 32), and the treatment of the agricultural buildings allowances has been stated in the preceding paragraphs. If a farming tenant vacates his holding and does not receive any consideration for his unrelieved agricultural buildings expenditure from the incoming tenant, the landlord is entitled to relief for the balance over the remaining writing-down period.

The occupation of land managed on a commercial basis is treated as a trade, thus applying where an agricultural landlord receives income from grazing. It follows that the land arguably qualifies as a business asset on which rollover relief for capital gains tax is available if it is sold and the proceeds reinvested in a qualifying replacement asset within one year before and three years after the sale (see chapter 4).

Although gifts relief for capital gains tax normally applies only to business assets or to gifts that are immediately chargeable to inheritance tax, it applies to agricultural property held as an investment providing the conditions for inheritance tax agricultural property relief are satisfied (see page 71).

Value added tax (VATA 1983, Sch 5, Group 8, Sch 6, Group 1, Sch 6A; F(No 2)A 1992, s 16)

From 1 January 1993, farmers will be able to opt to become 'flat rate farmers' for VAT purposes, regardless of their turnover. They will not need to register for VAT, but will be able to add a fixed flat rate compensation percentage to their sale prices when they sell to VAT registered businesses, which they will keep to offset the input tax they have suffered. The registered businesses will be able to reclaim the compensation amount on their VAT returns. Farmers below the registration threshold will not need to become flat rate farmers.

Grants of long or short leases of agricultural land and buildings, and rents received therefrom, are exempt from VAT, but since 1 August 1989 the landlord has had the option to charge VAT. Written notice must be given to Customs within 30 days. VAT is then charged from the day the landlord exercises his option, or any later date he specifies. (If the landlord is not already VAT registered, he will have to become registered to take this option.) If the option is taken it cannot later be changed. Where a landlord has interests in several different estates, one election covers all the land and buildings owned, leased or licensed by him that form a single estate. The landlord will be able to increase existing rents by the VAT charged if the lease allows VAT to be added or is silent as to VAT. If not, the rent will have to be treated as VAT inclusive.

VAT will have to be charged not only on rents and lease premiums, but also on any sale proceeds as and when any of the land and buildings are sold (subject to what is said on page 368). An apportionment will be made in each case, however, to exclude the private dwelling/charitable element. Making the election will enable the landlord to recover any VAT he suffers, for example on the acquisition of the property, or on repairs, and the farmer tenants will usually be VAT registered and will therefore be able to recover the VAT charged.

Small agricultural holdings

The profits of a commercial smallholding are assessed as trading profits under Schedule D, Case I, but, if losses arise, the Revenue may contend that the trade is not conducted on a commercial basis with a view to profit, so that the losses may only be carried forward against future income from the smallholding and not set against any other income. This is quite separate from their right to disallow farming losses from the sixth year onwards.

The smallholder may seek voluntary VAT registration even though his taxable supplies are less than £36,600 p.a., because he will then be able to reclaim input tax on his expenditure and he will have no liability on his supplies, which are zero-rated. Customs and Excise are required to register anyone making taxable supplies who seeks voluntary registration.

The farmhouse (TCGA 1992, ss 222–224)

The restriction of agricultural buildings allowances on a farmhouse to a maximum of one-third of the expenditure recognises that the domestic and business activities overlap. In arriving at the farm profits, an appropriate part of the establishment charges of the farmhouse is allowed. This will not jeopardise the capital gains tax private residence exemption (see chapter 30) provided that no part of the farmhouse has been used exclusively for business purposes. Where part is so used and a chargeable gain arises, rollover relief may be claimed if the farmhouse is replaced (see page 48). If the farmhouse is disposed of on retirement over age 55 (60 for disposals before 19 March 1991) or as a result of ill-health, the gain may be reduced by retirement relief (see page 49).

The capital gains tax exemption usually extends to grounds up to half a hectare (previously one acre), but for a farmhouse a larger area may be allowed because of the situation and character of the farmhouse and immediately surrounding grounds.

The capital gains tax exemptions and reliefs are dealt with in chapter 4.

Land let by partners to farming partnership, or by directors to farming company (TCGA 1992, ss 152–158, 164 and Sch 6)

Where land is owned personally by a partner or director, and let to the farming business, any rent paid is allowed as an expense of the business and treated as unearned income in the partner's or director's hands. If interest is paid on a loan to buy the land, it may be deducted from the rent (or any other rent) so long as the letting is on a commercial basis (see chapter 32 for the detailed treatment of let property).

The charging of a commercial rent will, however, affect retirement relief when the land is disposed of by an individual aged over 55 or retiring earlier through ill-health. If no rent is charged, then retirement relief is available provided that the land is disposed of in conjunction with the disposal of an interest in the partnership or shares in the company. Proportionate relief will be given where a rent below the market rent is charged.

Capital gains tax rollover relief may sometimes be claimed if the land is disposed of and the proceeds used to acquire a qualifying asset within one year before and three years after the sale. The charging or not of rent does not affect this relief. See page 48.

Inheritance tax (IHTA 1984, ss 115–124)

When agricultural property is transferred, agricultural property relief is given on the agricultural value, and where the property is also business property, business property relief is given on the non-agricultural value. The detailed rules for each relief are in chapter 5.

The rate of relief for tenanted agricultural property is 50%, as against 100% for owner-occupied land, so a farmer who grants a lease to his farming partnership or to a farm company will on a subsequent disposal only get relief at the 50% rate. The grant itself is specifically exempt from inheritance tax so long as it is made for full consideration. Although tenanted property normally has to be owned for seven years to qualify for agricultural property relief (see page 71), the period is only two years where the tenant is a partnership in which the donor is a partner or a company controlled by the donor.

The relief applies to lifetime transfers which are not potentially exempt, or which, having been so, become chargeable because the donor dies within seven years, and to transfers on death. The relief is only available in calculating the tax or additional tax payable as a result of the donor's death within seven years if the donee still owns the property (or qualifying replacement property) when the donor dies, or if earlier, when the donee dies.

Where relief at the time of the transfer is at 100%, there will be neither a chargeable transfer nor a potentially exempt transfer at that time, but the transfer will be counted at death if the donor does not survive the seven-year period. Where relief is at the 50% rate, and two years' annual exemptions are available (see pages 60 and 72), a combination of the 50% relief and the annual exemptions totalling £6,000 will eliminate a transfer of £12,000.

The introduction of the 100% rate of agricultural property relief has changed the effect of making lifetime gifts, because a lifetime gift will attract capital gains tax (although payment can be deferred by claiming gifts relief), whereas on death there is a capital gains tax free uplift in asset values. The previous compensating benefit of the lifetime gift in terms of the gifted assets not forming part of the death estate if the donor survived for seven years no longer applies, since the 100% relief has reduced the taxable amount to nil. There is, of course, no certainty that the present generous regime will continue.

Stamp duty

Stamp duty is payable on the sale of farm land and buildings. It is not usually payable on a gift, but if say mortgaged farmland was transferred from a farmer to a family farming partnership, or from one family partnership to another, and the transferee took over liability for the mortgage, the amount of the mortgage would be subject to stamp duty (unless it was £30,000 or less (£250,000 or less for documents executed between 20 December 1991 and 19 August 1992 inclusive) and the transaction was certified not liable to duty).

Woodlands

Income tax (FA 1988, s 65 and Sch 6)

There is no longer any income tax charge on woodlands, either by way of a fixed annual sum or on profits from felling and selling the trees, whether or not the extent of the forestry operations is such as to constitute a trade (subject to the transitional provisions outlined below).

Before 6 April 1988, commercially managed woodlands were charged to income tax under Schedule B on one-third of the gross annual value of the land, unless an election was made within two years after the end of the tax year for the profits or losses to be dealt with as those of a trade under Schedule D, Case I. The charge on commercially managed woodlands was abolished from 6 April 1988 subject to certain transitional provisions in respect of Schedule D, Case I elections either already made or capable of being made, or in respect of expenditure contracted for, before 15 March 1988. An election for Schedule D to apply, where permitted, will usually be appropriate where losses are being incurred, or interest is being paid. The treatment as a trade is, in any event, to cease on 5 April 1993.

An election under Schedule D enables loss relief to be claimed either against the total income (and, from 6 April 1991, capital gains) of the same tax year or the next tax year under TA 1988, s 380, or against subsequent income from the woodlands under TA 1988, s 385, but it does not enable losses of the first four tax years to be carried back against the income of the previous three tax years under TA 1988, s 381. (See chapter 25 for details of loss reliefs available.) In the case of a company, loss relief is available against the total profits of the same year or the previous three years, or by carry-forward against later assessable profits from the woodlands. (See chapter 26.)

The abolition of the income tax charge means that for newly acquired land, relief for losses incurred and interest paid in the initial planting period can no longer be claimed. There is, however, no income tax charge on any profits arising and there has been an increase in the Government grants given for investment in woodlands.

Agricultural buildings allowances were available for expenditure on buildings and works on forestry land, but they were withdrawn from 20 June 1989. Where an election has been made for woodlands to be taxed under Schedule D, Case I, the allowances will not be withdrawn until 6 April 1993.

Capital gains tax (TCGA 1992, ss 158, 250)

There is no charge to capital gains tax on trees that are standing or felled. Proceeds of sale of timber will therefore not be charged to tax at all, unless exceptionally an income tax charge arises before 6 April 1993 where a Schedule D election is in force. The land is, however, a chargeable asset for capital gains purposes. It is therefore important on acquisition and disposal to establish the different values applicable to the timber and the land.

For commercially run woodlands, gains on sale of the land may be deferred by rolling them over against the cost of replacement assets where the land sale proceeds are reinvested in qualifying business assets within one year before and three years after the sale. If a gain is made on a disposal by way of gift, it will not qualify for gifts relief (see page 52) unless the woodlands operation is a trade. For a disposal by someone over 55, or retiring earlier through ill health, retirement relief (see page 49) is also only available if the business constitutes a trade.

Where woodlands are owned by a company, the land is a qualifying asset for rollover relief as far as the company is concerned, but an individual will not get rollover relief when he sells his shares and reinvests the proceeds. He will not be entitled to gifts relief or retirement relief in respect of the shares unless the company is a trading company and the other conditions for relief are satisfied (see pages 49–53).

Value added tax (VATA 1983, Sch 1.5A)

A commercially run woodland is within the net of VAT, the supply or granting of any right to fell and remove standing timber being standard-rated. It is possible to register for VAT before making taxable supplies, the intention to make taxable supplies being sufficient for registration purposes even though they will not be made for some years. Having registered, you can recover input tax on goods and services in connection with the woodlands operation.

Inheritance tax (IHTA 1984, ss 125–130)

Where an estate on death includes growing timber, an election may be made to leave the timber (but not the land on which it stands) out of account in valuing the estate at death. The election must be made within two years of the date of death and is only available if the deceased either had been beneficially entitled to the land throughout the previous five years or had become entitled to it without consideration (for example by gift or inheritance).

The election may not be made if the occupation of the woodlands is subsidiary to the occupation of agricultural land, but agricultural relief would be given if the necessary conditions were fulfilled.

Following the election, when the timber is later disposed of by sale or gift, there will be a charge to inheritance tax on the sale price or, if the disposal is for less than full consideration, the market value, less allowable expenses in both cases. Allowable expenses are the costs of sale and expenses of replanting within three years of disposal, or such longer time as the Revenue allows (but excluding allowable expenses for income tax—this will only be relevant where, up to 5 April 1993, a Schedule D election remains in force, see page 354).

The net disposal proceeds or market value are treated as value transferred at the date of death, forming the top slice of the property passing on death, but using the scale and rates current at the time of disposal to find a notional liability on the estate first excluding and then including the timber proceeds, the tax on the timber proceeds being the difference between the two. The tax is due six months after the end of the month in which the disposal takes place, with interest on overdue tax at the death rate. The person entitled to the sale proceeds is liable for the tax. Where there are no proceeds because the disposal is by way of gift, the tax arising out of this disposal may be paid by instalments over ten years.

A lifetime gift of woodlands either attracts inheritance tax or is a potentially exempt transfer (see chapter 5). Where the disposal is one on which tax is payable following its being left out of account on an earlier death, the value transferred by the lifetime transfer is reduced by the tax charge arising out of the previous death.

If the person who inherits woodlands on which an election has been made dies before the timber is disposed of, no inheritance tax charge can arise in respect of the first death. Furthermore, a new election may then be made on the second death.

Where woodlands are managed on a commercial basis, despite there being no income tax charge, they qualify for 100% business property relief so long as they have been owned for two years (see chapter 5). Where tax is payable, it may be paid by instalments in the case of a death transfer where the value has not been left out of account and where, exceptionally, a lifetime transfer is not potentially exempt. If an election is made to leave the timber out of account on a death, business property relief is given on the net sale proceeds when it is disposed of. This will be relevant where the election has already been made, but clearly no new elections will be made where the 100% business property relief is available, because that relief eliminates the tax on death as distinct from deferring it.

Poll tax and business rates

Agricultural land and buildings are exempt from business rates. Any buildings or parts of buildings that are for domestic rather than agricultural use will attract the standard community charge if the building or part is no-one's only or main home. If it is someone's only or main home, poll tax will be payable by the occupants. In Scotland only, unoccupied, unfurnished property previously used in connection with agricultural land or woodlands etc. is exempt from the standard charge. Such property in England is subject to a maximum standard charge multiplier of one half if occupation is restricted to those working in agriculture.

Tax Points

- If you have a smallholding which is likely to show consistent losses, you are unlikely to be able to relieve them against other income, and treating the smallholding as a trade may prejudice your capital gains tax private residence exemption. It may be preferable to make a yearly note in your tax return that the working of the holding is not by way of trade but only for the maintenance of the holding and that no profits arise.

- If you are making losses and are in danger of falling foul of the six-year rule (see page 346), see if you can show a small profit in one year, perhaps by delaying repairs or other expenses. The six-year cycle will then start again. If you are caught by the six-year rule, there is a useful concession (extra-statutory concession B5) enabling you to set some of your unrelieved farm expenses against other income.

- Where a smallholding or market garden is clearly a trade, make sure if possible that no part of the dwelling house is used exclusively for business, to avoid any possible loss of the private residence exemption.

- When buying a holding with agricultural buildings, remember that what you pay for them does not necessarily entitle you to any relief. You cannot get relief on any more than that part of the seller's expenditure for which relief has not yet been given.

- If you are an agricultural landlord and have incurred expenditure on agricultural buildings, you can set the available allowances against any income to the extent that your agricultural income is insufficient. Relief can be given in the tax year itself or the following year.

- Owning agricultural land personally and renting it to your partnership or company will not stop you getting capital gains tax rollover relief if the land is sold and replaced, but the payment of rent does affect your entitlement to retirement relief (see page 353).

- Rollover relief (page 48) is not available to agricultural landlords except in the circumstances indicated above.

- Gifts relief *is* available to agricultural landlords if the conditions are satisfied (see page 52).

- A farmer's averaging election will affect income for two or more years. As well as the effect on the tax calculation, there is also a cash flow benefit in delayed tax payments if a good year is followed by a bad one. Remember, however, that the election will affect the permissible levels of personal pension contributions for the years concerned.

- There are a number of specialist organisations ready to advise on an investment in woodlands, not only from the taxation point of view but also on the question of cash grants through the Forestry Commission, and on estate management.

- The characteristics of farming often influence the treatment of matters affecting taxation. To give two examples, the valuation of cattle bred on the farm can be included at 60% of market value, and likewise that of home-reared sheep and pigs at 75% of market value, but no reduction is permissible for mature bought-in animals; amounts received for loss of milk, beet or potato quota will be treated as income or capital depending on whether they are compensation for loss of profit or of the quota itself. In the event of receipts for loss of milk and potato quotas being treated as capital, rollover relief (page 48) is available. The content of the chapter and these examples illustrate that it is essential that proper professional advice is sought on the agreement of taxation liabilities.

32
Investing in land and buildings

Introduction (TA 1988, s 354)

The provisions in this chapter apply to both commercial and private investment properties in the UK. The detailed treatment of let agricultural buildings is, however, covered in chapter 31. The tax advantages of investing in enterprise zone buildings are dealt with in chapter 22.

In some circumstances, where your letting income is small, you need only include total figures of rent, expenses and net income on your tax return—see page 109—and if you let furnished rooms in your own home, rent of up to £3,250 is exempt from 1992/93 onwards—see page 334.

If you buy investment property abroad, rents are income from a foreign possession and are charged under Schedule D, Case V (see chapter 41). Foreign rental income is calculated in a similar way to UK rental income, but an individual cannot get tax relief on borrowing to acquire the property (unless it is in the Republic of Ireland, which is not treated as 'abroad' for this purpose). If the foreign property is acquired by a UK company, interest on money borrowed to finance the acquisition is usually allowed as a charge on income (see page 24).

Income from land

Income from UK land and buildings is usually charged to income tax as investment income under Schedule A (or Schedule D, Case VI for furnished lettings). There are some exceptions, such as furnished holiday lettings, which are dealt with on page 365, or where one of the privileges of an employment or the holding of an office is the entitlement to rent from a particular property, in which case although the income is calculated using the rules of Schedule A, it is treated as earned income from the office or employment. The distinction between earned and unearned income is important in relation to relief for contributions to provide your own pension. It is also important for capital gains purposes because a property that provides you with investment income will not qualify for rollover relief (see page 48) when it is replaced (unless it is compulsorily purchased—see page 366) nor retirement relief if the property is sold after you reach age 55 (see page 49), and gifts relief (see page 52) will not usually be available either.

The following provisions apply to income from unfurnished lettings. The rules for furnished lettings are dealt with on page 364. As indicated on page 364, however, a landlord may choose to have the part of his furnished lettings rent that relates to the property rather than the furniture charged under the following rules instead of the furnished lettings rules.

Calculation of rent (TA 1988, ss 15, 41)

Rent is taken into account for tax purposes when it is due and payable, the date when it is actually received not being relevant and no apportionment being made over the period which it covers. See example 1. Anti-avoidance provisions have been introduced to prevent connected persons, such as companies in the same group, exploiting these provisions by getting a deduction for the payment in an earlier period than that in which the rent is charged to tax. If rent due from a connected person accrues in an earlier period than that in which it is payable, it is treated, for rent accruing on or after 10 March 1992, as income of the period in which it accrues.

You can deduct rent not received from the amount chargeable if you have tried but failed to collect the rent, or if you have not enforced your right to the rent in order to avoid hardship to the tenant.

Allowable expenses (TA 1988, s 25)

Allowable expenses include business rates or standard community charge if appropriate (see pages 369 and 370), rent payable to a superior landlord, maintenance, repairs and redecorations, insurance and management expenses, including advertising for tenants, and any other expenses which under the terms of the lease are to be met out of the rent. Improvement expenditure, on for example building extensions or installing central heating or double glazing, is not allowable in calculating income, although it will be counted as part of the cost for capital gains purposes. Where repair and maintenance expenditure is made unnecessary because of improvements, additions and alterations, a deduction from rent is allowed by Revenue concession B4 for the estimated amount that would have been spent on the repairs. No similar concession applies to deductions for repairs against trading profits.

Where the rent is sufficient, taking one year with another, to meet the landlord's outgoings, the lease is called a 'full rent lease'.

Normally, expenses incurred when a property is not let would not be allowed, but, for leases at a full rent, periods when a property is empty between the time of acquisition and being let at a full rent, and between full-rent leases, are regarded as part of a continuing lease, enabling expenses during the void periods to be deducted against rents as if the property had been let continuously. This does not apply, however, to expenditure on newly acquired property to rectify dilapidations arising before you bought it. Such expenditure will form part of the cost for capital gains purposes and is not allowable for income tax.

Example 1

Rent of £2,000 per quarter is due in advance on the usual quarter days under a seven-year lease commencing on 29 September 1992.

The rent to be included as income of 1992/93 is:

29 September 1992	2,000
25 December 1992	2,000
25 March 1993	2,000
	£6,000

even though on a day to day basis only a little over £4,000 relates to 1992/93, and whether or not rent is in fact received on those dates.

Several properties (TA 1988, s 25)

Where you have several let properties, whether the expenses of each have to be isolated against the rent of each depends on the type of lease.

For full-rent leases under which you are responsible for the repairs (known as landlord's repairing leases), you can set total expenses against total rents to arrive at the net income from the properties. If expenses exceed rents, the excess is carried forward to set against later rents on such properties. Expenses of any property let at a full rent under a tenant's repairing lease are first set against the rent of that property, and then against the surplus on landlord's repairing lease properties (if any), any balance being carried forward to set against a future profit on the same tenant's repairing lease property, and indeed this may be the only way of getting relief if it is the only property involved.

Where properties are let below a full rent, for example to a relative or friend for an insignificant return, losses arising may only be set against any future profit on that particular property and only while it is let to the same tenant under the same lease. If the rent is increased to a full rent, brought forward losses cannot be set off.

The total of the income less expenses from all properties can conveniently be called the 'net rents'.

Capital allowances (TA 1988, s 32; CAA 1990, ss 51–59)

The capital allowances available on let agricultural buildings are dealt with in chapter 31, and chapter 22 deals with allowances on industrial buildings, hotels and buildings in enterprise zones.

As far as plant and machinery is concerned, allowances are available where expenditure is incurred on machinery or plant for the maintenance, repair or management of premises where the rents are charged under Schedule A—see chapter 22, and also page 365 for furnished holiday lettings.

A tenant may claim allowances on expenditure he incurs on such items as lifts, heating and ventilating equipment etc. even though in law they become landlord's fixtures. Where such fixtures are not bought outright but are acquired on lease, either by a landlord or a tenant, an election may be made for allowances to be given to the equipment lessor, instead of to the landlord or the tenant as the case may be. Appropriate adjustments are made when rights under the equipment lease are transferred. The lessor will be taxed on the payments he receives under the lease, with those payments being allowed in calculating the rent income of the lessee.

Relief for interest (TA 1988, ss 25, 75, 338, 354, 355)

Interest on borrowing by companies to buy or improve property for letting is a 'charge on income' (see page 24) and is deducted from the company's total profits from all sources.

Interest on borrowing by individuals for the purchase or improvement of property let unfurnished is allowable, provided that the property has been let at a commercial rent for at least 26 weeks out of 52 and, when not so let, was available for letting or was being repaired or improved or was used as the only or main residence of the borrower. No relief is available for interest on money borrowed by individuals to repair rather than improve property (but Revenue booklet IR 11 interprets 'improvements' quite generously). Relief for qualifying interest is given against income from any let property, including furnished lettings, not just that to which the borrowing relates. The rules for interest paid in connection with furnished holiday lettings are less stringent. See page 365. They are also less stringent for other furnished lettings, on which relief is available if the interest is wholly and exclusively for the purposes of the letting.

If interest paid exceeds the rental income, individuals can carry the excess forward to set against later rents of any property so long as the property to which the interest relates is still held. They cannot, however, deduct rolled-up interest from a capital gain on sale of the property. An investment company, on the other hand, may carry forward unrelieved charges to set against any later profits, including capital gains.

Relief for interest is not available if the borrowing is by way of overdraft rather than a specific loan.

Payment of tax (TMA 1970, s 29(1)(c)(1A); TA 1988, ss 10, 22 and Sch 30)

Income tax under Schedule A is payable on 1 January in the tax year. Since the assessment is based on the net rents less allowable interest of the tax year, which still has three months to run, an adjustment of the tax payable is required after each 5 April. A provisional assessment is made in time for payment on the due date, based on the finally agreed assessment for the previous tax year. This is then amended to the actual net rents less interest after the end of the tax year.

If one or more of the properties has been disposed of since the beginning of the previous year, the taxpayer can apply to have the provisional assessment for the current year reduced.

The rules for payment of corporation tax on a company's Schedule A income are the same as those for all other company profits—normally nine months after the end of the accounting period (see page 28).

Where a premium is charged (TA 1988, ss 34, 37, 87; TCGA 1992, Sch 8(5))

There are two sorts of premium, one where an existing leasehold interest is assigned, the other where a lease or sublease is granted. The first is wholly a capital gains tax matter, being the disposal of a chargeable asset.

The treatment of the second depends on the length of the lease. If a lease is granted for more than 50 years, it is wholly a capital gains tax matter. There are both capital and income aspects if the lease is of 50 years duration or less (known as a short lease), in that the premium is partly charged to income tax and partly to capital gains tax. The income portion is treated as additional rent and is the amount of the premium less 2% for each complete year of the lease except the first. The amount by which the premium is reduced is treated as the proceeds of a part disposal for capital gains tax, the cost of the part disposed of being the proportion of the total cost that the capital portion of the premium bears to the full premium plus the value of the freehold reversion. See example 2.

Since the income part of the premium is treated as additional rent, any expenses of the letting can be relieved against it. The premium might in fact have been charged to recover some extraordinary expenses, perhaps necessitated by a previous defaulting tenant.

The income tax portion of a premium on a short lease is wholly assessed in the year the lease is granted, although the lease may run for anything up to 50 years.

Where a premium on a short lease is paid by a business tenant, he may deduct the income tax portion as a business expense, but spread over the term of the lease rather than in a single sum (see example 2). A similar deduction could be claimed by a tenant who sublets, his deduction depending on the length of the sublease. Any deductions allowed for income tax are not allowed in calculating the capital gain if the lease is disposed of.

Any expenditure on the acquisition of a lease is treated for capital gains tax as wasting away during the last 50 years (or shorter period for which the lease was granted) and only the depreciated cost (using a special table in TCGA 1992, Sch 8) may be used. If a lease is held for its full term, no allowable loss may be claimed for the unrelieved expenditure on acquisition, so that any expenditure for which relief has not been given for income tax will not have been allowed for tax at all.

Example 2

Lease is granted for 21 years commencing 25 March 1993 at a rent of £5,000 per annum, payable quarterly in advance, together with a premium of £8,000. The cost of the freehold was £15,000 in 1984. The value of the freehold reversion after the grant of the lease was £24,000.

The assessable rent for 1992/93 is: £

25 March 1993 1 quarter's rent due		1,250
Premium	8,000	
Less Treated as part disposal for capital gains (21–1) = 20 years at 2% = 40%	3,200	
Amount treated as additional rent		4,800
Assessable rent for 1992/93 (before expenses)		£6,050

The chargeable gain (before indexation allowance) is:

Capital proportion of premium	3,200
Less Allowable proportion of cost	
$15,000 \times \dfrac{3,200}{(8,000 + 24,000)}$	1,500
	£1,700

If the tenant was a business tenant, he could claim a deduction for £4,800 spread over 21 years, i.e. £229 per annum, in addition to the deduction for rent. If he assigned the lease within the 21 years, the allowable cost for capital gains tax would be the premium paid of £8,000 less depreciation under TCGA 1992, Sch 8, less the total annual deductions allowed.

Furnished lettings (TA 1988, s 15)

Since Schedule A is concerned with letting of land, it does not cover lettings where furnishings and services are included. A new relief has been introduced from 6 April 1992 for those who let furnished rooms in their homes—'rent a room' relief. If the total gross rents, before expenses, are not more than £3,250 per year, they are exempt from tax. For details see page 334. Where the relief is not available, or where the taxpayer does not want to claim it, the following provisions apply.

Furnished lettings of UK property are assessed under Schedule D, Case VI, but the taxpayer may choose to have the property rent element included under Schedule A, leaving only the payment in respect of the furnishings and/or services to be charged under Schedule D, Case VI. The advantage of separating the furnishings rent and the property rent is that the property rent may enable a set-off to be made for losses on unfurnished properties that would otherwise have to be carried forward.

The expenses of furnished lettings are, as with Schedule A, allowed broadly on a common-sense basis. See page 362 as to relief for interest. Additionally, relief is given for wear and tear on furnishings, as distinct from normal repairs. The Revenue usually accept a figure of 10% of the rent for this purpose, but additions to rent for rates and other sums for services which would normally be borne by a tenant have been deducted, if material, before the 10% deduction. Now that rates are not payable on domestic property, landlords should be reducing rates-inclusive rents accordingly, their tenants being liable to the personal community charge instead (unless exceptionally the property is not the tenant's only or main home, in which case the landlord will be liable to the standard community charge). The 10% deduction should now be based on the rent less water rates and any other material payments for services.

Income tax under Schedule D, Case VI on the full amount of the net income of the tax year, or on the furnishings element as the case may be, is due on 1 January in the tax year. As with Schedule A, an estimated assessment is made to enable a payment on 1 January, an adjustment being made after 5 April when the actual position is known. The normal corporation tax payment rules apply to Schedule D, Case VI income of a company (see page 28).

The Revenue will rarely accept that a furnished letting amounts to a trade, and their attitude has been supported by the courts. Income from furnished holiday lettings is, however, generally treated as trading income (see below).

Even though the letting is not treated as a trade, Class 2 national insurance contributions (but not Class 4 contributions) may be payable, because Class 2 contributions apply to a 'business', which is a wider term and would almost certainly include letting that was undertaken on a commercial basis.

Furnished holiday lettings (TA 1988, ss 503, 504; TCGA 1992, s 241)

As with other furnished lettings, the new 'rent a room' relief exempting gross rent of up to £3,250 a year for those who let rooms in their homes may be more beneficial than the furnished holiday lettings treatment described below (see page 334).

Income from furnished holiday lettings of UK property is broadly treated as trading income (although it remains chargeable under Schedule D, Case VI, and not Case I). If interest is paid on a loan to purchase or improve the property, it will be allowed as a trading expense (restricted if necessary by any private use proportion). Capital allowances (see chapter 22) on plant and machinery, such as furniture and kitchen equipment, and loss relief (see chapters 25 and 26) may be claimed, and the income qualifies as relevant earnings for personal pension purposes (see chapter 17). Income tax is payable by equal instalments on 1 January in the tax year and 1 July following. Corporation tax is payable on the normal due dates. The property is eligible for capital gains tax rollover relief either when it is itself replaced, or as a qualifying purchase against which gains on other assets may be set, and for retirement and business gifts reliefs (see pages 48–53). Despite the trading treatment, Class 4 national insurance contributions are not payable, because they only apply where profits are charged under Schedule D, Case I or II, not Case VI. Class 2 contributions would, however, almost certainly be payable (see above).

To qualify, the accommodation must be let on a commercial basis; it must be available as holiday accommodation for at least 140 days in the tax year, and actually let as such for at least 70 of those days. The 70 days test may be satisfied by averaging periods of occupation of any or all of the holiday accommodation let furnished by the same person. The accommodation must not normally be in the same occupation for a continuous period of more than 31 days during at least seven months of the year, which need not be continuous but includes any months containing any of the 70 let days. Where only part of the let accommodation is holiday accommodation, apportionments are made on a just and reasonable basis.

The letting of holiday caravans is, depending on the scale, either treated as a trade or charged under Case VI as a furnished letting. In the latter case, the income may be treated as trading income from furnished holiday accommodation if the conditions are satisfied. Long-term lets would accordingly not qualify. Caravans occupying holiday sites are treated as plant and machinery qualifying for capital allowances, even if they are on hard standings and not required to be moved.

Income from letting caravan sites is charged as unearned income under Schedule A, unless the activity really amounts to a trade, embracing services, shops, restaurants, etc. in which case the whole income will be treated as earned income from a trade.

For the treatment of furnished property, including holiday property and caravans, in relation to poll tax and business rates, see page 369.

Capital gains on sale of investment properties (TCGA 1992, ss 243–248, Revenue Statement of Practice SP 7/90)

The usual capital gains tax principles apply (see chapter 4), including the relief dealt with in chapter 30 (page 335) where part of the property is owner-occupied, and that dealt with above where the property is let as furnished holiday accommodation. Apart from those instances, there is no rollover relief on disposal of investment properties except where the disposal is occasioned by compulsory purchase. In this case, there is no tax charge if the proceeds are reinvested in another property, provided that the reinvestment is made within the period beginning one year before and ending three years after the disposal. The replacement property cannot, however, be the investor's capital gains tax exempt dwelling house at any time within six years after its acquisition. As an alternative to rollover relief where part of a holding of land is compulsorily purchased, small proceeds (not defined but probably not exceeding 5% of the value of the holding) may be treated as reducing the capital gains tax cost of the holding rather than being charged as a part disposal.

Compulsory purchase includes not only purchase by an authority but also (for claims made after 28 October 1990) purchase of the freehold by a tenant exercising his right to buy.

If a lease is surrendered and replaced by a new lease on similar terms except as to duration and rent payable, the surrender is, by concession, not treated as a disposal for capital gains tax.

See page 351 for the availability of capital gains tax gifts relief for agricultural landlords.

Property dealing, etc.

Although the income from letting is assessed under Schedule A or Schedule D, Case VI as the case may be, any surplus on disposal of a property may even so be liable to income tax, either specifically under TA 1988, s 776 (see page 502), or as a trading transaction, instead of as a chargeable gain. Whether or not a trade may be inferred is dealt with in chapter 20, but the letting, whilst not conclusive, will at least indicate an investment motive and be influential in the surplus being treated as a capital gain.

VAT (VATA 1983, Sch 5, Group 8, Sch 6, Group 1, Sch 6A)

The VAT position on land and buildings has had to be changed as a result of EC regulations and is now very complex. Sales of new commercial buildings and commercial buildings that are less than three years old are standard-rated from 1 April 1989. The first sale on or after 1 April 1989 of a new commercial building completed but not fully occupied before 1 April 1989 is standard-rated (thus enabling the vendor to recover VAT suffered) but later sales are exempt (subject to the vendor's option to tax—see page 368). Sales or leases for more than 21 years of new residential properties and new buildings occupied by charities for charitable purposes are zero-rated. (Shorter leases are exempt and cannot be subject to the option to tax—see page 368.)

Unless the vendor opts to tax (see page 368), all sales of buildings that are more than three years old are exempt, and grants of long or short leases (other than those mentioned above) are also exempt, except for holiday accommodation (see page 368). Rents received, some of which were zero-rated before 1 April 1989, are now all exempt from that date (except where the landlord has taken the option to tax).

Most landlords letting domestic property will be exempt from VAT. Any VAT they are charged will therefore form part of their costs, and must be taken into account in their rents. Landlords letting commercial property will be in the same position, unless they opt to tax (see below). If the expenditure is revenue expenditure, such as repairs, the unrecovered VAT may be claimed as part of the expense against the rent. If it is capital expenditure, such as on property conversion, reconstruction, extension, improvement etc., no deduction can be claimed against the rent, but the unrecovered VAT will form part of the capital cost in a capital gains computation when the property is disposed of.

Option to tax

In all situations where exemption applies (other than leases of residential/ charitable property for less than 21 years), the owner/landlord has an option to charge VAT from 1 August 1989 (but if he is not already VAT registered he has to become registered in order to take this option). VAT is then charged not only on rents and lease premiums but also on any sale proceeds when buildings are sold. Although the sale of tenanted property may represent the disposal of part of a business, the provisions relating to the sale of a going concern do not apply to land on which the seller has exercised the option to tax unless the buyer notifies Customs before the sale that he has also exercised the option. In the absence of such an election, the going concern treatment is not available and VAT must be charged on the sale (see page 89).

Making the election enables the landlord to recover any VAT he suffers, and could be particularly beneficial where he has to incur substantial repair expenditure. But if most of his tenants are partially exempt, part of the VAT will be an extra cost to them, so the overall effect needs to be considered carefully. Following the election, the landlord will be able to add VAT to the rent unless the lease specifically prevents him from doing so. In that event, the rent he receives will have to be treated as VAT inclusive until such time as it may be increased on a rent review.

The option may be exercised separately in relation to each building (but not separate parts of a building), except for agricultural land, where the election applies to all land that constitutes a single estate (see page 352). Once taken, the option cannot be revoked by that owner, but a new owner may or may not opt to tax as he wishes. Where the option is taken on a building completed before 1 August 1989, special provisions apply to rent payable by charities (see page 487).

Holiday accommodation etc.

The provision of short-term holiday accommodation in hotels, boarding houses, caravans etc. is charged to VAT at the standard rate but reduced charges apply if a tenant stays for more than four weeks. If you sell or lease holiday accommodation, including time share accommodation, that is less than three years old, then both the initial charges and any periodic charges, such as ground rent and service charges, are also standard-rated. If the property is over three years old, the initial charges are exempt from VAT but periodic charges are still standard-rated. The standard rate applies to charges for pitching tents and to seasonal pitch charges for caravans (charges for non-seasonal pitches being exempt). If the pitch charges to the caravan owners include water, gas and electricity and the landlord can ascertain how much is provided to the caravans as distinct from the rest of the site (shops, swimming pools etc.), this can be divided by the number of caravans and shown separately on the bills, and VAT need not then be charged on those services. VAT is also not charged on any part of the pitch charge that represents business rates on the individual caravans (but it is charged on any business rates element that relates to the rest of the site).

The sale of building plots for holiday accommodation is standard-rated.

'Self-supply' provisions

For commercial buildings on which construction commenced on or after 1 August 1989, there are special provisions to charge VAT if, within the period from the time the building is first planned to ten years after its completion, it is either occupied by the person who had it built or is leased rather than sold. The provisions are rather complex, but they broadly ensure that those who are partly exempt from VAT cannot avoid a VAT cost by having a building built on their own land (unless the original cost of the land plus the construction expenditure is less than £100,000). From 1 January 1992, the provisions are extended to cover certain reconstructions, extensions and enlargements of existing buildings.

Stamp duty on buying

When property is purchased for £30,000 or less (£2500,000 between 20 December 1991 and 19 August 1992 inclusive), no stamp duty arises. If the purchase price exceeds that amount, duty is payable on the whole of the purchase price at 1%. Any stamp duty paid forms part of the cost for capital gains tax purposes on a subsequent disposal.

Where VAT is included in the cost of property, stamp duty is charged on the VAT inclusive amount.

Poll tax and business rates

When considering liability to poll tax and/or business rates, each self-contained unit is looked at separately. Where there is mixed business and domestic use, business rates will be payable even if there is no separate business part of the property, unless the business use does not materially detract from the domestic use. Any charges that fall on a landlord will be allowable according to the normal expenses rules.

Let property that is domestic property and is not someone's only or main home is liable to the standard community charge. Where let property is someone's only or main home, that person will be liable to the personal poll tax and there will be no poll tax or rates implications for the landlord (unless the property is designated for the collective community charge—see page 99). If, however, such property is empty for a period of time, the landlord is liable to the standard community charge for the appropriate number of days (subject to available exemptions—see page 98). (Where property is let at a ground rent, the leaseholder would be liable rather than the ground landlord.)

Non-domestic property, such as commercial property, boarding houses etc., is liable to business rates. Staff accommodation, however, is domestic property and staff would be liable to personal poll tax if it was their only or main home, or the owner would be liable to the standard community charge if it was not. In the case of self-catering holiday accommodation, business rates are payable if it is available for short-term letting for 140 days or more in a year. This is independent of the number of days for which the property is actually let. Bed and breakfast accommodation is not subject to business rating providing it is not offered for more than six people, the provider lives there at the same time and the bed and breakfast activity is only a subsidiary use of the home. Where holiday property is not business rated, the standard community charge is payable on any self-contained accommodation that is not someone's only or main home.

Caravans are not subject to the standard community charge. If someone lives in a caravan as his or her only or main home, he or she will pay the personal poll tax. No charge is made while such a caravan is not lived in if it will again be someone's only or main home when next used. For other caravans, the site owner will pay business rates on the caravans and pitches, passing on the charge to the caravan owner in the site rents. (Note that this part of the site rent is not liable to VAT—see page 369). Originally, certain caravans on protected sites were to have been liable to the standard community charge. Anyone who has already paid standard community charge on a caravan is entitled to recover it.

Time shares

If you buy a time share, you may be concerned with taxation in respect of income from it, or on a capital gain when you sell it.

The nature of the rights acquired depends on the particular agreement, but most time share agreements do not give you any rights of ownership over the property itself, but merely a right to occupy it at a certain time.

If you let your time share, you will be liable to tax on the income less expenses under Schedule D, Case VI, the tax being due on 1 January in the tax year (tax being estimated initially and adjusted to the correct figures later). Where time share property is abroad, income is still usually charged under Case VI, unless under the particular agreement you are regarded as having rights over the property itself, or your rights are enforceable abroad rather than in the UK, in which case the time share would be a foreign possession charged under Case V (see page 459). Many people will not have any time share income, but will sometimes exchange time shares. If this is done on a temporary basis, there are no tax implications, but a long-term arrangement could be treated as a part disposal for capital gains tax.

When you sell a time share, you will be liable to capital gains tax on the profit, after taking into account the cost and indexation allowance in the usual way. If the time share has less than 50 years to run, a depreciated cost must be used (on a straight line basis).

Time share property is usually business rated and is not subject to the standard community charge (unless exceptionally it is available for letting commercially for less than 140 days a year). The owner of time share property charges value added tax on the selling price for the time share if it is less than three years old and on any service charges made, including business rates (or exceptionally, standard community charge). If the property is over three years old, the sale proceeds, but not the service charges, are exempt from VAT.

Assured tenancy scheme (CAA 1990, ss 84–97)

Until 15 March 1988, capital allowances were available for expenditure on dwellings for letting under the assured tenancy scheme. The scheme was introduced by the Housing Act 1980 to enable bodies approved by the Secretary of State for the Environment to let dwellings at freely negotiated rents that are not subject to the Rent Acts. The allowances have been available on new buildings and, in the case of lettings after 6 January 1987, on those substantially repaired or improved where the expenditure was incurred in the two years preceding the letting.

The allowances were to be available for expenditure up to 1 April 1992, but they have been generally withdrawn for expenditure on and after 15 March 1988. They will continue to be available for expenditure on contracts entered into before that date, and on expenditure incurred before 1 April 1992 on land or property that was acquired or contracted for before 15 March 1988.

The allowances broadly follow the industrial buildings allowances rules (see chapter 22). The expenditure on the building (excluding the amount paid for the land) qualified for an initial allowance of 50% in respect of expenditure incurred between 14 March 1984 and 31 March 1985, and of 25% for expenditure in the year ended 31 March 1986. In addition writing-down allowances at 4% of cost p.a. are allowed provided that the dwelling is let under an assured tenancy at the end of the basis period. There was a limit on the amount which qualified for relief in respect of each dwelling, being £60,000 if the dwelling was in Greater London and £40,000 if it was elsewhere. Where a dwelling formed only part of the building (for example a flat or maisonette) the expenditure was apportioned appropriately along with expenditure on any common parts of the building.

Balancing adjustments are made if the dwelling is disposed of within 25 years and a second-hand purchaser gets writing-down allowances based on the residue of expenditure after the sale, split over the remainder of the 25 years.

There are provisions for dwellings not to qualify for the allowances in certain circumstances, for example where landlord and tenant are connected persons.

The allowances are given by discharge or repayment of tax, primarily against Schedule A income from qualifying dwelling houses or balancing charges relating to qualifying dwelling houses, but then against income generally.

To encourage investment in the private rented sector, relief is currently available under the Business Expansion Scheme for investment in companies that provide property for letting on assured tenancies—see chapter 29.

Tax points

- Although you can get relief against *any* rent income for allowable interest on borrowing to purchase property for letting unfurnished at a commercial rent, the interest is not allowable unless the property is actually let for the appropriate period. This is particularly important for industrial buildings, which may at times be difficult to let.

- If interest paid cannot be relieved against rents, individuals cannot set it against a capital gain on disposal of the property but investment companies can—see page 362.

- In the current economic climate you may be incurring losses on furnished holiday accommodation that you want to set against other income. Make sure that you can demonstrate to the Revenue that the letting is in fact commercial and that all the various conditions are satisfied.

- The fact that property is being let does not of itself prevent an income tax charge instead of a chargeable gain on a disposal. Whilst an investment motive is most important in establishing that a trade has not been carried on, in a 1986 tax case the lack of yield did not prevent the surplus being taxed as a capital gain. With facilities for sheltering income being available (see chapter 29), whereas no such facilities usually exist for capital gains on investment properties (rollover relief applying only to properties used in a trade and in the event of compulsory purchase), a trading assessment may sometimes be more acceptable than the previously preferred capital gain.

- The value added tax provisions relating to property letting, including holiday letting, are extremely complex. Make sure you look carefully at the appropriate Customs and Excise booklets relating to your circumstances.

- If you normally let your property for long-term residential use but it is empty for a period of time, you will be liable to the standard community charge on it (see page 370).

- Bed and breakfast providers can escape business rates if they offer the facility as a subsidiary use of their own homes for not more than six people. Otherwise, business rates are payable.

- If you borrow to assist in the purchase of property for letting, make sure the borrowing is by way of loan. Interest on a bank overdraft is never allowable in calculating net rents for tax purposes.

- If you borrow to buy property abroad (other than in the Republic of Ireland), whether by loan or overdraft, no income tax relief is available on the interest.

33
Husband, wife and children

General

From 6 April 1990, the incomes of husband and wife are taxed independently. Each is entitled to a personal allowance and the husband gets a married couple's allowance (see below). From 6 April 1993, a wife will be able to claim half the married couple's allowance as of right, and all of it if both agree.

A married couple's gains are also now taxed independently, each being entitled to the annual exemption, currently £5,800. Losses of one spouse may no longer be set against gains of the other, but transfers of assets between husband and wife who are living together are not chargeable to capital gains tax. Any indexation allowance arising to the date of transfer increases the original cost for the purpose of calculating the gain on an eventual disposal. This provision enables couples to plan in advance and make appropriate transfers one to the other before negotiating disposals to third parties, so that one spouse does not have gains in excess of the exempt threshold while the other has unrelieved losses. Where losses are brought forward from before 6 April 1990, each spouse's losses must be separately identified so that they are set only against that person's gains.

From April 1991, husband and wife are each responsible for completion of tax returns and for payment of the tax.

For inheritance tax purposes, husband and wife have always been treated as separate taxable persons, each having separate exemptions and a separate nil rate threshold. Transfers between the two are exempt unless one of them is not domiciled in the United Kingdom, in which case the transfers to the other spouse are exempt up to £55,000, and potentially chargeable after that amount should the donor not survive for seven years.

Stamp duty is not normally charged on the value of assets transferred between husband and wife, but see page 377 re mortgaged property.

Married couple's allowance (TA 1988, ss 257A, 257B, 257BA, 257BB, 257C; F(No 2)A 1992, s 20 and Sch 5)

The married couple's allowance is currently given in the first instance to the husband. If the husband's income is too low to use it, he may ask the

374

Revenue to transfer the excess to the wife. It is not transferred automatically. There is a provision on tax returns for you to apply for a transfer notice form (form 575) if you think you will need it.

In working out a husband's income to see if any of the allowance is unused, you do not deduct MIRAS interest, premiums under occupational or personal pension schemes where paid net of tax, private medical insurance premiums if you pay them net (because the insured person or one of an insured married couple is over 60), relief under the business expansion scheme and payments after 5 April 1992 by trainees for their own vocational training where paid net (see page 135).

The married couple's allowance is given in full in the year of separation or death of either spouse, but it is reduced in the year of marriage (see page 378).

A wife can use the transferred allowance against any of her income for the year, even if it arose before marriage or after the date of separation or of her husband's death.

From 6 April 1993, a married woman may claim half the basic married couple's allowance (not any age addition for the over 65s) as of right, and the couple may jointly claim for the wife to get the whole of the basic allowance, providing in each case the claim is made *before* the tax year in which it is first to apply, except in the year of marriage, when the claim may be made within that year (see page 14 for the detailed provisions). This will enable their joint tax to be reduced if a wife pays tax at a higher rate than the husband. But the need to claim or revoke the claim in advance means that you may end up jointly paying more tax if your circumstances change. As with the present position, if income is too low to use the full allowance, the person entitled to it may elect to transfer the surplus to the other.

Example 1

Assume that 1993/94 tax rates and allowances remain the same as for 1992/93 (although they will in fact be increased). If a husband's income in 1993/94 after allowances is just below the basic rate limit while his wife's is above it, electing to transfer the married couple's allowance will save (40% − 25%) on the excess of her income over the basic rate limit, giving a maximum saving of £1,720 @ 15% = £258. If, however, having made the transfer claim, the couple find that the husband's income exceeds the basic rate limit while the wife's is below it, they will be worse off.

If the wife's income should fall below (£3,445 + £1,720), she can ask the Revenue to transfer the surplus up to £1,720 back to her husband.

Transitional provisions (TA 1988, ss 257D, 257E, 257F)

In a few cases, independent taxation gives a worse position than the previous rules, for example where a husband has a very low income and most of the married man's allowance was being given against the wife's income or where a man has an older wife and received age allowance based on her age. There are transitional provisions to cover these situations and these are dealt with on pages 15 and 390.

There are special transitional provisions to cover the situation of a couple who were separated before 6 April 1990 but the husband was wholly maintaining his wife by voluntary payments in 1989/90 (see page 380).

Using available allowances and the lower rate band

Some people on low incomes, particularly married women with only unearned income, will need to make sure that they make the best use of their allowances and the new 20% tax rate band.

You will get a cash flow advantage if you receive income equal to your available personal allowance in full, without tax being deducted by the payer. Investments that always pay interest gross are national savings bank accounts and offshore accounts with banks and building societies. If you will not be liable to tax at all, you can claim to receive interest from other banks and from building societies without tax being deducted rather than having to reclaim the tax later (see chapter 37). The claim to receive it in full cannot be made if you expect some of your income to be liable to tax, even if you will be entitled to get back all or most of the tax deducted by the bank or building society.

Transferring property from one spouse to another (TA 1988, ss 282A, 282B, 683–685)

In order to take best advantage of the independent taxation provisions, it may be sensible for property to be transferred from husband to wife or vice versa. Any such transfers are fully effective for tax purposes providing the transfer is an outright gift of the property with no question of the transferring spouse controlling it or deriving a benefit from it. It is not possible to transfer a right to income while retaining a right to the capital (but see below re jointly owned property). The rules do not prevent the spouse who gave the property getting it back later as a gift, or after the other spouse's death, providing there were no 'strings' on the transfer in the first place. And where property is transferred into the joint names of husband and wife and they own it under the normal 'joint tenants' provisions, under which the property goes automatically to the survivor when one dies (see below), the Revenue do not regard this as breaching the 'outright gift' rules.

Such transfers will be beneficial where a wife or husband would otherwise waste their personal allowance or 20% rate band, or where one spouse would be paying higher rate tax while the other did not fully use the basic rate band. It is essential that transfers are appropriately documented in the proper legal form.

Jointly owned property

Husband and wife are normally treated as owning joint property as 'joint tenants', which means that each has equal rights over the property and when one dies, it goes automatically to the other. The joint tenancy can, however, be severed, and replaced by a 'tenancy in common', in which the share of each is separate, and may be unequal, and may be disposed of in lifetime or on death as the spouse wishes. If you do this, make sure you have proper documentary evidence of what you have done.

Where property is in joint names, it is deemed to be owned equally for income tax purposes unless it is actually owned in some different proportions and you make a declaration to that effect. Such a declaration takes effect from the date it is made, providing notice of the declaration is given to the Revenue (on form 17) within 60 days. The form only covers the assets listed on it. Any new assets must be covered by a separate form. Special provisions apply to joint mortgage interest on your home (see page 337).

The tax treatment of joint ownership may be useful to overcome one practical difficulty of maximising the benefits of independent taxation—that the richer spouse may be unwilling to transfer property to the other. The reluctant spouse could retain ownership of 95% of an asset and transfer 5%; if no declaration to that effect is notified to the Revenue, the tax law treats the income as being shared equally.

Any sort of property may be transferred—land and buildings, shares, bank accounts etc. When you open joint bank and building society accounts, you normally declare that they are in your joint beneficial ownership. You can still later change your ownership to tenants in common, although the bank or building society are likely to act on the basis of your original declaration, so that they would treat the account as belonging to the survivor when one dies. The personal representatives would then need to make appropriate adjustments. Another point that needs to be watched is in relation to mortgaged property. If the spouse to whom the property is transferred takes over responsibility for the mortgage, the mortgage debt is treated as consideration for the transfer and is liable to stamp duty (unless covered by the £30,000 limit for certified transactions—see page 79). This will not apply if the spouse who is transferring the property undertakes to pay the mortgage. (See also page 385 re separation and divorce.)

Regardless of the way income is treated for income tax purposes, it is the underlying beneficial ownership of assets that determines the capital gains tax treatment. Again, it is essential to have evidence of the shares in which property is held.

Children (TA 1988, s 663)

The income of your children is theirs in their own right, no matter how young they are. For a child under 18 and unmarried, this does not apply to income that comes directly or indirectly from you, which is still treated as your own income with the following exceptions.

Each parent can give a child a capital sum that produces no more than £100 income per annum.

The new national savings 'children's bonus bonds' for under 16-year olds (see page 409) can be given in addition.

A parent may pay premiums (maximum £200 per annum) on a qualifying friendly society policy for a child under 18 (see page 453).

It used to be tax-efficient for parents to covenant income to their student children, because such covenants could be paid net of tax by the parents and the child could then recover the tax deducted provided that he or she had available personal allowances to cover the gross covenanted sum. Tax relief is no longer available for covenants made on or after 15 March 1988 unless they are to charities.

Relief for covenants existing at 15 March 1988 is not affected, but the following points are relevant.

Where your child has other sources of income, such as vacation earnings, the personal allowances available will be reduced by those earnings, reducing the available repayment accordingly.

A covenant providing income to an adult child will usually be expressed as ceasing when full-time education ceases. The Revenue have regarded a deed as lapsing when a sandwich course period of employment starts and recommencing when the full-time education resumes. Now that covenants are no longer tax effective, it is open to question whether a pre-15 March 1988 covenant can be revived. It is considered that the Revenue would accept that it could, providing the gap was 'reasonable', which would presumably cover the normal one-year working period.

Student grants

The parental contribution to student grants depends on the parents' income and although broadly the same rules apply as for income tax, it is worth finding out the detailed provisions and taking steps where appropriate to reduce the income of years that count for grant purposes, e.g. by making maximum payments into a personal pension plan. Any covenanted payment you make to your child neither reduces your income nor counts as the child's income for grant purposes.

Year of marriage (TA 1988, ss 257A, 257D)

If a couple marry in 1992/93, the husband is entitled to the married couple's allowance of £1,720, reduced by £143.33 for each complete tax month prior

378

to the date of marriage. Thus if you marry on 25 January 1993, the allowance is reduced by 9 × £143.33, i.e. by £1,290, giving a married couple's allowance of £430. From 1993/94, the new provisions enabling all or half of the married couple's allowance to be transferred to the wife will apply to the reduced amount.

For the 1992/93 transitional relief where a couple married in 1989/90, and the husband's 1990/91 income was too low to use his allowances, see page 15.

The additional personal allowance (see page 17) is not available in the year of marriage in respect of a child born after the marriage, although this allowance can continue in the year of marriage for a child of either husband or wife before marriage. In the case of a child of the husband, the proportion of the married couple's allowance could not be claimed as well (see page 14).

Death of the husband

In the year of her husband's death, a widow is entitled to a widow's bereavement allowance, which continues for the next tax year provided that she has not remarried before the start of it. If the widow has a qualifying child living with her (see page 18), she may claim the additional personal allowance in the year of her husband's death, and it continues for so long as there is a dependent child or children living with her and she remains unmarried at the beginning of the tax year.

In the year of her husband's death, the widow can also receive the benefit of any of the married couple's allowance which cannot be used against the husband's income up to the date of death. This might be particularly relevant where the husband died early in the tax year. The husband's executors must ask the Revenue to transfer the surplus married couple's allowance to the widow—it is not automatic.

All the allowances available to a widow in the year of her husband's death may be given against income arising both before and after the date of death.

Her income will include any she is entitled to from the assets in her husband's estate. By Revenue concession A7, a widow who acquires from her husband's estate a business or other source of income (such as a national savings bank account) normally charged to tax on a previous year basis can continue to be taxed on the previous year basis unless she wishes the closing and opening year rules to apply (for those rules see chapter 21 and page 417).

From 1993/94 onwards, a woman who has claimed all or half of the basic married couple's allowance will get the widow's bereavement allowance instead in the year of her husband's death, the married couple's allowance being automatically transferred back to set against the husband's income. If his income is insufficient to use his allowances, the widow will automatically get the benefit of any surplus married couple's allowance, without the need for a claim.

Some of the state benefits a widow gets are taxable and some are not (see table on page 126). If a widow qualifies for any of the non-taxable benefits, she may be better having her widow's pension reduced and drawing the non-taxable benefits in full instead. A widow who remarries before age 60 may also be worse off in terms of her state retirement pension—see page 170.

Death of the wife

The husband is entitled to the full married couple's allowance for the tax year in which his wife dies. For later years until remarriage, he loses his entitlement, but he may claim the additional personal allowance if he has a qualifying child living with him (see page 17). Investment income arising on the wife's assets following death will be assessed through her estate and will form part of the husband's income to the extent that he is the ultimate beneficiary. Revenue concession A7 outlined above also applies to a husband taking over sources of income from his deceased wife.

If, from 1993/94, all or half of the husband's basic married couple's allowance has been claimed by the wife, and her income in the year of her death is insufficient to cover her allowances, any surplus married couple's allowance can be transferred back to the husband, providing the wife's personal representatives notify the Revenue accordingly.

Separation (TA 1988, ss 257F, 259, 260, 261A; F(No 2)A 1992, s 20 and Sch 5)

If husband and wife separate in such circumstances as are likely to be permanent, the husband is currently entitled to the married couple's allowance (in full) for the year of separation but not in later years. The date of separation is a question of fact.

Before 6 April 1990, a husband could continue to get married man's allowance up to the year of divorce if he wholly maintained his separated wife by unenforceable payments, but this does not apply to the married couple's allowance. Where, however, a couple separated before 6 April 1990 and the husband was entitled to the married man's allowance under the old provisions, he will continue to get married couple's allowance so long as the conditions are satisfied.

A wife is entitled to the additional personal allowance from the tax year of separation onwards if she has a qualifying child resident with her (see page 17). The husband may also claim the additional personal allowance if the conditions are satisfied, but not in any year when he is entitled to the married couple's allowance. If they both claim in respect of the same child the allowance is apportioned between them, but if each has a different qualifying child resident with him or her for at least part of the year each can claim the allowance in full. If, however, they remain apart but either or both of them live with someone else as man and wife, only one additional personal allowance is available per household. So if, say, two unmarried people live with each other and each has a qualifying child from a former marriage, only one additional personal allowance will be available and it will be given in respect of the youngest qualifying child.

From 1993/94 onwards, additional personal allowance may be claimed by both husband and wife in the year of separation if each has a qualifying child resident with him or her for all or part of the remainder of the year (the allowance being split as indicated above if they both claim in respect of the same child). The available allowance is, however, reduced by any married couple's allowance to which he or she is entitled. If half of the basic married couple's allowance has been claimed by each, each can only claim half of the additional personal allowance. If the couple have claimed that the wife should get all of the married couple's allowance she cannot claim the additional allowance at all in that year. In that case, if the husband has a qualifying child resident with him for all or part of the remainder of the year, he will be entitled to a full additional personal allowance, unless he is over 65, in which case the age addition to the married couple's allowance will reduce his additional personal allowance.

Example 2

Husband aged 66 and wife aged 48 have two children in full-time education. Wife is liable to higher rate tax and husband's income is below £14,200. Assume that for 1993/94 a claim is made for basic married couple's allowance to go to the wife, and that personal allowances remain the same as in 1992/93.

Available allowances where each has a qualifying child resident with him or her following separation:

If they separate in	1992/93 £	1993/94 £
Husband:		
Personal allowance	4,200	4,200
Married couple's allowance	2,465	745
Additional personal allowance		975
Wife:		
Personal allowance	3,445	3,445
Married couple's allowance		1,720
Additional personal allowance	1,720	
Joint allowances	£11,830	£11,085

Allowances are £745 lower in 1993/94, because husband loses additional personal allowance to the extent that he has age-related married couple's allowance.

Reconciliation

If a couple become reconciled in a later tax year, the full married couple's allowance is available in the year of reconciliation (unless they had divorced). If the reconciliation takes place in the same tax year as the separation, they will be taxed as if they had not been separated.

Maintenance payments to spouse (TA 1988, ss 347A, 347B; FA 1988, s 38)

The tax treatment of maintenance payments depends on whether the obligation was in existence at 15 March 1988, with certain transitional provisions.

Payments made after 14 March 1988, other than payments under existing obligations (see below) (TA 1988, s 347B; F(No 2)A 1992, s 61)

Where you pay maintenance to your separated or divorced spouse by court order or agreement, you can claim a maintenance relief deduction from your taxable income of £1,720, or the amount paid if less. You cannot deduct more than £1,720 even if you pay maintenance to more than one person. Your spouse is not taxed on the amount received. The full allowance is available in the year of separation, as well as the married couple's allowance. Payments due after your spouse remarries do not qualify for relief. From 1992/93, maintenance relief is available to EC nationals resident in the UK and to UK nationals paying maintenance by order or written agreement of an EC country.

Payments under existing obligations (FA 1988, ss 38–40)

Special provisions apply to payments you make under existing obligations, which means payments that are enforceable:

By a court order made before 15 March 1988, or
By a deed or written agreement made before 15 March 1988 and received by the Revenue on or before 30 June 1988, or
Under an oral agreement made before 15 March 1988, written particulars of which were received by the Revenue on or before 30 June 1988, or
By a court order made on or before 30 June 1988 on an application made on or before 15 March 1988.

You can deduct these payments in calculating your taxable income, and the amount taxable on your spouse is reduced, in 1992/93, by £1,720 (or the amount received if less). The balance is charged to tax by direct assessment and the tax is payable on 1 January in the tax year. In many cases where your spouse is working, however, tax is collected by means of an adjustment to the PAYE coding.

Where maintenance has been increased, the amount you are entitled to deduct is limited to the maintenance paid in 1988/89, and your spouse pays tax only on that amount, less £1,720 or whatever the maintenance relief then is.

If the 1988/89 maintenance figure has been increased to more than the current maintenance relief limit, you may be better off claiming under the new rules, and you can make a claim to do this within twelve months after the end of the tax year to which you want the new rules first to apply. If, for example, the maintenance paid in 1988/89 was £1,500 and it is later increased to £2,000, with the current maintenance relief limit being £1,720, switching to the new rules would allow you relief on £1,720 instead of £1,500.

How payment is made

All maintenance payments to your former spouse, whether under new or existing obligations, are paid in full and you get relief at your top tax rate either on £1,720 (new arrangements) or for an amount not exceeding the amount paid in 1988/89 (existing obligations) in a PAYE coding or in an assessment.

Maintenance payments to children (TA 1988, ss 347A, 347B, 348, 683; FA 1988, s 38)

Relief is not available for maintenance payments to children unless they are made under a pre-existing obligation at 15 March 1988 (see page 382).

Income tax relief at your highest tax rate may be obtained on payments of maintenance direct to children, if paid under a court order made before 15 March 1988 or on or before 30 June 1988 where the application for the order was made on or before 15 March 1988. The maintenance is treated as your child's income, against which the child's personal allowance may be used. Relief for maintenance to a child over 21 is only available if the amount payable under the court order as at 15 March 1988 remains unchanged. Relief for younger children is restricted to the maintenance paid in 1988/89.

Where you pay maintenance under a pre-15 March 1988 agreement, rather than a court order, it is only effective if the child is over 18 or married, and even then saves you tax only at the basic rate and not the higher rate. Relief on such agreements is only available on the amount payable under the agreement at 15 March 1988 and only so long as that agreement remains in force. Later variations are ineffective.

How payment is made for arrangements on and after 15 March 1988

Children receiving maintenance under arrangements made on or after 15 March 1988, or increases over and above the maintenance due for 1988/89, receive it in full and are exempt from tax on it. No tax relief is available to the payer.

How payment is made under obligations existing at 15 March 1988

Children under 21 who receive maintenance under a court order receive it in full without tax being deducted. Children over 18 who receive maintenance under an agreement, and all children over 21 who receive maintenance, whether by court order or agreement, receive it after deduction of basic rate tax. However the payment is made, the maintenance is liable to tax, but may be covered by the child's personal allowance. If it is, and tax has been deducted, the child can claim a refund.

Where the child is liable to tax on payments made gross, the tax will be collected either by adjusting a PAYE coding or by direct assessment, the tax being due on 1 January in the tax year. If a child over 21 is liable at the higher rate on payments made net under a court order, the higher rate tax is due on 1 December following the end of the tax year, his basic rate liability being covered by the tax deducted from the payment. For maintenance paid by agreement to a child over 18 and thus paid net, the child's liability is restricted to the basic rate and will be covered by the tax deducted.

You get relief at your top tax rate, in a PAYE coding or in an assessment, for maintenance paid gross. Where payment is made net, basic rate relief is obtained by retaining the tax deducted. Higher rate relief on payments made net is due only on court order payments to children over 21 and not on any payments under an agreement. The higher rate relief is given by adjustment to a PAYE coding or in an assessment.

Divorce

The tax position of divorced couples is the same as that of separated couples, except that the married couple's allowance given to some married men who were separated before 6 April 1990 (see page 380) is not available in any circumstances in tax years after that in which the divorce occurs.

For policies entered into before 14 March 1984, a divorced wife continues to be entitled to life assurance relief on a policy on her husband's life taken out before the divorce. If she wishes to protect herself against the loss of maintenance on her husband's death, this can be done with her husband's co-operation if he takes out a policy on his own life in trust for her, or she herself takes out a policy on his life. There will be no tax relief on the premium unless the policy was taken out before 14 March 1984.

Separation and divorce—the family home (TCGA 1992, ss 222, 223; FA 1985, s 83; TA 1988, ss 354, 355; FA 1988, s 44; Stamp Duty (Exempt Instruments) Regulations 1987)

Two aspects are important—relief for mortgage interest paid and the capital gains tax position.

Where your former or separated spouse occupies the family home, relief for mortgage interest paid by you is not available unless the loan existed (or was under written offer), and the former or separated spouse was resident in the property, at 5 April 1988. Replacement loans do not qualify for relief. The £30,000 umbrella for mortgage interest relief (see chapter 2) has, however, to cover the borrowing on your own home, on that occupied rent-free by a dependent relative at 5 April 1988 and on the home provided for a divorced or separated spouse.

You are each entitled to relief on up to £30,000 in respect of borrowing for your separate houses following separation or divorce.

For capital gains tax, the family home will cease to be the main residence of the spouse who leaves it. His or her share of any calculated gain on a subsequent sale will therefore be chargeable to the extent that it relates to the period of non-residence, subject to any available exemptions or reliefs. The last three years of ownership (two years for disposals before 19 March 1991) always count as a period of residence, even if a new qualifying residence has been acquired. If the property is disposed of more than three years after a spouse leaves it, part of the calculated gain will be assessable, but only in the proportion that the excess period over three years bears to the total period of ownership since 31 March 1982. Even then the chargeable gain may be covered by the annual exemption of £5,800. There is a Revenue concession (concession D6) covering absences of more than three years following separation or divorce, but only where the property is eventually transferred to the spouse remaining in it as part of the financial settlement, and an election for a new qualifying residence has not been made by the spouse moving out in the meantime.

If property is transferred from one spouse to another on break-up of a marriage, stamp duty is not payable, even if the acquiring spouse takes over a mortgage. This exemption applies to all property, not just the family home.

Capital gains tax—other chargeable assets (TCGA 1992, ss 58, 165)

The inter-spouse exemption only applies to assets transferred in a tax year when you are living together. In later tax years, capital gains tax is chargeable in the normal way, and this must be remembered when considering a matrimonial settlement following separation. In the case of certain assets transferred from one to the other before the divorce, it may be possible to avoid gains being charged to tax at that time if husband and wife elect, under the 'business gifts relief', for the recipient to adopt the original cost plus indexation allowance to date in calculating the tax payable on an eventual disposal (see chapter 4). Gifts relief used to be available for all assets, but the general gifts relief was withdrawn for disposals after 5 April 1989. Even the business gifts relief will not usually be available after divorce since the transfer of assets will then be regarded as being for consideration and therefore not subject to gifts relief.

Inheritance tax (IHTA 1984, s 18(1))

The spouse exemption for inheritance tax is not lost on separation but continues until the time of divorce. Even then there is an exemption for transfers to former spouses for the maintenance of themselves and the children. See chapter 5.

Living together without being married

Whereas high income unmarried couples used to have tax advantages over married couples because of their entitlement to two basic rate bands against any income, whether earned or unearned, and two capital gains exemptions, the balance has now swung the other way, because married couples get the same treatment and also get the married couple's allowance.

An unmarried couple can get the equivalent of the married couple's allowance in the form of the additional personal allowance if they have a qualifying child (see page 17). But whereas they used to be able to claim two additional personal allowances if each had a qualifying child, only one claim may be made from 1989/90. The allowance is given in respect of the youngest qualifying child. When two people claim the relief for the same child, the relief is apportioned, the split being made according to how long the child resides with each claimant in the tax year, unless they have agreed some other split. Claimants other than the child's own parent are not entitled to the relief unless they maintain the child.

An unmarried person is not entitled to tax relief on payments under a maintenance order awarded to a cohabitee in respect of their children.

Poll tax

Couples who are living together as husband and wife, whether married or not, may have to pay one another's poll tax. This only applies for any part of the year when they are living together, and would not apply after separation or divorce. A partner is not liable unless the authority has issued a bill to him or her, which cannot be done unless the other has failed to pay.

You cannot be obliged to pay the poll tax of anyone else, such as an adult son or daughter or other relative living with you.

Tax points

- If all or half of the 1993/94 married couple's allowance is to be transferred to the wife, you must claim *before* 6 April 1993. The claim form is available from your tax office. Wives can claim half the allowance as of right, and all of it with the husband's agreement.

- The Revenue require a separate form 17 (notification of unequal shares) for any new assets. This needs to be borne in mind if you have a joint share portfolio, where there may be frequent changes.

- If you change your ownership of bank and building society accounts so that you hold them as tenants in common rather than joint tenants, make sure you have proper evidence that you have done so.

- Although the capital gains tax private residence exemption does not apply to a second home, if you own the second home jointly you will be entitled to two annual exemptions when you sell it (unless otherwise used).

- In a bona fide husband and wife partnership where both play a significant role in the business, profits can be shared so as to maximise the benefit of independent taxation.

- If your joint wealth is substantial, you may be able to save inheritance tax by rearranging the ownership of assets between you. See chapter 35 for details.

- If you are cohabiting, remember that the social security regulations are different from those relating to tax. They should be researched before making financial arrangements between you and for children.

34
Especially for the senior citizen

General (TA 1988, ss 257, 257A–257F)

Married couples

From 6 April 1990, the incomes of husband and wife are taxed independently. Each is entitled to a personal allowance based on their age, available against any income, earned or unearned. The allowances for 1992/93 are as follows:

Under 65	£3,445
65 to 74	£4,200
75 and over	£4,370

Note that even if a wife gets state pension at 60, she does not get the higher tax allowance until she is 65.

In addition, the husband gets a married couple's allowance, based on the age of the older spouse, as follows:

Both under 65	£1,720
Elder 65 to 74	£2,465
Elder 75 or over	£2,505

The entitlement to age allowances is subject to an income restriction—see page 389.

From 1993/94 a wife will be able to claim half of the basic married couple's allowance (not any addition for those over 65) as of right, and all of it if both agree. For the detailed provisions, see chapter 33. Note particularly page 381 on the possible adverse effect if a couple entitled to increased allowances for those over 65 become separated or divorced.

There are transitional provisions for certain husbands with older wives to prevent their allowances being lower with independent taxation—see page 390.

If the husband's income is lower than his total allowances, any excess married couple's allowance may be transferred to the wife. You have to

388

make a specific claim to do this—it is not automatic. There is a box to fill in on your tax return if you want the Revenue to send you the necessary form.

Single people

Single people are entitled to personal allowance at the same levels as those stated above for married people, and are subject to the same income limit (see below). A single woman gets state pension at age 60, but is not entitled to a higher tax allowance until she is 65.

Income limit for age allowances

The benefit of higher personal allowances, and higher married couple's allowances where applicable, is withdrawn to the extent that income exceeds a specified limit, £14,200 for 1992/93. Each of a married couple has his or her own limit.

The personal allowance is reduced by half the excess of income over that limit until it reaches the normal personal allowance level, currently £3,445. The married couple's age allowance depends on the husband's income only, even if the extra allowance is being given because of his wife's age rather than his. After the personal allowance has been reduced to £3,445, the married couple's allowance is similarly reduced by half of the excess of his total income over £14,200 which has not already been taken into account to reduce his personal allowance, until it reaches the normal married couple's allowance, currently £1,720 (which may, from 1993/94, have been transferred to the wife).

Once income reaches a certain level, all the benefit of the increased personal allowances, and increased married couple's allowances where relevant, is lost and only normal allowances are given. The maximum income levels at which age allowance and married couple's allowance are available are shown on page 15.

Example 1

	(a)	(b)
Single person aged 67 has income in 1992/93 of:	14,200	14,400
Personal allowance (over 65)		
Unrestricted	4,200	
Restricted by ½ of £200		4,100
Taxable income	£10,000	£10,300
Tax thereon: 2,000 @ 20%	400	400
8,000/8,300 @ 25%	£2,400	£2,475

Additional tax payable on extra £200 is £75, i.e. 37½%.

The reduction of the age allowance by £1 for every £2 of income over £14,200 is sometimes called the age allowance trap, because it has the effect of costing you tax at 37½% on the excess over £14,200, as shown in example 1 on page 389.

If you are in this position, you should consider reducing your taxable income by switching to tax-exempt investments such as Tax Exempt Special Savings Accounts and national savings certificates. In both cases, maximum returns are obtained by leaving the money invested for the prescribed period, but some withdrawal of funds is possible, particularly with savings certificates. For details, see chapters 36 and 37.

Where mortgage interest is paid jointly, but only one of you has income above the age allowance income limit, it will reduce your tax if you claim to have the interest treated as paid by that person alone—see page 337.

Transitional provisions (TA 1988, s 257E)

If the husband is under 65 in 1992/93 and received the age allowance for 1989/90 because his wife was then over 75, he can claim a personal allowance of £3,540 instead of £3,445, subject to the income limit of £14,200.

Pensions and state benefits

There are various points you need to know about pensions, both from employers and from the state. An increase in state pension will result in increased tax on an occupational pension. This is because the state pension increase takes up another slice of your tax allowances, reducing the amount available to set against your occupational pension. You are still better off over all. Some people with small occupational pensions may not get the full benefit of the new 20% tax rate band and will need to claim a refund—see below. Some state benefits are taxable and others, including some widows' benefits, are not (see Table on page 126), so you need to take care where you have a choice. For general points on state benefits see chapter 13.

Tax refunds

If you pay too much tax, you will be entitled to a refund. Although state pensions are received in full, and take up the first slice of your allowances, the remainder of your income might have been received net of 25% tax, so that you have not had the benefit of the balance of your allowances, or of the new 20% rate of tax on the first £2,000 of taxable income. Alternatively, the balance of your age allowance may have been given against, say, an occupational pension, but the remaining pension may be below £2,000, so that you will not have had the full benefit of the 20% rate of tax. In these circumstances, you will need to claim a refund. For an illustration, see page 21. You may be able to avoid overpaying tax by registering to receive bank and building society interest in full, but only if you will not be liable to pay tax at all—see page 415. You can, however, claim a refund of tax deducted from bank and building society interest without waiting till the end of the tax year if the refund is £50 or more.

Providing a home for a dependent relative (IHTA 1984, s 53; TCGA 1992, ss 73, 225)

A gain on the disposal of a property provided rent-free for a dependent relative, such as a parent over 65, used to be exempt from capital gains tax but this no longer applies unless the relative was in the property on 5 April 1988 and still lives there. It is, however, possible to acquire a property, put it into trust and allow an elderly relative to live in it rent-free for life, the property then reverting to you when the relative dies. There would be no income from the property, therefore no income tax problems, capital gains tax would not be payable when you reacquired the property, and providing the relative does not outlive you, inheritance tax would not be chargeable either. If the property was already owned for a time before it was put in trust, there would be a chargeable gain at that time equal to the difference between its value when transferred to the trust and the indexed cost. Professional advice is essential.

Maximising investment income

People with high incomes often used to look for capital growth instead of income. With the basic rate of income tax applying to £21,700 of income after personal allowances and the 20% rate band of £2,000, and with capital gains now being taxed at income tax rates, it may be sensible for you to reappraise your investments following retirement with a view to maximising income instead of concentrating on capital growth. You should, however, remember that each of husband and wife is exempt from capital gains tax on the first £5,800 of chargeable gains, so that investments with the potential of realising such gains should not be ignored.

Purchased life annuities

A purchased life annuity is where you receive an annual sum for your lifetime in exchange for a capital payment. The characteristic of a purchased life annuity is that part of it is regarded as a return of capital and thus escapes tax; the older you are the greater the tax-free capital element. You do, of course, sacrifice the capital required to buy the annuity, and this loss of capital must be weighed against the greater income arising. You may think the loss of capital is worthwhile to enable you to improve your standard of living, particularly if you have no dependants or others you want to leave your capital to. See example 2.

Making the most of the dwelling house

Your home is often your most significant asset, yet it can be your biggest liability in the sense that you have to maintain it, and in most cases it does not produce income.

If you decide to let part of it, you will not have to pay income tax on the rent from 6 April 1992 unless it exceeds £62.50 a week—see page 334. The

---

Example 2

	Tax calculation	Cash available
Income of a single taxpayer aged 75 is	4,500	4,500
Personal allowance (75 and over)	4,370	
Tax at 20% on	130	26
Net spendable income		£4,474

A life annuity is purchased for £16,000. Suppose it produces £2,800 for the taxpayer's lifetime, of which £1,750 is regarded by the Revenue as a return of capital.

The effect on the net spendable income is:

Net spendable income as before		4,474
Capital element of annuity received in full		1,750
Income element of annuity	1,050	
Less tax at 20%	210	840
Net spendable income increases to		£7,064

The net spendable income has been increased by £2,590.

---

letting will not cause you to lose your capital gains tax private residence exemption (see chapter 30) on disposal of the property provided that the gain on the let part does not exceed that on the exempt part, subject to a maximum exempt gain on the let part of £40,000. Taking in boarders who live as part of the family does not affect your capital gains tax exemption at all.

Another possibility is a home reversion scheme, under which you sell all or part of your house to the reversion company for much less than its value (the discount usually being at least 50%) in return for the right to live in it until you die. Some schemes give you a lower initial sum but give you a share in future increases in value of the property. The initial cash sum does not attract capital gains tax but shares of future increases in value may be liable. The investment of the initial capital sum gives you extra spendable income.

There are numerous life assurance/annuity schemes, some of them involving the value of your home. Proper financial advice is essential and you must also be sure that the scheme gives you security of income and does not put your home at risk.

Helping the family

You may be in a position to give financial help to your family rather than requiring help from them.

Before 15 March 1988, you would have been able to obtain income tax relief at the basic rate by covenanting income gifts to, say, your grandchildren or adult children, providing you had enough income over and above your available tax allowances. Tax relief on covenants to individuals was withdrawn from 15 March 1988 but is still available on covenants made before that date, and the recipient is still entitled to an income tax repayment if the covenanted income is covered by his tax allowances.

Even though covenanting is no longer tax-effective, except for charitable covenants, you may be thinking of making gifts to reduce the inheritance tax on your estate. The following gifts may be made without inheritance tax consequences:

(a)   habitual gifts out of income that leave you with enough income to maintain your usual standard of living;

(b)   gifts of not more than £250 per donee in each tax year;

(c)   the first £3,000 of total gifts in each tax year, plus any unused part of the £3,000 exemption for the previous tax year. This exemption applies to gifts on an 'earliest first' basis, so if you gave away nothing last year and give £5,000 in May and £5,000 in June, the May gift is exempt and £1,000 of the June gift is exempt.

Even if none of the exemptions is available, there is still no immediate inheritance tax problem since lifetime gifts (other than to discretionary trusts) are initially treated as potentially exempt transfers, only to be brought into account for inheritance tax if you do not survive the gift by seven years. If you do not survive the seven-year period, there is still no question of inheritance tax being payable if the gift is within the nil rate band for inheritance tax, currently £150,000. This nil band is used against the earliest gifts in the seven years before death. Any gifts over and above the nil band are chargeable, but the tax is reduced on a sliding scale if you have survived the gift by more than three years. All non-exempt gifts within the seven years before death do, however, affect how much of the nil rate band is available against the death estate.

Husband and wife have always been treated separately for inheritance tax, each being entitled to the available exemptions.

Tax position on your death

When you die, your wealth at death and the chargeable transfers you have made in the previous seven years will determine whether any, and if so how much, inheritance tax is payable (see chapter 5). There is no inheritance tax on assets passing to your husband or wife. There is no liability to capital gains tax on your estate, and those who acquire your assets are deemed to have bought them at their market value at the date of your death. Further details on the position at death are in chapters 33 and 35.

If capital gains have been made in that part of the tax year before the date of death, they will be chargeable if they exceed the annual exemption of £5,800. Any capital losses in the tax year of death may be carried back to set against gains on which tax has been paid in the three previous tax years, and, in that event, tax will be repayable to the estate.

As far as income tax is concerned, the income to the date of death is charged to tax in the usual way, with a full personal allowance against it. In the case of a married couple, the married couple's allowance is available in full in the year of the wife's death but not in later years. If the husband dies first, any part of the married couple's allowance that is not used against his income may be transferred to the widow, and she can use it against any of her income for the year, both before and after her husband's death. A widow is also entitled to a deduction from her taxable income of £1,720 (called the widow's bereavement allowance) in the year of her husband's death (the allowance being given against income both before and after the death), and in the following year unless she has remarried before the beginning of it. On remarriage she cannot transfer any unused allowance to her new husband. See page 379 for the treatment of married couple's allowance and widow's bereavement allowance from 1993/94.

A widow with a qualifying child may claim additional personal allowance (see page 17), commencing in the year of her husband's death. A widower can only claim for years after that in which his wife died.

Private medical insurance (FA 1989, ss 54–57)

Tax relief at the payer's highest rate of tax is available for premiums paid for private medical insurance, where the insured person is over 60, or, if the insurance relates to a married couple, where one of them is over 60, at the time of payment. Basic rate relief is deducted when you pay the premium, so that you pay a net sum. If you are entitled to relief at the higher rate of tax, the extra relief will be given by adjusting your PAYE code or in an assessment. If your income is too low to attract tax, you will still be entitled to retain the basic rate relief.

Relief at the payer's highest tax rate will also be available to someone else, such as your son or daughter, if they pay premiums on your behalf.

The person who is to pay the premium must complete a declaration of eligibility for tax relief on a form supplied by the insurer.

Poll tax

You are exempt from personal poll tax if you are a long-term hospital patient, or are being looked after in a residential care home (see page 97). If as a result your home is left unoccupied you will not be liable to the standard community charge.

People on low incomes are entitled to community charge benefit of up to
80% (see page 100).

Relief under the community charge reduction scheme is available to a man
over 65 or a woman over 60, or someone of either sex who is disabled, if that
person did not pay rates (and was not married to someone who did). Relief
under the scheme is also available to certain former ratepayers. See page 101.

Tax points

- The marginal tax rate for those over 65 with income over £14,200 is
37½%, so that investments that produce tax-free income or capital
gains should be considered in those circumstances.

- There is no point in increasing available income now if this jeopardises
your capital and causes worry and uncertainty for the future.

- Payments under covenants made before 15 March 1988 from adult
children to their dependent parents, and from grandparents to grandchildren, can still utilise available personal allowances and enable the
recipient to receive a tax refund, but there are no tax advantages to be
gained from covenants made after 14 March 1988.

- Now that lifetime transfers are potentially exempt and no longer have
to be reported, it is more important than ever to keep accurate records
of gifts out of income and capital so that there can be no doubt about
dates and amounts of gifts. Personal representatives are responsible
for enquiries about transfers in the seven years before death and carefully kept records will be essential for the avoidance of doubt.

- If, because of disability, you have to provide, adapt or extend a bath-
room, washroom or lavatory in your private residence, the cost is not
liable to VAT. There is, however, no income tax relief on the cost, nor
any income tax relief on interest you pay on money borrowed to pay
for the work, where the loan was made after 5 April 1988. Relief for
income tax on interest paid after 5 April 1988 on loans made before
then continues to be available (but not on replacement loans).

- In reckoning the income for age allowances, any investment bond
withdrawals over the 5% limit have to be taken into account even
though there is no tax to pay on that excess at the higher rate (see
chapter 40). Conversely, an amount paid under a deed of covenant to
a charity, or under a covenant made before 15 March 1988 to an
individual, will reduce the income for age allowances even though
there is no tax relief on the covenant at the higher rate in the case of
the deed in favour of the individual.

- If your wife is over 65 and does not have enough income of her own to
cover her personal allowance, you should consider transferring some

of your assets to her if this is practicable, so that the income from them will then be hers and not yours (see page 376). Interest on national savings bank accounts is paid gross, and the wife's allowance can be used to cover interest she has from such accounts. Interest on other bank and building society accounts can only be paid gross if you are able to register because you will not be liable to tax at all (see chapter 37). If you cannot do this, there will be a cash flow advantage with national savings bank interest, but you need to compare the rates of interest on offer as well.

- The income limit for age-related married couple's allowance depends on the husband's income, even if the allowance is given because of the wife's age. It does not matter how high the wife's income is.

- If a husband's income is too low to use the age-related married couple's allowance, the unused amount can be transferred to his wife and the full amount transferred is available against her income, with no income restriction.

35
Tax considerations in making a will

If you die without making a will

If you die without making a will, the rules of intestacy require your estate to be divided in a particular way. If you are married, your spouse automatically acquires the matrimonial home if you own as joint tenants (see page 399), and the intestacy rules apply only to the remainder of your estate. If, on the other hand, the house was owned either by you alone or jointly with your spouse as tenants in common (see page 399), your share would form part of your estate and would be subject to the intestacy rules. The intestacy rules applicable in England and Wales are set out in the following table.

Where there is a surviving spouse Are there any:			Spouse takes:	Remainder
Children and their issue*	Parents	Brothers and sisters and their issue*		
No	No	No	Whole estate	
Yes			Personal chattels + £75,000 + life interest in half of residue	Children (or their issue*) share half residue and take spouse's share on his or her death
No	Yes		Personal chattels + £125,000 + half of residue absolutely	Parents share half of residue absolutely
No	No	Yes	,,	Brothers and sisters (or their issue*) share half of residue absolutely

Where there is no surviving spouse

If there are children, or their issue*, they take the whole estate absolutely.

If there are no children or their issue*, the whole estate goes to surviving relatives in the following order of precedence, each category taking the whole estate to the exclusion of any later category:

> Parents
> Brothers and sisters (or their issue*)
> Half brothers and sisters (or their issue*)
> Grandparents
> Uncles and aunts (or their issue*)
> Parents' half brothers and sisters (or their issue*)

If there are none of these relatives, the estate goes to the Crown.

* 'Issue' means children and their children, grandchildren, great grandchildren etc., issue being entitled to an appropriate proportion of the deceased parent's share.

The share of anyone under 18 is held on trust to age 18.

It is possible for those entitled under an intestacy to vary their entitlement (see page 401), but if there are beneficiaries under 18, this cannot be done without court consent.

General considerations

In making the best arrangements from a taxation point of view, you should not forget that the prime objective is to ensure that those left behind are properly provided for in a sensible, practical and acceptable way. There are important tax implications, which it can be expensive to ignore, but they should not be allowed to override the main aim.

Inheritance tax: spouse exemption (IHTA 1984, s 18; TCGA 1992, s 58)

Gifts between husband and wife are exempt from inheritance tax for both lifetime and death transfers (unless the donee is not domiciled in the UK, in which case gifts are exempt up to a limit of £55,000—see chapter 5). Transfers between husband and wife in a tax year when they are living together are also exempt from capital gains tax, and there is no stamp duty on gifts.

Since husband and wife are each entitled to the inheritance tax nil rate threshold (currently £150,000) before transfers become chargeable, it is clearly sensible for the joint wealth to be arranged in such a way that each takes advantage of it. The tax advantage may, however, be lost on death if the estate is then left to the surviving spouse. If, say, each had £150,000 wealth and made no transfers in the seven years before death, no tax would arise if each left the wealth to the next generation, because it would be covered by the nil rate threshold. But if the wealth were left to the surviving spouse, that spouse would then have £300,000 (ignoring any capital variation in the meantime) which would attract a tax liability of £60,000 (at current rates) on the second death.

Bypassing your spouse will not be practicable if he/she is left with inadequate assets to maintain his/her standard of living. The surviving spouse can still have the benefit of the joint capital during his/her lifetime whilst preserving the family wealth for the next generation through the use of life assurance to cover the tax liability on the second death. This is dealt with later in the chapter.

Providing the nil rate threshold is used, there is no inheritance tax incentive to equalise estates in lifetime, and indeed it may be better to leave the excess over the nil rate threshold to the surviving spouse so that tax would be paid later rather than earlier, and the surviving spouse would be able to make further tax-exempt gifts and gifts within the nil rate threshold as it increased year by year. But for income tax, it will be tax-efficient for each spouse to have sufficient income to use the lower and basic rate bands, capital gains also being charged at marginal income tax rates, so the overall position needs to be looked at.

Jointly owned assets

There are two ways in which assets may be held jointly—as joint tenants or as tenants in common. If you hold an asset with someone else as a joint tenant, it automatically passes to the other joint tenant(s) when you die. With a tenancy in common, each has a separate share which can be disposed of in lifetime or on death as the person wishes. Husband and wife are presumed to own assets as joint tenants, and other people are presumed to own them as tenants in common, but if they want to vary the normal presumption this can be done. It must, however, be done in the proper legal manner appropriate to the asset.

Jointly held assets still form part of a person's estate for inheritance tax whether they are held on a joint tenancy or as tenants in common, but where they are held jointly by husband and wife, any assets passing to the spouse are covered in any event by the spouse exemption. Holding as joint tenants has the advantage in the case of a joint bank or building society account that when your spouse dies, all that is needed to enable you to take over sole ownership of the account is production of the death certificate. You do not have to wait for grant of probate or administration. But a joint account has other tax implications, particularly in relation to independent taxation of husband and wife since in many cases the share of income accruing to the wife will not give the best income tax position.

The joint ownership principles must be borne in mind when planning the use of the nil rate threshold for inheritance tax, and proper action taken to vary the normal presumptions where necessary.

Legacies and their effect on the spouse exemption

Unless a will states otherwise, legacies are payable out of the residue of an estate, after inheritance tax has been paid, and they thus reduce the amount available to the person entitled to the balance of the estate—called the residuary legatee. The legacies are not themselves reduced by inheritance tax unless the will specifically says so. It follows that the amount available to a residuary legatee is often less than is apparent at first sight.

If the residuary legatee is the surviving spouse, this has an effect on the tax payable because the exempt part of the estate (which goes to the spouse) is first reduced by the tax. In example 1, out of a gross estate of £300,000, B, C and D receive legacies totalling £180,000, leaving an apparent residue of £120,000 for the widow. She does not, however, get £120,000, but only that amount less the tax on the rest of the estate, calculated by working out the tax on a figure sufficient to leave the legacies intact, called grossing-up. The tax amounts to £20,000 as shown in example 1. If the will had provided that the donees B, C and D should pay the tax on their legacies, the widow would have received £120,000 and the total tax payable by the legatees on £180,000 would have been £12,000 (40% of the £30,000 excess over £150,000). The legatees could have provided for this liability by insuring the life of the person from whose will they were going to benefit, using the proceeds of the policy to pay the tax on the legacy.

Example 1

A has made no transfers in the seven years before his death in 1992/93. He leaves an estate of £300,000 as follows:
  £60,000 to each of B, C and D = £180,000
  Residue to his wife E

The inheritance tax position on A's death is as follows:

	Gross £	Tax £	Net £
Net legacies			180,000
Gross equivalent and tax thereon	200,000	20,000	

The estate will accordingly be divided as follows:

Gross estate	300,000
Legacies to B, C and D	(180,000)
Inheritance tax payable out of residue	(20,000)
Remainder to widow E, covered by spouse exemption	£100,000

Where there are deaths in quick succession (IHTA 1984, s 141)

Where someone's estate on death has been increased by a lifetime or death gift made to him within the previous five years, the tax charge on the second transfer is reduced by quick succession relief. Although the relief is deducted from the tax payable on the second transfer, it is calculated as a percentage of the tax paid on the earlier transfer (see chapter 5).

Quick succession relief is therefore not relevant in the case of assets acquired from a spouse, in lifetime or on death, or where they have been acquired in lifetime but no tax has been paid by reference to that transfer. While not losing sight of the overriding principle of family provision, there are cases where it is clearly not sensible to increase a person's estate by incoming transfers, if they have adequate resources already. Thus it will often be more tax-efficient to leave to grandchildren instead of to children. This gives the added advantage that the income arising is then that of the grandchildren in their own right against which their income tax allowances are available.

Simultaneous deaths and survivorship clauses (IHTA 1984, s 92)

Where two closely related people die at the same time, or in circumstances in which it is impossible to decide who died first, neither estate has to be increased by any entitlement from the other in calculating the inheritance tax payable. This is not so if it is clear who died first. It is therefore often advisable to include a survivorship clause in a will making a bequest conditional on the beneficiary outliving the deceased by a given period, and this is effective for inheritance tax providing the period does not exceed six months. This is particularly useful to a husband and wife who wish to leave their estates to each other to make sure that there is adequate provision for the survivor's lifetime. If the wills include an appropriate survivorship clause, then if they both die within six months, the estate of the first will not pass to the second, inheritance tax being payable at each death on the value of the separate estates. This will often attract less tax than if no tax was paid on the first death, but tax was calculated on the combined estates for the second, with the second spouse to die having had little or no benefit from the assets in the meantime. The assets in each estate and the extent to which the inheritance tax nil rate band is available need to be taken into account.

Deeds of family arrangement (IHTA 1984, ss 17, 142, 143; TCGA 1992, s 62)

It is possible for those entitled to a deceased's estate (either under a will or on an intestacy) to vary the way in which it is distributed, or to disclaim their entitlement, provided that they do so within two years after the death and notify the Revenue within six months of the date of the variation or disclaimer. (Court consent is needed if there are beneficiaries under 18.) Inheritance tax is then charged as if the revised distribution had operated at death. Such a variation or disclaimer can also be effective for capital gains tax purposes if an appropriate claim is made, and the ultimate beneficiary takes the asset at the market value at the date of death, so that any increase in value since death is not charged until the beneficiary disposes of the asset. As far as income derived from the assets is concerned, the personal representatives will have paid basic rate tax thereon, but the income is regarded as having been received not by the person who actually receives it but by the original beneficiary, and any tax arising in excess of the basic rate on the income up to the date of variation or disclaimer will be calculated by reference to his tax rates. It may be appropriate for the person actually receiving the income to agree to pay any income tax at the higher rate. Where a variation includes the setting up of a trust, those whose entitlement goes into the trust will be regarded as settlors of the trust fund, both for income tax and capital gains tax, so that for example parents whose share is given up in favour of infant children will still be taxed on the income so long as the children are under 18 and unmarried.

A deed of variation or disclaimer could be used to advantage where, for example, an estate has been left to the surviving spouse without the deceased's nil rate threshold having been used. If the surviving spouse is already adequately provided for, part of the estate could be diverted to, say, the children. It could also be useful where, for example, children have sufficient assets of their own and would prefer legacies to go to their own children, subject to what is said above about trusts.

Deeds of variation and disclaimer can therefore be used to lessen the overall tax burden, but it is necessary for all concerned to consent to the arrangement, and they should be regarded as something in reserve rather than a substitute for appropriate planning.

Two other ways of building flexibility into a will are worth consideration. It is possible for someone making a will to leave a 'letter of wishes' asking the personal representatives to give effect to the requests in the letter. This is particularly useful for dealing with chattels and personal effects, and is treated for inheritance tax purposes as if it had been part of the will. The other useful provision is the ability to create a discretionary trust by will, out of which the trustees can make distributions within two years of the death, which are again treated as having been made by the will.

Insurance

Life assurance may often be useful in planning for inheritance tax. It is not always possible to reconcile making adequate provision for the family with reducing the tax liability, and insurance may then be used to cover the anticipated liability.

There is no point in insuring your own life for the benefit of your estate, because the proceeds would then form part of the estate and attract inheritance tax. Furthermore, they would not be available until the grant of probate or administration is obtained. If, however, a policy on your life is arranged by someone with an insurable interest, say your children, or you take out a policy yourself and pay the premiums, with the proceeds in trust for someone else, again say your children, the funds will not be taxable in your estate. If you pay the premiums on a trust policy, each payment is a separate gift, but you will usually be able to show that it is normal expenditure out of income, and thus exempt from inheritance tax, or, if not, covered by the annual exemption of £3,000 for transfers out of capital.

Tax points

- Equalising estates of husband and wife was previously sound practice in most cases to make use of lower inheritance tax rates, making sure that the benefit was not then lost on the first death by bringing the estates together again. Now that there is only a single 40% rate above the exempt threshold of £150,000, no extra savings will be made once each has used that nil threshold. It may be better to leave most of the excess over the nil threshold to the surviving spouse, to avoid tax on the first death and give maximum flexibility for the future. The income tax and capital gains tax position needs to be looked at as well.

- Whilst it is beyond the scope of this book to deal in detail with discretionary trusts, it is possible, in order to use up the £150,000 nil threshold, to leave £150,000 or other appropriate amount to a trust where the trustees have a discretion as to what they do with the income. You could include your wife/husband as one of the beneficiaries. The supporting capital is thus not transferred to your spouse directly to swell his/her estate for tax purposes on eventual death, but any shortage of income may be made good by the trustees exercising their discretion to pay income to him/her. Professional advice is absolutely essential since this is a very complicated area.

- A discretionary trust is also useful where there is some uncertainty at the time of making the will as to who should benefit. A transfer of the capital to one or more individuals by the trustees within two years after your death will be treated for tax purposes as having been made by your will, and will have the same effect.

- Where tax at death cannot be avoided, consider covering the liability through life assurance, the proceeds of which belong to those who will have to bear the tax.

- If you leave your entire estate to your spouse, he/she can make lifetime transfers out of your combined wealth to an extent which he/she sees as sensible depending on the family circumstances from time to time. Those transfers may be completely exempt if they are covered by annual or marriage exemptions, or potentially exempt, becoming completely exempt if your spouse survives for seven years after making them (and where they exceed the nil rate threshold they would be subject to tapering relief on survival for three years). Unless you use appropriate trust provisions, you cannot ensure that your

spouse will carry out your wishes, since if it is left to him/her uncon-
ditionally, it is up to the spouse what he/she does with it.

- Although those entitled to your estate have the right to vary the way it
  is to be distributed, it is useful for your will to contain authority for a
  deed of variation, since this makes it clear to the beneficiaries that they
  would not be acting against your wishes.

- If you are apprehensive about leaving outright bequests to certain
  people, but still want them to benefit, you could leave an amount in
  trust for them to receive the income it produces, and in certain circumstances, the capital. There are only minimal, if any, taxation disadvantages and it may give you the comfort of knowing that, for example,
  an adult child, whilst able to benefit immediately from the income,
  does not have an outright capital sum until a later stage when he/she
  is better able to manage it.

- Since all gifts to your spouse are exempt from inheritance tax, it will
  often be more tax effective to leave agricultural and/or business
  property to someone else, otherwise agricultural and business
  property relief will be wasted. The tax position should not, however,
  override family and commercial considerations.

- Where business property and agricultural property reliefs are at the
  rate of 100%, deferring gifts of such property until your death avoids
  any charge to capital gains tax and also any problems of the relief
  being withdrawn at death because the donee has disposed of the
  property. But today's reliefs may not be available tomorrow, and you
  may still prefer to make lifetime gifts now, deferring any capital gains
  tax under the gifts relief provisions (see page 52).

- Although wealth left to the next generation will be liable to inheritance
  tax on your death, whereas it will not be liable if left to your spouse,
  tax is avoided on any increase in value between your death and that of
  your spouse, if the next generation inherits at the death of the first
  rather than the second parent.

- Changing legislation, as well as family circumstances, make it important to review wills regularly.

36
Tax on your investments

Introduction

This chapter outlines the tax position on the main forms of investment available to the majority of taxpayers. More detailed information is given in chapter 37 on investing in banks and building societies and in chapter 38 on stocks and shares. The following investments are not dealt with in this chapter but are covered in the chapters indicated:

(a) Industrial buildings (chapter 22).
(b) Unquoted trading companies through the business expansion scheme (chapter 29).
(c) Single premium life assurance policies-investment bonds (chapter 40).
(d) Chattels and valuables (chapter 39).

The information given on each type of investment is so that you can see the effect of taxation on the income and capital growth. It is not intended to replace advice on the investments themselves, which you should seek from appropriate sources.

Investing in building societies and banks (other than the National Savings Bank)

Most people who invest in building societies and banks invest in normal interest-bearing accounts. From 6 April 1991 the interest on such accounts is received after deduction of basic rate tax, unless you are able to register to receive interest in full because your total income is expected to be below the tax threshold. If after the end of the tax year the tax deducted is more than your liability, you may claim a repayment of tax from the Revenue. You can claim a repayment before the end of the year if it amounts to £50 or more. If you have received interest in full and it is found at the end of the tax year that some tax is due, the tax will have to be paid. There are other types of investment on offer—for example, the Tax Exempt Special Savings Account (TESSA) which has been available since 1 January 1991. For details on the tax treatment of the various accounts, see chapter 37.

National Savings Bank accounts

The National Savings Bank operates both ordinary and investment accounts. Interest on both types of account is credited annually on 31 December without deduction of income tax. Any tax payable is then collected from you by the Revenue by adjusting your PAYE coding or in an assessment.

The first £70 of interest on ordinary accounts is exempt from tax (for husband and wife, £70 each). The rate of interest is, however, too low to make the exemption worthwhile, being 5% on balances of £500 or more and 2½% on lower balances. Ordinary accounts do have the convenience of allowing you to withdraw up to £250 cash straight away.

The investment account usually pays interest at a competitive rate and will give you a cash flow advantage compared with investing in other banks or building societies if you have spare personal allowances to cover the interest received but are not completely exempt from tax, so that you would have to wait for a tax repayment where tax had been deducted. One month's notice is required for withdrawals.

Fixed interest national savings certificates

These certificates are issued in £25 units. They may be attractive to those paying income tax at the higher rate, since the interest, at rates guaranteed for five years, accumulates over the period of the investment, and when the certificates are cashed the capital appreciation is totally free from income tax and capital gains tax. They may also be attractive to someone whose income would otherwise exceed the age allowance income limit (see page 389). New issues are made fairly frequently, so you need to check the details of the issue currently on offer. A maximum holding of certificates is prescribed for each issue, that for the 37th issue being £7,500, but an additional £10,000 may be held if existing matured certificates (including index-linked and yearly plan certificates) are reinvested. The certificates may be wholly or partly repaid (in £25 units). They are repaid at their purchase price if encashed during the first year (except for reinvested certificates, which carry interest at 5.5% per annum for each complete three months in the first year), but after that, the tax-free yield rises each year. The compound tax-free annual interest rates for the 37th issue are 5.5% if held for one year, 5.85% for two years, 6.56% for three years, 7.26% for four years and 8% if held for the full five years. After five years, the certificates only earn interest at the lower general extension rate, so they should be reinvested into other issues.

National savings index-linked certificates

As with the fixed interest certificates, index-linked certificates are issued in £25 units. The current fifth issue of these certificates provides inflation proofing over five years, plus guaranteed extra interest on an increasing scale each year, but biased to discourage early encashment. The original purchase price is index-linked in line with the increase in the retail prices index, and the index linking and extra interest are earned monthly from the date of purchase (subject to the rules for early encashment). At the end of each year, the index increases and extra interest are capitalised, and the total amount then qualifies for index-linking and extra interest in the following year. The compound extra interest over the full five years is 4.5% in addition to the inflation proofing.

The certificates are repayable in £25 units. If they are cashed within the first year, only the amount invested is repaid. If they are cashed after the first year, they qualify for the index increases but no extra interest. If they are cashed after two years, then in addition to the index increases, they attract extra interest for each complete month they have been held since the date of purchase. Although the extra interest rates are guaranteed for only five years, the certificates may be held for longer, and after the fifth year they attract interest at an indexed extension rate. You need to check whether there is a better rate on offer by reinvesting in a current issue. Any increase in the value when the certificates are cashed is free of income tax and capital gains tax.

There is a limit on the holding of certificates in each issue, a maximum of £7,500 being prescribed for the fifth issue, but an additional £10,000 may be held if existing matured certificates (including fixed interest and yearly plan certificates) are reinvested.

These certificates are suitable for taxpayers who are prepared to forgo immediate income to protect their capital in real terms, and the extra interest improves the return and is itself fully index-linked once earned. Those who want regular income could make partial withdrawals of their investment, but at a lower rate of return.

National savings yearly plan

Monthly contributions (minimum £20, maximum £400) by bank standing order can be made to buy a Yearly Plan Savings Certificate at the end of the year. You can then buy further Yearly Plan Certificates by continuing your payments. Tax-free interest is paid at rates guaranteed for five years, the rates at the time of writing being 6.25% per annum on the individual monthly payments in the year of purchase, then 8.25% per annum over the next four years, giving an overall five-year return of 8% per annum. Lower rates apply if the certificates are cashed in early. Repayment is made after 14 days' notice. The rates for early cashing, at the time of writing, payable for each complete month from the day of issue, are 6.75% if the certificate is held for less than two years and 7.5% if held for at least two but less than four years.

Save As You Earn (SAYE)

Regular savings contracts may be made with building societies and banks, under which tax-free bonuses are added to the amount invested at the 5th and 7th anniversaries. The maximum monthly investment is £20.

 A separate SAYE contract may be taken out with a building society, bank or the Department of National Savings if the account is linked to a share option scheme, with the deductions being made from your pay—see chapter 11.

National savings capital bonds

Capital bonds may be purchased in multiples of £100, with an upper limit of £100,000 (excluding any holdings in Series A). The bonds are for a five-year period at a guaranteed rate of interest, which works out at 10.75% per annum compound on Series D if you hold the bonds for the full five years. The interest is added to the bond each year. They may be cashed in early on eight working days' notice (previously three months) but there will be no interest if they are repaid in the first year, and you will earn a lower rate unless you hold the bonds for the full five years.

Repayments of less than £100 will not be made and at least £100 must remain invested.

Although the interest is taxable, tax is paid annually on 1 January rather than being deducted when the interest is credited. The disadvantage for taxpayers is that tax is payable every year even though no income is received from the bond until the end of the five-year period, unless it is wholly or partly cashed in, in which case lower interest rates apply.

National savings income bonds

National savings income bonds are intended for those who wish to invest lump sums at a high rate of interest, and to receive a regular income from their capital. Interest is paid by monthly instalments, either by post or direct to a bank account. Although the interest is taxable, tax is paid annually on 1 January rather than being deducted at the time the interest is received, so there is a cash flow advantage. The bonds are particularly beneficial for those whose income is not high enough for tax to have to be paid. The minimum holding is £2,000 and the maximum £50,000 (in units of £1,000), or £100,000 for a joint holding. Three months notice is required to obtain repayment.

National savings guaranteed growth bonds

The new 'first option' bonds offer fixed rates of interest guaranteed for a year at a time. Unlike other national savings products, tax at the basic rate is deducted from the interest, which is added to the bond annually. Those liable to higher rate tax will have further tax to pay, and those not liable to the 25% rate wil be able to claim a refund. The minimum holding is £1,000 and the maximum £250,000, and bonds can be held indefinitely or cashed at any anniversary date without penalty. Bonds cashed between anniversary dates attract half the normal interest rate from the previous anniversary date. The rate of interest for the first year is 7.25% net (9.67% gross). There is an increased rate of 7.55% net (10.07% gross) for balances of £20,000 or more.

Premium savings bonds

Any person over 16 can buy these bonds. The current maximum holding is £10,000. They do not carry interest, but, once a bond has been held for three calendar months, it is included in a regular monthly draw for prizes of various amounts. All prizes are free of income tax and capital gains tax and the bond itself can be encashed at face value at any time. This gives you the chance to win a tax-free prize, but at the cost of not receiving any income or protection of the real value of your capital.

Children's bonus bonds

National Savings Children's bonus bonds for children under 16 were introduced on 8 July 1991. They are in units of £25 and the maximum holding per child is £1,000. The current issue B attracts daily interest at a flat rate of 5% per annum compound for five years and a bonus of 40.12% of the purchase price on the fifth anniversary, giving an overall guaranteed return over the first five years of 10.9% per annum compound. They may be cashed in before the end of the five years on one month's notice. At the end of five years they may be held for a further five years at revised guaranteed rates of interest, except that they mature at the holder's 21st birthday and no further returns are earned after that time.

All returns are exempt from tax, and parents may provide the funds without affecting their own tax liability.

Local authority stock, bonds and loans

Some local authority stocks are quoted on the Stock Exchange and interest on the stocks is paid after deduction of income tax. Local authorities also raise money by unquoted temporary loans, mortgages and non-negotiable bonds. Interest on these items will usually be paid after deduction of basic rate income tax from 6 April 1991, although if your income is not more than your available personal allowance you can register to receive interest gross in the same way as with bank and building society interest.

Local authority stocks, bonds and loans that are transferable are subject to the accrued income provisions described below (page 410). They are also within the definition of 'qualifying corporate bonds' and are exempt from capital gains tax. See page 436.

Government stocks

These represent borrowings by the British government, and they vary considerably in terms of interest. Some are issued on an index-linked basis so that the interest paid while the stock is held and the capital payment when it is redeemed are dependent on increases in the retail prices index. With the exception of 3½% War Loan, basic rate income tax is usually deducted at source. It is possible, however, to purchase stocks that are on the National Savings Stock Register through your local post office, and thereby to receive interest without deduction of tax although tax has to be paid in due course (on 1 January in the tax year for individuals and on the normal due date for companies). Where appropriate, higher rate tax will be charged on the interest, whether it is first received in full or after deduction of basic rate tax.

Most of the stocks have a redemption date upon which the par value, or index-linked value as the case may be, is paid to the holder, so if you buy them below par you will have a guaranteed capital gain at a given date, which is exempt from capital gains tax. The gain on non-index-linked stock will be fixed in money terms whereas on index-linked stock it is fixed in real terms. In the meantime, the value of the stock will fluctuate with market conditions, so that there may be opportunities to make capital gains before the redemption date. If, however, you make losses they are not allowable for set-off against chargeable gains.

Government stocks can be useful as a means of providing for future known commitments, such as school fees, and if you are inclined to overspend, the government stock is not as readily accessible as a building society account.

Looked at on a pure money return basis, however, a purchase for capital growth may sometimes be no better for a higher rate taxpayer than an investment producing a greater income with no growth prospects. It depends upon the rates of interest being paid from time to time, and the price at which government stock can be purchased.

Interest on government stocks is subject to the accrued income scheme.

Company loan stock

Company loan stock is normally within the definition of 'qualifying corporate bonds' and exempt from capital gains tax in the same way as government stocks (see page 436). Company loan stock is not likely to be so attractive to the individual taxpayer, however, because it is not so readily marketable, there is a greater degree of risk, brokers' commission charges are higher and it is not possible to acquire it through the post office and thus receive interest without deduction of tax. The 'accrued income' rules for reckoning interest on a day to day basis apply (see below).

Accrued income scheme (TA 1988, ss 710–722)

The accrued income scheme applies to interest-bearing marketable securities such as government stocks and to most local authority and company loan stock. It also applies to building society permanent interest bearing shares (see page 416). It does not apply to ordinary or preference shares in a company, units in unit trusts or bank deposits. Nor does it apply to an individual if the nominal value of all securities held does not exceed £5,000 at any time either in the tax year in which the next interest payment on the securities falls due or in the previous tax year (see illustration on pages 423). There are some other limited exceptions.

Interest received is included in income according to the amount accrued on a day to day basis, so that selling just before an interest date does not enable income tax to be avoided on the interest by effectively receiving it as part of the sales proceeds. If you sell before a security goes 'ex dividend', you will be taxed on the accrued interest to the settlement date and the buyer's taxable income will be correspondingly reduced. If you sell ex dividend (so that you get the full interest at the payment date), your taxable income will be reduced and the buyer's increased by the interest applicable to the period between the settlement date and the interest payment date. See example 1.

Example 1

An investor has owned £10,000 12% stock for some years. Interest is payable half-yearly on 12 June and 12 December. Stock goes ex dividend on 6 May 1992.

If sold for settlement on 28 April 1992 (i.e. sold cum dividend)

Buyer receives the full 6 months' interest on 12 June 1992, but effectively 'bought' part of this within his purchase price. Interest accrued due from 13 December 1991 to 28 April 1992 is:

$$£600 \times \frac{138}{183} = \underline{£452.46}$$

Seller's taxable income is increased (by an accrued income charge) and buyer's taxable income reduced (by accrued income relief) of £452.46.

If sold for settlement on 13 May 1992 (i.e. sold ex dividend)

Seller receives the full 6 months' interest on 12 June 1992, but effectively 'bought' part of this by receiving reduced sale proceeds. The interest from 14 May 1992 to 12 June 1992 when he did not own the stock amounts to:

$$£600 \times \frac{30}{183} = \underline{£98.36}$$

Seller's taxable income is reduced (by accrued income relief) and buyer's taxable income increased (by an accrued income charge) of £98.36.

The accrued income adjustments are made in the tax year in which the next interest payment date falls, 1992/93 in this example.

TAX ON YOUR INVESTMENTS 36

Where a sale is through a bank or stockbroker, the accrued interest is shown on the contract note.

Accrued income charges and reliefs must be shown in your tax return (see chapter 9, pages 111 and 113). Most securities covered by the accrued income scheme are exempt from capital gains tax (see page 436).

Ordinary shares in quoted companies

Ordinary shares are 'risk capital' and investors have to be prepared to accept the risk element in return for seeking rising income and capital appreciation. Although quoted shares are readily marketable, the price can fluctuate considerably, so they are not recommended if you may need to make an unplanned sale to meet unexpected commitments.

Dividends attract a tax credit (effectively a proportion of the company's corporation tax, passed on with the dividend) which satisfies basic rate tax liability and is repayable to non-taxpayers. If you are liable to tax above the basic rate you must pay the extra higher rate tax of 15% on the total of the cash received and the tax credit. Gains on disposal are chargeable to capital gains tax in the usual way.

Dividends are included in your income as they arise and are not subject to the 'accrued income' provisions that apply to government, local authority and company loan stocks.

Investment in ordinary shares can be free of income tax and capital gains tax if you invest through a Personal Equity Plan—see page 440.

The detailed treatment of shares, and further information on company loan stock and government stocks, is in chapter 38.

Purchased life annuities

If you pay a lump sum to a life assurance company to get a fixed annual sum in return, the annual sum is partly regarded as a non-taxable return of capital, thus giving a comparatively high after-tax income. You have, however, effectively spent your capital to secure the annual income and thus at the end of the annuity term the capital is exhausted.

It is therefore common for purchased life annuities to be acquired in conjunction with life assurance policies, part of the annual income being used to fund the life assurance premium so that at the end of the annuity period the life assurance policy proceeds can replace the purchase price of the annuity. There are numerous variations on this sort of arrangement—see chapter 40.

Tax points

- If you have spare personal allowances, national savings bank accounts still have a cash flow advantage over other bank accounts and building

412

society accounts unless you can register to receive the bank or building society interest in full, without tax being deducted. This needs to be weighed against the interest rates on offer. See chapter 37.

- Index-linked national savings certificates offer inflation proofing plus some guaranteed extra interest, the best return being available if you invest for a full five years.

- Although investing for the full term shows the highest returns with national savings certificates, they can be repaid gradually over the period in £25 units, giving the opportunity to draw a tax-free income. The increased investment limits for the latest issues make this more attractive.

- Some of the National Savings products are attractive to higher rate taxpayers because of the tax-exempt receipts. The Department of National Savings issues a booklet describing its products, which is useful to have so that you can keep up to date with what is on offer.

- Once your national savings certificates have matured they attract the general extension rate of interest, which is lower than other rates available. Make sure you reinvest matured certificates into one of the current issues.

- If you are a small investor, you can benefit from a wide range of investments through a unit or investment trust. The trust is exempt from tax on its gains. You pay tax on income and gains in the normal way. See pages 434–436.

- If you have a reasonable amount of capital, you can use the certain increase in the value of dated Government stocks to hedge the maximum loss on the purchase of ordinary shares. Suppose that safety of capital was all that mattered and you had £10,000 to invest.

Invest in £10,000 nominal of dated Government stock at £75 per £100		7,500
Invest in ordinary shares		2,500
		10,000
Surplus on Government stock if held to redemption	2,500	
Less maximum loss on ordinary shares	2,500	—
Original investment intact		£10,000

Income will have been received in the meantime, with the possibility of capital appreciation on the ordinary shares.

- For those who are liable to tax, capital bonds (see page 408) have the disadvantage of tax being payable every year even though no income is received until the end of the investment period.

37
Investing in banks and building societies

Investing in building societies and banks (other than the National Savings Bank) (TA 1988, ss 477A, 480A, 481, 482)

Investing in building societies and banks is usually regarded as a low risk investment. If the bank or building society should fail, however, the maximum compensation is currently 75% of £20,000 for investment in a bank and 90% of £20,000 for a building society investment.

Building societies and banks, including the National Savings Bank, used to report customers' interest to the Revenue only if it exceeded a certain level, but the limits have been removed and all interest, no matter how small, is now reported.

From 6 April 1991, interest from building societies and from banks other than the National Savings Bank is paid after deduction of basic rate tax unless either you can register to receive it in full (see below) or the interest arises under one of the following headings.

(a) Certificates of deposit and sterling or foreign currency time deposits, providing the loan is not less than £50,000 and is repayable within five years.
(b) Bank and building society accounts in the names of charities.
(c) Bank accounts in the names of companies (but tax is deducted from interest on company building society accounts).
(d) General client deposit accounts with building societies or banks operated by solicitors and estate agents.
(e) Accounts held at overseas branches of UK and foreign banks and building societies.
(f) Bank and building society accounts held by someone who is not ordinarily resident in the UK and has provided a declaration to that effect.
(g) Accounts held by Personal Equity Plan managers (see page 441).

The interest under these headings is paid in full and is charged to tax at the appropriate rates in the tax year or company accounting period in which it is received.

414

Where basic rate tax has been deducted by the payer and your tax rate is above or below 25%, you will have to pay the extra or claim some back.

Receiving bank and building society interest in full (TMA 1970, s 99A; TA 1988, ss 477A, 480A, 480B)

Although basic rate tax is now normally deducted from interest paid by banks and building societies, you can register to receive the interest in full if you expect your total taxable income to be below your available allowances. The relevant forms may be obtained from banks, building societies and local authorities (see page 409) or from your tax office. A separate form is needed for each account. A parent can register the account of a child under 16 if the child's total income will be less than the personal allowance (£3,445 for 1992/93), providing not more than £100 income arises from parental gifts (a separate £100 limit applying to income from gifts from each parent).

Even though the interest is received in full, the special rules for charging National Savings Bank interest outlined on page 417 do not apply and the interest is taxed as income of the year in which it is credited to your account.

You are required to give written notice straight away to banks and building societies who are paying you interest in full if your circumstances change and you are no longer eligible to receive gross interest. You should also let your tax office know about any tax you may have to pay. Where tax has been underpaid, it will be collected either by adjustment to a PAYE coding or by assessment. A penalty of up to £3,000 may be imposed if you fraudulently or negligently certify that you are entitled to register to receive interest in full, or if you fail to notify that you are no longer entitled to receive interest in full.

It is not possible to register some accounts and not others. You must expect to have *no tax liability at all* in order to be eligible. If you cannot register, say because your income is just above your available allowances, you will be entitled to a refund of any tax overpaid, and a refund can be claimed as soon as at least £50 tax is owing to you. You do not have to wait until the end of the tax year.

Building societies: change of status

Building societies are now able to convert to companies under the Building Societies Act 1986. If they do, they will be subject to normal company and bank legislation. Possible adverse consequences of conversion on building society members were removed by the Finance Act 1988, which provided that members are not liable to capital gains tax on rights to acquire shares in the company in priority to other subscribers, or at a discount, or rights to acquire shares free of charge; these provisions apply whether the rights are obtained directly or through trustees. If any cash payment is made to the members (for example as compensation for not being allowed to vote on conversion), it will be liable to capital gains tax, and free shares will be similarly liable as and when they are disposed of. Such gains may, however, be covered by the annual capital gains tax exemption if not already used.

Building society permanent interest bearing shares (FA 1991, ss 51, 52, Schs 10 & 11)

Where you have a share account in a building society, it is a chargeable asset for capital gains tax but indexation allowance is not available. When you close a share account, you normally draw out only what you put in (plus interest that has been charged to income tax), so there is no capital gain and the denial of indexation allowance means that you cannot create an allowable capital loss.

From 1 June 1991, building societies are able to issue a new type of share—permanent interest bearing shares (PIBS). These shares are acquired through and quoted on the Stock Exchange and are freely transferable, dealing charges being incurred on buying and selling. You are not entitled to compensation if the building society fails, and the shares are irredeemable, so what you get back on sale will depend on prevailing interest rates and the soundness of the building society. The tax treatment of the shares is different from that of other building society shares. Tax is deducted from interest on the shares by the building society (except for certain interest to non-residents) and you cannot register to receive it in full. The shares are within the definition of qualifying corporate bonds (see page 436) and are exempt from capital gains tax, so that no allowable losses may be created. They are also within the accrued income scheme (see page 410), so that adjustments for accrued interest are made when they are transferred.

Where the shares are issued to existing members in priority to other people this will not result in a capital gains tax charge.

Tax Exempt Special Savings Accounts (TESSA) (TA 1988, ss 326A, 326B, 326C)

Since 1 January 1991, anyone over 18 has been able to open a tax exempt special savings account (TESSA) with a bank or building society, husband and wife being entitled to one each. If the qualifying conditions are satisfied for five years (or until death if earlier), the interest earned during that period is totally tax-free.

Not more than £3,000 may be deposited during the first twelve months from the date the account is opened, nor more than £1,800 in any later year, nor more than £9,000 in total. Depositors may withdraw interest credited, providing an amount out of the interest equivalent to basic rate tax is left in the account. Such withdrawals need not be declared on tax returns.

The tax-exempt status is lost if the balance on the account falls below an amount equal to the sums deposited plus basic rate tax at the appropriate rate on all interest credited, or if the account is assigned or used as security for a loan. If the tax-exempt status is lost, all interest credited to that point is treated as income of the year in which the rules were breached, even though some of it may relate to earlier years. Such interest would have to be declared on your tax return and would be liable to tax at your highest rate, unless it was covered by available allowances.

After five years, the investment may be withdrawn if you wish. Any later interest on the account is fully taxable in the normal way. A new TESSA may then be opened, with the same investment limits as the original account.

Investing in the National Savings Bank (TA 1988, s 325)

Interest on accounts with the National Savings Bank is received in full and is charged to tax under the provisions of Schedule D, Case III. The first £70 of interest received on *ordinary* accounts is exempt from tax. Husband and wife get an exemption of £70 each. Any unused part of the £70 exemption cannot be transferred to the other spouse. There is no exemption for interest on investment accounts.

Date on which interest arises

Interest arises for tax purposes on the date when it is credited to your account. It is not apportioned over the period when it accrues.

Basis of assessment (TA 1988, ss 64, 66, 67)

The rules of Schedule D, Case III provide that tax is normally charged on the interest arising in the previous income tax year. In the first and second tax years in which interest arises, however, tax is charged on the interest arising in the tax year itself, and it is also open to the taxpayer (but not to the Revenue) to elect for the charge for the third tax year to be based on the interest arising in the third year itself. The choice for the taxpayer is thus whether the second or the third year's interest is charged to tax twice. See example 1, in which such an election by the taxpayer would be unfavourable, as it would cause £130 to be taxed twice (in 1989/90 and 1990/91) rather than £80 (in 1988/89 and 1989/90).

Tax cannot normally be charged for a period after a source of interest ceases, so the charge for the tax year when you close an account is based on the interest arising in that year. It is open to the Revenue to charge tax for the last year but one on the interest arising in that year, if it is greater than that arising in the previous year. In example 1, the Revenue would not do so, as the assessment for 1991/92 would be reduced from £178 to £150. In any event, one year's interest will escape assessment, thus compensating for one year's interest in the opening years being taxed more than once.

Technically *each* deposit in a National Savings Bank account is a separate source of income, and *each* withdrawal the cessation of a source, requiring the opening and closing years' rules to be applied as necessary. The Revenue tend, however, to ignore the movement on accounts unless a

Example 1

A National Savings Bank investment account was opened in November 1987 and is closed on 5 August 1992. Interest credited and related assessments are as follows:

Interest credited		Assessments	
December 1987	£10	1987/88	£10
December 1988	£80	1988/89	£80
December 1989	£130	1989/90	£80
December 1990	£178	1990/91	£130
December 1991	£150	1991/92	£178
August 1992	£65	1992/93	£65

substantial tax advantage is being obtained by the movement of funds into and out of them, in which case the strict rules will be applied.

Date of payment of tax (TA 1988, s 5)

The due date of payment is 1 January within the tax year. The assessment on 1 January may cover tax at all rates, but sometimes the excess over the basic rate is included in the higher rate tax assessment on taxed income due on 1 December.

Death of account holder or spouse

When a single person or a married person with his/her own account dies, any interest credited between 6 April and the date of death is charged to tax in the tax year of death, with the Revenue option applying to the previous year. Interest credited after the date of death is charged on the personal representatives. By Revenue concession A7, these rules need not apply to an account if it is left to a surviving spouse, and the normal previous year basis will continue unless the Revenue are asked to apply the closing year rules. The interest assessable in the tax year of death will therefore be that of the previous year, split on a time basis between the deceased's estate and the survivor.

In the case of a joint account between husband and wife, Revenue concession A7 (outlined above) applies (unless the Revenue are asked not to apply it), so that the interest charged in the year of death is that of the previous year, an appropriate proportion applying to the estate of the deceased. If the concession does not apply, the surviving spouse will continue to be taxed on the previous year basis on his or her share of the interest, but the rules for new accounts will apply to the interest relating to the share acquired from the other spouse. See example 2.

Example 2

Husband and wife have longstanding joint National Savings Bank account and husband died on 5 August 1991. Interest was credited as follows:

	Husband's share	Wife's share		Total
		Own	From husband	
	£	£	£	£
Dec 1989	60	60		120
Dec 1990	75	75		150
Dec 1991	30	90	60	180
Dec 1992		100	100	200
Dec 1993		105	105	210

If concession A7 applies, previous year's interest will be taxed in 1991/92, i.e. £150, the proportion of the assessable interest from 6 April 1991 to 5 August 1991, i.e. £50, being split between husband and wife and the remaining £100 being taxed wholly on the wife, and assessments will be:

	Husband	Wife		Total
		Own	From husband	
	£	£	£	£
1990/91	60	60		120
1991/92	25	75	50	150
1992/93		90	90	180
1993/94		100	100	200
1994/95		105	105	210

If the concession had not been applied the husband's 1990/91 and 1991/92 assessments would have been increased to his actual shares of interest, and the wife would be charged according to the new source rules on the share she inherited from him, so the assessments would have been:

	Husband	Wife		Total
		Own	From husband	
	£	£	£	£
1990/91	75	60		135
1991/92	30	75	60	165
1992/93		90	100	190
1993/94		100	100	200
1994/95		105	105	210

Partners and other joint owners

The assessment is not joint. Each partner or co-owner is assessed on his share. The rules for new and discontinued sources apply to each person's share.

Tax points

- If you close your National Savings Bank investment account, try to time it so that you maximise the saving from one year's interest escaping tax.

- The rules of assessment for National Savings Bank accounts set out on page 417 also apply to interest paid by the National Savings Bank on capital bonds, income bonds and deposit bonds.

- If you do not register to receive bank and building society interest in full, even though you are entitled to do so, you will still get the overpaid tax back. You can claim before the end of the tax year if you are owed £50 or more. If you do not know your tax office, fill in form R95 in leaflet IR 111 (which is obtainable from any tax office or tax enquiry centre).

- Make sure you do not register to receive bank and building society interest in full unless you expect all your income to be covered by your available allowances. Even if some tax will be repayable, you are not eligible to register unless you will have no tax liability at all.

- If you have registered to receive bank and building society interest in full because your income is less than your available tax allowances, there is now no difference between investing in the National Savings Bank and investing in other banks and building societies. You need to compare the rates of interest on offer. If you cannot register but have allowances available to set against interest, you will still get a cash flow benefit from a National Savings Bank account, because for other accounts you will usually have to wait for a tax refund.

- Even if most of your bank and building society interest will be covered by your allowances, you cannot register some accounts and not others. It is all or nothing.

- It is only the general client deposit accounts maintained by solicitors and estate agents on which interest is received without tax being deducted, and not their normal accounts for office monies.

- A joint bank or building society account of husband and wife is normally treated as owned in equal shares, with the survivor automatically entitled to take over the whole account when the other dies, and it is unlikely that banks and building societies would be prepared to vary this treatment. It is, however, possible for the underlying beneficial ownership to be altered, so that specific action could be taken to sever the joint tenancy and the account could be held as tenants in common (see page 377) in whatever proportions you wish, providing the spouse giving up part of his or her share does so as an outright gift. If the account continued to be treated as a common pool from which each could and did draw freely, the Revenue would be unlikely to accept that an outright gift had been made.

- If you do take specific action to hold a bank or building society account as tenants in common, then although the bank may regard the account as going automatically to the survivor when the other died, the survivor would have to account to the personal representatives for the deceased spouse's share.

38
Investing in stocks and shares

Background

When you invest through the Stock Exchange, the principal securities you may acquire are company shares or loan stock, government stocks, local authority loan stock and building society permanent interest bearing shares (see page 416). You may also invest in unquoted company stocks and shares and unquoted local authority loans. Unquoted local authority loans are dealt with on page 409. Unquoted company stocks and shares are dealt with in this chapter.

Income tax treatment of dividends and interest

Dividends paid by companies on their shares represent a distribution of profits to the members. The company pays part of its corporation tax – called advance corporation tax – when it pays a dividend, and an equivalent amount – called a tax credit – is passed on to the shareholder at the same time. This tax credit covers the shareholder's liability to tax at the basic rate.

If you take scrip shares instead of a dividend (a scrip option), the cash dividend forgone is treated as your income, unless it is substantially different from the market value of the shares, 'substantially' being interpreted by the Revenue as 15% or more either way. In that event your deemed income is the market value of the shares on the first day of dealing. Basic rate tax on the notional dividend is treated as paid (but you cannot claim a refund if you are a non-taxpayer). Those liable to higher rate tax will pay tax at 15% on the grossed up amount (TA 1988, ss 249–251). The capital gains tax effect is dealt with on page 434. Where scrip dividends are issued to a corporate shareholder, they are not treated as income, and have a capital gains base cost of nil. As far as the company issuing the scrip dividend is concerned, the issue does not count as a distribution and therefore ACT does not have to be paid (TA 1988, s 230).

Interest paid by companies on both quoted and unquoted stocks, and by local authorities and the Government on quoted stocks, is paid after deduction of basic rate tax, except for interest on 3½% War Loan and on some other government stocks if they are on the National Savings Stock Register and are bought from the post office. The interest on these stocks is received without deduction of tax, and tax at lower, basic and higher rates as appropriate is due for payment on 1 January in the tax year.

The gross amount of interest from which tax is deducted, and dividends plus their accompanying tax credits, are shown on your tax return as income of the tax year in which they are received. The income is included in your income of that year for tax purposes, except for sales of marketable securities other than shares, when interest for the period which spans the date of sale is apportioned so that the seller is taxed on that part of the interest accruing up to the date of sale, and the buyer on interest accruing after that date. This apportionment does not, however, apply if the nominal value of all the securities held by you does not exceed £5,000 either in the tax year in which the next interest payment on the securities falls due or in the previous tax year (see page 411). If, for example, you buy or sell securities in February 1992 on which interest is paid in June and December, the two tax years to look at are 1992/93 (in which the June interest date falls) and 1991/92 (the previous year). If the interest had been payable in March and September the two tax years to look at would have been 1991/92 (the interest date year) and 1990/91.

Where tax is due at the higher rate on dividend income and on interest where basic rate tax has been deducted at source, it is charged in a single assessment covering all sources of income from which tax has been deducted before receipt. The tax is due for payment on 1 December following the relevant tax year.

If you are either not liable to tax or liable wholly or partly at the 20% lower rate, you can claim a refund of tax deducted from interest and tax credits on dividends.

There are some special provisions covering 'deep discounted stocks' (see page 437).

Capital gains tax treatment of stocks and shares

For capital gains tax, shares and interest-bearing stocks are treated differently. Government stocks, qualifying corporate bonds and local authority stocks are exempt from capital gains tax (subject to some special rules for losses on qualifying corporate bonds—see page 436). Where interest-bearing stocks are chargeable to capital gains tax, they are subject to different rules for identifying disposals with acquisitions from those relating to shares. The provisions are outlined below, but this area has become one of the most complicated in the tax legislation and it is not possible to deal with all the complexities.

Capital gains tax when shares are disposed of (TCGA 1992, ss 35, 53–55, 104–110 and Sch 2)

When shares are disposed of, a capital gains tax computation is made. The

423

general rules for calculating gains and losses outlined in chapter 4 apply, but because of the special problems associated with shares (bonus and rights issues, takeovers, mergers etc.), the need to deal with shares already on hand on 6 April 1965 when capital gains tax started, and with those on hand when indexation was introduced, there are inevitable complications for shareholders with even a modest portfolio.

Shares acquired before the commencement of indexation

From 6 April 1988, taxpayers have been able to make a single irrevocable election (a rebasing election) to treat all assets owned on 31 March 1982 (except plant and machinery) as having been acquired on that day for their 31 March 1982 market value (see page 41). This means that valuations are needed for all assets held on that day. Where valuations of unquoted holdings are needed by several shareholders, the Revenue Shares Valuation Division will open negotiations with the shareholders or their advisers before being asked by a tax office, providing all shareholders with similar holdings will accept the value agreed. Someone with pre- and post-6 April 1965 unquoted holdings may, by concession, have them valued as a single holding, which may give a higher value per share. This does not affect the rules for matching disposals with acquisitions.

If the rebasing election has been made, taxpayers can effectively treat all such shares of the same class in the same company as a single asset, called the 1982 holding. (Strictly shares acquired before 6 April 1965 do not merge with those acquired afterwards, but since they are all regarded as costing the same amount it is considered that they need not be kept separate.)

If the rebasing election has not been made, unquoted shares acquired before 6 April 1965 must be kept separate from the 1982 holding. Quoted shares are treated in the same way unless an election has been made to treat them as acquired at their value on 6 April 1965, in which case they form part of the 1982 holding. For this purpose shares are divided into two categories, one covering preference shares and the other ordinary shares, and separate elections can be made for each category. The time limit for bringing pre-6 April 1965 quoted shares into the 1982 holding is two years from the end of the tax year in which the first disposal occurs after 5 April 1985 (31 March 1985 for companies).

Where the rebasing election is not made, the 31 March 1982 value is still used to calculate the gain or loss unless using the previous rules would show a lower gain or loss. If one method shows a loss and the other a gain, the transaction is treated as giving neither gain nor loss. If, however, the previous rules would already have given neither a loss nor a gain (see page 431), that result will not be disturbed.

Shares acquired after indexation was introduced

Quoted or unquoted shares of the same company and class acquired on or after 6 April 1982 (1 April 1982 for companies) are regarded as a single asset from 6 April 1985 (1 April 1985), called the 'new holding'. It grows with acquisitions and is depleted by disposals (see identification rules below) on or after 6 April 1985.

Identification of disposals

There are two identification rules that override the normal rules dealt with below. Shares of the same company and class that are purchased and sold on the same day are matched with each other. If the 'same day' rule does not apply, disposals by a company that owns 2% or more of the issued shares of a particular class are matched with acquisitions in the previous month (latest first) then with acquisitions in the following month (earliest first).

Where neither of these special rules applies, disposals on or after 6 April 1985 (1 April 1985 for companies) are identified as follows.

(a)   First with acquisitions within the previous nine days (and no indexation allowance is available).
(b)   Second with those in the 'new holding'.
(c)   Third with those in the '1982 holding'.
(d)   Fourth with those acquired before 6 April 1965 (unless, in the case of quoted shares, they are included in the '1982 holding' because of an election to include them at 6 April 1965 values) taking each acquisition separately and treating later acquisitions as sold before earlier acquisitions, i.e. 'last in, first out'.

See examples 1 to 6 and refer to the general computation rules in chapter 4.

Indexation allowance

For shares held at 6 April 1982 (1 April 1982 for companies), the indexation allowance is calculated by taking the increase in the retail prices index between March 1982 and the month of disposal. Where the rebasing election has been made to treat all assets acquired before 31 March 1982 as being acquired at their market value on that date, the indexation allowance is based on that 31 March 1982 value. Where the election has not been made, the indexation calculation is based on the higher of the value of the shares at 31 March 1982 and their cost or, for shares held at 6 April 1965, their 6 April 1965 market value when using that value to calculate the gain or loss (see page 430).

Indexation allowance on the 'new holding' is worked out from the date expenditure is incurred. The holding is maintained at an indexed value, and that value is uplifted by further indexation every time an event occurs that alters the value of the holding (such as a purchase or a sale). Strictly, the legislation requires a record to be kept of the unindexed value of the holding as well, but this is not necessary. The 'new holding' rules were introduced on 6 April 1985 (1 April 1985 for companies) and an opening figure for the indexed value was required at that date, working out indexation allowance on each acquisition from 6 April 1982 (1 April 1982) onwards. (If the calcula-

Example 1

Quoted shares acquired:	Number	Cost
		£
1.1.59	2,000	10,400
10.9.64	500	1,000
Between 6.4.65 and 5.4.82 (1982 holding)	5,000	35,000
New holding:		
Between 6.4.82 and 5.4.85	4,000⎫	12,000⎫
31.5.85	2,000⎭	18,000⎭

Sales	Number	Consideration
30.4.90	2,000	11,000
28.4.92	10,000	80,000

Market value £3 per share at 6 April 1965 and £5 per share at 31 March 1982. No election had been made to include shares acquired before 6 April 1965 in the 1982 holding nor a rebasing election to treat all assets acquired before 31 March 1982 as being acquired at 31 March 1982 value.

Retail price index at April 1992 is 138.8, so that the increase from March 1982 is 74.7%.

Sales identified on 'last in, first out' basis (see page 425)

	£	Gain (loss) £
Sale of 2,000 on 30.4.90 out of 'new holding'	11,000	
Indexed cost (see example 2)	(13,695)	(2,695)
Sale of 10,000 on 28.4.92:		
Sale out of 'new holding' 4,000/10,000 × 80,000	32,000	
Indexed cost (see example 2)	(30,402)	(1,598)
Sale of 5,000 shares in '1982 holding' Allowable loss (see example 3)		(11,145)
Sale of 500 shares acquired 10.9.64 and of 500 shares out of 2,000 acquired 1.1.59 both treated as giving neither gain nor loss (see example 4)		—
Giving total allowable loss of		£(12,242)

tion was delayed until the time of the first event affecting the value of the holding, it would not significantly affect the figures.)

Where the rebasing election has been made, the 'indexed value' approach can be used for the 1982 holding, although this is not provided for in the legislation. Even where there is no rebasing election, the 1982 holding could stil be maintained on an indexed basis, but figures would be required both for indexed cost and indexed 31 March 1982 value (basing indexation allowance in both cases on the higher of those two figures). (For an illustration see page 434.)

If the index has fallen since the previous event, no adjustment is made to the indexed value. Where partly paid shares are acquired, the instalments of the purchase price qualify for indexation allowance from the date the shares

---

Example 2

	Number of shares	Indexed pool of expenditure £
New holding at 6.4.85 per example 1 (acquisitions between 6.4.82 and 5.4.85)	4,000	12,000
If at 6.4.85 the entire holding had been sold, the indexation allowance would have been, say		1,200
Giving indexed pool of expenditure at 6.4.85 of		13,200
Indexed rise 6.4.85–31.5.85 (.005)		66
Addition 31.5.85	2,000	18,000
	6,000	31,266
Indexed rise 31.5.85–30.4.90 (.314)		9,818
		41,084
Indexed cost of shares sold $\frac{2,000}{6,000} \times 41,084$	2,000	13,695
	4,000	27,389
Indexed rise 30.4.90—28.4.92 (.110)		3,013
		30,402
Indexed cost of shares sold	4,000	30,402

Example 3

'1982 holding' per example 1
5,000 shares cost £35,000, value at 31.3.82
£5 each = £25,000.

	£	£
Sale proceeds 28.4.92 5,000/10,000 × 80,000	40,000	40,000
Cost	(35,000)	
31.3.82 value		(25,000)
Indexation allowance 74.7% on cost (being higher than 31.3.82 value)	(26,145)	(26,145)
	(21,145) or	(11,145)
Lower loss allowed		£11,145

Example 4

	Number of shares	Cost (£)
Pre 6.4.65 acquisitions per example 1:		
1.1.59	2,000	10,400
10.9.64	500	1,000

Identified with sales on 'last in, first out' basis.
Sale 28.4.92 of 500 shares acquired 10.9.64:

Using old 6.4.65 rules

	£	£
Sale proceeds 500/10,000 × 80,000	4,000	4,000
Cost 10.9.64	(1,000)	
6.4.65 value		(1,500)
Indexation allowance 74.7% on 31.3.82 value (500 @ £5 each = £2,500, which is higher than both cost, £1,000 and 6.4.65 value, £1,500)	(1,868)	(1,868)
or	1,132	632
Lower gain is		£632

Using 31.3.82 value

	£
Sale proceeds	4,000
31.3.82 value	(2,500)
Indexation allowance (as above)	(1,868)
Loss	£(368)

Transaction treated as at neither gain nor loss

example 4 continued

Sale 28.4.92 of 500 shares acquired
  1.1.59:

Using old 6.4.65 rules	£	£
Sale proceeds 500/10,000 × 80,000	4,000	4,000
Cost 1.1.59 500/2,000 × 10,400	(2,600)	
6.4.65 value		(1,500)
Indexation allowance 74.7% on:		
£2,600 (being higher than 31.3.82		
value of £2,500)	(1,942)	
£2,500 31.3.82 value (being higher		
than 6.4.65 value of		
£1,500)		(1,868)
Loss	£(542)	or gain £632

Transaction treated as no gain/no loss. This result stands and the
calculation using 31.3.82 value is not made.

Example 5

Facts as in example 1, but rebasing election has been made to use
31.3.82 value for all pre-31.3.82 acquisitions.

Treatment of sale of 2,000 shares on 30.4.90 and of 4,000 out of
10,000 shares sold on 28.4.92 is unchanged, since they comprise
the 'new holding'.

Since the '1982 holding' and the shares acquired before 6 April
1965 are all treated as acquired at their 31.3.82 value of £5, the gain
or loss on the remaining 6,000 shares sold on 28.4.92 can be
worked out in a single calculation as follows:

	£	£	£
Sale proceeds 6,000 shares 6,000/			
10,000 × 80,000		48,000	
31.3.82 value (£5 each)	30,000		
Indexation allowance 74.7%	22,410	52,410	
Allowable loss			(4,410)
The loss on 2,000 'new holding'			
shares sold on 30.4.90 was			(2,695)
The gain on 4,000 'new holding'			
shares sold on 28.4.92 was			1,598
Overall loss			
(compared with loss of £12,242 without election)			£(5,507)

are issued, unless they are paid more than twelve months later, in which case they qualify from the date they are paid. This does not apply to the privatisation issues, which qualify for indexation from the date of issue even if some instalments are paid more than twelve months later. (Any privatisation issue vouchers that are used to reduce bills are deducted from the allowable cost. Any free shares acquired later are added to the holding and treated as acquired at market value on the first day of dealing in them.)

See example 5 for the computation if the rebasing election had been made to use 31 March 1982 value for all pre-31 March 1982 acquisitions.

The figures used in the examples are not intended to be indicative of probable values and are used merely to illustrate the rules. In many cases, 31 March 1982 values will be higher than earlier costs and the irrevocable election will be made. But the election needs to be considered in the light of all the chargeable assets held on 31 March 1982 and not just the particular asset sold.

Shares held on 6 April 1965 (TCGA 1992, Sch 2, Parts I and III)

If the rebasing election has been made to treat all assets acquired before 31 March 1982 as acquired at their market value on that day, gains and losses will be computed on that basis for both quoted and unquoted shares (see example 5). Where the election has not been made, the procedure is as follows.

For unquoted securities, two computations are made, as follows.

(a) (i) Calculate the gain or loss over the whole period of ownership, then calculate the proportion of that gain or loss that relates to the period after 6 April 1965 (but ignoring any period of ownership before 6 April 1945).

(ii) Adjust for indexation allowance (based either on cost or 31 March 1982 value, whichever is higher).

(iii) As an alternative to the result in (ii), the taxpayer may make an irrevocable election to have the result computed by reference to the value of the asset on 6 April 1965, with indexation allowance based on the higher of 6 April 1965 value and 31 March 1982 value. If this would give a loss instead of a gain, the transaction is deemed to give neither gain nor loss. The election cannot give a greater loss than the amount by which the cost plus indexation allowance exceeds the sale proceeds.

(Losses are unlikely to arise under the first calculation because the costs of many years ago are being compared with current sale proceeds.)

(b) Calculate the gain or loss as if the shares had been bought on 31 March 1982 at their market value on that date, but calculating indexation allowance on the higher of 31 March 1982 value and either cost or 6 April 1965 value according to which was used to give the result in the first computation.

430

Example 6

1,500 unquoted shares acquired 6 April 1957 for £2 per share.
Market value considered to be £4 per share at 6 April 1965 and £8
per share at 31 March 1982. No rebasing election had been made to
treat all assets acquired before 31 March 1982 as being acquired at
31 March 1982 value.
The shares were sold 6 April 1992 for £15 per share.
Increase in retail prices index from March 1982 to April 1992 74.7%.

First computation

Using time apportionment		Using 6 April 1965 market value	
Sale 1,500 shares @ £15	22,500	Sale	22,500
Cost 6.4.57 @ £2	(3,000)	6.4.65 MV 1,500 @ £4	(6,000)
Overall gain	19,500		16,500

Proportion after 6.4.65

$$\frac{6.4.65 - 6.4.92}{6.4.57 - 6.4.92} = \frac{27}{35} \quad 15,043$$

Indexation allowance*	(8,964)		(8,964)
Gain	6,079		7,536

Therefore, election not made to use 6.4.65 value
and gain is £6,079

Second computation

Sale 1,500 shares @ £15	22,500
31.3.82 value @ £8	(12,000)
Indexation allowance 74.7% on 31.3.82 value (being higher than 6.4.65 value)	(8,964)
Gain is	£1,536

Chargeable gain is lower of £6,079 and £1,536 £1,536

*Indexation allowance is 74.7% on March 1982 value of £8 per
share. See page 432 for Revenue view on treatment of indexation
allowance.

If both computations show a loss, the lower loss is taken, and if both show a
gain, the lower gain is taken. See example 6. If one computation shows a
gain and the other a loss, the result is treated as neither gain nor loss. If,
however, the first computation has already resulted in no gain, no loss, that

result is taken and the 31 March 1982 value calculation is not made. It is the view of the Revenue that indexation allowance should be deducted *before* the time apportionment calculation, but they have lost a case on the point in the Court of Appeal, and it is now going to the House of Lords. The opportunity to use 31 March 1982 value from 6 April 1988 has made the point irrelevant in most cases, but for disposals before that date the Revenue view often gives a much worse result for the taxpayer. For any such computations that are not yet settled, the position needs to be kept open until the outcome of the case is known.

For quoted securities, unless the shares on hand at 6 April 1965 are included at their value at that date in the '1982 holding', two computations are also made. The procedure is the same as for unquoted securities, except that time apportionment does not apply. In the first computation, the sale proceeds are compared with both the cost and the 6 April 1965 value, the indexation allowance is deducted in each case (based on the higher of the cost/6 April 1965 value and 31 March 1982 value) and the lower gain or lower loss is taken. If one method shows a gain and the other a loss, the computation is treated as giving rise to neither gain nor loss. The second computation treats the shares as acquired at 31 March 1982 value (but indexation allowance is nonetheless based on cost/6 April 1965 value if it exceeds 31 March 1982 value). The lower gain or lower loss produced by the two computations is then taken. If one computation shows a loss and the other a gain, the result is neither gain nor loss. If the first computation has already given a no gain/no loss result, then the second computation is not made. See example 4 on page 428.

The above examples show that where a taxpayer has acquired shares at various times before and after 31 March 1982 the rules require several calculations to be made. These calculations can be simplified by using publications such as Extel and D & B Securities Taxation (formerly Stubbs) to obtain 31.3.82 values and information on scrip and bonus issues, takeovers etc.

Scrip and rights issues (TCGA 1992, ss 57, 122, 123, 126–132)

Scrip and rights issues are identified with the shares out of which they arise, although the amount paid for a rights issue only attracts indexation allowance from the time of payment.

If rights are sold nil paid, the proceeds are treated as a part disposal of the holding, unless they do not exceed 5% of the value of the holding, in which case they may be deducted from the cost instead. (The value of the holding is arrived at by taking the ex-rights value of the existing shares plus the proceeds for the rights shares sold. If not all the rights shares were sold, those retained would also be valued at nil paid price in this calculation.) For 'new holding' calculations (see page 425), the indexed pool is increased by indexation before making the deduction. For the '1982 holding' and other acquisitions (see page 425), the legislation provides that the indexation allowance on a later disposal is first calculated on the full cost then reduced by an indexation amount on the rights sale proceeds from the date of receipt. This ensures that the correct amount of indexation allowance is given. It is, however, more straightforward to operate the 1982 holding on an indexed basis (see page 427), so that the sale of rights nil paid can be treated in the same way as for the new holding.

Although examples 7 and 8 show small proceeds on a sale of rights being deducted from the value of the holding, if treating them as a part disposal would produce a gain covered by the annual exemption, the part disposal treatment would be better. The part of the cost of the holding that is taken into account against the cash proceeds is arrived at in the same way as for cash on a takeover (see page 438).

Example 7

A taxpayer acquired 2,000 shares on 23 February 1986 for £4,000. On 10 December 1987 there was a scrip issue of 1 for 2. On 19 April 1992 there was a rights issue of 1 for 6 at £3 per share. The ex-rights value of the shares was £3.40, giving a value of £10,200 for 3,000 shares.

Rights taken up:

	Shares	Indexed pool £
23.2.86	2,000	4,000
10.12.87 Scrip	1,000	
	3,000	
19.4.92 Rights	500	
Indexed rise February 1986 to		
April 1992 (.437)		1,748
Rights cost		1,500
	3,500	£7,248

Rights sold nil paid for 40p per share = £200, which is less than 5% of (£10,200 + £200):

	Shares	Indexed pool £
As above	3,000	5,748
Rights proceeds		(200)
	3,000	£5,548

Example 8

Facts as in example 7 but, in addition to the 'new holding', the taxpayer acquired 3,000 shares for £3,000 on 11 April 1979. These shares comprise the '1982 holding'. The 31 March 1982 value of the shares was £1.20 per share. Rebasing election not made.

Rights taken up:

	Shares	Indexed Cost	Indexed 31.3.82 value
		£	£
At 31.3.82	3,000	3,000	3,600
10.12.87 Scrip	1,500		
	4,500		
19.4.92 Rights	750		
Indexed rise March 1982 to			
April 1992 (.747 × £3,600)		2,689	2,689
Rights cost		2,250	2,250
	5,250	£7,939	£8,539

Rights sold nil paid for 40p per share:

	Shares	Indexed Cost	Indexed 31.3.82 value
		£	£
At 31.3.82,			
adjusted for scrip as above	4,500	5,689	6,289
19.4.92 rights proceeds		(300)	(300)
	4,500	£5,389	£5,989

Scrip dividend options (TCGA 1992, s 141)

If you take scrip shares instead of a dividend, the capital gains tax cost is the amount treated as your net income (see page 422), not the grossed up equivalent (there being a nil capital gains tax cost where the recipient is a company). That amount is treated in the same way as a rights issue, i.e. the shares increase existing holdings proportionately, and the deemed cost attracts indexation allowance from the month of issue.

Unit and investment trusts

Unit trusts (TA 1988, ss 468–470; FA 1989, s 80; TCGA 1992, ss 100, 103)

Unit trusts enable an investor to obtain a wide spread of investments, within a fund which is professionally managed. There are various types of funds to suit particular circumstances, for example some aimed at capital growth and some at maximising income. Most unit trusts are authorised unit trusts (i.e. authorised under the Financial Services Act 1986, which places certain restrictions on the investments the trust is able to make).

From 1 January 1991, authorised unit trusts pay corporation tax on their income at the same rate as the basic rate of income tax, i.e. 25%, and obtain relief for management expenses and interest. They are exempt from tax on capital gains. Individual investors are broadly taxed on their unit trust income and gains as if they had invested the funds directly, except that gains on sales of gilt units are taxable, whereas gains on gilts themselves are not (see page 436). Individuals investing directly could not, of course, obtain tax relief on the costs of managing their portfolio.

Units in unit trusts and offshore funds that are, at any time during the ownership of the units, 90% or more invested in assets such as sterling bank deposits or gilts, or in building society shares, do not qualify for indexation allowance, since no indexation allowance would have been due on such assets if the unitholder had owned them directly.

Companies that invest in authorised unit trusts will be charged to corporation tax on the gross income, less a credit for basic rate income tax. This does not apply to unit trust managers holding units in the ordinary course of their management business, to authorised unit trusts investing in other authorised unit trusts, or to certain holdings by investment trusts. Any income in these cases will be received as franked investment income and thus not be liable to corporation tax.

Investment trusts (TA 1988, s 842; TCGA 1992, s 100)

Investment trusts are actually companies and not trusts, and you buy shares in them in the usual way. Some trusts with a limited life are split level trusts, i.e. they have income shares that receive most of the trust's income and a fixed capital sum on liquidation, and capital shares that receive little or no income but get most of the capital surplus on a liquidation.

Investment trusts are exempt from tax on their capital gains if they are approved investment trusts (approval has to be given every year by the Inland Revenue) but the gains may only be reinvested and cannot be distributed as dividends. They are charged to corporation tax in the normal way, which puts them at a disadvantage as against unit trusts.

Savings schemes

Both unit trusts and investment trusts operate monthly savings schemes, which give the investor the advantage of 'pound cost averaging', i.e. fluctuations in prices will be evened out because overall you will get more units/shares when the price is low and less when it is high. Such schemes give calculation problems for capital gains tax, because the indexed pool cost needs to be increased every month (see page 425). Investors may, however, apply to be treated as if they had made a single annual investment in the seventh month of the trusts' accounting year, which cuts the calculations down significantly.

Personal Equity Plans (PEPs)

Investors can invest up to £6,000 (£3,000 before 6 April 1992) in unit and investment trusts through PEPs, providing the trust holds at least half of its own investments in UK ordinary shares or broadly comparable European Community shares.

As an alternative, PEP investments may be made in trusts that do not meet the investment requirement, but subject to a limit of £1,500.

The amount invested in unit and investment trusts is subject to the overall £6,000 maximum PEP investment. For details of the PEP scheme, see page 440.

Relief against income for losses on shares in unquoted companies (TA 1988, ss 574–576)

Where shares are sold at a loss, the loss is normally relievable, like any other capital loss, against gains on other assets. Where, however, the shares are in an unquoted UK trading company and were acquired by subscription as distinct from transfer, relief is available instead against any other *income* of the year of loss or of the following year, in the same way as an individual's or partner's trading loss.

This is not normally relevant to a loss on qualifying shares acquired under the business expansion scheme (see chapter 29), since the whole of the cost of the shares will usually have been relieved at the time of acquisition in that case. If, however, the relief has been withdrawn for some reason, relief for a loss on disposal, or because the shares become worthless due to a winding-up, can be given under this section.

Capital gains tax on government, local authority and company loan stocks (TCGA 1992, ss 104–106, 108, 115–117, 134 and Sch 9)

No chargeable gains or allowable losses arise on disposals of British Government stock and qualifying corporate bonds (with the exception of certain losses as indicated below). Qualifying corporate bonds are non-convertible sterling loan stock purchased or issued on commercial terms after 13 March 1984 in a body some or all of whose shares or securities are quoted on the Stock Exchange or dealt in on the Unlisted Securities Market, including local authority loan stock, and, for disposals after 13 March 1989, in a body all of whose shares and securities are unquoted. Building society permanent interest bearing shares (see page 416) are also within the definition of qualifying corporate bonds. There are special provisions for company reorganisations to ensure that the appropriate exemption is given on loan stock converted into shares or vice versa. The capital gains tax exemption for these stocks cannot be manipulated by selling just before an interest date, because of the accrued income provisions (see page 410).

Disposals of interest-bearing stocks that are not government stocks or qualifying corporate bonds (i.e. non-sterling loan stock, loan stock that may be converted into other securities (unless the other securities are also corporate bonds), loans that are not commercial loans and loan stock purchased before 14 March 1984) are subject to capital gains tax, but the computation differs from that for shares in the following respects.

The 'new holding' provisions dealt with on page 425 do not apply to these securities, nor to deep discount securities (see below), so that each acquisition of such securities is treated as a separate asset.

Disposals are not identified according to the rules on page 425. They are normally identified with acquisitions in the previous twelve months on a 'first in, first out' basis, then with any other acquisitions on a 'last in, first out' basis. These general rules are subject to certain anti-avoidance provisions. The same identification rules apply to deep discounted stock. Deep gain securities, however, are not chargeable to capital gains tax (see below).

If you receive Government stock in exchange for shares on nationalisation, the gain or loss arising at that time on the shares is held over until you sell the Government stock, at which time the nationalisation gain or loss crystallises. The provisions described on page 42, however, apply so that gains deferred before 31 March 1982 will not be charged and gains deferred between 31 March 1982 and 5 April 1988 that relate to acquisitions before 31 March 1982 will be halved.

Losses on qualifying corporate bonds (TCGA 1992, ss 251, 253–255)

Since qualifying corporate bonds are exempt from capital gains tax, no allowable loss can arise under the normal rules. For qualifying corporate bonds held on, or issued after, 14 March 1989, relief may be claimed according to the rules outlined on page 53 for losses (but without indexation allowance) if the claimant made the loan to a UK resident trader. A claim may be made when the value of the loan has become negligible, under the terms of Revenue concession D28 (see page 53). Where unquoted bonds were issued before 14 March 1989 in exchange for other shares or securities, and they do not strictly qualify for this loss relief because the money has not been used in a trade, the relief is given by Revenue concession (D38).

Deep discounted stock (TA 1988, s 57 and Sch 4; FA 1989, s 94 and Sch 11; FA 1990, ss 56–59 and Sch 10)

Where company loan stock is issued at a discount of up to ½% per year over the life of the stock (up to a maximum of 15%) the discount received on redemption will be subject only to capital gains tax and may be exempt as indicated on page 436. Where, however, company loan stock is issued at a deep discount (i.e. more than 15% of the amount payable on redemption, or if less, more than ½% for each complete year between issue and redemption) the discount will be treated as income accruing over the life of the stock on a compound yield basis. There will, however, be no charge to tax on the discount until the stock is disposed of, when the 'accrued income' deemed to have arisen will be charged as income of the year of disposal under Schedule D, Case III (or IV for foreign securities). The amount so charged will be excluded from the disposal proceeds in the capital gains tax computation. (If the stock comes within the definition of 'qualifying corporate bond'—see page 436—there will be no capital gains computation because it will be exempt.) If such stock is owned at death, then although death is not an occasion of charge for capital gains tax, the income tax charge will still be made.

Although you receive the accrued income and are charged to tax only when you dispose of the stock, the issuing company will normally be able to set the accrued income against its profits year by year. This may be useful to companies with current cash constraints or long-term projects that will not be profitable for some time.

These provisions led to a tax avoidance practice known as 'coupon stripping' and anti-avoidance provisions were introduced in the 1985 Finance Act to counter it (see page 499).

The deep discount provisions did not previously apply to similar securities issued by UK or foreign governments or other public bodies, nor to securities with variable features that made advance calculation of the discount impossible. From 14 March 1989, the deep discount provisions apply to securities issued by public bodies (but not to further tranches of existing issues).

Separate provisions impose an income tax charge on securities with variable features that fall outside the deep discount provisions but which nevertheless have similar features (called deep gain securities). As with deep discount securities, the charge is imposed at the time of disposal of the securities, but the charge is on the whole of the difference between acquisition cost and disposal or redemption proceeds and there is no separate capital gains tax charge.

Index-linked bonds and certain convertible securities are excluded from the deep discount provisions provided that various conditions are satisfied.

Takeovers, mergers and reconstructions (TCGA 1992, ss 57, 116, 126–131, 135; F(No 2)A 1992, s 35)

An exchange of new shares for old does not normally involve a chargeable gain, the new shares standing in the shoes of the old both as regards acquisition date and cost. This often happens when one company (whether or not its shares are quoted on the Stock Exchange) acquires another (either quoted or unquoted) by issuing its own shares to the holders of the shares in the company which is being taken over.

Where both cash and new shares are received, a partial disposal arises, in the proportion that the cash itself bears to the cash and market value of the securities acquired in exchange. See example 9.

438

Example 9

X owns 10,000 shares in a company, A, which cost £6,000 in August 1983.

Company A is taken over by company B on 6 September 1992.

(a) 12,000 shares in company B, valued at £15,000, are received in exchange for the 10,000 shares in company A.

No chargeable gain arises on the £9,000 excess value of the company B shares over the cost of the company A shares. Instead the 12,000 shares in company B are regarded as having the same £6,000 base value as the 10,000 company A shares which they replace.

(b) 12,000 shares in company B, valued at £11,250, together with £3,750 in cash received in exchange for the 10,000 shares in company A.

The 12,000 shares in company B have a base value of:

$$\begin{array}{l}\text{£6,000 cost of original} \\ \text{company A shares}\end{array} \times \frac{\begin{array}{l}\text{£11,250 value of shares} \\ \text{acquired in company B}\end{array}}{\begin{array}{l}\text{(£11,250 shares acquired} \\ \text{+ £3,750 cash =) £15,000}\end{array}} = \text{£4,500}$$

The cost to set off against the £3,750 cash received for the part disposal is likewise £1,500, using the same formula, plus indexation allowance from August 1983 on £1,500.

In the case of the 12,000 company B shares taken in part-exchange, indexation allowance will be given from August 1983 on £4,500 when they are disposed of.

When part of a takeover package takes the form of shares to be issued at some future date, the number of such shares depending for example on future profits, the current value of that future right should strictly be calculated and treated as part of the disposal proceeds, with an immediate capital gains tax liability arising. By Revenue concession D27, a taxpayer may elect for the normal takeover treatment in these circumstances. The concession does not apply if the future consideration is cash rather than shares. This can present a problem, because if the amount eventually received turns out to be less than the amount taken into account at the time of the takeover, losses will occur against which there may be no matching gains at that time. If, however, the takeover occurred before 26 April 1988, future cash that was limited to a specified maximum could be taken into account in the original computation at that maximum, then adjusted later if the amount proved not to be payable.

As indicated on page 436, qualifying corporate bonds are not chargeable assets for capital gains tax, and can create neither a chargeable gain nor allowable loss (subject to the special rules on page 437). Sometimes on a takeover or reorganisation qualifying corporate bonds may be exchanged for shares or vice versa. When qualifying corporate bonds are exchanged for shares, the normal rules outlined above do not apply and the shares are treated as acquired at their market value at the date of the exchange. If shares are exchanged for qualifying corporate bonds, the gain or loss at the date of the exchange is calculated and 'frozen' until the qualifying corporate bonds are disposed of, when the frozen gain or loss crystallises. From the date of the exchange, no further indexation allowance is available and no gain or loss can be established on the bonds themselves (with the exception stated on page 437). In some cases, this could mean that a gain is chargeable even though the qualifying corporate bonds have fallen dramatically in value. One solution is to give them to a charity. The frozen gain on the shares would not then be charged, nor would the charity have any tax liability when it disposed of the bonds.

Disposal by gift (TCGA 1992, ss 67, 165)

Where securities are disposed of by gift, the proceeds are regarded as being their open market value. If a gain arises, the donor and donee used to be able to make a joint election for the donee to adopt the donor's base cost for capital gains tax purposes, as increased by the indexation allowance to the date of the gift, but this right is only available in restricted circumstances for disposals after 13 March 1989 (see page 52).

If a loss arises on a transaction with a connected person (which broadly means close family of the donor and of his spouse) the loss is not allowed against gains generally but only against a gain on a subsequent transaction with the same person.

Stamp duty (FA 1990, s 108)

Stamp duty is currently payable on most transactions in stocks and shares, usually at ½%, but higher rates apply in some circumstances. The provisions are outlined in chapter 6. Stamp duty on share transactions is to be abolished from some time in 1993. The abolition will broadly coincide with the introduction of the system of paperless transactions (TAURUS) on the Stock Exchange.

Personal Equity Plans (PEPs) (TA 1988, s 333; TCGA 1992, s 151)

The Personal Equity Plan scheme was introduced by the government in 1987 to encourage savings through the purchase of shares. Every individual aged 18 and over who is resident and ordinarily resident in the UK is able to invest up to £6,000 in each tax year in a Personal Equity Plan (£6,000 each for a married couple). From 1 January 1992, a further £3,000 a year may be invested in a single-company PEP. Shares can be transferred free of capital gains tax into a single-company PEP from approved savings-related share option and profit sharing schemes (see chapter 11).

Any capital gains and dividends on the plan investments are entirely tax-free, and will remain so for as long as the investment is held within the plan. On the other hand, any losses arising on disposals within a plan are not allowable losses. The value of a plan is also increased because the plan managers are able to reclaim from the Revenue the tax credits on dividends. Dividends and credits may be retained within the plan or passed on to shareholders. Where gains, dividends and tax credits are reinvested, the total value of the plans held is permitted to go up to that extent each year by more than the annual limit. Investors may pay in cash to take up rights issues on shares they already hold in the plan but from 6 April 1991 this can only be done within the subscription limits and not in addition to them.

Subject to some special rules as to what part of the £6,000 investment may be in unit and investment trusts (see page 421), the plan managers are only allowed to invest the money in UK ordinary shares that are quoted on the Stock Exchange (listed securities) or on the Unlisted Securities Market or in comparable European Community shares. Investors (or plan managers on their behalf) are able to switch from one qualifying investment to another without any capital gains tax effect. Investors who acquire new issue shares outside the plan, including the privatisation issues and building society shares, are able, with the plan manager's approval, to transfer the shares into the plan, subject to the overall annual subscription limit.

When an investor wishes to withdraw all or part of his investment, the withdrawals may be either cash or the investments themselves. If investments are withdrawn, their base cost for capital gains tax purposes is their market value at the date of withdrawal. There is no loss of the tax advantages already obtained when funds or shares are withdrawn. If an investor dies, the personal representatives will be treated as acquiring the plan at its market value at the date of death.

Where plan managers hold cash on deposit within a plan before it is invested or reinvested in ordinary shares, tax is not deducted from any interest received and the interest is not subject to tax at all if it is reinvested in shares or unit trusts. Otherwise, it is taxed in full when withdrawn unless it is not more than £180.

Although a small investor's own capital gains tax exemption would usually cover gains he made if he invested other than through a PEP, the other tax advantages make them an attractive investment.

Groups of companies—anti-avoidance provisions (TCGA 1992, ss 182–184)

Anti-avoidance provisions have been introduced to prevent companies exploiting the indexation allowance through inter-group financing by way of shares or loans. The provisions apply to 'linked companies', i.e. companies in 51% groups and associated companies (where one controls the other or the same persons control both).

Tax points

- Selling quoted shares is often a convenient way to realise capital gains and use the annual exemption, currently £5,800. If you wish to continue to hold shares that offer such opportunities, you can arrange to buy them back again the next day (called 'bed and breakfast') but it is considered that this cannot be done without both the sale and purchase being fully completed, with the consequent costs involved, including the difference between buying and selling prices. Share portfolios should be looked at for suitable opportunities before the end of each tax year. The complicated calculation of the potential gain should be borne in mind when working out what can be sold without attracting tax.

- If you are a small investor, unit and investment trusts can be a useful way of getting the benefit of a wide spread of investments, with the added advantage of expert management. Such trusts are exempt from tax on their capital gains. You pay capital gains tax in the usual way when you dispose of your investment in the trust. The investment is particularly tax efficient when made through a personal equity plan.

- See page 440 re avoiding a frozen gain crystallising on qualifying corporate bonds that were acquired on a takeover etc. by giving them to a charity.

- If there is some control over the time of payment of a dividend, as with a family or other small company, watch that the date of payment does not aggravate an already high taxable income where the income of the major shareholders varies from year to year.

- When acquiring unquoted trading company shares not qualifying for relief under the business expansion scheme, ensure that they are subscribed for and not taken up by transfer, so that if a loss arises on disposal it may be relieved against income rather than against capital gains which are perhaps covered by the annual exemption.

- If you buy Government stocks on the National Savings Stock Register you will receive the interest in full and pay tax later, rather than receiving the interest net if you acquire the stocks on the Stock Exchange. The end result will be the same but your cash flow will be improved.

- Unless you hold not more than £5,000 nominal value of securities to which the accrued income scheme applies, you will need to consider what adjustment is required when you sell Government stock or other securities covered by the scheme. Details must be shown on your tax return. If you deal through a bank or stockbroker, the amount of accrued interest will be shown on your contract note. When you sell stock, you will be charged to income tax on any accrued interest that has been added to your proceeds, or entitled to relief for any accrued interest that has been deducted from your proceeds. When you buy stock, you will be entitled to relief for any accrued interest that has increased the price you pay, or charged to income tax on any accrued interest that has reduced the price you pay. The charges or reliefs are taken into account in the tax year in which the next interest payment is made on the stock.

- If you hold less than £5,000 nominal value of securities to which the accrued income scheme applies, remember that the accrued interest will not be charged to income tax (see page 411). The securities will usually be exempt from capital gains tax (see page 436). If they are not, the accrued interest will be taken into account for capital gains tax in arriving at the cost or proceeds as the case may be.

- Since each acquisition of shares before 6 April 1965 is a separate asset for capital gains tax purposes, unless an election has been made to include those holdings in the 1982 holding at their market value at 6 April 1965, or a rebasing election has been made to treat all assets owned on 31 March 1982 as acquired at their market value on that day, it follows that a disposal of a holding will often be treated as several disposals for capital gains tax purposes. If the disposal qualifies for the business gifts relief, this may give the opportunity of electing for the gifts rollover relief to apply to only some of the disposals, leaving the gain on others to be covered by the annual exemption if not otherwise used. Where there is only a new holding and/or a 1982 holding, gifts could be made at different times to enable the exemption to be used.

- With the rate at which you pay capital gains tax depending upon your level of income, the timing of disposals can be important where your level of income varies.

- Now that each of husband and wife is entitled to the annual capital gains tax exemption of £5,800, it may be appropriate to split share portfolios so that each may take advantage of it. Transfers between husband and wife are not chargeable disposals. If shares are held jointly in unequal shares, watch the provisions about notifying the Revenue for income tax purposes (see page 377).

39
Chattels and valuables

What are chattels? (TCGA 1992, ss 21, 263, 269)

Chattels are tangible movable property, for example coins, furniture, jewellery, works of art, motor vehicles. Although currency comes within the definition, sterling currency is specifically exempt from capital gains tax, as is foreign currency for personal use abroad. Motor cars (other than one-seater cars) are also specifically exempt from capital gains tax.

Income tax

Many people have turned to investing in valuable objects because money rates of interest have frequently barely kept up with inflation. This can be tax-efficient because the appreciation in value does not generally attract income tax (nor sometimes capital gains tax), but on the other hand there is no tax relief for expenses of ownership such as insurance or charges for safe custody.

A succession of profitable sales may suggest to the Revenue that chattels and valuables are held for trading purposes, particularly where the scale and frequency of the sales, or the way in which they are carried out, or the need for supplementary work between purchase and sale, suggest a trading motive. Indeed, even a single purchase and sale has on occasion been held to be a trading transaction. However, an important indicator of trading is the lack of significant investment value or pride of ownership. Where chattels have those qualities, a trading motive is more readily refuted.

Capital gains tax (TCGA 1992, ss 45, 262)

The capital gains tax treatment of a chattel depends on the nature of the chattel, and sometimes on its value.

Motor cars, sterling currency, and foreign currency for own use abroad are completely exempt, as indicated above. If other chattels have a predictable life of fifty years or less (called wasting assets), they are totally exempt from capital gains tax unless they are used in a business and capital allowances have been, or could have been, claimed on them. So privately owned items such as greyhounds and yachts are exempt because they are wasting assets. If an asset is exempt, there can be neither a chargeable gain nor an allowable loss. In many cases, therefore, the exemption denies you relief for a loss rather than exempting a gain.

In the case of chattels that are not wasting assets, and business chattels (whether they are wasting assets or not), any gain is exempt if the chattel is bought and sold for £6,000 or less.

Where the proceeds exceed £6,000, the chargeable gain cannot exceed 5/3rds of the excess proceeds over £6,000. See example 1.

Example 1

	£	£
Sale proceeds of antique clock are		7,200
Cost was	2,550	
Indexation allowance, say	1,020	3,570
Chargeable gain		£3,630
But limited to 5/3 × (7,200 − 6,000)		£2,000

Allowable losses can arise on business and non-wasting chattels whether the cost and/or sale proceeds is more or less than £6,000, but in calculating the allowable loss, proceeds of less than £6,000 are counted as £6,000.

Example 2

	£	£
Cost of painting	5,000	5,000
Indexation allowance, say	2,500	2,500
	7,500	7,500
Sale proceeds	4,500	
but counted as		6,000
Loss, although	£3,000, is limited to	£1,500

As far as business chattels are concerned, capital allowances are taken into account in computing income liable to income tax or corporation tax. If the chattel is sold for more than cost, the capital allowances will be withdrawn, so that they will not affect the computation of a capital gain or loss. Where a business chattel is sold for less than cost, the capital allowances computation will automatically give relief for the loss on sale. An allowable loss can even so arise for capital gains tax purposes, equivalent to the indexation allowance on the cost as reduced by capital allowances. See pages 254–256 for examples.

Items comprising a set or collection are treated as separate assets unless they are sold to the same or connected persons (as defined in TCGA 1992, s 286—see page 51), in which case the sales are added together and treated as arising on the occasion of the last sale. Splitting up a set and selling it to different unconnected people would usually not be sensible because it would substantially reduce its value.

Coins (TCGA 1992, ss 21, 262, 269)

Coins may either be currency, i.e. legal tender, or they may be demonetized. Coins are within the definition of a chattel, and if they have a predictable life or more than 50 years, which obviously applies to collectors' items, the exemption for chattels that are wasting assets is not available.

Foreign currency for your own personal use abroad is exempt from capital gains tax under a specific provision. The same applies to sterling currency (which includes post-1838 sovereigns). Demonetized coins (including pre-1838 sovereigns) are subject to the chattels rules and any gain is exempt if the coin is sold for £6,000 or less.

Where a coin is still legal tender, i.e. is currency, the £6,000 exemption is not available and the coin is chargeable to capital gains tax in the normal way. An example is Krugerrands, which are legal tender in South Africa.

Collectors' coins are normally liable to VAT at the standard rate, whether they are legal tender or not, unless they are dealt with under the special scheme for antiques and collectors' pieces.

Gifts of chattels

A gift of a chargeable asset is treated as a disposal at open market value at the date of the gift. In order to arrive at an estimated valuation, some evidence of the transaction in the form of correspondence etc. is advisable. If the value is below the £6,000 exempt level, no tax charge will arise, but the valuation at the time of the gift counts as the cost of the asset to the donee when calculating the gain on a subsequent disposal by him.

If the value of the gift exceeds the £6,000 exempt level and a chargeable gain arises, tax may not even so be payable because the gain, together with other gains, may be within the annual exemption of £5,800. Until 14 March 1989, it was possible for the donor and donee to elect that the gain be deducted from the market value of the gift in determining the cost to the donee for the purposes of a future sale by him. This is no longer possible from 14 March 1989 except for gifts of business assets, certain other gifts for public benefit etc. and gifts into and out of discretionary trusts (see page 52).

A gift of a chattel will initially be a potentially exempt transfer for inheritance tax purposes unless it is covered by the annual exemption or is to a discretionary trust, but if the donor does not survive the gift by seven years, the value at the time of the gift will be taken into account in calculating the inheritance tax payable at death. The person who received the gift will be primarily responsible for the inheritance tax triggered by the death within seven years, although the Revenue have the right to look to the estate of the donor if necessary. There may not be any potential liability because the gift was within the nil rate band, but, if there is, it may be worth insuring against by a term assurance policy on the life of the donor in favour of the donee.

Tax points

- Be aware of the trading trap if you engage in regular buying and selling.

- Details of chattel acquisitions are frequently required at a later date, perhaps for capital gains tax purposes or to demonstrate that funds for some other investment or business enterprise were available from their sale. Evidence can be provided by purchase invoices that identify the object, and/or by having substantial items included specifically on a household contents insurance policy when they are acquired.

- A profit on the sale of a vintage or classic car is exempt from capital gains tax (unless it is 'unsuitable to be used as a private vehicle') but if you buy and sell with the aim of making a profit rather than holding the car as an investment you are likely to be held to be trading and thus liable to income tax (or corporation tax).

40
Sensible use of life assurance

Background

You cannot now get tax relief on life assurance premiums (except as indicated below for term assurance within a personal pension plan) unless the policy was taken out before 14 March 1984 and has not subsequently been amended (whether or not by a clause in the policy) to increase the benefits or extend the term. There are, however, still tax advantages for qualifying policies, because of the treatment of the proceeds.

Relief for premium payments (TA 1988, s 274)

Where term assurance is included in a personal pension plan, you get relief at your highest tax rate (see chapter 17). Apart from that, the rate of relief available on a qualifying policy taken out before 14 March 1984, and not subsequently amended, is 12½% of the premiums paid, subject to maximum allowable premiums of either £1,500 or one-sixth of your total income, whichever is higher.

Qualifying policy (TA 1988, ss 266, 267, 272–274 and Sch 15)

The definition of 'qualifying policy' is complex, but broadly the policy must be on your own or your spouse's life, it must secure a capital sum on death, earlier disability or not earlier than ten years after the policy is taken out, the premiums must be reasonably even and paid at yearly or shorter intervals, and there are various requirements as to the amount of the sum assured and sometimes as to the surrender value. Providing these conditions are satisfied, the policy proceeds are tax-free (subject to what is said on page 449 as regards early surrender).

Purchased life annuities (TA 1988, ss 656–658)

A qualifying policy is sometimes useful to higher rate taxpayers in conjunction with a purchased life annuity (see chapter 36).

Only part of the purchased annuity is liable to income tax, the remainder being regarded as a return of capital.

Instead of making a conventional investment and losing a substantial part of the income in tax, a higher rate taxpayer could purchase a life annuity and use the net income arising to fund a qualifying life policy, the profits on maturity of the policy being tax-free. Whilst the reduction in tax rates has reduced the advantages of this form of investment, it can still be attractive in some circumstances, but specialist advice is essential.

If you are an older taxpayer, a variation is available under which only part of the net annual sum from the annuity is used to pay the premiums on a qualifying policy to replace the initial cost of the annuity, the remainder being retained as spendable income. It is also possible to use your house as security to borrow the money to buy an annuity if you are 65 or over but the annuity rates will often make this impracticable and specialist advice is again essential (see chapter 34).

Early surrender of qualifying policies (TA 1988, ss 540, 541, 547)

Where a qualifying policy is surrendered less than ten years after the policy is taken out (or, for endowment policies, before the expiry of three-quarters of the term if that amounts to less than ten years), any profit arising is charged to tax at the excess of higher rate tax over basic rate to the extent that the profit falls within the taxpayer's higher rate income tax band (but top-slicing relief is available—see page 450). There is no forfeiture of pre-mium relief where this was available, and there will be no tax liability at the higher rate if the proceeds are no greater than the gross premiums paid, because there has been no profit, the only benefit having been derived from any tax relief deducted when paying the premiums.

The surrender of the policy must still, however, be shown on your tax return, so that the Revenue can see whether any tax should be charged.

Non-qualifying policies (TA 1988, s 547)

If a policy is not a qualifying policy, there is no relief for premium payments even for policies taken out before 14 March 1984. Whenever the policy was taken out, the proceeds are not wholly tax-free. They are free of capital gains tax, but if the capital appreciation comes within the higher rate tax band when it is added to your income in the tax year of surrender or assignment, it is chargeable to income tax at the excess of higher rate tax over basic rate, subject to certain special provisions.

Investment bonds

A non-qualifying policy usually takes the form of a single premium invest-ment bond. When invested by the life office, the single premium should grow more rapidly than an equivalent amount in the hands of a higher rate taxpayer reinvesting net income from a conventional investment. You are able to make withdrawals of not more than 5% of the initial investment in each policy year (ending on the anniversary of the policy) without attracting a tax liability at that time, such withdrawals being treated as partial surrenders which are only taken into account in calculating the final profit on the bond when it is cashed in. The 5% is a cumulative figure and amounts unused in any year swell the tax-free withdrawal available in a later year, which could be useful if you want to save the withdrawal facility for some particularly heavy item of expenditure. If you withdraw more than the permitted 5% figure, you will be charged to tax on the excess, but only if, taking into account the excess, your taxable income exceeds the basic rate limit, so that if the excess occurs in a year when you are a basic rate taxpayer no charge will normally arise. The same applies to the position when you finally cash in the bond, because if this can be arranged in a year when your income, even with the addition of the bond profit, will not attract the higher rate, no tax will normally be payable (and see below as regards top-slicing relief). Thus it may be possible to surrender in a year when your income is low because of business losses, or tax efficient investment, or following retirement. If the bond is cashed in on your death, any mortality element of the profit as distinct from the surplus on the underlying investments is not taxable, and since the income of the year of death will usually not cover a full tax year, even on the taxable portion there may be little tax liability at the higher rate. There is no charge to tax if a new policy is issued under the terms of an option contained in the maturing policy and the whole of the proceeds under the maturing policy are retained by the insurance company and applied in paying one or more premiums under the new policy.

There is one instance where the cashing-in of a bond, or an earlier chargeable event, may result in a tax charge, even when you are not a higher rate taxpayer, and that is where you are entitled to a higher personal allowance because you are aged 65 or over, and/or a higher married couple's allowance because you or your wife is aged 65 or over. Although the bond profit or excess withdrawn is only chargeable to tax if your taxable income exceeds the basic rate limit, it still counts as part of your total income for the purposes of age-related allowances. Any loss of age-related allowances will thus indirectly result in a tax charge.

Top-slicing relief on policy surrenders (TA 1988, s 550)

In the tax year when you cash in the bond (or indeed when a chargeable event arises on a qualifying policy) top-slicing relief is available to lessen the impact of the higher rate charge. The surplus on the bond is divided by the number of complete policy years (ending on the anniversary of the policy) that the bond has been held, and the amount arrived at is treated as the top slice of your income, to ascertain the tax rate, which is then applied to the full profit. The longer the bond has been held the smaller the annual equivalent on which the tax charge is based. See example 1.

Top-slicing relief is only available when you pay tax above the basic rate. It does not enable you to avoid losing age-related allowances if the bond profit or excess withdrawal takes your income above £14,200.

Example 1

		£
Taxpayer purchases investment bond for		10,000
He takes annual withdrawals of £500 for six years (covered by 5% rule)	3,000	
He cashes in bond in 1992/93 for	11,800	14,800
Profit liable to tax in 1992/93		£4,800

His taxable income after all allowances and reliefs is £23,300, leaving £400 available within the basic rate limit.

Annual equivalent of bond profit (1/6th × £4,800)		800	
Tax thereon as extra income: 400 @ 25%		100	
400 @ 40%		160	260
Less basic rate tax on £800 @ 25%			200
Tax at excess rates on £800			£60
Tax charge on full profit of £4,800 is £60 × 6, i.e.			£360

An astute investor will usually want to switch investments from time to time, say from equities to properties, then to gilts and so on. For a small administration charge, a life office will let you switch the investments underlying your bond, and the switch has no adverse tax effect.

To give added flexibility in the timing of bond surrenders, it is possible to take out a number of smaller bonds, so that they need not all be cashed in the same tax year. Not only can the original investment be cashed over a number of years but the amount liable to tax in any year is itself top-sliced in arriving at the tax payable. This type of arrangement may be used as an alternative to a purchased life annuity in order to pay the premiums on a qualifying policy, and also to pay large items of recurrent expenditure such as school fees.

Trust policies

Where someone is entitled as of right to the income from a trust fund (called an interest in possession), the fund itself is regarded as belonging to that person for inheritance tax purposes.

If you take out a policy on your own life in trust for, say, your children, the policy is treated as belonging to them, and, when the proceeds are received, there is no inheritance tax charge because the child has held an interest in the trust fund throughout, which now comprises cash instead of a life policy. Nor is there any inheritance tax when the trustees pay the cash to the child, because the trust fund was always regarded as belonging to him. See example 2.

Example 2

In September 1992, a taxpayer takes out a qualifying policy on his own life assuring £100,000 on his death and pays the first annual premium of £5,000.

The policy is gifted to trustees for the benefit of his son, but he continues to pay the annual premiums of £5,000.

The effect is:

The gift of the annual premiums will be covered by the inheritance tax exemption for gifts out of income.
The son will receive the eventual proceeds without any tax charge whatsoever.

This is a useful way of providing for an anticipated inheritance tax liability by putting funds in the hands of those who will inherit the estate.

It is possible for husband and wife to arrange the policy so that the proceeds do not arise until the second death. The surviving spouse can then take the whole of the deceased's estate at the first death without inheritance tax, because of the surviving spouse exemption, and the liability to inheritance tax on the second death will be covered by the policy proceeds in the hands of the policy beneficiaries.

Endowment mortgages

Endowment mortgages are a combination of a loan on which you pay interest, plus a life assurance policy which pays off the loan when it matures. No capital repayments are made to the lender, so the interest cost never falls because of capital repaid. The profit element in the policy when it matures is not liable to tax.

Policies which were taken out before 14 March 1984 still attract 12½% life assurance tax relief on the premiums.

If the mortgage is repaid early, usually on change of residence, it is worth considering whether the existing endowment policy should be retained, if it is a pre-14 March 1984 policy, in order to preserve tax relief on the premiums, so that it will only be any new policy to support an additional amount of borrowing that will not attract the premium relief. If the existing policy were surrendered and a new policy taken out to cover the whole borrowing, no life assurance relief would be available.

Pension mortgages

Some building societies and banks will grant mortgages or loans with no capital repayments, but with an undertaking that the borrowing will eventually be repaid out of the capital sum received from a pension plan (see chapters 16 and 17), the borrowing in the meantime being covered by temporary life assurance. The lender cannot take a charge on the pension contract, but you can give an undertaking to use the lump sum from the plan to discharge the loan.

The effect is that tax relief at your various marginal rates over the period of your pension plan is obtained on the capital repayment since the fund used to make the repayment has been built up from premiums upon which the tax relief has been obtained at the time of payment. Unless these arrangements are part of an overall plan to provide adequately for your retirement, you will, however, have used part of the money that was intended to finance your retirement to pay off your mortgage.

Friendly societies (TA 1988, ss 459–467)

Whereas the profits of other life assurance companies are taxable (at 25% on income and gains attributable to policy holders), the profits of friendly societies arising from life or endowment business are generally exempt from income tax and corporation tax. The exemption applies where the premiums in respect of the policies issued by the friendly society do not exceed £200 p.a. (£222 if they are paid more often than once a year), or the annuities which they grant do not exceed £156 p.a.

Tax was previously charged on any profit on a friendly society policy taken out by someone under 18. From 25 July 1991, policies taken out by children under 18 are also tax-exempt and payment of the premiums by a parent will not contravene the income tax rules about parental gifts (see page 378); there will therefore be no tax charge on the parent.

The society's tax exemption gives an added advantage to a qualifying policy with a registered friendly society, although the restrictions on premiums and annuities limit the scope accordingly.

Friendly society annuity contracts made after 31 May 1984 are subject to the same surrender rules as life assurance policies.

Friendly Societies are currently unincorporated associations, but they may now become incorporated under the Friendly Societies Act 1992. This will not cause any changes in the tax treatment of their existing services.

Tax points

- With the abolition of premium relief for policies taken out after 13 March 1984, those who seek term assurance should consider arranging it under the personal pension provisions if they are self-employed or employees who have chosen to make personal pension provision (see chapter 17).

- A qualifying policy taken out before 14 March 1984 will continue to attract life assurance relief at 12½% on the premiums. Whether or not linked to a mortgage, this should be taken into account in considering early surrender.

- There is no point in taking out a policy on your own life to cover any inheritance tax arising on your death if the policy forms part of your estate. Although it will produce a capital sum, that sum will increase the taxable estate, and moreover will not be available until a grant of probate or administration has been obtained. A policy for the benefit of someone else will escape tax in your estate and the policy monies will be available to that person on production of the death certificate and appropriate claim form.

- A wide range of ways of investing through life assurance and purchased annuities is on offer by the various life offices, and an arrangement can often be tailored to your specific requirements. There are several schemes aimed at reducing inheritance tax. Specialist advice on what is available is essential.

- A single premium bond can be a simple and convenient way of investing without the need for any complex records such as those required when you invest on the Stock Exchange.

- Bonds are also a convenient way to get into and out of the property market by choice of appropriate funds, and you can give away one of a series of property fund supported bonds much more easily than giving land itself, with no inheritance tax charge if the gift is covered by exemptions, or if you survive for seven years after making it.

- There is no magic way of paying school fees. Sensible use of the types of life assurance contracts mentioned in this chapter will help, but early planning is essential, and contracts should be taken out soon after the child is born.

- There is a limit to the amount within a pension fund which can be taken as a lump sum. If you undertake to use your lump sum to repay a loan, the lender needs to be satisfied that the level of regular contributions is sufficient to produce a high enough lump sum to discharge or substantially reduce the debt (leaving you to draw the pension itself). The longer the period before retirement the bigger the fund that will be established.

- Friendly society policies for children are a tax-efficient way of using some of your income for your children's benefit. For other tax-efficient parent/child arrangements, see page 378.

41
The overseas element

Background

There are two main aspects to the overseas element: the tax treatment of UK citizens and UK resident companies with income or assets abroad; and the tax treatment of foreign nationals or foreign-resident companies with income or assets in the UK. In all cases, the tax liability may be affected by double taxation relief.

An individual's liability to UK tax depends on his country of residence, of ordinary residence and of domicile. For a company, ordinary residence and domicile are not normally significant, and the company's tax liability depends only on its residence. Within the scope of this book it is only possible to give a brief outline of the meaning of residence, ordinary residence and domicile. The Inland Revenue publishes a useful booklet IR 20, 'Residents and Non-residents—Liability to Tax in the United Kingdom', covering the provisions in more detail.

The overseas element also affects the taxation of trusts. This aspect is dealt with briefly on pages 472 and 473.

Residence and ordinary residence of individuals (TA 1988, ss 112, 207, 334–336; TCGA 1992, s 9)

Residence is a question of fact and usually requires physical presence in a country. It is possible for an individual to be resident in more than one country for tax purposes. Ordinary residence is broadly equivalent to habitual residence.

You are regarded as remaining resident and ordinarily resident in the UK despite a temporary absence abroad unless the absence spans a complete tax year. If you leave the UK to take up full-time employment abroad for a period which will span a complete tax year, you are regarded as not resident and not ordinarily resident from the day after you leave and as a new resident when you return. If you leave the UK for any other purpose you may be provisionally treated as not resident and not ordinarily resident if you can produce evidence of ceasing residence, e.g. selling your house here and buying one abroad, and the provisional ruling will be confirmed when your absence has spanned a complete tax year. If evidence is not available at the start of the absence, your residence status will be tested over three years, and if at the end of that time it is clear that you intend to remain out of the country, you will be treated as not resident and not ordinarily resident from the time of leaving.

New permanent residents are regarded as resident and ordinarily resident from the date of arrival in the UK. A visitor who does not know how long he is going to stay will be regarded as ordinarily resident from the beginning of the tax year after that in which the third anniversary of his arrival falls, or earlier if it becomes clear before then that he intends to stay on a long-term basis, or if he purchases accommodation in the UK.

Those who visit the UK without taking up permanent residence and who do not have accommodation available in the UK will be regarded as resident in any tax year in which their visits add up to six months in total. If UK visits, while not amounting to six months a year, average three months a year for four consecutive years (but excluding any days spent in the UK because of exceptional circumstances beyond the individual's control (SP 2/91)) a visitor is then regarded as becoming both resident and ordinarily resident in the UK. If it was clear at the outset that he was going to make such regular, substantial visits, he may be regarded as resident and ordinarily resident from the start. Former UK residents who have gone to live abroad are subject to these residence rules in the same way as foreigners, but it would be sensible to ensure that you were absent for a complete tax year before UK visits were made, so that you could demonstrate a clear break with the UK.

If a person has accommodation available in the UK, he is regarded as resident in any year when he visits the UK, no matter how short the visit, unless he works full-time in a business, profession or employment abroad, in which case the accommodation is disregarded in determining his status. Accommodation rented for use during a temporary stay is ignored if the rental period is less than two years for furnished accommodation or one year for unfurnished accommodation.

The residence of husband and wife is determined independently. If you accompany a spouse who goes abroad to work full-time but do not work yourself, the fact that you retain accommodation in the UK will mean that you normally will be treated as UK resident, although not ordinarily resident, in any complete tax year spent abroad during which you visit the UK. If you do not return to the UK in the tax year in which you leave, or make an earlier visit in the tax year when you finally return, you will be regarded as neither resident nor ordinarily resident for those parts of each of those years.

Where a business is carried on in partnership and the business is controlled and managed abroad, the partnership is deemed to reside abroad even though some of the partners are resident in the UK.

Residence of companies (FA 1988, s 66 and Sch 7)

A company used to be regarded as residing where its central management and control were situated, the place where the directors met being an important indicator. From 15 March 1988, any company that is incorporated in the UK is treated as being UK resident no matter where it is managed and controlled. Companies incorporated abroad will still be regarded as UK resident if they are managed and controlled here. There are therefore now two tests for company residence. Certain UK incorporated companies which had ceased to be UK resident before 15 March 1988 with Treasury consent, or had applied to be so treated at 15 March 1988 and obtained Treasury consent after that date, will not be treated as UK resident unless they cease business, or cease to be liable to overseas tax, in which case they will be treated as UK resident from that time or from 15 March 1993 if later. A UK incorporated company that was not resident at 15 March 1988, but had not become non-resident under a Treasury consent, will be treated as UK resident from 15 March 1993. If, however, a non-resident company transfers its central management and control to the UK it will be treated as resident from the time of the transfer. A company may have more than one country of residence. This has previously required some substantial business operations in each place as well as part of the management and control, but the new provisions make this irrelevant as far as the UK residence of UK registered companies is concerned. Anti-avoidance provisions were introduced in 1987 in relation to dual resident companies (see page 501).

Domicile

Domicile is different from nationality and residence and a person can only have one domicile at any one time. An individual's domicile is usually the country in which he has his permanent home. A domicile of origin is acquired at birth and under UK law this is the father's domicile for legitimate children and the mother's domicile for illegitimate children. A wife used to take her husband's domicile automatically, but since 1 January 1974 a wife's domicile is ascertained independently of her husband's. Women already married on 1 January 1974 retain the domicile they had on that date until action is taken to change it.

The domicile of origin may be abandoned and a domicile of choice acquired. This necessitates positive action, e.g. changing residence, making a will under the laws of the new country, obtaining citizenship of the new country. A high standard of proof is required to establish a change of domicile.

Domicile sometimes has an extended meaning for inheritance tax—see chapter 5.

The law of domicile is shortly to be changed, and the new rules will supersede the previous provisions. Under the new rules your domicile will broadly be the country with which you are most closely connected. A new domicile can be acquired if you move to another country and intend to stay there for an indefinite period. There will no longer be a specially high standard of proof to show a change of domicile and it will be decided on the balance of probabilities.

Effect of residence, ordinary residence and domicile on UK tax position for individuals

Income tax is charged broadly on the world income of UK residents, subject to certain deductions for earnings abroad and for individuals who are not ordinarily resident or not domiciled in the UK. Non-residents are liable to income tax only on income that arises in the UK. Where that income is high enough they pay higher rate tax. Non-residents are not usually entitled to personal allowances—see page 464.

Capital gains tax is charged on individuals who are resident *or* ordinarily resident in the UK—on world gains if domiciled in the UK, and on gains arising in or remitted to the UK if domiciled elsewhere. The gain or loss on the disposal of property abroad is arrived at by comparing the sterling equivalent of the cost at the date of purchase with the sterling equivalent of the proceeds at the date of sale (subject to indexation allowance). Non-residents carrying on business in the UK through a UK branch or agency are charged to tax on gains on assets used in the branch or agency—see page 466. Other non-residents who are not ordinarily resident in the UK are not charged to capital gains tax on the disposal of UK assets.

For the mortgage interest and capital gains position on your private residence when you are absent abroad, see pages 340 and 341.

If you are emigrating and you sell qualifying business assets (see page 48) in a tax year when you are UK resident, investing the proceeds in qualifying replacement assets abroad within three years, the gains on the UK assets may be rolled over against the cost of the replacement foreign assets (whether or not you are resident in the UK at the time of acquisition of the replacement assets). If the replacement assets are then sold in a tax year when you are not resident and not ordinarily resident in the UK (and are not carrying on a business in the UK through a branch or agency), you will escape UK tax on the rolled over gains. (You may, however, have a liability in your new country of residence.)

There are provisions to prevent a UK resident individual avoiding tax by transferring assets abroad while retaining a right to benefit from them (see page 502).

Residence has no bearing on inheritance tax, which applies to an individual's world-wide property if he is domiciled in the UK and to his UK property if he is domiciled elsewhere.

Basis of charge for foreign income of individuals (TA 1988, ss 17, 18, 19, 65–67, 192, 202A, 202B, 391)

The basis of charge under Schedule E for income from employment is the earnings received in the tax year. Deductions are available as indicated below.

Other income from abroad may be charged under Schedule C, Schedule D, Case IV or Schedule D, Case V.

Schedule C relates to the income from government securities, both UK and foreign, that is paid through a UK paying agent such as a bank. The paying agent deducts and accounts for tax at the basic rate, so that a basic rate taxpayer has no further liability, those liable at the higher rate are charged the excess and those not liable at the basic rate can claim a refund. The withholding of basic rate tax at source also applies to foreign dividends and interest chargeable under Schedule D where they are paid through a UK paying agent. Paying agents do not have to deduct tax from foreign dividends and interest paid into a recognised clearing system (such as Euroclear and CEDEL).

Schedule D, Case IV covers income from foreign securities, such as foreign debentures, and Schedule D, Case V charges income from foreign possessions, which covers all other income from abroad except that from employment (but see page 370 for foreign time shares). Anti-avoidance provisions have been introduced to counter the rolling-up of income in an offshore fund with the intention of realising it in a capital form. The provisions are dealt with briefly on page 501. Except where tax is deducted at source as explained above, tax under Schedule D, Cases IV and V is normally charged on the income arising in the previous tax year. For the first two years and the last year, however, tax is charged on the actual income of the tax year. For the third year the taxpayer may choose the actual basis instead of the previous year basis, and the Revenue may do likewise in the year before the last. The effect of the taxpayer or Revenue electing for the actual basis is that a different year's income is charged twice or escapes assessment as the case may be. By Revenue concession A7, where a surviving spouse inherits a source of income charged under Schedule D, Case IV or V, the previous year basis of charge will continue unless the Revenue are asked to apply the closing year rules. The charging provisions and the concession are the same as those for Schedule D, Case III, which are illustrated in chapter 37. The income to be brought into account is the sterling equivalent of the overseas amount at the date it arises. An average exchange rate for the year may be used, using rates published by the Revenue.

For individuals who are resident, ordinarily resident and domiciled in the UK, tax is charged on only 90% of foreign pensions (except where the pension is paid as a result of Nazi persecution, in which case it is not chargeable at all).

If you are resident but not ordinarily resident or not domiciled in the UK, you are not charged to tax on income from abroad unless you remit it to the

UK. If you do remit it, you are charged on the full amount remitted, with no percentage deduction. There are rules to decide whether you are remitting income or other sums.

Where you are charged on the amount remitted, the assessment rules outlined above for Schedule D, Cases IV and V apply to the amount remitted rather than to the income arising. The first year of charge is the year in which income is first remitted to the UK. Where you have earned income chargeable on the amount remitted under Schedule E, you are charged to tax in the year in which the earnings are remitted to the UK.

UK citizens with earnings from employment abroad (TA 1988, ss 19, 192 and Sch 12; FA 1991, ss 45, 46; F(No 2)A 1992, s 54)

If your employment abroad spans a complete tax year and all your duties are performed abroad, you will normally be treated as non-resident from the date of leaving and as a new resident when you return. Otherwise you will remain UK resident.

Notice that it is not the length of the absence but whether it spans a tax year that is important, so that if you were working away from 1 April 1991 to 30 April 1992, a period of thirteen months spanning a tax year, you would be non-resident for that period, but if you were working away from July 1991 to December 1992, a period of eighteen months that does not span a complete tax year, you would remain resident throughout.

If you are non-resident, you escape tax on all income other than that arising in the UK.

If you are resident, you are liable to tax on your earnings both in the UK and abroad, but a deduction of 100% is allowed for earnings during a long absence working abroad, which effectively makes the earnings exempt from UK tax. No deduction is available for short absences. The Revenue used to regard a period of non-residence as counting towards the qualifying period for the 100% deduction, but this has been found to be incorrect and such periods will no longer qualify from 6 April 1992 (although anyone who had already become resident and ordinarily resident again before that date may still count an earlier period of non-residence).

The 100% deduction is given in respect of earnings abroad during a qualifying period of at least 365 days. The 365 days do not have to coincide with a tax year. Thus the absence from July 1991 to December 1992 which *did not* establish non-residence for a tax year, *does* give an entitlement to the 100% deduction from the earnings abroad, but the non-resident period from 1 April 1991 to 30 April 1992 could not count as part of a qualifying absence for the 100% deduction if after again becoming resident you once more go to work abroad. A qualifying period is one consisting either wholly of days of absence or of days of absence linked by UK visits that do not overstep certain limits. A day does not count as a day of absence unless you are absent at the end of it, i.e. midnight. The limits are that UK visits must not exceed 62 consecutive days and that the days spent in the UK must not exceed one-sixth of the total days in the period. (More generous limits, of 183 consecutive days and one-half of the total days in the period, apply to seafarers. These limits apply for 1991/92 onwards providing at least one of the UK days falls after 5 April 1991. The previous seafarers' limits were 90 consecutive days and one-quarter of the total days.) This one-sixth rule cannot be calculated as a proportion of the total spell of employment abroad but must be considered at the end of each absence. See example 1.

Example 1

Two employees each spend fifteen months working abroad (not including a complete tax year), the time abroad and in the UK being as follows:

	1st employee Days	2nd employee Days	1/6th limit exceeded 1st employee	2nd employee
Abroad	100	100		
UK	10	60		
Abroad	150	150	No (10/260)	Yes (60/310)
UK	60	10		
Abroad	130	130	No (70/450)	No (10/290)
	450	450		

A deduction of 100% is given to first employee.

Second employee will not get the 100% deduction for the first absence, nor for the second and third absences unless he can link them to a further spell of overseas duty covering 365 days in all, with the UK visit limits not being breached.

If, although he satisfies the 365-day qualifying period rules, an employee has both overseas earnings and UK earnings, i.e. for work during his UK visits, the 100% deduction applies only to the overseas earnings.

The 100% deduction also applies to earnings in a period of paid leave at the end of the employment, but if the paid leave is spent in the UK it cannot be counted as part of the 365-day qualifying period. Thus a twelve-month contract abroad with the last month of it spent on leave in the UK would not qualify, whereas if the leave were spent abroad, or the contract was a thirteen-month contract with the last month as UK leave, it would qualify (provided that the 62 day and 1/6th rules were satisfied).

The 100% deduction is given where possible through the PAYE system, but where this is not possible a refund of income tax will be made by the

Revenue when summarising the position for the tax year. If the refund is made after the end of the next following tax year, it will attract a tax-free addition in the form of repayment supplement.

Owing to a defect in the definition of earnings for the 100% deduction, the earnings that qualify for relief are before deducting occupational pension contributions and other expenses. The defect is being corrected from 6 April 1992. For 1990/91 and 1991/92 overseas earnings can be calculated before deductions and a tax repayment may be available because the expenses may be set wholly against UK earnings.

Travelling and board and lodging expenses (TA 1988, ss 193, 194)

For an employee resident and ordinarily resident in the UK, the costs of travelling from and to the UK when taking up and ceasing an employment wholly abroad are allowed, and also the costs of travelling between a UK employment and a foreign employment and between foreign employments. The costs of any number of outward and return journeys whilst serving abroad are also allowed so long as the expense is met by the employer (thus offsetting the benefits charge on the expense). If the employer pays or reimburses the cost of board and lodging abroad, the amount paid or reimbursed is also offset by an equivalent expenses allowance, but no deduction is given for board and lodging payments that an employee bears himself.

If an absence lasts for sixty days or more (not necessarily in one tax year) an employee can claim a deduction for the travelling expenses of two outward and two return journeys per person in any tax year for his wife and children (under 18 at the start of the journey) to visit him, but only where the travelling expenses are paid or reimbursed by the employer (so that the deduction offsets the benefits charge on the expenses) and not where the employee bears them himself.

You can only offset a benefits charge on travelling and/or board and lodging expenses met by your employer if the expense is borne by the employer directly or you pay the expense yourself and are reimbursed. A round sum expenses allowance falls outside either provision, and care must be taken that the expenses are paid in a way that entitles you to the deduction.

Earned income from self-employment abroad (TA 1988, ss 80, 81, 112, 391)

If a business is controlled in the UK, the profits are assessable under the rules of Schedule D, Case I even though some of the profits are earned abroad.

If a business is controlled abroad, the profits are charged under Schedule D, Case V as income from a foreign possession.

A UK resident sole trader would find it virtually impossible to establish that his business was controlled abroad, so it is generally only the profits of partnerships that may be assessed under Case V instead of Case I.

Where a business is carried on wholly abroad, the expenses of travelling to and from it are allowed in computing its profits. Expenses of travelling between two or more overseas trades are similarly allowable, provided that either the business at the place of departure or that at the destination is carried on wholly abroad. A deduction is also allowable for board and lodging expenses at any place where the trade is carried on and, where the trader's absence spans sixty days or more, for not more than two visits in any tax year by wife and children (under 18 at the start of the journey).

If a business is controlled and carried on wholly abroad but has some UK resident partners, their profit shares are charged under Case V. The UK tax on a UK resident partner's share of the profits of a partnership resident abroad cannot be reduced or eliminated by double tax relief, even though the terms of the double tax agreement exempt the profits of the foreign partnership. If a foreign-controlled partnership carries on some trading operations in the UK, the UK activities are assessed under Case I and the foreign activities under Case V.

Other sources of foreign income (TA 1988, s 584)

For UK citizens who are resident and ordinarily resident in the UK, other sources of foreign income, such as dividends and interest, are charged on the full amount arising, with no percentage deduction available. There are provisions to treat income that is locked into a foreign country, and not capable of being extracted, as not arising until it is free to be brought to the UK.

Where the income is not received through a paying agent and thus not subject to deduction of tax at source, the tax charge for the current year is normally based on the previous tax year's income, as explained on page 459.

If you borrow money to buy a property abroad, you cannot claim tax relief on the interest on the borrowing (except for companies—see page 468).

Leaving and returning to the UK

In the tax year when you leave the UK to take up permanent or long-term residence abroad, you are treated as non-resident from the date of departure and get a full year's personal allowances against your income for the part of the year prior to your departure. See page 465 for the provisions exempting certain income of non-UK residents from tax.

If you are abroad for some period that includes a complete tax year and then become UK resident again, you are treated as resident for income tax from the date of arrival, with a full year's allowances on your income for the remainder of the year. If you have been away for at least thirty-six months, capital gains are subject to assessment only if they arise after your return (subject to certain anti-avoidance provisions). If you have been away for less than thirty-six months you will be charged on all gains in the tax year you return, whether they arise before or after your arrival.

Inheritance tax will continue to be chargeable so long as you remain or are regarded as UK domiciled (see chapter 5).

Non-residents and personal allowances (TA 1988, s 278)

Non-residents cannot normally claim UK personal allowances. Non-residents who are citizens of the UK, Commonwealth or Republic of Ireland, or are resident in the Isle of Man or the Channel Islands, and certain other categories of non-resident may do so. A claim for allowances may also be provided for by the terms of a double tax agreement. Where allowances are available, they are given in full against the UK income, regardless of the level of the overseas income.

Husband and wife (TA 1988, s 282)

As stated on page 456, the residence and ordinary residence status of a husband and wife is determined independently, although the rules are relaxed where a couple go abroad but only one works. If a wife remains in the UK while her husband is working abroad for a period which spans a tax year, she will be taxed as a UK resident on her UK and foreign income, and her husband will normally be exempt as a non-resident from UK tax on income arising outside the UK and will be able where appropriate (see above) to claim personal allowances as a non-resident against his UK income.

If a non-resident husband is entitled to personal allowances but his UK income is insufficient to absorb the married couple's allowance, he may transfer the surplus to his wife providing she is entitled to allowances either as a resident or a qualifying non-resident.

Earned income of visitors to the UK (TA 1988, ss 18, 19, 192, 195)

Income from employment

The treatment of a visitor's earnings depends on the length of his visit. A visitor to the UK who does not remain long enough to be classed as resident is nonetheless liable to UK tax on UK earnings (although sometimes he may be exempt under the provisions of a double tax treaty—see page 467). Non-residents cannot normally claim UK personal allowances (except as described above).

Expenses of travel and of visits by wives and children are allowed (thus offsetting the benefits assessment) in the same way as described above (on page 462) for a UK resident working abroad. This only applies, however, where the employee was either not resident in the UK in either of the two tax years before the tax year of his arrival in the UK, or was not in the UK at any time during the two years immediately preceding his arrival. Where this condition is satisfied, the expenses are allowed for a period of five years beginning with the date of arrival in the UK to perform the duties of the employment.

If a visitor is classed as resident but not ordinarily resident, he is still liable only on UK earnings unless he has earnings from abroad which he remits to the UK, in which case he will be taxed as well on the full amount remitted. It is important for visitors to keep records (for example, separate bank accounts for capital and for different sources of income) to enable them to demonstrate whether or not remittances out of foreign earnings have taken place.

Once a visitor has been in the UK long enough to be classed as ordinarily resident (or where he is ordinarily resident from the outset because of the length of his proposed stay—see page 456) he is charged to tax in the same way as a UK citizen.

Income from a UK branch or agency

Non-residents who carry on business in the UK through a branch or agency are charged to tax on the profits of the branch or agency in the same way as UK residents, the charge being under Schedule D, Case I for trades and under Schedule D, Case II for professions or vocations.

Non-resident entertainers and sportsmen (TA 1988, ss 555–558)

Basic rate tax may be deducted at source from the UK earnings of non-resident entertainers and sportsmen. Royalty payments received from the sale of records are excluded (as they are already exempt under many double taxation agreements).

Tax need not be deducted where the person making the payment does not expect to pay more than a total of £1,000 to the individual in question during that tax year. Where tax is deducted, the Revenue may agree a rate below the basic rate. The earnings will be charged to tax on a current year basis and the tax deducted will be set against the final tax liability for the year, or repaid to the extent that it exceeds that liability.

The rules are administered by a specialist department of the Revenue.

Other income, capital gains and capital transfers of visitors to the UK and non-residents (TCGA 1992, ss 2, 10, 12, 25)

Non-residents have no liability to UK tax on foreign income, but are fully liable to tax on income from UK sources, other than interest on various government securities that carry tax exemption if the holder is not ordinarily resident in the UK. The interest on such tax-exempt securities will be paid without deduction of tax if a claim is made to that effect. If you are not ordinarily resident in the UK and provide a bank or building society with a declaration to that effect, you will receive interest in full even though the income is chargeable to tax (see page 414). By Revenue concession, non-residents escape tax on bank and building society interest for any complete tax years of non-residence, unless the interest is taxed in the name of a UK agent or the UK tax is offset against relief due under a non-resident's claim for personal allowances (see page 464). It is understood that the

Revenue extend this concession in practice to state retirement pensions, although the published concession does not say so.

You do not escape liability to capital gains tax unless you are both not resident and not ordinarily resident in the UK. Even then, if you carry on business in the UK through a branch or agency, you are charged to capital gains tax on the disposal of assets in the UK used for the business or by the branch or agency. The charge was previously confined to those who trade in the UK, but it was extended to professions and vocations from 14 March 1989. Those caught by the change in the rules will, however, be treated as having acquired their assets at market value on 14 March 1989, so that only gains accruing subsequently will be charged.

If you cease to carry on the UK branch or agency, you will be treated as if you had disposed of all the assets, and charged to capital gains tax accordingly. If, while continuing to carry on the branch or agency, you remove any of the assets from the UK, you will be treated as if you had disposed of those assets.

If you are in the UK long enough to be classed as resident, you will be liable to income tax on foreign as well as UK sources of income. If, however, you are non-UK domiciled, or you are not ordinarily resident in the UK, you will only be liable on foreign income if you remit it to the UK. (See pages 464 and 465 for the position on income from employment.) As a resident, you are also liable to UK capital gains tax, but if you are non-UK domiciled you will only be liable to tax on chargeable gains arising in or remitted to the UK.

A gain on the disposal of your only or main residence is, subject to certain conditions, exempt from tax.

The treatment of income and gains may be varied by the provisions of a double tax treaty (see page 467).

The normal inheritance tax provisions apply to gifts of UK assets (see chapter 5).

Social security and national insurance contributions

If you leave the UK for permanent or semi-permanent residence abroad, your liability to pay national insurance contributions normally ceases when you leave, unless you work abroad for a UK employer, in which case contributions continue for the first 52 weeks. It may be to your advantage to pay voluntary contributions. Child benefit is not normally payable unless both parent and child are UK resident, but it may be paid for up to six months in some circumstances.

Visitors to the UK and new permanent residents are normally liable to pay national insurance contributions from the date of arrival, but exemption is often given for the first twelve months. Where an employee is liable, the employer will be liable to pay employer's secondary contributions unless he is not UK resident and does not have a place of business in the UK.

The general provisions are often varied by reciprocal social security arrangements and the position can be complex. Whether you are leaving or coming to the UK, it is advisable to contact the local social security office to establish your own liability to make contributions and your benefits position.

As far as state pension is concerned, if you emigrate, you are normally entitled to a pension based on the contributions you have made, but it is frozen at the rate payable when you leave the UK or when you first become entitled to it if later. This may be varied by the provisions of reciprocal social security agreements. Again, the position needs to be checked with your social security office.

Double taxation relief for individuals (TA 1988, ss 788–791; TCGA 1992, s 277)

Where the same income and gains are liable to tax in more than one country, relief for the double tax is given either under the provisions of a double tax agreement with the country concerned or unilaterally.

UK residents with foreign income and gains

Where there is a double tax agreement, it may provide for certain income and gains to be wholly exempt. If not, they are charged to UK tax, but a credit is given against the UK tax for the lower of the overseas tax liability and the UK tax liability.

Sometimes the agreements provide for a UK paying agent to adjust the UK tax he deducts to take account of the foreign tax, so that for example the deduction on a foreign dividend may be 15% overseas withholding tax and 10% UK tax, making 25% in all.

Where there is no double tax agreement, you may claim unilateral relief against the UK tax of the lower of the UK tax and the overseas tax. If double tax relief is not claimed, the income or gain is charged to UK tax net of the overseas tax suffered, but this would rarely be advantageous.

Non-residents with UK income and gains (TA 1988, ss 232, 233)

Income or gains may be exempt from UK tax under a double tax agreement.

Sometimes a double tax agreement may provide for income that is not exempt from UK tax to be charged at a reduced rate, for example interest may be taxed at only 10%. A non-resident will frequently be entitled to the tax credit on a dividend, and will be liable to tax at only 15% of the tax-credit inclusive amount, being entitled to a repayment accordingly (for example a dividend of £75 may be treated as income of £100, on which the tax payable would be £15, giving a repayment of £10). Where a non-resident's dividends are paid to UK nominees, the company may be authorised by the Revenue to pay the nominees the amount the shareholder would otherwise be entitled to have repaid. (So, in the above example the company would pay £85, with a tax credit of £15. The company would get a credit of £10 against their ACT liability.)

Non-residents who claim UK personal allowances (see page 464) are entitled to dividend tax credits whether or not they are entitled to them under a double tax agreement. If no claim for allowances is made, and there is no entitlement to a credit under a double tax agreement, a non-resident is liable to UK tax only on the amount of the dividend excluding the credit and then only to the extent of the excess, if any, of higher rate tax over the basic rate.

UK companies with interests abroad (TA 1988, ss 765–767, 788–795, 797, 799; TCGA 1992, s 140)

If a UK resident company has interests abroad, the company is liable to corporation tax on income received, before deduction of foreign taxes, the income being included either under Schedule C (interest received through paying agents), Schedule D, Case I (profits of foreign branch or agency), Case IV (foreign securities) or Case V (foreign possessions, which would include foreign subsidiaries), and also on any capital gains on the disposal of foreign assets. Interest on any borrowing to acquire foreign property would be deducted as a charge on income (see page 24).

If a UK resident company carries on business abroad through a branch or agency, it is usually charged under Schedule D, Case I on all the profits of the branch or agency, unless exceptionally the trade is carried on wholly abroad, in which case the charge would be under Case V. Where business is carried on through a foreign subsidiary, the UK company's liability would arise only on amounts received from the subsidiary by way of interest or dividends, which would be charged under Schedule D, Case V.

If an overseas branch is converted into a subsidiary, Treasury consent is required (unless the branch is in an EC country, but in that event the transaction may need to be reported to the Treasury). Stock has to be valued at open market value on the transfer, and there are balancing adjustments for capital allowances. Capital gains may usually be deferred until the parent company disposes of its shares in the subsidiary.

Double tax relief is available in respect of the foreign tax suffered on both income and gains.

Normally, only direct foreign taxes are taken into account for double tax relief but if a UK company receives dividends from a foreign company in which it owns 10% or more of the voting power, underlying taxes on the profits out of which the dividends are paid are taken into account as well. In this case the amount included in UK profits is the dividend plus both the direct and underlying foreign taxes.

Double tax relief is given either unilaterally or under the provisions of a double tax agreement.

The relief on overseas income cannot exceed the UK corporation tax payable on the overseas income, after all deductions other than advance corporation tax. It is, however, provided that in deciding how much corporation tax is attributable to the overseas income, charges such as debenture interest may

Example 2

		£
Company's profits for year to 31 March 1993 are:		
UK trading profits		450,000
Foreign trading profits £600,000 less overseas tax		
of £192,000		408,000
UK chargeable gains		30,000

The company paid debenture interest of £80,000
and ACT of £140,000.
Computation of double tax relief:

	Case I		
	UK profits	Foreign profits	Total
Case I profits	450,000	600,000	1,050,000
Chargeable gains	30,000		30,000
	480,000	600,000	1,080,000
Less charges — debenture interest	(80,000)		(80,000)
Profits chargeable to corporation tax	400,000	600,000	1,000,000
Corporation tax @ 33%	132,000	198,000	330,000
Less double tax relief		(192,000)	(192,000)
	132,000	6,000	138,000
Less ACT:			
Against UK profits (maximum)	(100,000)		(100,000)
Against foreign profits (maximum set-off £150,000 but restricted to balance of tax payable)		(6,000)	(6,000)
Final mainstream tax payable	£32,000		£32,000
Surplus ACT to be carried back or forward as the case may be (£140,000 – £106,000)			£34,000

be deducted against any source of profits in the most beneficial way. Since ACT may be set against corporation tax on both income and gains, the main point to bear in mind on charges is that they should be set against UK profits in priority to foreign profits. The set-off of ACT against any source of profits can never exceed the maximum, currently 25%.

Double tax relief in respect of foreign tax paid on chargeable gains is limited to the UK corporation tax payable thereon.

See example 2 on page 469.

If double tax relief is restricted because it exceeds the UK tax, the unrelieved foreign tax is wasted and cannot be carried forward or back.

Controlled foreign companies and dual resident companies

Complicated provisions outside the scope of this book enable the Revenue to direct in certain circumstances that tax be charged on a UK company in respect of profits of a foreign company in which the UK company has a 10% stake or more. They are outlined very briefly on page 501. There are also anti-avoidance provisions in relation to dual resident companies, which are also outlined on page 501.

European Economic Interest Groupings (TA 1988, s 510A)

A European Economic Interest Grouping (EEIG) is a new form of business entity that may be set up by enterprises of EC member states for activities such as packing, processing, marketing or research.

The EEIG's profits will be taxable and losses allowable only in the hands of the members. The EEIG cannot be formed to make profits for itself. Any trade or profession carried on by the members will be treated as carried on in partnership, with the normal rules of income tax (except those relating to joint assessment of individual partners), corporation tax and capital gains tax applying.

The 'fiscal transparency' of the EEIG will not apply to provisions other than charging tax on income and gains, so that an EEIG registered in the UK will be required to collect and account for tax on interest etc. and under PAYE.

Non-resident companies with interests in the UK (TA 1988, ss 6, 11, 100, 343; TCGA 1992, ss 25, 172)

If a non-resident company carries on business in the UK through a branch or agency, it is liable to corporation tax on the trading income from the branch, income from property or rights held by the branch and capital gains on the disposal of assets situated in the UK used for the trade or by the branch or agency. The company will be liable to income tax on other UK sources of income not connected with the branch or agency.

If the UK business ceases, or the assets are removed from the UK, the company is treated as if it had disposed of the assets, and gains are charged to tax accordingly. If, however, the branch is converted into a UK subsidiary, a claim may be made for the assets to be transferred from the parent to the subsidiary on a no gain/no loss basis. The subsidiary may also take over stock at cost, and be treated for losses and capital allowances as if there had been no change.

If a non-resident company does not carry on business in the UK through a branch or agency, it is not liable to corporation tax but is liable to income tax on UK sources of income, e.g. under Schedule A on rental income from UK property. A gain on the disposal of such a property would not be charged to tax.

UK subsidiaries of foreign companies (TA 1988, ss 14, 231, 238)

A UK resident subsidiary of a foreign company is liable to corporation tax in the same way as any other resident company, and an ACT liability arises on the payment of dividends. An overseas parent is not normally entitled to a tax credit on the dividend, although some double tax treaties provide for a limited credit.

Company ceasing to be resident (TA 1988, ss 765–767; TCGA 1992, ss 185–187)

A company incorporated in the UK cannot now cease to be resident in the UK, no matter where the business is carried on (see page 457). If a foreign registered company that is resident in the UK ceases to be so resident, it is charged to tax as if it had disposed of all its assets at that time, unless they are retained in a UK branch or agency. The tax charge is postponed if the company is a 75% subsidiary of a UK resident company and the two companies so elect within two years. The parent company is then charged to tax on the net gains on the deemed disposal as and when the subsidiary disposes of the assets, or ceases to be a subsidiary.

Transfer pricing (TA 1988, ss 770, 773)

Non-arm's length transactions between associated bodies where one is and one is not resident in the UK have to be adjusted for tax purposes to the normal arm's length price.

European Community changes

Corporation tax provisions (TCGA 1992, ss 140A–140D; F(No 2)A 1992 ss 44, 45)

From 1 January 1992, a claim may be made for the transfer of all or part of a UK trade between companies resident in different EC states, in exchange for shares or securities, to be treated as a no gain, no loss disposal provided certain conditions are satisfied. There are similar provisions to prevent a capital gains tax charge, or allow a tax credit for any tax paid, on the transfer of a non-UK trade between companies resident in different EC states.

As and when member states ratify the Arbitration Convention of 23 July 1990, a mechanism is to be set up for resolving transfer pricing disputes within the Community.

Value added tax

The VAT treatment of imports and exports will be changed in relation to European Community countries with the introduction of the Single Market from 1 January 1993. The new provisions are outlined on page 92. Customs and Excise are publishing a series of Information Sheets on detailed aspects of the new provisions and also provide information in their 'Single Market Report' and 'Customs News'.

Exchange rate fluctuations

Complex provisions apply to profits and losses arising from exchange rate fluctuations. In broad terms, such profits and losses are taken into account for tax purposes not only if they have been realised by the conversion of the relevant currency into sterling but also when, according to accepted accounting principles, they have been recognised in the company's accounts, except where they relate to capital items. The situation in relation to capital items is that capital gains and losses are arrived at by comparing the sterling value at the date of sale with the sterling value at the date of acquisition. The Revenue have published a detailed Statement of Practice (SP 1/87) setting out the treatment to be adopted in relation to trading profits. This statement does not have the force of law, but legislation to deal with this highly technical area is being considered and consultation papers have been published by the Revenue.

Trusts (TCGA 1992, ss 13(10), 69–73, 80–98, 168 and Sch 5)

A trust is treated as not resident and not ordinarily resident in the UK if the general administration of the trust is carried on abroad and a majority of the trustees are not resident and not ordinarily resident in the UK.

The use of non-resident trusts has enabled substantial tax benefits to be obtained, largely by transferring assets to resident trustees when the assets were low in value followed by the emigration of the trust. Gains held over on the transfer to the trust became chargeable at the time the trust became non-resident, but growth in value of the assets once they were in the trust escaped tax, except to the extent that capital payments were made to UK beneficiaries. The provisions were substantially altered by the Finance Act 1991 to minimise the loss of tax to the UK.

Exit charge when trust becomes non-resident

Where a trust becomes non-resident on or after 19 March 1991, all the trust assets (except any that remain within the scope of UK tax, for example assets that continue to be used in a UK trade) will be treated as disposed of and reacquired at market value, and gains will be charged to tax. The charge will be at the settlor's rate if he has a present or future right to the income or property of the trust (see page 479). Rollover relief on replacement of business assets cannot be claimed if the new assets are acquired after the trust becomes non-resident and are outside the UK tax charge. These provisions also apply to dual resident trusts that are exempt from UK tax on gains because of a double tax treaty.

Charge on settlor

Where a settlor who is UK domiciled and ordinarily resident has an interest in a non-resident trust (or a dual resident trust outside the UK capital gains charge), gains of the trust will be charged on the settlor (the settlor having the right to recover the tax from the trustees). A settlor will be treated as having an interest in a trust if his wife, children or their spouses have an interest, or an interest is held by a company controlled by him and/or them. These provisions apply to trusts created on or after 19 March 1991 and to existing settlements if funds are added or the beneficiaries are changed on or after that date.

Charge on beneficiaries

UK resident and domiciled beneficiaries are already charged to tax on their share of the gains of a non-resident trust if they receive capital payments from the trustees. A supplementary charge will now apply on payments made on or after 6 April 1992. The charge will run from 1 December in the tax year following that in which the trustees' gains arose (or 1 December 1991 if later) to 1 December in the tax year after that in which the charge on the beneficiary is made. The charge will not apply where gains are matched by capital payments in the same or following tax year. Gains made before 6 April 1990 are treated as made in 1990/91. Trustees could distribute such gains before 6 April 1992 without any supplementary charge on the beneficiary. Later gains can usually be distributed within the next following tax year without the supplementary charge becoming payable (but note that the 6 April 1990 fund of gains has to be matched with payments first). The charge is at an annual rate of 10% of the tax on the capital payment, with a maximum of six years, giving an overall maximum possible rate of 60% × 40% = 24%, in addition to the capital gains tax of up to 40% already payable.

Poll tax

Individuals are liable to personal poll tax if their only or main home is in the UK. It is a question of fact where your only or main home is. There will clearly be problems with those who go abroad from the UK and those who come to the UK from abroad. Short visits in either direction would not usually affect someone's status, but there is no definition to determine at what point someone would become or cease to be liable.

Students spending a year abroad as part of a full-time course are not liable during that period. On the other hand, students from overseas who are on full-time courses in the UK are liable to the 20% charge at their term-time address. Spouses of such students are liable to the full rate if they are regarded as having their only or main home in the UK.

If you are abroad long enough not to be liable to the personal poll tax, because your main home is elsewhere, you will be liable to the standard community charge if you retain a UK home that is not someone's only or main residence (subject to available exemptions—see page 98).

Overseas individuals or companies who own UK domestic property will be liable to the standard charge if the property is not someone's only or main residence.

Tax points

- Watch the timing of overseas work periods. Breaching the UK visit limits for long absences will deny you the 100% deduction.

- If you plan to obtain the 100% deduction for employment abroad or to have a period of non-UK residence, the situation may be changed by factors outside your control. Consider taking out insurance to cover the risk of extra tax liabilities through early return.

- Even though earnings abroad are covered by the 100% deduction, they still qualify as relevant earnings for pension purposes and could support a pension premium in the next six years.

- If you obtained the 100% deduction for 1990/91 and 1991/92 you may even so additionally be entitled to a tax refund in respect of expenses deductions because of a defect in the rules—see page 462. A refund may possibly be due for earlier years, but this has not yet been finally decided.

- Try to arrange for your employer to meet the cost of overseas board and lodging, so that the taxable benefit can then be offset by an expenses claim; otherwise, in addition to having to bear the cost yourself, you will get no tax relief on it.

- If your spouse accompanies you when you go to work abroad, the fact that he or she does not work will not prevent him or her being treated as non-resident, even if UK accommodation is retained, provided certain conditions are satisfied.

- If you are charged on the amount of income you remit to the UK, keep funds abroad separate where possible so that you can demonstrate for example that a remittance represents capital not income (but remember that a foreign capital gain will attract UK capital gains tax if remitted).

- If you are becoming non-resident, review your investments to make sure they are still tax effective. Interest on certain government securities is exempt from UK tax for a non-resident, and banks and building societies can pay interest gross to non-residents, the tax on which may, by concession, not be collected (see page 465).

- When rent of furnished or unfurnished accommodation is paid direct to someone resident abroad, an obligation arises to deduct tax at the basic rate (TA 1988, s 43). Other income is assessed on the UK agent, branch or other person responsible for the affairs of the non-resident (TMA 1970, s 78).

42
Trusts and estates

Background

The tax treatment of trusts is currently being reviewed with the aim of bringing it more closely into line with that of individuals. This chapter deals with the current position.

A trust is sometimes known as a settlement. It comes into being when someone transfers assets to trustees who hold those assets for the benefit of one or more persons who will receive income and/or capital from the trust.

A trust can be created in lifetime, or on death by a will or under the intestacy rules where a person does not leave a will (sometimes referred to as a statutory trust). Where the trust comes into being on death, the personal representatives must first complete the administration of the estate.

The overseas aspect of trusts is dealt with on pages 472 and 473.

Administration of an estate (TA 1988, ss 257A, 257B; TCGA 1992, s 62)

Personal representatives deal with the estate of a deceased either under the terms of his will or according to the rules of intestacy where there is no will. (For the way an intestate person's estate is distributed see page 397.) Income tax will be payable on the income of the deceased up to the date of death, with a full year's allowances, any unused married couple's allowance of a husband being transferable to the wife if the personal representatives notify the Revenue accordingly. (See pages 379 and 380 for the position on death from 1993/94 where married couple's allowance has been transferred to the wife.) If the deceased had capital gains in excess of the annual exemption in the tax year of his death, capital gains tax will also be payable. If there are capital losses in the year of death, they may be carried back to set against gains of the three previous years, latest first (ignoring any gains already covered by the annual exemption), and tax will be repaid accordingly. Inheritance tax will be payable on the estate if the transfers in the seven years before death which were either chargeable or potentially exempt, together with the estate at death, exceed the threshold (currently

£150,000). Property left to a surviving spouse on death is not counted in the taxable estate and business and agricultural property can also be excluded in some circumstances. The way in which the tax is calculated is dealt with in chapter 5. The administration period during which the personal representatives deal with the collection of assets and payment of liabilities and the distribution of the estate may last some months or even years if the estate is complex.

Income during the administration period (TA 1988, ss 695–701)

The personal representatives are liable to income tax at the basic rate of 25% on any income arising during the administration period (but not at the higher rate). There are no deductions for personal allowances. This income will be distributed to the beneficiaries entitled to it either because they are entitled absolutely to the assets or because, while the assets remain in trust, they are entitled to the income (known as a life interest or an interest in possession). Any payments to a beneficiary on account of income during the administration period are net of basic rate tax, the gross equivalent being included in the beneficiary's taxable income at that time. When the administration period is completed and the final amount of income due to each beneficiary ascertained, it is re-allocated over the administration period and the tax position of the beneficiaries for those years is recalculated. For someone with a life interest, the income is reallocated on a day-to-day basis. For someone with an absolute interest, the income is reallocated according to when it arose.

Capital gains during the administration period (TCGA 1992, ss 3(7), 62)

No capital gains tax arises on the transfer of assets to legatees, who are deemed to acquire them at market value at the date of death. Assets that pass to the personal representatives are also deemed to be acquired by them at market value at the date of death. Any gains arising on a disposal by the personal representatives are calculated by reference to their sales proceeds less the value at death as increased by the indexation allowance. The annual exemption, currently £5,800, is available against gains by the personal representatives in the tax year of death and the next two years, but not thereafter. Gains in excess of the exempt limit are charged at 25%. If any losses arise, they may only be set against gains of the personal representatives. They cannot be transferred to beneficiaries.

End of administration period

The administration period will end either when the whole estate is finally distributed if no trust has been created, or when the residue of the estate after payment of debts and legacies is transferred to a trust fund. The trustees and personal representatives are usually, but not necessarily, the same persons. There is no chargeable gain on personal representatives when they transfer assets to beneficiaries or trustees, the assets transferred being deemed to be acquired at market value at the date of death.

Tax liability on setting up a trust (IHTA 1984, s 200; TA 1988, ss 660–682; TCGA 1992, ss 165, 260)

The deceased's estate will be charged to inheritance tax before property is transferred to a trust created by his will.

Lifetime transfers to trusts for the disabled, or to accumulation and maintenance trusts for the settlor's children, are potentially exempt from inheritance tax and will only be taken into account if the settlor dies within seven years. For transfers on and after 17 March 1987, the same applies to other trusts created in lifetime in which someone is entitled to the income for life (known as an 'interest in possession') and to later transfers to that trust. For trusts created in lifetime in which no-one has a *right* to the income (known as 'discretionary trusts') the settlor is liable to inheritance tax at one half of the scale rate on the property transferred to the trust. The transfer has to be grossed up if the settlor also pays the tax (see chapter 5). If the settlor dies within seven years, tax is recalculated using the full rate and scale applicable at the date of death.

It is possible for the settlor to settle sums on himself, or his wife, any income arising then being assessable as his, or hers after his death. Such a settlement would be a chargeable disposal for capital gains tax, and tax would be payable accordingly, unless the gains were eligible for gifts relief (see below). Any gains arising to the trustees would be charged at the settlor's rate—see page 479. The transfer into the trust does not in these circumstances have to be reckoned for inheritance tax since the settlor or his wife is still enjoying the benefit of the capital.

A lifetime transfer into trust is deemed to be a disposal at open market value for capital gains tax. It used to be possible for the settlor to avoid paying tax at that time by electing for the gain to be rolled over and treated as reducing the trustees' base acquisition cost. This is only possible for gifts on or after 14 March 1989 if they are gifts of certain business assets or gifts into discretionary trusts. For the detailed provisions, see page 52.

As far as income tax is concerned, the settlor will continue to be liable for income tax on the trust income if:

(a) the period of the settlement does not exceed six years; or
(b) either the settlor or spouse has power to revoke the settlement within six years; or
(c) either the settlor or spouse retains any interest in or benefit from the income or the trust assets.

Further, where the settlor or his spouse creates a settlement in favour of their own children who are under 18 years of age and unmarried, the whole of the income will be regarded as that of the settlor except in the case of accumulation and maintenance trusts (see below) and the three situations outlined on page 378.

Types of trust

There are basically three types of trust.

(a) Trusts with an interest in possession, i.e. where someone has a right for the time being to receive the income of the trust, often called a life tenant.
(b) Discretionary trusts, in which no-one has a right to the income.
(c) Accumulation and maintenance trusts, under which income is, broadly, accumulated for minor children until they reach a specified age.

Trusts with an interest in possession

Income tax

Where there is an interest in possession, one or more beneficiaries has a right to the trust income.

The trustees are charged to tax on income arising in the trust fund at 25% and not to either the lower or the higher rate of tax. Income is calculated in the same way as for an individual, with deductions permitted for qualifying interest paid, say on a loan to buy property for letting. There are, however, no deductions for personal allowances. There is no relief for expenses of managing the trust, which are therefore paid out of the after-tax income.

The beneficiaries entitled to the income are personally liable to income tax on it, whether they draw the income or leave it in the trust fund. They are entitled to a credit for the basic rate tax paid by the trustees. If, say, the trust income is £1,000 gross, £750 net, and the trust expenses are £75, the beneficiary will receive £675, which is equivalent to a gross income of £900 with tax deducted of £225. If the tax deducted exceeds the beneficiary's liability, he may make an income tax repayment claim. But if he is liable at the higher rate of tax, he must pay the excess.

The need to pay expenses out of the taxed income of the trust may be minimised if specific income can be paid direct to the beneficiary, for example, by a mandate to a company to pay dividends direct, with a consequent saving in administration expenses.

Capital gains tax (TCGA 1992, ss 71–74, 165 and Schs 1, 7)

When the trustees dispose of any chargeable assets they are liable to capital gains tax thereon at 25%, subject to an annual exemption (£2,900 for 1992/93). Where there are a number of trusts created by the same settlor, the amount of £2,900 is divided equally between them, subject to a minimum exemption of £580 for each trust.

Where an individual has transferred assets to trustees, but he or his wife retains a present or future right to the income or property of the trust, any gains made by the trustees are taxed as if they were his personal gains rather than being allowed the trust's exemption and being taxed at the trust's fixed rate of 25%.

When a beneficiary becomes absolutely entitled to trust property following a life tenant's death, the trustees are regarded as disposing of the property to the beneficiary at its then market value, but no capital gains tax liability arises. Any increase in value up to that time escapes tax. A tax-free uplift also occurs on property that remains in the trust after a life tenant's death. In both cases, however, where the capital gains tax cost of the property had been reduced by gifts rollover relief (see page 52) there is a chargeable gain equal to the rolled over amount (subject to the special rules where gains relate wholly or partly to a period before 31 March 1982—see page 42).

When a life interest terminates other than on the death of a life tenant, for example because a widow remarries, but the property remains settled, there is neither a chargeable gain nor any change in the base value of the property for future capital gains tax disposals by the trustees.

When, however, a beneficiary becomes absolutely entitled to trust property other than on the death of a life tenant, this is regarded as a disposal at market value at that date, and tax will arise accordingly. If the property is a business asset qualifying for gifts rollover relief (see page 52), the trustees and the beneficiary may elect for the tax liability to be deferred by treating the gain as reducing the base acquisition cost of the beneficiary.

If a beneficiary under a trust transfers his interest to someone else, this is not normally treated as a chargeable disposal for capital gains tax, whether he is transferring a life interest or a reversionary interest (i.e. the right to the capital of the trust when those with life interests die or give up their interests). There is a chargeable disposal if the beneficiary had bought the interest from someone else, or had acquired it by gift from someone who had bought it.

Inheritance tax (IHTA 1984, Pt III)

Someone entitled to the income for the time being from a trust fund is regarded as entitled to the underlying capital, so that he will be treated as making a chargeable transfer of the underlying capital on his death. If he ceases to be entitled to the income in lifetime, with the trust assets passing either to someone else for life, or to someone else absolutely, or to an accumulation and maintenance or disabled trust, then with effect from 17 March 1987, the transfer is potentially exempt. It will only be chargeable if he dies within seven years. Although any tax arising is calculated by reference to his own chargeable position, the liability for payment rests with the trustees. The fact that trust funds are treated as belonging to the life tenant prevents wealth being protected from inheritance tax through the use of trusts. It may also result in inheritance tax being paid on the life tenant's own estate whereas his estate would have been below the nil band if the trust funds had not been included. See example 1.

Where there are successive charges on the trust property within five years, the tax payable on the later transfer is reduced by quick succession relief (see chapter 5).

Since the creation of a trust fund in which someone is entitled to the income for life is potentially exempt from inheritance tax, and will only attract tax if the settlor dies within seven years, such trusts provide an efficient means of inheritance tax planning and family provision. By the creation of the settlement you have transferred funds without giving the transferee absolute control over them. Any growth in the value of the assets will be within the trust fund and not in your personal estate. There is no tax charge if the life tenant receives a capital sum from the fund, since he is deemed to be entitled to the capital anyway. Tax may be attracted in the life tenant's estate if he continues to hold his interest until death, because the funds will be treated as part of his estate. If the interest comes to an end in his lifetime, other than by being transferred to a discretionary trust, potential exemption will again be available.

Example 1

A taxpayer died on 30 September 1992, having made no transfers in lifetime other than a potentially exempt transfer of £60,000 after annual exemptions of £6,000 in June 1990. At his death, his own assets less liabilities (called his free estate) were valued at £100,000. He was also entitled to the income from trust funds, the value of which were £50,000 and to which his daughter became absolutely entitled. He was a widower, his estate being left to his son.

The inheritance tax payable on his death is:

		Gross	Tax
Lifetime transfer*		60,000	—
Free estate at death	100,000		
Trust funds at death	50,000	150,000	24,000
		£210,000	£24,000

The tax is payable as follows:

From free estate	$\dfrac{100,000}{150,000}$ ×	£24,000	16,000
From trust funds	$\dfrac{50,000}{150,000}$ ×	£24,000	8,000
			£24,000

*Although potentially exempt in lifetime, the transfer must be taken into account at death because the taxpayer died within seven years of making it.

Discretionary trusts

Income tax (TA 1988, ss 686, 687, 832)

Where trustees have discretionary power as to the distribution of income and no-one is entitled to it as of right, the income tax treatment is the same as that for trusts with an interest in possession, except that the trustees are liable to tax both at the 25% rate and at an additional rate of 10%. They are, however, entitled to deduct their expenses in arriving at the amount charge-able at the additional 10% rate.

Any income paid to beneficiaries is deemed to be after deduction of 35% tax (basic rate of 25% plus additional rate of 10%), with the corresponding credit available to the beneficiary. Income of £130 net is thus equivalent to income of £200 from which £70 tax has been deducted.

Capital gains tax (TCGA 1992, ss 165, 260)

Capital gains tax is payable on disposals of chargeable assets by the trustees, subject to the annual exemption of £2,900 for 1992/93 (or proportionate part thereof where there are associated trusts). The rate of tax is 35%, i.e. the same rate as that payable on income. When a beneficiary becomes abso-lutely entitled to any chargeable assets of the trust, they will be deemed to be disposed of at market value at that date and capital gains tax will be payable accordingly, but the trustees and beneficiary may jointly elect for the tax liability to be deferred by treating the gains as reducing the benefi-ciary's deemed cost for capital gains tax (see page 52).

Inheritance tax (IHTA 1984, Pt III)

The inheritance tax position of discretionary trusts is complex and is to some extent dependent upon the position of the settlor. Since there is no interest in possession, no-one is treated as entitled to the underlying capital. In order to prevent the inheritance tax avoidance this would otherwise permit, there is a charge on the trust funds every ten years. A charge also arises when funds leave the trust (called an exit charge) and when a person becomes absolutely entitled to the fund or to an interest in possession. The ten-year and exit charges are, however, only at 15% of the scale rate, giving a maximum rate of 6% on the current scale. This makes a discretionary trust a useful vehicle where flexibility of beneficiary is required.

Accumulation and maintenance trusts

These are a special sort of discretionary trust to enable a parent or grand-parent to provide funds for the benefit of children without complete com-mitment on creation of the trust.

Income tax (TA 1988, ss 663–670)

The rule that a parent remains chargeable to income tax on income settled on his own unmarried children under age 18 does not apply where the

capital and income are required to be held on accumulation and maintenance trusts for the benefit of the children, except to the extent that trust
funds are used for the education and maintenance of the children.

Income accumulated within the fund is chargeable on the trustees at the
basic tax rate of 25% and, since the trust is a discretionary trust, at the
additional rate of 10%. When the accumulated income is transferred when
the child reaches the appropriate age, it does so as capital and thus does not
attract any further income tax at that time.

For settlements by a parent, the additional rate applicable to trustees is not
payable on any amounts paid out for the education or maintenance of the
children. Such amounts are treated as the parent's income and taxable at his
rate of tax, but he is entitled to recover from the trustees any tax paid by him
at the higher rate.

Capital gains tax (TCGA 1992, ss 165, 260)

The capital gains tax position of an accumulation and maintenance trust is
the same as that of any other discretionary trust (see above) except as
regards the availability of gifts relief when assets leave the trust. There is a
specific provision enabling gains on non-business assets to be held over and
treated as reducing a beneficiary's capital gains tax cost where the assets are
transferred out of an accumulation and maintenance trust, but this relief is
not available unless the beneficiary becomes entitled to both capital and
income of the trust at the same time. Where, as is often the case, the child
becomes entitled to income at 18 and capital at say 25, the relief is only
available on qualifying business assets.

Inheritance tax (IHTA 1984, s 71)

Accumulation and maintenance settlements receive favourable treatment
for inheritance tax where one or more of the beneficiaries will become
entitled to the property (or an interest in possession therein) not later than
age 25. To qualify for this treatment, the settlement must either terminate as
an accumulation and maintenance settlement not more than 25 years after
its creation (or 25 years from 15 April 1976 if later) or all the beneficiaries
must have a common grandparent. If such grandchildren fail to survive,
their children or widows/widowers qualify. 'Children' includes step-
children, adopted children and illegitimate children.

The advantages of such a settlement are that there is no ten-yearly charge
on the trust funds and no exit charges when a distribution is made to a
beneficiary or when a beneficiary becomes absolutely entitled to the trust
property or to a life interest in it. The transfer of property from the settlement to the beneficiaries is thus free of tax in these circumstances.

Position of infants

Where income is paid to beneficiaries, it is deemed to be after deduction of
tax at 25%, or, for discretionary trusts, 35%. If the beneficiaries are infants, a
repayment of tax will often be due. The parent or guardian can make the

appropriate claim, or the claim may be made by the beneficiary himself on
reaching age 18, in respect of the previous six years.

Stamp duty

No duty is payable where a trust is created by will or where a lifetime trust is
created, except for a 50p duty on the lifetime declaration of trust (and this is
to be abolished along with most other stamp duties around April 1993).
There is also no duty payable when trust property is transferred to a beneficiary.

Tax points

- Providing personal representatives have done everything possible to
  trace potentially exempt transfers made by the deceased in the seven
  years before his death and disclose them to the Revenue, they will not
  usually be asked to pay the tax on any untraced transfers that subsequently come to light.

- Where a person entitled to trust income has unused personal allowances, it is better to arrange for income to be paid direct to him,
  because the income will not then be depleted by trust expenses, and
  he will get a higher income tax repayment where tax has been deducted at source.

- Since inheritance tax is less where the value transferred is lower, it is
  usually beneficial in the case of appreciating assets to make transfers
  earlier rather than later, giving the intended beneficiary an interest for
  the time being in the income through an appropriately drawn trust. A
  transfer to such a trust will be potentially exempt, but even if the
  donor dies within seven years the benefit of transferring assets when
  their value was lower will be retained.

  The supporting capital can eventually be transferred free of inheritance tax to the person enjoying the income. To the extent that the
  trust assets qualify for business gifts rollover relief (see page 52), the
  value for capital gains tax purposes when the property was originally
  settled is also retained, but otherwise watch the capital gains tax liability which arises when chargeable assets are transferred to a trust.

- Where assets are put into a discretionary trust, the trustees may pay
  the inheritance tax arising because of doing so. If they do, and dependent upon the type of asset, the tax may be payable by instalments
  (see page 75). The grossing-up of the gift for tax calculation purposes
  where the donor pays the tax is also avoided.

- If you do not need the income you are entitled to from a life interest in
  a trust fund and would like some or all of the underlying capital to go
  to the person who will eventually be entitled to it, you could disclaim
  your entitlement to the income on the appropriate amount of capital.

Part of the disclaimed amount would be covered by inheritance tax annual exemptions if not otherwise used and the balance would be treated as a potentially exempt transfer, so there would be no immediate tax charge. If the potentially exempt transfer was within your nil rate band, no tax would be payable even if you died within seven years (although in that event the nil rate band available on your estate at death would be correspondingly reduced). If the potentially exempt transfer was above the nil band, tax would be payable by the donee if you did not survive the seven-year period, but it would be reduced if you had survived for more than three years (see page 64).

- For additional 'tax points' on trusts, see chapter 35.

43
Charities and charitable trusts

Formation and legal status

Many hundreds of new charities are set up and registered each year. In order to register a charity, it is necessary to satisfy the Charity Commissioners in England and Wales, or the Inland Revenue in Scotland and Northern Ireland, that the purposes or objects of the organisation fall entirely under one or more 'heads of charity'. These are as follows.

The relief of poverty.
The advancement of education.
The advancement of religion.
Other purposes beneficial to the community.

A charity may be a limited company with a separate legal existence independent of its members, or an unincorporated association which has no separate status so that assets must be held on its behalf by trustees.

Although charitable trusts are frequently national organisations, such as the Churches' children's organisations and bodies for medical research and care, there is nothing to prevent individuals creating and registering a charitable trust which remains under their control as trustees, so long as the 'heads of charity' are satisfied.

Tax status

Income tax and corporation tax (TA 1988, ss 505, 506)

Registered charities are exempt from tax on investment income used only for charitable purposes, including that derived from covenants. Trading profits are not automatically exempt but will be so where the trading is in the course of actually carrying out the charity's primary purpose. This includes trading that is mainly carried on by the beneficiaries of the charity.

Trading by the charity that is not within the exemption is often carried out by a separate trading organisation, which may be a conventional limited company. Although the trading organisation's profits will be liable to tax, they may be covenanted to the charity, so that the charity can reclaim the tax deducted (see page 488).

If a charity deposits money with a bank or building society, the bank or building society will pay the interest in full without deducting income tax.

Capital gains tax (TCGA 1992, s 256)

A charity is not liable to capital gains tax on gains arising on the disposal of assets where the gains are applied for charitable purposes.

Value added tax (VATA 1983, Sch 5, Groups 4, 14 and 16)

Where a charity makes taxable supplies it must register for VAT subject to the normal rules relating to exempt supplies and taxable turnover (see chapter 7). If a charity has a number of branches which are virtually autonomous, each branch having control over its own financial and other affairs, each branch will be regarded as a separate entity for VAT purposes and will be required to register only if its taxable supplies exceed £36,600.

Where a charity supplies goods or services consistently below cost for the relief of distressed persons, for example meals on wheels, such supplies are not regarded as being made in the course of business and hence are not liable to VAT. Sales of donated goods at a charity shop are zero-rated. Where, however, the charity sells used goods on behalf of others and charges a commission, VAT is chargeable on the commission but not on the actual sale proceeds.

Although newspaper, broadcast etc. advertising is normally standard-rated, it is zero-rated where it is for the charity's fund raising or for publicising the charity.

The VAT position on buildings was significantly changed from 1 April 1989. Zero-rating no longer applies to new buildings bought by charities or services provided in the construction of buildings for charities, unless the charity uses the building solely for charitable purposes (which means otherwise than in the course of a business), or as a village hall, or to provide social or recreational facilities for a local community. Any other use strictly falls foul of these provisions (for example allowing someone to rent a room for a children's party), but Customs and Excise have indicated that business use can be ignored where it is likely to be less than 10% of the total time that the building is normally available. Even if zero-rating applies, it does not apply to the services of architects and surveyors.

From 1 August 1989, landlords are able to opt to charge VAT on rents except for buildings or parts of buildings used for charitable purposes (but the exception does not cover the charity's offices). Where they take this option, the charge to charity tenants will be phased in as follows if the charity tenant occupied the building before 1 August 1989:

Year ended 31 July	Proportion of rent on which VAT is charged
1990	20%
1991	40%
1992	60%
1993	80%
1994 onwards	100%

The landlord is entitled to add VAT to existing rents unless the agreement specifically prevents him from doing so. In that event, the rent would have to be treated as VAT inclusive until such time as the landlord has a right under the agreement to increase it.

Customs & Excise have leaflets (701/1/92, 700/22/89 and 708/4/90) on the subject of charities, which are available from local VAT offices.

Stamp duty (FA 1982, s 129)

No stamp duty is payable on documents transferring assets to charities (including leases).

National insurance

Charities receive no special treatment. Employer's national insurance is dealt with in chapter 13.

Business rates

There is both mandatory and discretionary relief from business rates on premises occupied by a registered charity and used for charitable purposes. 'Charitable purposes' includes shops used for the sale of goods donated to the charity. The mandatory relief is 80% and discretionary relief can increase this to 100%, so that no rates are payable. Discretionary relief up to 100% may be awarded by local authorities to various non-profit-making organisations such as schools and colleges, societies concerned with literature and the arts, and recreational clubs and societies.

Giving to charity

Covenanting

A covenant is a legally binding settlement of income on one person by another. It signifies an enforceable obligation to make the payment, thus distinguishing it from a voluntary payment, and can be used to transfer income in a tax efficient way to charities, because the payer hands over an amount net of basic rate tax, and obtains tax relief on the payment, while the charity is entitled to repayment of the tax deducted on making a re-payment claim to the Revenue. Covenants have to be in the form of a deed, which means that the document must be signed in the presence of a witness.

Charity covenants need only be capable of exceeding three years, so that the most popular term is four years. Provided the covenant is *capable* of exceeding the stipulated period, it is immaterial whether it in fact does so. The covenant must, however, be irrevocable during the stipulated period. 'Escape clauses', allowing the covenantor to terminate the covenant in certain circumstances, will usually make it invalid.

Covenants by individuals (TA 1988, ss 660, 683, 685; FA 1989, s 59)

Relief is normally given to the payer at his top rate of tax. If, however, the charity abuses the tax reliefs available, higher rate relief may be restricted (see page 492).

The payer deducts basic rate income tax when he makes the covenanted payments, the net amount being sufficient to discharge his legal obligation under the covenant and basic rate tax relief being obtained by his retaining the tax deducted. An annual certificate R185 showing the amount of the covenanted payment and the tax deducted is given to the charity unless the Revenue agree to dispense with it.

Since only basic rate relief is retained when the payment is made, relief at the higher rate has to be given by the Revenue making a repayment of income tax or by their reducing the tax payable under direct assessments.

Should the payer for some reason not have sufficient taxable income in a tax year to make him an income tax payer, then, having deducted basic rate tax on making the payments, he will have to hand over the tax deducted to the Revenue, since to the extent that he is not a taxpayer, he is not entitled to tax relief. The Revenue will raise an assessment under TA 1988, s 350 in order to collect the tax from him. They do not always do this if the amount involved is insignificant.

The ability to recover tax deducted from payments substantially boosts covenanted income to charities. Since relief is normally given to the donor at his highest rate of tax on an unlimited amount of charity covenants, the higher rate taxpayer may be persuaded to increase his gross covenanted sum, thus making a larger contribution to the charity. See example 1.

Example 1

Taxpayer is prepared to contribute £1,200 per annum to a charity.

	Donor liable to tax at 25% £	Donor liable to tax at 40% £
Total income received by charity	1,600	2,000
Less tax deducted and repaid to charity	400	500
Net payment by donor	1,200	1,500
Higher rate relief to donor @ 15%	—	300
Net cost to donor	1,200	1,200

Charities usually have printed covenant forms available for intending donors.

Charities cannot reclaim tax on covenanted amounts that represent membership subscriptions, except to the extent that the subscription gives the right of free or cheap entry to view the charity's property. Relief will not be available if the subscription covers other benefits.

Covenants by limited companies (TA 1988, ss 338, 393, 423(1)(b)(ii))

Covenanted donations to charities are treated as a charge on the profits of a company for corporation tax purposes. The after-tax cost to the company in the year to 31 March 1993 may be either 67%, 75% or 65% depending on whether the company is paying tax at 33%, 25% or the marginal small companies rate of 35%. The cost may indeed be 100% if the company has no taxable profits to cover the covenant, because no loss relief is available for charitable covenants in excess of profits (except within a group of companies by way of group relief).

Deposited covenants

Both individuals and companies can give a charity the benefit of an immediate lump sum while retaining the tax advantages of covenants by means of a 'deposited covenant'. There are in effect two transactions:

 (i) An interest-free loan repayable in four equal instalments.
(ii) A deed of covenant for four annual payments, the net amount of each covenanted payment being equal to one-quarter of the loan.

The loans must not be made before the payer makes the deed of covenant.

The annual loan repayments are appropriated to satisfy the amount due under the covenant.

The charity benefits because it has the use of the money throughout the four years, and it can also reclaim tax on the four covenanted payments as and when they are made. For gifts of £400 net or more (or of any amount if made by non-close companies) the provisions outlined below will give the same tax effect without the delay in obtaining tax relief.

'Gift aid' for single gifts by individuals (FA 1990, s 25; F(No 2)A 1992, s 26)

Where an individual makes single gifts to charities of £400 net or more each (£600 for gifts before 7 May 1992), the payment will be treated in the same way as a charitable covenant, i.e. he will get higher rate relief where appropriate, or will have to account for tax to the extent that the payment is not out of taxed income. The individual gives the charity a certificate (R190(SD)) to enable the charity to get the tax back.

Non-covenanted donations by limited companies (TA 1988, ss 339, 339A; F(No 2)A 1992, s 26)

Both close and non-close companies (see chapter 3) may claim to treat one-off donations to a charity as a charge against profits, deducting and accounting to the Revenue for tax at the basic rate, which can then be recovered by the charity (the company supplying the charity with a certificate (form R240(SD)) for this purpose). For close companies, this relief is only available on gifts of not less than £400 net each (£600 for gifts before 7 May 1992). There is no minimum for a non-close company.

Payroll deduction scheme—Give As You Earn (TA 1988, s 202)

Employees can authorise participating employers to deduct up to £600 per annum from their earnings before tax, for passing on to charities chosen by the employee, through charity agencies with which the employer has made an arrangement. The employee thus receives full tax relief for the contributions made.

Capital gains tax (TCGA 1992, s 257)

Gifts of chargeable assets to charities are exempt from capital gains tax, so neither chargeable gain nor allowable loss will arise. Alternatively, the asset can be sold and the proceeds given to the charity. If a loss would arise, selling the asset would establish the allowable loss and the cash could then be given to the charity, either under the 'gift aid' provisions or, if the cash gift is less than £400, by way of deposited covenant (see above). Even if the sale of the asset would result in a chargeable gain, a tax saving would still be made if the charity was given the balance of the cash after payment of the capital gains tax, provided that the net gift was at least £400, because tax would be saved under gift aid on the amount of the gift. (The same saving could be made on a smaller gift by way of deposited covenant, but there would be a cash flow disadvantage both to the charity and to a higher rate taxpayer, who would only get the extra tax saving year by year rather than in the year the gift was made.)

Example 2

Chargeable asset would realise £3,000 net of expenses, and the gain would be £500. Assume taxpayer has a marginal tax rate of 40% and has used his annual exemption.

If asset is given to charity

Charity receives value of £3,000 (adjusted for expenses). Donor's tax position not affected.

If asset is sold and net proceeds given to charity under gift aid

Tax on gain is £500 @ 40% = £200, so net proceeds are £2,800. This represents a gift of £3,733 from which tax of £933 has been deducted, which the charity can reclaim. The donor is entitled to higher rate relief, less basic rate already retained, so he will save tax of £3,733 @ 15% = £560. Both the charity and the donor are better off than if the asset had been given.

Had the donor been a basic rate taxpayer, he would make no extra tax saving but the charity would still receive a larger sum.

Inheritance tax (IHTA 1984, ss 23, 58, 70, 76)

All gifts to charity are exempt whether made in lifetime, on death or out of a discretionary trust.

Where the charity is a discretionary trust, inheritance tax will not be payable by the trustees unless property leaving the trust is used for a non-charitable purpose.

Employees seconded to charities (TA 1988, s 86)

The salaries of employees temporarily seconded to charities, local education authorities or other approved educational bodies may be deducted as a business expense even though, because of the secondment, the salaries are not paid wholly and exclusively for the purposes of the trade.

Intermediary charities

Individuals and companies may want to give regularly to several charities, but may not want to commit themselves to a four-year covenant to any one of them. Apart from the 'gift aid' provisions (see above), there are two ways of achieving this and still retaining the advantages of covenanting. The simplest way is to enter into a covenant with an intermediary organisation such as the Charities Aid Foundation. You can tell the organisation which particular charity you want to benefit. Alternatively, and especially where the size of the covenant is more significant, it is possible for individuals or companies to set up their own intermediary charity. A simple charitable trust whose objects include all the four charitable heads can be set up relatively easily although it is essential to have proper professional advice. Additionally, for small amounts the payroll deduction scheme may enable the recipient charity to be varied.

Abuse of charity tax reliefs (TA 1988, ss 339, 427, 505, 506, 683 and Sch 20)

A charity's tax relief may be restricted if it uses its funds for non-charitable purposes, or makes payments to overseas bodies without taking reasonable steps to ensure that they are used for charitable purposes, or makes certain loans or investments for tax avoidance rather than for the benefit of the charity. Where a charity receives a grant from another charity, the grant is chargeable to tax, but will be exempt if used for charitable purposes. Covenanted payments by a company to its parent charity must be paid under deduction of tax, although the tax will be recoverable by the parent charity if the parent satisfies the conditions for exemption.

Where a charity's tax relief is restricted under these provisions, higher rate relief will be similarly restricted if your covenanted donations plus the gross equivalent of single gifts to the charity under the 'gift aid' provisions (see page 490) amount to £1,000 gross per annum or more.

Tax points

- If you set up your own charitable trust, the trustees must not profit from their position or allow their duties and responsibilities to conflict with their personal interests. You can, however, appoint a professional trustee, such as a solicitor or accountant, and an appropriate charging clause in the trust deed will enable his fees to be paid.

- If you are a higher rate taxpayer and make a deposited covenant, the relief at the higher rate is not given all at once but only as each annual payment is made by taking it from the loan. For a gift under the gift aid provisions, higher rate relief is given in the year in which the gift is made.

- Deeds of covenant from individuals will no longer need to be sent with a charity's claim for the refund of tax deducted at source from its income, but they must be kept for inspection by the Revenue.

- The Revenue will check that covenanted payments have actually been received by the charity. Charities receiving regular amounts in cash (notably church collections) must have a system that demonstrates that the covenanted amounts have been received.

- For the paying company to get relief from corporation tax for an accounting period on a covenanted payment, the payment must be made in that accounting period. Where a charity has a fund-raising subsidiary company that has covenanted its entire trading profit to the charity, the exact amount of that profit will not be known until after the end of the accounting period. The company will often make a payment during its accounting period that is more than the likely profit, paying tax to the Revenue on that amount and recovering the overpayment to the charity later. If the Revenue has made an excessive income tax repayment to a charity because of this, then unless it is a significant amount they are usually prepared to set it off against later repayments.

- A covenant is a legally binding obligation, and if it is not paid, the charity is entitled to take appropriate action for recovery. But where the covenantor's circumstances change, so that he has difficulty in meeting his obligations, the charity will not usually wish to pursue the right to payment, and is not obliged to do so.

  If a covenanted payment is not made, the covenantor cannot be called upon to account for the tax he would have deducted if he had made the payment, nor can the charity make a repayment claim.

- To get income tax relief for one-off gifts to charity under gift aid, you have to make a cash gift of at least £400 (treated as a gross amount of £533.33). For smaller gifts, you must still covenant for the minimum four-year term in order for the charity to get the tax benefit.

- If you have covenanted to a charity, you must be a taxpayer for at least as much tax as the amount you have deducted from the covenant. Tax paid by your spouse does not count. If you are caught by this, the charity will usually allow the covenant to lapse and your spouse can make a new covenant to replace it.

- 'Charity affinity cards', i.e. credit cards on which some of the money you spend goes to a charity, will not give the charity a tax liability if the money is channelled through a trading subsidiary that covenants its income to the charity. For VAT purposes, Customs and Excise has agreed that one-fifth of the income will usually be treated as liable to VAT as income from promotional activities and the remaining four-fifths will not attract VAT.

44
Subcontractors in the construction industry

Tax deduction scheme (TA 1988, ss 559–567)

The construction industry tax deduction scheme was introduced in 1975 to combat the widespread evasion of tax by itinerant construction workers, which was costing the Exchequer many millions of pounds in lost revenue, but inevitably the genuinely self-employed worker has also become enmeshed in the net. Some of the provisions of the scheme were strengthened in 1987 and 1988, particularly those in relation to control of companies. Further changes were announced in January 1990, most of which were effective from 6 April 1990. The paperwork has been reduced but the compliance rules have been strengthened.

Briefly, a contractor must deduct and pay over to the Collector each month tax at a prescribed rate from any labour payment made to a subcontractor, unless that person produces a valid 'exemption certificate' (form 714), when payment can be made gross. These rules apply whether the subcontractor is an individual, a partnership or a company. The prescribed rate is linked to the basic rate of income tax and is currently 25%. Contractors may pay the Collector quarterly rather than monthly if they expect their average payments of PAYE, national insurance contributions and sub-contractor deductions to be less than £450 a month (£400 before 6 April 1992).

Any person carrying on a business that includes construction operations is a contractor, and also any person whose expenditure on construction operations averages £250,000 per annum or more over three years.

The rules for obtaining an 'exemption certificate' are rigorous, but basically the Inspector of Taxes to whom an application is addressed must be satisfied that an individual applicant

(a) is working in the UK in the construction industry,
(b) is trading from identifiable premises,
(c) is keeping proper records to enable accounts to be prepared,
(d) has a continuous period of working in the UK of three years in the six years immediately prior to the application (but a six-month period of unemployment within the three-year qualifying period may be ignored),

(e) has a bank account through which the business is substantially conducted, and

(f) has paid all tax and national insurance due and has kept his tax affairs satisfactorily up-to-date.

A special certificate (form 714S) is available which allows payments of up to £150 per week to be made gross to individuals who may not satisfy condition (d) above because of their age, i.e. students leaving school, college or higher education, and to certain other individual applicants providing the Revenue with a bank guarantee in a standard form prescribed by the Revenue. The amount of the guarantee is £2,500 for each year in which the special certificate is valid.

Individuals who do not themselves satisfy the conditions cannot hide behind a limited company which has a clean taxation record. The legislation enables the Revenue to look behind the company to its shareholders and officers in determining whether a certificate should be issued.

There is a right of appeal against a Revenue refusal to issue a certificate.

Where a certificate is not forthcoming and deductions at source are made from the labour content of a payment to a subcontractor, the payer must issue a certificate of earnings and tax deducted (form SC60). The subcontractor is entitled to this certificate at the end of each of his contracts for his main contractor, and also at each 5 April for a contract that straddles that date. The certificate is important to him, because with it he may be able to support a postponement application if he receives an estimated assessment. The earnings are brought into the self-employed accounts of the subcontractor, and the tax deducted becomes a payment on account of the tax due. The deduction of tax at source does not absolve the subcontractor from preparing accounts and submitting returns, and if his liability is greater than the tax deducted there is the possibility of interest and penalties arising if he has not complied with time limits for submission of accounts.

Proposed changes

The Revenue have issued a consultation paper on possible changes to the scheme. The main suggestions are the introduction of a turnover threshold below which a sub-contractor's certificate would not be available, a tax deduction rate of less than 25% for those with certificates, all payments to be made by bank transfer (thus doing away with the need for vouchers), and an increase from £250,000 to £1,000,000 in the threshold for treating those outside the construction industry as contractors.

Tax points

• Since 25% tax is deducted from the full labour content of a payment to a subcontractor, an overpayment will normally arise because of the expenses of the trade and the personal allowances and 20% tax rate band available. This can only be obtained by the submission of accounts and returns.

- The definition of the construction industry is wide. Contractors who should have applied the scheme, but have not, may find themselves accountable for the tax which should have been deducted and may be charged interest thereon. Fringe trades should check the legislation to see if they are included.

- If you hold an exemption certificate you will have given your main contractor a receipt from the book supplied by the Revenue, giving details of his payments to you. Make sure that your annual trading accounts can be reconciled to those receipts.

- Although a subcontractor without an exemption certificate is not in the long run disadvantaged because any tax deducted from him is taken into account in what further tax he has to pay or what may be repaid to him, there is a short term cash-flow disadvantage which often discourages someone who is unemployed from taking up self-employment because condition (d) on page 495 cannot be satisfied. Whilst this is unfortunate, there is usually nothing which can be done about it.

- If you have an exemption certificate or are seeking one, it is imperative that you file your tax returns and business accounts promptly, since you may otherwise be disadvantaged when you apply for the renewal of your existing certificate or the issue of one for the first time, apart from the embarrassment of explaining yourself to the contractors for whom you work, who will have no alternative but to deduct the appropriate amount of tax.

45
Main anti-avoidance provisions

Background

The resistance to tax avoidance has increased considerably over recent years and in addition to the wide range of specific measures, the Revenue's powers have been significantly strengthened by various Court decisions. Schemes which include steps inserted purely for tax avoidance are almost certain to prove unsuccessful, although bona fide commercial arrangements will usually be effective provided that they do not breach any of the specific provisions.

The legislation relating to tax avoidance, and its interpretation in the courts, is necessarily complex, and what follows is only a brief indication. In addition to these specific provisions, much recent legislation granting reliefs has anti-avoidance measures within it, e.g. demergers, companies purchasing their own shares and the business expansion scheme. (These reliefs are dealt with in chapter 29.) Most anti-avoidance legislation enables the Revenue to obtain information from third parties.

A significant part of the legislation is intended to prevent what is really income being taxed as a capital gain. Despite capital gains now being taxed at income tax rates, the distinction between income and capital remains important (e.g. for capital gains tax retirement relief, exchange of shares when a company is taken over, etc.). On the other hand, however, income can be sheltered by a purchase of shares under the business expansion scheme (up to the end of 1993) or by a purchase of property in an enterprise zone, whereas a capital gain cannot, so that in certain circumstances, a capital gain may be less attractive than income, thereby turning some of the anti-avoidance legislation to the advantage of the taxpayer in appropriate cases.

Stripping income from securities (TA 1988, ss 703–709)

Where in consequence of a transaction in securities a person has obtained a tax advantage, then unless he shows that the transaction was for bona fide commercial reasons or in the course of making or managing investments, and that none of the transactions had as their main object, or one of their main objects, the realising of a tax advantage, that tax advantage may be nullified.

These provisions have been used particularly where elaborate schemes have been devised with the aim of extracting the undistributed profits of companies in a capital form. In view of the far reaching implications there is an appropriate clearance procedure which it is wise to follow wherever shares are being sold in closely controlled companies with significant distributable reserves.

The Revenue are also using either these provisions or the general 'series of transactions with a tax-avoidance motive' approach to attack schemes under which a group parent company seeks to avoid paying ACT that it will be unable to recover in the short term by arranging to receive dividends with tax credits attached, either from a newly acquired subsidiary with the facility to carry back ACT or from an existing subsidiary with such a facility.

Avoiding income on securities (TA 1988, ss 710–738)

Someone who habitually times their sales of securities so that income is not received but is reflected in a capital surplus on sale may be treated as having received the income that has accrued on a day-to-day basis, and be charged to tax at the excess of higher rate tax over the basic rate. These provisions, known as bondwashing, only apply to equities and preference shares, because interest is in any event treated as accruing on a day-to-day basis where other securities are sold, whether the sales have been habitual or not, under the provisions of the accrued income scheme—see page 410.

There are provisions to ensure that the legislation does not inhibit the properly controlled operation of the financial markets.

Deep discount securities and deep gain securities (TA 1988, s 57 and Sch 4; FA 1989, s 94 and Sch 11; F(No 2)A 1992, s 33 and Sch 7)

Deep discounted stock yields little or no income but gives a capital surplus on redemption. The surplus might itself escape tax if the stock is a 'qualifying corporate bond' (see page 436). It is therefore provided that deep discounted stock (i.e. with a discount of more than 15% of the redemption price, or, if less, more than ½% per year over the life of the stock) attracts an income tax charge when it is disposed of, on the 'accrued income' deemed to have arisen up to the time of disposal (see page 437). The charge will also arise if the holder dies. The issuing company is able to deduct the deemed 'accrued income' year by year against its profits even though the holder is only charged to income tax in the year of disposal or death. But to counter a practice known as coupon stripping, the holder is charged to tax annually on the income treated as accruing on a day-to-day basis if the assets of the issuing company are predominantly securities (other than UK corporate bonds). The total amount so charged will then be deducted from the accrued income chargeable on disposal or death.

The deep discount provisions were extended from 14 March 1989 to cover securities issued by UK or foreign governments and other public bodies.

New anti-avoidance provisions were also introduced from that date to catch securities that are outside the deep discount provisions because they have variable features that make the advance calculation of the discount impossible. Such securities, known as deep gain securities, suffer an income tax charge when they are disposed of, on the difference between the acquisition cost and the disposal or redemption proceeds.

Change in ownership of a company (TA 1988, ss 245, 245A, 245B, 768, 768A, 769)

Carry-forward of trading losses and surplus ACT is prevented where within a period of three years there is both a change in ownership of a company and a major change in the nature or conduct of its trade. The rules also apply where ownership changes after activities have sunk to a low level and before any significant revival. Where a change in ownership occurs on or after 14 June 1991, similar provisions apply to prevent trading losses in an accounting period ending *after* the change of ownership being carried back to an accounting period beginning *before* the change.

To prevent a company circumventing these rules by surrendering ACT to a subsidiary before the surrendering company's trade changes, the subsidiary cannot carry the surrendered ACT forward if a major change in the trade of the parent company occurs within the six years commencing three years before the change of ownership of the parent company.

A further restriction prevents a company buying a company with unrelieved ACT and transferring to it assets that are about to be sold at a capital gain. ACT on distributions made before the company is purchased cannot be set against tax on gains on assets transferred to the company on a no gain/no loss basis if they are disposed of within three years of the change of ownership. This provision is not linked to any major change in the business of either company.

The Revenue have issued a Statement of Practice (SP 10/91) giving their interpretation of a 'major change in the nature or conduct of a trade'.

Sale of subsidiaries (TCGA 1992, ss 31–33, 170; F(No 2)A 1992, s 24 and Sch 6)

There are provisions to prevent companies reducing or eliminating capital gains by reducing the value of a subsidiary before its sale. Where unrealised gains are distributed by a subsidiary to its parent company as group income (on which no ACT has to be accounted for) prior to the sale of the subsidiary, the parent company is treated as if it had received additional consideration of an equivalent amount.

There are also provisions to prevent companies retaining a subsidiary within a group for capital gains purposes by means of issuing special types of shares, while selling commercial control of the company.

Dual resident companies (TA 1988, s 404; TCGA 1992, ss 139, 160, 171, 175, 188)

Where an investment company is resident both in the UK and in another country, that company cannot surrender losses, charges etc. under the group relief provisions (see page 34). Such companies are also unable to take advantage of the various capital allowances provisions that would normally prevent transfers to them being treated as being at open market value.

The capital gains tax rules for transfers to be on a no gain/no loss basis on a company reconstruction or within a group are not available on a transfer to a dual resident company (whether it is an investment company or a trading company), nor can rollover relief on replacement of business assets (see page 48) be claimed where the new asset is acquired by a dual resident company.

Controlled foreign companies (TA 1988, ss 747–756 and Schs 24–26)

Complicated legislation was introduced in 1984 to enable the Board of Inland Revenue to direct that a UK resident company be charged to tax in respect of the profits of a foreign company if the foreign company is under overall UK control, and pays tax in its country of residence at less than half the amount that a UK resident company would pay, where the UK company and associates have at least a 10% stake in the foreign company. No Revenue direction will be made if the foreign company satisfies one or more of certain tests (as to acceptable distribution policy, exempt activities, public quotation or motive) or if its profits for a 12-month period were less than £20,000.

A dual resident company is treated as non-resident in the UK for the purpose of the controlled foreign company provisions.

Offshore funds (TA 1988, ss 757–764 and Schs 27, 28; FA 1989, s 140)

Gains on disposals of material interests in offshore funds by persons resident or ordinarily resident in the UK attract an income tax charge under Schedule D, Case VI instead of a capital gains tax charge, unless the offshore fund operates a full distribution policy (broadly 85% of its income). The income tax charge also arises on interests held at the taxpayer's death.

Where an investor switches from one class of investments to another, the switches are treated as disposals, and attract an income tax charge under Schedule D, Case VI or, where the fund operates a full distribution policy, a capital gains tax charge.

Transfer of assets abroad (TA 1988, ss 739–745)

The purpose of this legislation is to prevent a UK resident individual avoiding UK tax by transferring income-producing property abroad in circumstances which enable him to benefit from the property either immediately or in the future, such as a transfer to trustees of a foreign settlement made by him, of which he is a beneficiary.

Sales at artificial prices (TA 1988, ss 770–773)

Where any sales take place between persons connected with each other, including partnerships and companies, at a price other than open market value, then, if the Board of Inland Revenue so direct, the sale price of the one and purchase price of the other must be adjusted to the open market value for tax purposes. This is mainly directed at transfer pricing between the UK and overseas and does not apply where both parties are trading within the UK and the amount paid is a taxable receipt of one and allowable expense of the other. If the price is excessive, however, the payer may have difficulty proving that the expenditure is 'wholly and exclusively' for the purposes of the trade.

Transactions between associated dealing and non-dealing companies (TA 1988, s 774)

This section prevents abuse through transfer of assets by denying relief to one company where no taxable profit arises in the other.

Disguising income from personal activities as capital (TA 1988, s 775)

This prevents those with high personal earning potential, such as entertainers, contracting their services to a company in which they hold the shares and thereby turning income into capital by later selling the shares at a price reflecting the personal earnings.

Artificial transactions in land (TA 1988, ss 776–778)

The aim of this provision is 'to prevent the avoidance of income tax by persons connected with land or the development of land'. It enables land transactions to be taxed as trading or other income instead of as a capital gain.

Sale and lease-back of land (TA 1988, ss 779, 780)

Where land is sold and leased back, the deduction allowed for rent is limited to a commercial rent. A sale at an excessive price (subject to capital gains tax) cannot therefore be compensated by an excessive rent payment allowable for income tax.

Further, if a short lease (less than 50 years) is sold and leased back for fifteen years or less, part of the sale price is treated as income, that part being $(16 - n)/15$ where n is the term of the new lease.

Leases other than land (TA 1988, ss 781–785)

Capital gains may in certain circumstances be treated as income, and rent payable is limited to a commercial rent.

Individuals carrying on leasing trades (TA 1988, s 384; CAA 1990, s 42)

Losses arising from capital allowances in a leasing trade may only be set against non-leasing income if the loss arose in the course of a trade to which the individual devotes substantially the whole of his time and which has been carried on for a continuous period of six months.

Where assets are leased outside the UK, the writing-down allowance is reduced from the normal 25% to 10%. There are also limitations placed on the nature of the lease.

Relief for interest (TA 1988, ss 786, 787)

These provisions are aimed at blocking the artificial creation of allowable interest and preventing tax relief being obtained, on interest that would not otherwise qualify for tax relief, by means of various devices such as converting the interest into an annuity.

Other measures

There are also measures to counter avoidance in the following circumstances.

Companies leaving a group and taking out a chargeable asset acquired intra-group within the previous six years (TCGA 1992, ss 178–181; F(No 2)A 1992, s 25).

Claiming group relief for losses when arrangements exist where a company may leave the group (TA 1988, s 410).

Timing a company's entry to or exit from a group so that a time-apportioned split of the accounting period does not give a fair result in arriving at the set-off of profits/trading losses within the group under the group relief provisions (TA 1988, s 409).

Transfers of plant and machinery between associated persons in order to obtain capital allowances (CAA 1990, s 75).

Losses arising from depreciatory transactions, e.g. dividend-stripping (TCGA 1992, ss 176, 177).

Loss relief arising from dealings in commodity futures (TA 1988, s 399).

Value passing out of shares, which could have been avoided by a controlling shareholder (TCGA 1992, s 30).

Individuals realising capital gains abroad through a non-resident close company (TCGA 1992, s 13).

Transferring relief for partnership losses which would otherwise relate to a partner who is a company (TA 1988, s 116).

Annual payments for non-taxable consideration (TA 1988, s 125).

Transfer of chargeable assets on which holdover relief for capital gains tax is obtained into dual resident trusts (TCGA 1992, s 169).

Loans to participators in closely controlled companies (see chapter 12).

Abuse of life assurance reliefs and exemptions (see chapter 40).

Non-resident trusts (see chapter 41).

Residence of companies (see chapter 41).

Deemed disposal of assets at time of ceasing to be a UK resident company (see chapter 41).

Deemed disposal of assets when a non-resident carrying on business through a UK branch or agency removes assets from the UK, or ceases to carry on the branch or agency (see chapter 41).

Transferring income from parents to minor children (see chapters 33 and 42).

Subject index

This index lists the main subject matter referred to in the text. It does not include matters of general application (such as payment dates or bases of assessment) for which reference should be made to the Contents list at the front of the book for the chapter on the appropriate tax.

Page numbers in **bold type** indicate a chapter, or a substantial part thereof, dealing with the subject matter in question. Again, reference may be made to the Contents list for main headings within such chapters.

Reference should be made also to the 'Tax points' at the end of a chapter where appropriate.

SUBJECT INDEX

Cars
  benefits in kind xx–xxii, 133, 144
  capital allowances 251, 253
  capital gains exemption 444
  leasing 232
  mileage allowances xxiii, 128
  national insurance xxviii, xxix, 141, 171
  parking facilities 132
  severance payment, as part of 191
  VAT 233, 245
Casual income 222, 227
  losses 227
Certificates of tax deposit 20
Change of accounting date 243
Charges on income 10, 24, 35, 298
Charities Aid Foundation 492
Charities and charitable trusts 486
  building society interest 487
  business rates 488
  capital gains tax 487, 491
  covenants to 10, 488, 490
  donations 490
  employees seconded to 492
  gift aid 113, 490
  inheritance tax 61, 492
  investment income 486
  national insurance 488
  payroll deduction scheme 491
  rate relief 488
  single donations 490
  stamp duty 488
  trading profits 486
  VAT 487
Chattels and valuables 444
Child care facilities 132
Children 19, 374
  additional personal allowance 17
  community charge 97
  covenants to 378, 393
  friendly society policies 378, 453
  income of 19, 378, 478
  maintenance payments 383
  national savings bonus bonds 409
  poll tax 97
  school fees 454
  student grants 378
  trust income of 478, 482, 483
  working in family business 225, 236

Close companies 34
  charitable giving 490, 491
  family companies
  —directors of 156
  —selling 315
  loans to shareholders 164
  relief for interest paid 12
Close investment companies 34, 162
Coins 446
Commodity futures 55
Community charge 95
  absence abroad 473
  agricultural land 357
  appeals 103
  attachment of earnings 142
  benefit 100, 395
  caravans 340, 370
  children 97
  collective 96, 99
  exemptions 97
  farmland 357
  husband and wife 386
  hostels 97, 100
  job-related accommodation 340
  lodging houses 100
  payment 103
  personal 96
  reduction scheme 101, 395
  register 95
  Scotland, in 104
  senior citizens 394
  standard 96, 98, 340, 357
  students 102
  transitional reliefs 101
  unoccupied property 98
Company
  accounting periods 24
  building society interest 23
  capital gains 40
  change in ownership 500
  close 34, 164
  demergers 330
  dividends and other distributions 30, 422
  family
  —directors of 156
  —selling 315
  group 34, 301
  investigation cases 122
  liquidations 33, 34, 316
  loan stock 410, 436
  loans by 163

508

SUBJECT INDEX

Married persons *see* Husband and wife
Maternity allowance   126
Medical treatment   132
Medical insurance   112, 132, 394
Mileage allowances   xxiii, 128
Mineral extraction
 capital allowances   263
MIRAS   12, 112, 336
Mobile telephones   134
Mortgage
 endowment   339, 452
 funding of   339
 interest   12, 112, 134, 336
 deduction of tax at source   12, 112, 336
 personal equity plan linked   339
 pension plan linked   339, 452
 types of   339

National heritage property   52, 61
National insurance
 contributions   **169, 278**
 absence abroad   466
 agency workers   170
 benefits in kind and expenses
  payments   138, 142, 163, 171, 235
 —cars and fuel   xxviii, xxix, 141, 171
 charities   488
 Class 1   **169**
 Class 2   278
 Class 4   10, 280
 contracted-out employees   172, 207
 deferment of   282
 early retirement   202
 earnings, definition of   171
 employment, in   **169**
 losses, effect on   293
 rates, xxvii–xxix
 reduced rate   173, 279, 282
 residence   466
 self-employed, for the   **278**
National savings   406, 409
 bank   406, 417
 capital bonds   408
 certificates
 —fixed interest   406
 —index-linked   406
 children's bonus bonds   409
 'first option' bonds   408
 gauranteed growth bonds   408

income bonds   408
SAYE   408
stock register   410
yearly plan   407
Nationalisation   437
Negligent conduct   120
Negligible value, assets of   53
Non-residents
 capital gains tax   38, 458, 466
 companies   457, 471, 501
 entertainers and sportsmen   465
 national insurance contributions   466
 personal allowances   464
 remittances   458, 460, 466
 social security benefits   466
 trusts   472
 UK employment   126, 464
 UK income and gains   465, 467
Non-trading income   235

Occupational pension schemes   **193**
Official error, repayment and remission of tax   118
Offshore funds   501
Options (CGT)   55
Overdraft interest   13
Overseas matters   **455**

P11D employees   127, 129, 130, 131, 140
Part-time business   **222**
Partnerships   **265**
 agreements   275
 annuities to outgoing partners   270
 assets (CGT)   270
 bank interest   420
 basis of assessment   238, 265
 business rates   274
 capital allowances   268
 capital gains   270
 changes in partners   266
 company as partner   274, 504
 consultancy services   269
 continuation election   266, 273, 275
 death of partner   273
 farming   353
 funds, introducing   231, 269
 husband and wife   236, 274, 283
 inheritance tax   273
 joint liability   122

Tolley Publications

TAXATION PUBLICATIONS
Tax Reference Annuals
Tolley's Income Tax 1992-93 £27.95
Tolley's Corporation Tax 1992-93 £23.95
Tolley's Capital Gains Tax 1992-93 £24.95
Tolley's Inheritance Tax 1992-93 £21.95
Tolley's Value Added Tax 1992-93 £24.95
Tolley's National Insurance Contributions 1992-93 £29.95

Tolley's Tax Legislation Series
Income Tax, Corporation Tax and Capital Gains Tax Legislation 1992-93 (2 volumes) £29.95
Inheritance Tax Legislation 1992-93 £13.95
Value Added Tax Legislation 1992-93 £19.95
NIC Legislation 1992-93 £19.95

Tolley's Looseleaf Tax Service
Tolley's Tax Service Income Tax, Corporation Tax and Capital Gains Tax (4 binders) £295.00
Tolley's Inheritance Tax Service £75.00
Tolley's Value Added Tax Service (2 binders) £175.00

Other Annual Tax Books
Tolley's Taxwise No. I 1992-93 (IT/CT/CGT) £22.95
Tolley's Taxwise No. II 1992-93 (IHT/VAT/Trusts/Tax Planning £21.95
Tolley's Capital Allowances 1992-93 £27.95
Tolley's Estate Planning 1993 £27.95
Tolley's Official Tax Statements 1992-93 £32.95
Tolley's Tax Cases 1992 £28.95
Tolley's Tax Computations 1992-93 £31.95
Tolley's Tax Data 1992-93 £11.95
Tolley's Tax Guide 1992-93 £22.95
Tolley's Tax Office Directory 1992 £7.95
Tolley's Tax Planning 1993 (2 volumes) £tba
Tolley's Tax Tables 1992-93 £8.95
Tolley's Taxation in the Channel Islands and Isle of Man 1992-93 £21.95
Tolley's Taxation in the Republic of Ireland 1992-93 £21.95
Tolley's VAT Planning 1993 £29.95
Tolley's VAT Cases 1992 £55.00
Tolley's Personal Tax and Investment Planning 1992-93 £tba

Other Tax Books
Tolley's Tax Appeals to the Commissioners £14.95
Tolley's Anti-Avoidance Provisions 2nd Edition £44.95
Tolley's Tax Planning for Private Residences £29.95
Tolley's Taxation of Offshore Trusts and Funds £39.95
Tolley's Taxes Management Provisions £24.95
Tolley's Property Taxes 1992-93 £32.95
Tolley's Roll-over, Hold-over and Retirement Reliefs 2nd Edition £tba
Tolley's Taxation of Employments £29.95
Tolley's Stamp Duties and Stamp Duty Reserve Tax £16.95
Tolley's Trading in Europe £42.95
Tolley's Tax Havens £35.00
Tolley's International Tax Planning 2nd Edition £tba
Tolley's Tax Compliance and Investigations 3rd Edition £tba
Tolley's Tax Planning for New Businesses 3rd Edition £15.95

Tolley's UK Taxation of Trusts 2nd Edition £29.95
Tolley's Tax on Takeovers £19.95
Tolley's Indemnities and Warranties £34.95
Tolley's Taxation of Lloyd's Underwriters 3rd Edition £49.95
Tolley's VAT Compliance and Investigations 2nd Edition £22.95
Tolley's VAT on Construction, Land and Property 2nd Edition £23.95
Tolley's Purchase and Sale of a Private Company's Shares 4th Edition £24.95
Tolley's Taxation in Corporate Insolvency 2nd Edition £29.95
Tolley's Interest and Penalty Provisions £tba
Tolley's Partnership Taxation £tba
Tolley's Companies Purchasing Their Own Shares £tba
Tolley's Tax Planning for Post-Death Variations £tba
Tolley's Taxation of Trades and Professions £tba
Tolley's Tax Planning for Family Companies £tba

LEGAL PUBLICATIONS
Company Law and Practice
Tolley's Company Law (looseleaf) £95.00
Tolley's Business Administration (looseleaf) £75.00
Tolley's Index to Companies Legislation £9.95
Tolley's Practical Guide to Company Acquisitions 2nd Edition £29.95
Tolley's Company Secretary's Handbook 2nd Edition £tba
Tolley's Directors Handbook £24.95
Tolley's Companies Handbook £25.95

Employment Law and Social Security
Tolley's Employment Handbook 7th Edition £22.95
Tolley's Drafting Contracts of Employment £24.95
Tolley's Health and Safety at Work Handbook 1992-93 £tba
Tolley's Payroll Handbook 6th Edition £tba
Tolley's Social Security and State Benefits 1992-93 £32.95
Tolley's Guide to Statutory Sick Pay and Statutory Maternity Pay 2nd Edition £24.95
Tolley's Discrimination Law Handbook £19.95
Tolley's Employment Law £tba
Tolley's Personnel Procedures £tba
Tolley's Control of Chemicals at Work £tba
Tolley's Environmental Handbook £tba

BUSINESS PUBLICATIONS
Accounting and Finance
Tolley's Charities Manual (looseleaf) £65.00
Tolley's Manual of Accounting volume one £29.95
Tolley's Manual of Accounting volume two £19.95
Tolley's Manual of Accounting volume three £29.95
Tolley's Companies Accounts Check List 1992 £13.50 per pack of 5 (inc VAT)
Tolley's Commercial Loan Agreements £29.95
Tolley's Accounting for Pension Costs £22.95

Pensions
Tolley's Administration of Small Self-Administered Pension Schemes £29.95
Pensions Handbook £tba

Survey
Tolley's Survey of Employee Benefits £45.00
Survey of Company Car Schemes 1992-93 £tba

Please note: while every effort is made to ensure accuracy, information shown above is often compiled in advance of publication, and prices are subject to change without notice.

Order form*

To: Tolley Publishing Company Ltd., Tolley House, 2 Addiscombe Road, Croydon, Surrey CR9 5AF England.　　Telephone: 081-686 9141

Please send me the following book(s), as shown below. I understand that if, for any reason, I am not satisfied with my order and return the book(s) in saleable condition within 21 days, Tolley will refund my money in full.

If you wish to place a standing order for any book(s) and obtain the benefits of the Tolley Subscriber Service, please tick the relevant standing order box(es). All books placed on standing order are sent post-free within the U.K. Please add 5% towards postage and packing if not placed on standing order.

Title	Price per copy	No. of copies	Standing order	Amount £
			☐	
			☐	
			☐	
			☐	
			☐	
			☐	
	Plus VAT (if applicable)			
	Plus 5% postage and packing (if applicable)			
	Total £			

Cheque is enclosed for total amount of order £ _____

Please debit Access/Visa* account number

[_____]　　*VISA*　Signature _____

*Please delete as necessary

Please send me a copy of the full Tolley catalogue ☐

Name† _____

Firm _____

Position _____

Address† _____

_____

_____ Post Code _____

Telephone No _____ Date _____

†If paying by credit card, please enter name and address of cardholder

Registered No. 729731 England VAT No. 243 3583 67　　　　Code 262

Tolley

FREE PUBLICATIONS with
Tolley's Tax Guide 1992-93

Complete this order form for your *FREE* Publications

Two practical and convenient publications are available *free* to all purchasers of
Tolley's Tax Guide. Simply complete the coupon below, ticking the appropriate
boxes, cut out this page and return it to the address below.

Year-End Tax Planning Memorandum

Published in December, this useful tax planning aid highlights those
financial areas which should be reviewed before the end of the fiscal year
and restructured, if necessary, in order to minimise tax liabilities. ☐

1993 Spring Budget Summary

Produced immediately after the Chancellor's spring speech by Tolley's
in-house team of qualified experts, the summary uses clear, succinct
language to explain the impact of the Budget proposals and is highly
recommended by businessmen, taxpayers and advisers alike. ☐

Please enter Tolley Account Number *(if applicable)*

[   ] **[T]**

Surname_____ Initials_____ Title (Mr, Mrs, Miss, Ms)_____

Qualifications _____ Year of First Qualification 19_____

Job Title _____ Telephone _____

Number of Employees A☐1-5 B☐6-50 C☐51-200 D☐201-1000 E☐1000+

Full Name of Firm *(if applicable)* _____

Address_____

_____ Postcode _____

How to place a Standing Order

Tolley's Tax Guide is updated annually to take account of the numerous
important changes accross the whole range of UK taxes. To ensure that you
receive the next edition as soon as it is published simply tick this Standing Order
box. There is no long-standing commitment - we will write to you once a year to
give you the opportunity to confirm or amend your standing order. You may, of
course, cancel this arrangement at *any* time.

To request Further Information *(please tick the appropriate boxes)*

Tolley Catalogue ☐ Current Titles ☐ Tolley Conferences ☐ Client Services ☐

To: Customer Services Department,
     Tolley Publishing Co. Ltd.,
     FREEPOST,
     Tolley House, 2 Addiscombe Road,
     Croydon, Surrey
     CR9 9EA

Tolley

Telephone: 081-686 9141